Matthew Arnold was born in England in 1822. His father was Thomas Arnold, a noted historian and renowned educator, in the shadow of whose fame Matthew was to live for many years. Raised in an atmosphere of intense intellectual activity, educated at Oxford, the young Arnold published his first poems in 1849, and over the next twenty years earned a distinguished place in English poetry. Increasingly, however, his energy was devoted to literary criticism, and after the 1869 publication of his *Collected Poems,* he became almost exclusively a critic, working both to set standards of quality for the literature of his day and to widen the horizons of popular taste. His output was major, his influence immense, and by the time of his death in 1883, his reputation as one of the foremost of English men of letters was secure.

SELECTED

CRITICISM

OF

Matthew Arnold

EDITED

AND WITH AN INTRODUCTION BY

CHRISTOPHER RICKS

PREPARED UNDER THE EDITORIAL SUPERVISION
OF HAROLD BLOOM

A SIGNET CLASSIC from
NEW AMERICAN LIBRARY
TIMES MIRROR
New York and Scarborough, Ontario
The New English Library Limited, London

ACKNOWLEDGMENTS: For permission to quote from Arnold's
letters, we are grateful to Oxford University Press (for *The Letters
of Matthew Arnold to Arthur Hugh Clough*, ed. H. F. Lowry, 1932);
to Yale University Press (for *Unpublished Letters of Matthew
Arnold*, ed. A. Whitridge, 1923); and to Macmillan and Company
Limited (for *Letters of Mattthew Arnold*, ed. G. W. E. Russell, 1895).

SIGNET TRADEMARK REG. U.S. PAT. OFF. AND FOREIGN COUNTRIES
REGISTERED TRADEMARK—MARCA REGISTRADA
HECHO EN CHICAGO, U.S.A.

Signet, Signet Classics, Signette, Mentor and Plume Books

are published IN THE UNITED STATES by

The New American Library, Inc.,

1301 Avenue of the Americas, New York, New York 10019,

IN CANADA by The New American Library of Canada Limited,

81 Mack Avenue, Scarborough, 704, Ontario,

IN THE UNITED KINGDOM by The New English Library Limited,

Barnard's Inn, Holborn, London, E.C. 1, England

First Printing, April, 1972

PRINTED IN THE UNITED STATES OF AMERICA

CONTENTS

INTRODUCTION

JUST AS there is a certain kind of political activist who prefers to be out of office, the obligation to persuade being far more onerous than the pleasure of fulminating, so there is a certain kind of literary critic for whom it is so important to preach to the converted that it doesn't much matter if the only converted person is the critic himself. Matthew Arnold saw his duties, and found his pleasures, differently—not in self-gratification or in solipsism, but in debate. He was sufficiently in earnest about his beliefs to care whether people could be won to them—not for his sake but for theirs, and for truth's. He would not perhaps have minded that T. S. Eliot called him "rather a propagandist for criticism than a critic"; at least he might have retorted equably that it was perfectly possible to be both, as, of all people, the author of *After Strange Gods* and *Notes Towards a Definition of Culture* would come to know.

A scornful attitude toward the propagandist could be rather a luxury, and Arnold was perfectly willing to use a word such as "propagandism" in praise of the contemporary critic whom he admired most, Sainte-Beuve. Writing a tribute in 1869 soon after Sainte-Beuve's death, Arnold saw nothing disrespectful in speaking of the way in which the French critic respected "the ideas and methods of scientific natural inquiry . . . while keeping in perfection the ease of movement and charm of touch which belong to letters properly so called, and which give them their unique power of universal penetration and of propagandism." T. S. Eliot's words were framed as an accusation against Arnold, but it is a less grave one than that which Eliot made against Arnold's contemporary, Poe: "all of his ideas seem to be *entertained* rather than believed." Arnold not only believed his ideas, he paid them the compliment of thinking that it mattered whether other people believed them. What mattered most, indeed, was to remind people of those things which the spirit of the age conspired to forget or to stifle. So that when Arnold praised Sainte-Beuve's life's work, he would himself have wished to earn the same tribute to a commitment at once unpretentious and ambitious: "He did but follow his instinct, however, of opposing in whatever medium he was, the current of that medium when it seemed excessive and tyrannous."

It was therefore essential that the critic should not himself lapse into being excessive and tyrannous. If Arnold devised a style which knew how to win friends, that is because he cared, in the right way, about influencing people. Winning people, not winning them over, because Arnold's charm is not a pretty purring.

> Partly nature, partly time and study, have also by this time taught me thoroughly the precious truth that everything turns upon one's exercising the power of *persuasion,* of *charm;* that without this all fury, energy, reasoning power, acquirement, are thrown away and only render their owner more miserable. Even in one's ridicule one must preserve a sweetness and good-humour . . . I really want to *persuade* on this subject, and I have felt how necessary it was to keep down many and many sharp and telling things that rise to one's lips, and which one would gladly utter if one's object was to show one's own abilities.[1]

Arnold saw—as Carlyle and Ruskin, for all their coruscations, did not—the vital connection between the two senses of the word *articulate:* "to pronounce distinctly" and "to connect in a series." He saw that the writing of poetry—or rather the writing of such poetry as the Victorians had encouraged to evade some of poetry's responsibilities—did not demand the same articulation as discursive prose:

> How difficult it is to write prose: and why? because of the *articulations of the discourse:* one leaps these over in Poetry —places one thought cheek by jowl with another without introducing them and leaves them—but in prose this will not do. It is of course not right in poetry either—but we all do it.[2]

Persuading takes trouble—just how much trouble has been made clear by John Holloway's excellent analysis (in *The Victorian Sage*) of how Arnold's style works, the gentle pressures which it exerts, the directions to which it inclines us so subtly and justly as to make it seem that we are doing

[1] *Letters of Matthew Arnold, 1848-88,* ed. G. W. E. Russell (1895), i.201, 219-20.
[2] *The Letters of Matthew Arnold to Clough,* ed. H. F. Lowry (1932), p. 144.

no more than follow our own inclination. Even Arnold's banter and ridicule were to serve a worthy purpose. Max Beerbohm could caricature Arnold's niece, Mrs. Humphry Ward, inquiring of the great man: "Why, Uncle Matthew, oh, why, will you not be always wholly serious?" But Arnold's seriousness felt under the obligation to veer neither toward the grim nor the flippant. Not the flippant, because "there is a levity which is altogether evil."[3] Not the grim, because in the seventeenth century

> the great English middle class, the kernel of the nation, the class whose intelligent sympathy had upheld a Shakespeare, entered the prison of Puritanism, and had the key turned on its spirit there for two hundred years. [*Heinrich Heine*]

Whatever might be true of other kinds of argument, the manner of a cultural argument is inseparable from its matter, and tact becomes indispensable, that delicacy of touch which can warn us against the impending moment when our legitimate commitment of self is degenerating into self-will, the moment when our quest for the truth is hardening into obstinacy or arrogance:

> To try and approach truth on one side after another, not to strive or cry, nor to persist in pressing forward, on any one side, with violence and self-will,—it is only thus, it seems to me, that mortals may hope to gain any vision of the mysterious Goddess, whom we shall never see except in outline, but only thus even in outline. He who will do nothing but fight impetuously towards her on his own, one, favourite, particular line, is inevitably destined to run his head into the folds of the black robe in which she is wrapped. [Preface to *Essays in Criticism*]

The prison of Puritanism was ruled over by Hebraism, "the tendency to cultivate strictness of conscience rather than spontaneity of consciousness."[4] A critic who set himself to awaken and encourage Hellenism, spontaneity of consciousness, could not but see that tone was irreducibly important. The spokesman for culture would need to speak in the accents of culture, of suppleness, magnanimity, "sweetness and light." The modern Englishman who had pledged himself "to pull out a few more stops in that powerful but at present somewhat narrow-toned organ, the modern Englishman"[5] would have to be audibly richer and finer in tone. So it is not surprising that Arnold is the first literary-social critic

[3] *Letters*, ii.120.
[4] *Culture and Anarchy (Porro Unum est Necessarium)*.
[5] Preface to *Essays in Criticism*.

in English for whom tone and style had become an overtly moral matter, moral in the spirit of the question "how to live?"

> In Sophocles what is valuable is not so much his contributions to psychology and the anatomy of sentiment, as the grand moral effects produced by *style*. For the style is the expression of the nobility of the poet's character, as the matter is the expression of the richness of his mind: but on men character produces as great an effect as mind.[6]

That is from a letter to Clough, and Arnold had not yet worked out precisely how he could best make his point; "not so much this as that" is never quite satisfactory as a way of putting it, since it evades too many of the difficulties. The question, after all, can hardly be seen as one of proportions; it is rather one of relationship. Arnold himself was to speak of relations: "The *ethical* influences of style in language,— its close relations, so often pointed out, with character,—are most important" (*The Literary Influence of Academies*).

What was wrong with Victorian England could not be discerned if the only standards that a society had to meet were "Hebraic" standards of conduct. For Arnold—as for many social critics since but rather few before—the essential political questions had become inseparable from cultural questions. What had come to matter more than laws or kings was quality of life, or—in more ancient and more resonant terms —having life and having it more abundantly. Style as a moral matter: perhaps this has become all too accepted a part of our consciousness, with the result that the word *style* has bred its own empty travesties: *stylish, stylishness*. That cultural differences may constitute very painful and implacable critiques of each other; that there is more in style than meets the ear, since there is much that meets the mind and heart: these are now well known. That radical beard constitutes a criticism of my way of life. But then so does that bowler hat. Our poets have evoked the association of the style of a hat with a style of thinking, an allegiance:

> Rationalists, wearing square hats,
> Think, in square rooms,
> Looking at the floor,
> Looking at the ceiling.
> They confine themselves
> To right-angled triangles.
> If they tried rhomboids,
> Cones, waving lines, ellipses—

[6] *Letters to Clough*, p. 101.

As, for example, the ellipse of the half-moon—
Rationalists would wear sombreros.
[Wallace Stevens, "Six Significant Landscapes"]

Well known to the point of platitude. But what is well
known may not be known well. The enduringly valuable
thing about Arnold's exposition is his scrupulous justice.
Never evading the claims of conduct, of institutions, of his
conviction that it may be urgently better to have one system
(say, of schooling) than another since systems undeniably
make a difference; never thinking us all soul—or all culture;
never brandishing "style," even "the grand style," with the
cry "In this sign shalt thou conquer": Arnold, as literary
critic and as cultural critic, did not ever make things easy for
himself by opting for a "one thing needful." For, as he said
in *Culture and Anarchy,*

> There is no *unum necessarium,* or one thing needful, which
> can free human nature from the obligation of trying to come
> to its best at all these points. The real *unum necessarium* for
> us is to come to our best at all points.

As a literary critic Arnold was at his most cogent on style,
whether it was the style of Homer and the inadequacies of
Homer's translators, the development of English prose style,
or a consummate formulation on the nature of style itself,
such as the following, at once fluent and compact:

> We may add yet further, what is in itself evident, that to the
> style and manner of the best poetry their special character,
> their accent, is given by their diction, and, even yet more, by
> their movement. And though we distinguish between the two
> characters, the two accents, of superiority, yet they are never-
> theless vitally connected one with the other. The superior
> character of truth and seriousness, in the matter and substance
> of the best poetry, is inseparable from the superiority of dic-
> tion and movement marking its style and manner. [*The Study
> of Poetry*]

This is supremely perceptive, both in its firmness and in its
discrimination. It is only in "the best poetry," not in all
poetry, that substance and style are inseparable; we may find
it useful tentatively to distinguish the one from the other,
but we should never forget that they are "vitally connected."
Arnold here treads surefootedly, tempted by neither of the
precipitous errors to left and right. The same is true of his
inquiry into what it would truly mean to say that Addison's
style had "never been surpassed"; ought this not to imply
that Addison is the greatest of writers? What is the nature of

the reciprocity between style and force of thought? Arnold holds fast, rightly, to the idea that we can usefully speak of "style" in isolation, at a certain level of accomplishment, and yet that the limits of that level then themselves become the point at issue:

> But to say of Addison's style, that 'in its varied cadence and subtle ease it has never been surpassed', seems to me to be going a little too far. One could not say more of Plato's. Whatever his services to his time, Addison is for us now a writer whose range and force of thought are not considerable enough to make him interesting; and his style cannot equal in varied cadence and subtle ease the style of a man like Plato, because without range and force of thought all the resources of style, whether in cadence or in subtlety, are not and cannot be brought out. [*A Guide to English Literature*]

A certain kind of literary theorist might say that all we have here is Arnold contradicting himself. But to discriminate between the two kinds of thing one might mean by saying such-and-such, and to help us see their different kinds of critical usefulness: this is not contradiction but contradistinction. Again and again one finds in Arnold a succinct and authoritative statement of a critical crux, as in the profound dexterity with which he characterizes the greatest symbolic effects in literature. He is contrasting Eugénie de Guérin with her brother Maurice:

> She never, indeed, expresses herself without grace and intelligence; but her words, when she speaks of the life and appearances of nature, are in general but intellectual signs; they are not like her brother's—symbols equivalent with the thing symbolised. They bring the notion of the thing described to the mind, they do not bring the feeling of it to the imagination. [*Eugénie de Guérin*]

Arnold has here pinpointed, without fuss and without fustian, the tantalizing success of the finest symbolic effects, the disappearance of the symbolized into the symbol, so that when the symbols of Shakespeare or Chekhov or D. H. Lawrence are at their best, their perfect tact must bring hauntingly into question whether anything which we can without damage call "symbolic" is going on at all.

Arnold is similarly discriminating on the question of how much should be claimed for literary criticism at all. The trouble with claiming too little is that before long this will impel somebody to claim too much. It may well be that too much is claimed these days, and that it would not hurt if for a generation or so we reverted to thinking of the critic as a humble handmaid. But qualms about critics' megalomania ought not to be vented on Arnold, despite the strong claims which he made for the critic. On the contrary, the sane limits set by Arnold are the best protection against exorbitance. Arnold never encouraged as promiscuous a use of the word "genius" as John Stuart Mill allowed himself in 1832:

> If the genius which *discovers* is no peculiar faculty, neither is the genius which *creates*. It was genius which produced the Prometheus Vinctus, the Oration on the Crown, the Minerva, or the Transfiguration; and is it not genius which *comprehends* them? Without genius, a work of genius may be felt, but it cannot possibly be understood. [*On Genius*]

It is true that Mill made a concession with the words "in an inferior degree": "An exercise of the same powers of imagination, abstraction, and discrimination (though in an inferior degree) which would have enabled ourselves to produce the selfsame work." But his ardor rekindled: "Do we not accordingly see that as much genius is often displayed in explaining the design and bringing out the hidden significance of a work of art, as in creating it?"

Arnold was more cool and more cogent. Praising Sainte-Beuve, he observed that "Excellent work in a lower kind counts in the long run above work which is short of excellence in a higher; first-rate criticism has a permanent value greater than that of any but first-rate works of poetry and art." Notice the tentativeness, the deliberate holding open of the question "At what point then? . . . ," the absence of a "precision" which in the circumstances could not but be spurious. (It is only a particular instance which could make precision possible.) It is the same with Arnold's insistence that "Magic of style is creative: its possessor himself creates, and he inspires and enables his reader in some sort to create after him" (*Amiel*). This both insists that a reader too creates, and also insists—by saying "in some sort"—that this creativity is not amenable to too confident a claim and must remain mysterious, a starting point for discussion rather than the clinching of it.

It is characteristic of Arnold to see that the abstract proposition has to be brought into relationship with the vital instance. "Everybody, too, would be willing to admit, as a general proposition, that the critical faculty is lesser than the inventive." But it remains a proposition, not a law:

> Is it true that Johnson had better have gone on producing more *Irenes* instead of writing his *Lives of the Poets;* nay, is it certain that Wordsworth himself was better employed in

making his Ecclesiastical Sonnets than when he made his celebrated Preface, so full of criticism, and criticism of the works
of others? [*The Function of Criticism at the Present Time*]

Arnold achieved much by his dextrous insistence on the
word "adequacy." For to ask that literature be adequate
does not sound like an exorbitant demand; the word is
modest and uninflamed. But the concept is suitably demanding, totally demanding, since what would it be for a work of
literature to be adequate, given all that Arnold (rightly)
hopes from literature? Arnold's adequacy resembles T. S.
Eliot's simplicity:

> A condition of complete simplicity
> (Costing not less than everything).

Arnold saw English culture as continually satisfied with the
second-rate. Grateful for the second-rate—that would have
been different. But satisfied: such satisfaction is inseparable
from self-satisfaction. It made the good into the enemy of
the great, and in the long run the good itself could not but
suffer if a society failed to discriminate between the kind of
gratitude due to, say, Thackeray ("certainly a first-rate
journeyman though not a great artist"), and that due to
Wordsworth.

> Charlatanism is for confusing or obliterating the distinctions
> between excellent and inferior, sound and unsound or only
> half-sound, true and untrue or only half-true. It is charlatan-
> ism, conscious or unconscious, whenever we confuse or ob-
> literate these. And in poetry, more than anywhere else, it is
> unpermissible to confuse or obliterate them. For in poetry
> the distinction between excellent and inferior, sound and un-
> sound or only half-sound, true and untrue or only half-true, is
> of paramount importance. [*The Study of Poetry*]

Arnold does not say that it is the half-sound or half-true
works of literature themselves which constitute charlatanism;
the charlatanism is in the beholder, who protects himself
against what the very greatest literature can do—search him
out and know him—by resting content with the half-sound.
Arnold is aware that the virtues of much good (as distinct
from great) literature are not nothing, but his persistent
question is "Are they enough? Are they everything?" To
cease asking for everything, for adequacy, in those works of
literature which we will call great, would not only be to
abandon any chance of gaining everything, it would in the
long run sap our chances of gaining anything much. Good
literature cannot but be parasitic upon great literature—the

essential thing is to see that it does not batten upon great literature.

For the first time "centrality" emerges as an essential critical concept, and a paramount duty of the critic becomes "to ascertain the master-current in the literature of an epoch, and to distinguish this from all minor currents" (*Heinrich Heine*). Arnold might have appealed to the dictionary to support him, since how can one understand what a tributary is without realizing that it pays tribute to the great river?

Hence Arnold's warning about American literature; he feared that in their gratitude at the fact that their writers had recently done much, Americans might forget to ask whether their writers had done enough:

> Theodore Parker, born an American, is as a preacher and writer a genuine American voice, not an echo of English pulpits and books; that is much. In the same way, Mr. Walt Whitman, born an American, is as a poet a genuine American voice, not an echo of English poetry; that, too, is much. But the admirers of Theodore Parker or of Mr. Walt Whitman easily make more of it than it is worth. At this time of day it is not enough to be an American voice, or an English voice, or a French voice; for a real spiritual lead it is necessary to be a European voice. [*Pall Mall Gazette*, August 24, 1867; reprinted in Fraser Neiman's *Essays, Letters, and Reviews by Matthew Arnold,* 1960]

An American may resent the hint of cultural snobbery which hangs around that use of *European,* but it is to be remembered that Arnold was willing to bring the same accusation against a fellow-Englishman when he called Tennyson's *Maud* "a lamentable production, and like so much of our literature thoroughly and intensely *provincial,* not European."[7] Moreover Arnold's point might still constitute a valid warning about American literature, where a novelist's ambition is apparently not, as it is in England or France, to write a great novel, but to write the great American novel.

Arnold's plea for centrality and sanity was not that of a man unaware of what is darkly inaccessible and uncontrollable. His best poems, disturbed and disturbing, give us warrant for taking him at his word when he insists:

> No one has a stronger and more abiding sense than I have of the "daemonic" element—as Goethe called it—which underlies and encompasses our life; but I think, as Goethe thought, that the right thing is, while conscious of this element, and of all that there is inexplicable round one, to keep

---

[7] *Letters to Clough,* p. 147.

pushing on one's posts into the darkness, and to establish no post that is not perfectly in light and firm. One gains nothing on the darkness by being, like Shelley, as incoherent as the darkness itself.[8]

That tart remark about Shelley is a reminder that though Arnold was without rancor he was not deferential. It is good to be transported back to a time when Shakespeare was honored this—and not that—side of idolatry.

His workmanship is often far from being pure and flawless.

> "Till that Bellona's bridegroom, lapp'd in proof,
> Confronted him with self-comparisons—"

There is but one name for such writing as that, if Shakespeare had signed it a thousand times,—it is detestable. And it is too frequent in Shakespeare. [*A Guide to English Literature*]

Such independence of mind is salutary even when it is insufficiently substantiated. Moreover, Arnold was willing to substantiate his general position as to adverse criticism. Sentimentalists are always with us, urging critics to speak only of what they love, and to remain silent about those works of literature with which they are "out of sympathy." And since Arnold's day, such sentimentalists have been joined by those with a vested professional interest in advancing claims for a "hitherto neglected" or "underrated" figure—the establishment of English Literature as a major academic discipline has made it even more imperative than it was in Arnold's day to see how indispensable, and how "positive," a well-argued and well-informed negative criticism may be. Arnold set out the principles calmly and keenly, with a sure sense of the interdependence of all our judgments, an interdependence which means that an unjustified or exaggerated admiration will not stay quietly out on its own but will be bound to seep into and affect other judgments, other comprehensions, with which it might seem to have little connection. Arnold the social critic made similar points about the ugliness and vulgarity of so much in our modern environment and culture—the environment refuses to stay out there as merely environment; it doesn't just environ us, it enters us. Our critical judgments too constitute an environment.

It is a mistake to think that the judgment of mature reason on our favourite author, even if it abates considerably our high-raised estimate of him, is not a gain to us. Admiration

[8] *Letters*, i.249.

is positive, say some people, disparagement is negative; from what is negative we can get nothing. But is it no advantage, then, to the youthful enthusiast for Chateaubriand, to come to know that 'the Eternal did *not* create Chateaubriand to be a guide to the universe'? It is a very great advantage, because these over-charged admirations are always exclusive, and prevent us from giving heed to other things which deserve admiration. Admiration is salutary and formative, true; but things admirable are sown wide, and are to be gathered here and gathered there, not all in one place; and until we have gathered them wherever they are to be found, we have not known the true salutariness and formativeness of admiration. The quest is large; and occupation with the unsound or half-sound, delight in the not good or less good, is a sore let and hindrance to us. Release from such occupation and delight sets us free for ranging farther, and for perfecting our sense of beauty. He is the happy man, who encumbering himself with the love of nothing which is not beautiful, is able to embrace the greatest number of things beautiful in his love.

It is an excellent and wholesome discipline for a student of Goethe to be brought face to face with such opposite judgments concerning his chief productions. It compels us to rouse ourselves out of the passiveness with which we in general read a celebrated work, to open our eyes wide, to ask ourselves frankly how, according to our genuine feeling, the truth stands. [*A French Critic on Goethe*]

For what can it mean to a work of literature, to be admired by somebody to whom all works of literature are to be admired? Arnold is in a proper position to indict the wrong kind of "passiveness," since he was himself a patient man and a patient critic, not one likely to mistake bustle for activity. His objection to most readers and to most critics of literature is that they do not truly read—they take it as read.

Yet Arnold had to pay a price for his commitment to persuasion. Brawling and violence seemed to him fatal to the disinterestedness of culture—and yet how could the literature of one's own day be discussed without the note of brawling and violence? "No man can trust himself to speak of his own time and his own contemporaries with the same sureness of judgment and the same proportion as of times and men gone by" (*A Guide to English Literature*). Perhaps not, though some of the best criticism by Coleridge and by Hazlitt would suggest otherwise. But are not the risks which are endemic in this less sure judgment, this less sure sense of proportion, exceeded by the risks which are endemic in an abdication of judgment altogether, in letting the literature of one's contemporaries do as it likes? *He never spoke out:* it is a severe charge which Arnold brings against Thomas Gray, and it tolls through that essay—tolls often enough to suggest that Arnold here was manifesting some unease beyond the apparent occasion. Certainly it could not simply be said of Arnold that he never spoke out—but at what point does persuasion become compromise? At what point does charm become too accommodating?

For it was not that Arnold had nothing to say about his contemporaries. His letters, which have brilliant critical flashes similar to those in the letters of Gerard Manley Hopkins or Edward FitzGerald, show that his public abstention was a self-denying ordinance. "One cannot change English ideas so much as, if I live, I hope to change them, without saying imperturbably what one thinks and making a good many people uncomfortable."[9] Pithy and firm in grip, his critical asides show us an Arnold less imperturbable than his public self, less elegant, but no less acute. One need not agree with his judgments to feel that they invariably embody a critical point with which it would be essential for any subsequent critic scrupulously to work out his agreement or disagreement. On Charlotte Brontë and her "hideous undelightful convulsed constricted novel . . . one of the most utterly disagreeable books I ever read"[10]:

> Why is *Villette* disagreeable? Because the writer's mind contains nothing but hunger, rebellion, and rage, and therefore that is all she can, in fact, put into her book. No fine writing can hide this thoroughly, and it will be fatal to her in the long run.[11]

A critic who describes himself as "determined in print to be always scrupulously polite"[12] will hardly be able to utter such sentiments in print. Nor will he be able, unfortunately, to refer publicly to "moral desperadoes like Carlyle":

> I never much liked Carlyle. He seemed to me to be "carrying coals to Newcastle," as our proverb says; preaching earnestness to a nation which has plenty of it by nature, but was less abundantly supplied with several other useful things.[13]

Nor will the scrupulously polite critic say publicly of Elizabeth Barrett Browning what he might say privately: that she

[9] *Letters*, i.194.
[10] *Letters to Clough*, p. 132.
[11] *Letters*, i.29.
[12] *Letters*, i.58.
[13] *Letters to Clough*, p. 111; *Letters*, ii.191.

was "hopelessly confirmed in her aberration from health, nature, beauty, and truth."[14]

For the public Arnold was committed, on principle, to the belief that "the great thing is to speak without a particle of vice, malice, or rancour."[15] If Arnold had indeed been without a particle of malice, he would have been as insufferable as some of his contemporaries found him. His letters glitter with the salty particles. But he knew that what contemporary culture most needed was sane, flexible argument, not particles or aperçus; indeed, one of his own aperçus both admires and sets limit to its admiration:

> There is nothing here in literature worth speaking of—except that the National Review is doing well—that Ruskin has published a new volume of *Modern Painters* even fuller than the others of true 'aperçus', even more than the others deprived of the '*ordo concatenatioque veri*' which is the one thing needful. However to have good and faithful 'aperçus' is a great thing.[16]

A great thing, but not the great thing: this is generous and discriminating, and it is so partly because Arnold knew that on the subject of Ruskin he was himself no more capable of *ordo concatenatioque veri*, the order and concatenation of the true, than was Ruskin on any subject whatsoever.

Most of these strictures by Arnold turn upon the question of discipline, that artistic self-discipline which both creates and is created by a sense of other disciplines which do not belong to oneself: of tradition, of fact. At what point—such a phrase characterizes Arnold's sense that the crucial critical question again and again crystallizes into something which might be crudely summarized as "How can we tell where to draw the line?"—at what point does self-expression become self-indulgence? Arnold the social critic pointed out that though it is a notable thing to be able to say what you like, an important question remains: what you then say. There is a clear enough link between the social critic who speaks in such a way about liberty, the Englishman's boon, and the literary critic who found that the "fatal habit of using one hundred words where one would suffice"[17] made Swinburne merely a "pseudo-Shelley."

It was all the more important to be without shadow of

[14] *Letters*, i.61.
[15] *Letters*, i.194.
[16] *Unpublished Letters of Matthew Arnold*, ed. A. Whitridge (1923), p. 33.
[17] *Letters*, ii.200.

rancor when dealing with contemporary poets, since here
Arnold could have been impugned as being not disinterested
but in competition. His reluctance to articulate his objections
to Tennyson publicly and at some length stems from this
likelihood of being misconstrued. "But is it possible or
proper for me to say this about Tennyson, when my saying
it would inevitably be attributed to odious motives?"[18] A
pity, since Arnold's asides about Tennyson, whether public
or private, are by no means casual. A letter speaks disparag-
ingly of "the 'In Memoriam' type of poems; poems which
have no beginning, middle or end, but are holdings forth in
verse, which, for anything in the nature of the composition
itself, may perfectly well go on for ever."[19]

Arnold's judgments on Victorian poetry are an extension
of his judgment, less harsh but equally firm, on Romantic
poetry. But what of the novel? Like T. S. Eliot (and like
Dr. Johnson and Coleridge), Arnold seems to have been not
so much disinterested as uninterested when it came to the
novel. It might be said of both Johnson and Coleridge that
they preceded the great age of the novel, but Arnold and
T. S. Eliot did not, and the fact that they had no more than
a mild concern with the novel makes their critical influence
the more striking as an achievement. That this is a striking
deficiency is clear enough; but so too is the decisive influence
wielded by Arnold, an authority all the more impressive in
that though he saw literature steadily he did not see it whole.
Arnold's only extended discussion of novelists is wrung from
him by his duties as a social critic or a religious critic. So
that *David Copperfield* does important social work on Arnold's behalf when he is pondering Irish attitudes toward
the English. And Tolstoi the novelist gains admission because of Tolstoi the religious thinker, as Arnold conceded:

> I had a special reason for writing about Tolstoi, because of
> his religious ideas; in general I do not write about the literary
> performances of living contemporaries or contemporaries only
> recently dead. Therefore I am not likely to write about Tour-
> guenieff, though I admire him greatly, and am going to read
> two of his novels this very year.[20]

Arnold came to set more and more store by being of use,
and it is not surprising that he came to speak sharply of
some writers who might, in airier days, have meant much to

[18] *Letters*, i.239.
[19] A letter of July 21, 1860; quoted by R. H. Super, *Times Literary Supplement*, October 28, 1960.
[20] *Letters*, ii.376.

him. One such was the Swiss writer Amiel, about whom he wrote in 1887:

> The thoughts which have positive truth and value, the thoughts to be lived with and dwelt upon, the thoughts which are a real acquisition for our minds, are precisely thoughts which counteract the 'vague aspiration and indeterminate desire' possessing Amiel and filling his Journal: they are thoughts insisting on the need of limit, the feasibility of performance. . . . The ideas to live with, the ideas of sterling value to us, are, I repeat, ideas of this kind: ideas staunchly counteracting and reducing the power of the infinite and indeterminate, not paralysing us with it. [*Amiel*]

"The need of limit, the feasibility of performance": such strictures on Romanticism are an attempt to distinguish Arnold's own kind of generality from what he saw as a pernicious kind. "Criticism of life," "sweetness and light," "high seriousness," "the grand style": these are certainly general enough, but John Holloway succeeds in demonstrating that the function of these phrases in Arnold is precisely to discourage philosophical speculation. Such phrases have none of the curt precision of "objective correlative" or "dissociation of sensibility," phrases which prick us into thought but may not be such as to sustain thought. Arnold's phrases are not vacant, but they are deliberately not at all provocative—both as not being tendentious and as not provoking thought.

For Arnold believed that the highest claim on our thought was elsewhere than in critical theory or aesthetics. So that our judgment as to who gets the worst of it when René Wellek grapples with Arnold will be inseparable from our judgment as to whether critics gain or lose by possessing a literary theory, an aesthetic. Like Dr. Johnson and like Dr. Leavis (both of whom are found deficient as theoreticians by Professor Wellek, but only one of whom was in any position to publish in reply an argument as to why critical theory was more likely to impede rather than aid a critic), Arnold did not have a theory but he did have critical principles. For Professor Wellek, as for any thorough-going critical theorist, the alternatives are stark: a critic either has a literary theory, or he has caprices. But just as all intelligent men think about the terms they use, yet not all intelligent men are philosophers; so it seemed to Dr. Johnson or to Arnold that the crucial question was one about priorities, about emphases. The dictionary provided enough for Johnson to know initially what Nature or Novelty was, as it provided enough for Arnold to know what "high seriousness" was; neither Johnson nor Arnold thereupon set himself to mine away at the concept, but instead to mine away at the instances.

None of our great critics has had an adequate "theory of literature," and this must call in question whether such a theory is actively hostile to, and not merely inessential to, great criticism. That Arnold was not a philosopher is clear enough. What is by no means clear is that his not being a philosopher in any way invalidated or limited his criticism. "A disinterested attempt to learn and propagate the best that is known and thought in the world"—Arnold's own work has taken its place among the best that is known and thought.

CHRONOLOGY

1822   Matthew Arnold born.

1828   His father, Thomas Arnold, made Headmaster of Rugby School.

1841   Enters Balliol College, Oxford.

1845   Elected Fellow of Oriel College, Oxford.

1849   *The Strayed Reveller, and Other Poems.*

1851   Appointed Inspector of Schools. Marries Frances Lucy Wightman.

1852   *Empedocles on Etna, and Other Poems.*

1853   *Poems. A New Edition.*

1854   *Poems, Second Series.*

1857   Elected Professor of Poetry at Oxford. Inaugural lecture, "On the Modern Element in Literature." After his first five-year term, Arnold was re-elected.

1861   *On Translating Homer.*

1864   *A French Eton.*

1865   *Essays in Criticism* [First Series].

1867   *On the Study of Celtic Literature. New Poems* (reprinting "Empedocles on Etna").

1869   *Culture and Anarchy.* Collected edition of *Poems.*

NOTE

ARNOLD's literary criticism is here arranged in three sections: first, criticism of a general nature, or which ranges widely, here given in chronological order of publication; second, criticism of particular authors or topics, given in the historical order of the authors discussed; third, extracts from Arnold's letters, given in chronological order of composition.

The date at the head of an essay is of publication, not of composition and not—in the case of a lecture—of delivery. The text, though, is that finally adopted by Arnold. For full details of composition, for the many changes which he made, and for comprehensive annotation, see R. H. Super's excellent edition of *The Complete Prose Works of Matthew Arnold,* in progress (1960–).

It is worth noting that many of Arnold's best *aperçus* occur in unexpected contexts—or, rather, in contexts not perhaps to be divined from an essay's title. An example is his comment on Tennyson in *On Translating Homer.* The index at the end of this volume should help.

Footnotes by Arnold are asterisked and followed by his initials, thus: [M.A.]. Editor's footnotes are numbered and appear at the end of each selection. Omissions made for this volume are indicated by asterisks (***), leaving Arnold's own occasional use of ellipsis (. . .).

PREFACE
TO FIRST EDITION
OF *POEMS*

1853

IN TWO small volumes of Poems, published anonymously, one in 1849, the other in 1852, many of the poems which compose the present volume have already appeared. The rest are now published for the first time.

I have, in the present collection, omitted the poem from which the volume published in 1852 took its title. I have done so, not because the subject of it was a Sicilian Greek born between two and three thousands years ago, although many persons would think this a sufficient reason. Neither have I done so because I had, in my own opinion, failed in the delineation which I intended to effect. I intended to delineate the feelings of one of the last of the Greek religious philosophers, one of the family of Orpheus and Musæus, having survived his fellows, living on into a time when the habits of Greek thought and feeling had begun fast to change, character to dwindle, the influence of the Sophists to prevail. Into the feelings of a man so situated there entered much that we are accustomed to consider as exclusively modern; how much, the fragments of Empedocles himself which remain to us are sufficient at least to indicate. What those who are familiar only with the great monuments of early Greek genius supposed to be its exclusive characteristics, have disappeared: the calm, the cheerfulness, the disinterested objectivity have disappeared; the dialogue of the mind with itself has commenced; modern problems have presented themselves; we hear already the doubts, we witness the discouragement, of Hamlet and of Faust.

The representation of such a man's feelings must be interesting, if consistently drawn. We all naturally take pleasure, says Aristotle,[1] in any imitation or representation whatever: this is the basis of our love of poetry; and we take pleasure in them, he adds, because all knowledge is naturally agreeable to us; not to the philosopher only, but to mankind at large. Every representation, therefore, which is consistently drawn may be supposed to be interesting, inasmuch as it gratifies this natural interest in knowledge of all kinds. What is *not* interesting, is that which does not add to our knowledge of any kind; that which is vaguely conceived and loosely drawn; a representation which is general, indeterminate, and faint, instead of being particular, precise, and firm.

Any accurate representation may therefore be expected to be interesting; but, if the representation be a poetical one, more than this is demanded. It is demanded, not only that it shall interest, but also that it shall inspirit and rejoice the reader; that it shall convey a charm, and infuse delight. For the Muses, as Hesiod[2] says, were born that they might be 'a forgetfulness of evils, and a truce from cares:' and it is not enough that the poet should add to the knowledge of men, it is required of him also that he should add to their happiness. 'All art,' says Schiller,[3] 'is dedicated to Joy, and there is no higher and no more serious problem, than how to make men happy. The right art is that alone, which creates the highest enjoyment.'

A poetical work, therefore, is not yet justified when it has been shown to be an accurate, and therefore interesting representation; it has to be shown also that it is a representation from which men can derive enjoyment. In presence of the most tragic circumstances, represented in a work of art, the feeling of enjoyment, as is well known, may still subsist; the representation of the most utter calamity, of the liveliest anguish, is not sufficient to destroy it; the more tragic the situation, the deeper becomes the enjoyment; and the situation is more tragic in proportion as it becomes more terrible.

What then are the situations, from the representation of which, though accurate, no poetical enjoyment can be derived? They are those in which the suffering finds no vent in action; in which a continuous state of mental distress is prolonged, unrelieved by incident, hope, or resistance; in which there is everything to be endured, nothing to be done. In such situations there is inevitably something morbid, in the description of them something monotonous. When they occur in actual life, they are painful, not tragic; the representation of them in poetry is painful also.

To this class of situations, poetically faulty as it appears to me, that of Empedocles, as I have endeavoured to represent him, belongs; and I have therefore excluded the poem from the present collection.

And why, it may be asked, have I entered into this explanation respecting a matter so unimportant as the admission or exclusion of the poem in question? I have done so, because I was anxious to avow that the sole reason for its exclusion was that which has been stated above; and that it has not been excluded in deference to the opinion which many critics of the present day appear to entertain against subjects chosen from distant times and countries: against the choice, in short, of any subjects but modern ones.

'The poet,' it is said,* and by an intelligent critic, 'the poet who would really fix the public attention must leave the exhausted past, and draw his subjects from matters of present import, and *therefore* both of interest and novelty.'

Now this view I believe to be completely false. It is worth examining, inasmuch as it is a fair sample of a class of critical dicta everywhere current at the present day, having a philosophical form and air, but no real basis in fact; and which are calculated to vitiate the judgment of readers of poetry, while they exert, so far as they are adopted, a misleading influence on the practice of those who make it.

What are the eternal objects of poetry, among all nations, and at all times? They are actions; human actions; possessing an inherent interest in themselves, and which are to be communicated in an interesting manner by the art of the poet. Vainly will the latter imagine that he has everything in his own power; that he can make an intrinsically inferior action equally delightful with a more excellent one by his treatment of it. He may indeed compel us to admire his skill, but his work will possess, within itself, an incurable defect.

The poet, then, has in the first place to select an excellent action; and what actions are the most excellent? Those, certainly, which most powerfully appeal to the great primary human affections: to those elementary feelings which subsist permanently in the race, and which are independent of

* In the *Spectator* of April 2, 1853. The words quoted were not used with reference to poems of mine. [M. A.]

time. These feelings are permanent and the same; that which
interests them is permanent and the same also. The modern-
ness or antiquity of an action, therefore, has nothing to do
with its fitness for poetical representation; this depends upon
its inherent qualities. To the elementary part of our nature,
to our passions, that which is great and passionate is eternally interesting; and interesting solely in proportion to its
greatness and to its passion. A great human action of a
thousand years ago is more interesting to it than a smaller
human action of to-day, even though upon the representation of this last the most consummate skill may have been
expended, and though it has the advantage of appealing by
its modern language, familiar manners, and contemporary
allusions, to all our transient feelings and interests. These,
however, have no right to demand of a poetical work that it
shall satisfy them; their claims are to be directed elsewhere.
Poetical works belong to the domain of our permanent passions; let them interest these, and the voice of all subordinate claims upon them is at once silenced.

Achilles, Prometheus, Clytemnestra, Dido,—what modern
poem presents personages as interesting, even to us moderns,
as these personages of an 'exhausted past'? We have the
domestic epic dealing with the details of modern life which
pass daily under our eyes; we have poems representing
modern personages in contact with the problems of modern
life, moral, intellectual, and social; these works have been
produced by poets the most distinguished of their nation and time; yet I fearlessly assert that *Hermann and
Dorothea, Childe Harold, Jocelyn, The Excursion,*[4] leave
the reader cold in comparison with the effect produced upon
him by the latter books of the *Iliad,* by the *Oresteia,* or by
the episode of Dido.[5] And why is this? Simply because in
the three last-named cases the action is greater, the personages nobler, the situations more intense: and this is the true
basis of the interest in a poetical work, and this alone.

It may be urged, however, that past actions may be interesting in themselves, but that they are not to be adopted
by the modern poet, because it is impossible for him to have
them clearly present to his own mind, and he cannot therefore feel them deeply, nor represent them forcibly. But this
is not necessarily the case. The externals of a past action,
indeed, he cannot know with the precision of a contemporary; but his business is with its essentials. The outward
man of Œdipus or of Macbeth, the houses in which they
lived, the ceremonies of their courts, he cannot accurately
figure to himself; but neither do they essentially concern

him. His business is with their inward man; with their feelings and behaviour in certain tragic situations, which engage their passions as men; these have in them nothing local and casual; they are as accessible to the modern poet as to a contemporary.

The date of an action, then, signifies nothing: the action itself, its selection and construction, this is what is all-important. This the Greeks understood far more clearly than we do. The radical difference between their poetical theory and ours consists, as it appears to me, in this: that, with them, the poetical character of the action in itself, and the conduct of it, was the first consideration; with us, attention is fixed mainly on the value of the separate thoughts and images which occur in the treatment of an action. They regarded the whole; we regard the parts. With them, the action predominated over the expression of it; with us, the expression predominates over the action. Not that they failed in expression, or were inattentive to it; on the contrary, they are the highest models of expression, the unapproached masters of the *grand style*. But their expression is so excellent because it is so admirably kept in its right degree of prominence; because it is so simple and so well subordinated; because it draws its force directly from the pregnancy of the matter which it conveys. For what reason was the Greek tragic poet confined to so limited a range of subjects? Because there are so few actions which unite in themselves, in the highest degree, the conditions of excellence: and it was not thought that on any but an excellent subject could an excellent poem be constructed. A few actions, therefore, eminently adapted for tragedy, maintained almost exclusive possession of the Greek tragic stage. Their significance appeared inexhaustible; they were as permanent problems, perpetually offered to the genius of every fresh poet. This too is the reason of what appears to us moderns a certain baldness of expression in Greek tragedy; of the triviality with which we often reproach the remarks of the chorus, where it takes part in the dialogue: that the action itself, the situation of Orestes, or Merope, or Alcmæon,[6] was to stand the central point of interest, unforgotten, absorbing, principal; that no accessories were for a moment to distract the spectator's attention from this; that the tone of the parts was to be perpetually kept down, in order not to impair the grandiose effect of the whole. The terrible old mythic story on which the drama was founded stood, before he entered the theatre, traced in its bare outlines upon the spectator's mind; it stood in his memory, as a group of statuary, faintly seen, at the end of a long and dark vista: then came the poet, embodying outlines, developing situations, not a word wasted, not a sentiment capriciously thrown in: stroke upon stroke, the drama proceeded: the light deepened upon the group; more and more it revealed itself to the riveted gaze of the spectator: until at last, when the final words were spoken, it stood before him in broad sunlight, a model of immortal beauty.

This was what a Greek critic demanded; this was what a Greek poet endeavoured to effect. It signified nothing to what time an action belonged. We do not find that the *Persæ* occupied a particularly high rank among the dramas of Æschylus, because it represented a matter of contemporary interest; this was not what a cultivated Athenian required. He required that the permanent elements of his nature should be moved; and dramas of which the action, though taken from a long-distant mythic time, yet was calculated to accomplish this in a higher degree than that of the *Persæ*, stood higher in his estimation accordingly. The Greeks felt, no doubt, with their exquisite sagacity of taste, that an action of present times was too near them, too much mixed up with what was accidental and passing, to form a sufficiently grand, detached, and self-subsistent object for a tragic poem. Such objects belonged to the domain of the comic poet, and of the lighter kinds of poetry. For the more serious kinds, for *pragmatic* poetry, to use an excellent expression of Polybius, they were more difficult and severe in the range of subjects which they permitted. Their theory and practice alike, the admirable treatise of Aristotle, and the unrivalled works of their poets, exclaim with a thousand tongues—'All depends upon the subject; choose a fitting action, penetrate yourself with the feeling of its situations; this done, everything else will follow.'

But for all kinds of poetry alike there was one point on which they were rigidly exacting: the adaptability of the subject to the kind of poetry selected, and the careful construction of the poem.

How different a way of thinking from this is ours! We can hardly at the present day understand what Menander meant, when he told a man who enquired as to the progress of his comedy that he had finished it, not having yet written a single line, because he had constructed the action of it in his mind. A modern critic would have assured him that the merit of his piece depended on the brilliant things which arose under his pen as he went along. We have poems which seem to exist merely for the sake of single lines and passages; not for the sake of producing any total impression. We have critics who seem to direct their attention merely to detached expressions, to the language about the action, not to the action itself. I verily think that the majority of them do not in their hearts believe that there is such a thing as a total impression to be derived from a poem at all, or to be demanded from a poet; they think the term a commonplace of metaphysical criticism. They will permit the poet to select any action he pleases, and to suffer that action to go as it will, provided he gratifies them with occasional bursts of fine writing, and with a shower of isolated thoughts and images. That is, they permit him to leave their poetical sense ungratified, provided that he gratifies their rhetorical sense and their curiosity. Of his neglecting to gratify these, there is little danger. He needs rather to be warned against the danger of attempting to gratify these alone; he needs rather to be perpetually reminded to prefer his action to everything else; so to treat this, as to permit its inherent excellences to develop themselves, without interruption from the intrusion of his personal peculiarities; most fortunate, when he most entirely succeeds in effacing himself, and in enabling a noble action to subsist as it did in nature.

But the modern critic not only permits a false practice; he absolutely prescribes false aims.—'A true allegory of the state of one's own mind in a representative history,' the poet is told, 'is perhaps the highest thing that one can attempt in the way of poetry.'[7] And accordingly he attempts it. An allegory of the state of one's own mind, the highest problem of an art which imitates actions! No assuredly, it is not, it never can be so: no great poetical work has ever been produced with such an aim. *Faust*[8] itself, in which something of the kind is attempted, wonderful passages as it contains, and in spite of the unsurpassed beauty of the scenes which relate to Margaret, *Faust* itself, judged as a whole, and judged strictly as a poetical work, is defective: its illustrious author, the greatest poet of modern times, the greatest critic of all times, would have been the first to acknowledge it; he only defended his work, indeed, by asserting it to be 'something incommensurable.'

The confusion of the present times is great, the multitude of voices counselling different things bewildering, the number of existing works capable of attracting a young writer's attention and of becoming his models, immense. What he wants is a hand to guide him through the confusion, a voice to prescribe to him the aim which he should keep in view, and to explain to him that the value of the literary works

which offer themselves to his attention is relative to their
power of helping him forward on his road towards this aim.
Such a guide the English writer at the present day will
nowhere find. Failing this, all that can be looked for, all
indeed that can be desired, is, that his attention should be
fixed on excellent models; that he may reproduce, at any
rate, something of their excellence, by penetrating himself
with their works and by catching their spirit, if he cannot
be taught to produce what is excellent independently.

Foremost among these models for the English writer
stands Shakespeare: a name the greatest perhaps of all
poetical names; a name never to be mentioned without
reverence. I will venture, however, to express a doubt,
whether the influence of his works, excellent and fruitful
for the readers of poetry, for the great majority, has been
of unmixed advantage to the writers of it. Shakespeare indeed chose excellent subjects; the world could afford no
better than Macbeth, or Romeo and Juliet, or Othello; he
had no theory respecting the necessity of choosing subjects
of present import, or the paramount interest attaching to
allegories of the state of one's own mind; like all great poets,
he knew well what constituted a poetical action; like them,
wherever he found such an action, he took it; like them, too,
he found his best in past times. But to these general characteristics of all great poets he added a special one of his
own; a gift, namely, of happy, abundant, and ingenious
expression, eminent and unrivalled: so eminent as irresistibly to strike the attention first in him, and even to throw
into comparative shade his other excellences as a poet. Here
has been the mischief. These other excellences were his
fundamental excellences *as a poet;* what distinguishes the
artist from the mere amateur, says Goethe, is *Architectonicè*
in the highest sense; that power of execution, which creates,
forms, and constitutes: not the profoundness of single
thoughts, not the richness of imagery, not the abundance
of illustration. But these attractive accessories of a poetical
work being more easily seized than the spirit of the whole,
and these accessories being possessed by Shakespeare in an
unequalled degree, a young writer having recourse to Shakespeare as his model runs great risk of being vanquished and
absorbed by them, and, in consequence, of reproducing, according to the measure of his power, these, and these alone.
Of this preponderating quality of Shakespeare's genius, accordingly, almost the whole of modern English poetry has,
it appears to me, felt the influence. To the exclusive atten-

tion on the part of his imitators to this it is in a great degree owing, that of the majority of modern poetical works the details alone are valuable, the composition worthless. In reading them one is perpetually reminded of that terrible sentence on a modern French poet:—*Il dit tout ce qu'il veut, mais malheureusement il n'a rien à dire.*[9]

Let me give an instance of what I mean. I will take it from the works of the very chief among those who seem to have been formed in the school of Shakespeare: of one whose exquisite genius and pathetic death render him for ever interesting. I will take the poem of *Isabella, or the Pot of Basil,* by Keats. I choose this rather than the *Endymion,* because the latter work (which a modern critic[10] has classed with the *Fairy Queen!*), although undoubtedly there blows through it the breath of genius, is yet as a whole so utterly incoherent, as not strictly to merit the name of a poem at all. The poem of *Isabella,* then, is a perfect treasure-house of graceful and felicitous words and images: almost in every stanza there occurs one of those vivid and picturesque turns of expression, by which the object is made to flash upon the eye of the mind, and which thrill the reader with a sudden delight. This one short poem contains, perhaps, a greater number of happy single expressions which one could quote than all the extant tragedies of Sophocles. But the action, the story? The action in itself is an excellent one; but so feebly is it conceived by the poet, so loosely constructed, that the effect produced by it, in and for itself, is absolutely null. Let the reader, after he has finished the poem of Keats, turn to the same story in the *Decameron:* he will then feel how pregnant and interesting the same action has become in the hands of a great artist, who above all things delineates his object; who subordinates expression to that which it is designed to express.

I have said that the imitators of Shakespeare, fixing their attention on his wonderful gift of expression, have directed their imitation to this, neglecting his other excellences. These excellences, the fundamental excellences of poetical art, Shakespeare no doubt possessed them,—possessed many of them in a splendid degree; but it may perhaps be doubted whether even he himself did not sometimes give scope to his faculty of expression to the prejudice of a higher poetical duty. For we must never forget that Shakespeare is the great poet he is from his skill in discerning and firmly conceiving an excellent action, from his power of intensely feeling a situation, of intimately associating himself with a character;

not from his gift of expression, which rather even leads him astray, degenerating sometimes into a fondness for curiosity of expression, into an irritability of fancy, which seems to make it impossible for him to say a thing plainly, even when the press of the action demands the very directest language, or its level character the very simplest. Mr. Hallam,[11] than whom it is impossible to find a saner and more judicious critic, has had the courage (for at the present day it needs courage) to remark, how extremely and faultily difficult Shakespeare's language often is. It is so: you may find main scenes in some of his greatest tragedies, *King Lear* for instance, where the language is so artificial, so curiously tortured, and so difficult, that every speech has to be read two or three times before its meaning can be comprehended. This over-curiousness of expression is indeed but the excessive employment of a wonderful gift,—of the power of saying a thing in a happier way than any other man; nevertheless, it is carried so far that one understands what M. Guizot[12] meant, when he said that Shakespeare appears in his language to have tried all styles except that of simplicity. He has not the severe and scrupulous self-restraint of the ancients, partly, no doubt, because he had a far less cultivated and exacting audience. He has indeed a far wider range than they had, a far richer fertility of thought; in this respect he rises above them. In his strong conception of his subject, in the genuine way in which he is penetrated with it, he resembles them, and is unlike the moderns. But in the accurate limitation of it, the conscientious rejection of superfluities, the simple and rigorous development of it from the first line of his work to the last, he falls below them, and comes nearer to the moderns. In his chief works, besides what he has of his own, he has the elementary soundness of the ancients; he has their important action and their large and broad manner; but he has not their purity of method. He is therefore a less safe model; for what he has of his own is personal, and inseparable from his own rich nature; it may be imitated and exaggerated, it cannot be learned or applied as an art. He is above all suggestive; more valuable, therefore, to young writers as men than as artists. But clearness of arrangement, rigour of development, simplicity of style,—these may to a certain extent be learned; and these may, I am convinced, be learned best from the ancients, who, although infinitely less suggestive than Shakespeare, are thus, to the artist, more instructive.

What then, it will be asked, are the ancients to be our sole models? the ancients with their comparatively narrow range of experience, and their widely different circumstances? Not, certainly, that which is narrow in the ancients, nor that in which we can no longer sympathise. An action like the action of the *Antigone* of Sophocles, which turns upon the conflict between the heroine's duty to her brother's corpse and that to the laws of her country, is no longer one in which it is possible that we should feel a deep interest. I am speaking too, it will be remembered, not of the best sources of intellectual stimulus for the general reader, but of the best models of instruction for the individual writer. This last may certainly learn of the ancient, better than anywhere else, three things which it is vitally important for him to know:—the all-importance of the choice of a subject; the necessity of accurate construction; and the subordinate character of expression. He will learn from them how unspeakably superior is the effect of the one moral impression left by a great action treated as a whole, to the effect produced by the most striking single thought or by the happiest image. As he penetrates into the spirit of the great classical works, as he becomes gradually aware of their intense significance, their noble simplicity, and their calm pathos, he will be convinced that it is this effect, unity and profoundness of moral impression, at which the ancient poets aimed; that it is this which constitutes the grandeur of their works, and which makes them immortal. He will desire to direct his own efforts towards producing the same effect. Above all, he will deliver himself from the jargon of modern criticism, and escape the danger of producing poetical works conceived in the spirit of the passing time, and which partake of its transitoriness.

The present age makes great claims upon us: we owe it service, it will not be satisfied without our admiration. I know not how it is, but their commerce with the ancients appears to me to produce, in those who constantly practise it, a steadying and composing effect upon their judgment, not of literary works only, but of men and events in general. They are like persons who have had a very weighty and impressive experience: they are more truly than others under the empire of facts, and more independent of the language current among those with whom they live. They wish neither to applaud nor to revile their age; they wish to know what it is, what it can give them, and whether this is what they want. What they want, they know very well; they want to educe and cultivate what is best and noblest in themselves; they know, too, that this is no easy task—χαλεπόν, as Pittacus said, χαλεπὸν ἐσθλὸν ἔμμεναι[13]—and they ask themselves sincerely whether their age and its literature can assist

them in the attempt. If they are endeavouring to practise
any art, they remember the plain and simple proceedings
of the old artists, who attained their grand results by penetrating themselves with some noble and significant action,
not by inflating themselves with a belief in the pre-eminent
importance and greatness of their own times. They do not
talk of their mission, nor of interpreting their age, nor of the
coming poet; all this, they know, is the mere delirium of
vanity; their business is not to praise their age, but to afford
to the men who live in it the highest pleasure which they are
capable of feeling. If asked to afford this by means of subjects drawn from the age itself, they ask what special fitness
the present age has for supplying them. They are told that it
is an era of progress, an age commissioned to carry out the
great ideas of industrial development and social ameliora-
tion. They reply that with all this they can do nothing; that
the elements they need for the exercise of their art are great
actions, calculated powerfully and delightfully to affect what
is permanent in the human soul; that so far as the present
age can supply such actions, they will gladly make use of
them; but that an age wanting in moral grandeur can with
difficulty supply such, and an age of spiritual discomfort
with difficulty be powerfully and delightfully affected by
them.

A host of voices will indignantly rejoin that the present
age is inferior to the past neither in moral grandeur nor in
spiritual health. He who possesses the discipline I speak of
will content himself with remembering the judgments passed
upon the present age, in this respect, by the men of strongest
head and widest culture whom it has produced; by Goethe
and by Niebuhr.[14] It will be sufficient for him that he knows
the opinions held by these two great men respecting the
present age and its literature; and that he feels assured in his
own mind that their aims and demands upon life were such
as he would wish, at any rate, his own to be; and their judgment as to what is impeding and disabling such as he may
safely follow. He will not, however, maintain a hostile attitude towards the false pretensions of his age: he will content himself with not being overwhelmed by them. He will
esteem himself fortunate if he can succeed in banishing from
his mind all feelings of contradiction, and irritation, and impatience; in order to delight himself with the contemplation
of some noble action of a heroic time, and to enable others,
through his representation of it, to delight in it also.

I am far indeed from making any claim, for myself, that
I possess this discipline; or for the following poems, that

they breathe its spirit. But I say, that in the sincere en-deavour to learn and practise, amid the bewildering confu-sion of our times, what is sound and true in poetical art, I seemed to myself to find the only sure guidance, the only solid footing, among the ancients. They, at any rate, knew what they wanted in art, and we do not. It is this uncertainty which is disheartening, and not hostile criticism. How often have I felt this when reading words of disparagement or of cavil: that it is the uncertainty as to what is really to be aimed at which makes our difficulty, not the dissatisfaction of the critic, who himself suffers from the same uncertainty! *Non me tua fervida terrent Dicta; . . . Dii me terrent, et Jupiter hostis.*[15]

Two kinds of *dilettanti,* says Goethe, there are in poetry: he who neglects the indispensable mechanical part, and thinks he has done enough if he shows spirituality and feel-ing; and he who seeks to arrive at poetry merely by mech-anism, in which he can acquire an artisan's readiness, and is without soul and matter. And he adds, that the first does most harm to art, and the last to himself. If we must be *dilettanti:* if it is impossible for us, under the circumstances amidst which we live, to think clearly, to feel nobly, and to delineate firmly: if we cannot attain to the mastery of the great artists;—let us, at least, have so much respect for our art as to prefer it to ourselves. Let us not bewilder our suc-cessors; let us transmit to them the practice of poetry, with its boundaries and wholesome regulative laws, under which excellent works may again, perhaps, at some future time, be produced, not yet fallen into oblivion through our neglect, not yet condemned and cancelled by the influence of their eternal enemy, caprice.

NOTES

Preface to First Edition of Poems: Reprinted in *Irish Essays* (1882). Arnold had published *The Strayed Reveller* (1849), and *Empedocles on Etna* (1852). For his 1853 volume, he withdrew the dramatic poem "Empedocles on Etna," and was not to reprint it till 1867.

1. *Poetics,* alluded to by Arnold throughout the Preface.
2. One of the earliest of Greek poets (8th century B.C.?).
3. J. C. F. von Schiller (1759–1805), German dramatist and poet.
4. By, respectively, Goethe (1797), Byron (1812–18), A. de Lamartine (1836), and Wordsworth (1814).
5. Aeschylus's tetralogy; and Virgil, *Aeneid* IV.
6. Orestes, whose mother Clytemnestra killed his father Aga-memnon; Orestes revenged his father by killing his mother. Merope: see pp. 46–47. Alcmaeon, at the urging of his father Amphiaraus, killed his mother Eriphyle because she had sent Amphiaraus to war knowing he would be killed.

7. From an article apparently by David Masson (though sometimes attributed to J. M. Ludlow), "Theories of Poetry," *North British Review* (August, 1853).

8. Goethe (Part I, 1808; Part II, 1832).

9. *He says all he means to, but unfortunately he has nothing to say.*

10. Masson; see p. 33.

11. Henry Hallam, *Introduction to the Literature of Europe* (1837–39; 2nd ed., 1843).

12. François Guizot's book on Shakespeare (1852).

13. Plato, *Protagoras* 343 C: *It is hard to be good.*

14. B. G. Niebuhr (1766–1831), historian.

15. *Aeneid,* xii.894–95: *Thy fierce words dismay me not . . . the gods dismay me, and Jupiter's enmity.*

PREFACE

TO SECOND EDITION

OF *POEMS*

1854

I HAVE ALLOWED the Preface to the former edition of these Poems to stand almost without change, because I still believe it to be, in the main, true. I must not, however, be supposed insensible to the force of much that has been alleged against portions of it, or unaware that it contains many things incompletely stated, many things which need limitation. It leaves, too, untouched the question, how far and in what manner the opinions there expressed respecting the choice of subjects apply to lyric poetry,—that region of the poetical field which is chiefly cultivated at present. But neither do I propose at the present time to supply these deficiencies, nor, indeed, would this be the proper place for attempting it. On one or two points alone I wish to offer, in the briefest possible way, some explanation.

An objection has been warmly urged to the classing together, as subjects equally belonging to a past time, Œdipus and Macbeth. And it is no doubt true that to Shakespeare, standing on the verge of the middle ages, the epoch of Macbeth was more familiar than that of Œdipus. But I was speaking of actions as they presented themselves to us moderns: and it will hardly be said that the European mind, in our day, has much more affinity with the times of Macbeth than with those of Œdipus. As moderns, it seems to me, we have no longer any direct affinity with the circumstances and feelings of either. As individuals, we are attracted towards this or that personage, we have a capacity for imagining him, irrespective of his times, solely according to a law of personal sympathy; and those subjects for which we feel this personal attraction most strongly, we may hope to treat successfully. Prometheus or Joan or Arc, Charlemagne or Agamemnon,—one of these is not really nearer to us now than another. Each can be made present only by an act of poetic imagination; but this man's imagination has an affinity for one of them, and that man's for another.

It has been said that I wish to limit the poet, in his choice of subjects, to the period of Greek and Roman antiquity; but it is not so. I only counsel him to choose for his subjects great actions, without regarding to what time they belong. Nor do I deny that the poetic faculty can and does manifest itself in treating the most trifling action, the most hopeless subject. But it is a pity that power should be wasted; and that the poet should be compelled to impart interest and force to his subject, instead of receiving them from it, and thereby doubling his impressiveness. There is, it has been excellently said, an immortal strength in the stories of great actions; the most gifted poet, then, may well be glad to supplement with it that mortal weakness, which, in presence of the vast spectacle of life and the world, he must for ever feel to be his individual portion.

Again, with respect to the study of the classical writers of antiquity: it has been said that we should emulate rather than imitate them. I make no objection; all I say is, let us study them. They can help to cure us of what is, it seems to me, the great vice of our intellect, manifesting itself in our incredible vagaries in literature, in art, in religion, in morals: namely, that it is *fantastic*, and wants *sanity*. Sanity,—that is the great virtue of the ancient literature; the want of that is the great defect of the modern, in spite of all its variety and power. It is impossible to read carefully the great ancients, without losing something of our caprice and eccentricity; and to emulate them we must at least read them.

NOTES

Preface to Second Edition of Poems: Reprinted in *Irish Essays* (1882).

"THE GREEK TRAGIC FORMS": *from* PREFACE TO *MEROPE*

1858

I AM NOT about to defend myself for having taken the story of the following tragedy from classical antiquity. On this subject I have already said all which appears to me to be necessary. For those readers to whom my tragedy will give pleasure, no argument on such a matter is required: one critic, whose fine intelligence it would have been an honour to convince, lives, alas! no longer: there are others, upon whom no arguments which I could possibly use would produce any impression. The Athenians fined Phrynichus[1] for representing to them their own sufferings: there are critics who would fine us for representing to them anything else.

But, as often as it has happened to me to be blamed or praised for my supposed addiction to the classical school in poetry, I have thought, with real humiliation, how little any works of mine were entitled to rank among the genuine works of that school; how little they were calculated to give, to readers unacquainted with the great creations of classical antiquity, any adequate impression of their form or of their spirit. And yet, whatever the critics may say, there exists, I am convinced, even in England, even in this stronghold of the romantic school, a wide though an ill-informed curiosity on the subject of the so-called classical school, meriting a more complete satisfaction than it has hitherto obtained. Greek art—the antique—classical beauty—a nameless hope

and interest attaches, I can often see, to these words, even
in the minds of those who have been brought up among the
productions of the romantic school; of those who have been
taught to consider classicalism as inseparable from coldness,
and the antique as another phrase for the unreal. So immortal, so indestructible is the power of true beauty, of consummate form: it may be submerged, but the tradition of it
survives: nations arise which know it not, which hardly believe in the report of it; but they, too, are haunted with an
indefinable interest in its name, with an inexplicable curiosity as to its nature.

But however the case may be with regard to the curiosity
of the public, I have long had the strongest desire to attempt,
for my own satisfaction, to come to closer quarters with the
form which produces such grand effects in the hands of the
Greek masters; to try to obtain, through the medium of a
living, familiar language, a fuller and more intense feeling of
that beauty, which, even when apprehended through the
medium of a dead language, so powerfully affected me. In
his delightful *Life of Goethe*,[2] Mr. Lewes has most truly observed that Goethe's *Iphigeneia* enjoys an inestimable advantage in being written in a language which, being a modern
language, is in some sort our own. Not only is it vain to
expect that the vast majority of mankind will ever undertake
the toil of mastering a dead language, above all, a dead
language so difficult as the Greek; but it may be doubted
whether even those, whose enthusiasm shrinks from no toil,
can ever so thoroughly press into the intimate feeling of
works composed in a dead language as their enthusiasm
would desire.

I desired to try, therefore, how much of the effectiveness
of the Greek poetical forms I could retain in an English
poem constructed under the conditions of those forms; of
those forms, too, in their severest and most definite expression, in their application to dramatic poetry.

I thought at first that I might accomplish my object by a
translation of one of the great works of Æschylus or Sophocles. But a translation is a work not only inferior to the
original by the whole difference of talent between the first
composer and his translator: it is even inferior to the best
which the translator could do under more inspiring circumstances. No man can do his best with a subject which does
not penetrate him: no man can be penetrated by a subject
which he does not conceive independently.

Should I take some subject on which we have an extant

work by one of the great Greek poets, and treat it independently? Something was to be said for such a course: in antiquity, the same tragic stories were handled by all the tragic poets: Voltaire says truly that to see the same materials differently treated by different poets is most interesting; accordingly, we have an *Œdipus* of Corneille, an *Œdipus* of Voltaire: innumerable are the *Agamemnons,* the *Electras,* the *Antigones,* of the French and Italian poets from the sixteenth to the nineteenth century. But the same disadvantage which we have in translating clings to us in our attempt to treat these subjects independently: their treatment by the ancient masters is so overwhelmingly great and powerful that we can henceforth conceive them only as they are there treated: an independent conception of them has become impossible for us: in working upon them we are still, therefore, subject to conditions under which no man can do his best.

It remained to select a subject among those which had been considered to possess the true requisites of good tragic subjects; on which great works had been composed, but had not survived to chill emulation by their grandeur. Of such subjects there is, fortunately, no lack. In the writings of Hyginus, a Latin mythographer of uncertain date, we possess a large stock of them. The heroic stories in Hyginus, Maffei,[3] the reformer of the Italian theatre, imagined rightly or wrongly to be the actual summaries of lost Greek dramas: they are, at any rate, subjects on which lost dramas were founded. Maffei counsels the poets of his nation to turn from the inferior subjects on which they were employing themselves, to this *"miniera di tragici argomenti,"* this rich mine of subjects for tragedy. Lessing, the great German critic, echoes Maffei's counsel, but adds a warning. "Yes," he cries, "the great subjects are there, but they await an intelligent eye to regard them: they can be handled, not by the great majority of poets, but only by the small minority."

Among these subjects presented in the collection of Hyginus, there is one which has long attracted my interest, from the testimony of the ancients to its excellence, and from the results which that testimony has called forth from the emulation of the moderns. That subject is the story of Merope. To the effectiveness of the situations which this story offered, Aristotle and Plutarch have borne witness: a celebrated tragedy upon it, probably by Euripides, existed in antiquity. "The *Cresphontes* of Euripides is lost," exclaims the reviewer of Voltaire's *Merope,* a jesuit, and not unwilling to conciliate the terrible pupil of his order; "the *Cresphontes*

of Euripides is lost: M. de Voltaire has restored it to us."
"Aristotle," says Voltaire, "Aristotle, in his immortal work
on Poetry, does not hesitate to affirm that the recognition
between Merope and her son was the most interesting moment of the Greek stage." Aristotle affirms no such thing;
but he *does* say that the story of Merope, like the stories of
Iphigeneia and Antiope, supplies an example of a recognition of the most affecting kind. And Plutarch says: "Look at
Merope in the tragedy, lifting up the axe against her own
son as being the murderer of her own son, and crying—

> ὁσιωτέραν δὴ τήνδ' ἐγὼ δίδωμί σοι
> πληγήν ——

> A more just stroke than that thou gav'st my son,
> Take—

What an agitation she makes in the theatre! how she fills the
spectators with terror lest she should be too quick for the old
man who is trying to stop her, and should strike the lad!"

It is singular that neither Aristotle nor Plutarch names the
author of the tragedy: scholiasts and other late writers quote
from it as from a work of Euripides; but the only writer of
authority who names him as its author is Cicero. About fifty
lines of it have come down to us: the most important of
these remains are the passage just quoted, and a choral address to Peace; of these I have made use in my tragedy,
translating the former, and of the latter adopting the general
thought, that of rejoicing at the return of peace: the other
fragments consist chiefly of detached moral sentences, of
which I have not made any use.

It may be interesting to give some account of the more
celebrated of those modern works which have been founded
upon this subject. But before I proceed to do this, I will state
what accounts we have of the story itself.

These proceed from three sources—Apollodorus, Pausanias, and Hyginus. Of their accounts that of Apollodorus is
the most ancient, that of Pausanias the most historically
valuable, and that of Hyginus the fullest. I will begin with
the last-named writer.

Hyginus says:—

"Merope sent away and concealed her infant son. Polyphontes sought for him everywhere, and promised gold to
whoever should slay him. He, when he grew up, laid a plan
to avenge the murder of his father and brothers. In pursuance of this plan he came to king Polyphontes and asked

for the promised gold, saying that he had slain the son of Cresphontes and Merope. The king ordered him to be hospitably entertained, intending to inquire further of him. He, being very tired, went to sleep, and an old man, who was the channel through whom the mother and son used to communicate, arrives at this moment in tears, bringing word to Merope that her son had disappeared from his protector's house. Merope, believing that the sleeping stranger is the murderer of her son, comes into the guest-chamber with an axe, not knowing that he whom she would slay was her son: the old man recognised him, and withheld Merope from slaying him. After the recognition had taken place, Merope, to prepare the way for her vengeance, affected to be reconciled with Polyphontes. The king, overjoyed, celebrated a sacrifice: his guest, pretending to strike the sacrificial victim, slew the king, and so got back his father's kingdom."

* * *

What is the real merit of Voltaire's tragedy? We must forget the rhymed Alexandrines; that metre, faulty not so much because it is disagreeable in itself, as because it has in it something which is essentially unsuited to perfect tragedy; that metre which is so indefensible, and which Voltaire has so ingeniously laboured to defend. He takes a noble passage from Racine's *Phèdre*, alters words so as to remove the rhyme, and asks if the passage now produces as good an effect as before. But a fine passage which we are used to we like in the form in which we are used to it, with all its faults. Prose is, undoubtedly, a less noble vehicle for tragedy than verse; yet we should not like the fine passages in Goethe's prose tragedy of *Egmont* the better for having them turned into verse. Besides, it is not clear that the unrhymed Alexandrine is a better tragic metre than the rhymed. Voltaire says that usage has now established the metre in France, and that the dramatic poet has no escape from it. For him and his contemporaries this is a valid plea; but how much one regrets that the poetical feeling of the French nation did not, at a period when such an alteration was still possible, change for a better this unsuitable tragic metre, as the Greeks, in the early period of their tragic art, changed for the more fitting iambus their trochaic tetrameter.

To return to Voltaire's *Merope*. It is admirably constructed, and must have been most effective on the stage. One feels, as one reads it, that a poet gains something by living amongst a population who have the nose of the rhinoceros: his ingenuity becomes sharpened. This work has, be-

sides, that stamp of a prodigious talent which none of
Voltaire's works are without; it has vigour, clearness, rapid
movement; it has lines which are models of terse observation—

> Le premier qui fut roi fut un soldat heureux:
> Qui sert bien son pays n'a pas besoin d'aïeux."[4]

It has lines which are models of powerful, animated, rhetoric—

MÉROPE

"Courons à Polyphonte—implorons son appui."

NARBAS

"N'implorez que les dieux, et ne craignez que lui."[5]

What it wants is a charm of poetical feeling, which Racine's
tragedies possess, and which has given to them the decisive
superiority over those of Voltaire. He has managed his story
with great adroitness; but he has departed from the original
tradition yet further than Maffei. He has avoided several of
Maffei's faults: why has he not avoided his fault of omitting
to introduce, at the moment of recognition, a scene between
the mother and son? Lessing thinks that he wanted the double recognition in order to enable him to fill his prescribed
space, that terrible "carrière de cinq actes" of which he so
grievously complains. I believe, rather, that he cut the recognition in two, in order to produce for his audience two distinct shocks of surprise: for to inspire *surprise,* Voltaire considered the dramatic poet's true aim; an opinion which, as
we shall hereafter see, sometimes led him astray.

*   *   *

A mistake, a grave mistake it seems to me, in the treatment of their subject, is common to Maffei, Voltaire, and
Alfieri. They have abandoned the tradition where they had
better have followed it; they have followed it, where they
had better have abandoned it.

The tradition is a great matter to a poet; it is an unspeak-
able support; it gives him the feeling that he is treading on
solid ground. Aristotle tells the tragic poet that he must not
destroy the received stories.[6] A noble and accomplished living poet, M. Manzoni,[7] has, in an admirable dissertation, developed this thesis of the importance to the poet of a basis of
tradition. Its importance I feel so strongly, that, where driven
to invent in the false story told by Merope's son, as by
Orestes in the *Electra,* of his own death, I could not satisfy
myself until I discovered in Pausanias a tradition, which I

took for my basis, of an Arcadian hunter drowned in the lake Stymphalus, down one of those singular Katabothra, or chasms in the limestone rock, so well known in Greece, in a manner similar to that in which Æpytus is represented to have perished.

Maffei did right, I think, in altering the ancient tradition where it represents Merope as actually the wife of Polyphontes. It revolts our feeling to consider her as married to her husband's murderer; and it is no great departure from the tradition to represent her as sought in marriage by him, but not yet obtained. But why did Maffei (for he, it will be remembered, gave the story its modern arrangement, which Voltaire and Alfieri have, in all its leading points, followed), why did Maffei abandon that part of the tradition which represents Æpytus, the Messenian prince, as acquainted with his own origin? Why did he and his followers prefer to attribute to curiosity a return which the tradition attributed to a far more tragic motive? Why did they compel themselves to invent a machinery of robbers, assassins, guards, rings, girdles, and I know not what, to effect that which the tradition effects in a far simpler manner, to place Æpytus before his mother as his own murderer? Lessing imagines that Maffei, who wished to depict, above all, the maternal anxiety of Merope, conceived that this anxiety would be more naturally and powerfully awakened by the thought of her child reared in hardship and obscurity as a poor man's son, than by the thought of him reared in splendour as a prince in the palace of her own father. But what a conception of the sorrow of a queen, whose husband has been murdered, and whose son is an exile from his inheritance, to suppose that such a sorrow is enhanced by the thought that her child is rudely housed and plainly fed; to assume that it would take a less tragic complexion if she knew that he lived in luxury! No; the true tragic motive of Merope's sorrow is elsewhere: the tradition amply supplied it.

Here, then, the moderns have invented amiss, because they have invented needlessly; because, on this point, the tradition, as it stood, afforded perfect materials to the tragic poet: and, by Maffei's change, not a higher tragic complication, but merely a greater puzzle and intricacy is produced. I come now to a point on which the tradition might with advantage, as I think, have been set aside; and that is, the character of Polyphontes.

Yet, on this point, to speak of *setting aside the tradition* is to speak too strongly; for the tradition is here not complete. Neither Pausanias nor Apollodorus mention circumstances which definitely fix the character of Polyphontes; Hyginus, no doubt, represents him as a villain, and, if Hyginus follows Euripides, Euripides also thus represented him. Euripides may possibly have done so; yet a purer tragic feeling, it seems to me, is produced, if Polyphontes is represented as not wholly black and inexcusable, than if he is represented as a mere monster of cruelty and hypocrisy. Aristotle's profound remark is well known, that the tragic personage whose ruin is represented, should be a personage neither eminently good, nor yet one brought to ruin by sheer iniquity; nay, that his character should incline rather to good than to bad, but that he should have some fault which impels him to his fall. For, as he explains, the two grand tragic feelings, pity and terror, which it is the business of tragedy to excite, will not be excited by the spectacle of the ruin of a mere villain; since pity is for those who suffer undeservedly, and such a man suffers deservedly: terror is excited by the fall of one of like nature with ourselves, and we feel that the mere villain is not as ourselves. Aristotle, no doubt, is here speaking, above all, of the Protagonist, or principal personage of the drama; but the noblest tragic poets of Greece rightly extended their application of the truth on which his remark is based to all the personages of the drama: neither the Creon of Sophocles, nor the Clytemnestra of Æschylus, are wholly inexcusable; in none of the extant dramas of Æschylus or Sophocles is there a character which is entirely bad. For such a character we must go to Euripides; we must go to an art—wonderful indeed, for I entirely dissent from the unreserved disparagers of this great poet—but an art of less moral significance than the art of Sophocles and Æschylus; we must go to tragedies like the *Hecuba*, for villains like Polymestor.

What is the main dramatic difficulty of the story of Merope, as usually treated? It is, as Alfieri rightly saw, that the interest naturally declines from the moment of Merope's recognition of her son; that the destruction of the tyrant is not, after this, matter of interest enough to affect us deeply. This is true, if Polyphontes is a mere villain. It is not true, if he is one for the ruin of whom we may, in spite of his crime, feel a profound compassion. Then our interest in the story lasts to the end: for to the very end we are inspired with the powerful tragic emotions of commiseration and awe. Pausanias states circumstances which suggest the possibility of representing Polyphontes, not as a mere cruel and selfish tyrant, but as a man whose crime was a truly tragic fault, the error of a noble nature. Assume such a nature in him, and the turn of circumstances in the drama takes a new aspect: Merope and her son triumph, but the fall of their foe leaves us awestruck and compassionate: the story issues *tragically*, as Aristotle has truly said that the best tragic stories ought to issue.

Neither Maffei, nor Voltaire, nor Alfieri have drawn Polyphontes with a character to inspire any feeling but aversion, with any traits of nobleness to mitigate our satisfaction at his death. His character being such, it is difficult to render his anxiety to obtain Merope's hand intelligible, for Merope's situation is not such as to make her enmity really dangerous to Polyphontes; he has, therefore, no sufficient motive of self-interest, and the nobler motives of reparation and pacification could have exercised, on such a character, no force. Voltaire accordingly, whose keen eye no weak place of this kind escaped, felt his difficulty. "Neither M. Maffei nor I," he confesses, "have assigned any sufficient motives for the desire of Polyphontes to marry Merope."

To criticise is easier than to create; and if I have been led, in this review of the fortunes of my story, to find fault with the works of others, I do not on that account assume that I have myself produced a work which is not a thousand times more faulty.

It remains to say something, for those who are not familiar with the Greek dramatic forms, of the form in which this tragedy is cast. Greek tragedy, as is well known, took its origin from the songs of a chorus, and the stamp of its origin remained for ever impressed upon it. A chorus, or band of dancers, moving around the altar of Bacchus, sang the adventures of the god. To this band Thespis joined an actor, who held dialogue with the chorus, and who was called ὑποκριτὴς, *the answerer*, because he answered the songs of the chorus. The drama thus commenced; for the dialogue of this actor with the chorus brought before the audience some action of Bacchus, or of one of the heroes; this action, narrated by the actor, was commented on in song, at certain intervals, by the chorus alone. Æschylus added a second actor, thus making the character of the representation more *dramatic*, for the chorus was never itself so much an actor as a hearer and observer of the actor: Sophocles added a third. These three actors might successively personate several characters in the same piece; but to three actors and a chorus the dramatic poet limited himself: only in a single piece of Sophocles,[8] not brought out until after his death, was the employment of a fourth actor, it appears, necessary.

The chorus consisted, in the time of Sophocles, of fifteen

persons. After their first entrance they remained before the spectators, without withdrawing, until the end of the piece. Their place was in the orchestra; that of the actors was upon the stage. The orchestra was a circular space, like the pit of our theatres: the chorus arrived in it by side-entrances, and not by the stage. In the centre of the orchestra was the altar of Bacchus, around which the chorus originally danced; but in dramatic representations their place was between this altar and the stage: here they stood, a little lower than the persons on the stage, but looking towards them, and holding, through their leaders, conversation with them: then, at pauses in the action, the united chorus sang songs expressing their feelings at what was happening upon the stage, making, as they sang, certain measured stately movements between the stage and the altar, and occasionally standing still. Steps led from the orchestra to the stage, and the chorus, or some members of it, might thus, if necessary, join the actors on the stage; but this seldom happened, the proper place for the chorus was the orchestra. The dialogue of the chorus with the actors on the stage passed generally in the ordinary form of dramatic dialogue; but, on occasions where strong feeling was excited, the dialogue took a lyrical form. Long dialogues of this kind sometimes took place between the leaders of the chorus and one of the actors upon the stage, their burden being a lamentation for the dead.

The Greek theatres were vast, and open to the sky; the actors, masked, and in a somewhat stiff tragic costume, were to be regarded from a considerable distance: a solemn, clearly marked style of gesture, a sustained tone of declamation, were thus rendered necessary. Under these conditions, intricate by-play, rapid variations in the action, requiring great mobility, ever-changing shades of tone and gesture in the actor, were impossible. Broad and simple effects were, under these conditions, above all to be aimed at; a profound and clear impression was to be effected. Unity of plan in the action, and symmetry in the treatment of it, were indispensable. The action represented, therefore, was to be a single, rigorously developed action; the masses of the composition were to be balanced, each bringing out the other into stronger and distincter relief. In the best tragedies, not only do the divisions of the full choral songs accurately correspond to one another, but the divisions of the lyrical dialogue, nay, even the divisions of the regular dramatic dialogue, form corresponding members, of which one member is the answer, the counter-stroke to the other; and an indescribable sense of distinctness and depth of impression is thus produced.

From what has been said, the reader will see that the Greek tragic forms were not chosen as being, in the nature of things, the best tragic forms; such would be a wholly false conception of them. They are an adaptation to dramatic purposes, under certain theatrical conditions, of forms previously existing for other purposes; that adaptation at which the Greeks, after several stages of improvement, finally rested. The laws of Greek tragic art, therefore, are not exclusive; they are for Greek dramatic art itself, but they do not pronounce other modes of dramatic art unlawful; they are, at most, *prophecies of the improbability of dramatic success under other conditions.* "Tragedy," says Aristotle, in a remarkable passage, "after going through many changes, got the nature which suited it, and there it stopped. Whether or no the kinds of tragedy are yet exhausted," he presently adds, "tragedy being considered either in itself, or in respect to the stage, I shall not now inquire." Travelling in a certain path, the spirit of man arrived at Greek tragedy; travelling in other paths, it may arrive at other kinds of tragedy.

But it cannot be denied that the Greek tragic forms, although not the only possible tragic forms, satisfy, in the most perfect manner, some of the most urgent demands of the human spirit. If, on the one hand, the human spirit demands variety and the widest possible range, it equally demands, on the other hand, depth and concentration in its impressions. Powerful thought and emotion, flowing in strongly marked channels, make a stronger impression: this is the main reason why a metrical form is a more effective vehicle for them than prose: in prose there is more freedom, but, in the metrical form, the very limit gives a sense of precision and emphasis. This sense of emphatic distinctness in our impressions rises, as the thought and emotion swell higher and higher without over-flowing their boundaries, to a lofty sense of the mastery of the human spirit over its own stormiest agitations; and this, again, conducts us to a state of feeling which it is the highest aim of tragedy to produce, to *a sentiment of sublime acquiescence in the course of fate, and in the dispensations of human life.*

What has been said explains, I think, the reason of the effectiveness of the severe forms of Greek tragedy, with its strongly marked boundaries, with its recurrence, even in the most agitating situations, of mutually replying masses of metrical arrangement. Sometimes the agitation becomes overwhelming, and the correspondence is for a time lost, the torrent of feeling flows for a space without check: this disorder amid the general order produces a powerful effect; but the balance is restored before the tragedy closes: the final sentiment in the mind must be one not of trouble, but of acquiescence.

This sentiment of acquiescence is, no doubt, a sentiment of *repose;* and, therefore, I cannot agree with Mr. Lewes when he says, in his remarks on Goethe's *Iphigeneia,* that "the Greek Drama is distinguished by its absence of repose; by the currents of passion being for ever kept in agitation." I entirely agree, however, in his criticism of Goethe's tragedy; of that noble poem which Schiller so exactly characterised when he said that it was "full of soul:" I entirely agree with him when he says that "the tragic situation in the story of Iphigeneia is not touched by Goethe; that his tragedy addresses the conscience rather than the emotions." But Goethe does not err from Greek ideas when he thinks that there is repose in tragedy: he errs from Greek practice in the mode in which he strives to produce that repose. Sophocles does not produce the sentiment of repose, of acquiescence, by inculcating it, by avoiding agitating circumstances: he produces it by exhibiting to us the most agitating matter under the conditions of the severest form. Goethe has truly recognised that this sentiment is the grand final effect of Greek tragedy: but he produces it, not in the manner of Sophocles, but, as Mr. Lewes has most ably pointed out, in a manner of his own; he produces it by inculcating it; by avoiding agitating matter; by keeping himself in the domain of the soul and conscience, not in that of the passions.

I have now to speak of the chorus; for of this, as of the other forms of Greek tragedy, it is not enough, considering how Greek tragedy arose, to show that the Greeks used it; it is necessary to show that it is effective. Johnson[9] says, that "it could only be by long prejudice and the bigotry of learning that Milton could prefer the ancient tragedies, with their encumbrance of a chorus, to the exhibitions of the French and English stages:" and his tragedy of *Irene* sufficiently proves that he himself, in his practice, adopted Greek art as arranged at Paris, by those

> "Juges plus éclairés que ceux qui dans Athène
> Firent naître et fleurir les lois de Melpomène;"[10]

as Voltaire calls them in the prologue to his *Éryphile.* Johnson merely calls the chorus an encumbrance. Voltaire, who, in his *Œdipus,* had made use of the chorus in a singular manner, argued, at a later period, against its introduction. Voltaire is always worth listening to, because his keenness of remark is always suggestive. "In an interesting piece the intrigue generally requires," says Voltaire, "that the principal actors should have secrets to tell one another—*Eh! le moyen de dire son secret à tout un peuple*. And, if the songs of the chorus allude to what has already happened, they must," he says, "be tiresome; if they allude to what is about to happen, their effect will be to *dérober le plaisir de la surprise*." How ingenious, and how entirely in Voltaire's manner! The sense to be appealed to in tragedy is *curiosity;* the impression to be awakened in us is *surprise*. But the Greeks thought differently. For them, the aim of tragedy was *profound moral impression:* and the ideal spectator, as Schlegel and Müller have called the chorus, was designed to enable the actual spectator to feel his own impressions more distinctly and more deeply. The chorus was, at each stage in the action, to collect and weigh the impressions which the action would at that stage naturally make on a pious and thoughtful mind; and was at last, at the end of the tragedy, when the issue of the action appeared, to strike the final balance. If the feeling with which the actual spectator regarded the course of the tragedy could be deepened by reminding him of what was past, or by indicating to him what was to come, it was the province of the ideal spectator so to deepen it. To combine, to harmonise, to deepen for the spectator the feelings naturally excited in him by the sight of what was passing upon the stage—this is one grand effect produced by the chorus in Greek tragedy.

There is another. Coleridge observes that Shakespeare, after one of his grandest scenes, often plunges, as if to relax and relieve himself, into a scene of buffoonery. After tragic situations of the greatest intensity, a desire for relief and relaxation is no doubt natural, both to the poet and to the spectator; but the finer feeling of the Greeks found this relief, not in buffoonery, but in lyrical song. The noble and natural relief from the emotion produced by tragic events is in the transition to the emotion produced by lyric poetry, not in the contrast and shock of a totally opposite order of feelings. The relief afforded to excited feeling by lyrical song every one has experienced at the opera: the delight and facility of this relief renders so universal the popularity of the opera, of this *"beau monstre,"* which still, as in Voltaire's time, *"étouffe Melpomène."*[11] But in the opera, the lyrical element, the element of feeling and relaxation, is in excess: the dramatic element, the element of intellect and labour, is in defect. In the best Greek tragedy, the lyrical element occupies its true place; it is the relief and solace in the stress and conflict of the action; it is not the substantive business.

Few can have read the *Samson Agonistes* of Milton without feeling that the chorus imparts a peculiar and noble effect to that poem; but I regret that Milton determined, induced probably by his preference for Euripides, to adopt, in the songs of the chorus, "the measure," as he himself says, "called by the Greeks Monostrophic, or rather Apolelymenon, without regard had to Strophe, Antistrophe, or Epode." In this relaxed form of the later Greek tragedy, the means are sacrificed by which the chorus could produce, within the limits of a single choric song, the same effect which it was their business, as we have seen, to produce in the tragedy as a whole. The regular correspondence of part with part, the antithesis, in answering stanzas, of thought to thought, feeling to feeling, with the balance of the whole struck in one independent final stanza or epode, is lost; something of the peculiar distinctness and symmetry, which constitute the vital force of the Greek tragic forms, is thus forfeited. The story of Samson, although it has no mystery or complication, to inspire, like tragic stories of the most perfect kind, a foreboding and anxious gloom in the mind of him who hears it, is yet a truly dramatic and noble one; but the forms of Greek tragedy, which are founded on Greek manners, on the practice of chorus-dancing, and on the ancient habitual transaction of affairs in the open air in front of the dwellings of kings, are better adapted to Greek stories than to Hebrew or any other. These reserves being made, it is impossible to praise the *Samson Agonistes* too highly: it is great with all the greatness of Milton. Goethe might well say to Eckermann, after re-reading it, that hardly any work had been composed so entirely in the spirit of the ancients.

Milton's drama has the true oratorical flow of ancient tragedy, produced mainly, I think, by his making it, as the Greeks made it, the rule, not the exception, to put the pause at the end of the line, not in the middle. Shakespeare has some noble passages, particularly in his *Richard the Third,* constructed with this, the true oratorical rhythm; indeed, that wonderful poet, who has so much besides rhetoric, is also the greatest poetical rhetorician since Euripides: still, it is to the Elizabethan poets that we owe the bad habit, in dramatic poetry, of perpetually dividing the line in the middle. Italian tragedy has the same habit: in Alfieri's plays it is intolerable. The constant occurrence of such lines produces, not a sense of variety, but a sense of perpetual interruption.

Some of the measures used in the choric songs of my tragedy are ordinary measures of English verse: others are not so; but it must not be supposed that these last are the reproduction of any Greek choric measures. So to adapt Greek measures to English verse is impossible: what I have done is to try to follow rhythms which produced on my own feeling a similar impression to that produced on it by the rhythms of Greek choric poetry. In such an endeavour, when the ear is guided solely by its own feeling, there is, I know, a continual risk of failure and of offence. I believe, however, that there are no existing English measures which produce the same effect on the ear, and therefore on the mind, as that produced by many measures indispensable to the nature of Greek lyric poetry. He, therefore, who would obtain certain effects obtained by that poetry, is driven to invent new measures, whether he will or no.

Pope and Dryden felt this. Pope composed two choruses for the Duke of Buckingham's *Brutus,* a tragedy altered from Shakespeare, and performed at Buckingham-house. A short specimen will show what these choruses were—

> "Love's purer flames the Gods approve:
> The Gods and Brutus bend to love:
> Brutus for absent Portia sighs,
> And sterner Cassius melts at Junia's eyes."

In this style he proceeds for eight lines more, and then the antistrophe duly follows. Pope felt that the peculiar effects of Greek lyric poetry were here missed; the measure in itself makes them impossible: in his ode on St. Cecilia's day, accordingly, he tries to come nearer to the Greeks. Here is a portion of his fourth stanza; of one of those stanzas in which Johnson thinks that "we have all that can be performed by sweetness of diction, or elegance of versification:"[12]

> "Dreadful gleams,
> Dismal screams,
> Fires that glow,
> Shrieks of woe,
> Sullen moans,
> Hollow groans,
> And cries of tortured ghosts."

Horrible! yet how dire must have been the necessity, how strong the feeling of the inadequacy of existing metres to produce effects demanded, which could drive a man of Pope's taste to such prodigies of invention! Dryden in his "Alexander's Feast" deviates less from ordinary English measures; but to deviate from them in some degree he was compelled. My admiration for Dryden's genius is warm: my delight in this incomparable ode, the mighty son of his old age, is unbounded: but it seems to me that in only one stanza and chorus of the "Alexander's Feast," the fourth, does the rhythm from first to last completely satisfy the ear.

I must have wearied my reader's patience: but I was desirous, in laying before him my tragedy, that it should not lose what benefit it can derive from the foregoing explanations. To his favourable reception of it there will still be obstacles enough, in its unfamiliar form, and in the incapacity of its author.

How much do I regret that the many poets of the present day who possess that capacity which I have not, should not have forestalled me in an endeavour far beyond my powers! How gladly should I have applauded their better success in the attempt to enrich with what, in the forms of the most perfectly-formed literature in the world, is most perfect, our noble English literature; to extend its boundaries in the one direction, in which, with all its force and variety, it has not yet advanced! They would have lost nothing by such an attempt, and English literature would have gained much.

Only their silence could have emboldened to undertake it one with inadequate time, inadequate knowledge, and a talent, alas! still more inadequate: one who brings to the task none of the requisite qualifications of genius or learning: nothing but a passion for the great Masters, and an effort to study them without fancifulness.

NOTES

"*The Greek Tragic Forms*": from *Preface to* Merope: Arnold's classical verse-tragedy was published in December, 1857 (title-page "1858"), with this Preface, which was not reprinted by Arnold. He compares his treatment of the legend with that in Maffei's *Merope* (1713), Voltaire's *Mérope* (1743), and Alfieri's *Merope* (1785).

1. Herodotus tells that this happened to the dramatist Phrynichus (R. H. Super).
2. G. H. Lewes (1855).
3. F. S. Maffei (1675–1755), Italian scholar and dramatist.
4. I. iii: *The first man who became king was a successful soldier; a man who serves his country well has no need of ancestors.*
5. III. v: "*Let us run to Polyphonte—let us beseech his support.*" "*Beseech none but the gods, and fear none but him.*"

6. R. H. Super notes: "Aristotle did not say this explicitly; his remarks on the use of 'received stories' are made in *Poetics* 9.6-9 and 13.5."

7. Alessandro Manzoni (1785–1873).

8. *Oedipus at Colonus.*

9. *Life of Milton.*

10. *Judges more enlightened than those who in Athens made the laws of Melpomene (the muse of tragedy) to be born and flourish.*

11. *Beautiful monster (which) stifles Melpomene.*

12. *Life of Pope* (transposing "sweetness" and "elegance," as R. H. Super notes).

"THE HIGHEST POWERS OF POETRY": *from* MAURICE DE GUÉRIN

1863

THE GRAND power of poetry is its interpretative power; by which I mean, not a power of drawing out in black and white an explanation of the mystery of the universe, but the power of so dealing with things as to awaken in us a wonderfully full, new, and intimate sense of them, and of our relations with them. When this sense is awakened in us, as to objects without us, we feel ourselves to be in contact with the essential nature of those objects, to be no longer bewildered and oppressed by them, but to have their secret, and to be in harmony with them; and this feeling calms and satisfies us as no other can. Poetry, indeed, interprets in another way besides this; but one of its two ways of interpreting, of exercising its highest power, is by awakening this sense in us. I will not now inquire whether this sense is illusive, whether it can be proved not to be illusive, whether it does absolutely make us possess the real nature of things; all I say is, that poetry can awaken it in us, and that to awaken it is one of the highest powers of poetry. The interpretations of science do not give us this intimate sense of objects as the interpretations of poetry give it; they appeal to a limited faculty, and not to the whole man. It is not Linnæus or Cavendish or Cuvier who gives us the true sense of animals, or water, or plants, who seizes their secret for us, who makes us participate in their life; it is Shakespeare, with his

> "daffodils
> That come before the swallow dares, and take
> The winds of March with beauty;"[1]

it is Wordsworth, with his

> "voice . . . heard
> In spring-time from the cuckoo-bird,
> Breaking the silence of the seas
> Among the farthest Hebrides;"[2]

it is Keats, with his

> "moving waters at their priestlike task
> Of cold ablution round Earth's human shores;"[3]

it is Chateaubriand,[4] with his *"cîme indéterminée des forêts"*; it is Senancour,[5] with his mountain birch-tree: *"Cette écorce blanche, lisse et crevassée; cette tige agreste; ces branches qui s'inclinent vers la terre; la mobilité des feuilles, et tout cet abandon, simplicité de la nature, attitude des déserts."*

Eminent manifestations of this magical power of poetry are very rare and very precious: the compositions of Guérin manifest it, I think, in singular eminence. Not his poems, strictly so called,—his verse,—so much as his prose; his poems in general take for their vehicle that favourite metre of French poetry, the Alexandrine; and, in my judgment, I confess they have thus, as compared with his prose, a great disadvantage to start with. In prose, the character of the vehicle for the composer's thoughts is not determined beforehand; every composer has to make his own vehicle; and who has ever done this more admirably than the great prose-writers of France,—Pascal, Bossuet, Fénelon, Voltaire? But in verse the composer has (with comparatively narrow liberty of modification) to accept his vehicle ready-made; it is therefore of vital importance to him that he should find at his disposal a vehicle adequate to convey the highest matters of poetry. We may even get a decisive test of the poetical power of a language and nation by ascertaining how far the principal poetical vehicle which they have employed, how far (in plainer words) the established national metre for high poetry, is adequate or inadequate. It seems to me that the established metre of this kind in France,—the Alexandrine,—is inadequate; that as a vehicle for high poetry it is greatly inferior to the hexameter or to the iambics of Greece (for example), or to the blank verse of England. Therefore the man of genius who uses it is at a disadvantage as compared with the man of genius who has for conveying his thoughts a more adequate vehicle, metrical or not. Racine is at a disadvantage as compared with Sophocles or Shakespeare, and he is likewise at a disadvantage as compared with Bossuet.

The same may be said of our own poets of the eighteenth century, a century which gave them as the main vehicle for their high poetry a metre inadequate (as much as the French Alexandrine, and nearly in the same way) for this poetry,— the ten-syllable couplet. It is worth remarking, that the English poet of the eighteenth century whose compositions wear best and give one the most entire satisfaction,—Gray,— hardly uses that couplet at all: this abstinence, however, limits Gray's productions to a few short compositions, and (exquisite as these are) he is a poetical nature repressed and without free issue. For English poetical production on a great scale, for an English poet deploying all the forces of his genius, the ten-syllable couplet was, in the eighteenth century, the established, one may almost say the inevitable, channel. Now this couplet, admirable (as Chaucer uses it) for story-telling not of the epic pitch, and often admirable for a few lines even in poetry of a very high pitch, is for continuous use in poetry of this latter kind inadequate. Pope, in his *Essay on Man*, is thus at a disadvantage compared with Lucretius in his poem on Nature: Lucretius has an adequate vehicle, Pope has not. Nay, though Pope's genius for didactic poetry was not less than that of Horace, while his satirical power was certainly greater, still one's taste receives, I cannot but think, a certain satisfaction when one reads the Epistles and Satires of Horace, which it fails to receive when one reads the Satires and Epistles of Pope. Of such avail is the superior adequacy of the vehicle used to compensate even an inferiority of genius in the user! In the same way Pope is at a disadvantage as compared with Addison. The best of Addison's composition (the "Coverley Papers" in the *Spectator*, for instance) wears better than the best of Pope's, because Addison has in his prose an intrinsically better vehicle for his genius than Pope in his couplet. But Bacon has no such advantage over Shakespeare; nor has Milton, writing prose (for no contemporary English prose-writer must be matched with Milton except Milton himself), any such advantage over Milton writing verse: indeed, the advantage here is all the other way.

*   *   *

In few natures, however, is there really such essential consistency as in Guérin's. He says of himself, in the very beginning of his journal: "I owe everything to poetry, for there is no other name to give to the sum total of my thoughts; I owe to it whatever I now have pure, lofty, and solid in my soul; I owe to it all my consolations in the past; I shall probably owe to it my future." Poetry, the poetical instinct, was indeed the basis of his nature; but to say so thus absolutely is not quite enough. One aspect of poetry fascinated Guérin's imagination and held it prisoner. Poetry is the interpretress of the natural world, and she is the interpretress of the moral world; it was as the interpretress of the natural world that she had Guérin for her mouthpiece. To make magically near and real the life of Nature, and man's life only so far as it is a part of that Nature, was his faculty; a faculty of naturalistic, not of moral interpretation. This faculty always has for its basis a peculiar temperament, an extraordinary delicacy of organisation and susceptibility to impressions; in exercising it the poet is in a great degree passive (Wordsworth thus speaks of a *wise passiveness*); he aspires to be a sort of human Æolian harp,[6] catching and rendering every rustle of Nature. To assist at the evolution of the whole life of the world is his craving, and intimately to feel it all:

> . . . "the glow, the thrill of life,
> Where, where do these abound?"[7]

is what he asks: he resists being riveted and held stationary by any single impression, but would be borne on for ever down an enchanted stream. He goes into religion and out of religion, into society and out of society, not from the motives which impel men in general, but to feel what it is all like; he is thus hardly a moral agent, and, like the passive and ineffectual Uranus of Keats's poem, he may say:

> . . . . . . "I am but a voice;
> My life is but the life of winds and tides;
> No more than winds and tides can I avail."[8]

He hovers over the tumult of life, but does not really put his hand to it.

No one has expressed the aspirations of this temperament better than Guérin himself. In the last year of his life he writes:—

"I return, as you see, to my old brooding over the world of Nature, that line which my thoughts irresistibly take; a sort of passion which gives me enthusiasm, tears, bursts of joy, and an eternal food for musing; and yet I am neither philosopher nor naturalist, nor anything learned whatsoever. There is one word which is the God of my imagination, the tyrant, I ought rather to say, that fascinates it, lures it onward, gives it work to do without ceasing, and will finally carry it I know not where; the word *life*."

And in one place in his journal he says:—

"My imagination welcomes every dream, every impression, without attaching itself to any, and goes on for ever seeking something new."

And again in another:—

"The longer I live, and the clearer I discern between true and false in society, the more does the inclination to live, not as a savage or a misanthrope, but as a solitary man on the frontiers of society, on the outskirts of the world, gain strength and grow in me. The birds come and go and make nests around our habitations, they are fellow-citizens of our farms and hamlets with us; but they take their flight in a heaven which is boundless, but the hand of God alone gives and measures to them their daily food, but they build their nests in the heart of the thick bushes, or hang them in the height of the trees. So would I, too, live, hovering round society, and having always at my back a field of liberty vast as the sky."

In the same spirit he longed for travel. "When one is a wanderer," he writes to his sister, "one feels that one fulfils the true condition of humanity." And the last entry in his journal is,—"The stream of travel is full of delight. Oh, who will set me adrift on this Nile!"

Assuredly it is not in this temperament that the active virtues have their rise. On the contrary, this temperament, considered in itself alone, indisposes for the discharge of them. Something morbid and excessive, as manifested in Guérin, it undoubtedly has. In him, as in Keats, and as in another youth of genius, whose name, but the other day unheard of, Lord Houghton has so gracefully written in the history of English poetry,—David Gray,[9]—the temperament, the talent itself, is deeply influenced by their mysterious malady; the temperament is *devouring;* it uses vital power too hard and too fast, paying the penalty in long hours of unutterable exhaustion and in premature death. The intensity of Guérin's depression is described to us by Guérin himself with the same incomparable touch with which he describes happier feelings; far oftener than any pleasurable sense of his gift he has "the sense profound, near, immense, of my misery, of my inward poverty." And again: "My inward misery gains upon me; I no longer dare look within." And on another day of gloom he does look within, and here is the terrible analysis:—

"Craving, unquiet, seeing only by glimpses, my spirit is

stricken by all those ills which are the sure fruit of a youth doomed never to ripen into manhood. I grow old and wear myself out in the most futile mental strainings, and make no progress. My head seems dying, and when the wind blows I fancy I feel it, as if I were a tree, blowing through a number of withered branches in my top. Study is intolerable to me, or rather it is quite out of my power. Mental work brings on, not drowsiness, but an irritable and nervous disgust which drives me out, I know not where, into the streets and public places. The Spring, whose delights used to come every year stealthily and mysteriously to charm me in my retreat, crushes me this year under a weight of sudden hotness. I should be glad of any event which delivered me from the situation in which I am. If I were free I would embark for some distant country where I could begin life anew."

Such is this temperament in the frequent hours when the sense of its own weakness and isolation crushes it to the ground. Certainly it was not for Guérin's happiness, or for Keats's, as men count happiness, to be as they were. Still the very excess and predominance of their temperament has given to the fruits of their genius a unique brilliancy and flavour. I have said that poetry interprets in two ways; it interprets by expressing with magical felicity the physiognomy and movement of the outward world, and it interprets by expressing, with inspired conviction, the ideas and laws of the inward world of man's moral and spiritual nature. In other words, poetry is interpretative both by having *natural magic* in it, and by having *moral profundity*. In both ways it illuminates man; it gives him a satisfying sense of reality; it reconciles him with himself and the universe. Thus Æschylus's "δράσαντι παθεῖν" and his "ἀνήριθμον γέλασμα"[10] are alike interpretative. Shakespeare interprets both when he says,

> "Full many a glorious morning have I seen,
> Flatter the mountain-tops with sovran eye;"[11]

and when he says,

> "There's a divinity that shapes our ends,
> Rough-hew them as we will."[12]

These great poets unite in themselves the faculty of both kinds of interpretation, the naturalistic and the moral. But it is observable that in the poets who unite both kinds, the latter (the moral) usually ends by making itself the master. In Shakespeare the two kinds seem wonderfully to balance one another; but even in him the balance leans; his expression tends to become too little sensuous and simple, too much intellectualised. The same thing may be yet more strongly affirmed of Lucretius and of Wordsworth. In Shelley there is not a balance of the two gifts, nor even a co-existence of them, but there is a passionate straining after them both, and this is what makes Shelley, as a man, so interesting: I will not now inquire how much Shelley achieves as a poet, but whatever he achieves, he in general fails to achieve natural magic in his expression; in Mr. Palgrave's charming *Treasury*[13] may be seen a gallery of his failures.* But in Keats and Guérin, in whom the faculty of naturalistic interpretation is overpoweringly predominant, the natural magic is perfect; when they speak of the world they speak like Adam naming by divine inspiration the creatures; their expression corresponds with the thing's essential reality. Even between Keats and Guérin, however, there is a distinction to be drawn. Keats has, above all, a sense of what is pleasurable and open in the life of Nature; for him she is the *Alma Parens:* his expression has, therefore, more than Guérin's, something genial, outward, and sensuous. Guérin has, above all, a sense of what there is adorable and secret in the life of Nature; for him she is the *Magna Parens;*[14] his expression has, therefore, more than Keats's, something mystic, inward, and profound.

* Compare, for example, his "Lines Written in the Euganean Hills," with Keats's "Ode to Autumn" *(Golden Treasury,* pp. 256, 284). The latter piece *renders* Nature; the former *tries to render* her. I will not deny, however, that Shelley has natural magic in his rhythm; what I deny is, that he has it in his language. It always seems to me that the right sphere for Shelley's genius was the sphere of music, not of poetry; the medium of sounds he can master, but to master the more difficult medium of words he has neither intellectural force enough nor sanity enough. [M. A.]

NOTES

"The Highest Powers of Poetry": from *Maurice de Guérin:* Delivered at Oxford, November, 1862; published in *Fraser's Magazine* (January, 1863); *Essays in Criticism* (1865). Maurice de Guérin (1810–39), French poet.

1. *The Winter's Tale,* IV.iv.118–20.
2. "The Solitary Reaper."
3. "Bright star" ("pure ablution").
4. From *Atala* (1801), by Chateaubriand (1768–1848): *the indeterminate summit of the forests.*
5. From *Obermann* (1804), by E. P. de Senancour (1770–1846), a psychological romance much praised by Arnold both in his verse and prose: *this white bark, smooth and cracked; this rustic trunk; these branches which bend towards the earth; the mobility of the*

leaves, and all this solitariness, simplicity of nature, attitude of deserts.

6. On the appeal of the Aeolian harp to the Romantic sensibility, see M. H. Abrams, *The Mirror and the Lamp* (1953).

7. Arnold, "Stanzas in Memory of the Author of 'Obermann'" (1852).

8. *Hyperion,* i.340–42.

9. Posthumous poems by David Gray (1838–61) were published in 1862, prefaced by Lord Houghton (Richard Monckton Milnes).

10. *The Libation-Bearers,* line 313: *To him that doeth, it shall be done by;* and *Prometheus Bound,* line 90: *multitudinous laughter.*

11. Sonnet 33.

12. *Hamlet,* V.ii. 10–11 ("how we").

13. F. T. Palgrave, *The Golden Treasury* (1861).

14. *Alma Parens* (*Aeneid,* x.252) *and Magna Parens:* "The one is warm and fostering, the other great and unapproachable" (R. H. Super).

THE
LITERARY INFLUENCE
OF ACADEMIES

1864

IT IS IMPOSSIBLE to put down a book like the history of the French Academy, by Pellisson and D'Olivet,[1] which M. Charles Livet has lately re-edited, without being led to reflect upon the absence, in our own country, of any institution like the French Academy, upon the probable causes of this absence, and upon its results. A thousand voices will be ready to tell us that this absence is a signal mark of our national superiority; that it is in great part owing to this absence that the exhilarating words of Lord Macaulay, lately given to the world by his very clever nephew, Mr. Trevelyan,[2] are so profoundly true: "It may safely be said that the literature now extant in the English language is of far greater value than all the literature which three hundred years ago was extant in all the languages of the world together." I daresay this is so; only, remembering Spinoza's maxim that the two great banes of humanity are self-conceit and the laziness coming from self-conceit, I think it may do us good, instead of resting in our pre-eminence with perfect security, to look a little more closely why this is so, and whether it is so without any limitations.

But first of all I must give a very few words to the out-ward history of the French Academy. About the year 1629, seven or eight persons in Paris, fond of literature, formed themselves into a sort of little club to meet at one another's houses and discuss literary matters. Their meetings got talked of, and Cardinal Richelieu, then minister and all-powerful, heard of them. He himself had a noble passion for letters, and for all fine culture; he was interested by what he heard of the nascent society. Himself a man in the grand style, if ever man was, he had the insight to perceive what a potent instrument of the grand style was here to his hand. It was the beginning of a great century for France, the seventeenth; men's minds were working, the French language was forming. Richelieu sent to ask the members of the new society whether they would be willing to become a body with a public character, holding regular meetings. Not without a little hesitation,—for apparently they found themselves very well as they were, and these seven or eight gentlemen of a social and literary turn were not perfectly at their ease as to what the great and terrible minister could want with them, —they consented. The favours of a man like Richelieu are not easily refused, whether they are honestly meant or no; but this favour of Richelieu's was meant quite honestly. The Parliament, however, had its doubts of this. The Parliament had none of Richelieu's enthusiasm about letters and culture; it was jealous of the apparition of a new public body in the State; above all, of a body called into existence by Richelieu. The King's letters-patent, establishing and authorising the new society, were granted early in 1635; but, by the old constitution of France, these letters-patent required the verification of the Parliament. It was two years and a half—towards the autumn of 1637—before the Parliament would give it; and it then gave it only after pressing solicitations, and earnest assurances of the innocent intentions of the young Academy. Jocose people said that this society, with its mission to purify and embellish the language, filled with terror a body of lawyers like the French Parliament, the stronghold of barbarous jargon and of chicane.

This improvement of the language was in truth the declared grand aim for the operations of the Academy. Its statutes of foundation, approved by Richelieu before the royal edict establishing it was issued, say expressly: "The Academy's principal function shall be to work with all the care and all the diligence possible at giving sure rules to our language, and rendering it pure, eloquent, and capable of treating the arts and sciences." This zeal for making a nation's great instrument of thought,—its language,—correct and worthy, is undoubtedly a sign full of promise,— a weighty earnest of future power. It is said that Richelieu had it in his mind that French should succeed Latin in its general ascendency, as Latin had succeeded Greek; if it was so, even this wish has to some extent been fulfilled. But, at any rate, the *ethical* influences of style in language,—its close relations, so often pointed out, with character,—are most important. Richelieu, a man of high culture, and, at the same time, of great character, felt them profoundly; and that he should have sought to regularise, strengthen, and perpetuate them by an institution for perfecting language, is alone a striking proof of his governing spirit and of his genius.

This was not all he had in his mind, however. The new Academy, now enlarged to a body of forty members, and meant to contain all the chief literary men of France, was to be a *literary tribunal.* The works of its members were to be brought before it previous to publication, were to be criticised by it, and finally, if it saw fit, to be published with its declared approbation. The works of other writers, not members of the Academy, might also, at the request of these writers themselves, be passed under the Academy's review. Besides this, in essays and discussions the Academy examined and judged works already published, whether by living or dead authors, and literary matters in general. The celebrated opinion on Corneille's *Cid,* delivered in 1637 by the Academy at Richelieu's urgent request, when this poem, which strongly occupied public attention, had been attacked by M. de Scudéry, shows how fully Richelieu designed his new creation to do duty as a supreme court of literature, and how early it in fact began to exercise this function. One* who had known Richelieu declared, after the Cardinal's death, that he had projected a yet greater institution than the Academy, a sort of grand European college of art, science, and literature, a Prytaneum, where the chief authors of all Europe should be gathered together in one central home, there to live in security, leisure, and honour;—that was a dream which will not bear to be pulled about too roughly. But the project of forming a high court of letters for France was no dream; Richelieu in great measure fulfilled it. This is what the Academy, by its idea, really is; this is what it has always tended to become; this is what it has, from time to time, really been; by being, or tending to be this, far more than even by what it has done for the language, it is of such importance in France. To give the law, the tone to literature, and that tone a high one, is its business. "Richelieu meant it," says M. Sainte-Beuve, "to be a *haut jury,*"—a jury the most choice and authoritative that

* La Mesnardière. [M. A.]

could be found on all important literary matters in question before the public; to be, as it in fact became in the latter half of the eighteenth century, "a sovereign organ of opinion." "The duty of the Academy is," says M. Renan, *"maintenir la délicatesse de l'esprit français"*—to keep the fine quality of the French spirit unimpaired; it represents a kind of *"maîtrise en fait de bon ton"*—the authority of a recognised master in matters of tone and taste. "All ages," says M. Renan again, "have had their inferior literature; but the great danger of our time is that this inferior literature tends more and more to get the upper place. No one has the same advantage as the Academy for fighting against this mischief;" the Academy, which, as he says elsewhere, has even special facilities for "creating a form of intellectual culture *which shall impose itself on all around.*" M. Sainte-Beuve and M. Renan are, both of them, very keen-sighted critics; and they show it signally by seizing and putting so prominently forward this character of the French Academy.

Such an effort to set up a recognised authority, imposing on us a high standard in matters of intellect and taste, has many enemies in human nature. We all of us like to go our own way, and not to be forced out of the atmosphere of commonplace habitual to most of us;—*"was uns alle bändigt,"* says Goethe, *"das Gemeine."*[3] We like to be suffered to lie comfortably in the old straw of our habits, especially of our intellectual habits, even though this straw may not be very clean and fine. But if the effort to limit this freedom of our lower nature finds, as it does and must find, enemies in human nature, it finds also auxiliaries in it. Out of the four great parts, says Cicero,[4] of the *honestum*, or good, which forms the matter on which *officium*, or human duty, finds employment, one is the fixing of a *modus* and an *ordo*, a measure and an order, to fashion and wholesomely constrain our action, in order to lift it above the level it keeps if left to itself, and to bring it nearer to perfection. Man alone of living creatures, he says, goes feeling after *"quid sit* ordo, *quid sit quod* deceat, *in factis dictisque qui* modus—the discovery of an *order*, a law of *good taste*, a *measure* for his words and actions." Other creatures submissively follow the law of their nature; man alone has an impulse leading him to set up some other law to control the bent of his nature.

This holds good, of course, as to moral matters, as well as intellectual matters: and it is of moral matters that we are generally thinking when we affirm it. But it holds good as to intellectual matters too. Now, probably, M. Sainte-Beuve had not these words of Cicero in his mind when he made, about the French nation, the assertion I am going to quote; but, for all that, the assertion leans for support, one may say, upon the truth conveyed in those words of Cicero, and wonderfully illustrates and confirms them. "In France," says M. Sainte-Beuve, "the first consideration for us is not whether we are amused and pleased by a work of art or mind, nor is it whether we are touched by it. What we seek above all to learn is, whether *we were right* in being amused with it, and in applauding it, and in being moved by it." Those are very remarkable words, and they are, I believe, in the main quite true. A Frenchman has, to a considerable degree, what one may call a conscience in intellectual matters; he has an active belief that there is a right and a wrong in them, that he is bound to honour and obey the right, that he is disgraced by cleaving to the wrong. All the world has, or professes to have, this conscience in moral matters. The word *conscience* has become almost confined, in popular use, to the moral sphere, because this lively susceptibility of feeling is, in the moral sphere, so far more common than in the intellectual sphere; the livelier, in the moral sphere, this susceptibility is, the greater becomes a man's readiness to admit a high standard of action, an ideal authoritatively correcting his everyday moral habits; here, such willing admission of authority is due to sensitiveness of conscience. And a like deference to a standard higher than one's own habitual standard in intellectual matters, a like respectful recognition of a superior ideal, is caused, in the intellectual sphere, by sensitiveness of intelligence. Those whose intelligence is quickest, openest, most sensitive, are readiest with this deference; those whose intelligence is less delicate and sensitive are less disposed to it. Well, now we are on the road to see why the French have their Academy and we have nothing of the kind.

What are the essential characteristics of the spirit of our nation? Not, certainly, an open and clear mind, not a quick and flexible intelligence. Our greatest admirers would not claim for us that we have these in a pre-eminent degree; they might say that we had more of them than our detractors gave us credit for; but they would not assert them to be our essential characteristics. They would rather allege, as our chief spiritual characteristics, energy and honesty; and, if we are judged favourably and positively, not invidiously and negatively, our chief characteristics are, no doubt, these:— energy and honesty, not an open and clear mind, not a quick and flexible intelligence. Openness of mind and flexibility of intelligence were very signal characteristics of the Athenian people in ancient times; everybody will feel that. Openness of mind and flexibility of intelligence are remarkable characteristics of the French people in modern times; at any rate, they strikingly characterise them as compared with us; I think everybody, or almost everybody, will feel that. I will not now ask what more the Athenian or the French spirit has than this, nor what shortcomings either of them may have as a set-off against this; all I want now to point out is that they have this, and that we have it in a much lesser degree.

Let me remark, however, that not only in the moral sphere, but also in the intellectual and spiritual sphere, energy and honesty are most important and fruitful qualities; that, for instance, of what we call genius energy is the most essential part. So, by assigning to a nation energy and honesty as its chief spiritual characteristics,—by refusing to it, as at all eminent characteristics, openness of mind and flexibility of intelligence,—we do not by any means, as some people might at first suppose, relegate its importance and its power of manifesting itself with effect from the intellectual to the moral sphere. We only indicate its probable special line of successful activity in the intellectual sphere, and, it is true, certain imperfections and failings to which, in this sphere, it will always be subject. Genius is mainly an affair of energy, and poetry is mainly an affair of genius; therefore, a nation whose spirit is characterised by energy may well be eminent in poetry;—and we have Shakespeare. Again, the highest reach of science is, one may say, an inventive power, a faculty of divination, akin to the highest power exercised in poetry; therefore, a nation whose spirit is characterised by energy may well be eminent in science;—and we have Newton. Shakespeare and Newton: in the intellectual sphere there can be no higher names. And what that energy, which is the life of genius, above everything demands and insists upon, is freedom; entire independence of all authority, prescription, and routine,—the fullest room to expand as it will. Therefore, a nation whose chief spiritual characteristic is energy, will not be very apt to set up, in intellectual matters, a fixed standard, an authority, like an academy. By this it certainly escapes certain real inconveniences and dangers, and it can, at the same time, as we have seen, reach undeniably splendid heights in poetry and science. On the other hand, some of the requisites of intellectual work are specially the affair of quickness of mind and flexibility of intelligence. The form, the method of evolution, the precision, the proportions, the relations of the parts to the whole, in an intellectual work, depend mainly upon them. And these are the elements of an intellectual work which are really most communicable from it, which can most be learned and adopted from it, which have, therefore, the greatest effect upon the intellectual performance of others. Even in poetry, these requisites are very important; and the poetry of a nation, not eminent for the gifts on which they depend, will, more or less, suffer by this shortcoming. In poetry, however, they are, after all, secondary, and energy is the first thing; but in prose they are of first-rate importance. In its prose literature, therefore, and in the routine of intellectual work generally, a nation with no particular gifts for these will not be so successful. These are what, as I have said, can to a certain degree be learned and appropriated, while the free activity of genius cannot. Academies consecrate and maintain them, and, therefore, a nation with an eminent turn for them naturally establishes academies. So far as routine and authority tend to embarrass energy and inventive genius, academies may be said to be obstructive to energy and inventive genius, and, to this extent, to the human spirit's general advance. But then this evil is so much compensated by the propagation, on a large scale, of the mental aptitudes and demands which an open mind and a flexible intelligence naturally engender, genius itself, in the long run, so greatly finds its account in this propagation, and bodies like the French Academy have such power for promoting it, that the general advance of the human spirit is perhaps, on the whole, rather furthered than impeded by their existence.

How much greater is our nation in poetry than prose! how much better, in general, do the productions of its spirit show in the qualities of genius than in the qualities of intelligence! One may constantly remark this in the work of individuals; how much more striking, in general, does any Englishman, —of some vigour of mind, but by no means a poet,—seem in his verse than in his prose! His verse partly suffers from his not being really a poet, partly, no doubt, from the very same defects which impair his prose, and he cannot express himself with thorough success in it. But how much more powerful a personage does he appear in it, by dint of feeling, and of originality and movement of ideas, than when he is writing prose! With a Frenchman of like stamp, it is just the reverse: set him to write poetry, he is limited, artificial, and impotent; set him to write prose, he is free, natural, and effective. The power of French literature is in its prose-writers, the power of English literature is in its poets. Nay, many of the celebrated French poets depend wholly for their fame upon the qualities of intelligence which they exhibit,—qualities which are the distinctive support of prose; many of the celebrated English prose-writers depend wholly for their fame upon the qualities of genius and imagination which they exhibit,—qualities which are the distinctive support of poetry. But, as I have said, the qualities of genius are less transferable than the qualities of intelligence; less can be immediately learned and appropriated from their product; they are less direct and stringent intellectual agencies, though they may be more beautiful and divine. Shakespeare and our great Elizabethan group were certainly more gifted writers than Corneille and his group; but what was the sequel to this great literature, this literature of genius, as we may call it, stretching from Marlowe to Milton? What did it lead up to in English literature? To our provincial and second-rate literature of the eighteenth century. What, on the other hand, was the sequel to the literature of the French "great century," to this literature of intelligence, as, by comparison with our Elizabethan literature, we may call it; what did it lead up to? To the French literature of the eighteenth century, one of the most powerful and pervasive intellectual agencies that have ever existed,—the greatest European force of the eighteenth century. In science, again, we had Newton, a genius of the very highest order, a type of genius in science, if ever there was one. On the continent, as a sort of counterpart to Newton, there was Leibnitz; a man, it seems to me (though on these matters I speak under correction), of much less creative energy of genius, much less power of divination than Newton, but rather a man of admirable intelligence, a type of intelligence in science, if ever there was one. Well, and what did they each directly lead up to in science? What was the intellectual generation that sprang from each of them? I only repeat what the men of science have themselves pointed out. The man of genius was continued by the English analysts of the eighteenth century, comparatively powerless and obscure followers of the renowned master. The man of intelligence was continued by successors like Bernouilli, Euler, Lagrange, and Laplace, the greatest names in modern mathematics.

What I want the reader to see is, that the question as to the utility of academies to the intellectual life of a nation is not settled when we say, for instance: "Oh, we have never had an academy, and yet we have, confessedly, a very great literature." It still remains to be asked: "What sort of a great literature? a literature great in the special qualities of genius, or great in the special qualities of intelligence?" If in the former, it is by no means sure that either our literature, or the general intellectual life of our nation, has got already, without academies, all that academies can give. Both the one and the other may very well be somewhat wanting in those qualities of intelligence out of a lively sense for which a body like the French Academy, as I have said, springs, and which such a body does a great deal to spread and confirm. Our literature, in spite of the genius manifested in it, may fall short in form, method, precision, proportions, arrangement,—all of them, I have said, things where intelligence proper comes in. It may be comparatively weak in prose, that branch of literature where intelligence proper is, so to speak, all in all. In this branch it may show many grave faults to which the want of a quick, flexible intelligence, and of the strict standard which such an intelligence tends to impose, makes it liable; it may be full of hap-hazard, crudeness, provincialism, eccentricity, violence, blundering. It may be a less stringent and effective intellectual agency, both upon our own nation and upon the world at large, than other literatures which show less genius, perhaps, but more intelligence.

The right conclusion certainly is that we should try, so far as we can, to make up our shortcomings; and that to this end, instead of always fixing our thoughts upon the points in which our literature, and our intellectual life generally, are strong, we should, from time to time, fix them upon those in which they are weak, and so learn to perceive clearly what we have to amend. What is our second great spiritual characteristic,—our honesty,—good for, if it is not good for this? But it will,—I am sure it will,—more and more, as time goes on, be found good for this.

Well, then, an institution like the French Academy,—an institution owing its existence to a national bent towards the things of the mind, towards culture, towards clearness, correctness, and propriety in thinking and speaking, and, in its turn, promoting this bent,—sets standards in a number of directions, and creates, in all these directions, a force of educated opinion, checking and rebuking those who fall below these standards, or who set them at nought. Educated opinion exists here as in France; but in France the Academy serves as a sort of centre and rallying-point to it, and gives it a force which it has not got here. Why is all the *journeyman-work* of literature, as I may call it, so much worse done here than it is in France? I do not wish to hurt any one's feelings; but surely this is so. Think of the difference between our books of reference and those of the French, between our biographical dictionaries (to take a striking instance) and theirs; think of the difference between the translations of the classics turned out for Mr. Bohn's library and those turned out for M. Nisard's collection![5] As a general rule, hardly any one amongst us, who knows French and German well, would use an English book of reference when he could get a French or German one; or would look at an English prose translation of an ancient author when he could get a French or German one. It is not that there do not exist in England, as in France, a number of people perfectly well able to discern what is good, in these things, from what is bad, and preferring what is good; but they are isolated, they form no powerful body of opinion, they are not strong enough to set a standard, up to which even the journeyman-work of literature must be brought, if it is to be vendible. Ignorance and charlatanism in work of this kind are always trying to pass off their wares as excellent, and to cry down criticism as the voice of an insignificant, over-fastidious minority; they easily persuade the multitude that this is so when the minority is scattered about as it is here; not so easily when it is banded together as in the French Academy. So, again, with freaks in dealing with language; certainly all such freaks tend to impair the power and beauty of language; and how far more common they are with us than with the French! To take a very familiar instance. Every one has noticed the way in which the *Times* chooses to spell the word "diocese;" it always spells it diocess,* deriving it, I suppose, from *Zeus* and *census*. The *Journal des Débats* might just as well write "diocess" instead of "diocèse," but imagine the *Journal des Débats*[7] doing so! Imagine an educated Frenchman indulging himself in an orthographical antic of this sort, in face of the grave respect with which the Academy and its dictionary invest the French language! Some people will say these are little things; they are not; they are of bad example. They tend to spread the baneful notion that there is no such thing as a high, correct standard in intellectual matters; that every one may as well take his own way; they are at variance with the severe discipline necessary for all real culture; they confirm us in habits of wilfulness and eccentricity, which hurt our minds, and damage our credit with serious people. The late Mr. Donaldson was certainly a man of great ability, and I, who am not an Orientalist, do not pretend to judge his *Jashar*:[8]

* The *Times* has now (1868) abandoned this spelling and adopted the ordinary one. [M. A.][6]

but let the reader observe the form which a foreign Orientalist's judgment of it naturally takes. M. Renan calls it a *tentative malheureuse,* a failure, in short; this it may be, or it may not be; I am no judge. But he goes on: "It is astonishing that a recent article" (in a French periodical, he means) "should have brought forward as the last word of German exegesis a work like this, composed by a doctor of the University of Cambridge, and universally condemned by German critics." You see what he means to imply: an extravagance of this sort could never have come from Germany, where there is a great force of critical opinion controlling a learned man's vagaries, and keeping him straight; it comes from the native home of intellectual eccentricity of all kinds,*—from England, from a doctor of the University of Cambridge;—and I daresay he would not expect much better things from a doctor of the University of Oxford. Again, after speaking of what Germany and France have done for the history of Mahomet: "America and England," M. Renan goes on, "have also occupied themselves with Mahomet." He mentions Washington Irving's *Life of Mahomet,* which does not, he says, evince much of an historical sense, a *sentiment historique fort élevé;* "but," he proceeds, "this book shows a real progress, when one thinks that in 1829 Mr. Charles Forster published two thick volumes, which enchanted the English *révérends,* to make out that Mahomet was the little horn of the he-goat that figures in the eighth chapter of Daniel, and that the Pope was the great horn. Mr. Forster founded on this ingenious parallel a whole philosophy of history, according to which the Pope represented the Western corruption of Christianity, and Mahomet the Eastern; thence the striking resemblances between Mahometanism and Popery." And in a note M. Renan adds: "This is the same Mr. Charles Forster who is the author of a mystification about the Sinaitic inscriptions, in which he declares he finds the primitive language." As much as to say: "It is an Englishman, be surprised at no extravagance." If these innuendoes had no ground, and were made in hatred and malice, they would not be worth a moment's attention; but they come from a grave Orientalist, on his own subject, and they point to a real fact;—the absence, in this country, of any force of educated literary and scientific

* A critic declares I am wrong in saying that M. Renan's language implies this. I still think that there is a shade, a *nuance* of expression, in M. Renan's language, which does imply this; but, I confess, the only person who can really settle such a question is M. Renan himself. [M. A.]

opinion, making aberrations like those of the author of *The One Primeval Language* out of the question. Not only the author of such aberrations, often a very clever man, suffers by the want of check, by the not being kept straight, and spends force in vain on a false road, which, under better discipline, he might have used with profit on a true one; but all his adherents, both "reverends" and others, suffer too, and the general rate of information and judgment is in this way kept low.

In a production which we have all been reading lately,[9] a production stamped throughout with a literary quality very rare in this country, and of which I shall have a word to say presently—*urbanity;* in this production, the work of a man never to be named by any son of Oxford without sympathy, a man who alone in Oxford of his generation, alone of many generations, conveyed to us in his genius that same charm, that same ineffable sentiment which this exquisite place itself conveys,—I mean Dr. Newman,—an expression is frequently used which is more common in theological than in literary language, but which seems to me fitted to be of general service; the *note* of so and so, the note of catholicity, the note of antiquity, the note of sanctity, and so on. Adopting this expressive word, I say that in the bulk of the intellectual work of a nation which has no centre, no intellectual metropolis like an academy, like M. Sainte-Beuve's "sovereign organ of opinion," like M. Renan's "recognised authority in matters of tone and taste,"—there is observable a *note of provinciality*. Now to get rid of provinciality is a certain stage of culture; a stage the positive result of which we must not make of too much importance, but which is, nevertheless, indispensable, for it brings us on to the platform where alone the best and highest intellectual work can be said fairly to begin. Work done after men have reached this platform is *classical;* and that is the only work which, in the long run, can stand. All the *scoriæ*[10] in the work of men of great genius who have not lived on this platform are due to their not having lived on it. Genius raises them to it by moments, and the portions of their work which are immortal are done at these moments; but more of it would have been immortal if they had not reached this platform at moments only, if they had had the culture which makes men live there.

The less a literature has felt the influence of a supposed centre of correct information, correct judgment, correct taste, the more we shall find in it this note of provinciality. I have shown the note of provinciality as caused by remoteness from a centre of correct information. Of course the note of provinciality from the want of a centre of correct taste is still more visible, and it is also still more common. For here great—even the greatest—powers of mind most fail a man. Great powers of mind will make him inform himself thoroughly, great powers of mind will make him think profoundly, even with ignorance and platitude all round him; but not even great powers of mind will keep his taste and style perfectly sound and sure, if he is left too much to himself, with no "sovereign organ of opinion" in these matters near him. Even men like Jeremy Taylor and Burke suffer here. Take this passage from Taylor's funeral sermon[11] on Lady Carbery:—

"So have I seen a river, deep and smooth, passing with a still foot and a sober face, and paying to the *fiscus*, the great exchequer of the sea, a tribute large and full; and hard by it a little brook, skipping and making a noise upon its unequal and neighbour bottom; and after all its talking and bragged motion, it paid to its common audit no more than the revenues of a little cloud or a contemptible vessel: so have I sometimes compared the issues of her religion to the solemnities and famed outsides of another's piety."

That passage has been much admired, and, indeed, the genius in it is undeniable. I should say, for my part, that genius, the ruling divinity of poetry, had been too busy in it, and intelligence, the ruling divinity of prose, not busy enough. But can any one, with the best models of style in his head, help feeling the note of provinciality there, the want of simplicity, the want of measure, the want of just the qualities that make prose classical? If he does not feel what I mean, let him place beside the passage of Taylor this passage from the Panegyric of St. Paul, by Taylor's contemporary, Bossuet:[12]—

"Il ira, cet ignorant dans l'art de bien dire, avec cette locution rude, avec cette phrase qui sent l'étranger, il ira en cette Grèce polie, la mère des philosophes et des orateurs; et malgré la résistance du monde, il y établira plus d'Eglises que Platon n'y a gagné de disciples par cette éloquence qu'on a crue divine."

There we have prose without the note of provinciality— classical prose, prose of the centre.

Or take Burke, our greatest English prose-writer, as I think; take expressions like this:[13]—

"Blindfold themselves, like bulls that shut their eyes when they push, they drive, by the point of their bayonets, their slaves, blindfolded, indeed, no worse than their lords, to

take their fictions for currencies, and to swallow down paper
pills by thirty-four millions sterling at a dose."

Or this:—

"They used it" (the royal name) "as a sort of navel-
string, to nourish their unnatural offspring from the bowels
of royalty itself. Now that the monster can purvey for its
own subsistence, it will only carry the mark about it, as a
token of its having torn the womb it came from."

Or this:—

"Without one natural pang, he" (Rousseau) "casts away,
as a sort of offal and excrement, the spawn of his disgust-
ful amours, and sends his children to the hospital of found-
lings."

Or this:—

"I confess I never liked this continual talk of resistance
and revolution, or the practice of making the extreme medicine of the constitution its daily bread. It renders the habit
of society dangerously valetudinary; it is taking periodical
doses of mercury sublimate, and swallowing down repeated
provocatives of cantharides to our love of liberty."

I say that is extravagant prose; prose too much suffered
to indulge its caprices; prose at too great a distance from the
centre of good taste; prose, in short, with the note of provinciality. People may reply, it is rich and imaginative; yes,
that is just it, it is *Asiatic* prose, as the ancient critics would
have said; prose somewhat barbarously rich and overloaded.
But the true prose is Attic prose.[14]

Well, but Addison's prose is Attic prose. Where, then, it
may be asked, is the note of provinciality in Addison? I answer, in the commonplace of his ideas.* This is a matter
worth remarking. Addison claims to take leading rank as a
moralist. To do that, you must have ideas of the first order
on your subject—the best ideas, at any rate, attainable in

---

* A critic says this is paradoxical, and urges that many second-
rate French academicians have uttered the most commonplace ideas
possible. I agree that many second-rate French academicians have
uttered the most commonplace ideas possible; but Addison is not a
second-rate man. He is a man of the order, I will not say of Pascal,
but at any rate of La Bruyère and Vauvenargues; why does he not
equal them? I say because of the medium in which he finds himself,
the atmosphere in which he lives and works; an atmosphere which
tells unfavourably, or rather *tends* to tell unfavourably (for that is
the truer way of putting it) either upon style or else upon ideas;
tends to make even a man of great ability either a Mr. Carlyle or
else a Lord Macaulay. [M. A.]

It is to be observed, however, that Lord Macaulay's style has in
its turn suffered by his failure in ideas, and this cannot be said of
Addison's. [M. A.]

your time—as well as be able to express them in a perfectly sound and sure style. Else you show your distance from the centre of ideas by your matter; you are provincial by your matter, though you may not be provincial by your style. It is comparatively a small matter to express oneself well, if one will be content with not expressing much, with expressing only trite ideas; the problem is to express new and profound ideas in a perfectly sound and classical style. He is the true classic, in every age, who does that. Now Addison has not, on his subject of morals, the force of ideas of the moralists of the first class—the classical moralists; he has not the best ideas attainable in or about his time, and which were, so to speak, in the air then, to be seized by the finest spirits; he is not to be compared for power, searchingness, or delicacy of thought to Pascal[15] or La Bruyère[16] or Vauvenargues;[17] he is rather on a level, in this respect, with a man like Marmontel.[18] Therefore, I say, he has the note of provinciality as a moralist; he is provincial by his matter, though not by his style.

To illustrate what I mean by an example. Addison, writing as a moralist on fixedness in religious faith, says:—

"Those who delight in reading books of controversy do very seldom arrive at a fixed and settled habit of faith. The doubt which was laid revives again, and shows itself in new difficulties; and that generally for this reason,—because the mind, which is perpetually tossed in controversies and disputes, is apt to forget the reasons which had once set it at rest, and to be disquieted with any former perplexity when it appears in a new shape, or is started by a different hand."[19]

It may be said, that is classical English, perfect in lucidity, measure, and propriety. I make no objection; but, in my turn, I say that the idea expressed is perfectly trite and barren, and that it is a note of provinciality in Addison, in a man whom a nation puts forward as one of its great moralists, to have no profounder and more striking idea to produce on this great subject. Compare, on the same subject, these words of a moralist really of the first order, really at the centre by his ideas,—Joubert:—

"L'expérience de beaucoup d'opinions donne à l'esprit beaucoup de flexibilité et l'affermit dans celles qu'il croit les meilleures."[20]

With what a flash of light that touches the subject! how it sets us thinking! what a genuine contribution to moral science it is!

In short, where there is no centre like an academy, if you

have genius and powerful ideas, you are apt not to have the best style going; if you have precision of style and not genius, you are apt not to have the best ideas going.

The provincial spirit, again, exaggerates the value of its ideas for want of a high standard at hand by which to try them. Or rather, for want of such a standard, it gives one idea too much prominence at the expense of others; it orders its ideas amiss; it is hurried away by fancies; it likes and dislikes too passionately, too exclusively. Its admiration weeps hysterical tears, and its disapprobation foams at the mouth. So we get the *eruptive* and the *aggressive* manner in literature; the former prevails most in our criticism, the latter in our newspapers. For, not having the lucidity of a large and centrally placed intelligence, the provincial spirit has not its graciousness; it does not persuade, it makes war; it has not urbanity, the tone of the city, of the centre, the tone which always aims at a spiritual and intellectual effect, and not excluding the use of banter, never disjoins banter itself from politeness, from felicity. But the provincial tone is more violent, and seems to aim rather at an effect upon the blood and senses than upon the spirit and intellect; it loves hard-hitting rather than persuading. The newspaper, with its party spirit, its thorough-goingness, its resolute avoidance of shades and distinctions, its short, highly-charged, heavy-shotted articles, its style so unlike that style *lenis minimèque pertinax*[21]—easy and not too violently insisting,—which the ancients so much admired, is its true literature; the provincial spirit likes in the newspaper just what makes the newspaper such bad food for it,—just what made Goethe say, when he was pressed hard about the immorality of Byron's poems, that, after all, they were not so immoral as the newspapers. The French talk of the *brutalité des journaux anglais*. What strikes them comes from the necessary inherent tendencies of newspaper-writing not being checked in England by any centre of intelligent and urbane spirit, but rather stimulated by coming in contact with a provincial spirit. Even a newspaper like the *Saturday Review*, that old friend of all of us, a newspaper expressly aiming at an immunity from the common newspaper-spirit, aiming at being a sort of organ of reason,—and, by thus aiming, it merits great gratitude and has done great good,— even the *Saturday Review*, replying to some foreign criticism on our precautions against invasion, falls into a strain of this kind:—

"To do this" (to take these precautions) "seems to us eminently worthy of a great nation, and to talk of it as unworthy of a great nation, seems to us eminently worthy of a great fool."

There is what the French mean when they talk of the *brutalité des journaux anglais;* there is a style certainly as far removed from urbanity as possible,—a style with what I call the note of provinciality. And the same note may not unfrequently be observed even in the ideas of this newspaper, full as it is of thought and cleverness: certain ideas allowed to become fixed ideas, to prevail too absolutely. I will not speak of the immediate present, but, to go a little while back, it had the critic who so disliked the Emperor of the French; it had the critic who so disliked the subject of my present remarks—academies; it had the critic who was so fond of the German element in our nation, and, indeed, everywhere; who ground his teeth if one said *Charlemagne* instead of *Charles the Great,* and, in short, saw all things in Teutonism, as Malebranche[22] saw all things in God. Certainly any one may fairly find faults in the Emperor Napoleon or in academies, and merit in the German element; but it is a note of the provincial spirit not to hold ideas of this kind a little more easily, to be so devoured by them, to suffer them to become crotchets.

In England there needs a miracle of genius like Shakespeare's to produce balance of mind, and a miracle of intellectual delicacy like Dr. Newman's to produce urbanity of style. How prevalent all round us is the want of balance of mind and urbanity of style! How much, doubtless, it is to be found in ourselves,—in each of us! but, as human nature is constituted, every one can see it clearest in his contemporaries. There, above all, we should consider it, because they and we are exposed to the same influences; and it is in the best of one's contemporaries that it is most worth considering, because one then most feels the harm it does, when one sees what they would be without it. Think of the difference between Mr. Ruskin exercising his genius, and Mr. Ruskin exercising his intelligence; consider the truth and beauty of this:—

"Go out, in the spring-time, among the meadows that slope from the shores of the Swiss lakes to the roots of their lower mountains. There, mingled with the taller gentians and the white narcissus, the grass grows deep and free; and as you follow the winding mountain paths, beneath arching boughs all veiled and dim with blossom,—paths that for ever droop and rise over the green banks and mounds sweeping down in scented undulation, steep to the blue water, studded here and there with new-mown heaps, filling all the air with fainter sweetness,—look up towards the higher hills, where the waves of everlasting green roll silently into their long inlets among the shadows of the pines. . . . . ."23

There is what the genius, the feeling, the temperament in Mr. Ruskin, the original and incommunicable part, has to do with; and how exquisite it is! All the critic could possibly suggest, in the way of objection, would be, perhaps, that Mr. Ruskin is there trying to make prose do more than it can perfectly do; that what he is there attempting he will never, except in poetry, be able to accomplish to his own entire satisfaction: but he accomplishes so much that the critic may well hesitate to suggest even this. Place beside this charming passage another,—a passage about Shakespeare's names, where the intelligence and judgment of Mr. Ruskin, the acquired, trained, communicable part in him, are brought into play,—and see the difference:—

"Of Shakespeare's names I will afterwards speak at more length; they are curiously—often barbarously—mixed out of various traditions and languages. Three of the clearest in meaning have been already noticed. Desdemona —'δυσδαιμονία,' *miserable fortune*—is also plain enough. Othello is, I believe, 'the careful;' all the calamity of the tragedy arising from the single flaw and error in his magnificently collected strength. Ophelia, 'serviceableness,' the true, lost wife of Hamlet, is marked as having a Greek name by that of her brother, Laertes; and its signification is once exquisitely alluded to in that brother's last word of her, where her gentle preciousness is opposed to the uselessness of the churlish clergy:—'A *ministering* angel shall my sister be, when thou liest howling.' Hamlet is, I believe, connected in some way with 'homely,' the entire event of the tragedy turning on betrayal of home duty. Hermione (ἕρμα), 'pillar-like' (ἡ εἶδος ἔχε χρυσέης 'Αφροδίτης); Titania (τιτήνη), 'the queen;' Benedick and Beatrice, 'blessed and blessing;' Valentine and Proteus, 'enduring or strong' (*valens*), and 'changeful.' Iago and Iachimo have evidently the same root—probably the Spanish Iago, Jacob, 'the supplanter.' "24

Now, really, what a piece of extravagance all that is! I will not say that the meaning of Shakespeare's names (I put aside the question as to the correctness of Mr. Ruskin's etymologies) has no effect at all, may be entirely lost sight of; but to give it that degree of prominence is to throw the reins to one's whim, to forget all moderation and proportion, to lose the balance of one's mind altogether. It is to show in one's criticism, to the highest excess, the note of provinciality.

Again, there is Mr. Palgrave, certainly endowed with a very fine critical tact: his *Golden Treasury* abundantly proves it. The plan of arrangement which he devised for that work, the mode in which he followed his plan out, nay, one might even say, merely the juxtaposition, in pursuance of it, of two such pieces as those of Wordsworth and Shelley which form the 285th and 286th in his collection,[25] show a delicacy of feeling in these matters which is quite indisputable and very rare. And his notes are full of remarks which show it too. All the more striking, conjoined with so much justness of perception, are certain freaks and violences in Mr. Palgrave's criticism, mainly imputable, I think, to the critic's isolated position in this country, to his feeling himself too much left to take his own way, too much without any central authority representing high culture and sound judgment, by which he may be, on the one hand, confirmed as against the ignorant, on the other, held in respect when he himself is inclined to take liberties. I mean such things as this note on Milton's line,—

"The great Emathian conqueror bade spare" . . .[26]

"When Thebes was destroyed, Alexander ordered the house of Pindar to be spared. *He was as incapable of appreciating the poet as Louis XIV. of appreciating Racine; but even the narrow and barbarian mind of Alexander could understand the advantage of a showy act of homage to poetry.*" A note like that I call a freak or a violence; if this disparaging view of Alexander and Louis XIV., so unlike the current view, is wrong,—if the current view is, after all, the truer one of them,—the note is a freak. But, even if its disparaging view is right, the note is a violence; for, abandoning the true mode of intellectual action—persuasion, the instilment of conviction,—it simply astounds and irritates the hearer by contradicting, without a word of proof or preparation, his fixed and familiar notions; and this is mere violence. In either case, the fitness, the measure, the centrality, which is the soul of all good criticism, is lost, and the note of provinciality shows itself.

Thus, in the famous *Handbook*,[27] marks of a fine power of perception are everywhere discernible, but so, too, are marks of the want of sure balance, of the check and support afforded by knowing one speaks before good and severe judges. When Mr. Palgrave dislikes a thing, he feels no pressure constraining him either to try his dislike closely or to express it moderately; he does not mince matters, he gives his dislike all its own way; both his judgment and his style would gain if he were under more restraint. "The style which has filled London with the dead monotony of Gower or Harley Streets, or the pale commonplace of Belgravia, Tyburnia, and Kensington; which has pierced Paris and Madrid with the feeble frivolities of the Rue Rivoli and the Strada de Toledo." He dislikes the architecture of the Rue Rivoli, and he puts it on a level with the architecture of Belgravia and Gower Street; he lumps them all together in one condemnation, he loses sight of the shade, the distinction, which is everything here; the distinction, namely, that the architecture of the Rue Rivoli expresses show, splendour, pleasure,—unworthy things, perhaps, to express alone and for their own sakes, but it expresses them; whereas the architecture of Gower Street and Belgravia merely expresses the impotence of the architect to express anything. Then, as to style: "sculpture which stands in a contrast with Woolner hardly more shameful than diverting," . . . "passing from Davy or Faraday to the art of the mountebank or the science of the spirit-rapper," . . . "it is the old, old story with Marochetti, the frog trying to blow himself out to bull dimensions. He may puff and be puffed, but he will never do it."[28] We all remember that shower of amenities on poor M. Marochetti. Now, here Mr. Palgrave himself enables us to form a contrast which lets us see just what the presence of an academy does for style; for he quotes a criticism by M. Gustave Planche on this very M. Marochetti. M. Gustave Planche was a critic of the very first order, a man of strong opinions, which he expressed with severity; he, too, condemns M. Marochetti's work, and Mr. Palgrave calls him as a witness to back what he has himself said; certainly Mr. Palgrave's translation will not exaggerate M. Planche's urbanity in dealing with M. Marochetti, but, even in this translation, see the difference in sobriety, in measure, between the critic writing in Paris and the critic writing in London:—

"These conditions are so elementary, that I am at a perfect loss to comprehend how M. Marochetti has neglected them. There are soldiers here like the leaden playthings of the nursery: it is almost impossible to guess whether there is a body beneath the dress. We have here no question of style, not even of grammar; it is nothing beyond mere matter of the alphabet of art. To break these conditions is the same as to be ignorant of spelling."

That is really more formidable criticism than Mr. Palgrave's, and yet in how perfectly temperate a style! M. Planche's advantage is, that he feels himself to be speaking before competent judges, that there is a force of cultivated opinion for him to appeal to. Therefore, he must not be extravagant, and he need not storm; he must satisfy the reason and taste,—that is his business. Mr. Palgrave, on the other hand, feels himself to be speaking before a promiscuous multitude, with the few good judges so scattered through it as to be powerless; therefore, he has no calm confidence and no self-control; he relies on the strength of his lungs; he knows that big words impose on the mob, and that, even if he is outrageous, most of his audience are apt to be a great deal more so.*

Again, the first two volumes of Mr. Kinglake's *Invasion of the Crimea*[29] were certainly among the most successful and renowned English books of our time. Their style was one of the most renowned things about them, and yet how conspicuous a fault in Mr. Kinglake's style is this overcharge of which I have been speaking! Mr. James Gordon Bennett, of the *New York Herald,* says, I believe, that the highest achievement of the human intellect is what he calls "a good editorial." This is not quite so; but, if it were so, on what a height would these two volumes by Mr. Kinglake stand! I have already spoken of the Attic and the Asiatic styles; besides these, there is the Corinthian style.[30] That is the style for "a good editorial," and Mr. Kinglake has really reached perfection in it. It has not the warm glow, blithe movement, and soft pliancy of life, as the Attic style has; it has not the over-heavy richness and encumbered gait of the Asiatic style; it has glitter without warmth, rapidity without ease, effectiveness without charm. Its characteristic is, that it has no *soul;* all it exists for, is to get its ends, to make its points, to damage its adversaries, to be admired, to triumph. A style so bent on effect at the expense of soul, simplicity, and delicacy; a style so little studious of the charm of the great models; so far from classic truth and grace, must surely be said to have the note of provinciality. Yet Mr. Kinglake's talent is a really eminent one, and so in harmony with our intellectual habits and tendencies, that, to the great bulk of English people, the faults of his style seem its merits; all the more needful that criticism should not be dazzled by them.

We must not compare a man of Mr. Kinglake's literary talent with French writers like M. de Bazancourt.[31] We must

* When I wrote this I had before me the first edition of Mr. Palgrave's *Handbook.* I am bound to say that in the second edition much strong language has been expunged, and what remains, softened. [M. A.]

compare him with M. Thiers.[32] And what a superiority in style has M. Thiers from being formed in a good school, with severe traditions, wholesome restraining influences! Even in this age of Mr. James Gordon Bennett, his style has nothing Corinthian about it; its lightness and brightness make it almost Attic. It is not quite Attic, however; it has not the infallible sureness of Attic taste. Sometimes his head gets a little hot with the fumes of patriotism, and then he crosses the line, he loses perfect measure, he declaims, he raises a momentary smile. France condemned "à être l'effroi du monde *dont elle pourrait être l'amour*,"[33]—Cæsar, whose exquisite simplicity M. Thiers so much admires, would not have written like that. There is, if I may be allowed to say so, the slightest possible touch of fatuity in such language,—of that failure in good sense which comes from too warm a self-satisfaction. But compare this language with Mr. Kinglake's Marshal St. Arnaud—"dismissed from the presence" of Lord Raglan or Lord Stratford, "cowed and pressed down" under their "stern reproofs," or under "the majesty of the great Elchi's[34] Canning brow and tight, merciless lips!" The failure in good sense and good taste there reaches far beyond what the French mean by *fatuity;* they would call it by another word, a word expressing blank defect of intelligence, a word for which we have no exact equivalent in English,—*bête*. It is the difference between a venial, momentary, good-tempered excess, in a man of the world, of an amiable and social weakness,—vanity; and a serious, settled, fierce, narrow, provincial misconception of the whole relative value of one's own things and the things of others. So baneful to the style of even the cleverest man may be the total want of checks.

In all I have said, I do not pretend that the examples given prove my rule as to the influence of academies; they only illustrate it. Examples in plenty might very likely be found to set against them; the truth of the rule depends, no doubt, on whether the balance of all the examples is in its favour or not; but actually to strike this balance is always out of the question. Here, as everywhere else, the rule, the idea, if true, commends itself to the judicious, and then the examples make it clearer still to them. This is the real use of examples, and this alone is the purpose which I have meant mine to serve. There is also another side to the whole question,—as to the limiting and prejudicial operation which academies may have; but this side of the question it rather behoves the French, not us, to study.

The reader will ask for some practical conclusion about

the establishment of an Academy in this country, and perhaps I shall hardly give him the one he expects. But nations have their own modes of acting, and these modes are not easily changed; they are even consecrated, when great things have been done in them. When a literature has produced Shakespeare and Milton, when it has even produced Barrow[35] and Burke, it cannot well abandon its traditions; it can hardly begin, at this late time of day, with an institution like the French Academy. I think academies with a limited, special, scientific scope, in the various lines of intellectual work,—academies like that of Berlin, for instance,—we with time may, and probably shall, establish. And no doubt they will do good; no doubt the presence of such influential centres of correct information will tend to raise the standard amongst us for what I have called the *journeyman-work* of literature, and to free us from the scandal of such biographical dictionaries as Chalmers's,[36] or such translations as a recent one of Spinoza,[37] or perhaps, such philological freaks as Mr. Forster's about the one primeval language. But an academy quite like the French Academy, a sovereign organ of the highest literary opinion, a recognised authority in matters of intellectual tone and taste, we shall hardly have, and perhaps we ought not to wish to have it. But then every one amongst us with any turn for literature will do well to remember to what shortcomings and excesses, which such an academy tends to correct, we are liable; and the more liable, of course, for not having it. He will do well constantly to try himself in respect of these, steadily to widen his culture, severely to check in himself the provincial spirit; and he will do this the better the more he keeps in mind that all mere glorification by ourselves of ourselves or our literature, in the strain of what, at the beginning of these remarks, I quoted from Lord Macaulay, is both vulgar, and, besides being vulgar, retarding.

NOTES

The Literary Influence of Academies: Delivered at Oxford, June, 1864; published in *Cornhill Magazine* (August, 1864); *Essays in Criticism* (1865).

1. P. Pellisson (continued by P. J. T. d'Olivet), *Histoire de l'Académie Française* (Paris, 1858). It prompted an essay (known to Arnold) by the critic whom Arnold held in the greatest respect, C. A. Sainte-Beuve (1804–69), and one by Ernest Renan (1823–92).
2. See p. 331.
3. "Epilog zu Schillers Glocke": *What holds us all down, the common and mean.*

4. *De Officiis,* I.iv-v.

5. H. G. Bohn's Classical Library and Philosophical Library, as against a comparable French series edited by Désiré Nisard.

6. "It was the only form recognized by Dr. Johnson . . . and was retained by some (notably by the *Times* newspaper) in the nineteenth century" *(Oxford English Dictionary).* R. H. Super unfolds Arnold's further gibe: "Δίς, Διός was a synonym for Zeus, whose Latin name, Jupiter, was a common nickname of the *Times.*"

7. A Parisian newspaper.

8. J. W. Donaldson's Biblical reconstruction (1854).

9. John Henry Newman's *Apologia* was first published April-June, 1864.

10. *Dross.*

11. October, 1650, by Jeremy Taylor (1613–67).

12. J. B. Bossuet (1627–1704).

13. *Reflections on the Revolution in France* (1790), and *Letter to a Member of the National Assembly* (1791).

14. Attic and Asiatic: the concise and the inflated styles mentioned by Quintilian.

15. Blaise Pascal (1623–62).

16. Jean de la Bruyère (1645–96), author of *Caractères.*

17. Marquis de Vauvenargues (1715–47), French moralist.

18. J. F. Marmontel (1723–99), French novelist and dramatist.

19. *The Spectator* No. 465 (August 23, 1712), slightly misquoted and with cuts.

20. *Experiencing many opinions gives the mind much flexibility and steadies it in those which it believes the best.* For Joubert, see p. 390.

21. Cicero, *De Officiis,* I.xxvii.

22. Nicolas Malebranche (1638–1715), theologian.

23. *Modern Painters,* Part IV (1856), chapter xiv.

24. *Munera Pulveris* (1872), chapter v. Ruskin quotes *Odyssey,* iv.14 (R. H. Super). Ruskin subsequently modified the opening of this paragraph.

25. Shelley's "A Lament" and Wordsworth's "My heart leaps up."

26. Sonnet, "When the assault was intended to the city" ("bid spare").

27. *Handbook to the Fine Art Collection in the International Exhibition of 1862.*

28. Thomas Woolner (1826–92), sculptor. Sir Humphry Davy (1778–1829), scientist. Michael Faraday (1791–1867), scientist. Carlo Marochetti (1805–67), sculptor.

29. A. W. Kinglake (1863).

30. A style of muddled affectation mentioned by Quintilian.

31. César de Bazancourt, author of *L'Expédition de Crimée* (1856).

32. Louis Adolphe Thiers (1797–1877), historian and statesman.

33. *To be the terror of the world of which she could have been the love.*

34. Ambassador's.

35. Isaac Barrow (1630–77), notable for his sermons.

36. Alexander Chalmers, the *General Biographical Dictionary* (1812–17).

37. Robert Willis' translation (1862), which Arnold reviewed.

THE FUNCTION OF
CRITICISM AT THE
PRESENT TIME

1864

MANY OBJECTIONS have been made to a proposition which, in some remarks of mine on translating Homer,[1] I ventured to put forth; a proposition about criticism, and its importance at the present day. I said: "Of the literature of France and Germany, as of the intellect of Europe in general, the main effort, for now many years, has been a critical effort; the endeavour, in all branches of knowledge, theology, philosophy, history, art, science, to see the object as in itself it really is." I added, that owing to the operation in English literature of certain causes, "almost the last thing for which one would come to English literature is just that very thing which now Europe most desires,—criticism;" and that the power and value of English literature was thereby impaired. More than one rejoinder declared that the importance I here assigned to criticism was excessive, and asserted the inherent superiority of the creative effort of the human spirit over its critical effort. And the other day, having been led by a Mr. Shairp's[2] excellent notice of Wordsworth* to

* I cannot help thinking that a practice, common in England during the last century, and still followed in France, of printing a notice of this kind,—a notice by a competent critic,—to serve as an introduction to an eminent author's works, might be revived among us with advantage. To introduce all succeeding editions of Wordsworth, Mr. Shairp's notice might, it seems to me, excellently serve; it is written

turn again to his biography, I found, in the words of this great man, whom I, for one, must always listen to with the profoundest respect, a sentence passed on the critic's business, which seems to justify every possible disparagement of it. Wordsworth says in one of his letters:—

"The writers in these publications" (the Reviews), "while they prosecute their inglorious employment, can not be supposed to be in a state of mind very favourable for being affected by the finer influences of a thing so pure as genuine poetry."

And a trustworthy reporter of his conversation quotes a more elaborate judgment to the same effect:—

"Wordsworth holds the critical power very low, infinitely lower than the inventive; and he said to-day that if the quantity of time consumed in writing critiques on the works of others were given to original composition, of whatever kind it might be, it would be much better employed; it would make a man find out sooner his own level, and it would do infinitely less mischief. A false or malicious criticism may do much injury to the minds of others; a stupid invention, either in prose or verse, is quite harmless."[3]

It is almost too much to expect of poor human nature, that a man capable of producing some effect in one line of literature, should, for the greater good of society, voluntarily doom himself to impotence and obscurity in another. Still less is this to be expected from men addicted to the composition of the "false or malicious criticism" of which Wordsworth speaks. However, everybody would admit that a false or malicious criticism had better never have been written. Everybody, too, would be willing to admit, as a general proposition, that the critical faculty is lower than the inventive. But is it true that criticism is really, in itself, a baneful and injurious employment; is it true that all time given to writing critiques on the works of others would be much better employed if it were given to original composition, of whatever kind this may be? Is it true that Johnson had better have gone on producing more *Irenes*[4] instead of writing his *Lives of the Poets;* nay, is it certain that Wordsworth himself was better employed in making his Ecclesiastical Sonnets than when he made his celebrated Preface, so full of criticism, and criticism of the works of others?

from the point of view of an admirer, nay, of a disciple, and that is right; but then the disciple must be also, as in this case he is, a critic, a man of letters, not, as too often happens, some relation or friend with no qualification for his task except affection for his author. [M. A.]

Wordsworth was himself a great critic, and it is to be sincerely regretted that he has not left us more criticism;
Goethe was one of the greatest of critics, and we may sincerely congratulate ourselves that he has left us so much
criticism. Without wasting time over the exaggeration which
Wordsworth's judgment on criticism clearly contains, or
over an attempt to trace the causes,—not difficult, I think,
to be traced,—which may have led Wordsworth to this exaggeration, a critic may with advantage seize an occasion
for trying his own conscience, and for asking himself of
what real service at any given moment the practice of criticism either is or may be made to his own mind and spirit,
and to the minds and spirits of others.

The critical power is of lower rank than the creative.
True; but in assenting to this proposition, one or two things
are to be kept in mind. It is undeniable that the exercise of
a creative power, that a free creative activity, is the highest
function of man; it is proved to be so by man's finding in
it his true happiness. But it is undeniable, also, that men
may have the sense of exercising this free creative activity
in other ways than in producing great works of literature
or art; if it were not so, all but a very few men would be
shut out from the true happiness of all men. They may have
it in well-doing, they may have it in learning, they may
have it even in criticising. This is one thing to be kept in
mind. Another is, that the exercise of the creative power in
the production of great works of literature or art, however
high this exercise of it may rank, is not at all epochs and
under all conditions possible; and that therefore labour may
be vainly spent in attempting it, which might with more
fruit be used in preparing for it, in rendering it possible.
This creative power works with elements, with materials;
what if it has not those materials, those elements, ready for
its use? In that case it must surely wait till they are ready.
Now, in literature,—I will limit myself to literature, for it is
about literature that the question arises,—the elements with
which the creative power works are ideas; the best ideas, on
every matter which literature touches, current at the time.
At any rate we may lay it down as certain that in modern
literature no manifestation of the creative power not working with these can be very important or fruitful. And I say
current at the time, not merely accessible at the time, for
creative literary genius does not principally show itself in
discovering new ideas, that is rather the business of the
philosopher. The grand work of literary genius is a work of
synthesis and exposition, not of analysis and discovery; its

gift lies in the faculty of being happily inspired by a certain intellectual and spiritual atmosphere, by a certain order of ideas, when it finds itself in them; of dealing divinely with these ideas, presenting them in the most effective and attractive combinations,—making beautiful works with them, in short. But it must have the atmosphere, it must find itself amidst the order of ideas, in order to work freely; and these it is not so easy to command. This is why great creative epochs in literature are so rare, this is why there is so much that is unsatisfactory in the productions of many men of real genius; because for the creation of a master-work of literature two powers must concur, the power of the man and the power of the moment, and the man is not enough without the moment; the creative power has, for its happy exercise, appointed elements, and those elements are not in its own control.

Nay, they are more within the control of the critical power. It is the business of the critical power, as I said in the words already quoted, "in all branches of knowledge, theology, philosophy, history, art, science, to see the object as in itself it really is." Thus it tends, at last, to make an intellectual situation of which the creative power can profitably avail itself. It tends to establish an order of ideas, if not absolutely true, yet true by comparison with that which it displaces; to make the best ideas prevail. Presently these new ideas reach society, the touch of truth is the touch of life, and there is a stir and growth everywhere; out of this stir and growth come the creative epochs of literature.

Or, to narrow our range, and quit these considerations of the general march of genius and of society,—considerations which are apt to become too abstract and impalpable,— every one can see that a poet, for instance, ought to know life and the world before dealing with them in poetry; and life and the world being in modern times very complex things, the creation of a modern poet, to be worth much, implies a great critical effort behind it; else it must be a comparatively poor, barren, and short-lived affair. This is why Byron's poetry had so little endurance in it, and Goethe's so much; both Byron and Goethe had a great productive power, but Goethe's was nourished by a great critical effort providing the true materials for it, and Byron's was not; Goethe knew life and the world, the poet's necessary subjects, much more comprehensively and thoroughly than Byron. He knew a great deal more of them, and he knew them much more as they really are.

It has long seemed to me that the burst of creative activity in our literature, through the first quarter of this century, had about it in fact something premature; and that from this cause its productions are doomed, most of them, in spite of the sanguine hopes which accompanied and do still accompany them, to prove hardly more lasting than the productions of far less splendid epochs. And this prematureness comes from its having proceeded without having its proper data, without sufficient materials to work with. In other words, the English poetry of the first quarter of this century, with plenty of energy, plenty of creative force, did not know enough. This makes Byron so empty of matter, Shelley so incoherent, Wordsworth even, profound as he is, yet so wanting in completeness and variety. Wordsworth cared little for books, and disparaged Goethe. I admire Wordsworth, as he is, so much that I cannot wish him different; and it is vain, no doubt, to imagine such a man different from what he is, to suppose that he *could* have been different. But surely the one thing wanting to make Wordsworth an even greater poet than he is,—his thought richer, and his influence of wider application,—was that he should have read more books, among them, no doubt, those of that Goethe whom he disparaged without reading him.

But to speak of books and reading may easily lead to a misunderstanding here. It was not really books and reading that lacked to our poetry at this epoch; Shelley had plenty of reading, Coleridge had immense reading. Pindar and Sophocles—as we all say so glibly, and often with so little discernment of the real import of what we are saying—had not many books; Shakespeare was no deep reader. True; but in the Greece of Pindar and Sophocles, in the England of Shakespeare, the poet lived in a current of ideas in the highest degree animating and nourishing to the creative power; society was, in the fullest measure, permeated by fresh thought, intelligent and alive. And this state of things is the true basis for the creative power's exercise, in this it finds its data, its materials, truly ready for its hand; all the books and reading in the world are only valuable as they are helps to this. Even when this does not actually exist, books and reading may enable a man to construct a kind of semblance of it in his own mind, a world of knowledge and intelligence in which he may live and work. This is by no means an equivalent to the artist for the nationally diffused life and thought of the epochs of Sophocles or Shakespeare; but, besides that it may be a means of preparation for such epochs, it does really constitute, if many share in it, a quick-

ening and sustaining atmosphere of great value. Such an atmosphere the many-sided learning and the long and widely-
combined critical effort of Germany formed for Goethe,
when he lived and worked. There was no national glow of
life and thought there as in the Athens of Pericles or the
England of Elizabeth. That was the poet's weakness. But
there was a sort of equivalent for it in the complete culture
and unfettered thinking of a large body of Germans. That
was his strength. In the England of the first quarter of this
century there was neither a national glow of life and thought,
such as we had in the age of Elizabeth, nor yet a culture
and a force of learning and criticism such as were to be
found in Germany. Therefore the creative power of poetry
wanted, for success in the highest sense, materials and a
basis; a thorough interpretation of the world was necessarily
denied to it.

At first sight it seems strange that out of the immense stir
of the French Revolution and its age should not have come
a crop of works of genius equal to that which came out of
the stir of the great productive time of Greece, or out of
that of the Renascence, with its powerful episode the Reformation. But the truth is that the stir of the French Revolution took a character which essentially distinguished it from
such movements as these. These were, in the main, dis-
interestedly intellectual and spiritual movements; movements
in which the human spirit looked for its satisfaction in itself
and in the increased play of its own activity. The French
Revolution took a political, practical character. The movement which went on in France under the old *régime*,
from 1700 to 1789, was far more really akin than that of
the Revolution itself to the movement of the Renascence;
the France of Voltaire and Rousseau told far more powerfully upon the mind of Europe than the France of the
Revolution. Goethe reproached this last expressly with having "thrown quiet culture back." Nay, and the true key to
how much in our Byron, even in our Wordsworth, is this!
—that they had their source in a great movement of feeling, not in a great movement of mind. The French Revolution, however,—that object of so much blind love and
so much blind hatred,—found undoubtedly its motive-
power in the intelligence of men, and not in their practical
sense; this is what distinguishes it from the English Revolution of Charles the First's time. This is what makes it a more
spiritual event than our Revolution, an event of much more
powerful and world-wide interest, though practically less

successful; it appeals to an order of ideas which are universal, certain, permanent. 1789 asked of a thing, Is it rational? 1642 asked of a thing, Is it legal? or, when it went furthest, Is it according to conscience? This is the English fashion, a fashion to be treated, within its own sphere, with the highest respect; for its success, within its own sphere, has been prodigious. But what is law in one place is not law in another; what is law here to-day is not law even here tomorrow; and as for conscience, what is binding on one man's conscience is not binding on another's. The old woman[5] who threw her stool at the head of the surpliced minister in St. Giles's Church at Edinburgh obeyed an impulse to which millions of the human race may be permitted to remain strangers. But the prescriptions of reason are absolute, unchanging, of universal validity; *to count by tens is the easiest way of counting*—that is a proposition of which every one, from here to the Antipodes, feels the force; at least I should say so if we did not live in a country where it is not impossible that any morning we may find a letter in the *Times* declaring that a decimal coinage is an absurdity. That a whole nation should have been penetrated with an enthusiasm for pure reason, and with an ardent zeal for making its prescriptions triumph, is a very remarkable thing, when we consider how little of mind, or anything so worthy and quickening as mind, comes into the motives which alone, in general, impel great masses of men. In spite of the extravagant direction given to this enthusiasm, in spite of the crimes and follies in which it lost itself, the French Revolution derives from the force, truth, and universality of the ideas which it took for its law, and from the passion with which it could inspire a multitude for these ideas, a unique and still living power; it is—it will probably long remain—the greatest, the most animating event in history. And as no sincere passion for the things of the mind, even though it turn out in many respects an unfortunate passion, is ever quite thrown away and quite barren of good, France has reaped from hers one fruit—the natural and legitimate fruit, though not precisely the grand fruit she expected: she is the country in Europe where *the people* is most alive.

But the mania for giving an immediate political and practical application to all these fine ideas of the reason was fatal. Here an Englishman is in his element: on this theme we can all go on for hours. And all we are in the habit of saying on it has undoubtedly a great deal of truth. Ideas cannot be too much prized in and for themselves, cannot be too much lived with; but to transport them abruptly into the world of politics and practice, violently to revolutionise this world to their bidding,—that is quite another thing. There is the world of ideas and there is the world of practice; the French are often for suppressing the one and the English the other; but neither is to be suppressed. A member of the House of Commons said to me the other day: "That a thing is an anomaly, I consider to be no objection to it whatever." I venture to think he was wrong; that a thing is an anomaly *is* an objection to it, but absolutely and in the sphere of ideas: it is not necessarily, under such and such circumstances, or at such and such a moment, an objection to it in the sphere of politics and practice. Joubert[6] has said beautifully: "C'est la force et le droit qui règlent toutes choses dans le monde; la force en attendant le droit." (Force and right are the governors of this world; force till right is ready.) *Force till right is ready;* and till right is ready, force, the existing order of things, is justified, is the legitimate ruler. But right is something moral, and implies inward recognition, free assent of the will; we are not ready for right,—*right,* so far as we are concerned, *is not ready,* —until we have attained this sense of seeing it and willing it. The way in which for us it may change and transform force, the existing order of things, and become, in its turn, the legitimate ruler of the world, should depend on the way in which, when our time comes, we see it and will it. Therefore for other people enamoured of their own newly discerned right, to attempt to impose it upon us as ours, and violently to substitute their right for our force, is an act of tyranny, and to be resisted. It sets at nought the second great half of our maxim, *force till right is ready.* This was the grand error of the French Revolution; and its movement of ideas, by quitting the intellectual sphere and rushing furiously into the political sphere, ran, indeed, a prodigious and memorable course, but produced no such intellectual fruit as the movement of ideas of the Renascence, and created, in opposition to itself, what I may call an *epoch of concentration.* The great force of that epoch of concentration was England; and the great voice of that epoch of concentration was Burke. It is the fashion to treat Burke's writings on the French Revolution as superannuated and conquered by the event; as the eloquent but unphilosophical tirades of bigotry and prejudice. I will not deny that they are often disfigured by the violence and passion of the moment, and that in some directions Burke's view was bounded, and his observation therefore at fault. But on the whole, and for those who can make the needful corrections, what distinguishes these writings is their profound, permanent, fruitful, philosophical truth. They contain the true philosophy of an epoch of concentration, dissipate the heavy atmosphere which its own nature is apt to engender round it, and make its resistance rational instead of mechanical.

But Burke is so great because, almost alone in England, he brings thought to bear upon politics, he saturates politics with thought. It is his accident that his ideas were at the service of an epoch of concentration, not of an epoch of expansion; it is his characteristic that he so lived by ideas, and had such a source of them welling up within him, that he could float even an epoch of concentration and English Tory politics with them. It does not hurt him that Dr. Price[7] and the Liberals were enraged with him; it does not even hurt him that George the Third and the Tories were enchanted with him. His greatness is that he lived in a world which neither English Liberalism nor English Toryism is apt to enter;—the world of ideas, not the world of catchwords and party habits. So far is it from being really true of him that he "to party gave up what was meant for mankind,"[8] that at the very end of his fierce struggle with the French Revolution, after all his invectives against its false pretensions, hollowness, and madness, with his sincere conviction of its mischievousness, he can close a memorandum on the best means of combating it, some of the last pages he ever wrote,—the *Thoughts on French Affairs,* in December 1791, —with these striking words:—

"The evil is stated, in my opinion, as it exists. The remedy must be where power, wisdom, and information, I hope, are more united with good intentions than they can be with me. I have done with this subject, I believe, for ever. It has given me many anxious moments for the last two years. *If a great change is to be made in human affairs, the minds of men will be fitted to it; the general opinions and feelings will draw that way. Every fear, every hope will forward it; and then they who persist in opposing this mighty current in human affairs, will appear rather to resist the decrees of Providence itself, than the mere designs of men. They will not be resolute and firm, but perverse and obstinate.*"

That return of Burke upon himself has always seemed to me one of the finest things in English literature, or indeed in any literature. That is what I call living by ideas: when one side of a question has long had your earnest support, when all your feelings are engaged, when you hear all round you no language but one, when your party talks this language like a steam-engine and can imagine no other,— still to be able to think, still to be irresistibly carried, if so it be, by the current of thought to the opposite side of the question, and, like Balaam, to be unable to speak anything *but what the Lord has put in your mouth.*[9] I know nothing more striking, and I must add that I know nothing more un-English.

For the Englishman in general is like my friend the Member of Parliament, and believes, point-blank, that for a thing to be an anomaly is absolutely no objection to it whatever. He is like the Lord Auckland of Burke's day, who, in a memorandum on the French Revolution, talks of "certain miscreants, assuming the name of philosophers, who have presumed themselves capable of establishing a new system of society." The Englishman has been called a political animal, and he values what is political and practical so much that ideas easily become objects of dislike in his eyes, and thinkers "miscreants," because ideas and thinkers have rashly meddled with politics and practice. This would be all very well if the dislike and neglect confined themselves to ideas transported out of their own sphere, and meddling rashly with practice; but they are inevitably extended to ideas as such, and to the whole life of intelligence; practice is everything, a free play of the mind is nothing. The notion of the free play of the mind upon all subjects being a pleasure in itself, being an object of desire, being an essential provider of elements without which a nation's spirit, whatever compensations it may have for them, must, in the long run, die of inanition, hardly enters into an Englishman's thoughts. It is noticeable that the word *curiosity*, which in other languages is used in a good sense, to mean, as a high and fine quality of man's nature, just this disinterested love of a free play of the mind on all subjects, for its own sake,—it is noticeable, I say, that this word has in our language no sense of the kind, no sense but a rather bad and disparaging one. But criticism, real criticism, is essentially the exercise of this very quality. It obeys an instinct prompting it to try to know the best that is known and thought in the world, irrespectively of practice, politics, and everything of the kind; and to value knowledge and thought as they approach this best, without the intrusion of any other considerations whatever. This is an instinct for which there is, I think, little original sympathy in the practical English nature, and what there was of it has undergone a long benumbing period of blight and suppression in the epoch of concentration which followed the French Revolution.

But epochs of concentration cannot well endure for ever; epochs of expansion, in the due course of things, follow them. Such an epoch of expansion seems to be opening in this country. In the first place all danger of a hostile forcible pressure of foreign ideas upon our practice has long disappeared; like the traveller in the fable, therefore, we begin to wear our cloak a little more loosely. Then, with a long peace, the ideas of Europe steal gradually and amicably in, and mingle, though in infinitesimally small quantities at a time, with our own notions. Then, too, in spite of all that is said about the absorbing and brutalising influence of our passionate material progress, it seems to me indisputable that this progress is likely, though not certain, to lead in the end to an apparition of intellectual life; and that man, after he has made himself perfectly comfortable and has now to determine what to do with himself next, may begin to remember that he has a mind, and that the mind may be made the source of great pleasure. I grant it is mainly the privilege of faith, at present, to discern this end to our railways, our business, and our fortune-making; but we shall see if, here as elsewhere, faith is not in the end the true prophet. Our ease, our travelling, and our unbounded liberty to hold just as hard and securely as we please to the practice to which our notions have given birth, all tend to beget an inclination to deal a little more freely with these notions themselves, to canvass them a little, to penetrate a little into their real nature. Flutterings of curiosity, in the foreign sense of the word, appear amongst us, and it is in these that criticism must look to find its account. Criticism first; a time of true creative activity, perhaps,—which, as I have said, must inevitably be preceded amongst us by a time of criticism,—hereafter, when criticism has done its work.

It is of the last importance that English criticism should clearly discern what rule for its course, in order to avail itself of the field now opening to it, and to produce fruit for the future, it ought to take. The rule may be summed up in one word,—*disinterestedness*. And how is criticism to show disinterestedness? By keeping aloof from what is called "the practical view of things;" by resolutely following the law of its own nature, which is to be a free play of the mind on all subjects which it touches. By steadily refusing to lend itself to any of those ulterior, political, practical considerations about ideas, which plenty of people will be sure to attach to them, which perhaps ought often to be attached to them, which in this country at any rate are certain to be attached to them quite sufficiently, but which criticism has really nothing to do with. Its business is, as I have said, simply to know the best that is known and thought in the world, and by in its turn making this known, to create a current of true and fresh ideas. Its business is to do this with inflexible honesty, with due ability; but its business is to do no more, and to leave alone all questions of practical consequences and applications, questions which will never fail to have due prominence given to them. Else criticism, besides being really false to its own nature, merely continues in the old rut which it has hitherto followed in this country, and will certainly miss the chance now given to it. For what is at present the bane of criticism in this country? It is that practical considerations cling to it and stifle it. It subserves interests not its own. Our organs of criticism are organs of men and parties having practical ends to serve, and with them those practical ends are the first thing and the play of mind the second; so much play of mind as is compatible with the prosecution of those practical ends is all that is wanted. An organ like the *Revue des Deux Mondes,* having for its main function to understand and utter the best that is known and thought in the world, existing, it may be said, as just an organ for a free play of the mind, we have not. But we have the *Edinburgh Review,* existing as an organ of the old Whigs, and for as much play of the mind as may suit its being that; we have the *Quarterly Review,* existing as an organ of the Tories, and for as much play of mind as may suit its being that; we have the *British Quarterly Review,* existing as an organ of the political Dissenters, and for as much play of mind as may suit its being that; we have the *Times,* existing as an organ of the common, satisfied, well-to-do Englishman, and for as much play of mind as may suit its being that. And so on through all the various fractions, political and religious, of our society; every fraction has, as such, its organ of criticism, but the notion of combining all fractions in the common pleasure of a free disinterested play of mind meets with no favour. Directly this play of mind wants to have more scope, and to forget the pressure of practical considerations a little, it is checked, it is made to feel the chain. We saw this the other day in the extinction, so much to be regretted, of the *Home and Foreign Review.* Perhaps in no organ of criticism in this country was there so much knowledge, so much play of mind; but these could not save it. The *Dublin Review* subordinates play of mind to the practical business of English and Irish Catholicism, and lives. It must needs be that men should act in sects and parties, that each of these sects and parties should have its organ, and should make this organ subserve the interests of its action; but it would be well, too, that there should be a criticism, not the minister of these interests, not their enemy, but absolutely and entirely independent of them. No other criticism will ever attain any real authority or make any real way towards its end,—the creating a current of true and fresh ideas.

It is because criticism has so little kept in the pure intellectual sphere, has so little detached itself from practice, has been so directly polemical and controversial, that it has so ill accomplished, in this country, its best spiritual work; which is to keep man from a self-satisfaction which is retarding and vulgarising, to lead him towards perfection, by making his mind dwell upon what is excellent in itself, and the absolute beauty and fitness of things. A polemical practical criticism makes men blind even to the ideal imperfection of their practice, makes them willingly assert its ideal perfection, in order the better to secure it against attack; and clearly this is narrowing and baneful for them. If they were reassured on the practical side, speculative considerations of ideal perfection they might be brought to entertain, and their spiritual horizon would thus gradually widen. Sir Charles Adderley[10] says to the Warwickshire farmers:—

"Talk of the improvement of breed! Why, the race we ourselves represent, the men and women, the old Anglo-Saxon race, are the best breed in the whole world. . . . The absence of a too enervating climate, too unclouded skies, and a too luxurious nature, has produced so vigorous a race of people, and has rendered us so superior to all the world."

Mr. Roebuck[11] says to the Sheffield cutlers:—

"I look around me and ask what is the state of England? Is not property safe? Is not every man able to say what he likes? Can you not walk from one end of England to the other in perfect security? I ask you whether, the world over or in past history, there is anything like it? Nothing. I pray that our unrivalled happiness may last."

Now obviously there is a peril for poor human nature in words and thoughts of such exuberant self-satisfaction, until we find ourselves safe in the streets of the Celestial City.

"Das wenige verschwindet leicht dem Blicke
Der vorwärts sieht, wie viel noch übrig bleibt—"[12]

says Goethe; "the little that is done seems nothing when we look forward and see how much we have yet to do." Clearly this is a better line of reflection for weak humanity, so long as it remains on this earthly field of labour and trial.

But neither Sir Charles Adderley nor Mr. Roebuck is by nature inaccessible to considerations of this sort. They only lose sight of them owing to the controversial life we all lead, and the practical form which all speculation takes with us. They have in view opponents whose aim is not ideal, but practical; and in their zeal to uphold their own practice against these innovators, they go so far as even to attribute to this practice an ideal perfection. Somebody has been wanting to introduce a six-pound franchise, or to abolish church-rates, or to collect agricultural statistics by force, or to diminish local self-government. How natural, in reply to such proposals, very likely improper or ill-timed, to go a little beyond the mark, and to say stoutly, "Such a race of people as we stand, so superior to all the world! The old Anglo-Saxon race, the best breed in the whole world! I pray that our unrivalled happiness may last! I ask you whether, the world over or in past history, there is anything like it?" And so long as criticism answers this dithyramb by insisting that the old Anglo-Saxon race would be still more superior to all others if it had no church-rates, or that our unrivalled happiness would last yet longer with a six-pound franchise, so long will the strain, "The best breed in the whole world!" swell louder and louder, everything ideal and refining will be lost out of sight, and both the assailed and their critics will remain in a sphere, to say the truth, perfectly unvital, a sphere in which spiritual progression is impossible. But let criticism leave church-rates and the franchise alone, and in the most candid spirit, without a single lurking thought of practical innovation, confront with our dithyramb this paragraph on which I stumbled in a newspaper immediately after reading Mr. Roebuck:—

"A shocking child murder has just been committed at Nottingham. A girl named Wragg left the workhouse there on Saturday morning with her young illegitimate child. The child was soon afterwards found dead on Mapperly Hills, having been strangled. Wragg is in custody."

Nothing but that; but, in juxtaposition with the absolute eulogies of Sir Charles Adderley and Mr. Roebuck, how eloquent, how suggestive are those few lines! "Our old Anglo-Saxon breed, the best in the whole world!"—how much that is harsh and ill-favoured there is in this best! *Wragg!* If we are to talk of ideal perfection, of "the best in the whole world," has any one reflected what a touch of grossness in our race, what an original shortcoming in the more delicate spiritual perceptions, is shown by the natural growth amongst us of such hideous names,—Higginbottom, Stiggins, Bugg! In Ionia and Attica they were luckier in this respect than "the best race in the world;" by the Ilissus there was no Wragg, poor thing! And "our unrivalled happiness;"—what an element of grimness, bareness, and hideousness mixes with it and blurs it; the workhouse, the dismal Mapperly Hills,—how dismal those who have seen them will remember;—the gloom, the smoke, the cold, the strangled illegitimate child! "I ask you whether, the world over or in past history, there is anything like it?" Perhaps not, one is inclined to answer; but at any rate, in that case, the world is very much to be pitied. And the final touch,— short, bleak, and inhuman: *Wragg is in custody.* The sex lost in the confusion of our unrivalled happiness; or (shall I say?) the superfluous Christian name lopped off by the straight-forward vigour of our old Anglo-Saxon breed! There is profit for the spirit in such contrasts as this; criticism serves the cause of perfection by establishing them. By eluding sterile conflict, by refusing to remain in the sphere where alone narrow and relative conceptions have any worth and validity, criticism may diminish its momentary importance, but only in this way has it a chance of gaining admittance for those wider and more perfect conceptions to which all its duty is really owed. Mr. Roebuck will have a poor opinion of an adversary who replies to his defiant songs of triumph only by murmuring under his breath, *Wragg is in custody;* but in no other way will these songs of triumph be induced gradually to moderate themselves, to get rid of what in them is excessive and offensive, and to fall into a softer and truer key.

It will be said that it is a very subtle and indirect action which I am thus prescribing for criticism, and that, by embracing in this manner the Indian virtue of detachment and abandoning the sphere of practical life, it condemns itself to a slow and obscure work. Slow and obscure it may be, but it is the only proper work of criticism. The mass of mankind will never have any ardent zeal for seeing things as they are; very inadequate ideas will always satisfy them. On these inadequate ideas reposes, and must repose, the general practice of the world. That is as much as saying that whoever sets himself to see things as they are will find himself one of a very small circle; but it is only by this small circle resolutely doing its own work that adequate ideas will ever get current at all. The rush and roar of practical life will always have a dizzying and attracting effect upon the most collected spectator, and tend to draw him into its vortex; most of all will this be the case where that life is so powerful as it is in England. But it is only by remaining collected, and refusing to lend himself to the point of view of the practical man, that the critic can do the practical man any service; and it is only by the greatest sincerity in pursuing his own course, and by at last convincing even the practical man of his sincerity, that he can escape misunderstandings which perpetually threaten him.

For the practical man is not apt for fine distinctions, and yet in these distinctions truth and the highest culture greatly find their account. But it is not easy to lead a practical man, —unless you reassure him as to your practical intentions, you have no chance of leading him,—to see that a thing which he has always been used to look at from one side only, which he greatly values, and which, looked at from that side, quite deserves, perhaps, all the prizing and admiring which he bestows upon it,—that this thing, looked at from another side, may appear much less beneficent and beautiful, and yet retain all its claims to our practical allegiance. Where shall we find language innocent enough, how shall we make the spotless purity of our intentions evident enough, to enable us to say to the political Englishman that the British Constitution itself, which, seen from the practical side, looks such a magnificent organ of progress and virtue, seen from the speculative side,—with its compromises, its love of facts, its horror of theory, its studied avoidance of clear thoughts,—that, seen from this side, our august Constitution sometimes looks,—forgive me, shade of Lord Somers![13]—a colossal machine for the manufacture of Philistines? How is Cobbett[14] to say this and not be misunderstood, blackened as he is with the smoke of a life-long conflict in the field of political practice? how is Mr. Carlyle to say it and not be misunderstood, after his furious raid into this field with his *Latter-day Pamphlets?* how is Mr. Ruskin, after his pugnacious political economy? I say, the critic must keep out of the region of immediate practice in the political, social, humanitarian sphere, if he wants to make a beginning for that more free speculative treatment of things, which may perhaps one day make its benefits felt even in this sphere, but in a natural and thence irresistible manner.

Do what he will, however, the critic will still remain exposed to frequent misunderstandings, and nowhere so much as in this country. For here people are particularly indisposed even to comprehend that without this free disinterested treatment of things, truth and the highest culture are out of the question. So immersed are they in practical life, so accustomed to take all their notions from this life and its processes, that they are apt to think that truth and culture themselves can be reached by the processes of this life, and that it is an impertinent singularity to think of reaching them in any other. "We are all *terræ filii*,"[15] cries their eloquent advocate; "all Philistines together. Away with the notion of proceeding by any other course than the course dear to the Philistines; let us have a social movement, let us organise and combine a party to pursue truth and new thought, let us call it *the liberal party*, and let us all stick to each other, and back each other up. Let us have no nonsense about independent criticism, and intellectual delicacy, and the few and the many. Don't let us trouble ourselves about foreign thought; we shall invent the whole thing for ourselves as we go along. If one of us speaks well, applaud him; if one of us speaks ill, applaud him too; we are all in the same movement, we are all liberals, we are all in pursuit of truth." In this way the pursuit of truth becomes really a social, practical, pleasurable affair, almost requiring a chairman, a secretary, and advertisements; with the excitement of an occasional scandal, with a little resistance to give the happy sense of difficulty overcome; but, in general, plenty of bustle and very little thought. To act is so easy, as Goethe says; to think is so hard! It is true that the critic has many temptations to go with the stream, to make one of the party movement, one of these *terræ filii*; it seems ungracious to refuse to be a *terræ filius*, when so many excellent people are; but the critic's duty is to refuse, or, if resistance is vain, at least to cry with Obermann: *Périssons en résistant.*[16]

How serious a matter it is to try and resist, I had ample opportunity of experiencing when I ventured some time ago to criticise the celebrated first volume of Bishop Colenso.*

---

* So sincere is my dislike to all personal attack and controversy, that I abstain from reprinting, at this distance of time from the occasion which called them forth, the essays in which I criticised Dr. Colenso's book; I feel bound, however, after all that has passed, to make here a final declaration of my sincere impenitence for having published them. Nay, I cannot forbear repeating yet once more, for his benefit and that of his readers, this sentence from my original

The echoes of the storm which was then raised I still, from time to time, hear grumbling round me. That storm arose out of a misunderstanding almost inevitable. It is a result of no little culture to attain to a clear perception that science and religion are two wholly different things. The multitude will for ever confuse them; but happily that is of no great real importance, for while the multitude imagines itself to live by its false science, it does really live by its true religion. Dr. Colenso,[17] however, in his first volume did all he could to strengthen the confusion,* and to make it dangerous. He did this with the best intentions, I freely admit, and with the most candid ignorance that this was the natural effect of what he was doing; but, says Joubert, "Ignorance, which in matters of morals extenuates the crime, is itself, in intellectual matters, a crime of the first order." I criticised Bishop Colenso's speculative confusion. Immediately there was a cry raised: "What is this? here is a liberal attacking a liberal. Do not you belong to the movement? are not you a friend of truth? Is not Bishop Colenso in pursuit of truth? then speak with proper respect of his book. Dr. Stanley[18] is another friend of truth, and you speak with proper respect of his book; why make these invidious differences? both books are excellent, admirable, liberal; Bishop Colenso's perhaps the most so, because it is the boldest, and will have the best practical consequences for the liberal cause. Do you want to encourage to the attack of a brother liberal his, and your, and our implacable enemies, the *Church and State Review* or the *Record*,—the High Church rhinoceros and the Evangelical hyæna? Be silent, therefore; or rather speak, speak as loud as ever you can! and go into ecstasies over the eighty and odd pigeons."[19]

But criticism cannot follow this coarse and indiscriminate method. It is unfortunately possible for a man in pursuit of truth to write a book which reposes upon a false conception. Even the practical consequences of a book are to genuine criticism no recommendation of it, if the book is, in the highest sense, blundering. I see that a lady who her-

---

remarks upon him: *There is truth of science and truth of religion; truth of science does not become truth of religion till it is made religious.* And I will add: Let us have all the science there is from the men of science; from the men of religion let us have religion. [M. A.]

* It has been said I make it "a crime against literary criticism and the higher culture to attempt to inform the ignorant." Need I point out that the ignorant are not informed by being confirmed in a confusion? [M. A.]

self, too, is in pursuit of truth, and who writes with great ability, but a little too much, perhaps, under the influence of the practical spirit of the English liberal movement, classes Bishop Colenso's book and M. Renan's together, in her survey of the religious state of Europe, as facts of the same order, works, both of them, of "great importance;" "great ability, power, and skill;" Bishop Colenso's, perhaps, the most powerful; at least, Miss Cobbe[20] gives special expression to her gratitude that to Bishop Colenso "has been given the strength to grasp, and the courage to teach, truths of such deep import." In the same way, more than one popular writer has compared him to Luther. Now it is just this kind of false estimate which the critical spirit is, it seems to me, bound to resist. It is really the strongest possible proof of the low ebb at which, in England, the critical spirit is, that while the critical hit in the religious literature of Germany is Dr. Strauss's book, in that of France M. Renan's book, the book of Bishop Colenso is the critical hit in the religious literature of England. Bishop Colenso's book reposes on a total misconception of the essential elements of the religious problem, as that problem is now presented for solution. To criticism, therefore, which seeks to have the best that is known and thought on this problem, it is, however well meant, of no importance whatever. M. Renan's book attempts a new synthesis of the elements furnished to us by the Four Gospels. It attempts, in my opinion, a synthesis, perhaps premature, perhaps impossible, certainly not successful. Up to the present time, at any rate, we must acquiesce in Fleury's sentence on such recastings of the Gospel-story: *Quiconque s'imagine la pouvoir mieux écrire, ne l'entend pas.*[21] M. Renan had himself passed by anticipation a like sentence on his own work, when he said: "If a new presentation of the character of Jesus were offered to me, I would not have it; its very clearness would be, in my opinion, the best proof of its insufficiency." His friends may with perfect justice rejoin that at the sight of the Holy Land, and of the actual scene of the Gospel-story, all the current of M. Renan's thoughts may have naturally changed, and a new casting of that story irresistibly suggested itself to him; and that this is just a case for applying Cicero's maxim: Change of mind is not inconsistency—*nemo doctus unquam mutationem consilii inconstantiam dixit esse.*[22] Nevertheless, for criticism, M. Renan's first thought must still be the truer one, as long as his new casting so fails more fully to commend itself, more fully (to use Coleridge's[23] happy phrase about the Bible) to *find* us. Still M. Renan's attempt is, for criticism, of the most real interest and importance, since, with all its difficulty, a fresh synthesis of the New Testament *data*,—not a making war on them, in Voltaire's fashion, not a leaving them out of mind, in the world's fashion, but the putting a new construction upon them, the taking them from under the old, traditional, conventional point of view and placing them under a new one,—is the very essence of the religious problem, as now presented; and only by efforts in this direction can it receive a solution.

Again, in the same spirit in which she judges Bishop Colenso, Miss Cobbe, like so many earnest liberals of our practical race, both here and in America, herself sets vigorously about a positive reconstruction of religion, about making a religion of the future out of hand, or at least setting about making it. We must not rest, she and they are always thinking and saying, in negative criticism, we must be creative and constructive; hence we have such works as her recent *Religious Duty,* and works still more considerable, perhaps, by others, which will be in every one's mind. These works often have much ability; they often spring out of sincere convictions, and a sincere wish to do good; and they sometimes, perhaps, do good. Their fault is (if I may be permitted to say so) one which they have in common with the British College of Health, in the New Road. Every one knows the British College of Health; it is that building with the lion and the statue of the Goddess Hygeia before it; at least I am sure about the lion, though I am not absolutely certain about the Goddess Hygeia. This building does credit, perhaps, to the resources of Dr. Morrison[24] and his disciples; but it falls a good deal short of one's idea of what a British College of Health ought to be. In England, where we hate public interference and love individual enterprise, we have a whole crop of places like the British College of Health; the grand name without the grand thing. Unluckily, creditable to individual enterprise as they are, they tend to impair our taste by making us forget what more grandiose, noble, or beautiful character properly belongs to a public institution. The same may be said of the religions of the future of Miss Cobbe and others. Creditable, like the British College of Health, to the resources of their authors, they yet tend to make us forget what more grandiose, noble, or beautiful character properly belongs to religious constructions. The historic religions, with all their faults, have had this; it certainly belongs to the religious sentiment, when it truly flowers, to have this; and we impoverish our spirit if we allow a religion of the future without it. What then is the duty of criticism here? To take the practical point of view, to applaud the liberal movement and all its works,—its New Road religions of the future into the bargain,—for their general utility's sake? By no means; but to be perpetually dissatisfied with these works, while they perpetually fall short of a high and perfect ideal.

For criticism, these are elementary laws; but they never can be popular, and in this country they have been very little followed, and one meets with immense obstacles in following them. That is a reason for asserting them again and again. Criticism must maintain its independence of the practical spirit and its aims. Even with well-meant efforts of the practical spirit it must express dissatisfaction, if in the sphere of the ideal they seem impoverishing and limiting. It must not hurry on to the goal because of its practical importance. It must be patient, and know how to wait; and flexible, and know how to attach itself to things and how to withdraw from them. It must be apt to study and praise elements that for the fulness of spiritual perfection are wanted, even though they belong to a power which in the practical sphere may be maleficent. It must be apt to discern the spiritual shortcomings or illusions of powers that in the practical sphere may be beneficent. And this without any notion of favouring or injuring, in the practical sphere, one power or the other; without any notion of playing off, in this sphere, one power against the other. When one looks, for instance, at the English Divorce Court,—an institution which perhaps has its practical conveniences, but which in the ideal sphere is so hideous; an institution which neither makes divorce impossible nor makes it decent, which allows a man to get rid of his wife, or a wife of her husband, but makes them drag one another first, for the public edification, through a mire of unutterable infamy,—when one looks at this charming institution, I say, with its crowded trials, its newspaper reports, and its money compensations, this institution in which the gross unregenerate British Philistine has indeed stamped an image of himself,—one may be permitted to find the marriage theory of Catholicism refreshing and elevating. Or when Protestantism, in virtue of its supposed rational and intellectual origin, gives the law to criticism too magisterially, criticism may and must remind it that its pretensions, in this respect, are illusive and do it harm; that the Reformation was a moral rather than an intellectual event; that Luther's theory of grace no more exactly reflects the mind of the spirit than Bossuet's[25] philosophy of history reflects it; and that there is no more antecedent probability of the Bishop of Durham's stock of ideas being agreeable to perfect reason than of Pope Pius the Ninth's. But criticism will not on that account forget the achievements of Protestantism in the practical and moral sphere; nor that, even in the intellectual sphere, Protestantism, though in a blind and stumbling manner, carried forward the Renascence, while Catholicism threw itself violently across its path.

I lately heard a man of thought and energy contrasting the want of ardour and movement which he now found amongst young men in this country with what he remembered in his own youth, twenty years ago. "What reformers we were then!" he exclaimed; "what a zeal we had! how we canvassed every institution in Church and State, and were prepared to remodel them all on first principles!" He was inclined to regret, as a spiritual flagging, the lull which he saw. I am disposed rather to regard it as a pause in which the turn to a new mode of spiritual progress is being accomplished. Everything was long seen, by the young and ardent amongst us, in inseparable connection with politics and practical life. We have pretty well exhausted the benefits of seeing things in this connection, we have got all that can be got by so seeing them. Let us try a more disinterested mode of seeing them; let us betake ourselves more to the serener life of the mind and spirit. This life, too, may have its excesses and dangers; but they are not for us at present. Let us think of quietly enlarging our stock of true and fresh ideas, and not, as soon as we get an idea or half an idea, be running out with it into the street, and trying to make it rule there. Our ideas will, in the end, shape the world all the better for maturing a little. Perhaps in fifty years' time it will in the English House of Commons be an objection to an institution that it is an anomaly, and my friend the Member of Parliament will shudder in his grave. But let us in the meanwhile rather endeavour that in twenty years' time it may, in English literature, be an objection to a proposition that it is absurd. That will be a change so vast, that the imagination almost fails to grasp it. *Ab integro sæclorum nascitur ordo.*[26]

If I have insisted so much on the course which criticism must take where politics and religion are concerned, it is because, where these burning matters are in question, it is most likely to go astray. I have wished, above all, to insist on the attitude which criticism should adopt towards things in general; on its right tone and temper of mind. But then comes another question as to the subject-matter which literary criticism should most seek. Here, in general, its course is determined for it by the idea which is the law of its being; the idea of a disinterested endeavour to learn and propagate the best that is known and thought in the world, and thus to establish a current of fresh and true ideas. By the very nature of things, as England is not all the world, much of the best that is known and thought in the world cannot be of English growth, must be foreign; by the nature of things, again, it is just this that we are least likely to know, while English thought is streaming in upon us from all sides, and takes excellent care that we shall not be ignorant of its existence. The English critic of literature, therefore, must dwell much on foreign thought, and with particular heed on any part of it, which, while significant and fruitful in itself, is for any reason specially likely to escape him. Again, judging is often spoken of as the critic's one business, and so in some sense it is; but the judgment which almost insensibly forms itself in a fair and clear mind, along with fresh knowledge, is the valuable one; and thus knowledge, and ever fresh knowledge, must be the critic's great concern for himself. And it is by communicating fresh knowledge, and letting his own judgment pass along with it,—but insensibly, and in the second place, not the first, as a sort of companion and clue, not as an abstract lawgiver,—that the critic will generally do most good to his readers. Sometimes, no doubt, for the sake of establishing an author's place in literature, and his relation to a central standard (and if this is not done, how are we to get at our *best in the world?*) criticism may have to deal with a subject-matter so familiar that fresh knowledge is out of the question, and then it must be all judgment; an enunciation and detailed application of principles. Here the great safeguard is never to let oneself become abstract, always to retain an intimate and lively consciousness of the truth of what one is saying, and, the moment this fails us, to be sure that something is wrong. Still, under all circumstances, this mere judgment and application of principles is, in itself, not the most satisfactory work to the critic; like mathematics, it is tautological, and cannot well give us, like fresh learning, the sense of creative activity.

But stop, some one will say; all this talk is of no practical use to us whatever; this criticism of yours is not what we have in our minds when we speak of criticism; when we speak of critics and criticism, we mean critics and criticism of the current English literature of the day; when you offer to tell criticism its function, it is to this criticism that we expect you to address yourself. I am sorry for it, for I am afraid I must disappoint these expectations. I am bound by my own definition of criticism: *a disinterested endeavour to learn and propagate the best that is known and thought in the world.* How much of current English literature comes into this "best that is known and thought in the world?" Not very much, I fear; certainly less, at this moment, than of the current literature of France or Germany. Well, then, am I to alter my definition of criticism, in order to meet the requirements of a number of practising English critics, who, after all, are free in their choice of a business? That would be making criticism lend itself just to one of those alien practical considerations, which, I have said, are so fatal to it. One may say, indeed, to those who have to deal with the mass—so much better disregarded—of current English literature, that they may at all events endeavour, in dealing with this, to try it, so far as they can, by the standard of the best that is known and thought in the world; one may say, that to get anywhere near this standard, every critic should try and possess one great literature, at least, besides his own; and the more unlike his own, the better. But, after all, the criticism I am really concerned with,—the criticism which alone can much help us for the future, the criticism which, throughout Europe, is at the present day meant, when so much stress is laid on the importance of criticism and the critical spirit,—is a criticism which regards Europe as being, for intellectual and spiritual purposes, one great confederation, bound to a joint action and working to a common result; and whose members have, for their proper outfit, a knowledge of Greek, Roman, and Eastern antiquity, and of one another. Special, local, and temporary advantages being put out of account, that modern nation will in the intellectual and spiritual sphere make most progress, which most thoroughly carries out this programme. And what is that but saying that we too, all of us, as individuals, the more thoroughly we carry it out, shall make the more progress?

There is so much inviting us!—what are we to take? what will nourish us in growth towards perfection? That is the question which, with the immense field of life and of literature lying before him, the critic has to answer; for himself first, and afterwards for others. In this idea of the critic's business the essays brought together in the following pages[27] have had their origin; in this idea, widely different as are their subjects, they have, perhaps, their unity.

I conclude with what I said at the beginning: to have the sense of creative activity is the great happiness and the great proof of being alive, and it is not denied to criticism to have it; but then criticism must be sincere, simple, flexible, ardent, ever widening its knowledge. Then it may have, in no contemptible measure, a joyful sense of creative activity; a sense which a man of insight and conscience will prefer to what he might derive from a poor, starved, fragmentary, inadequate creation. And at some epochs no other creation is possible.

Still, in full measure, the sense of creative activity belongs only to genuine creation; in literature we must never forget that. But what true man of letters ever can forget it? It is no such common matter for a gifted nature to come into possession of a current of true and living ideas, and to produce amidst the inspiration of them, that we are likely to underrate it. The epochs of Æschylus and Shakespeare make us feel their pre-eminence. In an epoch like those is, no doubt, the true life of literature; there is the promised land, towards which criticism can only beckon. That promised land it will not be ours to enter, and we shall die in the wilderness: but to have desired to enter it, to have saluted it from afar, is already, perhaps, the best distinction among contemporaries; it will certainly be the best title to esteem with posterity.

NOTES

The Function of Criticism at the Present Time: Delivered at Oxford, October, 1864; published in *National Review* (November,1864); *Essays in Criticism* (1865).

1. See pp. 232–3.
2. J. C. Shairp, in *North British Review* (August, 1864).
3. Christopher Wordsworth, *Memoirs of Wordsworth* (1851), ii.53, 439 (R. H. Super).
4. Johnson's tragedy *Irene* (1749).
5. "Jenny Geddes, on July 23, 1637; see *Dictionary of National Biography*" (R. H. Super).
6. See p. 390.
7. R. H. Super notes: "Richard Price (1723–91), Nonconformist minister whose sermon of November 4, 1789, in praise of the French Revolution stirred Burke to the writing of his *Reflections on the Revolution in France*."
8. Goldsmith, "Retaliation."
9. *Numbers,* xxii.38.
10. M. P. for North Staffordshire.
11. M. P. for Sheffield.

12. *Iphigenie auf Tauris,* I.ii.91–92.

13. R. H. Super notes: "John, Lord Somers (1651–1716) presided over the drafting of the Declaration of Rights after the abdication of James II."

14. William Cobbett (1763–1835), political writer.

15. Persius, vi.59: *Sons of (mother) earth.*

16. Senancour, *Obermann,* Letter xc: *Let us die in resisting.*

17. J. W. Colenso (1814–83), bishop of Natal, whose study of the Pentateuch (1862–79) excited great controversy and caused him to be deposed from his See.

18. A. P. Stanley (1815–81).

19. In his essay "The Bishop and the Philosopher" (January, 1863), Arnold had ridiculed Colenso's arithmetical scholarship: "as to the account in Leviticus of the provision made for the priests: 'If three priests have to eat 264 pigeons a day, how many must each priest eat?'"

20. Frances Cobbe, *Broken Lights* (1864).

21. *Anyone who supposes he could write it better does not understand it;* Claude Fleury, 18th-century ecclesiastical historian.

22. *Ad Atticum,* XVI vii: *No philosopher ever called a change of plan inconsistency.*

23. *Confessions of an Inquiring Spirit* (posthumously published, 1840).

24. R. H. Super corrects to "Morison": "Founded by James Morison (1770–1840), self-styled 'the Hygeist,' in 1828 for the dispensing of his vegetable pills."

25. J. B. Bossuet (1627–1704), for whom history was Providence.

26. Virgil, *Eclogues,* iv.5: *The order of the ages is born anew.*

27. "The Function of Criticism" opened *Essays in Criticism* (1865).

from ON THE STUDY OF
CELTIC LITERATURE

1866

SENTIMENTAL,—*always ready to react against the despotism of fact;* that is the description a great friend* of the Celt gives of him; and it is not a bad description of the sentimental temperament; it lets us into the secret of its dangers and of its habitual want of success. Balance, measure, and patience, these are the eternal conditions, even supposing the happiest temperament to start with, of high success; and balance, measure, and patience are just what the Celt has never had. Even in the world of spiritual creation, he has never, in spite of his admirable gifts of quick perception and warm emotion, succeeded perfectly, because he never has had steadiness, patience, sanity enough to comply with the conditions under which alone can expression be perfectly given to the finest perceptions and emotions. The Greek has the same perceptive, emotional temperament as the Celt; but he adds to this temperament the sense of *measure;* hence his admirable success in the plastic arts, in which the Celtic genius, with its chafing against the despotism of fact, its perpetual straining after mere emotion, has accomplished nothing. In the comparatively petty art of ornamentation, in rings, brooches, crosiers, relic-cases, and so on, he has done just enough to show his delicacy of taste, his happy temperament; but the grand difficulties of painting and sculpture, the prolonged dealings of spirit with

* Monsieur Henri Martin, whose chapters on the Celts, in his *Histoire de France*, are full of information and interest. [M. A.]

matter, he has never had patience for. Take the more spiritual arts of music and poetry. All that emotion alone can do in music the Celt has done; the very soul of emotion breathes in the Scotch and Irish airs; but with all this power of musical feeling, what has the Celt, so eager for emotion that he has not patience for science, effected in music, to be compared with what the less emotional German, steadily developing his musical feeling with the science of a Sebastian Bach or a Beethoven, has effected? In poetry, again,—poetry which the Celt has so passionately, so nobly loved; poetry where emotion counts for so much, but where reason, too, reason, measure, sanity, also count for so much,—the Celt has shown genius, indeed, splendid genius; but even here his faults have clung to him, and hindered him from producing great works, such as other nations with a genius for poetry,—the Greeks, say, or the Italians,—have produced. The Celt has not produced great poetical works, he has only produced poetry with an air of greatness investing it all, and sometimes giving, moreover, to short pieces, or to passages, lines, and snatches of long pieces, singular beauty and power. And yet he loved poetry so much that he grudged no pains to it; but the true art, the *architectonicé* which shapes great works, such as the *Agamemnon* or the *Divine Comedy*, comes only after a steady, deep-searching survey, a firm conception of the facts of human life, which the Celt has not patience for. So he runs off into technic, where he employs the utmost elaboration, and attains astonishing skill; but in the contents of his poetry you have only so much interpretation of the world as the first dash of a quick, strong perception, and then sentiment, infinite sentiment, can bring you. Here, too, his want of sanity and steadfastness has kept the Celt back from the highest success.

* * *

If I were asked where English poetry got these three things, its turn for style, its turn for melancholy, and its turn for natural magic, for catching and rendering the charm of nature in a wonderfully near and vivid way,—I should answer, with some doubt, that it got much of its turn for style from a Celtic source; with less doubt, that it got much of its melancholy from a Celtic source; with no doubt at all, that from a Celtic source it got nearly all its natural magic.

Any German with penetration and tact in matters of literary criticism will own that the principal deficiency of German poetry is in style; that for style, in the highest

sense, it shows but little feeling. Take the eminent masters
of style, the poets who best give the idea of what the peculiar
power which lies in style is,—Pindar, Virgil, Dante, Milton.
An example of the peculiar effect which these poets produce, you can hardly give from German poetry. Examples
enough you can give from German poetry of the effect
produced by genius, thought, and feeling expressing themselves in clear language, simple language, passionate language, eloquent language, with harmony and melody; but
not of the peculiar effect exercised by eminent power of
style. Every reader of Dante can at once call to mind what
the peculiar effect I mean is; I spoke of it in my lectures on
translating Homer,[1] and there I took an example of it from
Dante, who perhaps manifests it more eminently than any
other poet. But from Milton, too, one may take examples of
it abundantly; compare this from Milton:—

> . . . . . nor sometimes forget
> Those other two equal with me in fate,
> So were I equall'd with them in renown,
> Blind Thamyris and blind Mæonides—[2]

with this from Goethe:—

> Es bildet ein Talent sich in der Stille,
> Sich ein Character in dem Strom der Welt.[3]

Nothing can be better in its way than the style in which
Goethe there presents his thought, but it is the style of prose
as much as of poetry; it is lucid, harmonious, earnest, eloquent, but it has not received that peculiar kneading, heightening, and recasting which is observable in the style of the
passage from Milton,—a style which seems to have for its
cause a certain pressure of emotion, and an ever-surging, yet
bridled, excitement in the poet, giving a special intensity to
his way of delivering himself. In poetical races and epochs
this turn for style is peculiarly observable; and perhaps it is
only on condition of having this somewhat heightened and
difficult manner, so different from the plain manner of
prose, that poetry gets the privilege of being loosed, at its
best moments, into that perfectly simple, limpid style, which
is the supreme style of all, but the simplicity of which is still
not the simplicity of prose. The simplicity of Menander's[4]
style is the simplicity of prose, and is the same kind of simplicity as that which Goethe's style, in the passage I have
quoted, exhibits; but Menander does not belong to a great
poetical moment, he comes too late for it; it is the simple
passages in poets like Pindar or Dante which are perfect,

being masterpieces of *poetical* simplicity. One may say the same of the simple passages in Shakespeare; they are perfect, their simplicity being a *poetical* simplicity. They are the golden, easeful, crowning moments of a manner which is always pitched in another key from that of prose, a manner changed and heightened; the Elizabethan style, regnant in most of our dramatic poetry to this day, is mainly the continuation of this manner of Shakespeare's. It was a manner much more turbid and strewn with blemishes than the manner of Pindar, Dante, or Milton; often it was detestable; but it owed its existence to Shakespeare's instinctive impulse towards *style* in poetry, to his native sense of the necessity for it; and without the basis of style everywhere, faulty though it may in some places be, we should not have had the beauty of expression, unsurpassable for effectiveness and charm, which is reached in Shakespeare's best passages. The turn for style is perceptible all through English poetry, proving, to my mind, the genuine poetical gift of the race; this turn imparts to our poetry a stamp of high distinction, and sometimes it doubles the force of a poet not by nature of the very highest order, such as Gray, and raises him to a rank beyond what his natural richness and power seem to promise. Goethe, with his fine critical perception, saw clearly enough both the power of style in itself, and the lack of style in the literature of his own country; and perhaps if we regard him solely as a German, not as a European, his great work was that he laboured all his life to impart style into German literature, and firmly to establish it there. Hence the immense importance to him of the world of classical art, and of the productions of Greek or Latin genius, where style so eminently manifests its power. Had he found in the German genius and literature an element of style existing by nature and ready to his hand, half his work, one may say, would have been saved him, and he might have done much more in poetry. But as it was, he had to try and create, out of his own powers, a style for German poetry, as well as to provide contents for this style to carry; and thus his labour as a poet was doubled.

It is to be observed that power of style, in the sense in which I am here speaking of style, is something quite different from the power of idiomatic, simple, nervous, racy expression, such as the expression of healthy, robust natures so often is, such as Luther's was in a striking degree. Style, in my sense of the world, is a peculiar recasting and heightening, under a certain condition of spiritual excitement, of what a man has to say, in such a manner as to add dignity and distinction to it; and dignity and distinction are not terms which suit many acts or words of Luther. Deeply touched with the *Gemeinheit*[5] which is the bane of his nation, as he is at the same time a grand example of the honesty which is his nation's excellence, he can seldom even show himself brave, resolute, and truthful, without showing a strong dash of coarseness and commonness all the while; the right definition of Luther, as of our own Bunyan, is that he is a Philistine of genius. So Luther's sincere idiomatic German,—such language as this: "Hilf lieber Gott, wie manchen Jammer habe ich gesehen, dass der gemeine Mann doch so gar nichts weiss won der christlichen Lehre!"[6]—no more proves a power of style in German literature, than Cobbett's sinewy idiomatic English proves it in English literature. Power of style, properly so called, as manifested in masters of style like Dante or Milton in poetry, Cicero, Bossuet or Bolingbroke[7] in prose, is something quite different, and has, as I have said, for its characteristic effect, this: to add dignity and distinction.

Style, then, the Germans are singularly without, and it is strange that the power of style should show itself so strongly as it does in the Icelandic poetry, if the Scandinavians are such genuine Teutons as is commonly supposed. Fauriel[8] used to talk of the Scandinavian Teutons and the German Teutons, as if they were two divisions of the same people, and the common notion about them, no doubt, is very much this. Since the war in Schleswig-Holstein, however, all one's German friends are exceedingly anxious to insist on the difference of nature between themselves and the Scandinavians; when one expresses surprise that the German sense of nationality should be so deeply affronted by the rule over Germans, not of Latins or Celts, but of brother Teutons or next door to it, a German will give you I know not how long a catalogue of the radical points of unlikeness, in genius and disposition, between himself and a Dane. This emboldens me to remark that there is a fire, a sense of style, a distinction, in Icelandic poetry, which German poetry has not. Icelandic poetry, too, shows a powerful and developed technic; and I wish to throw out, for examination by those who are competent to sift the matter, the suggestion that this power of style and development of technic in the Norse poetry seems to point towards an early Celtic influence or intermixture. It is curious that Zeuss, in his grammar, quotes a text which gives countenance to this notion; as late as the ninth century, he says, there were Irish Celts in Iceland; and the text he quotes to show this, is as follows:—"In 870 A.D., when the Norwegians came to Iceland, there were Christians there, who departed, and left behind them Irish books, bells, and other things; from whence it may be inferred that these Christians were Irish." I speak, and ought to speak, with the utmost diffidence on all these questions of ethnology; but I must say that when I read this text in Zeuss, I caught eagerly at the clue it seemed to offer; for I had been hearing the *Nibelungen* read and commented on in German schools (German schools have the good habit of reading and commenting on German poetry, as we read and comment on Homer and Virgil, but do *not* read and comment on Chaucer and Shakespeare), and it struck me how the fatal humdrum and want of style of the Germans had marred their way of telling this magnificent tradition of the *Nibelungen*, and taken half its grandeur and power out of it; while in the Icelandic poems which deal with this tradition, its grandeur and power are much more fully visible, and everywhere in the poetry of the Edda there is a force of style and a distinction as unlike as possible to the want of both in the German *Nibelungen*.* At the same time the Scandinavians have a realism, as it is called, in their genius, which abundantly proves their relationship with the Germans; any one whom Mr. Dasent's[9] delightful books have made acquainted with the prose tales of the Norsemen, will be struck with the stamp of a Teutonic nature in them; but the Norse poetry seems to have something which from Teutonic sources alone it could not have derived; which the Germans have not, and which the Celts have.

This something is *style*, and the Celts certainly have it in a wonderful measure. Style is the most striking quality of their poetry. Celtic poetry seems to make up to itself for being unable to master the world and give an adequate interpretation

* Lord Strangford's note on this is:—"The Irish monks whose bells and books were found in Iceland could not have contributed anything to the old Norse spirit, for they had perished before the first Norsemen had set foot on the island. The form of the old Norse poetry known to us as Icelandic, from the accident of its preservation in that island alone, is surely Pan-Teutonic from old times; the art and method of its strictly literary cultivation must have been much influenced by the contemporary Old-English national poetry, with which the Norsemen were in constant contact; and its larger, freer, and wilder spirit must have been owing to their freer and wilder life, to say nothing of their roused and warring paganism. They could never have known any Celts save when living in embryo with other Teutons."

Very likely Lord Strangford is right, but the proposition with which he begins is at variance with what the text quoted by Zeuss alleges. [M. A.]

of it, by throwing all its force into style, by bending language at any rate to its will, and expressing the ideas it has with unsurpassable intensity, elevation, and effect. It has all through it a sort of intoxication of style,—a *Pindarism,* to use a word formed from the name of the poet, on whom, above all other poets, the power of style seems to have exercised an inspiring and intoxicating effect; and not in its great poets only, in Taliesin, or Llywarch Hen, or Ossian, does the Celtic genius show this Pindarism, but in all its productions:—

> "The grave of March is this, and this the grave of Gwythyr;
> Here is the grave of Gwgawn Gleddyfreidd;[10]
> But unknown is the grave of Arthur."

That comes from the Welsh *Memorials of the Graves of the Warriors,* and if we compare it with the familiar memorial inscriptions of an English churchyard (for we English have so much Germanism in us that our productions offer abundant examples of German want of style as well as of its opposite):—

> "Afflictions sore long time I bore,
> Physicians were in vain,
> Till God did please Death should me seize
> And ease me of my pain"—

if, I say, we compare the Welsh memorial lines with the English, which in their *Gemeinheit* of style are truly Germanic, we shall get a clear sense of what that Celtic talent for style I have been speaking of is.

Or take this epitaph of an Irish Celt, Angus the Culdee, whose *Félire,* or festology, I have already mentioned;—a festology in which, at the end of the eighth or beginning of the ninth century, he collected from "the countless hosts of the illuminated books of Erin" (to use his own words) the festivals of the Irish saints, his poem having a stanza for every day in the year. The epitaph on Angus, who died at Cluain Eidhnech, in Queen's County, runs thus:—

> "Angus in the assembly of Heaven,
> Here are his tomb and his bed;
> It is from hence he went to death,
> In the Friday, to holy Heaven.
>
> "It was in Cluain Eidhnech he was rear'd;
> It was in Cluain Eidhnech he was buried;
> In Cluain Eidhnech, of many crosses,
> He first read his psalms."

That is by no eminent hand; and yet a Greek epitaph could not show a finer perception of what constitutes propriety and felicity of style in compositions of this nature. Take the well-known Welsh prophecy about the fate of the Britons:—

> "Their Lord they will praise,
> Their speech they will keep,
> Their land they will lose,
> Except wild Wales."

To however late an epoch that prophecy belongs, what a feeling for style, at any rate, it manifests! And the same thing may be said of the famous Welsh triads. We may put aside all the vexed questions as to their greater or less antiquity, and still what important witness they bear to the genius for literary style of people who produced them!

Now we English undoubtedly exhibit very often the want of sense for style of our German kinsmen. The churchyard lines I just now quoted afford an instance of it; but the whole branch of our literature,—and a very popular branch it is, our hymnology,—to which those lines are to be referred, is one continued instance of it. Our German kinsmen and we are the great people for hymns. The Germans are very proud of their hymns, and we are very proud of ours; but it is hard to say which of the two, the German hymn-book or ours, has least poetical worth in itself, or does least to prove genuine poetical power in the people producing it. I have not a word to say against Sir Roundell Palmer's choice and arrangement of materials for his *Book of Praise;* I am content to put them on a level (and that is giving them the highest possible rank) with Mr. Palgrave's choice and arrangement of materials for his *Golden Treasury;* but yet no sound critic can doubt that, so far as poetry is concerned, while the *Golden Treasury* is a monument of a nation's strength, the *Book of Praise* is a monument of a nation's weakness. Only the German race, with its want of quick instinctive tact, of delicate, sure perception, could have invented the hymn as the Germans and we have it; and our non-German turn for style,—style, of which the very essence is a certain happy fineness and truth of poetical perception,—could not but desert us when our German nature carried us into a kind of composition which can please only when the perception is somewhat blunt. Scarcely any one of us ever judges our hymns fairly, because works of this kind have two sides,—their side for religion and their side for poetry. Everything which has helped a man in his religious life, everything which associates itself in his mind with the

growth of that life, is beautiful and venerable to him; in this
way, productions of little or no poetical value, like the German hymns and ours, may come to be regarded as very
precious. Their worth in this sense, as means by which we
have been edified, I do not for a moment hold cheap; but
there is an edification proper to all our stages of development, the highest as well as the lowest, and it is for man to
press on towards the highest stages of his development, with
the certainty that for those stages, too, means of edification
will not be found wanting. Now certainly it is a higher state
of development when our fineness of perception is keen than
when it is blunt. And if,—whereas the Semitic genius placed
its highest spiritual life in the religious sentiment, and made
that the basis of its poetry,—the Indo-European genius
places its highest spiritual life in the imaginative reason, and
makes that the basis of its poetry, we are none the better for
wanting the perception to discern a natural law, which is,
after all, like every natural law, irresistible; we are none the
better for trying to make ourselves Semitic, when Nature has
made us Indo-European, and to shift the basis of our poetry.
We may mean well; all manner of good may happen to us
on the road we go; but we are not on our real right road, the
road we must in the end follow.

That is why, when our hymns betray a false tendency by
losing a power which accompanies the poetical work of our
race on our other more suitable lines, the indication thus
given is of great value and instructiveness for us. One of our
main gifts for poetry deserts us in our hymns, and so gives
us a hint as to the one true basis for the spiritual work of an
Indo-European people, which the Germans, who have not
this particular gift of ours, do not and cannot get in this
way, though they may get it in others. It is worth noticing
that the masterpieces of the spiritual work of Indo-Euro-
peans taking the pure religious sentiment, and not the imaginative reason, for their basis, are works like the *Imitation,*
the *Dies Iræ,* the *Stabat Mater,*—works clothing themselves
in the Middle-Age Latin, the genuine native voice of no
Indo-European nation. The perfection of their kind, but that
kind not perfectly legitimate, they take a language not perfectly legitimate; as if to show, that when mankind's Semitic
age is once passed, the age which produced the great incomparable monuments of the pure religious sentiment, the
books of Job and Isaiah, the Psalms,—works truly to be
called inspired, because the same divine power which
worked in those who produced them works no longer,—as
if to show us, that, after this primitive age, we Indo-Euro-

peans must feel these works without attempting to remake them; and that our poetry, if it tries to make itself simply the organ of the religious sentiment, leaves the true course, and must conceal this by not speaking a living language. The moment it speaks a living language, and still makes itself the organ of the religious sentiment only, as in the German and English hymns, it betrays weakness;—the weakness of all false tendency.

But if, by attending to the Germanism in us English and to its works, one has come to doubt whether we, too, are not thorough Germans by genius and with the German deadness to style, one has only to repeat to oneself a line of Milton, —a poet intoxicated with the passion for style as much as Taliesin or Pindar,—to see that we have another side to our genius beside the German one. Whence do we get it? The Normans may have brought in among us the Latin sense for rhetoric and style,—for, indeed, this sense goes naturally with a high spirit and a strenuousness like theirs,—but the sense for style which English poetry shows is something finer than we could well have got from a people so positive and so little poetical as the Normans; and it seems to me we may much more plausibly derive it from a root of the poetical Celtic nature in us.

Its chord of penetrating passion and melancholy, again, its *Titanism* as we see it in Byron,—what other European poetry possesses that like the English, and where do we get it from? The Celts, with their vehement reaction against the despotism of fact, with their sensuous nature, their manifold striving, their adverse destiny, their immense calamities, the Celts are the prime authors of this vein of piercing regret and passion,—of this Titanism in poetry. A famous book, Macpherson's *Ossian*, carried in the last century this vein like a flood of lava through Europe. I am not going to criticise Macpherson's *Ossian* here. Make the part of what is forged, modern, tawdry, spurious, in the book, as large as you please; strip Scotland, if you like, of every feather of borrowed plumes which on the strength of Macpherson's *Ossian* she may have stolen from that *vetus et major Scotia*,[11] the true home of the Ossianic poetry, Ireland; I make no objection. But there will still be left in the book a residue with the very soul of the Celtic genius in it, and which has the proud distinction of having brought this soul of the Celtic genius into contact with the genius of the nations of modern Europe, and enriched all our poetry by it. Woody Morven, and echoing Sora,[12] and Selma with its silent halls!—we all owe them a debt of gratitude, and when we are unjust enough to forget it, may the Muse forget us! Choose any one of the better passages in Macpherson's *Ossian* and you can see even at this time of day what an apparition of newness and power such a strain must have been to the eighteenth century:—

"I have seen the walls of Balclutha, but they were desolate. The fox looked out from the windows, the rank grass of the wall waved round her[13] head. Raise the song of mourning, O bards, over the land of strangers. They have but fallen before us, for one day we must fall. Why dost thou build the hall, son of the winged days? Thou lookest from thy towers to-day; yet a few years, and the blast of the desert comes; it howls in thy empty court, and whistles round thy half-worn shield. Let the blast of the desert come! we shall be renowned in our day."

All Europe felt the power of that melancholy; but what I wish to point out is, that no nation of Europe so caught in its poetry the passionate penetrating accent of the Celtic genius, its strain of Titanism, as the English. Goethe, like Napoleon, felt the spell of Ossian very powerfully, and he quotes a long passage from him in his *Werther*. But what is there Celtic, turbulent, and Titanic about the German Werther, that amiable, cultivated, and melancholy young man, having for his sorrow and suicide the perfectly definite motive that Lotte cannot be his? Faust, again, has nothing unaccountable, defiant, and Titanic in him; his knowledge does not bring him the satisfaction he expected from it, and meanwhile he finds himself poor and growing old, and baulked of the palpable enjoyment of life; and here is the motive for Faust's discontent. In the most energetic and impetuous of Goethe's creations,—his *Prometheus,*—it is not Celtic self-will and passion, it is rather the Germanic sense of justice and reason, which revolts against the despotism of Zeus. The German *Sehnsucht* itself is a wistful, soft, tearful longing, rather than a struggling, fierce, passionate one. But the Celtic melancholy is struggling, fierce, passionate; to catch its note, listen to Llywarch Hen[14] in old age, addressing his crutch:—

"O my crutch! is it not autumn, when the fern is red, the waterflag yellow? Have I not hated that which I love?

"Oh my crutch! is it not winter-time now, when men talk together after that they have drunken? Is not the side of my bed left desolate?

"O my crutch! is it not spring, when the cuckoo passes through the air, when the foam sparkles on the sea? The young maidens no longer love me.

"O my crutch! is it not the first day of May? The furrows,

are they not shining; the young corn, is it not springing? Ah! the sight of thy handle makes me wroth.

"O my crutch! stand straight, thou wilt support me the better; it is very long since I was Llywarch.

"Behold old age, which makes sport of me, from the hair of my head to my teeth, to my eyes, which women loved.

"The four things I have all my life most hated fall upon me together,—coughing and old age, sickness and sorrow.

"I am old, I am alone, shapeliness and warmth are gone from me; the couch of honour shall be no more mine; I am miserable, I am bent on my crutch.

"How evil was the lot allotted to Llywarch, the night when he was brought forth! sorrows without end, and no deliverance from his burden."

There is the Titanism of the Celt, his passionate, turbulent, indomitable reaction against the despotism of fact; and of whom does it remind us so much as of Byron?

> "The fire which on my bosom preys
> Is lone as some volcanic isle;
> No torch is kindled at its blaze;
> A funeral pile!"[15]

Or, again:—

> "Count o'er the joys thine hours have seen,
> Count o'er thy days from anguish free,
> And know, whatever thou hast been,
> 'Tis something better not to be."[16]

One has only to let one's memory begin to fetch passages from Byron striking the same note as that passage from Llywarch Hen, and she will not soon stop. And all Byron's heroes, not so much in collision with outward things, as breaking on some rock of revolt and misery in the depths of their own nature; Manfred, self-consumed, fighting blindly and passionately with I know not what, having nothing of the consistent development and intelligible motive of Faust, —Manfred, Lara, Cain,[17] what are they but Titanic? Where in European poetry are we to find this Celtic passion of revolt so warm-breathing, puissant, and sincere; except perhaps in the creation of a yet greater poet than Byron, but an English poet, too, like Byron,—in the Satan of Milton?

> . . . . "What though the field be lost?
> All is not lost; the unconquerable will,
> And study of revenge, immortal hate,
> And courage never to submit or yield,
> And what is else not to be overcome?"[18]

There, surely, speaks a genius to whose composition the Celtic fibre was not wholly a stranger!

And as, after noting the Celtic Pindarism or power of style present in our poetry, we noted the German flatness coming in in our hymns, and found here a proof of our compositeness of nature; so, after noting the Celtic Titanism or power of rebellious passion in our poetry, we may also note the Germanic patience and reasonableness in it, and get in this way a second proof how mixed a spirit we have. After Llywarch Hen's:—

> "How evil was the lot allotted to Llywarch, the night when he was brought forth"—

after Byron's:—

> "Count o'er the joys thine hours have seen"—

take this of Southey's, in answer to the question whether he would like to have his youth over again:—

> "Do I regret the past?
> Would I live o'er again
> The morning hours of life?
> Nay, William, nay, not so!
> Praise be to God who made me what I am,
> Other I would not be."[19]

There we have the other side of our being; the Germanic goodness, docility, and fidelity to nature, in place of the Celtic Titanism.

The Celt's quick feeling for what is noble and distinguished gave his poetry style; his indomitable personality gave it pride and passion; his sensibility and nervous exaltation gave it a better gift still, the gift of rendering with wonderful felicity the magical charm of nature. The forest solitude, the bubbling spring, the wild flowers, are everywhere in romance. They have a mysterious life and grace there; they are Nature's own children, and utter her secret in a way which makes them something quite different from the woods, waters, and plants of Greek and Latin poetry. Now of this delicate magic, Celtic romance is so pre-eminent a mistress, that it seems impossible to believe the power did not come into romance from the Celts.* Magic is just the

---

* Rhyme,—the most striking characteristic of our modern poetry as distinguished from that of the ancients, and a main source, to our poetry, of its magic and charm, of what we call its *romantic element*,—rhyme itself, all the weight of evidence tends to show, comes into our poetry from the Celts. [M. A.]

word for it,—the magic of nature; not merely the beauty of nature,—that the Greeks and Latins had; not merely an honest smack of the soil, a faithful realism,—that the Germans had; but the intimate life of Nature, her weird power and her fairy charm. As the Saxon names of places, with the pleasant wholesome smack of the soil in them,—Weathersfield, Thaxted, Shalford,—are to the Celtic names of places, with their penetrating, lofty beauty,—Velindra, Tyntagel, Caernarvon,—so is the homely realism of German and Norse nature to the fairy-like loveliness of Celtic nature. Gwydion wants a wife for his pupil: "Well," says Math, "we will seek, I and thou, by charms and illusions, to form a wife for him out of flowers. So they took the blossoms of the oak, and the blossoms of the broom, and the blossoms of the meadow-sweet, and produced from them a maiden, the fairest and most graceful that man ever saw. And they baptized her, and gave her the name of Flower-Aspect."[20] Celtic romance is full of exquisite touches like that, showing the delicacy of the Celt's feeling in these matters, and how deeply Nature lets him come into her secrets. The quick dropping of blood is called "faster than the fall of the dewdrop from the blade of reed-grass upon the earth, when the dew of June is at the heaviest." And thus is Olwen described: "More yellow was her hair than the flower of the broom, and her skin was whiter than the foam of the wave, and fairer were her hands and her fingers than the blossoms of the wood-anemony amidst the spray of the meadow fountains."[21] For loveliness it would be hard to beat that; and for magical clearness and nearness take the following:—

"And in the evening Peredur entered a valley, and at the head of the valley he came to a hermit's cell, and the hermit welcomed him gladly, and there he spent the night. And in the morning he arose, and when he went forth, behold, a shower of snow had fallen the night before, and a hawk had killed a wild-fowl in front of the cell. And the noise of the horse scared the hawk away, and a raven alighted upon the bird. And Peredur stood and compared the blackness of the raven, and the whiteness of the snow, and the redness of the blood, to the hair of the lady whom best he loved, which was blacker than the raven, and to her skin, which was whiter than the snow, and to her two cheeks, which were redder than the blood upon the snow appeared to be."

And this, which is perhaps less striking, is not less beautiful:—

"And early in the day Geraint and Enid left the wood, and they came to an open country, with meadows on one hand and mowers mowing the meadows. And there was a river before them, and the horses bent down and drank the water. And they went up out of the river by a steep bank, and there they met a slender stripling with a satchel about his neck; and he had a small blue pitcher in his hand, and a bowl on the mouth of the pitcher."

And here the landscape, up to this point so Greek in its clear beauty, is suddenly magicalised by the romance touch:—

"And they saw a tall tree by the side of the river, one-half of which was in flames from the root to the top, and the other half was green and in full leaf."

Magic is the word to insist upon,—a magically vivid and near interpretation of nature; since it is this which constitutes the special charm and power of the effect I am calling attention to, and it is for this that the Celt's sensibility gives him a peculiar aptitude. But the matter needs rather fine handling, and it is easy to make mistakes here in our criticism. In the first place, Europe tends constantly to become more and more one community, and we tend to become Europeans instead of merely Englishmen, Frenchmen, Germans, Italians; so whatever aptitude or felicity one people imparts into spiritual work, gets imitated by the others, and thus tends to become the common property of all. Therefore anything so beautiful and attractive as the natural magic I am speaking of, is sure nowadays, if it appears in the productions of the Celts, or of the English, or of the French, to appear in the productions of the Germans also, or in the productions of the Italians; but there will be a stamp of perfectness and inimitableness about it in the literatures where it is native, which it will not have in the literatures where it is not native. Novalis[22] or Rückert,[23] for instance, have their eye fixed on nature, and have undoubtedly a feeling for natural magic; a rough-and-ready critic easily credits them and the Germans with the Celtic fineness of tact, the Celtic nearness to Nature and her secret; but the question is whether the strokes in the German's picture of nature* have ever the

---

* Take the following attempt to render the natural magic supposed to pervade Tieck's poetry:—"In diesen Dichtungen herrscht eine geheimnissvolle Innigkeit, ein sonderbares Einverständniss mit der Natur, besonders mit dem Pflanzen- und Steinreich. Der Leser fühlt sich da wie in einem verzauberten Walde; er hört die unterirdischen Quellen melodisch rauschen; wildfremde Wunderblumen schauen ihn an mit ihren bunten sehnsüchtigen Augen; unsichtbare Lippen küssen seine Wangen mit neckender Zärtlichkeit; *hohe Pilze, wie goldne Glocken, wachsen klingend empor am Fusse der Bäume;*"

indefinable delicacy, charm, and perfection of the Celt's touch in the pieces I just now quoted, or of Shakespeare's touch in his daffodil, Wordsworth's in his cuckoo, Keats's in his Autumn, Obermann's in his mountain birch-tree or his Easter-daisy among the Swiss farms. To decide where the gift for natural magic originally lies, whether it is properly Celtic or Germanic, we must decide this question.

In the second place, there are many ways of handling nature, and we are here only concerned with one of them; but a rough-and-ready critic imagines that it is all the same so long as nature is handled at all, and fails to draw the needful distinction between modes of handling her. But these modes are many; I will mention four of them now: there is the conventional way of handling nature, there is the faithful way of handling nature, there is the Greek way of handling nature, there is the magical way of handling nature. In all these three last the eye is on the object, but with a difference; in the faithful way of handling nature, the eye is on the object, and that is all you can say; in the Greek, the eye is on the object, but lightness and brightness are added; in the magical, the eye is on the object, but charm and magic are added. In the conventional way of handling nature, the eye is not on the object; what that means we all know, we have only to think of our eighteenth-century poetry:—

"As when the moon, refulgent lamp of night"—25

to call up any number of instances. Latin poetry supplies plenty of instances too; if we put this from Propertius's *Hylas:*—

. . . "manus heroum . . . .
Mollia composita litora fronde tegit"—26

side by side with the line of Theocritus by which it was suggested:—

"λειμὼν γάρ σφιν ἔκειτο μέγας, στιβάδεσσιν ὄνειαρ"—27

we get at the same moment a good specimen both of the conventional and of the Greek way of handling nature. But

---

and so on. Now that stroke of the *hohe Pilze*, the great funguses, would have been impossible to the tact and delicacy of a born lover of nature like the Celt, and could only have come from a German who has *hineinstudirt* himself into natural magic. It is a crying false note, which carries us at once out of the world of nature-magic and the breath of the woods, into the world of theatre-magic and the smell of gas and orange-peel. [M. A.]24

from our own poetry we may get specimens of the Greek
way of handling nature, as well as of the conventional: for
instance, Keats's:—

> "What little town, by river or seashore,
>   Or mountain-built with quiet citadel,
> Is emptied of its folk, this pious morn?"[28]

is Greek, as Greek as a thing from Homer or Theocritus; it
is composed with the eye on the object, a radiancy and light
clearness being added. German poetry abounds in specimens
of the faithful way of handling nature; an excellent example
is to be found in the stanzas called *Zueignung,* prefixed to
Goethe's poems; the morning walk, the mist, the dew, the
sun, are as faithful as they can be, they are given with the
eye on the object, but there the merit of the work, as a handling of nature, stops; neither Greek radiance nor Celtic
magic is added; the power of these is not what gives the
poem in question its merit, but a power of quite another
kind, a power of moral and spiritual emotion. But the power
of Greek radiance Goethe could give to his handling of nature, and nobly too, as any one who will read his *Wanderer,*
—the poem in which a wanderer falls in with a peasant
woman and her child by their hut, built out of the ruins of a
temple near Cuma,—may see. Only the power of natural
magic Goethe does not, I think, give; whereas Keats passes
at will from the Greek power to that power which is, as I
say, Celtic; from his:—

> "What little town, by river or seashore"—

to his:—

> "White hawthorn and the pastoral eglantine,
>   Fast-fading violets cover'd up in leaves"—[29]

or his:—

> . . . "magic casements, opening on the foam
>   Of perilous seas, in fairy lands forlorn"—

in which the very same note is struck as in those extracts
which I quoted from Celtic romance, and struck with au-
thentic and unmistakable power.

Shakespeare, in handling nature, touches this Celtic note
so exquisitely, that perhaps one is inclined to be always looking for the Celtic note in him, and not to recognise his
Greek note when it comes. But if one attends well to the
difference between the two notes, and bears in mind, to

guide one, such things as Virgil's "moss-grown springs and grass softer than sleep:"—

"Muscosi fontes et somno mollior herba"—[30]

as his charming flower-gatherer, who:—

"Pallentes violas et summa papavera carpens
Narcissum et florem jungit bene olentis anethi"—

as his quinces and chestnuts:—

... "cana legam tenera lanugine mala
Castaneasque nuces" ....[31]

then, I think, we shall be disposed to say that in Shakespeare's:—

"I know a bank where the wild thyme blows,
Where oxlips and the nodding violet grows,
Quite over-canopied with luscious woodbine,
With sweet musk-roses and with eglantine"—[32]

it is mainly a Greek note which is struck. Then, again in his:—

..... "look how the floor of heaven
Is thick inlaid with patines of bright gold!"[33]

we are at the very point of transition from the Greek note to the Celtic; there is the Greek clearness and brightness, with the Celtic aërialness and magic coming in. Then we have the sheer, inimitable Celtic note in passages like this:—

"Met we on hill, in dale, forest or mead,
By paved fountain or by rushy brook,
Or in the beached margent of the sea"—[34]

or this, the last I will quote:—

"The moon shines bright. In such a night as this,
When the sweet wind did gently kiss the trees,
And they did make no noise, in such a night
Troilus, methinks, mounted the Trojan walls—

...... "in such a night
Did Thisbe fearfully o'ertrip the dew—

...... "in such a night
Stood Dido, with a willow in her hand,
Upon the wild sea-banks, and waved her love
To come again to Carthage."[35]

And those last lines of ali are so drenched and intoxicated with the fairy-dew of that natural magic which is our theme, that I cannot do better than end with them.

And now, with the pieces of evidence in our hand, let us go to those who say it is vain to look for Celtic elements in any Englishman, and let us ask them, first, if they seize what we mean by the power of natural magic in Celtic poetry; secondly, if English poetry does not eminently exhibit this power; and, thirdly, where they suppose English poetry got it from?

I perceive that I shall be accused of having rather the air, in what I have said, of denying this and that gift to the Germans, and of establishing our difference from them a little ungraciously and at their expense. The truth is, few people have any real care to analyse closely in their criticism; they merely employ criticism as a means for heaping all praise on what they like, and all blame on what they dislike. Those of us (and they are many) who owe a great debt of gratitude to the German spirit and to German literature, do not like to be told of any powers being lacking there; we are like the young ladies who think the hero of their novel is only half a hero unless he has all perfections united in him. But nature does not work, either in heroes or races, according to the young ladies' notion. We all are what we are, the hero and the great nation are what they are, by our limitations as well as by our powers, by lacking something as well as by possessing something. It is not always gain to possess this or that gift, or loss to lack this or that gift. Our great, our only first-rate body of contemporary poetry is the German; the grand business of modern poetry,—a moral interpretation, from an independent point of view, of man and the world, —it is only German poetry, Goethe's poetry, that has, since the Greeks, made much way with. Campbell's[36] power of style, and the natural magic of Keats and Wordsworth, and Byron's Titanic personality, may be wanting to this poetry; but see what it has accomplished without them! How much more than Campbell with his power of style, and Keats and Wordsworth with their natural magic, and Byron with his Titanic personality! Why, for the immense serious task it had to perform, the steadiness of German poetry, its going near the ground, its patient fidelity to nature, its using great plainness of speech, poetical drawbacks in one point of view, were safeguards and helps in another. The plainness and earnestness of the two lines I have already quoted from Goethe:—

"Es bildet ein Talent sich in der Stille,
  Sich ein Character in dem Strom der Welt"——[37]

compared with the play and power of Shakespeare's style or
Dante's, suggest at once the difference between Goethe's task
and theirs, and the fitness of the faithful laborious German
spirit for its own task. Dante's task was to set forth the lesson of the world from the point of view of mediæval Catholicism; the basis of spiritual life was given, Dante had not
to make this anew. Shakespeare's task was to set forth the
spectacle of the world when man's spirit re-awoke to the
possession of the world at the Renaissance. The spectacle of
human life, left to bear its own significance and tell its own
story, but shown in all its fulness, variety, and power, is at
that moment the great matter; but, if we are to press deeper,
the basis of spiritual life is still at that time the traditional
religion, reformed or unreformed, of Christendom, and
Shakespeare has not to supply a new basis. But when Goethe came, Europe had lost her basis of spiritual life; she had
to find it again; Goethe's task was,—the inevitable task for
the modern poet henceforth is,—as it was for the Greek poet
in the days of Pericles, not to preach a sublime sermon on a
given text like Dante, not to exhibit all the kingdoms of human life and the glory of them like Shakespeare, but to interpret human life afresh, and to supply a new spiritual basis
to it. This is not only a work for style, eloquence, charm,
poetry; it is a work for science; and the scientific, serious
German spirit, not carried away by this and that intoxication
of ear, and eye, and self-will, has peculiar aptitudes for it.

We, on the other hand, do not necessarily gain by the
commixture of elements in us; we have seen how the clash-
ing of natures in us hampers and embarrasses our behaviour;
we might very likely be more attractive, we might very likely
be more successful, if we were all of a piece. Our want of
sureness of taste, our eccentricity, come in great measure, no
doubt, from our not being all of a piece, from our having no
fixed, fatal, spiritual centre of gravity. The Rue de Rivoli is
one thing, and Nuremberg is another, and Stonehenge is another; but we have a turn for all three, and lump them all up
together. Mr. Tom Taylor's translations from Breton poetry[38] offer a good example of this mixing; he has a genuine
feeling for these Celtic matters, and often, as in the "Evil
Tribute of Nomenoë," or in "Lord Nann and the Fairy," he
is, both in movement and expression, true and appropriate;
but he has a sort of Teutonism and Latinism in him too, and

so he cannot forbear mixing with his Celtic strain such disparates as:—

> " 'Twas mirk, mirk night, and the water bright
> Troubled and drumlie flowed"—

which is evidently Lowland-Scotchy; or as:—

> "Foregad, but thou'rt an artful hand!"

which is English-stagey; or as:—

> "To Gradlon's daughter, bright of blee,
> Her lover he whispered tenderly—
> *Bethink thee, sweet Dahut! the key!*"

which is Anacreontic in the manner of Tom Moore.[39] Yes, it is not a sheer advantage to have several strings to one's bow! if we had been all German, we might have had the science of Germany; if we had been all Celtic, we might have been popular and agreeable; if we had been all Latinised, we might have governed Ireland as the French govern Alsace, without getting ourselves detested. But now we have Germanism enough to make us Philistines, and Normanism enough to make us imperious, and Celtism enough to make us self-conscious and awkward; but German fidelity to Nature, and Latin precision and clear reason, and Celtic quick-wittedness and spirituality, we fall short of. Nay, perhaps, if we are doomed to perish (Heaven avert the omen!), we shall perish by our Celtism, by our self-will and want of patience with ideas, our inability to see the way the world is going; and yet those very Celts, by our affinity with whom we are perishing, will be hating and upbraiding us all the time.

NOTES

From *On the Study of Celtic Literature:* Delivered at Oxford, December, 1865–May, 1866; published in *Cornhill Magazine* (March, April, May, and July, 1866); as a book, 1866. For a discussion of Arnold's ideas of race, see F. E. Faverty, *Matthew Arnold, the Ethnologist* (1951).

1. See pp. 229–30.
2. *Paradise Lost,* iii. 32–35 (*"other two equall'd"*).
3. *Torquato Tasso,* I. ii. 66–67: *Talent develops in retirement, but character in the stream of the world.*
4. Athenian poet and playwright (c. 342–292 B.C.).
5. *Vulgarity.*
6. Preface to *Catechismus fur die gemeine Pfarrherr: Oh, God! how much misery I have seen from the common man's understanding nothing at all about Christian teaching!*

7. Henry St. John, Viscount Bolingbroke (1678–1751), political and philosophical writer.

8. Claude Fauriel (1772–1844), French historian.

9. G. W. Dasent's books include *The Story of Burnt Njal* (1861).

10. R. H. Super notes that Lady Charlotte Guest's *Mabinogion* has "Gleddyfrudd."

11. *The ancient and greater Scotia.*

12. R. H. Super notes that Macpherson has "Lora."

13. R. H. Super notes that Macpherson has "his" ("Carthon: a Poem").

14. Sixth-century Welsh leader; the Welsh poems associated with his name are ninth-century.

15. "On This Day I Complete My Thirty-Sixth Year" ("fire that").

16. "Euthanasia".

17. The central figures in three poems by Byron.

18. *Paradise Lost,* i. 105–9.

19. Slightly misquoting (as R. H. Super notes) "To a Friend."

20. From the *Mabinogion,* as are the five excerpts which follow.

21. R. H. Super notes that the *Mabinogion* has "fountain."

22. "Novalis," F. L. von Hardenberg (1772–1801), German romantic poet.

23. J. M. F. Rückert (1788–1866), German poet notable particularly for his translations and imitations of Oriental poetry.

24. Heine, *Die Romantische Schule* (1836), Book II: *In these compositions we feel a mysterious depth of meaning, a marvellous union with Nature, especially with the realm of plants and stones. The reader seems to be in the enchanted forest; he hears subterranean springs and streams rustling melodiously, and his own name whispered by the trees. Broad-leaved clinging plants wind vexingly about his feet, wild and strange wonder-flowers look at him with vari-coloured longing eyes, invisible lips kiss his cheeks with mocking tenderness, tall mushrooms like golden bells grow singing about the roots of trees.*

25. Pope's *Iliad,* viii. 637.

26. *Elegies,* I. xx. 21–22: *Here the band of heroes carpeted the ground with a soft coverlet of leaves.*

27. *Idyls,* xiii. 34: *for they found to their hand a meadow that furnished good store of litter.*

28. "Ode on a Grecian Urn" ("peaceful citadel").

29. "Ode to a Nightingale."

30. *Eclogues,* vii. 45.

31. *Eclogues,* ii. 47–48: *cropping pale violets and poppy tops, to which she joins the narcissus, and the flower of the sweet-scented dill;* ii. 51–52: *I will gather quinces, heavy with tender bloom, and chestnuts.*

32. *Midsummer Night's Dream,* II. i. 249–52.

33. *Merchant of Venice,* v. i. 58–59.

34. *Midsummer Night's Dream,* II. i. 83–85.

35. *Merchant of Venice,* V. i. 1–12.

36. Thomas Campbell (1777–1844).

37. See p. 120.

38. *Ballads and Songs of Brittany* (1865).

39. Thomas Moore (1779–1852) translated Anacreon's Odes (1800).

ON
THE MODERN ELEMENT
IN LITERATURE

1869

[What follows was delivered as an inaugural lecture in the Poetry Chair at Oxford. It was never printed, but there appeared at the time several comments on it from critics who had either heard it, or heard reports about it. It was meant to be followed and completed by a course of lectures developing the subject entirely, and some of these were given. But the course was broken off because I found my knowledge insufficient for treating in a solid way many portions of the subject chosen. The inaugural lecture, however, treating a portion of the subject where my knowledge was perhaps less insufficient, and where besides my hearers were better able to help themselves out from their own knowledge, is here printed. No one feels the imperfection of this sketchy and generalizing mode of treatment more than I do; and not only is this mode of treatment less to my taste now than it was eleven years ago, but the style too, which is that of the doctor rather than the explorer, is a style which I have long since learnt to abandon. Nevertheless, having written much of late about Hellenism and Hebraism,[1] and Hellenism being to many people almost an empty name compared with Hebraism, I print this lecture with the hope that it may serve, in the absence of other and fuller illustrations, to give some notion of the Hellenic spirit and its works, and of their significance in the history of the evolution of the human spirit in general.   M. A.]

IT IS RELATED in one of those legends which illustrate the history of Buddhism, that a certain disciple once presented himself before his master, Buddha, with the desire to be permitted to undertake a mission of peculiar difficulty. The compassionate teacher represented to him the obstacles to be surmounted and the risks to be run. Pourna—so the disciple was called—insisted, and replied, with equal humility and adroitness, to the successive objections of his adviser. Satisfied at last by his answers of the fitness of his disciple, Buddha accorded to him the desired permission; and dismissed him to his task with these remarkable words, nearly identical with those in which he himself is said to have been admonished by a divinity at the outset of his own career:—"Go then, O Pourna," are his words; "having been delivered, deliver; having been consoled, console; being arrived thyself at the farther bank, enable others to arrive there also."

It was a moral deliverance, eminently, of which the great Oriental reformer spoke; it was a deliverance from the pride, the sloth, the anger, the selfishness, which impair the moral activity of man—a deliverance which is demanded of all individuals and in all ages. But there is another deliverance for the human race, hardly less important, indeed, than the first —for in the enjoyment of both united consists man's true freedom—but demanded far less universally, and even more rarely and imperfectly obtained; a deliverance neglected, apparently hardly conceived, in some ages, while it has been pursued with earnestness in others, which derive from that very pursuit their peculiar character. This deliverance is an intellectual deliverance.

An intellectual deliverance is the peculiar demand of those ages which are called modern; and those nations are said to be imbued with the modern spirit most eminently in which the demand for such a deliverance has been made with most zeal, and satisfied with most completeness. Such a deliverance is emphatically, whether we will or no, the demand of the age in which we ourselves live. All intellectual pursuits our age judges according to their power of helping to satisfy this demand; of all studies it asks, above all, the question, how far they can contribute to this deliverance.

I propose, on this my first occasion of speaking here, to attempt such a general survey of ancient classical literature and history as may afford us the conviction—in presence of the doubts so often expressed of the profitableness, in the present day, of our study of this literature—that, even admitting to their fullest extent the legitimate demands of our age, the literature of ancient Greece is, even for modern times, a mighty agent of intellectual deliverance; even for modern times, therefore, an object of indestructible interest.

But first let us ask ourselves why the demand for an intellectual deliverance arises in such an age as the present, and in what the deliverance itself consists? The demand arises, because our present age has around it a copious and complex present, and behind it a copious and complex past; it arises, because the present age exhibits to the individual man who contemplates it the spectacle of a vast multitude of facts awaiting and inviting his comprehension. The deliverance consists in man's comprehension of this present and past. It begins when our mind begins to enter into possession of the general ideas which are the law of this vast multitude of facts. It is perfect when we have acquired that harmonious acquiescence of mind which we feel in contemplating a grand spectacle that is intelligible to us; when we have lost that impatient irritation of mind which we feel in presence of an immense, moving, confused spectacle which, while it perpetually excites our curiosity, perpetually baffles our comprehension.

This, then, is what distinguishes certain epochs in the history of the human race, and our own amongst the number; —on the one hand, the presence of a significant spectacle to contemplate; on the other hand, the desire to find the true point of view from which to contemplate this spectacle. He who has found that point of view, he who adequately comprehends this spectacle, has risen to the comprehension of his age: he who communicates that point of view to his age, he who interprets to it that spectacle, is one of his age's intellectual deliverers.

The spectacle, the facts, presented for the comprehension of the present age, are indeed immense. The facts consist of the events, the institutions, the sciences, the arts, the literatures, in which human life has manifested itself up to the present time: the spectacle is the collective life of humanity. And everywhere there is connexion, everywhere there is illustration: no single event, no single literature, is adequately comprehended except in its relation to other events, to other literatures. The literature of ancient Greece, the literature of the Christian Middle Age, so long as they are regarded as two isolated literatures, two isolated growths of the human spirit, are not adequately comprehended; and it is adequate comprehension which is the demand of the present age. "We

must compare,"—the illustrious Chancellor of Cambridge*
said the other day to his hearers at Manchester,—"we must
compare the works of other ages with those of our own age
and country; that, while we feel proud of the immense development of knowledge and power of production which we
possess, we may learn humility in contemplating the refinement of feeling and intensity of thought manifested in the
works of the older schools." To know how others stand, that
we may know how we ourselves stand; and to know how we
ourselves stand, that we may correct our mistakes and
achieve our deliverance—that is our problem.

But all facts, all the elements of the spectacle before us,
have not an equal value—do not merit a like attention: and
it is well that they do not, for no man would be adequate
to the task of thoroughly mastering them all. Some have
more significance for us, others have less; some merit our
utmost attention in all their details, others it is sufficient to
comprehend in their general character, and then they may be
dismissed.

What facts, then, let us ask ourselves, what elements of
the spectacle before us, will naturally be most interesting to
a highly developed age like our own, to an age making the
demand which we have described for an intellectual deliverance by means of the complete intelligence of its own situation? Evidently, the other ages similarly developed, and
making the same demand. And what past literature will
naturally be most interesting to such an age as our own?
Evidently, the literatures which have most successfully
solved for *their* ages the problem which occupies ours: the
literatures which in their day and for their own nation have
adequately comprehended, have adequately represented, the
spectacle before them. A significant, a highly-developed, a
culminating epoch, on the one hand,—a comprehensive, a
commensurate, an adequate literature, on the other,—these
will naturally be the objects of deepest interest to our modern age. Such an epoch and such a literature are, in fact,
modern, in the same sense in which our own age and literature are modern; they are founded upon a rich past and
upon an instructive fulness of experience.

It may, however, happen that a great epoch is without a
perfectly adequate literature; it may happen that a great age,
a great nation, has attained a remarkable fulness of political
and social development, without intellectually taking the
complete measure of itself, without adequately representing

* The late Prince Consort. [M. A.][2]

that development in its literature. In this case, the *epoch,* the *nation* itself, will still be an object of the greatest interest to us; but the *literature* will be an object of less interest to us: the facts, the material spectacle, are there; but the contemporary view of the facts, the intellectual interpretation, are inferior and inadequate.

It may happen, on the other hand, that great authors, that a powerful literature, are found in an age and nation less great and powerful than themselves; it may happen that a literature, that a man of genius, may arise adequate to the representation of a greater, a more highly developed age than that in which they appear; it may happen that a literature completely interprets its epoch, and yet has something over; that it has a force, a richness, a geniality, a power of view which the materials at its disposition are insufficient adequately to employ. In such a case, the literature will be more interesting to us than the epoch. The interpreting power, the illuminating and revealing intellect, are there; but the spectacle on which they throw their light is not fully worthy of them.

And I shall not, I hope, be thought to magnify too much my office if I add, that it is to the poetical literature of an age that we must, in general, look for the most perfect, the most adequate interpretation of that age,—for the performance of a work which demands the most energetic and harmonious activity of all the powers of the human mind. Because that activity of the whole mind, that genius, as Johnson nobly describes it, "without which judgment is cold and knowledge is inert; that energy which collects, combines, amplifies, and animates,"[3] is in poetry at its highest stretch and in its most energetic exertion.

What we seek, therefore, what will most enlighten us, most contribute to our intellectual deliverance, is the union of two things; it is the coexistence, the simultaneous appearance, of a great epoch and a great literature.

Now the culminating age in the life of ancient Greece I call, beyond question, a great epoch; the life of Athens in the fifth century before our era I call one of the highly developed, one of the marking, one of the modern periods in the life of the whole human race. It has been said that the "Athens of Pericles was a vigorous man, at the summit of his bodily strength and mental energy." There was the utmost energy of life there, public and private; the most entire freedom, the most unprejudiced and intelligent observation of human affairs. Let us rapidly examine some of the characteristics which distinguish modern epochs; let us see how far the culminating century of ancient Greece exhibits them; let us compare it, in respect of them, with a much later, a celebrated century; let us compare it with the age of Elizabeth in our own country.

To begin with what is exterior. One of the most characteristic outward features of a *modern* age, of an age of advanced civilization, is the banishment of the ensigns of war and bloodshed from the intercourse of civil life. Crime still exists, and wars are still carried on; but within the limits of civil life a circle has been formed within which man can move securely, and develop the arts of peace uninterruptedly. The private man does not go forth to his daily occupation prepared to assail the life of his neighbour or to have to defend his own. With the disappearance of the constant means of offence the occasions of offence diminish; society at last acquires repose, confidence, and free activity. An important inward characteristic, again, is the growth of a tolerant spirit; that spirit which is the offspring of an enlarged knowledge; a spirit patient of the diversities of habits and opinions. Other characteristics are the multiplication of the conveniences of life, the formation of taste, the capacity for refined pursuits. And this leads us to the supreme characteristic of all: the intellectual maturity of man himself; the tendency to observe facts with a critical spirit; to search for their law, not to wander among them at random; to judge by the rule of reason, not by the impulse of prejudice or caprice.

Well, now, with respect to the presence of all these characteristics in the age of Pericles, we possess the explicit testimony of an immortal work,—of the history of Thucydides. "The Athenians first," he says—speaking of the gradual development of Grecian society up to the period when the Peloponnesian war commenced—"the Athenians first left off the habit of wearing arms:" that is, this mark of superior civilization had, in the age of Pericles, become general in Greece, had long been visible at Athens. In the time of Elizabeth, on the other hand, the wearing of arms was universal in England and throughout Europe. Again, the conveniences, the ornaments, the luxuries of life, had become common at Athens at the time of which we are speaking. But there had been an advance even beyond this; there had been an advance to that perfection, that propriety of taste which proscribes the excess of ornament, the extravagance of luxury. The Athenians had given up, Thucydides says, had given up, although not very long before, an extravagance of dress and an excess of personal ornament which, in the first flush of newly-discovered luxury, had been adopted by some of the richer classes. The height of civilization in this respect seems to have been attained; there was general elegance and refinement of life, and there was simplicity. What was the case in this respect in the Elizabethan age? The scholar Casaubon, who settled in England in the reign of James I, bears evidence to the want here, even at that time, of conveniences of life which were already to be met with on the continent of Europe. On the other hand, the taste for fantastic, for excessive personal adornment, to which the portraits of the time bear testimony, is admirably set forth in the work of a great novelist, who was also a very truthful antiquarian—in the *Kenilworth* of Sir Walter Scott. We all remember the description, in the thirteenth and fourteenth chapters of the second volume of *Kenilworth,* of the barbarous magnificence, the "fierce vanities," of the dress of the period.

Pericles praises the Athenians that they had discovered sources of recreation for the spirit to counterbalance the labours of the body: compare these, compare the pleasures which charmed the whole body of the Athenian people through the yearly round of their festivals with the popular shows and pastimes in *Kenilworth*. "We have freedom," says Pericles, "for individual diversities of opinion and character; we do not take offence at the tastes and habits of our neighbour if they differ from our own." Yes, in Greece, in the Athens of Pericles, there is toleration; but in England, in the England of the sixteenth century?—the Puritans are then in full growth. So that with regard to these characteristics of civilization of a modern spirit which we have hitherto enumerated, the superiority, it will be admitted, rests with the age of Pericles.

Let us pass to what we said was the supreme characteristic of a highly developed, a modern age—the manifestation of a critical spirit, the endeavour after a rational arrangement and appreciation of facts. Let us consider one or two of the passages in the masterly introduction which Thucydides, the contemporary of Pericles, has prefixed to his history. What was his motive in choosing the Peloponnesian War for his subject? Because it was, in his opinion, the most important, the most instructive event which had, up to that time, happened in the history of mankind. What is his effort in the first twenty-three chapters of his history? To place in their correct point of view all the facts which had brought Grecian society to the point at which that dominant event found it; to strip these facts of their exaggeration, to examine them critically. The enterprises undertaken in the early times of Greece were on a much smaller scale than had been commonly supposed. The Greek chiefs were induced to combine in the expedition against Troy, not by their respect for an oath taken by them all when suitors to Helen, but by their respect for the preponderating influence of Agamemnon; the siege of Troy had been protracted not so much by the valour of the besieged as by the inadequate mode of warfare necessitated by the want of funds of the besiegers. No doubt Thucydides' criticism of the Trojan war is not perfect; but observe how in these and many other points he labours to correct popular errors, to assign their true character to facts, complaining, as he does so, of men's habit of *uncritical* reception of current stories. "So little a matter of care to most men," he says, "is the search after truth, and so inclined are they to take up any story which is ready to their hand." "He himself," he continues, "has endeavoured to give a true picture, and believes that in the main he has done so. For some readers his history may want the charm of the uncritical, half-fabulous narratives of earlier writers; but for such as desire to gain a clear knowledge of the past, and thereby of the future also, which will surely, after the course of human things, represent again hereafter, if not the very image, yet the near resemblance of the past—if such shall judge my work to be profitable, I shall be well content."

What language shall we properly call this? It is *modern* language; it is the language of a thoughtful philosophic man of our own days; it is the language of Burke or Niebuhr[4] assigning the true aim of history. And yet Thucydides is no mere literary man; no isolated thinker, speaking far over the heads of his hearers to a future age—no: he was a man of action, a man of the world, a man of his time. He represents, at its best indeed, but he represents, the general intelligence of his age and nation; of a nation the meanest citizens of which could follow with comprehension the profoundly thoughtful speeches of Pericles.

Let us now turn for a contrast to a historian of the Elizabethan age, also a man of great mark and ability, also a man of action, also a man of the world, Sir Walter Ralegh. Sir Walter Ralegh writes the *History of the World*, as Thucydides has written the *History of the Peloponnesian War;* let us hear his language; let us mark his point of view; let us see what problems occur to him for solution. "Seeing," he says, "that we digress in all the ways of our lives—yea, seeing the life of man is nothing else but digression—I may "be the better excused in writing their lives and actions." What are the preliminary facts which he discusses, as Thucydides discusses the Trojan War and the early naval power of Crete, and which are to lead up to his main inquiry? Open the table of contents of his first volume. You will find: —"Of the firmament, and of the waters above the firmament, and whether there be any crystalline Heaven, or any primum mobile." You will then find —"Of Fate, and that the stars have great influence, and that their operations may diversely be prevented or furthered." Then you come to two entire chapters on the place of Paradise, and on the two chief trees in the garden of Paradise. And in what style, with what power of criticism, does Ralegh treat the subjects so selected? I turn to the 7th section of the third chapter of his first book, which treats "Of their opinion which make Paradise as high as the moon, and of others which make it higher than the middle region of the air." Thus he begins the discussion of this opinion·—"Whereas Beda saith, and as the schoolmen affirm Paradise to be a place altogether removed from the knowledge of men ('locus a cognitione hominum remotissimus'), and Barcephas conceived that Paradise was far in the east, but mounted above the ocean and all the earth, and near the orb of the moon (which opinion, though the schoolmen charge Beda withal, yet Pererius lays it off from Beda, upon Strabus, and his "master Rabanus); and whereas Rupertus in his geography of Paradise doth not much differ from the rest, but finds it seated next or nearest Heaven—" So he states the error, and now for his own criticism of it. "First, such a place cannot be commodious to live in, for being so near the moon it had been too near the sun and other heavenly bodies. Secondly, it must have been too joint a neighbour to the element of fire. Thirdly, the air in that region is so violently moved and carried about with such swiftness as nothing in that place can consist or have abiding. Fourthly,"—but what has been quoted is surely enough, and there is no use in continuing.

Which is the ancient here, and which is the modern? Which uses the language of an intelligent man of our own days? which a language wholly obsolete and unfamiliar to us? Which has the rational appreciation and control of his facts? Which wanders among them helplessly and without a clue? Is it our own countryman, or is it the Greek? And the language of Ralegh affords a fair sample of the critical power, of the point of view, possessed by the majority of intelligent men of his day; as the language of Thucydides affords us a fair sample of the critical power of the majority of intelligent men in the age of Pericles.

Well, then, in the age of Pericles we have, in spite of its antiquity, a highly-developed, a modern, a deeply interesting epoch. Next comes the question: Is this epoch adequately interpreted by its highest literature? Now, the peculiar characteristic of the highest literature—the poetry—of the fifth century in Greece before the Christian era, is its *adequacy;* the peculiar characteristic of the poetry of Sophocles is its consummate, its unrivalled *adequacy;* that it represents the highly developed human nature of that age—human nature developed in a number of directions, politically, socially, religiously, morally developed—in its completest and most harmonious development in all these directions; while there is shed over this poetry the charm of that noble serenity which always accompanies true insight. If in the body of Athenians of that time there was, as we have said, the utmost energy of mature manhood, public and private; the most entire freedom, the most unprejudiced and intelligent observation of human affairs—in Sophocles there is the same energy, the same maturity, the same freedom, the same intelligent observation; but all these idealized and glorified by the grace and light shed over them from the noblest poetical feeling. And therefore I have ventured to say of Sophocles, that he "saw life steadily, and saw it whole."5 Well may we understand how Pericles—how the great statesman whose aim was, it has been said, "to realize in Athens the idea which he had conceived of human greatness," and who partly succeeded in his aim—should have been drawn to the great poet whose works are the noblest reflection of his success.

I assert, therefore, though the detailed proof of the assertion must be reserved for other opportunities, that, if the fifth century in Greece before our era is a significant and modern epoch, the poetry of that epoch—the poetry of Pindar, Æschylus, and Sophocles—is an adequate representation and interpretation of it.

The poetry of Aristophanes is an adequate representation of it also. True, this poetry regards humanity from the comic side; but there is a comic side from which to regard humanity as well as a tragic one; and the distinction of Aristophanes is to have regarded it from the true point of view on the comic side. He too, like Sophocles, regards the human nature of his time in its fullest development; the boldest creations of a riotous imagination are in Aristophanes, as has been justly said, based always upon the foundation of a serious thought: politics, education, social life, literature—all the great modes in which the human life of his day manifested itself—are the subjects of his thoughts, and of his penetrating comment. There is shed, therefore, over his poetry the charm, the vital freshness, which is felt when man and his relations are from any side adequately, and therefore genially, regarded. Here is the true difference between Aristophanes and Menander.[6] There has been preserved an epitome of a comparison by Plutarch between Aristophanes and Menander, in which the grossness of the former, the exquisite truth to life and felicity of observation of the latter, are strongly insisted upon; and the preference of the refined, the learned, the intelligent men of a later period for Menander loudly proclaimed. "What should take a man of refinement to the theatre," asks Plutarch, "except to see one of Menander's plays? When do you see the theatre filled with cultivated persons, except when Menander is acted? and he is the favourite refreshment," he continues, "to the overstrained mind of the laborious philosopher" And every one knows the famous line of tribute to this poet by an enthusiastic admirer in antiquity:— "O Life and Menander, which of you painted the other?" We remember, too, how a great English statesman is said to have declared that there was no lost work of antiquity which he so ardently desired to recover as a play of Menander. Yet Menander has perished, and Aristophanes has survived. And to what is this to be attributed? To the instinct of self-preservation in humanity. The human race has the strongest, the most invincible tendency to *live*, to *develop* itself. It retains, it clings to what fosters its life, what favours its development, to the literature which exhibits it in its vigour; it rejects, it abandons what does not foster its development, the literature which exhibits it arrested and decayed. Now, between the times of Sophocles and Menander a great check had befallen the development of Greece;—the failure of the Athenian expedition to Syracuse, and the consequent termination of the Peloponnesian War in a result unfavourable to Athens. The free expansion of her growth was checked; one of the noblest channels of Athenian life, that of political activity, had begun to narrow and to dry up. That was the true catastrophe of the ancient world; it was then that the oracles of the ancient world should have become silent, and that its gods should have forsaken their temples; for from that date the intellectual and spiritual life of Greece was left without an adequate material basis of political and practical life; and both began inevitably to decay. The opportunity of the ancient world was then lost, never to return; for neither the Macedonian nor the Roman world, which possessed an adequate material basis, possessed, like the Athens of earlier times, an adequate intellect and soul to inform and inspire them; and there was left of the ancient world, when Christianity arrived, of Greece only a head without a body, and of Rome only a body without a soul.

It is Athens after this check, after this diminution of vitality,—it is man with part of his life shorn away, refined and intelligent indeed, but sceptical, frivolous, and dissolute,—which the poetry of Menander represented. The cultivated, the accomplished might applaud the dexterity, the perfection of the representation—might prefer it to the free genial delineation of a more living time with which they were no longer in sympathy. But the instinct of humanity taught it, that in the one poetry there was the seed of life, in the other poetry the seed of death; and it has rescued Aristophanes, while it has left Menander to his fate.

In the flowering period of the life of Greece, therefore, we have a culminating age, one of the flowering periods of the life of the human race: in the poetry of that age we have a literature commensurate with its epoch. It is most perfectly commensurate in the poetry of Pindar, Æschylus, Sophocles, Aristophanes; these, therefore, will be the supremely interesting objects in this literature; but the stages in literature which led up to this point of perfection, the stages in literature which led downward from it, will be deeply interesting also. A distinguished person,* who has lately been occupying himself with Homer, has remarked that an undue preference is given, in the studies of Oxford, to these poets over Homer. The justification of such a preference, even if we put aside all philological considerations, lies, perhaps, in what I have said. Homer himself is eternally interesting; he is a greater poetical power than even Sophocles or Æschylus; but his age is less interesting than himself. Æschylus and Sophocles represent an age as interesting as themselves; the names, indeed, in their dramas are the names of the old heroic world, from which they were far separated; but these names are taken, because the use of them permits to the poet that free and ideal treatment of his characters which the highest tragedy demands; and into these figures of the old world is poured all the fulness of life and of thought which the new world had accumulated. This new world in its maturity of reason resembles our own; and the

* Mr. Gladstone. [M. A.][7]

advantage over Homer in their greater significance for *us*, which Æschylus and Sophocles gain by belonging to this new world, more than compensates for their poetical inferiority to him.

Let us now pass to the Roman world. There is no necessity to accumulate proofs that the culminating period of Roman history is to be classed among the leading, the significant, the modern periods of the world. There is universally current, I think, a pretty correct appreciation of the high development of the Rome of Cicero and Augustus; no one doubts that material civilization and the refinements of life were largely diffused in it; no one doubts that cultivation of mind and intelligence were widely diffused in it. Therefore, I will not occupy time by showing that Cicero corresponded with his friends in the style of the most accomplished, the most easy letter-writers of modern times; that Cæsar did not write history like Sir Walter Ralegh. The great period of Rome is, perhaps, on the whole, the greatest, the fullest, the most significant period on record; it is certainly a greater, a fuller period than the age of Pericles. It is an infinitely larger school for the men reared in it; the relations of life are immeasurably multiplied, the events which happen are on an immeasurably grander scale. The facts, the spectacle of this Roman world, then, are immense: let us see how far the literature, the interpretation of the facts, has been adequate.

Let us begin with a great poet, a great philosopher, Lucretius. In the case of Thucydides I called attention to the fact that his habit of mind, his mode of dealing with questions, were modern; that they were those of an enlightened, reflecting man among ourselves. Let me call attention to the exhibition in Lucretius of a modern *feeling* not less remarkable than the modern *thought* in Thucydides. The predominance of thought, of reflection, in modern epochs is not without its penalties; in the unsound, in the overtasked, in the over-sensitive, it has produced the most painful, the most lamentable results; it has produced a state of feeling unknown to less enlightened but perhaps healthier epochs—the feeling of depression, the feeling of *ennui*. Depression and *ennui;* these are the characteristics stamped on how many of the representative works of modern times! they are also the characteristics stamped on the poem of Lucretius. One of the most powerful, the most solemn passages of the work of Lucretius, one of the most powerful, the most solemn passages in the literature of the whole world, is the well-known conclusion of the third book. With masterly touches he exhibits the lassitude, the incurable tedium which pursue men in their amusements; with indignant irony he upbraids them for the cowardice with which they cling to a life which for most is miserable; to a life which contains, for the most fortunate, nothing but the old dull round of the same unsatisfying objects for ever presented. "A man rushes abroad," he says, "because he is sick of being at home; and suddenly comes home again because he finds himself no whit easier abroad. He posts as fast as his horses can take him to his country-seat: when he has got there he hesitates what to do; or he throws himself down moodily to sleep, and seeks forgetfulness in that; or he makes the best of his way back to town again with the same speed as he fled from it. Thus every one flies from himself." What a picture of *ennui!* of the disease of the most modern societies, the most advanced civilizations! "O man," he exclaims again, "the lights of the world, Scipio, Homer, Epicurus, are dead; wilt thou hesitate and fret at dying, whose life is well-nigh dead whilst thou art yet alive; who consumest in sleep the greater part of thy span, and when awake dronest and ceasest not to dream; and carriest about a mind troubled with baseless fear, and canst not find what it is that aileth thee when thou staggerest like a drunken wretch in the press of thy cares, and welterest hither and thither in the unsteady wandering of thy spirit!" And again: "I have nothing more than you have already seen," he makes Nature say to man, "to invent for your amusement; *eadem sunt omnia semper*—all things continue the same for ever."

Yes, Lucretius is modern; but is he adequate? And how can a man adequately interpret the activity of his age when he is not in sympathy with it? Think of the varied, the abundant, the wide spectacle of the Roman life of his day; think of its fulness of occupation, its energy of effort. From these Lucretius withdraws himself, and bids his disciples to withdraw themselves; he bids them to leave the business of the world, and to apply themselves "*naturam cognoscere rerum*—to learn the nature of things;" but there is no peace, no cheerfulness for him either in the world from which he comes, or in the solitude to which he goes. With stern effort, with gloomy despair, he seems to rivet his eyes on the elementary reality, the naked framework of the world, because the world in its fulness and movement is too exciting a spectacle for his discomposed brain. He seems to feel the spectacle of it at once terrifying and alluring; and to deliver himself from it he has to keep perpetually repeating his formula of disenchantment and annihilation. In reading him, you understand the tradition which represents him as having been driven mad by a poison administered as a love-charm by his mistress, and as having composed his great work in the intervals of his madness. Lucretius is, therefore, overstrained, gloom-weighted, morbid; and he who is morbid is no adequate interpreter of his age.

I pass to Virgil; to the poetical name which of all poetical names has perhaps had the most prodigious fortune; the name which for Dante, for the Middle Age, represented the perfection of classical antiquity. The perfection of classical antiquity Virgil does not represent; but far be it from me to add my voice to those which have decried his genius: nothing that I shall say is, or can ever be, inconsistent with a profound, an almost affectionate veneration for him. But with respect to him, as with respect to Lucretius, I shall freely ask the question, *Is he adequate?* Does he represent the epoch in which he lived, the mighty Roman world of his time, as the great poets of the great epoch of Greek life represented theirs, in all its fulness, in all its significance?

From the very form itself of his great poem, the *Æneid,* one would be led to augur that this was impossible. The epic form, as a form for representing contemporary or nearly contemporary events, has attained, in the poems of Homer, an unmatched, an immortal success; the epic form as employed by learned poets for the reproduction of the events of a past age has attained a very considerable success. But for *this* purpose, for the poetic treatment of the events of a *past* age, the epic form is a less vital form than the dramatic form. The great poets of the modern period of Greece are accordingly, as we have seen, the *dramatic* poets. The chief of these—Æschylus, Sophocles, Euripides, Aristophanes—have survived: the distinguished epic poets of the same period—Panyasis, Chœrilus, Antimachus—though praised by the Alexandrian critics, have perished in a common destruction with the undistinguished. And what is the reason of this? It is, that the dramatic form exhibits, above all, *the actions of man as strictly determined by his thoughts and feelings;* it exhibits, therefore, what may be always accessible, always intelligible, always interesting. But the epic form takes a wider range; it represents not only the thought and passion of man, that which is universal and eternal, but also the forms of outward life, the fashion of manners, the aspects of nature, that which is local or transient. To exhibit adequately what is local and transient, only a witness, a contemporary, can suffice. In the *reconstruction*, by learning and antiquarian ingenuity, of the local and transient features of a past age, in their representation by one who is not a witness or contemporary, it is impossible to feel the liveliest kind of interest. What, for instance, is the most interesting portion of the *Æneid*,—the portion where Virgil seems to be moving most freely, and therefore to be most animated, most forcible? Precisely that portion which has most a *dramatic* character; the episode of Dido; that portion where locality and manners are nothing—where persons and characters are everything. We might presume beforehand, therefore, that if Virgil, at a time when contemporary epic poetry was no longer possible, had been inspired to represent human life in its fullest significance, he would not have selected the epic form. Accordingly, what is, in fact, the character of the poem, the frame of mind of the poet? Has the poem the depth, the completeness of the poems of Æschylus or Sophocles, of those adequate and consummate representations of human life? Has the poet the serious cheerfulness of Sophocles, of a man who has mastered the problem of human life, who knows its gravity, and is therefore serious, but who knows that he comprehends it, and is therefore cheerful? Over the whole of the great poem of Virgil, over the whole *Æneid*, there rests an ineffable melancholy: not a rigid, a moody gloom, like the melancholy of Lucretius; no, a sweet, a touching sadness, but still a sadness; a melancholy which is at once a source of charm in the poem, and a testimony to its incompleteness. Virgil, as Niebuhr has well said, expressed no affected self-disparagement, but the haunting, the irresistible self-dissatisfaction of his heart, when he desired on his deathbed that his poem might be destroyed. A man of the most delicate genius, the most rich learning, but of weak health, of the most sensitive nature, in a great and overwhelming world; conscious, at heart, of his inadequacy for the thorough spiritual mastery of that world and its interpretation in a work of art; conscious of this inadequacy—the one inadequacy, the one weak place in the mighty Roman nature! This suffering, this graceful-minded, this finely-gifted man is the most beautiful, the most attractive figure in literary history; but he is not the adequate interpreter of the great period of Rome.

We come to Horace: and if Lucretius, if Virgil want cheerfulness, Horace wants seriousness. I go back to what I said of Menander: as with Menander so it is with Horace: the men of taste, the men of cultivation, the men of the world are enchanted with him; he has not a prejudice, not an illusion, not a blunder. True! yet the best men in the best ages have never been thoroughly satisfied with Horace. If human life were complete without faith, without enthusiasm, without energy, Horace, like Menander, would be the perfect interpreter of human life: but it is not; to the best, to the most living sense of humanity, it is not; and because it is not, Horace is inadequate. Pedants are tiresome, men of reflection and enthusiasm are unhappy and morbid; therefore Horace is a sceptical man of the world. Men of action are without ideas, men of the world are frivolous and sceptical; therefore Lucretius is plunged in gloom and in stern sorrow. So hard, nay, so impossible for most men is it to develop themselves in their entireness; to rejoice in the variety, the movement of human life with the children of the world; to be serious over the depth, the significance of human life with the wise! Horace warms himself before the transient fire of human animation and human pleasure while he can, and is only serious when he reflects that the fire must soon go out:—

"Damna tamen celeres reparant cœlestia lunæ:
 Nos, ubi decidimus—"[8]

'For nature there is renovation, but for man there is none!' —it is exquisite, but it is not interpretative and fortifying.

In the Roman world, then, we have found a highly modern, a deeply significant, an interesting period—a period more significant and more interesting, because fuller, than the great period of Greece; but we have not a commensurate literature. In Greece we have seen a highly modern, a most significant and interesting period, although on a scale of less magnitude and importance than the great period of Rome; but then, coexisting with the great epoch of Greece there is what is wanting to that of Rome, a commensurate, an interesting literature.

The intellectual history of our race cannot be clearly understood without applying to other ages, nations, and literatures the same method of inquiry which we have been here imperfectly applying to what is called classical antiquity. But enough has at least been said, perhaps, to establish the absolute, the enduring interest of Greek literature, and, above all, of Greek poetry.

NOTES

On the Modern Element in Literature: Delivered at Oxford, November 1857; published in *Macmillan's Magazine* (February, 1869); not reprinted by Arnold.

1. *Culture and Anarchy* (January, 1869).
2. Speaking in May, 1857.
3. *Life of Pope.*
4. See p. 40.
5. Sonnet, "To a Friend" (1849).
6. Aristophanes, *c.* 448–*c.* 380 B.C. Menander, *c.* 342–292 B.C.
7. *Homer and the Homeric Age* (1858), from *Oxford Essays* (1857) as R. H. Super notes.
8. *Odes,* IV. vii. 13–14: *Yet the swiftly changing moons repair their losses in the sky. We, when we have descended—.*

WHAT HAVE WE to unlearn?[1] Are we to unlearn our
old estimate of serious French poetry and drama? For every
lover of poetry and of the drama, this is a very interesting
question. In the great and serious kinds of poetry, we used
to think that the French genius, admirable as in so many
other ways it is, showed radical weakness. But there is a
new generation growing up amongst us,—and to this young
and stirring generation who of us would not gladly belong,
even at the price of having to catch some of its illusions
and to pass through them?—a new generation which takes
French poetry and drama as seriously as Greek, and for
which M. Victor Hugo is a great poet of the race and lineage of Shakespeare.

M. Victor Hugo is a great romance-writer. There are
people who are disposed to class all imaginative producers
together, and to call them all by the name of poet. Then a
great romance-writer will be a great poet. Above all are the
French inclined to give this wide extension to the name
poet, and the inclination is very characteristic of them. It
betrays that very defect which we have mentioned, the inadequacy of their genius in the higher regions of poetry.
If they were more at home in those regions, they would feel
the essential difference between imaginative production in
verse, and imaginative production in prose, too strongly, to
be ever inclined to call both by the common name of poetry.
They would perceive with us, that M. Victor Hugo, for

instance, or Sir Walter Scott, may be a great romance-writer, and may yet be by no means a great poet.

Poetry is simply the most delightful and perfect form of utterance that human words can reach. Its rhythm and measure, elevated to a regularity, certainty, and force very different from that of the rhythm and measure which can pervade prose, are a part of its perfection. The more of genius that a nation has for high poetry, the more will the rhythm and measure which its poetical utterance adopts be distinguished by adequacy and beauty. That is why M. Henry Cochin's remark on Shakespeare, which I have elsewhere quoted,[2] is so good: 'Shakespeare is not only,' says M. Henry Cochin, 'the king of the realm of thought, he is also the king of poetic rhythm and style. Shakespeare has succeeded in giving us the most varied, the most harmonious verse, which has ever sounded upon the human ear since the verse of the Greeks.'

Let us have a line or two of Shakespeare's verse before us, just to supply the mind with a standard of reverence in the discussion of this matter. We may take the lines from him almost at random:—

> Five hundred poor I have in yearly pay,
> Who twice a day their wither'd hands hold up
> Toward heaven, to pardon blood; and I have built
> Two chantries, where the sad and solemn priests
> Sing still for Richard's soul.[3]

Yes, there indeed is the verse of Shakespeare, the verse of the highest English poetry; there is what M. Henry Cochin calls 'the majestic English iambic!' We will not inflict Greek upon our readers, but every one who knows Greek will remember that the iambic of the Attic tragedians is a rhythm of the same high and splendid quality.

Which of us doubts that imaginative production, uttering itself in such a form as this, is altogether another and a higher thing from imaginative production uttering itself in any of the forms of prose? And if we find a nation doubting whether there is any great difference between imaginative and eloquent production in verse and imaginative and eloquent production in prose, and inclined to call all imaginative producers by the common name of poets, then we may be sure of one thing: namely, that this nation has never yet succeeded in finding the highest and most adequate form for poetry. Because, if it had, it could never have doubted of the essential superiority of this form to all prose forms of utterance. And if a nation has never succeeded in creating this high and adequate form for its poetry, then we may conclude that it is not gifted with the genius for high poetry; since the genius for high poetry calls forth the high and adequate form, and is inseparable from it. So that, on the one hand, from the absence of conspicuous genius in a people for poetry, we may predict the absence of an adequate poetical form; and on the other hand, again, from the want of an adequate poetical form, we may infer the want of conspicuous national genius for poetry.

And we may proceed, supposing that our estimate of a nation's success in poetry is said to be much too low, and is called in question, in either of two ways. If we are said to underrate, for instance, the production of Corneille and Racine in poetry, we may compare this production in power, in penetrativeness, in criticism of life, in ability to call forth our energy and joy, with the production of Homer and Shakespeare. M. Victor Hugo is said to be a poet of the race and lineage of Shakespeare, and I hear astonishment expressed at my not ranking him much above Wordsworth. Well, then, compare their production, in cases where it lends itself to a comparison. Compare the poetry of the moonlight scene in *Hernani*,[4] really the most poetical scene in that play, with the poetry of the moonlight scene in the *Merchant of Venice*. Compare

> . . . Sur nous, tout en dormant,
> La nature à demi veille amoureusement—

with

> Sit, Jessica; look how the floor of heaven
> Is thick inlaid with patines of bright gold![5]

Compare the laudation of their own country, an inspiring but also a trying theme for a poet, by Shakespeare and Wordsworth on the one hand, and by M. Victor Hugo on the other. Compare Shakespeare's

> This precious stone set in the silver sea,
> This blessed plot, this earth, this realm, this England—[6]

or compare Wordsworth's

> We must be free or die, who speak the tongue
> Which Shakespeare spake, the faith and morals hold
> Which Milton held . . . .[7]

with M. Victor Hugo's

> Non, France, l'univers a besoin que tu vives!
> Je le redis, la France est un besoin des hommes.[8]

Who does not recognise the difference in spirit here? And the difference is, that the English lines have the distinctive spirit of high poetry, and the French lines have not.

Here we have been seeking to attend chiefly to the contents and spirit of the verses chosen. Let us now attend, so far as we can, to form only, and the result will be the same. We will confine ourselves, since our subject is the French play in London, to dramatic verse. We require an adequate form of verse for high poetic drama. The accepted form with the French is the rhymed Alexandrine. Let us keep the iambic of the Greeks or of Shakespeare, let us keep such verse as,

> This precious stone set in a silver sea

present to our minds. Then let us take such verse as this from *Hernani:*—

> Le comte d'Onate, qui l'aime aussi, la garde
> Et comme un majordome et comme un amoureux.
> Quelque reître, une nuit, *gardien peu langoureux,*
> Pourrait bien, &c. &c.[9]

or as this, from the same:—

> Quant à lutter ensemble
> Sur le terrain d'amour, *beau champ qui toujours tremble,*
> De fadaises, mon cher, je sais mal faire assaut.[10]

The words in italics will suffice to give us, I think, the sense of what constitutes the fatal fault of the rhyming Alexandrine of French tragedy,—its incurable artificiality, its want of the fluidity, the naturalness, the rapid forward movement of true dramatic verse. M. Victor Hugo is said to be a cunning and mighty artist in Alexandrines, and so unquestionably he is; but he is an artist in a form radically inadequate and inferior, and in which a drama like that of Sophocles or Shakespeare is impossible.

It happens that in our own language we have an example of the employment of an inadequate form in tragedy and in elevated poetry, and can see the result of it. The rhymed ten-syllable couplet, the heroic couplet as it is often called, is such a form. In the earlier work of Shakespeare, work adopted or adapted by him even if not altogether his own work, we find this form often employed:—

> Alas! what joy shall noble Talbot have
> To bid his young son welcome to his grave?
> Away! vexation almost stops my breath
> That sundered friends greet in the hour of death.

> Lucy, farewell; no more my future can
> But curse the cause I cannot aid the man.
> Maine, Blois, Poitiers and Tours are won away
> 'Long all of Somerset and his delay.[11]

Traces of this form remain in Shakespeare's work to the last, in the rhyming of final couplets. But because he had so great a genius for true tragic poetry, Shakespeare dropped this necessarily inadequate form and took a better. We find the rhymed couplet again in Dryden's tragedies. But this vigorous rhetorical poet had no real genius for true tragic poetry, and his form is itself a proof of it. True tragic poetry is impossible with this inadequate form. Again, all through the eighteenth century this form was dominant as the main form for high efforts in English poetry; and our serious poetry of that century, accordingly, has something inevitably defective and unsatisfactory. When it rises out of this, it at the same time adopts instinctively a true form, as Gray does in the *Elegy*. The just and perfect use of the ten-syllable couplet is to be seen in Chaucer. As a form for tragedy, and for poetry of the most serious and elevated kind, it is defective. It makes real adequacy in poetry of this kind impossible; and its prevalence, for poetry of this kind, proves that those amongst whom it prevails have for poetry of this kind no signal gift.

The case of the great Molière himself will illustrate the truth of what I say. Molière is by far the chief name in French poetry; he is one of the very greatest names in all literature. He has admirable and delightful power, penetrativeness, insight; a masterly criticism of life. But he is a comic poet. Why? Had he no seriousness and depth of nature? He had profound seriousness. And would not a dramatic poet with this depth of nature be a tragedian if he could? Of course he would. For only by breasting in full the storm and cloud of life, breasting it and passing through it and above it, can the dramatist who feels the weight of mortal things liberate himself from the pressure, and rise, as we all seek to rise, to content and joy. Tragedy breasts the pressure of life. Comedy eludes it, half liberates itself from it by irony. But the tragedian, if he has the sterner labour, has also the higher prize. Shakespeare has more joy than Molière, more assurance and peace. *Othello,* with all its passion and terror, is on the whole a work animating and fortifying; more so a thousand times than *George Dandin,* which is mournfully depressing. Molière, if he could, would have given us Othellos instead of George Dandins; let us not doubt it. If he did not give Othellos to us, it was because the highest sort of poetic power was wanting to him. And if the highest sort of poetic power had been not wanting to him but present, he would have found no adequate form of dramatic verse for conveying it, he would have had to create one. For such tasks Molière had not power; and this is only another way of saying that for the highest tasks in poetry the genius of his nation appears to have not power. But serious spirit and great poet that he was, Molière had far too sound an instinct to attempt so earnest a matter as tragic drama with inadequate means. It would have been a heart-breaking business for him. He did not attempt it, therefore, but confined himself to comedy.

The *Misanthrope* and the *Tartuffe* are comedy, but they are comedy in verse, poetic comedy. They employ the established verse of French dramatic poetry, the Alexandrine. Immense power has gone to the making of them; a world of vigorous sense, piercing observation, pathetic meditation, profound criticism of life. Molière had also one great advantage as a dramatist over Shakespeare; he wrote for a more developed theatre, a more developed society. Moreover he was at the same time, probably, by nature a better *theatre-poet* than Shakespeare; he had a keener sense for theatrical situation. Shakespeare is not rightly to be called, as Goethe calls him, an epitomator rather than a dramatist; but he may rightly be called rather a dramatist than a theatre-poet. Molière,—and here his French nature stood him in good stead,—was a theatre-poet of the very first order. Comedy, too, escapes, as has been already said, the test of entire seriousness; it remains, by the law of its being, in a region of comparative lightness and of irony. What is artificial can pass in comedy more easily. In spite of all these advantages, the *Misanthrope* and the *Tartuffe* have, and have by reason of their poetic form, an artificiality which makes itself too much felt, and which provokes weariness. The freshness and power of Molière are best felt when he uses prose, in pieces such as the *Avare,* or the *Fourberies de Scapin,* or *George Dandin.* How entirely the contrary is the case with Shakespeare; how undoubtedly is it his verse which shows his power most! But so inadequate a vehicle for dramatic poetry is the French Alexandrine, that its sway hindered Molière, one may think, from being a tragic poet at all, in spite of his having gifts for this highest form of dramatic poetry which are immeasurably superior to those of any other French poet. And in comedy, where Molière thought he could use the Alexandrine, and where he did use it with splendid power, it yet in a considerable degree hampered and lamed him, so that this true and great poet is actually most satisfactory in his prose.

If Molière cannot make us insensible to the inherent defects of French dramatic poetry, still less can Corneille and Racine. Corneille has energy and nobility, Racine an often Virgilian sweetness and pathos. But while Molière, in depth, penetrativeness, and powerful criticism of life, belongs to the same family as Sophocles and Shakespeare, Corneille and Racine are quite of another order. We must not be misled by the excessive estimate of them among their own countrymen. I remember an answer of M. Sainte-Beuve, who always treated me with great kindness, and to whom I once ventured to say that I could not think Lamartine[12] a poet of very high importance. 'He was important to *us,*' answered M. Sainte-Beuve. In a far higher degree can a Frenchman say of Corneille and Racine: 'They were important to *us.*' Voltaire pronounces of them: 'These men taught our nation to think, to feel, and to express itself' *Ces hommes enseignèrent à la nation à penser, à sentir et à s'exprimer.* They were thus the instructors and formers of a society in many respects the most civilised and consummate that the world has ever seen, and which certainly has not been inclined to underrate its own advantages. How natural, then, that it should feel grateful to its formers, and should extol them! 'Tell your brother Rodolphe,' writes Joseph de Maistre[13] from Russia to his daughter at home, 'to get on with his French poets; let him have them by heart, —the inimitable Racine above all; never mind whether he understands him or not. I did not understand him, when my mother used to come and sit on my bed, and repeat from him, and put me to sleep with her beautiful voice to the sound of this incomparable music. I knew hundreds of lines of him before I could read; and that is why my ears, having drunk in this ambrosia betimes, have never been able to endure common stuff since.' What a spell must such early use have had for riveting the affections; and how civilising are such affections, how honourable to the society which can be imbued with them, to the literature which can inspire them! Pope was in a similar way, though not at all in the same degree, a forming and civilising influence to our grandfathers, and limited their literary taste while he stimulated and formed it. So, too, the Greek boy was fed by his mother and nurse with Homer; but then in this case it was Homer!

We English had Shakespeare waiting to open our eyes, whensoever a favourable moment came, to the insufficiencies of Pope. But the French had no Shakespeare to open their eyes to the insufficiencies of Corneille and Racine. Great artists like Talma[14] and Rachel,[15] whose power, as actors, was far superior to the power, as poets, of the dramatists whose work they were rendering, filled out with their own life and warmth the parts into which they threw themselves, gave body to what was meagre, fire to what was cold, and themselves supported the poetry of the French classic drama rather than were supported by it. It was easier to think the poetry of Racine inimitable, when Talma and Rachel were seen producing in it such inimitable effects. Indeed French acting is so good, that there are few pieces, excepting always those of Molière, in the repertory of a company such as that which we have just seen, where the actors do not show themselves to be superior to the pieces they render, and to be worthy of pieces which are better. *Phèdre* is a work of much beauty, yet certainly one felt this in seeing Rachel in the part of Phèdre. I am not sure that one feels it in seeing Mdlle. Sarah Bernhardt[16] as Phèdre, but I am sure that one feels it in seeing her as Doña Sol.[17]

The tragedy of M. Victor Hugo has always, indeed, stirring events in plenty; and so long as the human nerves are what they are, so long will things like the sounding of the horn, in the famous fifth act of *Hernani*, produce a thrill in us. But so will Werner's *Twenty-fourth of February*,[18] or Scott's *House of Aspen*.[19] A thrill of this sort may be raised in us, and yet our poetic sense may remain profoundly dissatisfied. So it remains in *Hernani*. M. Sarcey,[20] a critic always acute and intelligent, and whom one reads with profit and pleasure, says that we English are fatigued by the long speeches in *Hernani*, and that we do not appreciate what delights French people in it, the splendour of the verse, the wondrous beauty of the style, the poetry. Here recurs the question as to the adequacy of the French Alexandrine as tragic verse. If this form is vitally inadequate for tragedy, then to speak absolutely of splendour of verse and wondrous beauty of style in it when employed for tragedy, is misleading. Beyond doubt M. Victor Hugo has an admirable gift for versification. So had Pope. But to speak absolutely of the splendour of verse and wondrous beauty of style of the *Essay on Man* would be misleading. Such terms can be properly used only of verse and style of an altogether higher and more adequate kind, a verse and style like that of Dante, Shakespeare, or Milton. Pope's brilliant gift for versification is exercised within the limits of a form inadequate for true philosophic poetry, and by its very presence excluding it. M. Victor Hugo's brilliant gift for versification is exercised

within the limits of a form inadequate for true tragic poetry,
and by its very presence excluding it.

But, if we are called upon to prove this from the poetry
itself, instead of inferring it from the form, our task, in the
case of *Hernani*, is really only too easy. What is the poetical
value of this famous fifth act of *Hernani?* What poetical
truth, or verisimilitude, or possibility has Ruy Gomez, this
chivalrous old Spanish grandee, this venerable nobleman,
who, because he cannot marry his niece, presents himself to
her and her husband upon their wedding night, and insists
on the husband performing an old promise to commit suicide if summoned by Ruy Gomez to do so? Naturally the
poor young couple raise difficulties, and the venerable nobleman keeps plying them with: *Bois! Allons! Le sépulcre est
ouvert, et je ne puis attendre! J'ai hâte! Il faut mourir!*[21]
This is a mere character of Surrey melodrama.[22] And
Hernani, who, when he is reminded that it is by his father's
head that he has sworn to commit suicide, exclaims:

Mon père! mon père!—Ah! j'en perdrai la raison![23]

and who, when Doña Sol gets the poison away from him,
entreats her to return it:

> Par pitié, ce poison,
> Rends-le-moi! Par l'amour, par notre âme immortelle![24]

because

Le duc a ma parole, et mon père est là-haut![25]

The *poetry!* says M. Sarcey;—and one thinks of the poetry
of *Lear!* M. Sarcey must pardon me for saying, that in

> Le duc a ma parole, et mon père est là-haut!

we are not in the world of poetry at all, hardly even in the
world of literature, unless it be the literature of *Bombastes
Furioso*.[26]

Our sense, then, for what is poetry and what is not, the
attractiveness of the French plays and players must not
make us unlearn. We may and must retain our old conviction of the fundamental insufficiency, both in substance and
in form, of the rhymed tragedy of the French. We are to
keep, too, what in the main has always been the English
estimate of Molière: that he is a man of creative and splendid power, a dramatist whose work is truly delightful, is
edifying and immortal; but that even Molière in poetic
drama is hampered and has not full swing, and, in conse-

quence, leaves us somewhat dissatisfied. Finally, we poor old
people should pluck up courage to stand out yet, for the
few years of life which yet remain to us, against that passing
illusion of the confident young generation who are newly
come out on the war-path, that M. Victor Hugo is a poet of
the race and lineage of Shakespeare.

What, now, are we to say of the prose drama of modern
life, the drama of which the *Sphinx*[27] and the *Étrangère* and
the *Demi-Monde*[28] are types, and which was the most
strongly attractive part, probably, of the feast offered to us
by the French company? The first thing to be said of these
pieces is that they are admirably acted. But then constantly,
as I have already said, one has the feeling that the French
actors are better than the pieces which they play. What are
we to think of this modern prose drama in itself, the drama
of M. Octave Feuillet, and M. Alexandre Dumas the
younger, and M. Augier?[29] Some of the pieces composing it
are better constructed and written than others, and much
more effective. But this whole drama has one character
common to it all. It may be best described as the theatre of
the *homme sensuel moyen,* the average sensual man, whose
country is France, and whose city is Paris, and whose ideal
is the free, gay, pleasurable life of Paris,—an ideal which
our young literary generation, now out on the war-path here
in England, seek to adopt from France, and which they
busily preach and work for. Of course there is in Paris much
life of another sort too, as there are in France many men
of another type than that of the *homme sensuel moyen.* But
for many reasons, which I need not enumerate here, the life
of the free, confident, harmonious development of the
senses, all round, has been able to establish itself among the
French and at Paris, as it has established itself nowhere else:
and the ideal life of Paris is this sort of life triumphant.
And of this ideal the modern French drama, works like the
Sphinx and the *Étrangère* and the *Demi-Monde,* are the
expression. It is the drama, I say, this drama now in question, of the *homme sensuel moyen,* the average sensual man.
It represents the life of the senses developing themselves all
round without misgiving; a life confident, fair and free, with
fireworks of fine emotions, grand passions and devotedness,
—or rather, perhaps, we should say *dévouement,*—lighting
it up when necessary.

We in England have no modern drama at all. We have
our Elizabethan drama. We have a drama of the last century and of the latter part of the century preceding, a drama

which may be called our drama of *the town,* when *the town* was an entity powerful enough, because homogeneous enough, to evoke a drama embodying its notions of life. But we have no modern drama. Our vast society is not at present homogeneous enough for this,—not sufficiently united, even any large portion of it, in a common view of life, a common ideal, capable of serving as basis for a modern English drama. We have apparitions of poetic and romantic drama (as the French, too, have their charming *Gringoire*),[30] which are always possible, because man has always in his nature the poetical fibre. Then we have numberless imitations and adaptations from the French. All of these are at the bottom fantastic. We may truly say of them, that 'truth and sense and liberty are flown.' And the reason is evident. They are pages out of a life which the ideal of the *homme sensuel moyen* rules, transferred to a life where this ideal, notwithstanding the fervid adhesion to it of our young generation, does not reign. For the attentive observer the result is a sense of incurable falsity in the piece as adapted. Let me give an example. Everybody remembers *Pink Dominoes.*[31] The piece turns upon an incident possible and natural enough in the life of Paris. Transferred to the life of London the incident is altogether unreal, and its unreality makes the whole piece, in its English form, fantastic and absurd.

Still that does not prevent such pieces, and the theatre generally, from now exercising upon us a great attraction. For we are at the end of a period, and have to deal with the facts and symptoms of a new period on which we are entering; and prominent among these fresh facts and symptoms is the irresistibility of the theatre. We know how the Elizabethan theatre had its cause in an ardent zest for life and living, a bold and large curiosity, a desire for a fuller, richer existence, pervading this nation at large, as they pervaded other nations, after the long mediæval time of obstruction and restraint. But we know, too, how the great middle class of this nation, alarmed at grave symptoms which showed themselves in the new movement, drew back; made choice for its spirit to live at one point, instead of living, or trying to live, at many; entered, as I have so often said, the prison of Puritanism, and had the key turned upon its spirit there for two hundred years. Our middle class forsook the theatre. The English theatre reflected no more the aspiration of a great community for a fuller and richer sense of human existence.

This theatre came afterwards, however, to reflect the aspirations of 'the town.' It developed a drama to suit these aspirations; while it also brought back and re-exhibited the Elizabethan drama, so far as 'the town' wanted it and liked it. Finally, as even 'the town' ceased to be homogeneous, the theatre ceased to develop anything expressive. It still repeated what was old with more or less of talent. But the mass of our English community, the mass of the middle class, kept aloof from the whole thing.

NOTES

from *The French Play in London:* Published in *Nineteenth Century* (August, 1879); *Irish Essays* (1882).

1. As a result of the successful visit by the Comédie-Française to London in 1879.
2. See p. 369.
3. *Henry V*, IV. i. 304–8.
4. (1830): *Nature, even in her sleep, half watches over us with loving care.*
5. *Merchant of Venice*, V. i. 58–59.
6. *Richard II*, II. i. 46, 50 (Arnold leaves out three lines).
7. "It is not to be thought of that the Flood" ("That Shakespeare").
8. *No, France, the universe has need that you live! I say it again, France is a need to men.*
9. *The count of Onate, who loves her too, guards her both as a steward and as a lover. Some trooper, one night—a not very languorous warder—could well, etc.*
10. *As for jousting together in the lists of love—a fair terrain which always trembles—I am scarcely versed, my dear, in the art of duelling with trifles.*
11. *1 Henry VI*, IV. iii. 39–46.
12. Alphonse de Lamartine (1790–1869).
13. (1753–1821), thinker and ambassador at St. Petersburg.
14. François Joseph Talma (1763–1826), tragic actor.
15. Élisa Felix (Rachel), actress (1821–58).
16. (1844–1923), tragic actress.
17. A character in *Hernani*.
18. A one-act tragedy (1810) by the German Zacharias Werner (1768–1823).
19. A tragedy (1829) by Sir Walter Scott.
20. Francisque Sarcey (1827–99), dramatic critic.
21. *Drink up! Hurry! The tomb lies open, and I cannot wait! Time presses! You must die!*
22. The Surrey Theatre in London was notable in the 19th century for sensational dramas.
23. *My father! My father! Ah, I shall go mad at the thought!*
24. *For pity's sake, give me the poison! For the sake of our love, of our immortal soul!*
25. *The duke has my word of honour, and my father is above!*
26. Burlesque (1810) by W. B. Rhodes.

27. (1874), by Octave Feuillet (1821–90).

28. Plays (1876 and 1855), by Alexandre Dumas the younger (1824–95).

29. Émile Augier (1820–89).

30. Sentimental comedy (1866), by Théodore de Banville.

31. (1877), by James Albery, from the French *Les Dominos Roses* of A.-N. Hennequin.

THE STUDY OF POETRY

1880

'THE FUTURE of poetry is immense, because in poetry, where it is worthy of its high destinies, our race, as time goes on, will find an ever surer and surer stay. There is not a creed which is not shaken, not an accredited dogma which is not shown to be questionable, not a received tradition which does not threaten to dissolve. Our religion has materialised itself in the fact, in the supposed fact; it has attached its emotion to the fact, and now the fact is failing it. But for poetry the idea is everything; the rest is a world of illusion, of divine illusion. Poetry attaches its emotion to the idea; the idea *is* the fact. The strongest part of our religion to-day is its unconscious poetry.'

Let me be permitted to quote these words of my own,[1] as uttering the thought which should, in my opinion, go with us and govern us in all our study of poetry. In the present work it is the course of one great contributory stream to the world-river of poetry that we are invited to follow. We are here invited to trace the stream of English poetry. But whether we set ourselves, as here, to follow only one of the several streams that make the mighty river of poetry, or whether we seek to know them all, our governing thought should be the same. We should conceive of poetry worthily, and more highly than it has been the custom to conceive of it. We should conceive of it as capable of higher uses, and called to higher destinies, than those which in general men have assigned to it hitherto. More and more mankind will discover that we have to turn to poetry to interpret life for us, to console us, to sustain us. Without poetry, our science will appear incomplete; and most of what now passes with us for religion and philosophy will be replaced by poetry. Science, I say, will appear incomplete without it. For finely and truly does Wordsworth[2] call poetry 'the impassioned expression which is in the countenance of all science'; and what is a countenance without its expression? Again, Wordsworth finely and truly calls poetry 'the breath and finer spirit of all knowledge': our religion, parading evidences such as those on which the popular mind relies now; our philosophy, pluming itself on its reasonings about causation and finite and infinite being; what are they but the shadows and dreams and false shows of knowledge? The day will come when we shall wonder at ourselves for having trusted to them, for having taken them seriously; and the more we perceive their hollowness, the more we shall prize 'the breath and finer spirit of knowledge' offered to us by poetry.

But if we conceive thus highly of the destinies of poetry, we must also set our standard for poetry high, since poetry, to be capable of fulfilling such high destinies, must be poetry of a high order of excellence. We must accustom ourselves to a high standard and to a strict judgment. Sainte-Beuve relates that Napoleon one day said, when somebody was spoken of in his presence as a charlatan: 'Charlatan as much as you please; but where is there *not* charlatanism?'—'Yes,' answers Sainte-Beuve, 'in politics, in the art of governing mankind, that is perhaps true. But in the order of thought, in art, the glory, the eternal honour is that charlatanism shall find no entrance; herein lies the inviolableness of that noble portion of man's being.' It is admirably said, and let us hold fast to it. In poetry, which is thought and art in one, it is the glory, the eternal honour, that charlatanism shall find no entrance; that this noble sphere be kept inviolate and inviolable. Charlatanism is for confusing or obliterating the distinctions between excellent and inferior, sound and unsound or only half-sound, true and untrue or only half-true. It is charlatanism, conscious or unconscious, whenever we confuse or obliterate these. And in poetry, more than anywhere else, it is unpermissible to confuse or obliterate them. For in poetry the distinction between excellent and inferior, sound and unsound or only half-sound, true and untrue or only half-true, is of paramount importance. It is of paramount importance because of the high destinies of poetry. In poetry, as a criticism of life under the conditions fixed for such a criticism by the laws of poetic truth and poetic beauty, the spirit of our race will find, we have said, as time goes on and as other helps fail, its consolation and stay. But the consolation and stay will be of power in proportion to the power of the criticism of life. And the criticism of life will be of power in proportion as the poetry conveying it is excellent rather than inferior, sound rather than unsound or half-sound, true rather than untrue or half-true.

The best poetry is what we want; the best poetry will be found to have a power of forming, sustaining, and delighting us, as nothing else can. A clearer, deeper sense of the best in poetry, and of the strength and joy to be drawn from it, is the most precious benefit which we can gather from a poetical collection such as the present. And yet in the very nature and conduct of such a collection there is inevitably something which tends to obscure in us the consciousness of what our benefit should be, and to distract us from the pursuit of it. We should therefore steadily set it before our minds at the outset, and should compel ourselves to revert constantly to the thought of it as we proceed.

Yes; constantly in reading poetry, a sense for the best, the really excellent, and of the strength and joy to be drawn from it, should be present in our minds and should govern our estimate of what we read. But this real estimate, the only true one, is liable to be superseded, if we are not watchful, by two other kinds of estimate, the historic estimate and the personal estimate, both of which are fallacious. A poet or a poem may count to us historically, they may count to us on grounds personal to ourselves, and they may count to us really. They may count to us historically. The course of development of a nation's language, thought, and poetry, is profoundly interesting; and by regarding a poet's work as a stage in this course of development we may easily bring ourselves to make it of more importance as poetry than in itself it really is, we may come to use a language of quite exaggerated praise in criticising it; in short, to over-rate it. So arises in our poetic judgments the fallacy caused by the estimate which we may call historic. Then, again, a poet or a poem may count to us on grounds personal to ourselves. Our personal affinities, likings, and circumstances, have great power to sway our estimate of this or that poet's work, and to make us attach more importance to it as poetry than in itself it really possesses, because to us it is, or has been, of high importance. Here also we over-rate the object of our interest, and apply to it a language of praise which is quite exaggerated. And thus we get the source of a second fallacy in our poetic judgments—the fallacy caused by an estimate which we may call personal.

Both fallacies are natural. It is evident how naturally the

study of the history and development of a poetry may incline a man to pause over reputations and works once conspicuous but now obscure, and to quarrel with a careless
public for skipping, in obedience to mere tradition and habit,
from one famous name or work in its national poetry to
another, ignorant of what it misses, and of the reason for
keeping what it keeps, and of the whole process of growth
in its poetry. The French have become diligent students of
their own early poetry, which they long neglected; the study
makes many of them dissatisfied with their so-called classical
poetry, the court-tragedy of the seventeenth century, a poetry which Pellisson[3] long ago reproached with its want of
the true poetic stamp, with its *politesse stérile et rampante,*
but which nevertheless has reigned in France as absolutely
as if it had been the perfection of classical poetry indeed.
The dissatisfaction is natural; yet a lively and accomplished
critic, M. Charles d'Héricault, the editor of Clément Marot,[4]
goes too far when he says that 'the cloud of glory playing
round a classic is a mist as dangerous to the future of a
literature as it is intolerable for the purposes of history.' 'It
hinders,' he goes on, 'it hinders us from seeing more than
one single point, the culminating and exceptional point; the
summary, fictitious and arbitrary, of a thought and of a
work. It substitutes a halo for a physiognomy, it puts a
statue where there was once a man, and hiding from us all
trace of the labour, the attempts, the weaknesses, the failures,
it claims not study but veneration; it does not show us how
the thing is done, it imposes upon us a model. Above all, for
the historian this creation of classic personages is inadmissible; for it withdraws the poet from his time, from his
proper life, it breaks historical relationships, it blinds criticism by conventional admiration, and renders the investiga-
tion of literary origins unacceptable. It gives us a human personage no longer, but a God seated immovable amidst His
perfect work, like Jupiter on Olympus; and hardly will it be
possible for the young student, to whom such work is exhibited at such a distance from him, to believe that it did not
issue ready made from that divine head.'

All this is brilliantly and tellingly said, but we must plead
for a distinction. Everything depends on the reality of a
poet's classic character. If he is a dubious classic, let us sift
him; if he is a false classic, let us explode him. But if he is a
real classic, if his work belongs to the class of the very best
(for this is the true and right meaning of the word *classic,
classical*), then the great thing for us is to feel and enjoy his

work as deeply as ever we can, and to appreciate the wide difference between it and all work which has not the same high character. This is what is salutary, this is what is formative; this is the great benefit to be got from the study of poetry. Everything which interferes with it, which hinders it, is injurious. True, we must read our classic with open eyes, and not with eyes blinded with superstition; we must perceive when his work comes short, when it drops out of the class of the very best, and we must rate it, in such cases, at its proper value. But the use of this negative criticism is not in itself, it is entirely in its enabling us to have a clearer sense and a deeper enjoyment of what is truly excellent. To trace the labour, the attempts, the weaknesses, the failures of a genuine classic, to acquaint oneself with his time and his life and his historical relationships, is mere literary dilettantism unless it has that clear sense and deeper enjoyment for its end. It may be said that the more we know about a classic the better we shall enjoy him; and, if we lived as long as Methuselah and had all of us heads of perfect clearness and wills of perfect steadfastness, this might be true in fact as it is plausible in theory. But the case here is much the same as the case with the Greek and Latin studies of our schoolboys. The elaborate philological groundwork which we require them to lay is in theory an admirable preparation for appreciating the Greek and Latin authors worthily. The more thoroughly we lay the groundwork, the better we shall be able, it may be said, to enjoy the authors. True, if time were not so short, and schoolboys' wits not so soon tired and their power of attention exhausted; only, as it is, the elaborate philological preparation goes on, but the authors are little known and less enjoyed. So with the investigator of 'historic origins' in poetry. He ought to enjoy the true classic all the better for his investigations; he often is distracted from the enjoyment of the best, and with the less good he overbusies himself, and is prone to over-rate it in proportion to the trouble which it has cost him.

The idea of tracing historic origins and historical relationships cannot be absent from a compilation like the present. And naturally the poets to be exhibited in it will be assigned to those persons for exhibition who are known to prize them highly, rather than to those who have no special inclination towards them. Moreover the very occupation with an author, and the business of exhibiting him, disposes us to affirm and amplify his importance. In the present work, therefore, we are sure of frequent temptation to adopt the historic estimate, or the personal estimate, and to forget the real estimate; which latter, nevertheless, we must employ if we are to make poetry yield us its full benefit. So high is that benefit, the benefit of clearly feeling and of deeply enjoying the really excellent, the truly classic in poetry, that we do well, I say, to set it fixedly before our minds as our object in studying poets and poetry, and to make the desire of attaining it the one principle to which, as the *Imitation* says, whatever we may read or come to know, we always return. *Cum multa legeris et cognoveris, ad unum semper oportet redire principium.*[5]

The historic estimate is likely in especial to affect our judgment and our language when we are dealing with ancient poets; the personal estimate when we are dealing with poets our contemporaries, or at any rate modern. The exaggerations due to the historic estimate are not in themselves, perhaps, of very much gravity. Their report hardly enters the general ear; probably they do not always impose even on the literary men who adopt them. But they lead to a dangerous abuse of language. So we hear Cædmon,[6] amongst our own poets, compared to Milton. I have already noticed the enthusiasm of one accomplished French critic for 'historic origins.' Another eminent French critic, M. Vitet, comments upon that famous document of the early poetry of his nation, the *Chanson de Roland*. It is indeed a most interesting document. The *joculator* or *jongleur* Taillefer, who was with William the Conqueror's army at Hastings, marched before the Norman troops, so said the tradition, singing 'of Charlemagne and of Roland and of Oliver, and of the vassals who died at Roncevaux'; and it is suggested that in the *Chanson de Roland* by one Turoldus or Théroulde, a poem preserved in a manuscript of the twelfth century in the Bodleian Library at Oxford, we have certainly the matter, perhaps even some of the words, of the chant which Taillefer sang. The poem has vigour and freshness; it is not without pathos. But M. Vitet is not satisfied with seeing in it a document of some poetic value, and of very high historic and linguistic value; he sees in it a grand and beautiful work, a monument of epic genius. In its general design he finds the grandiose conception, in its details he finds the constant union of simplicity with greatness, which are the marks, he truly says, of the genuine epic, and distinguish it from the artificial epic of literary ages. One thinks of Homer; this is the sort of praise which is given to Homer, and justly given. Higher praise there cannot well be, and it is the praise due to epic poetry of the highest order only, and to no other. Let us try, then, the *Chanson de Roland* at its best. Roland, mortally wounded, lays himself down under a pine-tree, with his face turned towards Spain and the enemy—

> 'De plusurs choses à remembrer li prist,
> De tantes teres cume li bers cunquist,
> De dulce France, des humes de sun lign,
> De Carlemagne sun seignor ki l'nurrit.'*

That is primitive work, I repeat, with an undeniable poetic quality of its own. It deserves such praise, and such praise is sufficient for it. But now turn to Homer—

> Ὣς φάτο· τοὺς δ᾽ ἤδη κατέχεν φυσίζοος αἶα
> ἐν Λακεδαίμονι αὖθι, φίλῃ ἐν πατρίδι γαίῃ.†

We are here in another world, another order of poetry altogether; here is rightly due such supreme praise as that which M. Vitet gives to the *Chanson de Roland*. If our words are to have any meaning, if our judgments are to have any solidity, we must not heap that supreme praise upon poetry of an order immeasurably inferior.

Indeed there can be no more useful help for discovering what poetry belongs to the class of the truly excellent, and can therefore do us most good, than to have always in one's mind lines and expressions of the great masters, and to apply them as a touchstone to other poetry. Of course we are not to require this other poetry to resemble them; it may be very dissimilar. But if we have any tact we shall find them, when we have lodged them well in our minds, an infallible touchstone for detecting the presence or absence of high poetic quality, and also the degree of this quality, in all other poetry which we may place beside them. Short passages, even single lines, will serve our turn quite sufficiently. Take the two lines which I have just quoted from Homer, the poet's comment on Helen's mention of her brothers;—or take his

> Ἆ δειλώ, τί σφῶϊ δόμεν Πηλῆϊ ἄνακτι
> θνητᾷ; ὑμεῖς δ᾽ ἐστὸν ἀγήρω τ᾽ ἀθανάτω τε.
> ἦ ἵνα δυστήνοισι μετ᾽ ἀνδράσιν ἄλγε᾽ ἔχητον;‡

---

* 'Then began he to call many things to remembrance,—all the lands which his valour conquered, and pleasant France, and the men of his lineage, and Charlemagne his liege lord who nourished him.' —*Chanson de Roland*, iii. 939–942 [M. A.]

† 'So said she; they long since in Earth's soft arms were reposing,
   There, in their own dear land, their fatherland, Lacedæmon.'
   Iliad, iii. 243–44 (translated by Dr. Hawtrey). [M. A.]⁷

‡ 'Ah, unhappy pair, why gave we you to King Peleus, to a mortal? but ye are without old age, and immortal. Was it that with men born to misery ye might have sorrow?'—*Iliad*, xvii. 443–45. [M. A.]

the address of Zeus to the horses of Peleus;—or take finally his

Καὶ σέ, γέρον, τὸ πρὶν μὲν ἀκούομεν ὄλβιον εἶναι.*

the words of Achilles to Priam, a suppliant before him. Take that incomparable line and a half of Dante, Ugolino's tremendous words—

> 'Io no piangeva; sì dentro impietrai.
> Piangevan elli . . .'†

take the lovely words of Beatrice to Virgil—

> 'Io son fatta da Dio, sua mercè, tale,
> Che la vostra miseria non mi tange,
> Nè fiamma d'esto incendio non m'assale . . .'‡

take the simple, but perfect, single line—

> 'In la sua volontade è nostra pace.'§

Take of Shakespeare a line or two of Henry the Fourth's expostulation with sleep—

> 'Wilt thou upon the high and giddy mast
> Seal up the ship-boy's eyes, and rock his brains
> In cradle of the rude imperious surge . . .'⁸

and take, as well, Hamlet's dying request to Horatio—

> 'If thou didst ever hold me in thy heart,
> Absent thee from felicity awhile,
> And in this harsh world draw thy breath in pain
> To tell my story . . .'⁹

Take of Milton that Miltonic passage—

> 'Darken'd so, yet shone
> Above them all the archangel; but his face
> Deep scars of thunder had intrench'd, and care
> Sat on his faded cheek. . . .'

add two such lines as—

> 'And courage never to submit or yield:
> And what is else not to be overcome . . .'

---

* 'Nay, and thou too, old man, in former days wast, as we hear, happy.'—*Iliad*, xxiv. 543. [M. A.]

† 'I wailed not, so of stone grew I within;—*they* wailed.'—*Inferno*, xxxiii. 39–40. [M. A.]

‡ 'Of such sort hath God, thanked be His mercy, made me, that your misery toucheth me not, neither doth the flame of this fire strike me.'—*Inferno*, ii. 91–93. [M. A.]

§ 'In His will is our peace.'—*Paradiso*, iii. 85. [M. A.]

and finish with the exquisite close to the loss of Proserpine,
the loss

> '. . . which cost Ceres all that pain
> To seek her through the world.'[10]

These few lines, if we have tact and can use them, are
enough even of themselves to keep clear and sound our
judgments about poetry, to save us from fallacious estimates
of it, to conduct us to a real estimate.

The specimens I have quoted differ widely from one another, but they have in common this: the possession of the
very highest poetical quality. If we are thoroughly penetrated
by their power, we shall find that we have acquired a sense
enabling us, whatever poetry may be laid before us, to feel
the degree in which a high poetical quality is present or
wanting there. Critics give themselves great labour to draw
out what in the abstract constitutes the characters of a high
quality of poetry. It is much better simply to have recourse
to concrete examples;—to take specimens of poetry of the
high, the very highest quality, and to say: The characters
of a high quality of poetry are what is expressed *there*. They
are far better recognised by being felt in the verse of the
master, than by being perused in the prose of the critic.
Nevertheless if we are urgently pressed to give some critical
account of them, we may safely, perhaps, venture on laying
down, not indeed how and why the characters arise, but
where and in what they arise. They are in the matter and
substance of the poetry, and they are in its manner and style.
Both of these, the substance and matter on the one hand, the
style and manner on the other, have a mark, an accent, of
high beauty, worth, and power. But if we are asked to define
this mark and accent in the abstract, our answer must be:
No, for we should thereby be darkening the question, not
clearing it. The mark and accent are as given by the substance and matter of that poetry, by the style and manner of
that poetry, and of all other poetry which is akin to it in
quality.

Only one thing we may add as to the substance and matter of poetry, guiding ourselves by Aristotle's profound
observation that the superiority of poetry over history consists in its possessing a higher truth and a higher seriousness
(φιλοσοφώτερον καὶ σπουδαιότερον). Let us add, therefore, to
what we have said, this: that the substance and matter of
the best poetry acquire their special character from possessing, in an eminent degree, truth and seriousness. We may
add yet further, what is in itself evident, that to the style

and manner of the best poetry their special character, their accent, is given by their diction, and, even yet more, by their movement. And though we distinguish between the two characters, the two accents, of superiority, yet they are nevertheless vitally connected one with the other. The superior character of truth and seriousness, in the matter and substance of the best poetry, is inseparable from the superiority of diction and movement marking its style and manner. The two superiorities are closely related, and are in steadfast proportion one to the other. So far as high poetic truth and seriousness are wanting to a poet's matter and substance, so far also, we may be sure, will a high poetic stamp of diction and movement be wanting to his style and manner. In proportion as this high stamp of diction and movement, again, is absent from a poet's style and manner, we shall find, also, that high poetic truth and seriousness are absent from his substance and matter.

So stated, these are but dry generalities; their whole force lies in their application. And I could wish every student of poetry to make the application of them for himself. Made by himself, the application would impress itself upon his mind far more deeply than made by me. Neither will my limits allow me to make any full application of the generalities above propounded; but in the hope of bringing out, at any rate, some significance in them, and of establishing an important principle more firmly by their means, I will, in the space which remains to me, follow rapidly from the commencement the course of our English poetry with them in my view.

Once more I return to the early poetry of France, with which our own poetry, in its origins, is indissolubly connected. In the twelfth and thirteenth centuries, that seed-time of all modern language and literature, the poetry of France had a clear predominance in Europe. Of the two divisions of that poetry, its productions in the *langue d'oil* and its productions in the *langue d'oc,* the poetry of the *langue d'oc,* of southern France, of the troubadours, is of importance because of its effect on Italian literature;—the first literature of modern Europe to strike the true and grand note, and to bring forth, as in Dante and Petrarch it brought forth, classics. But the predominance of French poetry in Europe, during the twelfth and thirteenth centuries, is due to its poetry of the *langue d'oil,* the poetry of northern France and of the tongue which is now the French language. In the twelfth century the bloom of this romance-poetry was earlier and stronger in England, at the court of our Anglo-Norman kings, than in France itself. But it was a bloom of French poetry; and as our native poetry formed itself, it formed itself out of this. The romance-poems which took possession of the heart and imagination of Europe in the twelfth and thirteenth centuries are French; 'they are,' as Southey justly says, 'the pride of French literature, nor have we anything which can be placed in competition with them.' Themes were supplied from all quarters; but the romance-setting which was common to them all, and which gained the ear of Europe, was French. This constituted for the French poetry, literature, and language, at the height of the Middle Age, an unchallenged predominance. The Italian Brunetto Latini, the master of Dante, wrote his *Treasure* in French because, he says, 'la parleure en est plus délitable et plus commune à toutes gens.'[11] In the same century, the thirteenth, the French romance-writer, Christian of Troyes, formulates the claims, in chivalry and letters, of France, his native country, as follows:—

'Or vous ert par ce livre apris,
Que Gresse ot de chevalerie
Le premier los et de clergie;
Puis vint chevalerie à Rome,
Et de la clergie la some,
Qui ore est en France venue.
Diex doinst qu'ele i soit retenue,
Et que li lius li abelisse
Tant que de France n'isse
L'onor qui s'i est arestée!'

'Now by this book you will learn that first Greece had the renown for chivalry and letters; then chivalry and the primacy in letters passed to Rome, and now it is come to France. God grant it may be kept there; and that the place may please it so well, that the honour which has come to make stay in France may never depart thence!'

Yet it is now all gone, this French romance-poetry, of which the weight of substance and the power of style are not unfairly represented by this extract from Christian of Troyes. Only by means of the historic estimate can we persuade ourselves now to think that any of it is of poetical importance.

But in the fourteenth century there comes an Englishman nourished on this poetry, taught his trade by this poetry, getting words, rhyme, metre from this poetry; for even of that stanza which the Italians used, and which Chaucer derived immediately from the Italians, the basis and suggestion was probably given in France. Chaucer (I have already named him) fascinated his contemporaries, but so too did Christian of Troyes and Wolfram of Eschenbach.[12] Chaucer's power of fascination, however, is enduring; his poetical importance does not need the assistance of the historic estimate; it is real. He is a genuine source of joy and strength, which is flowing still for us and will flow always. He will be read, as time goes on, far more generally than he is read now. His language is a cause of difficulty for us; but so also, and I think in quite as great a degree, is the language of Burns. In Chaucer's case, as in that of Burns, it is a difficulty to be unhesitatingly accepted and overcome.

If we ask ourselves wherein consists the immense superiority of Chaucer's poetry over the romance-poetry—why it is that in passing from this to Chaucer we suddenly feel ourselves to be in another world, we shall find that his superiority is both in the substance of his poetry and in the style of his poetry. His superiority in substance is given by his large, free, simple, clear yet kindly view of human life,—so unlike the total want, in the romance-poets, of all intelligent command of it. Chaucer has not their helplessness; he has gained the power to survey the world from a central, a truly human point of view. We have only to call to mind the Prologue to *The Canterbury Tales*. The right comment upon it is Dryden's:[13] 'It is sufficient to say, according to the proverb, that *here is God's plenty*.' And again: 'He is a perpetual fountain of good sense.' It is by a large, free, sound representation of things, that poetry, this high criticism of life, has truth of substance; and Chaucer's poetry has truth of substance.

Of his style and manner, if we think first of the romance-poetry and then of Chaucer's divine liquidness of diction, his divine fluidity of movement, it is difficult to speak temperately. They are irresistible, and justify all the rapture with which his successors speak of his 'gold dew-drops of speech.' Johnson[14] misses the point entirely when he finds fault with Dryden for ascribing to Chaucer the first refinement of our numbers, and says that Gower[15] also can show smooth numbers and easy rhymes. The refinement of our numbers means something far more than this. A nation may have versifiers with smooth numbers and easy rhymes, and yet may have no real poetry at all. Chaucer is the father of our splendid English poetry; he is our 'well of English undefiled,'[16] because by the lovely charm of his diction, the

lovely charm of his movement, he makes an epoch and
founds a tradition. In Spenser, Shakespeare, Milton, Keats,
we can follow the tradition of the liquid diction, the fluid
movement, of Chaucer; at one time it is his liquid diction of
which in these poets we feel the virtue, and at another time
it is his fluid movement. And the virtue is irresistible.

Bounded as is my space, I must yet find room for an example of Chaucer's virtue, as I have given examples to show
the virtue of the great classics. I feel disposed to say that a
single line is enough to show the charm of Chaucer's verse;
that merely one line like this—

> 'O martyr souded* in virginitee!'

has a virtue of manner and movement such as we shall not
find in all the verse of romance-poetry;—but this is saying
nothing. The virtue is such as we shall not find, perhaps, in
all English poetry, outside the poets whom I have named as
the special inheritors of Chaucer's tradition. A single line,
however, is too little if we have not the strain of Chaucer's
verse well in our memory; let us take a stanza. It is from
The Prioress's Tale, the story of the Christian child murdered
in a Jewry—

> 'My throte is cut unto my nekke-bone
> Saidè this child, and as by way of kinde
> I should have deyd, yea, longè time agone;
> But Jesu Christ, as ye in bookès finde,
> Will that his glory last and be in minde,
> And for the worship of his mother dere
> Yet may I sing *O Alma* loud and clere.'

Wordsworth has modernised this Tale, and to feel how delicate and evanescent is the charm of verse, we have only to
read Wordsworth's first three lines of this stanza after
Chaucer's—

> 'My throat is cut unto the bone, I trow
> Said this young child, and by the law of kind
> I should have died, yea, many hours ago.'

The charm is departed. It is often said that the power of
liquidness and fluidity in Chaucer's verse was dependent
upon a free, a licentious dealing with language, such as is
now impossible; upon a liberty, such as Burns too enjoyed,
of making words like *neck, bird,* into a dissyllable by adding
to them, and words like *cause, rhyme,* into a dissyllable by

---

* The French *soudé;* soldered, fixed fast. [M. A.][17]

sounding the *e* mute. It is true that Chaucer's fluidity is conjoined with this liberty, and is admirably served by it; but
we ought not to say that it was dependent upon it. It was
dependent upon his talent. Other poets with a like liberty do
not attain to the fluidity of Chaucer; Burns himself does not
attain to it. Poets, again, who have a talent akin to Chaucer's,
such as Shakespeare or Keats, have known how to attain to
his fluidity without the like liberty.

And yet Chaucer is not one of the great classics. His
poetry transcends and effaces, easily and without effort, all
the romance-poetry of Catholic Christendom; it transcends
and effaces all the English poetry contemporary with it, it
transcends and effaces all the English poetry subsequent to
it down to the age of Elizabeth. Of such avail is poetic truth
of substance, in its natural and necessary union with poetic
truth of style. And yet, I say, Chaucer is not one of the
great classics. He has not their accent. What is wanting to
him is suggested by the mere mention of the name of the
first great classic of Christendom, the immortal poet who
died eighty years before Chaucer,—Dante. The accent of
such verse as

'In la sua volontade è nostra pace . . .'

is altogether beyond Chaucer's reach; we praise him, but we
feel that this accent is out of the question for him. It may
be said that it was necessarily out of the reach of any poet
in the England of that stage of growth. Possibly; but we are
to adopt a real, not a historic, estimate of poetry. However
we may account for its absence, something is wanting, then,
to the poetry of Chaucer, which poetry must have before it
can be placed in the glorious class of the best. And there is
no doubt what that something is. It is the σπουδαιότης, the
high and excellent seriousness, which Aristotle assigns as one
of the grand virtues of poetry. The substance of Chaucer's
poetry, his view of things and his criticism of life, has largeness, freedom, shrewdness, benignity; but it has not this
high seriousness. Homer's criticism of life has it, Dante's has
it, Shakespeare's has it. It is this chiefly which gives to our
spirits what they can rest upon; and with the increasing demands of our modern ages upon poetry, this virtue of giving
us what we can rest upon will be more and more highly
esteemed. A voice from the slums of Paris, fifty or sixty
years after Chaucer, the voice of poor Villon out of his life
of riot and crime, has at its happy moments (as, for instance,

in the last stanza of *La Belle Heaulmière**) more of this important poetic virtue of seriousness than all the productions of Chaucer. But its apparition in Villon, and in men like Villon, is fitful; the greatness of the great poets, the power of their criticism of life, is that their virtue is sustained.

To our praise, therefore, of Chaucer as a poet there must be this limitation; he lacks the high seriousness of the great classics, and therewith an important part of their virtue. Still, the main fact for us to bear in mind about Chaucer is his sterling value according to that real estimate which we firmly adopt for all poets. He has poetic truth of substance, though he has not high poetic seriousness, and corresponding to his truth of substance he has an exquisite virtue of style and manner. With him is born our real poetry.

For my present purpose I need not dwell on our Elizabethan poetry, or on the continuation and close of this poetry in Milton. We all of us profess to be agreed in the estimate of this poetry; we all of us recognise it as great poetry, our greatest, and Shakespeare and Milton as our poetical classics. The real estimate, here, has universal currency. With the next age of our poetry divergency and difficulty begin. An historic estimate of that poetry has established itself; and the question is, whether it will be found to coincide with the real estimate.

The age of Dryden, together with our whole eighteenth century which followed it, sincerely believed itself to have produced poetical classics of its own, and even to have made advance, in poetry, beyond all its predecessors. Dryden[18] regards as not seriously disputable the opinion 'that the

---

* The name *Heaulmière* is said to be derived from a headdress (helm) worn as a mark by courtesans. In Villon's ballad, a poor old creature of this class laments her days of youth and beauty. The last stanza of the ballad runs thus—

> 'Ainsi le bon temps regretons
> Entre nous, pauvres vieilles sottes,
> Assises bas, à croppetons,
> Tout en ung tas comme pelottes;
> A petit feu de chenevottes
> Tost allumées, tost estainctes.
> Et jadis fusmes si mignottes!
> Ainsi en prend à maintz et maintes.'

'Thus amongst ourselves we regret the good time, poor silly old things, low-seated on our heels, all in a heap like so many balls; by a little fire of hemp-stalks, soon lighted, soon spent. And once we were such darlings! So fares it with many and many a one.' [M. A.]

sweetness of English verse was never understood or practised by our fathers.' Cowley[19] could see nothing at all in Chaucer's poetry. Dryden heartily admired it, and, as we have seen, praised its matter admirably; but of its exquisite manner and movement all he can find to say is that 'there is the rude sweetness of a Scotch tune in it, which is natural and pleasing, though not perfect.' Addison, wishing to praise Chaucer's numbers, compares them with Dryden's own. And all through the eighteenth century, and down even into our own times, the stereotyped phrase of approbation for good verse found in our early poetry has been, that it even approached the verse of Dryden, Addison, Pope, and Johnson.

Are Dryden and Pope poetical classics? Is the historic estimate, which represents them as such, and which has been so long established that it cannot easily give way, the real estimate? Wordsworth and Coleridge, as is well known, denied it; but the authority of Wordsworth and Coleridge does not weigh much with the young generation, and there are many signs to show that the eighteenth century and its judgments are coming into favour again. Are the favourite poets of the eighteenth century classics?

It is impossible within my present limits to discuss the question fully. And what man of letters would not shrink from seeming to dispose dictatorially of the claims of two men who are, at any rate, such masters in letters as Dryden and Pope; two men of such admirable talent, both of them, and one of them, Dryden, a man, on all sides, of such energetic and genial power? And yet, if we are to gain the full benefit from poetry, we must have the real estimate of it. I cast about for some mode of arriving, in the present case, at such an estimate without offence. And perhaps the best way is to begin, as it is easy to begin, with cordial praise.

When we find Chapman, the Elizabethan translator of Homer, expressing himself in his preface thus: 'Though truth in her very nakedness sits in so deep a pit, that from Gades to Aurora and Ganges few eyes can sound her, I hope yet those few here will so discover and confirm that, the date being out of her darkness in this morning of our poet, he shall now gird his temples with the sun,'[20]—we pronounce that such a prose is intolerable. When we find Milton[21] writing: 'And long it was not after, when I was confirmed in this opinion, that he, who would not be frustrate of his hope to write well hereafter in laudable things, ought himself to be a true poem,'—we pronounce that such a prose has its own grandeur, but that it is obsolete and inconvenient. But when we find Dryden[22] telling us: 'What Virgil wrote in the vigour of his age, in plenty and at ease, I have undertaken to translate in my declining years; struggling with wants, oppressed with sickness, curbed in my genius, liable to be misconstrued in all I write,'—then we exclaim that here at last we have the true English prose, a prose such as we would all gladly use if we only knew how. Yet Dryden was Milton's contemporary.[23]

But after the Restoration the time had come when our nation felt the imperious need of a fit prose. So, too, the time had likewise come when our nation felt the imperious need of freeing itself from the absorbing preoccupation which religion in the Puritan age had exercised. It was impossible that this freedom should be brought about without some negative excess, without some neglect and impairment of the religious life of the soul; and the spiritual history of the eighteenth century shows us that the freedom was not achieved without them. Still, the freedom was achieved; the preoccupation, an undoubtedly baneful and retarding one if it had continued, was got rid of. And as with religion amongst us at that period, so it was also with letters. A fit prose was a necessity; but it was impossible that a fit prose should establish itself amongst us without some touch of frost to the imaginative life of the soul. The needful qualities for a fit prose are regularity, uniformity, precision, balance. The men of letters, whose destiny it may be to bring their nation to the attainment of a fit prose, must of necessity, whether they work in prose or in verse, give a predominating, an almost exclusive attention to the qualities of regularity, uniformity, precision, balance. But an almost exclusive attention to these qualities involves some repression and silencing of poetry.

We are to regard Dryden as the puissant and glorious founder, Pope as the splendid high priest, of our age of prose and reason, of our excellent and indispensable eighteenth century. For the purposes of their mission and destiny their poetry, like their prose, is admirable. Do you ask me whether Dryden's verse, take it almost where you will, is not good?

> 'A milk-white Hind, immortal and unchanged,
>   Fed on the lawns and in the forest ranged.'[24]

I answer: Admirable for the purposes of the inaugurator of

an age of prose and reason. Do you ask me whether Pope's verse, take it almost where you will, is not good?

> 'To Hounslow Heath I point, and Banstead Down;
> Thence comes your mutton, and these chicks my own.'[25]

I answer: Admirable for the purposes of the high priest of an age of prose and reason. But do you ask me whether such verse proceeds from men with an adequate poetic criticism of life, from men whose criticism of life has a high serious-ness, or even, without that high seriousness, has poetic large-ness, freedom, insight, benignity? Do you ask me whether the application of ideas to life in the verse of these men, often a powerful application, no doubt, is a powerful *poetic* application? Do you ask me whether the poetry of these men has either the matter or the inseparable manner of such an adequate poetic criticism; whether it has the accent of

> 'Absent thee from felicity awhile . . .'

or of

> 'And what is else not to be overcome . . .'

or of

> 'O martyr souded in virginitee!'

I answer: It has not and cannot have them; it is the poetry of the builders of an age of prose and reason. Though they may write in verse, though they may in a certain sense be masters of the art of versification, Dryden and Pope are not classics of our poetry, they are classics of our prose.

Gray is our poetical classic of that literature and age; the position of Gray is singular, and demands a word of notice here. He has not the volume or the power of poets who, coming in times more favourable, have attained to an inde-pendent criticism of life. But he lived with the great poets, he lived, above all, with the Greeks, through perpetually studying and enjoying them; and he caught their poetic point of view for regarding life, caught their poetic manner. The point of view and the manner are not self-sprung in him, he caught them of others; and he had not the free and abundant use of them. But whereas Addison and Pope never had the use of them, Gray had the use of them at times. He is the scantiest and frailest of classics in our poetry, but he is a classic.

And now, after Gray, we are met, as we draw towards the end of the eighteenth century, we are met by the great name of Burns. We enter now on times where the personal estimate of poets begins to be rife, and where the real estimate of them is not reached without difficulty. But in spite of the disturbing pressures of personal partiality, of national partiality, let us try to reach a real estimate of the poetry of Burns.

By his English poetry Burns in general belongs to the eighteenth century, and has little importance for us.

> 'Mark ruffian Violence, distain'd with crimes,
>   Rousing elate in these degenerate times;
>   View unsuspecting Innocence a prey,
>   As guileful Fraud points out the erring way;
>   While subtle Litigation's pliant tongue
>   The life-blood equal sucks of Right and Wrong!'[26]

Evidently this is not the real Burns, or his name and fame would have disappeared long ago. Nor is Clarinda's love-poet, Sylvander, the real Burns either. But he tells us himself: 'These English songs gravel me to death. I have not the command of the language that I have of my native tongue. In fact, I think that my ideas are more barren in English than in Scotch. I have been at "Duncan Gray" to dress it in English, but all I can do is desperately stupid.' We English turn naturally, in Burns, to the poems in our own language, because we can read them easily; but in those poems we have not the real Burns.

The real Burns is of course in his Scotch poems. Let us boldly say that of much of this poetry, a poetry dealing perpetually with Scotch drink,[27] Scotch religion, and Scotch manners, a Scotchman's estimate is apt to be personal. A Scotchman is used to this world of Scotch drink, Scotch religion, and Scotch manners; he has a tenderness for it; he meets its poet half way. In this tender mood he reads pieces like the "Holy Fair" or "Halloween." But this world of Scotch drink, Scotch religion, and Scotch manners is against a poet, not for him, when it is not a partial countryman who reads him; for in itself it is not a beautiful world, and no one can deny that it is of advantage to a poet to deal with a beautiful world. Burns's world of Scotch drink, Scotch religion, and Scotch manners, is often a harsh, a sordid, a repulsive world; even the world of his "Cotter's Saturday Night" is not a beautiful world. No doubt a poet's criticism of life may have such truth and power that it triumphs over its world and delights us. Burns may triumph over his world, often he does triumph over his world, but let us observe how and where. Burns is the first case we have had where the bias of the personal estimate tends to mislead; let us look at him closely, he can bear it.

Many of his admirers will tell us that we have Burns, convivial, genuine, delightful, here—

> 'Leeze me on drink! it gies us mair
> Than either school or college;
> It kindles wit, it waukens lair,
> It pangs us fou o' knowledge.
> Be 't whisky gill or penny wheep
> Or ony stronger potion,
> It never fails, on drinking deep,
> To kittle up our notion
>   By night or day.'[28]

There is a great deal of that sort of thing in Burns, and it is unsatisfactory, not because it is bacchanalian poetry, but because it has not that accent of sincerity which bacchanalian poetry, to do it justice, very often has. There is something in it of bravado, something which makes us feel that we have not the man speaking to us with his real voice; something, therefore, poetically unsound.

With still more confidence will his admirers tell us that we have the genuine Burns, the great poet, when his strain asserts the independence, equality, dignity, of men, as in the famous song *For a' that and a' that*—

> 'A prince can mak' a belted knight,
> A marquis, duke, and a' that;
> But an honest man's aboon his might,
> Guid faith he mauna fa'[29] that!
>   For a' that, and a' that,
>   Their dignities, and a' that,
>   The pith o' sense, and pride o' worth,
>   Are higher rank than a' that.'

Here they find his grand, genuine touches; and still more, when this puissant genius, who so often set morality at defiance, falls moralising—

> 'The sacred lowe o' weel-placed love
> Luxuriantly indulge it;
> But never tempt th' illicit rove,
> Tho' naething should divulge it.
>   I waive the quantum o' the sin,
>   The hazard o' concealing,
>   But och! it hardens a' within,
>   And petrifies the feeling.'[30]

Or in a higher strain—

> 'Who made the heart, 'tis He alone
> Decidedly can try us;
> He knows each chord, its various tone;
> Each spring, its various bias.
> Then at the balance let's be mute,
> We never can adjust it;
> What's *done* we partly may compute,
> But know not what's resisted.'[31]

Or in a better strain yet, a strain, his admirers will say, unsurpassable—

> 'To make a happy fire-side clime
> To weans and wife,
> That's the true pathos and sublime
> Of human life.'[32]

There is criticism of life for you, the admirers of Burns will say to us; there is the application of ideas to life! There is, undoubtedly. The doctrine of the last-quoted line coincides almost exactly with what was the aim and end, Xenophon tells us, of all the teaching of Socrates. And the application is a powerful one; made by a man of vigorous understanding, and (need I say?) a master of language.

But for supreme poetical success more is required than the powerful application of ideas to life; it must be an application under the conditions fixed by the laws of poetic truth and poetic beauty. Those laws fix as an essential condition, in the poet's treatment of such matters as are here in question, high seriousness;—the high seriousness which comes from absolute sincerity. The accent of high seriousness, born of absolute sincerity, is what gives to such verse as

> 'In la sua volontade è nostra pace . . .'

to such criticism of life as Dante's, its power. Is this accent felt in the passages which I have been quoting from Burns? Surely not; surely, if our sense is quick, we must perceive that we have not in those passages a voice from the very inmost soul of the genuine Burns; he is not speaking to us from these depths, he is more or less preaching. And the compensation for admiring such passages less, from missing the perfect poetic accent in them, will be that we shall admire more the poetry where that accent is found.

No; Burns, like Chaucer, comes short of the high seriousness of the great classics, and the virtue of matter and manner which goes with that high seriousness is wanting to his work. At moments he touches it in a profound and passionate melancholy, as in those four immortal lines taken by Byron as a motto for *The Bride of Abydos,* but which have in them a depth of poetic quality such as resides in no verse of Byron's own—

> 'Had we never loved sae kindly,
> Had we never loved sae blindly,
> Never met, or never parted,
> We had ne'er been broken-hearted.'

But a whole poem of that quality Burns cannot make; the rest, in the "Farewell to Nancy,"[33] is verbiage.

We arrive best at the real estimate of Burns, I think, by conceiving his work as having truth of matter and truth of manner, but not the accent or the poetic virtue of the highest masters. His genuine criticism of life, when the sheer poet in him speaks, is ironic; it is not—

> 'Thou Power Supreme, whose mighty scheme
> These woes of mine fulfil,
> Here firm I rest, they must be best
> Because they are Thy will!'[34]

It is far rather: *Whistle owre the lave*[35] *o't!* Yet we may say of him as of Chaucer, that of life and of the world, as they come before him, his view is large, free, shrewd, benignant, —truly poetic, therefore; and his manner of rendering what he sees is to match. But we must note, at the same time, his great difference from Chaucer. The freedom of Chaucer is heightened, in Burns, by a fiery, reckless energy; the benignity of Chaucer deepens, in Burns, into an overwhelming sense of the pathos of things;—of the pathos of human nature, the pathos, also, of non-human nature. Instead of the fluidity of Chaucer's manner, the manner of Burns has spring, bounding swiftness. Burns is by far the greater force, though he has perhaps less charm. The world of Chaucer is fairer, richer, more significant than that of Burns; but when the largeness and freedom of Burns get full sweep, as in "Tam o' Shanter," or still more in that puissant and splendid production, "The Jolly Beggars," his world may be what it will, his poetic genius triumphs over it. In the world of "The Jolly Beggars" there is more than hideousness and squalor, there is bestiality; yet the piece is a superb poetic success. It has a breadth, truth, and power which make the famous scene in Auerbach's Cellar, of Goethe's *Faust,* seem artificial

and tame beside it, and which are only matched by Shakespeare and Aristophanes.

Here, where his largeness and freedom serve him so admirably, and also in those poems and songs where to shrewdness he adds infinite archness and wit, and to benignity infinite pathos, where his manner is flawless, and a perfect poetic
whole is the result,—in things like the address to the mouse
whose home he had ruined, in things like "Duncan Gray,"
"Tam Glen," "Whistle and I'll come to you my Lad," "Auld
Lang Syne" (this list might be made much longer),—here we
have the genuine Burns, of whom the real estimate must be
high indeed. Not a classic, nor with the excellent σπουδαιότης
of the great classics, nor with a verse rising to a criticism of
life and a virtue like theirs; but a poet with thorough truth of
substance and an answering truth of style, giving us a poetry
sound to the core. We all of us have a leaning towards the
pathetic, and may be inclined perhaps to prize Burns most
for his touches of piercing, sometimes almost intolerable,
pathos; for verse like—

> 'We twa hae paidl't i' the burn
> From mornin' sun till dine;
> But seas between us braid hae roar'd
> Sin auld lang syne . . .'

where he is as lovely as he is sound. But perhaps it is by the
perfection of soundness of his lighter and archer masterpieces that he is poetically most wholesome for us. For the
votary misled by a personal estimate of Shelley, as so many
of us have been, are, and will be,—of that beautiful spirit
building his many-coloured haze of words and images

> 'Pinnacled dim in the intense inane'—[36]

no contact can be wholesomer than the contact with Burns
at his archest and soundest. Side by side with the

> 'On the brink of the night and the morning
> My coursers are wont to respire,
> But the Earth has just whispered a warning
> That their flight must be swifter than fire . . .'

of *Prometheus Unbound*, how salutary, how very salutary,
to place this from "Tam Glen"—

> 'My minnie[37] does constantly deave[38] me
> And bids me beware o' young men;
> They flatter, she says, to deceive me;
> But wha can think sae o' Tam Glen?'

But we enter on burning ground as we approach the poetry of times so near to us—poetry like that of Byron, Shelley, and Wordsworth—of which the estimates are so often not only personal, but personal with passion. For my purpose, it is enough to have taken the single case of Burns, the first poet we come to of whose work the estimate formed is evidently apt to be personal, and to have suggested how we may proceed, using the poetry of the great classics as a sort of touchstone, to correct this estimate, as we had previously corrected by the same means the historic estimate where we met with it. A collection like the present,[39] with its succession of celebrated names and celebrated poems, offers a good opportunity to us for resolutely endeavouring to make our estimate of poetry real. I have sought to point out a method which will help us in making them so, and to exhibit it in use so far as to put any one who likes in a way of applying it for himself.

At any rate the end to which the method and the estimate are designed to lead, and from leading to which, if they do lead to it, they get their whole value,—the benefit of being able clearly to feel and deeply to enjoy the best, the truly classic, in poetry,—is an end, let me say it once more at parting, of supreme importance. We are often told that an era is opening in which we are to see multitudes of a common sort of readers, and masses of a common sort of literature; that such readers do not want and could not relish anything better than such literature, and that to provide it is becoming a vast and profitable industry. Even if good literature entirely lost currency with the world, it would still be abundantly worth while to continue to enjoy it by oneself. But it never will lose currency with the world, in spite of momentary appearances; it never will lose supremacy. Currency and supremacy are insured to it, not indeed by the world's deliberate and conscious choice, but by something far deeper,—by the instinct of self-preservation in humanity.

NOTES

The Study of Poetry: Published as an introduction to T. H. Ward's *The English Poets* (1880); *Essays in Criticism (Second Series)* (1888).

1. A revision of the final paragraph of Arnold's introduction to vol. i of *The Hundred Greatest Men* (1880).
2. Preface to *Lyrical Ballads.*
3. Paul Pellisson (1624–93): *sterile and tame refinement.*
4. (1496–1544), French poet.
5. *The Imitation of Christ,* by Thomas à Kempis (1380–1471).

6. Seventh-century poet, a hymn by whom is quoted by the historian Bede.

7. See p. 200.

8. *Henry IV, Part II,* III. i. 18–20.

9. V. ii. 333–36.

10. *Paradise Lost,* i. 599–602, 108–09; iv. 271–72.

11. *Its language is more pleasurable and more accessible to everybody.*

12. Bavarian poet, author of the early thirteenth-century epic *Parzival.*

13. Preface to *Fables* (1700).

14. "The History of the English Language," Johnson's *Dictionary.*

15. John Gower (1330?–1408), author of *Confessio Amantis.*

16. *Faerie Queene,* IV. ii. xxxii: "Dan Chaucer, well of English undefiled."

17. "The Prioress's Tale" ("to virginitee").

18. *Essay of Dramatic Poesy* (1668).

19. Reported in Dryden's Preface to *Fables* (1700). Cowley apparently said that Chaucer was "a dry, old-fashioned wit, not worth reviving" (A. H. Nethercot, *Abraham Cowley,* 1931, p. 226).

20. *Iliads* (complete 1611), commentary on Book I; Chapman wrote "confirm her" and "our Homer."

21. *Apology for Smectymnuus* (1642).

22. Dedication of the *Aeneis:* Postscript to the Reader (1697).

23. Dryden, 1631–1700; Milton, 1608–74.

24. *The Hind and the Panther* (1687).

25. *Imitations of Horace,* Satire II. ii (1734).

26. "On the death of the late Lord President Dundas" (died 1787).

27. Taking up Burns's poem "Scotch Drink": ". . . O thou, my Muse! guid, auld Scotch Drink!"

28. "The Holy Fair," stanza xix. (*Leeze me on:* lief is me, I am delighted by. *lair:* lore, learning.)

29. Lay claim to.

30. "Epistle to a Young Friend" (*lowe:* flame).

31. "Address to the Unco Guid."

32. "To Dr. Blacklock."

33. "Ae fond kiss, and then we sever."

34. "Winter, A Dirge."

35. Rest.

36. *Prometheus Unbound,* III. iv. 204; II. v. 1–4.

37. Mother.

38. Deafen.

39. See p. 194.

ON TRANSLATING HOMER

1861

. . . . Nunquamne reponam?[1]

I

IT HAS MORE than once been suggested to me that I
should translate Homer. That is a task for which I have
neither the time nor the courage; but the suggestion led me
to regard yet more closely a poet whom I had already long
studied, and for one or two years the works of Homer were
seldom out of my hands. The study of classical literature is
probably on the decline; but, whatever may be the fate of
this study in general, it is certain that, as instruction spreads
and the number of readers increases, attention will be more
and more directed to the poetry of Homer, not indeed as
part of a classical course, but as the most important poetical
monument existing. Even within the last ten years two fresh
translations of the *Iliad* have appeared in England: one by a
man of great ability and genuine learning, Professor Newman;[2] the other by Mr. Wright,[3] the conscientious and
painstaking translator of Dante. It may safely be asserted
that neither of these works will take rank as the standard
translation of Homer; that the task of rendering him will
still be attempted by other translators. It may perhaps be
possible to render to these some service, to save them some
loss of labour, by pointing out rocks on which their predecessors have split, and the right objects on which a translator of Homer should fix his attention.

It is disputed what aim a translator should propose to himself in dealing with his original. Even this preliminary is not
yet settled. On one side it is said that the translation ought to
be such 'that the reader should, if possible, forget that it is a

translation at all, and be lulled into the illusion that he is reading an original work,—something original' (if the translation be in English), 'from an English hand.' The real original is in this case, it is said, 'taken as a basis on which to rear a poem that shall affect our countrymen as the original may be conceived to have affected its natural hearers.' On the other hand, Mr. Newman, who states the foregoing doctrine only to condemn it, declares that he 'aims at precisely the opposite: to retain every peculiarity of the original, so far as he is able, *with the greater care the more foreign it may happen to be;*' so that it may 'never be forgotten that he is imitating, and imitating in a different material.' The translator's 'first duty,' says Mr. Newman, 'is a historical one: to be *faithful*.' Probably both sides would agree that the translator's 'first duty is to be faithful;' but the question at issue between them is, in what faithfulness consists.

My one object is to give practical advice to a translator; and I shall not the least concern myself with theories of translation as such. But I advise the translator not to try 'to rear on the basis of the *Iliad,* a poem that shall affect our countrymen as the original may be conceived to have affected its natural hearers;' and for this simple reason, that we cannot possibly tell *how* the *Iliad* 'affected its natural hearers.' It is probably meant merely that he should try to affect Englishmen powerfully, as Homer affected Greeks powerfully; but this direction is not enough, and can give no real guidance. For all great poets affect their hearers powerfully, but the effect of one poet is one thing, that of another poet another thing: it is our translator's business to reproduce the effect of Homer, and the most powerful emotion of the unlearned English reader can never assure him whether he has reproduced this, or whether he has produced something else. So, again, he may follow Mr. Newman's directions, he may try to be 'faithful,' he may 'retain every peculiarity of his original;' but who is to assure him, who is to assure Mr. Newman himself, that, when he has done this, he has done that for which Mr. Newman enjoins this to be done, 'adhered closely to Homer's manner and habit of thought'? Evidently the translator needs some more practical directions than these. No one can tell him how Homer affected the Greeks; but there are those who can tell him how Homer affects *them*. These are scholars; who possess, at the same time with knowledge of Greek, adequate poetical taste and feeling. No translation will seem to them of much worth compared with the original; but they alone can say whether the translation produces more or less the same effect upon them as the original. They are the only competent tribunal in this matter: the Greeks are dead; the unlearned Englishman has not the data for judging; and no man can safely confide in his own single judgment of his own work. Let not the translator, then, trust to his notions of what the ancient Greeks would have thought of him; he will lose himself in the vague. Let him not trust to what the ordinary English reader thinks of him; he will be taking the blind for his guide. Let him not trust to his own judgment of his own work; he may be misled by individual caprices. Let him ask how his work affects those who both know Greek and can appreciate poetry; whether to read it gives the Provost of Eton, or Professor Thompson at Cambridge, or Professor Jowett here in Oxford,[4] at all the same feeling which to read the original gives them. I consider that when Bentley[5] said of Pope's translation, 'It was a pretty poem, but must not be called Homer,' the work, in spite of all its power and attractiveness, was judged.

'Ὡς ἂν ὁ φρόνιμος ὁρίσειεν,—'as the judicious would determine,'[6]—that is a test to which every one professes himself willing to submit his works. Unhappily, in most cases, no two persons agree as to who 'the judicious' are. In the present case, the ambiguity is removed: I suppose the translator at one with me as to the tribunal to which alone he should look for judgment; and he has thus obtained a practical test by which to estimate the real success of his work. How is he to proceed, in order that his work, tried by this test, may be found most successful?

First of all, there are certain negative counsels which I will give him. Homer has occupied men's minds so much, such a literature has arisen about him, that every one who approaches him should resolve strictly to limit himself to that which may directly serve the object for which he approaches him. I advise the translator to have nothing to do with the questions, whether Homer ever existed; whether the poet of the *Iliad* be one or many; whether the *Iliad* be one poem or an *Achilleis* and an *Iliad* stuck together; whether the Christian doctrine of the Atonement is shadowed forth in the Homeric mythology; whether the Goddess Latona in any way prefigures the Virgin Mary, and so on. These are questions which have been discussed with learning, with ingenuity, nay, with genius; but they have two inconveniences, —one general for all who approach them, one particular for the translator. The general inconvenience is that there really exist no data for determining them. The particular inconvenience is that their solution by the translator, even were it possible, could be of no benefit to his translation.

I advise him, again, not to trouble himself with constructing a special vocabulary for his use in translation; with excluding a certain class of English words, and with confining himself to another class, in obedience to any theory about the peculiar qualities of Homer's style. Mr. Newman says that 'the entire dialect of Homer being essentially archaic, that of a translator ought to be as much Saxo-Norman as possible, and owe as little as possible to the elements thrown into our language by classical learning.' Mr. Newman is unfortunate in the observance of his own theory; for I continually find in his translation words of Latin origin, which seem to me quite alien to the simplicity of Homer,—'responsive,' for instance, which is a favourite word of Mr. Newman, to represent the Homeric ἀμειβόμενος:

Great Hector of the motley helm thus spake to her *responsive*.
But thus *responsively* to him spake god-like Alexander.

And the word 'celestial,' again, in the grand address of Zeus to the horses of Achilles.

You, who are born *celestial*, from Eld and Death exempted!

seems to me in that place exactly to jar upon the feeling as too bookish. But, apart from the question of Mr. Newman's fidelity to his own theory, such a theory seems to me both dangerous for a translator and false in itself. Dangerous for a translator; because, wherever one finds such a theory announced (and one finds it pretty often), it is generally followed by an explosion of pedantry; and pedantry is of all things in the world the most un-Homeric. False in itself; because, in fact, we owe to the Latin element in our language most of that very rapidity and clear decisiveness by which it is contradistinguished from the German, and in sympathy with the languages of Greece and Rome: so that to limit an English translator of Homer to words of Saxon origin is to deprive him of one of his special advantages for translating Homer. In Voss's well-known translation of Homer,[7] it is precisely the qualities of his German language itself, something heavy and trailing both in the structure of its sentences and in the words of which it is composed, which prevent his translation, in spite of the hexameters, in spite of the fidelity, from creating in us the impression created by the Greek. Mr. Newman's prescription, if followed, would just strip the English translator of the advantage which he has over Voss.

The frame of mind in which we approach an author influences our correctness of appreciation of him; and Homer should be approached by a translator in the simplest frame of mind possible. Modern sentiment tries to make the ancient not less than the modern world its own; but against modern sentiment in its applications to Homer the translator, if he would feel Homer truly—and unless he feels him truly, how can he render him truly?—cannot be too much on his guard. For example: the writer of an interesting article on English translations of Homer, in the last number of the *National Review*,[8] quotes, I see, with admiration, a criticism of Mr. Ruskin on the use of the epithet φυσίζοος, 'life-giving,' in that beautiful passage in the third book of the *Iliad*, which follows Helen's mention of her brothers Castor and Pollux as alive, though they were in truth dead:

> ὣς φάτο · τοὺς δ' ἤδη κάτεχεν φυσίζοος αἶα
> ἐν Λακεδαίμονι αὖθι, φίλῃ ἐν πατρίδι γαίῃ.*

'The poet,' says Mr. Ruskin,[10] 'has to speak of the earth in sadness; but he will not let that sadness affect or change his thought of it. No; though Castor and Pollux be dead, yet the earth is our mother still,—fruitful, life-giving.' This is a just specimen of that sort of application of modern sentiment to the ancients, against which a student, who wishes to feel the ancients truly, cannot too resolutely defend himself. It reminds one, as, alas! so much of Mr. Ruskin's writing reminds one, of those words of the most delicate of living critics: 'Comme tout genre de composition a son écueil particulier, *celui du genre romanesque, c'est le faux*.'[11] The reader may feel moved as he reads it; but it is not the less an example of 'le faux' in criticism; it is false. It is not true, as to that particular passage, that Homer called the earth φυσίζοος because, 'though he had to speak of the earth in sadness, he would not let that sadness change or affect his thought of it,' but consoled himself by considering that 'the earth is our mother still,—fruitful, life-giving.' It is not true, as a matter of general criticism, that this kind of sentimentality, eminently modern, inspires Homer at all. 'From Homer and Polygnotus[12] I every day learn more clearly,' says Goethe, 'that in our life here above ground we have, properly speaking, to enact Hell:'†—if the student must absolutely have a keynote to the *Iliad*, let him take this of Goethe, and see what he can do with it; it will not, at any

---

* *Iliad*, iii. 243. [M. A.][9]
† *Briefwechsel zwischen Schiller und Goethe*, vi. 230. [M. A.]

rate, like the tender pantheism of Mr. Ruskin, falsify for
him the whole strain of Homer.

These are negative counsels; I come to the positive. When
I say, the translator of Homer should above all be penetrated
by a sense of four qualities of his author:—that he is eminently rapid; that he is eminently plain and direct, both in
the evolution of his thought and in the expression of it, that
is, both in his syntax and in his words; that he is eminently
plain and direct in the substance of his thought, that is, in
his matter and ideas; and, finally that he is eminently noble;
—I probably seem to be saying what is too general to be of
much service to anybody. Yet it is strictly true that, for
want of duly penetrating themselves with the first-named
quality of Homer, his rapidity, Cowper[13] and Mr. Wright
have failed in rendering him; that, for want of duly appreciating the second-named quality, his plainness and directness of style and diction, Pope[14] and Mr. Sotheby[15] have
failed in rendering him; that for want of appreciating the
third, his plainness and directness of ideas, Chapman[16] has
failed in rendering him; while for want of appreciating the
fourth, his nobleness, Mr. Newman, who has clearly seen
some of the faults of his predecessors, has yet failed more
conspicuously than any of them.

Coleridge says, in his strange language, speaking of the
union of the human soul with the divine essence, that this
takes place

> Whene'er the mist, which stands 'twixt God and thee,
> Defecates to a pure transparency;[17]

and so, too, it may be said of that union of the translator
with his original, which alone can produce a good translation, that it takes place when the mist which stands between
them—the mist of alien modes of thinking, speaking, and
feeling on the translator's part—'defecates to a pure trans-
parency,' and disappears. But between Cowper and Homer
—(Mr. Wright repeats in the main Cowper's manner, as Mr.
Sotheby repeats Pope's manner, and neither Mr. Wright's
translation nor Mr. Sotheby's has, I must be forgiven for
saying, any proper reason for existing)—between Cowper
and Homer there is interposed the mist of Cowper's elaborate Miltonic manner, entirely alien to the flowing rapidity
of Homer; between Pope and Homer there is interposed the
mist of Pope's literary artificial manner, entirely alien to the
plain naturalness of Homer's manner; between Chapman
and Homer there is interposed the mist of the fancifulness of
the Elizabethan age, entirely alien to the plain directness of

Homer's thought and feeling; while between Mr. Newman and Homer is interposed a cloud of more than Egyptian thickness,—namely, a manner, in Mr. Newman's version, eminently ignoble, while Homer's manner is eminently noble.

I do not despair of making all these propositions clear to a student who approaches Homer with a free mind. First, Homer is eminently rapid, and to this rapidity the elaborate movement of Miltonic blank verse is alien. The reputation of Cowper, that most interesting man and excellent poet, does not depend on his translation of Homer; and in his preface to the second edition, he himself tells us that he felt, —he had too much poetical taste not to feel,—on returning to his own version after six or seven years, 'more dissatisfied with it himself than the most difficult to be pleased of all his judges.' And he was dissatisfied with it for the right reason,—that 'it seemed to him deficient *in the grace of ease.*' Yet he seems to have originally misconceived the manner of Homer so much, that it is no wonder he rendered him amiss. 'The similitude of Milton's manner to that of Homer is such,' he says, 'that no person familiar with both can read either without being reminded of the other; and it is in those breaks and pauses to which the numbers of the English poet are so much indebted, both for their dignity and variety, that he chiefly copies the Grecian.' It would be more true to say: 'The unlikeness of Milton's manner to that of Homer is such, that no person familiar with both can read either without being struck with his difference from the other; and it is in his breaks and pauses that the English poet is most unlike the Grecian.'

The inversion and pregnant conciseness of Milton or Dante are, doubtless, most impressive qualities of style; but they are the very opposites of the directness and flowingness of Homer, which he keeps alike in passages of the simplest narrative, and in those of the deepest emotion. Not only, for example, are these lines of Cowper un-Homeric:—

> So numerous seemed those fires the banks between
> Of Xanthus, blazing, and the fleet of Greece
> In prospect all of Troy;[18]

where the position of the word 'blazing' gives an entirely un-Homeric movement to this simple passage, describing the fires of the Trojan camp outside of Troy; but the following lines, in that very highly-wrought passage where the horse of Achilles answers his master's reproaches for having left Patroclus on the field of battle, are equally un-Homeric:—

For not through sloth or tardiness on us
Aught chargeable, have Ilium's sons thine arms
Stript from Patroclus' shoulders; but a God
Matchless in battle, offspring of bright-haired
Latona, him contending in the van
Slew, for the glory of the chief of Troy.[19]

Here even the first inversion, 'have Ilium's sons thine arms
Stript from Patroclus' shoulders,' gives the reader a sense of
a movement not Homeric; and the second inversion, 'a God
him contending in the van Slew,' gives this sense ten times
stronger. Instead of moving on without check, as in reading
the original, the reader twice finds himself, in reading the
translation, brought up and checked. Homer moves with the
same simplicity and rapidity in the highly-wrought as in the
simple passage.

It is in vain that Cowper insists on his fidelity: 'my chief
boast is that I have adhered closely to my original:'—'the
matter found in me, whether the reader like it or not, is
found also in Homer; and the matter not found in me, how
much soever the reader may admire it, is found only in Mr.
Pope.' To suppose that it is *fidelity* to an original to give its
matter, unless you at the same time give its manner; or,
rather, to suppose that you can really give its matter at all,
unless you can give its manner, is just the mistake of our
pre-Raphaelite school of painters, who do not understand
that the peculiar effect of nature resides in the whole and not
in the parts. So the peculiar effect of a poet resides in his
manner and movement, not in his words taken separately.
It is well known how conscientiously literal is Cowper in his
translation of Homer. It is well known how extravagantly
free is Pope.

So let it be!
Portents and prodigies are lost on me:

that is Pope's rendering of the words,

Ξάνθε, τί μοι θάνατον μαντεύεαι; οὐδέ τί σε χρή · *

Xanthus, why prophesiest thou my death to me? thou needest
not at all:—

yet, on the whole, Pope's translation of the *Iliad* is more
Homeric than Cowper's, for it is more rapid.

Pope's movement, however, though rapid, is not of the
same kind as Homer's; and here I come to the real objection

* *Iliad*, xix. 420. [M. A.]

to rhyme in a translation of Homer. It is commonly said that rhyme is to be abandoned in a translation of Homer, because 'the exigences of rhyme,' to quote Mr. Newman, 'positively forbid faithfulness;' because 'a just translation of any ancient poet in rhyme,' to quote Cowper, 'is impossible.' This, however, is merely an accidental objection to rhyme. If this were all, it might be supposed that if rhymes were more abundant, Homer could be adequately translated in rhyme. But this is not so; there is a deeper, a substantial objection to rhyme in a translation of Homer. It is, that rhyme inevitably tends to pair lines which in the original are independent, and thus the movement of the poem is changed. In these lines of Chapman, for instance, from Sarpedon's speech to Glaucus, in the twelfth book of the *Iliad:*—

> O friend, if keeping back
> Would keep back age from us, and death, and that we might
>   not wrack
> In this life's human sea at all, but that deferring now
> We shunned death ever,—nor would I half this vain valour
>   show,
> Nor glorify a folly so, to wish thee to advance;
> But since we *must* go, though not here, and that besides the
>   chance
> Proposed now, there are infinite fates, etc.

Here the necessity of making the line,

> Nor glorify a folly so, to wish thee to advance,

rhyme with the line which follows it, entirely changes and spoils the movement of the passage.

> οὔτε κεν αὐτὸς ἐνὶ πρώτοισι μαχοίμην,
> οὔτε κε σὲ στέλλοιμι μάχην ἐς κυδιάνειραν · *

> Neither would I myself go forth to fight with the foremost,
> Nor would I urge thee on to enter the glorious battle,

says Homer; there he stops, and begins an opposed movement:

> νῦν δ'—ἔμπης γὰρ Κῆρες ἐφεστᾶσιν θανάτοιο—

> But—for a thousand fates of death stand close to us always—

This line, in which Homer wishes to go away with the most marked rapidity from the line before, Chapman is forced by the necessity of rhyming, intimately to connect with the line before.

* *Iliad,* xii. 324. [M. A.]

But since we *must* go, though not here, and that besides the chance—

The moment the word *chance* strikes our ear, we are irresistibly carried back to *advance* and to the whole previous line, which, according to Homer's own feeling, we ought to have left behind us entirely, and to be moving farther and farther away from.

Rhyme certainly, by intensifying antithesis, can intensify separation, and this is precisely what Pope does; but this balanced rhetorical antithesis, though very effective, is entirely un-Homeric. And this is what I mean by saying that Pope fails to render Homer, because he does not render his plainness and directness of style and diction. Where Homer marks separation by moving away, Pope marks it by antithesis. No passage could show this better than the passage I have just quoted, on which I will pause for a moment.

Robert Wood, whose *Essay on the Genius of Homer* is mentioned by Goethe as one of the books which fell into his hands when his powers were first developing themselves, and strongly interested him, relates of this passage a striking story. He says that in 1762, at the end of the Seven Years' War, being then Under-Secretary of State, he was directed to wait upon the President of the Council, Lord Granville, a few days before he died, with the preliminary articles of the Treaty of Paris. 'I found him,' he continues, 'so languid, that I proposed postponing my business for another time; but he insisted that I should stay, saying, it could not prolong his life to neglect his duty; and repeating the following passage out of Sarpedon's speech, he dwelled with particular emphasis on the third line, which recalled to his mind the distinguishing part he had taken in public affairs:—

ὦ πέπον, εἰ μὲν γὰρ, πόλεμον περὶ τόνδε φυγόντε,
αἰεὶ δὴ μέλλοιμεν ἀγήρω τ' ἀθανάτω τε
ἔσσεσθ', οὔτε κεν αὐτὸς ἐνὶ πρώτοισι μαχοίμην,*
οὔτε κε σὲ στέλλοιμι μάχην ἐς κυδιάνειραν·
νῦν δ'—ἔμπης γὰρ Κῆρες ἐφεστᾶσιν θανάτοιο
μυρίαι, ἃς οὐκ ἔστι φυγεῖν βροτὸν, οὐδ' ὑπαλύξαι—
ἴομεν.

His Lordship repeated the last word several times with a calm and determinate resignation; and, after a serious pause of some minutes, he desired to hear the Treaty read, to which he listened with great attention, and recovered spirits

* These are the words on which Lord Granville 'dwelled with particular emphasis.' [M. A.]

enough to declare the approbation of a dying statesman (I use his own words) "on the most glorious war, and most honourable peace, this nation ever saw." [*]

I quote this story, first, because it is interesting as exhibiting the English aristocracy at its very height of culture, lofty spirit, and greatness, towards the middle of the last century. I quote it, secondly, because it seems to me to illustrate Goethe's saying which I mentioned, that our life, in Homer's view of it, represents a conflict and a hell; and it brings out, too, what there is tonic and fortifying in this doctrine. I quote it, lastly, because it shows that the passage is just one of those in translating which Pope will be at his best, a passage of strong emotion and oratorical movement, not of simple narrative or description.

Pope translates the passage thus:—

> Could all our care elude the gloomy grave
> Which claims no less the fearful than the brave,
> For lust of fame I should not vainly dare
> In fighting fields, nor urge thy soul to war:
> But since, alas! ignoble age must come,
> Disease, and death's inexorable doom;
> The life which others pay, let us bestow,
> And give to fame what we to nature owe.

Nothing could better exhibit Pope's prodigious talent; and nothing, too, could be better in its own way. But, as Bentley said, 'You must not call it Homer.' One feels that Homer's thought has passed through a literary and rhetorical crucible, and come out highly intellectualised; come out in a form which strongly impresses us, indeed, but which no longer impresses us in the same way as when it was uttered by Homer. The antithesis of the last two lines—

> The life which others pay, let us bestow,
> And give to fame what we to nature owe—

is excellent, and is just suited to Pope's heroic couplet; but neither the antithesis itself, nor the couplet which conveys it, is suited to the feeling or to the movement of the Homeric ἴομεν.[20]

A literary and intellectualised language is, however, in its own way well suited to grand matters; and Pope, with a language of this kind and his own admirable talent, comes off well enough as long as he has passion, or oratory, or a

---

[*] Robert Wood, *Essay on the Original Genius and Writings of Homer*, London, 1775, p. vii. [M. A.]

great crisis to deal with. Even here, as I have been pointing out, he does not render Homer; but he and his style are in themselves strong. It is when he comes to level passages, passages of narrative or description, that he and his style are sorely tried, and prove themselves weak. A perfectly plain direct style can of course convey the simplest matter as naturally as the grandest; indeed, it must be harder for it, one would say, to convey a grand matter worthily and nobly, than to convey a common matter, as alone such a matter should be conveyed, plainly and simply. But the style of *Rasselas*[21] is incomparably better fitted to describe a sage philosophising than a soldier lighting his camp-fire. The style of Pope is not the style of *Rasselas;* but it is equally a literary style, equally unfitted to describe a simple matter with the plain naturalness of Homer.

Every one knows the passage at the end of the eighth book of the *Iliad*, where the fires of the Trojan encampment are likened to the stars. It is very far from my wish to hold Pope up to ridicule, so I shall not quote the commencement of the passage, which in the original is of great and celebrated beauty, and in translating which Pope has been singularly and notoriously unfortunate. But the latter part of the passage, where Homer leaves the stars, and comes to the Trojan fires, treats of the plainest, most matter-of-fact subject possible, and deals with this, as Homer always deals with every subject, in the plainest and most straightforward style. 'So many in number, between the ships and the streams of Xanthus, shone forth in front of Troy the fires kindled by the Trojans. There were kindled a thousand fires in the plain; and by each one there sat fifty men in the light of the blazing fire. And the horses, munching white barley and rye, and standing by the chariots, waited for the bright-throned Morning.'*

In Pope's translation, this plain story becomes the following:—

> So many flames before proud Ilion blaze,
> And brighten[22] glimmering Xanthus with their rays;
> The long reflections of the distant fires
> Gleam on the walls, and tremble on the spires.
> A thousand piles the dusky horrors gild,
> And shoot a shady lustre o'er the field.
> Full fifty guards each flaming pile attend,
> Whose umbered arms, by fits, thick flashes send;
> Loud neigh the coursers o'er their heaps of corn,
> And ardent warriors wait the rising morn.

* *Iliad*, viii. 560. [M. A.]

It is for passages of this sort, which, after all, form the bulk of a narrative poem, that Pope's style is so bad. In elevated passages he is powerful, as Homer is powerful, though not in the same way; but in plain narrative, where Homer is still powerful and delightful, Pope, by the inherent fault of his style, is ineffective and out of taste. Wordsworth[23] says somewhere, that wherever Virgil seems to have composed 'with his eye on the object,' Dryden fails to render him. Homer invariably composes 'with his eye on the object,' whether the object be a moral or a material one: Pope composes with his eye on his style, into which he translates his object, whatever it is. That, therefore, which Homer conveys to us immediately, Pope conveys to us through a medium. He aims at turning Homer's sentiments pointedly and rhetorically; at investing Homer's description and ornament and dignity. A sentiment may be changed by being put into a pointed and oratorical form, yet may still be very effective in that form; but a description, the moment it takes its eyes off that which it is to describe, and begins to think of ornamenting itself, is worthless.

Therefore, I say, the translator of Homer should penetrate himself with a sense of the plainness and directness of Homer's style; of the simplicity with which Homer's thought is evolved and expressed. He has Pope's fate before his eyes, to show him what a divorce may be created even between the most gifted translator and Homer by an artificial evolution of thought and a literary cast of style.

Chapman's style is not artificial and literary like Pope's nor his movement elaborate and self-retarding like the Miltonic movement of Cowper. He is plain-spoken, fresh, vigorous, and, to a certain degree, rapid; and all these are Homeric qualities. I cannot say that I think the movement of his fourteen-syllable line, which has been so much commended, Homeric; but on this point I shall have more to say by and by, when I come to speak of Mr. Newman's metrical exploits. But it is not distinctly anti-Homeric, like the movement of Milton's blank verse; and it has a rapidity of its own. Chapman's diction, too, is generally good, that is, appropriate to Homer; above all, the syntactical character of his style is appropriate. With these merits, what prevents his translation from being a satisfactory version of Homer? Is it merely the want of literal faithfulness to his original, imposed upon him, it is said, by the exigences of rhyme? Has this celebrated version, which has so many advantages, no other and deeper defect than that? Its author is a poet, and a poet, too, of the Elizabethan age; the golden age of English literature as it is called, and on the whole truly called; for, whatever be the defects of Elizabethan literature (and they are great), we have no development of our literature to compare with it for vigour and richness. This age, too, showed what it could do in translating, by producing a master-piece, its version of the Bible.

Chapman's translation has often been praised as eminently Homeric. Keats's fine sonnet in its honour every one knows; but Keats could not read the original, and therefore could not really judge the translation. Coleridge, in praising Chapman's version, says at the same time, 'It will give you small idea of Homer.' But the grave authority of Mr. Hallam[24] pronounces this translation to be 'often exceedingly Homeric;' and its latest editor[25] boldly declares that by what, with a deplorable style, he calls 'his own innative Homeric genius,' Chapman 'has thoroughly identified himself with Homer;' and that 'we pardon him even for his digressions, for they are such as we feel Homer himself would have written.'

I confess that I can never read twenty lines of Chapman's version without recurring to Bentley's cry, 'This is not Homer!' and that from a deeper cause than any unfaithfulness occasioned by the fetters of rhyme.

I said that there were four things which eminently distinguished Homer, and with a sense of which Homer's translator should penetrate himself as fully as possible. One of these four things was, the plainness and directness of Homer's ideas. I have just been speaking of the plainness and directness of his style; but the plainness and directness of the contents of his style, of his ideas themselves, is not less remarkable. But as eminently as Homer is plain, so eminently is the Elizabethan literature in general, and Chapman in particular, fanciful. Steeped in humours and fantasticality up to its very lips, the Elizabethan age, newly arrived at the free use of the human faculties after their long term of bondage, and delighting to exercise them freely, suffers from its own extravagance in this first exercise of them, can hardly bring itself to see an object quietly or to describe it temperately. Happily, in the translation of the Bible, the sacred character of their original inspired the translators with such respect that they did not dare to give the rein to their own fancies in dealing with it. But, in dealing with works of profane literature, in dealing with poetical works above all, which highly stimulated them, one may say that the minds of the Elizabethan translators were *too* active; that they could not forbear importing so much of their own, and this of a most peculiar and Elizabethan character, into their original, that they effaced the character of the original itself.

Take merely the opening pages to Chapman's translation, the introductory verses, and the dedications. You will find:—

> An Anagram of the name of our Dread Prince,
> My most gracious and sacred Mæcenas,
> Henry, Prince of Wales,
> Our Sunn, Heyr, Peace, Life,—

Henry, son of James the First, to whom the work is dedicated. Then comes an address,

> To the sacred Fountain of Princes,
> Sole Empress of Beauty and Virtue, Anne, Queen
>   Of England, etc.

All the Middle Age, with its grotesqueness, its conceits, its irrationality, is still in these opening pages; they by themselves are sufficient to indicate to us what a gulf divides Chapman from the 'clearest-souled'[26] of poets, from Homer; almost as great a gulf as that which divides him from Voltaire. Pope has been sneered at for saying that Chapman writes 'somewhat as one might imagine Homer himself to have written before he arrived at years of discretion.' But the remark is excellent: Homer expresses himself like a man of adult reason, Chapman like a man whose reason has not yet cleared itself. For instance, if Homer had had to say of a poet, that he hoped his merit was now about to be fully established in the opinion of good judges, he was as incapable of saying this as Chapman[27] says it,—'Though truth in her very nakedness sits in so deep a pit, that from Gades to Aurora, and Ganges, few eyes can sound her, I hope yet those few here will so discover and confirm that, the date being out of her darkness in this morning of our poet, he shall now gird his temples with the sun,'—I say, Homer was as incapable of saying this in that manner, as Voltaire himself would have been. Homer, indeed, has actually an affinity with Voltaire in the unrivalled clearness and straightforwardness of his thinking; in the way in which he keeps to one thought at a time, and puts that thought forth in its complete natural plainness, instead of being led away from it by some fancy striking him in connection with it, and being beguiled to wander off with this fancy till his original thought, in its natural reality, knows him no more. What could better show us how gifted a race was this Greek race? The same member of it has not only the power of profoundly touching that natural heart of humanity which it is

Voltaire's weakness that he cannot reach, but can also address the understanding with all Voltaire's admirable simplicity and rationality.

My limits will not allow me to do more than shortly illustrate, from Chapman's version of the *Iliad*, what I mean when I speak of this vital difference between Homer and an Elizabethan poet in the quality of their thought; between the plain simplicity of the thought of the one, and the curious complexity of the thought of the other. As in Pope's case, I carefully abstain from choosing passages for the express purpose of making Chapman appear ridiculous; Chapman, like Pope, merits in himself all respect, though he too, like Pope, fails to render Homer.

In that tonic speech of Sarpedon, of which I have said so much, Homer, you may remember, has:—

> εἰ μὲν γὰρ, πόλεμον περὶ τόνδε φυγόντε,
> αἰεὶ δὴ μέλλοιμεν ἀγήρω τ' ἀθανάτω τε
> ἔσσεσθ',—

> if indeed, but once *this* battle avoided,
> We were for ever to live without growing old and immortal.

Chapman cannot be satisfied with this, but must add a fancy to it:—

> if keeping back
> Would keep back age from us, and death, and *that we might
> not wrack
> In this life's human sea at all;*

and so on. Again; in another passage which I have before quoted, where Zeus says to the horses of Peleus,

> τί σφῶϊ δόμεν Πηλῆϊ ἄνακτι
> θνητῷ; ὑμεῖς δ' ἐστον ἀγήρω τ' ἀθανάτω τε • *

> Why gave we you to royal Peleus, to a mortal? but ye are without old age, and immortal.

Chapman sophisticates this into:—

> Why gave we you t' a mortal king, when immortality
> And *incapacity of age so dignifies your states?*

Again; in the speech of Achilles to his horses,[28] where Achilles, according to Homer, says simply, 'Take heed that ye bring your master safe back to the host of the Danaans, in some other sort than the last time, when the battle is ended,' Chapman sophisticates this into:—

* *Iliad*, xvii. 443. [M. A.]

> *When with blood, for this day's fast observed, revenge shall*
>   *yield*
> *Our heart satiety, bring us off.*

In Hector's famous speech, again, at his parting from Andromache, Homer makes him say: 'Nor does my own heart
so bid me' (to keep safe behind the walls), 'since I have
learned to be staunch always, and to fight among the foremost
of the Trojans, busy on behalf of my father's great glory,
and my own.'* In Chapman's hands this becomes:—

>   The spirit I first did breathe
> Did never teach me that; much less, since the contempt of
>   death
> Was settled in me, *and my mind knew what a worthy was,*
> *Whose office is to lead in fight, and give no danger pass*
> *Without improvement. In this fire must Hector's trial shine:*
> *Here must his country, father, friends, be in him made divine.*

You see how ingeniously Homer's plain thought is *tor-
mented,* as the French would say, here. Homer goes on: 'For
well I know this in my mind and in my heart, the day will
be, when sacred Troy shall perish:'—

> ἔσσεται ἦμαρ, ὅτ' ἄν ποτ' ὀλώλῃ Ἴλιος ἱρή.

Chapman makes this:—

> And such a *stormy* day shall come, in mind and soul I
>   know,
> When sacred Troy *shall shed her towers, for tears of*
>   *overthrow.*

I might go on for ever, but I could not give you a better illustration than this last, of what I mean by saying that the
Elizabethan poet fails to render Homer because he cannot
forbear to interpose a play of thought between his object
and its expression. Chapman translates his object into Elizabethan, as Pope translates it into the Augustan of Queen
Anne; both convey it to us through a medium. Homer, on
the other hand, sees his object and conveys it to us immediately.

And yet, in spite of this perfect plainness and directness
of Homer's style, in spite of this perfect plainness and directness of his ideas, he is eminently *noble;* he works as entirely
in the grand style, he is as grandiose, as Phidias,[29] or Dante,
or Michael Angelo. This is what makes his translators despair. 'To give relief,' says Cowper, 'to prosaic subjects' (such
as dressing, eating, drinking, harnessing, travelling, going to
bed), that is to treat such subjects nobly, in the grand style,

---

* *Iliad,* vi. 444. [M. A.]

'without seeming unreasonably[30] tumid, is extremely difficult.' It *is* difficult, but Homer has done it. Homer is precisely the incomparable poet he is, because he has done it.
His translator must not be tumid, must not be artificial, must
not be literary; true: but then also he must not be commonplace, must not be ignoble. I have shown you how translators of Homer fail by wanting rapidity, by wanting simplicity of style, by wanting plainness of thought: in a second
lecture I will show you how a translator fails by wanting
nobility.

II

I must repeat what I said in beginning, that the translator
of Homer ought steadily to keep in mind where lies the real
test of the success of his translation, what judges he is to try
to satisfy. He is to try to satisfy *scholars*, because scholars
alone have the means of really judging him. A scholar may
be a pedant, it is true, and then his judgment will be
worthless; but a scholar may also have poetical feeling, and
then he can judge him truly; whereas all the poetical feeling
in the world will not enable a man who is not a scholar to
judge him truly. For the translator is to reproduce Homer,
and the scholar alone has the means of knowing that Homer
who is to be reproduced. He knows him but imperfectly, for
he is separated from him by time, race, and language; but
he alone knows him at all. Yet people speak as if there were
two real tribunals in this matter,—the scholar's tribunal, and
that of the general public. They speak as if the scholar's
judgment was one thing, and the general public's judgment
another; both with their shortcomings, both with their liabil-
ity to error; but both to be regarded by the translator. The
translator who makes verbal literalness his chief care 'will,'
says a writer in the *National Review,* whom I have already
quoted, 'be appreciated by the scholar accustomed to test a
translation rigidly by comparison with the original, to look
perhaps with excessive care to finish in detail rather than
boldness and general effect, and find pardon even for a
version that seems bare and bald, so it be scholastic and
faithful.' But, if the scholar in judging a translation looks to
detail rather than to general effect, he judges it pedantically
and ill. The appeal, however, lies not from the pedantic
scholar to the general public, which can only like or dislike
Chapman's version, or Pope's, or Mr. Newman's, but cannot *judge* them; it lies from the pedantic scholar to the
scholar who is not pedantic, who knows that Homer is
Homer by his general effect, and not by his single words,

and who demands but one thing in a translation,—that it shall, as nearly as possible, reproduce for him the *general effect* of Homer. This, then, remains the one proper aim of the translator: to reproduce on the intelligent scholar, as nearly as possible, the general effect of Homer. Except so far as he reproduces this, he loses his labour, even though he may make a spirited *Iliad* of his own, like Pope, or translate Homer's *Iliad* word for word, like Mr. Newman. If his proper aim were to stimulate in any manner possible the general public, he might be right in following Pope's example; if his proper aim were to help schoolboys to construe Homer, he might be right in following Mr. Newman's. But it is not: his proper aim is, I repeat it yet once more, to reproduce on the intelligent scholar, as nearly as he can, the general effect of Homer.

When, therefore, Cowper says, 'My chief boast is that I have adhered closely to my original;' when Mr. Newman says, 'My aim is to retain every peculiarity of the original, to be *faithful,* exactly as is the case with the draughtsman of the Elgin marbles;' their real judge only replies: 'It may be so: reproduce then upon us, reproduce the effect of Homer, as a good copy reproduces the effect of the Elgin marbles.'

When, again, Mr. Newman tells us that 'by an exhaustive process of argument and experiment' he has found a metre which is at once the metre of 'the modern Greek epic,' and a metre 'like in moral genius' to Homer's metre, his judge has still but the same answer for him: 'It may be so: reproduce then on our ear something of the effect produced by the movement of Homer.'

But what is the general effect which Homer produces on Mr. Newman himself? because, when we know this, we shall know whether he and his judges are agreed at the outset, whether we may expect him, if he can reproduce the effect he feels, if his hand does not betray him in the execution, to satisfy his judges and to succeed. If, however, Mr. Newman's impression from Homer is something quite different from that of his judges, then it can hardly be expected that any amount of labour or talent will enable him to reproduce for them *their* Homer.

Mr. Newman does not leave us in doubt as to the general effect which Homer makes upon him. As I have told you what is the general effect which Homer makes upon me,—that of a most rapidly moving poet, that of a poet most plain and direct in his style, that of a poet most plain and direct in his ideas, that of a poet eminently noble,—so Mr. Newman tells us his general impression of Homer. 'Homer's style,' he says, 'is direct, popular, forcible, quaint, flowing, garrulous.' Again: 'Homer rises and sinks with his subject, is prosaic when it is tame, is low when it is mean.'

I lay my finger on four words in these two sentences of Mr. Newman, and I say that the man who could apply those words to Homer can never render Homer truly. The four words are these: *quaint, garrulous, prosaic, low*. Search the English language for a word which does not apply to Homer, and you could not fix on a better than *quaint*, unless perhaps you fixed on one of the other three.

Again; 'to translate Homer suitably,' says Mr. Newman, 'we need a diction sufficiently antiquated to obtain pardon of the reader for its frequent homeliness.' 'I am concerned,' he says again, 'with the artistic problem of attaining a plausible aspect of moderate antiquity, while remaining easily intelligible.' And again, he speaks of 'the more antiquated style suited to this subject.' Quaint! antiquated!—but to whom? Sir Thomas Browne is quaint, and the diction of Chaucer is antiquated: does Mr. Newman suppose that Homer seemed quaint to Sophocles, when he read him, as Sir Thomas Browne seems quaint to us, when we read him? or that Homer's diction seemed antiquated to Sophocles, as Chaucer's diction seems antiquated to us? But we cannot really know, I confess, how Homer seemed to Sophocles: well then, to those who can tell us how he seems to them, to the living scholar, to our only present witness on this matter,—does Homer make on the Provost of Eton, when he reads him, the impression of a poet quaint and antiquated? does he make this impression on Professor Thompson or Professor Jowett? When Shakespeare[31] says, 'The princes *orgulous*,' meaning 'the proud princes,' we say, 'This is antiquated;' when he says of the Trojan gates, that they

> With massy staples
> And corresponsive and fulfilling bolts
> *Sperr* up the sons of Troy,

we say, 'This is both quaint and antiquated.' But does Homer ever compose in a language which produces on the scholar at all the same impression as this language which I have quoted from Shakespeare? Never once. Shakespeare is quaint and antiquated in the lines which I have just quoted; but Shakespeare—need I say it?—can compose, when he likes, in a language perfectly simple, perfectly intelligible; in a language which, in spite of the two centuries and a half which part its author from us, stops us or surprises us as little as the language of a contemporary.

And Homer has not Shakespeare's variations: Homer always composes as Shakespeare composes at his best; Homer is always simple and intelligible, as Shakespeare is often; Homer is never quaint and antiquated, as Shakespeare is sometimes.

When Mr. Newman says that Homer is garrulous, he seems, perhaps, to depart less widely from the common opinion than when he calls him quaint; for is there not Horace's authority for asserting that 'the good Homer sometimes nods,' *bonus dormitat Homerus?*[32] and a great many people have come, from the currency of this well-known criticism, to represent Homer to themselves as a diffuse old man, with the full-stocked mind, but also with the occasional slips and weaknesses, of old age. Horace has said better things than his 'bonus dormitat Homerus;' but he never meant by this, as I need not remind any one who knows the passage, that Homer was garrulous, or anything of the kind. Instead, however, of either discussing what Horace meant, or discussing Homer's garrulity as a general question, I prefer to bring to my mind some style which *is* garrulous, and to ask myself, to ask you, whether anything at all of the impression made by that style is ever made by the style of Homer. The mediæval romancers, for instance, are garrulous; the following, to take out of a thousand instances the first which comes to hand, is in a garrulous manner. It is from the romance of Richard Cœur de Lion.

> Of my tale be not a-wondered!
> The French says he slew an hundred
> (Whereof is made this English saw)
> Or he rested him any thraw.
> Him followed many an English knight
> That eagerly holp him for to fight,—

and so on. Now the manner of that composition I call garrulous; every one will feel it to be garrulous; every one will understand what is meant when it is called garrulous. Then I ask the scholar,—does Homer's manner ever make upon you, I do not say, the same impression of its garrulity as that passage, but does it make, ever for one moment, an impression in the slightest way resembling, in the remotest degree akin to, the impression made by that passage of the mediæval poet? I have no fear of the answer.

I follow the same method with Mr. Newman's two other epithets, *prosaic* and *low*. 'Homer rises and sinks with his subject,' says Mr. Newman; 'is prosaic when it is tame, is low when it is mean.' First I say, Homer is never, in any sense, to be with truth called prosaic; he is never to be called low. He does not rise and sink with his subject; on the contrary, his manner invests his subject, whatever his subject be, with nobleness. Then I look for an author of whom it may with truth be said, that he 'rises and sinks with his subject, is prosaic when it is tame, is low when it is mean.' Defoe is eminently such an author; of Defoe's manner it may with perfect precision be said, that it follows his matter; his lifelike composition takes its character from the facts which it conveys, not from the nobleness of the composer. In *Moll Flanders* and *Colonel Jack,* Defoe is undoubtedly prosaic when his subject is tame, low when his subject is mean. Does Homer's manner in the *Iliad,* I ask the scholar, ever make upon him an impression at all like the impression made by Defoe's manner in *Moll Flanders* and *Colonel Jack?* Does it not, on the contrary, leave him with an impression of nobleness, even when it deals with Thersites or with Irus?[33]

Well then, Homer is neither quaint, nor garrulous, nor prosaic, nor mean: and Mr. Newman, in seeing him so, sees him differently from those who are to judge Mr. Newman's rendering of him. By pointing out how a wrong conception of Homer affects Mr. Newman's translation, I hope to place in still clearer light those four cardinal truths which I pronounce essential for him who would have a right conception of Homer: that Homer is rapid, that he is plain and direct in word and style, that he is plain and direct in his ideas, and that he is noble.

Mr. Newman says that in fixing on a style for suitably rendering Homer, as he conceives him, he 'alights on the delicate line which separates the *quaint* from the *grotesque.*' 'I ought to be quaint,' he says, 'I ought not to be grotesque.' This is a most unfortunate sentence. Mr. Newman is grotesque, which he himself says he ought not to be; and he ought not to be quaint, which he himself says he ought to be.

'No two persons will agree,' says Mr. Newman, 'as to where the quaint ends and the grotesque begins;' and perhaps this is true. But, in order to avoid all ambiguity in the use of the two words, it is enough to say, that most persons would call an expression which produced on them a very strong sense of its incongruity, and which violently surprised them, *grotesque;* and an expression, which produced on them a slighter sense of its incongruity, and which more gently surprised them, *quaint.* Using the two words in this manner, I say, that when Mr. Newman translates Helen's words to Hector in the sixth book,

Δᾶερ ἐμεῖο, κυνὸς κακομηχάνου, ὀκρυοέσσης,*—

O, brother thou of me, who am a mischief-working vixen,
A numbing horror,—

he is grotesque; that is, he expresses himself in a manner
which produces on us a very strong sense of its incongruity,
and which violently surprises us. I say, again, that when
Mr. Newman translates the common line,

Τὴν δ᾽ ἠμείβετ᾽ ἔπειτα μέγας κορυθαίολος Ἕκτωρ,—

Great Hector of the motley helm then spake to her
responsive,—

or the common expression ἐϋκνήμιδες Ἀχαιοί, 'dapper-greaved
Achaians,' he is quaint; that is, he expresses himself in a
manner which produces on us a slighter sense of incongruity,
and which more gently surprises us. But violent and gentle
surprise are alike far from the scholar's spirit when he reads
in Homer κυνὸς κακομηχάνου, or κορυθαίολος Ἕκτωρ, or, ἐϋκνήμιδες
Ἀχαιοί. These expressions no more seem odd to him than the
simplest expressions in English. He is not more checked by
any feeling of strangeness, strong or weak, when he reads
them, than when he reads in an English book 'the painted
savage,' or, 'the phlegmatic Dutchman.' Mr. Newman's renderings of them must, therefore, be wrong expressions in a
translation of Homer, because they excite in the scholar,
their only competent judge, a feeling quite alien to that excited in him by what they profess to render.

Mr. Newman, by expressions of this kind, is false to his
original in two ways. He is false to him inasmuch as he is
ignoble; for a noble air, and a grotesque air, the air of the
address,

Δᾶερ ἐμεῖο, κυνὸς κακομηχάνου, ὀκρυοέσσης,—

and the air of the address,

O, brother thou of me, who am a mischief-working vixen,
A numbing horror,—

are just contrary the one to the other: and he is false to him
inasmuch as he is odd; for an odd diction like Mr. Newman's, and a perfectly plain natural diction like Homer's,
—'dapper-greaved Achaians' and ἐϋκνήμιδες Ἀχαιοί,—are also
just contrary the one to the other. Where, indeed, Mr. Newman got his diction, with whom he can have lived, what can
be his test of antiquity and rarity for words, are questions
which I ask myself with bewilderment. He has prefixed to

* *Iliad*, vi. 344. [M. A.]

his translation a list of what he calls 'the more antiquated or rarer words' which he has used. In this list appear, on the one hand, such words as *doughty, grisly, lusty, noisome, ravin,* which are familiar, one would think, to all the world; on the other hand such words as *bragly,* meaning, Mr. Newman tells us, 'proudly fine;' *bulkin,* 'a calf;' *plump,* 'a mass;' and so on. 'I am concerned,' says Mr. Newman, 'with the artistic problem of attaining a plausible aspect of moderate antiquity, while remaining easily intelligible.' But it seems to me that *lusty* is not antiquated: and that *bragly* is not a word readily understood. That this word, indeed, and *bulkin,* may have 'a plausible aspect of moderate antiquity,' I admit; but that they are 'easily intelligible,' I deny.

Mr. Newman's syntax has, I say it with pleasure, a much more Homeric cast than his vocabulary; his syntax, the mode in which his thought is evolved, although not the actual words in which it is expressed, seems to me right in its general character, and the best feature of his version. It is not artificial or rhetorical like Cowper's syntax or Pope's: it is simple, direct, and natural, and so far it is like Homer's. It fails, however, just where, from the inherent fault of Mr. Newman's conception of Homer, one might expect it to fail, —it fails in nobleness. It presents the thought in a way which is something more than unconstrained,—over-familiar; something more than easy,—free and easy. In this respect it is like the movement of Mr. Newman's version, like his rhythm, for this, too, fails, in spite of some good qualities, by not being noble enough; this, while it avoids the faults of being slow and elaborate, falls into a fault in the opposite direction, and is slip-shod. Homer presents his thought naturally; but when Mr. Newman has,

A thousand fires along the plain, *I say,* that night were burning,—

he presents his thought familiarly; in a style which may be the genuine style of ballad-poetry, but which is not the style of Homer. Homer moves freely; but when Mr. Newman has,

Infatuate! O that thou wert lord to some other army,—*

* From the reproachful answer of Ulysses to Agamemnon, who had proposed an abandonment of their expedition. This is one of the 'tonic' passages of the *Iliad,* so I quote it:—

Ah, unworthy king, some other inglorious army
Should'st thou command, not rule over *us,* whose portion for ever
Zeus hath made it, from youth right up to age, to be winding
Skeins of grievous wars, till every soul of us perish.
                                              Iliad, xiv. 84. [M. A.]

he gives himself too much freedom; he leaves us too much to do for his rhythm ourselves, instead of giving to us a rhythm like Homer's, easy indeed, but mastering our ear with a fulness of power which is irresistible.

I said that a certain style might be the genuine style of ballad-poetry, but yet not the style of Homer. The analogy of the ballad is ever present to Mr. Newman's thoughts in considering Homer; and perhaps nothing has more caused his faults than this analogy,—this popular, but, it is time to say, this erroneous analogy. 'The moral qualities of Homer's style,' says Mr. Newman, 'being like to those of the English ballad, we need a metre of the same genius. Only those metres, which by the very possession of these qualities are liable to degenerate into *doggerel,* are suitable to reproduce the ancient epic.' 'The style of Homer,' he says, in a passage which I have before quoted, 'is direct, popular, forcible, quaint, flowing, garrulous: in all these respects it is similar to the old English ballad.' Mr. Newman, I need not say, is by no means alone in this opinion. 'The most really and truly Homeric of all the creations of the English muse is,' says Mr. Newman's critic in the *National Review,* 'the ballad-poetry of ancient times; and the association between metre and subject is one that it would be true wisdom to preserve.' 'It is confessed,' says Chapman's last editor, Mr. Hooper, 'that the fourteen-syllable verse' (that is, a ballad-verse) "is peculiarly fitting for Homeric translation.' And the editor of Dr. Maginn's clever and popular *Homeric Ballads*[34] assumes it as one of his author's greatest and most undisputable merits, that he was 'the first who consciously realised to himself the truth that Greek ballads can be really represented in English only by a similar measure.'

This proposition that Homer's poetry is *ballad-poetry,* analogous to the well-known ballad-poetry of the English and other nations, has a certain small portion of truth in it, and at one time probably served a useful purpose, when it was employed to discredit the artificial and literary manner in which Pope and his school rendered Homer. But it has been so extravagantly over-used, the mistake which it was useful in combating has so entirely lost the public favour, that it is now much more important to insist on the large part of error contained in it, than to extol its small part of truth. It is time to say plainly that, whatever the admirers of our old ballads may think, the supreme form of epic poetry, the genuine Homeric mould, is not the form of the Ballad of Lord Bateman. I have myself shown the broad difference between Milton's manner and Homer's; but, after a course of Mr. Newman and Dr. Maginn, I turn around in desperation upon them and upon the balladists who have misled them, and I exclaim: 'Compared with you, Milton is Homer's double; there is, whatever you may think, ten thousand times more of the real strain of Homer in,

> Blind Thamyris, and blind Mæonides,
> And Tiresias, and Phineus, prophets old,—35

than in,

> Now Christ thee save, thou proud portèr,
> Now Christ thee save and see,*—

or in,

> While the tinker did dine, he had plenty of wine.†'

For Homer is not only rapid in movement, simple in style, plain in language, natural in thought; he is also, and above all, *noble*. I have advised the translator not to go into the vexed question of Homer's identity. Yet I will just remind him that the grand argument—or rather, not argument, for the matter affords no data for arguing, but the grand source from which conviction, as we read the *Iliad*, keeps pressing in upon us, that there is one poet of the *Iliad*, one Homer—is precisely this nobleness of the poet, this grand manner; we feel that the analogy drawn from other joint compositions does not hold good here, because those works do not bear, like the *Iliad,* the magic stamp of a master; and the moment you have *anything* less than a masterwork, the co-operation or consolidation of several poets becomes possible, for talent is not uncommon; the moment you have *much* less than a masterwork, they become easy, for mediocrity is everywhere. I can imagine fifty Bradies joined with as many Tates36 to make the New Version of the Psalms. I can imagine several poets having contributed to any one of the old English ballads in Percy's collection. I can imagine several poets, possessing, like Chapman, the Elizabethan vigour and the Elizabethan mannerism, united with Chapman to produce his version of the *Iliad*. I can imagine several poets, with the literary knack of the twelfth century, united to produce the *Nibelungen*

* From the ballad of *King Estmere*, in Percy's *Reliques of Ancient English Poetry*, i. 69 (edit. of 1767). [M. A.]

† *Reliques*, i. 241. [M. A.]

Lay in the form in which we have it,—a work which the Germans, in their joy at discovering a national epic of their own, have rated vastly higher than it deserves. And lastly, though Mr. Newman's translation of Homer bears the strong mark of his own idiosyncrasy, yet I can imagine Mr. Newman and a school of adepts trained by him in his art of poetry, jointly producing that work, so that Aristarchus[37] himself should have difficulty in pronouncing which line was the master's, and which a pupil's. But I cannot imagine several poets, or one poet, joined with Dante in the composition of his *Inferno,* though many poets have taken for their subject a descent into Hell. Many artists, again, have represented Moses; but there is only one Moses of Michael Angelo. So the insurmountable obstacle to believing the *Iliad* a consolidated work of several poets is this: that the work of great masters is unique; and the *Iliad* has a great master's genuine stamp, and that stamp is *the grand style.*

Poets who cannot work in the grand style instinctively seek a style in which their comparative inferiority may feel itself at ease, a manner which may be, so to speak, indulgent to their inequalities. The ballad-style offers to an epic poet, quite unable to fill the canvas of Homer, or Dante, or Milton, a canvas which he is capable of filling. The ballad-measure is quite able to give due effect to the vigour and spirit which its employer, when at his very best, may be able to exhibit; and, when he is not at his best, when he is a little trivial, or a little dull, it will not betray him, it will not bring out his weaknesses into broad relief. This is a convenience; but it is a convenience which the ballad-style purchases by resigning all pretensions to the highest, to the grand manner. It is true of its movement, as it is *not* true of Homer's, that it is 'liable to degenerate into doggerel.' It is true of its 'moral qualities,' as it is *not* true of Homer's, that 'quaintness' and 'garrulity' are among them. It is true of its employers, as it is *not* true of Homer, that they 'rise and sink with their subject, are prosaic when it is tame, are low when it is mean.' For this reason the ballad-style and the ballad-measure are eminently *in*appropriate to render Homer. Homer's manner and movement are always both noble and powerful: the ballad-manner and movement are often either jaunty and smart, so not noble; or jog-trot and humdrum, so not powerful.

The *Nibelungen Lay* affords a good illustration of the qualities of the ballad-manner. Based on grand traditions,

which had found expression in a grand lyric poetry, the
German epic poem of the *Nibelungen Lay*, though it is interesting, and though it has good passages, is itself anything
rather than a grand poem. It is a poem of which the composer is, to speak the truth, a very ordinary mortal, and
often, therefore, like other ordinary mortals, very prosy. It
is in a measure which eminently adapts itself to this commonplace personality of its composer, which has much the
movement of the well-known measures of Tate and Brady,
and can jog on, for hundreds of lines at a time, with a level
ease which reminds one of Sheridan's saying that easy writing may be often such hard reading. But, instead of occupying myself with the *Nibelungen Lay*, I prefer to look at
the ballad-style as directly applied to Homer, in Chapman's
version and Mr. Newman's, and in the *Homeric Ballads*
of Dr. Maginn.

First I take Chapman. I have already shown that Chapman's conceits are un-Homeric, and that his rhyme is un-
Homeric; I will now show how his manner and movement
are un-Homeric. Chapman's diction, I have said, is generally good; but it must be called good with this reserve, that,
though it has Homer's plainness and directness, it often of-
fends him who knows Homer, by wanting Homer's nobleness. In a passage which I have already quoted, the address
of Zeus to the horses of Achilles, where Homer has—

$$\text{ἆ δειλώ, τί σφῶϊ δόμεν Πηλῆϊ ἄνακτι}$$
$$\text{θνητῷ; ὑμεῖς δ' ἐστὸν ἀγήρω τ' ἀθανάτω τε!}$$
$$\text{ἦ ἵνα δυστήνοισι μετ' ἀνδράσιν ἄλγε' ἔχητον;}^*$$

Chapman has—

>   'Poor wretched beasts,' said he,
> 'Why gave we you to a mortal king, when immortality
> And incapacity of age so dignifies your states?
> Was it to haste† the miseries poured out on human fates?'

There are many faults in this rendering of Chapman's, but
what I particularly wish to notice in it is the expression
'Poor wretched beasts' for ἆ δειλώ. This expression just illustrates the difference between the ballad-manner and
Homer's. The ballad-manner—Chapman's manner—is, I
say, pitched sensibly lower than Homer's. The ballad-manner requires that an expression shall be plain and natural,

---

* *Iliad*, xvii. 443. [M. A.]

† All the editions which I have seen have 'haste,' but the right
reading must certainly be 'taste.' [M. A.][38]

and then it asks no more. Homer's manner requires that an
expression shall be plain and natural, but it also requires
that it shall be noble. Ἀ δειλώ is as plain, as simple as 'Poor
wretched beasts;' but it is also noble, which 'Poor wretched
beasts' is not. 'Poor wretched beasts' is, in truth, a little over-
familiar, but this is no objection to it for the ballad-manner;
it is good enough for the old English ballad, good enough
for the *Nibelungen Lay,* good enough for Chapman's *Iliad,*
good enough for Mr. Newman's *Iliad,* good enough for Dr.
Maginn's *Homeric Ballads;* but it is not good enough for
Homer.

To feel that Chapman's measure, though natural, is not
Homeric; that, though tolerably rapid, it has not Homer's
rapidity; that it has a jogging rapidity rather than a flowing
rapidity; and a movement familiar rather than nobly easy,
one has only, I think, to read half a dozen lines in any part of
his version. I prefer to keep as much as possible to passages
which I have already noticed, so I will quote the conclusion
of the nineteenth book, where Achilles answers his horse
Xanthus, who has prophesied his death to him.*

> Achilles, far in rage,
> Thus answered him:—It fits not thee thus proudly to presage
> My overthrow. I know myself it is my fate to fall
> Thus far from Phthia; yet that fate shall fail to vent her gall
> Till mine vent thousands.—These words said,[39] he fell to hor-
> rid deeds,
> Gave dreadful signal, and forthright made fly his one-hoofed
> steeds.

For what regards the manner of this passage, the words
'Achilles Thus answered him,' and 'I know myself it is my
fate to fall Thus far from Phthia,' are in Homer's manner,
and all the rest is out of it. But for what regards its movement, who, after being jolted by Chapman through such
verse as this,—

> These words said, he fell to horrid deeds,
> Gave dreadful signal, and forthright made fly his one-hoofed
> steeds,—

who does not feel the vital difference of the movement of
Homer,—

ἦ ῥα, καὶ ἐν πρώτοις ἰάχων ἔχε μώνυχας ἵππους?

To pass from Chapman to Dr. Maginn. His *Homeric*

* *Iliad,* xix. 419. [M. A.]

Ballads are vigorous and genuine poems in their own way; they are not one continual falsetto, like the pinchbeck *Roman Ballads* of Lord Macaulay;[40] but just because they are ballads in their manner and movement, just because, to use the words of his applauding editor, Dr. Maginn has 'consciously realised to himself the truth that Greek ballads can be really represented in English only by a similar manner,' —just for this very reason they are not at all Homeric, they have not the least in the world the manner of Homer. There is a celebrated incident in the nineteenth book of the *Odyssey*, the recognition by the old nurse Eurycleia of a scar on the leg of her master Ulysses, who has entered his own hall as an unknown wanderer, and whose feet she has been set to wash. 'Then she came near,' says Homer, 'and began to wash her master; and straightway she recognised a scar which he had got in former days from the white tusk of a wild boar, when he went to Parnassus unto Autolycus and the sons of Autolycus, his mother's father and brethren.'* This, 'really represented' by Dr. Maginn, in 'a measure similar' to Homer's, becomes:—

> And scarcely had she begun to wash
> Ere she was aware of the grisly gash
>   Above his knee that lay.
> It was a wound from a wild boar's tooth,
>   All on Parnassus' slope,
> Where he went to hunt in the days of his youth
> With his mother's sire,—

and so on. That is the true ballad-manner, no one can deny; 'all on Parnassus' slope' is, I was going to say, the true ballad-slang; but never again shall I be able to read,

> νίζε δ' ἄρ' ἆσσον ἰοῦσα ἄναχθ' ἑόν · αὐτίκα δ' ἔγνω
> οὐλήν,

without having the detestable dance of Dr. Maginn's,—

> And scarcely had she begun to wash
> Ere she was aware of the grisly gash,—

jigging in my ears, to spoil the effect of Homer, and to torture me. To apply that manner and that rhythm to Homer's incidents, is not to imitate Homer, but to travesty him.

Lastly I come to Mr. Newman. His rhythm, like Chapman's and Dr. Maginn's, is a ballad-rhythm, but with a modification of his own. 'Holding it,' he tells us, 'as an ax-

* *Odyssey*, xix. 392. [M. A.]

iom, that rhyme must be abandoned,' he found, on abandoning it, 'an unpleasant void until he gave a double ending to the verse.' In short, instead of saying,

> Good people all with one accord
> Give ear unto my *tale*,—

Mr. Newman would say,

> Good people all with one accord
> Give ear unto my *story*.

A recent American writer* gravely observes that for his countrymen this rhythm has a disadvantage in being like the rhythm of the American national air *Yankee Doodle*, and thus provoking ludicrous associations. *Yankee Doodle* is not our national air: for us Mr. Newman's rhythm has not this disadvantage. He himself gives us several plausible reasons why this rhythm of his really ought to be successful: let us examine how far it *is* successful.

Mr. Newman joins to a bad rhythm so bad a diction that it is difficult to distinguish exactly whether in any given passage it is his words or his measure which produces a total impression of such an unpleasant kind. But with a little attention we may analyse our total impression, and find the share which each element has in producing it. To take the passage which I have so often mentioned, Sarpedon's speech to Glaucus. Mr. Newman translates this as follows:—

> O gentle friend! if thou and I, from this encounter 'scaping,
> Hereafter might forever be from Eld and Death exempted
> As heavenly gods, not I in sooth would fight among the foremost,
> Nor liefly thee would I advance to man-ennobling battle.
> Now,—sith ten thousand shapes of Death do any-gait pursue us
> Which never mortal may evade, though sly of foot and nimble;—
> Onward! and glory let us earn, or glory yield to some one.—
>
> Could all our care elude the gloomy grave
> Which claims no less the fearful than the brave—

I am not going to quote Pope's version over again, but I must remark in passing, how much more, with all Pope's radical difference of manner from Homer, it gives us of the real effect of

εἰ μὲν γὰρ, πόλεμον περὶ τόνδε φυγόντε—

* Mr. Marsh, in his *Lectures on the English Language,* New York, 1860, p. 520. [M. A.]

than Mr. Newman's lines. And now, why are Mr. Newman's lines faulty? They are faulty, first, because, as a matter of diction, the expressions 'O gentle friend,' 'eld,' 'in
sooth,' 'liefly,' 'advance,' 'man-ennobling,' 'sith,' 'any-gait,'
and 'sly of foot,' are all bad; some of them worse than
others, but all bad: that is, they all of them as here used
excite in the scholar, their sole judge,—excite, I will boldly
affirm, in Professor Thompson or Professor Jowett,—a feeling totally different from that excited in them by the words
of Homer which these expressions profess to render. The
lines are faulty, secondly, because, as a matter of rhythm,
any and every line among them has to the ear of the same
judges (I affirm it with equal boldness) a movement as unlike Homer's movement in the corresponding line as the
single words are unlike Homer's words. Οὔτε κε σὲ στέλλοιμι
μάχην ἐς κυδιάνειραν,—'Nor liefly thee would I advance to
man-ennobling battle;'—for whose ears do those two
rhythms produce impressions of, to use Mr. Newman's own
words, 'similar moral genius'?

I will by no means make search in Mr. Newman's version
for passages likely to raise a laugh; that search, alas! would
be far too easy. I will quote but one other passage from
him, and that a passage where the diction is comparatively
inoffensive, in order that disapproval of the words may not
unfairly heighten disapproval of the rhythm. The end of the
nineteenth book, the answer of Achilles to his horse
Xanthus, Mr. Newman gives thus:—

'Chestnut! why bodest death to me? from thee this was not
    needed.
Myself right surely know alsó, that 't is my doom to perish,
From mother and from father dear apart, in Troy; but never
Pause will I make of war, until the Trojans be glutted.'
He spake, and yelling, held afront the single-hoofed horses.

Here Mr. Newman calls Xanthus *Chestnut,* indeed, as he
calls Balius *Spotted,* and Podarga *Spry-foot;* which is as if
a Frenchman were to call Miss Nightingale *Mdlle. Ros-
signol,* or Mr. Bright *M. Clair.* And several other expressions, too,—'yelling,' 'held afront,' 'single-hoofed,'—leave,
to say the very least, much to be desired. Still, for Mr. Newman, the diction of this passage is pure. All the more clearly
appears the profound vice of a rhythm, which, with comparatively few faults of words, can leave a sense of such incurable alienation from Homer's manner as, 'Myself right
surely know alsó that 't is my doom to perish,' compared

with the εὖ νυ τὸ οἶδα καὶ αὐτός, ὅ μοι μόρος ἐνθάδ' ὀλέσθαι of Homer.

But so deeply seated is the difference between the ballad-manner and Homer's, that even a man of the highest powers, even a man of the greatest vigour of spirit and of true genius,—the Coryphæus[41] of balladists, Sir Walter Scott,—fails with a manner of this kind to produce an effect at all like the effect of Homer. 'I am not so rash,' declares Mr. Newman, 'as to say that if *freedom* be given to rhyme as in Walter Scott's poetry,'—Walter Scott, 'by far the most Homeric of our poets,' as in another place he calls him,—'a genius may not arise who will translate Homer into the melodies of *Marmion*.' 'The *truly* classical and the *truly* romantic,' says Dr. Maginn, 'are one; the moss-trooping[42] Nestor reappears in the moss-trooping heroes of Percy's *Reliques*' and a description by Scott, which he quotes, he calls 'graphic, and therefore Homeric.' He forgets our fourth axiom,—that Homer is not *only* graphic; he is also noble, and has the grand style. Human nature under like circumstances is probably in all ages much the same; and so far it may be said that 'the truly classical and the truly romantic are one;' but it is of little use to tell us this, because we know the human nature of other ages only through the representations of them which have come down to us, and the classical and the romantic modes of representation are so far from being 'one,' that they remain eternally distinct, and have created for us a separation between the two worlds which they respectively represent. Therefore to call Nestor the 'moss-trooping Nestor' is absurd, because, though Nestor may possibly have been much the same sort of man as many a moss-trooper, he has yet come to us through a mode of representation so unlike that of Percy's *Reliques,* that instead of 'reappearing in the moss-trooping heroes' of these poems, he exists in our imagination as something utterly unlike them, and as belonging to another world. So the Greeks in Shakespeare's *Troilus and Cressida* are no longer the Greeks whom we have known in Homer, because they come to us through a mode of representation of the romantic world. But I must not forget Scott.

I suppose that when Scott is in what may be called full ballad swing, no one will hesitate to pronounce his manner neither Homeric nor the grand manner. When he says, for instance,

> I do not rhyme to that dull elf
> Who cannot image to himself,*

* *Marmion,* canto vi. 38. [M. A.]

and so on, any scholar will feel that *this* is not Homer's manner. But let us take Scott's poetry at its best; and when it is at its best, it is undoubtedly very good indeed:—

> Tunstall lies dead upon the field,
> His life-blood stains the spotless shield;
> Edmund is down,—my life is reft,—
> The Admiral alone is left.
> Let Stanley charge with spur of fire,—
> With Chester charge, and Lancashire,
> Full upon Scotland's central host,
> Or victory and England's lost.*

That is, no doubt, as vigorous as possible, as spirited as possible; it is exceedingly fine poetry. And still I say, it is not in the grand manner, and therefore it is not like Homer's poetry. Now, how shall I make him who doubts this feel that I say true; that these lines of Scott are essentially neither in Homer's style nor in the grand style? I may point out to him that the movement of Scott's lines, while it is rapid, is also at the same time what the French call *saccadé*, its rapidity is 'jerky;' whereas Homer's rapidity is a flowing rapidity. But this is something external and material; it is but the outward and visible sign of an inward and spiritual diversity. I may discuss what, in the abstract, constitutes the grand style; but that sort of general discussion never much helps our judgment of particular instances. I may say that the presence or absence of the grand style can only be spiritually discerned; and this is true, but to plead this looks like evading the difficulty. My best way is to take eminent specimens of the grand style, and to put them side by side with this of Scott. For example, when Homer says:—

> ἀλλά, φίλος, θάνε καὶ σύ · τίη ὀλυφύρεαι οὕτως;
> κάτθανε καὶ Πάτροκλος, ὅπερ σέο πολλὸν ἀμείνων,†

that is in the grand style. When Virgil says:—

> Disce, puer, virtutem ex me verumque laborem,
> Fortunam ex aliis,‡

that is in the grand style. When Dante says:—

---

* *Marmion*, canto vi. 29. [M. A.]
† 'Be content, good friend, die also thou! why lamentest thou thyself on this wise? Patroclus, too, died, who was a far better than thou.'—*Iliad*, xxi. 106. [M. A.]
‡ From me, young man, learn nobleness of soul and true effort: learn success from others.'—*Æneid*, xii. 435. [M. A.]

> Lascio lo fele, e vo per dolci pomi
> Promessi a me per lo verace Duca;
> Ma fino al centro pria convien ch' io tomi,*

that is in the grand style. When Milton says:—

> His form had yet not lost
> All her original brightness, nor appeared
> Less than archangel ruined, and the excess
> Of glory obscured,†

that, finally, is in the grand style. Now let any one, after repeating to himself these four passages, repeat again the passage of Scott, and he will perceive that there is something in style which the four first have in common, and which the last is without; and this something is precisely the grand manner. It is no disrespect to Scott to say that he does not attain to this manner in his poetry; to say so, is merely to say that he is not among the five or six supreme poets of the world. Among these he is not; but, being a man of far greater powers than the ballad-poets, he has tried to give to their instrument a compass and an elevation which it does not naturally possess, in order to enable him to come nearer to the effect of the instrument used by the great epic poets,—an instrument which he felt he could not truly use,—and in this attempt he has but imperfectly succeeded. The poetic style of Scott is—(it becomes necessary to say so when it is proposed to 'translate Homer into the melodies of *Marmion*')—it is, tried by the highest standards, a bastard epic style; and that is why, out of his own powerful hands, it has had so little success. It is a less natural, and therefore a less good style, than the original ballad-style; while it shares with the ballad-style the inherent incapacity of rising into the grand style, of adequately rendering Homer. Scott is certainly at his best in his battles. Of Homer you could not say this; he is not better in his battles than elsewhere; but even between the battle-pieces of the two there exists all the difference which there is between an able work and a masterpiece.

> Tunstall lies dead upon the field,
> His life-blood stains the spotless shield:
> Edmund is down,—my life is reft,—
> The Admiral alone is left.

* 'I leave the gall of bitterness, and I go for the apples of sweetness promised unto me by my faithful Guide; but far as the centre it behoves me first to fall.'—*Hell*, xvi. 61. [M. A.]
† *Paradise Lost*, i. 591. [M. A.]

—'For not in the hands of Diomede the son of Tydeus rages the spear, to ward off destruction from the Danaans; neither as yet have I heard the voice of the son of Atreus, shouting out of his hated mouth; but the voice of Hector the slayer of men bursts round me, as he cheers on the Trojans; and they with their yellings fill all the plain, overcoming the Achaians in the battle.'[43]—I protest that, to my feeling, Homer's performance, even through that pale and far-off shadow of a prose translation, still has a hundred times more of the grand manner about it, than the original poetry of Scott.

Well, then, the ballad-manner and the ballad-measure, whether in the hands of the old ballad poets, or arranged by Chapman, or arranged by Mr. Newman, or, even, arranged by Sir Walter Scott, cannot worthily render Homer. And for one reason: Homer is plain, so are they; Homer is natural, so are they; Homer is spirited, so are they; but Homer is sustainedly noble, and they are not. Homer and they are both of them natural, and therefore touching and stirring; but the grand style, which is Homer's, is something more than touching and stirring; it can form the character, it is edifying. The old English balladist may stir Sir Philip Sidney's heart like a trumpet,[44] and this is much: but Homer, but the few artists in the grand style, can do more; they can refine the raw natural man, they can transmute him. So it is not without cause that I say, and say again, to the translator of Homer: 'Never for a moment suffer yourself to forget our fourth fundamental proposition, *Homer is noble*.' For it is seen how large a share this nobleness has in producing that general effect of his, which it is the main business of a translator to *re*produce.

I shall have to try your patience yet once more upon this subject, and then my task will be completed. I have shown what the four axioms respecting Homer which I have laid down, exclude, what they bid a translator not to do; I have still to show what they supply, what positive help they can give to the translator in his work. I will even, with their aid, myself try my fortune with some of those passages of Homer which I have already noticed; not indeed with any confidence that I more than others can succeed in adequately rendering Homer, but in the hope of satisfying competent judges, in the hope of making it clear to the future translator, that I at any rate follow a right method, and that, in coming short, I come short from weakness of execution, not from original vice of design. This is why I have so long occupied myself with Mr. Newman's version; that, apart from all faults of execution, his original design was wrong, and that he has done us the good service of declaring that design in its naked wrongness. To bad practice he has prefixed the bad theory which made the practice bad; he has given us a false theory in his preface, and he has exemplified the bad effects of that false theory in his translation. It is because his starting-point is so bad that he runs so badly; and to save others from taking so false a starting-point, may be to save them from running so futile a course.

Mr. Newman, indeed, says in his preface, that if any one dislikes his translation, 'he has his easy remedy; to keep aloof from it.' But Mr. Newman is a writer of considerable and deserved reputation; he is also a Professor of the University of London, an institution which by its position and by its merits acquires every year greater importance. It would be a very grave thing if the authority of so eminent a Professor led his students to misconceive entirely the chief work of the Greek world; that work which, whatever the other works of classical antiquity have to give us, gives it more abundantly than they all. The eccentricity too, the arbitrariness, of which Mr. Newman's conception of Homer offers so signal an example, are not a peculiar failing of Mr. Newman's own; in varying degrees they are the great defect of English intellect, the great blemish of English literature. Our literature of the eighteenth century, the literature of the school of Dryden, Addison, Pope, Johnson, is a long reaction against this eccentricity, this arbitrariness; that reaction perished by its own faults, and its enemies are left once more masters of the field. It is much more likely that any new English version of Homer will have Mr. Newman's faults than Pope's. Our present literature, which is very far, certainly, from having the spirit and power of Elizabethan genius, yet has in its own way these faults, eccentricity and arbitrariness, quite as much as the Elizabethan literature ever had. They are the cause that, while upon none, perhaps, of the modern literatures has so great a sum of force been expended as upon the English literature, at the present hour this literature, regarded not as an object of mere literary interest but as a living intellectual instrument, ranks only third in European effect and importance among the literatures of Europe; it ranks after the literatures of France and Germany. Of these two literatures, as of the intellect of Europe in general, the main effort, for now many years, has been a *critical* effort; the endeavour, in all branches of knowledge,—theology, philosophy, history, art, science,—to see the object as in itself it really is. But, owing to the presence in English literature of this eccentric and arbitrary spirit, owing to the strong tendency of English writers to bring to the consideration of their object some individual fancy, almost the last thing for which one would come to English literature is just that very thing which now Europe most desires—*criticism*. It is useful to notice any signal manifestation of those faults, which thus limit and impair the action of our literature. And therefore I have pointed out how widely, in translating Homer, a man even of real ability and learning may go astray, unless he brings to the study of this clearest of poets one quality in which our English authors, with all their great gifts, are apt to be somewhat wanting—simple lucidity of mind.

III

Homer is rapid in his movement, Homer is plain in his words and style, Homer is simple in his ideas, Homer is noble in his manner. Cowper renders him ill because he is slow in his movement, and elaborate in his style; Pope renders him ill because he is artificial both in his style and in his words; Chapman renders him ill because he is fantastic in his ideas; Mr. Newman renders him ill because he is odd in his words and ignoble in his manner. All four translators diverge from their original at other points besides those named; but it is at the points thus named that their divergence is greatest. For instance, Cowper's diction is not as Homer's diction, nor his nobleness as Homer's nobleness; but it is in movement and grammatical style that he is most unlike Homer. Pope's rapidity is not of the same sort as Homer's rapidity, nor are his plainness of ideas and his nobleness as Homer's plainness of ideas and nobleness: but it is in the artificial character of his style and diction that he is most unlike Homer. Chapman's movement, words, style, and manner, are often far enough from resembling Homer's movement, words, style, and manner; but it is the fantasticality of his ideas which puts him farthest from resembling Homer. Mr. Newman's movement, grammatical style, and ideas, are a thousand times in strong contrast with Homer's; still it is by the oddness of his diction and the ignobleness of his manner that he contrasts with Homer the most violently.

Therefore the translator must not say to himself: 'Cowper is noble, Pope is rapid, Chapman has a good diction, Mr.

Newman has a good cast of sentence; I will avoid Cowper's slowness, Pope's artificiality, Chapman's conceits, Mr. Newman's oddity; I will take Cowper's dignified manner, Pope's impetuous movement, Chapman's vocabulary, Mr. Newman's syntax, and so make a perfect translation of Homer.' Undoubtedly in certain points the versions of Chapman, Cowper, Pope, and Mr. Newman, all of them have merit; some of them very high merit, others a lower merit; but even in these points they have none of them precisely the same kind of merit as Homer, and therefore the new translator, even if he can imitate them in their good points, will still not satisfy his judge, the scholar, who asks him for Homer and Homer's kind of merit, or, at least, for as much of them as it is possible to give.

So the translator really has no good model before him for any part of his work, and has to invent everything for himself. He is to be rapid in movement, plain in speech, simple in thought, and noble; and *how* he is to be either rapid, or plain, or simple, or noble, no one yet has shown him. I shall try to-day to establish some practical suggestions which may help the translator of Homer's poetry to comply with the four grand requirements which we make of him.

His version is to be rapid; and of course, to make a man's poetry rapid, as to make it noble, nothing can serve him so much as to have, in his own nature, rapidity and nobleness. *It is the spirit that quickeneth*,[45] and no one will so well render Homer's swift-flowing movement as he who has himself something of the swift-moving spirit of Homer. Yet even this is not quite enough. Pope certainly had a quick and darting spirit, as he had, also, real nobleness; yet Pope does not render the movement of Homer. To render this the translator must have, besides his natural qualifications, an appropriate metre.

I have sufficiently shown why I think all forms of our ballad-metre unsuited to Homer. It seems to me to be beyond question that, for epic poetry, only three metres can seriously claim to be accounted capable of the grand style. Two of these will at once occur to every one,—the ten-syllable, or so-called *heroic*, couplet, and blank verse. I do not add to these the Spenserian stanza, although Dr. Maginn, whose metrical eccentricities I have already criticised, pronounces this stanza the one right measure for a translation of Homer. It is enough to observe that if Pope's couplet, with the simple system of correspondences that its rhymes introduce, changes the movement of Homer, in which no such correspondences are found, and is therefore a bad measure for

a translator of Homer to employ, Spenser's stanza, with its
far more intricate system of correspondences, must change
Homer's movement far more profoundly, and must therefore be for the translator a far worse measure than the
couplet of Pope. Yet I will say, at the same time, that the
verse of Spenser is more fluid, slips more easily and quickly
along, than the verse of almost any other English poet.

> By this the northern wagoner had set
> His seven-fold team behind the steadfast star
> That was in ocean waves yet never wet,
> But firm is fixt, and sendeth light from far
> To all that in the wide deep wandering are.*

One cannot but feel that English verse has not often moved
with the fluidity and sweet ease of these lines. It is possible
that it may have been this quality of Spenser's poetry which
made Dr. Maginn think that the stanza of *The Faery Queen*
must be a good measure for rendering Homer. This it is not:
Spenser's verse is fluid and rapid, no doubt, but there are
more ways than one of being fluid and rapid, and Homer is
fluid and rapid in quite another way than Spenser. Spenser's
manner is no more Homeric than is the manner of the one
modern inheritor of Spenser's beautiful gift,—the poet, who
evidently caught from Spenser his sweet and easy-slipping
movement, and who has exquisitely employed it; a Spenserian genius, nay, a genius by natural endowment richer
probably than even Spenser; that light which shines so unexpected and without fellow in our century, an Elizabethan
born too late, the early lost and admirably gifted Keats.

I say then that there are really but three metres,—the ten-
syllable couplet, blank verse, and a third metre which I will
not yet name, but which is neither the Spenserian stanza nor
any form of ballad-verse,—between which, as vehicles for
Homer's poetry, the translator has to make his choice. Every
one will at once remember a thousand passages in which
both the ten-syllable couplet and blank verse prove themselves to have nobleness. Undoubtedly the movement and
manner of this,—

> Still raise for good the supplicating voice,
> But leave to Heaven the measure and the choice,—[46]

are noble. Undoubtedly, the movement and manner of
this:—

> High on a throne of royal state, which far
> Outshone the wealth of Ormus and of Ind,—[47]

---

* *The Faery Queen*, [Book I] Canto ii. stanza. I. [M. A.]

are noble also. But the first is in a rhymed metre; and the un-
fitness of a rhymed metre for rendering Homer I have already shown. I will observe, too, that the fine couplet which
I have quoted comes out of a satire, a didactic poem; and
that it is in didactic poetry that the ten-syllable couplet has
most successfully essayed the grand style. In narrative poetry
this metre has succeeded best when it essayed a sensibly
lower style, the style of Chaucer, for instance; whose narrative manner, though a very good and sound manner, is certainly neither the grand manner nor the manner of Homer.

The rhymed ten-syllable couplet being thus excluded,
blank verse offers itself for the translator's use. The first kind
of blank verse which naturally occurs to us is the blank verse
of Milton, which has been employed, with more or less modification, by Mr. Cary[48] in translating Dante, by Cowper and
by Mr. Wright in translating Homer. How noble this metre
is in Milton's hands, how completely it shows itself capable
of the grand, nay, of the grandest, style, I need not say. To
this metre, as used in the *Paradise Lost*, our country owes
the glory of having produced one of the only two poetical
works in the grand style which are to be found in the modern languages; the *Divine Comedy* of Dante is the other.
England and Italy here stand alone; Spain, France, and Germany have produced great poets, but neither Calderon, nor
Corneille, nor Schiller, nor even Goethe, has produced a
body of poetry in the true grand style, in the sense in which
the style of the body of Homer's poetry, or Pindar's, or
Sophocles's, is grand. But Dante has, and so has Milton; and
in this respect Milton possesses a distinction which even
Shakespeare, undoubtedly the supreme poetical power in our
literature, does not share with him. Not a tragedy of Shakespeare but contains passages in the worst of all styles, the
affected style; and the grand style, although it may be harsh,
or obscure, or cumbrous, or over-laboured, is never affected.
In spite, therefore, of objections which may justly be urged
against the plan and treatment of the *Paradise Lost*, in spite
of its possessing, certainly, a far less enthralling force of interest to attract and to carry forward the reader than the
Iliad or the *Divine Comedy*, it fully deserves, it can never
lose, its immense reputation; for, like the *Iliad* and the
Divine Comedy, nay, in some respects to a higher degree
than either of them, it is in the grand style.

But the grandeur of Milton is one thing, and the grandeur
of Homer is another. Homer's movement, I have said again
and again, is a flowing, a rapid movement; Milton's, on the

other hand, is a laboured, a self-retarding movement. In each case, the movement, the metrical cast, corresponds with the mode of evolution of the thought, with the syntactical cast, and is indeed determined by it. Milton charges himself so full with thought, imagination, knowledge, that his style will hardly contain them. He is too full-stored to show us in much detail one conception, one piece of knowledge; he just shows it to us in a pregnant allusive way, and then he presses on to another; and all this fulness, this pressure, this condensation, this self-constraint, enters into his movement, and makes it what it is,—noble, but difficult and austere. Homer is quite different; he says a thing, and says it to the end, and then begins another, while Milton is trying to press a thousand things into one. So that whereas, in reading Milton, you never lose the sense of laborious and condensed fulness, in reading Homer you never lose the sense of flowing and abounding ease. With Milton line runs into line, and all is straitly bound together: with Homer line runs off from line, and all hurries away onward. Homer begins, Μῆνιν ἄειδε, Θεά,[49]—at the second word announcing the proposed action: Milton begins:

> Of man's first disobedience, and the fruit
> Of that forbidden tree, whose mortal taste
> Brought death into the world, and all our woe,
> With loss of Eden, till one greater Man
> Restore us, and regain the blissful seat,
> Sing, heavenly muse.[50]

So chary of a sentence is he, so resolute not to let it escape him till he has crowded into it all he can, that it is not till the thirty-ninth word in the sentence that he will give us the key to it, the word of action, the verb. Milton says:

> O for that warning voice, which he, who saw
> The Apocalypse, heard cry in heaven aloud.[51]

He is not satisfied, unless he can tell us, all in one sentence, and without permitting himself to actually mention the name, that the man who had the warning voice was the same man who saw the Apocalypse. Homer would have said, 'O for that warning voice, which *John* heard'—and if it had suited him to say that John also saw the Apocalypse, he would have given us that in another sentence. The effect of this allusive and compressed manner of Milton is, I need not say, often very powerful; and it is an effect which other great poets have often sought to obtain much in the same way:

Dante is full of it, Horace is full of it; but wherever it exists, it is always an un-Homeric effect. 'The losses of the heavens,' says Horace, 'fresh moons speedily repair; we, when we have gone down where the pious Æneas, where the rich Tullus and Ancus are,—*pulvis et umbra sumus*.'* He never actually says *where* we go to; he only indicates it by saying that it is that place where Æneas, Tullus, and Ancus are. But Homer, when he has to speak of going down to the grave, says, definitely, ἐς Ἠλύσιον πεδίον—ἀθάνατοι πέμψουσιν,†—'The immortals shall send thee *to the Elysian plain;*' and it is not till after he has definitely said this, that he adds, that it is there that the abode of departed worthies is placed: ὅθι ξανθὸς 'Ραδάμανθυς—'Where the yellow-haired Rhadamanthus is.' Again; Horace, having to say that punishment sooner or later overtakes crime, says it thus:

> Raro antecedentem scelestum
> Deseruit pede Pœna claudo.‡

The thought itself of these lines is familiar enough to Homer and Hesiod; but neither Homer nor Hesiod, in expressing it, could possibly have so complicated its expression as Horace complicates it, and purposely complicates it, by his use of the word *deseruit*. I say that this complicated evolution of the thought necessarily complicates the movement and rhythm of a poet; and that the Miltonic blank verse, of course the first model of blank verse which suggests itself to an English translator of Homer, bears the strongest marks of such complication, and is therefore entirely unfit to render Homer.

If blank verse is used in translating Homer, it must be a blank verse of which English poetry, naturally swayed much by Milton's treatment of this metre, offers at present hardly any examples. It must not be Cowper's blank verse, who has studied Milton's pregnant manner with such effect, that, having to say of Mr. Throckmorton that he spares his avenue, although it is the fashion with other people to cut down theirs, he says that Benevolus 'reprieves The obsolete prolixity of shade'.[54] It must not be Mr. Tennyson's blank verse.

> For all experience is an arch, wherethrough
> Gleams that untravelled world, whose distance fades
> For ever and for ever, as we gaze.[55]

It is no blame to the thought of those lines, which belongs to

* *Odes*, IV. vii. 13. [M. A.][52]
† *Odyssey* iv. 563. [M. A.]
‡ *Odes*, III. ii. 31. [M. A.][53]

another order of ideas than Homer's, but it is true, that Homer would certainly have said of them, 'It is to consider too curiously to consider so.' It is no blame to their rhythm, which belongs to another order of movement than Homer's, but it is true that these three lines by themselves take up nearly as much time as a whole book of the *Iliad*. No; the blank verse used in rendering Homer must be a blank verse of which perhaps the best specimens are to be found in some of the most rapid passages of Shakespeare's plays,—a blank verse which does not dovetail its lines into one another, and which habitually ends its lines with monosyllables. Such a blank verse might no doubt be very rapid in its movement, and might perfectly adapt itself to a thought plainly and directly evolved; and it would be interesting to see it well applied to Homer. But the translator who determines to use it, must not conceal from himself that in order to pour Homer into the mould of this metre, he will have entirely to break him up and melt him down, with the hope of then successfully composing him afresh; and this is a process which is full of risks. It may, no doubt, be the real Homer that issues new from it; it is not certain beforehand that it cannot be the real Homer, as it is certain that from the mould of Pope's couplet or Cowper's Miltonic verse it cannot be the real Homer that will issue; still, the chances of disappointment are great. The result of such an attempt to renovate the old poet may be an Æson; but it may also, and more probably will, be a Pelias.[56]

When I say this, I point to the metre which seems to me to give the translator the best chance of preserving the general effect of Homer,—that third metre which I have not yet expressly named, the hexameter. I know all that is said against the use of hexameters in English poetry; but it comes only to this, that, among us, they have not yet been used on any considerable scale with success. *Solvitur ambulando:*[57] this is an objection which can best be met by *producing* good English hexameters. And there is no reason in the nature of the English language why it should not adapt itself to hexameters as well as the German language does; nay, the English language, from its greater rapidity, is in itself better suited than the German for them. The hexameter, whether alone or with the pentameter, possesses a movement, an expression, which no metre hitherto in common use amongst us possesses, and which I am convinced English poetry, as our mental wants multiply, will not always be content to forego. Applied to Homer, this metre affords to the translator the immense support of keeping him more nearly than any other metre to Homer's movement; and, since a poet's movement makes so large a part of his general effect, and to reproduce this general effect is at once the translator's indispensable business and so difficult for him, it is a great thing to have this part of your model's general effect already given you in your metre, instead of having to get it entirely for yourself.

These are general considerations; but there are also one or two particular considerations which confirm me in the opinion that for translating Homer into English verse the hexameter should be used. The most successful attempt hitherto made at rendering Homer into English, the attempt in which Homer's general effect has been best retained, is an attempt made in the hexameter measure. It is a version of the famous lines in the third book of the *Iliad,* which end with that mention of Castor and Pollux from which Mr. Ruskin extracts the sentimental consolation already noticed by me. The author is the accomplished Provost of Eton, Dr. Hawtrey; and this performance of his must be my excuse for having taken the liberty to single him out for mention, as one of the natural judges of a translation of Homer, along with Professor Thompson and Professor Jowett, whose connection with Greek literature is official. The passage is short;* and Dr. Hawtrey's version of it is suffused with a pensive grace which is, perhaps, rather more Virgilian than Homeric; still it is the one version of any part of the *Iliad* which in some degree reproduces for me the original effect of Homer: it is the best, and it is in hexameters.

This is one of the particular considerations that incline me to prefer the hexameter, for translating Homer, to our established metres. There is another. Most of you, probably, have some knowledge of a poem by Mr. Clough, *The Bothie of Toper-na-fuosich,*[58] a long-vacation pastoral, in hexameters. The general merits of that poem I am not going to discuss: it is a serio-comic poem, and, therefore, of essentially different nature from the *Iliad.* Still in two things it is, more than any other English poem which I can call to mind, like the *Iliad:* in the rapidity of its movement, and the plainness and directness of its style. The thought in this poem is often curious and subtle, and that is not Homeric; the diction is often grotesque, and that is not Homeric. Still, by its rapidity of movement, and plain and direct manner of presenting the

---

* So short, that I quote it entire:—

Clearly the rest I behold of the dark-eyed sons of Achaia;
Known to me well are the faces of all; their names I remember;
Two, two only remain, whom I see not among the commanders,

thought however curious in itself, this poem, which, being as
I say a serio-comic poem, has a right to be grotesque, is
grotesque *truly*, not, like Mr. Newman's version of the *Iliad*,
falsely. Mr. Clough's odd epithets, 'The grave man nick-
named Adam,' 'The hairy Aldrich,' and so on, grow vitally
and appear naturally in their place; while Mr. Newman's
'dapper-greaved Achaians,' and 'motley-helmed Hector,'
have all the air of being mechanically elaborated and arti-
ficially stuck in. Mr. Clough's hexameters are excessively,
needlessly rough; still, owing to the native rapidity of this
measure, and to the directness of style which so well allies
itself with it, his composition produces a sense in the reader
which Homer's composition also produces, and which
Homer's translator ought to *reproduce*,—the sense of having, within short limits of time, a large portion of human life
presented to him, instead of a small portion.

Mr. Clough's hexameters are, as I have just said, too

Castor fleet in the car,—Polydeukes brave with the cestus,—
Own dear brethren of mine,—one parent loved us as infants.
Are they not here in the host, from the shores of loved Lacedæmon,
Or, though they came with the rest in ships that bound through the
       waters,
Dare they not enter the fight or stand in the council of Heroes,
All for fear of the shame and the taunts my crime has awakened?
   So said she;—they long since in Earth's soft arms were reposing,
There, in their own dear land, their Fatherland, Lacedæmon.
       English Hexameter Translations; London, 1847; p. 242.

I have changed Dr. Hawtrey's 'Kastor,' 'Lakedaimon,' back to the
familiar 'Castor,' 'Lacedæmon,' in obedience to my own rule that
everything *odd* is to be avoided in rendering Homer, the most natural
and least odd of poets. I see Mr. Newman's critic in the *National
Review* urges our generation to bear with the unnatural effect of
these rewritten Greek names, in the hope that by this means the
effect of them may have to the next generation become natural. For
my part, I feel no disposition to pass all my own life in the wilderness of pedantry, in order that a posterity which I shall never see
may one day enter an orthographical Canaan; and, after all, the real
question is this: whether our living apprehension of the Greek world
is more checked by meeting in an English book about the Greeks,
names not spelt letter for letter as in the original Greek, or by meeting names which make us rub our eyes and call out, 'How exceedingly odd!'
The Latin names of the Greek deities raise in most cases the idea
of quite distinct personages from the personages whose idea is raised
by the Greek names. Hera and Juno are actually, to every scholar's
imagination, two different people. So in all these cases the Latin
names must, at any inconvenience, be abandoned when we are dealing with the Greek world. But I think it can be in the imagination
of Mr. Grote only, that 'Thucydides' raises the idea of a different
man from Θουκυδίδης [M. A.]

rough and irregular; and indeed a good model, on any considerable scale, of this metre, the English translator will nowhere find. He must not follow the model offered by Mr. Longfellow in his pleasing and popular poem of *Evangeline;* for the merit of the manner and movement of *Evangeline,* when they are at their best, is to be tenderly elegant; and their fault, when they are at their worst, is to be lumbering; but Homer's defect is not lumberingness, neither is tender elegance his excellence. The lumbering effect of most English hexameters is caused by their being much too dactylic;* the translator must learn to use spondees freely. Mr. Clough has done this, but he has not sufficiently observed another rule which the translator cannot follow too strictly; and that is, to have no lines which will not, as it is familiarly said, *read themselves.* This is of the last importance of rhythms with which the ear of the English public is not thoroughly acquainted. Lord Redesdale,[59] in two papers on the subject of Greek and Roman metres, has some good remarks on the outrageous disregard of quantity in which English verse, trusting to its force of accent, is apt to indulge itself. The predominance of accent in our language is so great, that it would be pedantic not to avail one's self of it; and Lord Redesdale suggests rules which might easily be pushed too far. Still, it is undeniable that in English hexameters we generally force the quantity far too much; we rely on justification by accent with a security which is excessive. But not only do we abuse accent by shortening long syllables and lengthening short ones; we perpetually commit a far worse fault, by requiring the removal of the accent from its natural place to an unnatural one, in order to make our line scan. This is a fault, even when our metre is one which every English reader knows, and when he can see what we want and can correct the rhythm according to our wish; although it is a fault which a great master may sometimes commit knowingly to produce a desired effect, as Milton changes the natural accent on the word *Tirésias* in the line:—

And Tíresias and Phineus, prophets old;

and then it ceases to be a fault, and becomes a beauty. But it is a real fault, when Chapman has:—

* For instance; in a version (I believe, by the late Mr. Lockhart) of Homer's description of the parting of Hector and Andromache, there occurs, in the first five lines, but one spondee besides the necessary spondees in the sixth place; in the corresponding five lines of Homer there occur ten. See *English Hexameter Translations,* 244. [M. A.]

> By him the golden-throned Queen slept, the Queen of
> Deities;[60]

for in this line, to make it scan, you have to take away the
accent from the word *Queen,* on which it naturally falls, and
to place it on *throned,* which would naturally be unaccented;
and yet, after all, you get no peculiar effect or beauty of
cadence to reward you. It is a real fault, when Mr. Newman
has:—

> Infatuate! O that thou wert lord to some other army—

for here again the reader is required, not for any special advantage to himself, but simply to save Mr. Newman trouble,
to place the accent on the insignificant word *wert,* where it
has no business whatever. But it is still a greater fault, when
Spenser has (to take a striking instance):—

> Wot ye why his mother with a veil hath covered his face?[61]

for a hexameter; because here not only is the reader cause-
lessly required to make havoc with the natural accentuation
of the line in order to get it to run as a hexameter; but also
he, in nine cases out of ten, will be utterly at a loss how to
perform the process required, and the line will remain a
mere monster for him. I repeat, it is advisable to construct
all verses so that by reading them naturally—that is, according to the sense and legitimate accent,—the reader gets the
right rhythm; but, for English hexameters, that they be so
constructed is indispensable.

If the hexameter best helps the translator to the Homeric
rapidity, what style may best help him to the Homeric plainness and directness? It is the merit of a metre appropriate to
your subject, that it in some degree suggests and carries with
itself a style appropriate to the subject; the elaborate and
self-retarding style, which comes so naturally when your
metre is the Miltonic blank verse, does not come naturally
with the hexameter; is, indeed, alien to it. On the other hand,
the hexameter has a natural dignity which repels both the
jaunty style and the jog-trot style, to both of which the ballad-measure so easily lends itself. These are great advantages; and, perhaps, it is nearly enough to say to the translator who uses the hexameter that he cannot too religiously
follow, in style, the inspiration of his metre. He will find that
a loose and idiomatic grammar—a grammar which follows
the essential rather than the formal logic of the thought—
allies itself excellently with the hexameter; and that, while
this sort of grammar ensures plainness and naturalness, it by

no means comes short in nobleness. It is difficult to pronounce, certainly, what is idiomatic in the ancient literature
of a language which, though still spoken, has long since entirely adopted, as modern Greek has adopted, modern id-
ioms. Still one may, I think, clearly perceive that Homer's
grammatical style is idiomatic,—that it may even be called,
not improperly, a loose grammatical style.* Examples, however, of what I mean by a loose grammatical style, will be of
more use to the translator if taken from English poetry than
if taken from Homer. I call it, then, a loose and idiomatic
grammar which Shakespeare uses in the last line of the following three:—

> He's here in double trust:
> First, as I am his kinsman and his subject,
> *Strong both against the deed;*—[62]

or in this:—

> Wit, *whither wilt?*[63]

What Shakespeare means is perfectly clear, clearer, probably, than if he had said it in a more formal and regular
manner; but his grammar is loose and idiomatic, because he
leaves out the subject of the verb 'wilt' in the second passage
quoted, and because, in the first, a prodigious addition to the
sentence has to be, as we used to say in our old Latin grammar days, *understood,* before the word 'both' can be properly parsed. So, again, Chapman's grammar is loose and idiomatic where he says,

> Even share hath he that keeps his tent, and *he to field* doth
> go,—[64]

because he leaves out, in the second clause, the relative
which in formal writing would be required. But Chapman
here does not lose dignity by this idiomatic way of expressing himself, any more than Shakespeare loses it by neglecting to confer on 'both' the blessings of a regular government: neither loses dignity, but each gives that impression
of a plain, direct, and natural mode of speaking, which Homer,
too, gives, and which it is so important, as I say, that

---

* See, for instance, in the *Iliad*, the loose construction of ὅστε, xvii.
658; that of ἴδοιτο, xvii. 681; that of οἵτε, xviii. 209; and the elliptical
construction at xix. 42, 43; also the idiomatic construction of ἐγὼν
ὅδε παρασχεῖν, xix. 140. These instances are all taken within a range
of a thousand lines; any one may easily multiply them for himself.
[M. A.]

Homer's translator should succeed in giving. Cowper calls blank verse 'a style farther removed than rhyme from the vernacular idiom, both in the language itself and in the arrangement of it;' and just in proportion as blank verse is removed from the vernacular idiom, from that idiomatic style which is of all styles the plainest and most natural, blank verse is unsuited to render Homer.

Shakespeare is not only idiomatic in his grammar or style, he is also idiomatic in his words or diction; and here too, his example is valuable for the translator of Homer. The translator must not, indeed, allow himself all the liberty that Shakespeare allows himself; for Shakespeare sometimes uses expressions which pass perfectly well as he uses them, because Shakespeare thinks so fast and so powerfully, that in reading him we are borne over single words as by a mighty current; but, if our mind were less excited,—and who may rely on exciting our mind like Shakespeare?—they would check us. 'To grunt and sweat under a weary load;'[65]—that does perfectly well where it comes in Shakespeare; but if the translator of Homer, who will hardly have wound our minds up to the pitch at which these words of Hamlet find them, were to employ, when he has to speak of one of Homer's heroes under the load of calamity, this figure of 'grunting' and 'sweating,' we should say, *He Newmanises,* and his diction would offend us. For he is to be noble; and no plea of wishing to be plain and natural can get him excused from being this: only, as he is to be also, like Homer, perfectly simple and free from artificiality, and as the use of idiomatic expressions undoubtedly gives this effect,* he should be as idiomatic as he can be without ceasing to be noble. Therefore the idiomatic language of Shakespeare[66]—such language as, 'prate of his *whereabout;*' '*jump* the life to come;' 'the damnation of his *taking-off;*' 'his *quietus make* with a bare *bodkin*'—should be carefully observed by the translator of Homer, although in every case he will have to decide for

---

* Our knowledge of Homer's Greek is hardly such as to enable us to pronounce quite confidently what is idiomatic in his diction, and what is not, any more than in his grammar; but I seem to myself clearly to recognise an idiomatic stamp in such expressions as τολυπεύειν πολέμους, xiv. 86; φάος ἐν νήεσσιν θῆς, xvi. 94; τιν' οἵω ἀσπασίως αὐτῶν γόνυ κάμψειν, xix. 71; κλοτοπεύειν, xix. 149; and many others. The first-quoted expression, τολυπεύειν ἀργαλέους πολέμους, seems to me to have just about the same degree of freedom as the '*jump* the life to come,' or the '*shuffle off* this mortal coil,' of Shakespeare. [M. A.]

himself whether the use, by him, of Shakespeare's liberty, will or will not clash with his indispensable duty of nobleness. He will find one English book and one only, where, as in the *Iliad* itself, perfect plainness of speech is allied with perfect nobleness; and that book is the Bible. No one could see this more clearly than Pope saw it: 'This pure and noble simplicity,' he says, 'is nowhere in such perfection as in the Scripture and Homer:' yet even with Pope a woman is a 'fair,' a father is a 'sire,' and an old man a 'reverend sage,' and so on through all the phrases of that pseudo-Augustan, and most unbiblical, vocabulary. The Bible, however, is undoubtedly the grand mine of diction for the translator of Homer; and, if he knows how to discriminate truly between what will suit him and what will not, the Bible may afford him also invaluable lessons of style.

I said that Homer, besides being plain in style and diction, was plain in the quality of his thought. It is possible that a thought may be expressed with idiomatic plainness, and yet not be in itself a plain thought. For example, in Mr. Clough's poem, already mentioned, the style and diction is almost always idiomatic and plain, but the thought itself is often of a quality which is not plain; it is *curious*. But the grand instance of the union of idiomatic expression with curious or difficult thought is in Shakespeare's poetry. Such, indeed, is the force and power of Shakespeare's idiomatic expression, that it gives an effect of clearness and vividness even to a thought which is imperfect and incoherent; for instance, when Hamlet says,—

> To take arms against a sea of troubles,—[67]

the figure there is undoubtedly most faulty, it by no means runs on four legs; but the thing is said so freely and idiomatically, that it passes. This, however, is not a point to which I now want to call your attention; I want you to remark, in Shakespeare and others, only that which we may directly apply to Homer. I say, then, that in Shakespeare the thought is often, while most idiomatically uttered, nay, while good and sound in itself, yet of a quality which is curious and difficult; and that this quality of thought is something entirely un-Homeric. For example, when Lady Macbeth says,—

> Memory, the warder of the brain,
> Shall be a fume, and the receipt of reason
> A limbeck only,—[68]

this figure is a perfectly sound and correct figure, no doubt;

Mr. Knight[69] even calls it a 'happy' figure; but it is a *difficult* figure: Homer would not have used it. Again, when Lady Macbeth says,—

> When you durst do it, then you were a man;
> And, to be more than what you were, you would
> Be so much more the man,—[70]

the thought in the two last of these lines is, when you seize it, a perfectly clear thought, and a fine thought; but it is a *curious* thought: Homer would not have used it. These are favourable instances of the union of plain style and words with a thought not plain in quality; but take stronger instances of this union,—let the thought be not only not plain in quality, but highly fanciful: and you have the Elizabethan conceits; you have, in spite of idiomatic style and idiomatic diction, everything which is most un-Homeric; you have such atrocities as this of Chapman:—

> Fate shall fail to vent her gall
> Till mine vent thousands.

I say, the poets of a nation which has produced such a conceit as that, must purify themselves seven times in the fire before they can hope to render Homer. They must expel their nature with a fork, and keep crying to one another night and day: 'Homer not only moves rapidly, not only speaks idiomatically; he is, also, *free from fancifulness.*'

So essentially characteristic of Homer is his plainness and naturalness of thought, that to the preservation of this in his own version the translator must without scruple sacrifice, where it is necessary, verbal fidelity to his original, rather than run any risk of producing, by literalness, an odd and unnatural effect. The double epithets so constantly occurring in Homer must be dealt with according to this rule; these epithets come quite naturally in Homer's poetry; in English poetry they, in nine cases out of ten, come, when literally rendered, quite unnaturally. I will not now discuss why this is so, I assume it as an indisputable fact that it is so; that Homer's μερόπων ἀνθρώπων comes to the reader as something perfectly natural, while Mr. Newman's 'voice-dividing mortals' comes to him as something perfectly unnatural. Well then, as it is Homer's general effect which we are to reproduce, it is to be false to Homer to be so verbally faithful to him as that we lose this effect: and by the English translator Homer's double epithets must be, in many places, renounced altogether; in all places where they are rendered, rendered by equivalents which come naturally. Instead of rendering Θέτι τανύπεπλε by Mr. Newman's 'Thetis trailing-robed,' which brings to one's mind long petticoats sweeping a dirty pavement, the translator must render the Greek by English words which come as naturally to us as Milton's words when he says, 'Let gorgeous Tragedy With sceptred pall come sweeping by.'[71] Instead of rendering μώνυχας ἵππους by Chapman's 'one-hoofed steeds,' or Mr. Newman's 'single-hoofed horses,' he must speak of horses in a way which surprises us as little as Shakespeare surprises us when he says, 'Gallop apace you fiery-footed steeds.'[72] Instead of rendering μελιηδέα θυμόν by 'life as honey pleasant,' he must characterise life with the simple pathos of Gray's 'warm precincts of the cheerful day.'[73] Instead of converting ποῖόν σε ἔπος φύγεν ἕρκος ὀδόντων,[74] into the portentous remonstrance, 'Betwixt the out-work of thy teeth what word hath slipt?' he must remonstrate in English as straightforward as this of St. Peter, 'Be it far from thee, Lord: this shall not be unto thee;'[75] or as this of the disciples, 'What is this that he saith, a little while? we cannot tell what he saith.'[76] Homer's Greek, in each of the places quoted, reads as naturally as any of those English passages: the expression no more calls away the attention from the sense in the Greek than in the English. But when, in order to render literally in English one of Homer's double epithets, a strange unfamiliar adjective is invented,—such as 'voice-dividing' for μέροψ,—an improper share of the reader's attention is necessarily diverted to this ancillary word, to this word which Homer never intended should receive so much notice; and a total effect quite different from Homer's is thus produced. Therefore Mr. Newman, though he does not purposely import, like Chapman, conceits of his own into the *Iliad,* does actually import them; for the result of his singular diction is to raise ideas, and odd ideas, not raised by the corresponding diction in Homer; and Chapman himself does no more. Cowper says: 'I have cautiously avoided all terms of new invention, with an abundance of which persons of more ingenuity than judgment have not enriched our language but encumbered it;' and this criticism so exactly hits the diction of Mr. Newman that one is irresistibly led to imagine his present appearance in the flesh to be at least his second.

A translator cannot well have a Homeric rapidity, style, diction, and quality of thought, without at the same time having what is the result of these in Homer,—nobleness. Therefore I do not attempt to lay down any rules for obtaining this effect of nobleness,—the effect, too, of all others the most impalpable, the most irreducible to rule, and which most depends on the individual personality of the artist. So I proceed at once to give you, in conclusion, one or two passages in which I have tried to follow those principles of Homeric translation which I have laid down. I give them, it must be remembered, not as specimens of perfect translation, but as specimens of an attempt to translate Homer on certain principles; specimens which may very aptly illustrate those principles by falling short as well as by succeeding.

I take first a passage of which I have already spoken, the comparison of the Trojan fires to the stars. The first part of that passage is, I have said, of splendid beauty; and to begin with a lame version of that would be the height of imprudence in me. It is the last and more level part with which I shall concern myself. I have already quoted Cowper's version of this part in order to show you how unlike his stiff and Miltonic manner of telling a plain story is to Homer's easy and rapid manner:—

> So numerous seemed those fires the banks between
> Of Xanthus, blazing, and the fleet of Greece,
> In prospect all of Troy—

I need not continue to the end. I have also quoted Pope's version of it, to show you how unlike his ornate and artificial manner is to Homer's plain and natural manner:

> So many flames before proud Ilion blaze,
> And brighten glimmering Xanthus with their rays;
> The long reflections of the distant fires
> Gleam on the walls, and tremble on the spires,—

and much more of the same kind. I want to show you that it is possible, in a plain language of this sort, to keep Homer's simplicity without being heavy and dull; and to keep his dignity without bringing in pomp and ornament. 'As numerous as are the stars on a clear night,' says Homer,

> So shone forth, in front of Troy, by the bed of Xanthus,
> Between that and the ships, the Trojans' numerous fires.
> In the plain there were kindled a thousand fires: by each one
> There sat fifty men, in the ruddy light of the fire:
> By their chariots stood the steeds, and champed the white
>   barley
> While their masters sat by the fire, and waited for Morning.

Here, in order to keep Homer's effect of perfect plainness and directness, I repeat the word 'fires' as he repeats πυρά, without scruple; although in a more elaborate and literary style of poetry this recurrence of the same word would be a fault to be avoided. I omit the epithet of Morning, and whereas Homer says that the steeds 'waited for Morning,' I prefer to attribute this expectation of Morning to the master and not to the horse. Very likely in this particular, as in any other single particular, I may be wrong: what I wish you to remark is my endeavour after absolute plainness of speech, my care to avoid anything which may the least check or surprise the reader, whom Homer does not check or surprise. Homer's lively personal familiarity with war, and with the war-horse as his master's companion, is such that, as it seems to me, his attributing to the one the other's feelings comes to us quite naturally; but, from a poet without this familiarity, the attribution strikes as a little unnatural; and therefore, as everything the least unnatural is un-Homeric, I avoid it.

Again, in the address of Zeus to the horses of Achilles,[77] Cowper has:

> Jove saw their grief with pity, and his brows
> Shaking, within himself thus, pensive, said.
>   'Ah hapless pair! wherefore by gift divine
> Were ye to Peleus given, a mortal king,
> Yourselves immortal and from age exempt?'

There is no want of dignity here, as in the versions of Chapman and Mr. Newman, which I have already quoted: but the whole effect is much too slow. Take Pope:—

> Nor Jove disdained to cast a pitying look
> While thus relenting to the steeds he spoke.
>   'Unhappy coursers of immortal strain!
> Exempt from age and deathless now in vain;
> Did we your race on mortal man bestow
> Only, alas! to share in mortal woe?'

Here there is no want either of dignity or rapidity, but all is too artificial. 'Nor Jove disdained,' for instance, is a very artificial and literary way of rendering Homer's words, and so is, 'coursers of immortal strain.'

Μυρομένω δ' ἄρα τώ γε ἰδὼν, ἐλέησε Κρονίων.—

And with pity the son of Saturn saw them bewailing,
And he shook his head, and thus addressed his own bosom:—
  'Ah, unhappy pair, to Peleus why did we give you,

To a mortal? but ye are without old age and immortal.
Was it that ye, with man, might have your thousands of
   sorrows?
For than man, indeed, there breathes no wretcheder creature,
Of all living things, that on earth are breathing and moving.'

Here I will observe that the use of 'own,' in the second line,
for the last syllable of a dactyl, and the use of 'To a,' in the
fourth, for a complete spondee, though they do not, I think,
actually spoil the run of the hexameter, are yet undoubtedly
instances of that over-reliance on accent, and too free disregard of quantity, which Lord Redesdale visits with just
reprehension.*

I now take two longer passages in order to try my method
more fully; but I still keep to passages which have already
come under our notice. I quoted Chapman's version of some
passages in the speech of Hector at his parting with Andromache. One astounding conceit will probably still be in your
remembrance,—

When sacred Troy shall *shed her tow'rs for tears of over-
   throw,*—

as a translation of ὅτ' ἄν ποτ' ὀλώλῃ Ἴλιος ἱρή. I will quote a
few lines which may give you, also, the key-note to the
Anglo-Augustan manner of rendering this passage and to
the Miltonic manner of rendering it. What Mr. Newman's
manner of rendering it would be, you can by this time sufficiently imagine for yourselves. Mr. Wright,—to quote for

* It must be remembered, however, that, if we disregard quantity
too much in constructing English hexameters, we also disregard accent
too much in reading Greek hexameters. We read every Greek dactyl
so as to make a pure dactyl of it; but, to a Greek, the accent must
have hindered many dactyls from sounding as pure dactyls. When we
read αἰόλος ἵππος, for instance, or αἰγιόχοιο, the dactyl in each
of these cases is made by us as pure a dactyl as 'Tityre,' or 'dignity;'
but to a Greek it was not so. To him αἰόλος must have been nearly as
impure a dactyl as 'death-destined' is to us; and αἰγιόχ nearly as impure as the 'dressed his own' of my text. Nor, I think, does this right
mode of pronouncing the two words at all spoil the run of the line as
a hexameter. The effect αἰόλλος ἵππος (or something like that),
though not *our* effect, is not a disagreeable one. On the other hand,
κορυθαιόλος as a paroxytonon, although it has the respectable authority of Liddell and Scott's *Lexicon* (following Heyne), is certainly
wrong; for then the word cannot be pronounced without throwing an accent on the first syllable as well as the third, and μέγας
κορρυθαιόλλος Ἕκτωρ would have been to a Greek as intolerable an ending for a hexameter line as 'accurst *orphanhood-destined*
houses' would be to us. The best authorities, accordingly, accent
κορυθαιόλος as a proparoxytonon. [M. A.]

once from his meritorious version instead of Cowper's,
whose strong and weak points are those of Mr. Wright also,
—Mr. Wright begins his version of this passage thus:

> All these thy anxious cares are also mine,
> Partner beloved; but how could I endure
> The scorn of Trojans and their long-robed wives,
> Should they behold their Hector shrink from war,
> And act the coward's part? Nor doth my soul
> Prompt the base thought.

Ex pede Herculem:[78] you see just what the manner is. Mr.
Sotheby, on the other hand (to take a disciple of Pope instead of Pope himself), begins thus:

> 'What moves thee, moves my mind,' brave Hector said,
> 'Yet Troy's upbraiding scorn I deeply dread,
> If, like a slave, where chiefs with chiefs engage,
> The warrior Hector fears the war to wage.
> Not thus my heart inclines.'

From that specimen, too, you can easily divine what, with
such a manner, will become of the whole passage. But
Homer has neither

> What moves thee, moves my mind,—

nor has he

> All these thy anxious cares are also mine.

> ῏Η καὶ ἐμοὶ τάδε πάντα μέλει, γύναι · ἀλλὰ μάλ' αἰνῶς,—

that is what Homer has, that is his style and movement, if
one could but catch it. Andromache, as you know, has been
entreating Hector to defend Troy from within the walls,
instead of exposing his life, and, with his own life, the safety
of all those dearest to him, by fighting in the open plain.
Hector replies:—

> Woman, I too take thought for this; but then I bethink me
> What the Trojan men and Trojan women might murmur,
> If like a coward I skulked behind, apart from the battle.
> Nor would my own heart let me; my heart, which has bid me
>   be valiant
> Always, and always fighting among the first of the Trojans,
> Busy for Priam's fame and my own, in spite of the future.
> For that day will come, my soul is assured of its coming,
> It will come, when sacred Troy shall go to destruction,
> Troy, and warlike Priam too, and the people of Priam.

And yet not that grief, which then will be, of the Trojans,
Moves me so much—not Hecuba's grief, nor Priam my
    father's,
Nor my brethren's, many and brave, who then will be lying
In the bloody dust, beneath the feet of their foemen—
As thy grief, when, in tears, some brazen-coated Achaian
Shall transport thee away, and the day of thy freedom be
    ended.
Then, perhaps, thou shalt work at the loom of another, in
    Argos,
Or bear pails to the well of Messeïs, or Hypereia,
Sorely against thy will, by strong Necessity's order.
And some man may say, as he looks and sees thy tears
    falling:
See, the wife of Hector, that great pre-eminent captain
Of the horsemen of Troy, in the day they fought for their
    city.
So some man will say; and then thy grief will redouble
At thy want of a man like me, to save thee from bondage.
But let me be dead, and the earth be mounded above me,
Ere I hear thy cries, and thy captivity told of.

The main question, whether or no this version reproduces
for him the movement and general effect of Homer better
than other versions* of the same passage, I leave for the
judgment of the scholar. But the particular points, in which
the operation of my own rules is manifested, are as follows.
In the second line I leave out the epithet of the Trojan
women, ἑλκεσιπέπλους, altogether. In the sixth line I put in
five words, 'in spite of the future,' which are in the original
by implication only, and are not there actually expressed.
This I do, because Homer, as I have before said, is so remote from one who reads him in English, that the English
translator must be even plainer, if possible, and more un-
ambiguous than Homer himself; the connection of meaning
must be even more distinctly marked in the translation than
in the original. For in the Greek language itself there is
something which brings one nearer to Homer, which gives
one a clue to his thought, which makes a hint enough; but in
the English language this sense of nearness, this clue, is gone;
hints are insufficient, everything must be stated with full distinctness. In the ninth line Homer's epithet for Priam is
ἐϋμμελίω,—'armed with good ashen spear,' say the dictionaries; 'ashen-speared,' translates Mr. Newman, following his

* Dr. Hawtrey also has translated this passage; but here, he has
not, I think, been so successful as in his 'Helen on the walls of Troy.'
[M. A.]

own rule to 'retain every peculiarity of his original,'—I say, on the other hand, that εὔμμελίω has not the effect of a 'peculiarity' in the original, while 'ashen-speared' has the effect of a 'peculiarity' in English; and 'warlike' is as marking an equivalent as I dare give for εὔμμελίω, for fear of disturbing the balance of expression in Homer's sentence. In the fourteenth line, again, I translate χαλκοχιτώνων by 'brazen-coated.' Mr. Newman, meaning to be perfectly literal, translates it by 'brazen-cloaked,' an expression which comes to the reader oddly and unnaturally, while Homer's word comes to him quite naturally; but I venture to go as near to a literal rendering as 'brazen-coated,' because a 'coat of brass' is familiar to us all from the Bible, and familiar, too, as distinctly specified in connection with the wearer. Finally, let me further illustrate from the twentieth line the value which I attach, in a question of diction, to the authority of the Bible. The word 'pre-eminent' occurs in that line; I was a little in doubt whether that was not too bookish an expression to be used in rendering Homer, as I can imagine Mr. Newman to have been a little in doubt whether his 'responsively accosted,' for ἀμειβόμενος προσέφη, was not too bookish an expression. Let us both, I say, consult our Bibles: Mr. Newman will nowhere find it in his Bible that David, for instance, 'responsively accosted Goliath;' but I do find in mine that 'the right hand of the Lord hath the pre-eminence;'[79] and forthwith I use 'pre-eminent,' without scruple. My Bibliolatry is perhaps excessive; and no doubt a true poetic feeling is the Homeric translator's best guide in the use of words; but where this feeling does not exist, or is at fault, I think he cannot do better than take for a mechanical guide Cruden's *Concordance*. To be sure, here as elsewhere, the consulter must know how to consult,—must know how very slight a variation of word or circumstance makes the difference between an authority in his favour, and an authority which gives him no countenance at all; for instance, the 'Great simpleton!' (for μέγα νήπιος) of Mr. Newman, and the 'Thou fool!' of the Bible, are something alike; but 'Thou fool!' is very grand, and 'Great simpleton!' is an atrocity. So, too, Chapman's 'Poor wretched beasts' is pitched many degrees too low; but Shakespeare's 'Poor venomous fool, Be angry and despatch!'[80] is in the grand style.

One more piece of translation and I have done. I will take the passage in which both Chapman and Mr. Newman have already so much excited our astonishment, the passage at the

end of the nineteenth book of the *Iliad,* the dialogue between
Achilles and his horse Xanthus, after the death of Patroclus.
Achilles begins:—

'Xanthus and Balius both, ye far-famed seed of Podarga!
See that ye bring your master home to the host of the Argives
In some other sort than your last, when the battle is ended;
And not leave him behind, a corpse on the plain, like
    Patroclus.'
        Then, from beneath the yoke, the fleet horse Xanthus
            addressed him:
Sudden he bowed his head, and all his mane, as he bowed it,
Streamed to the ground by the yoke, escaping from under
    the collar:
And he was given a voice by the white-armed Goddess Hera.
    'Truly, yet this time will we save thee, mighty Achilles!
But thy day of death is at hand; nor shall *we* be the reason—
No, but the will of heaven, and Fate's invincible power.
For by no slow pace or want of swiftness of ours
Did the Trojans obtain to strip the arms from Patroclus;
But that prince among Gods, the son of the lovely-haired
    Leto,
Slew him fighting in front of the fray, and glorified Hector.
But, for us, we vie in speed with the breath of the West-
    Wind,
Which, men say, is the fleetest of winds; 't is thou who art
    fated
To lie low in death, by the hand of a God and a Mortal.'
        Thus far he; and here his voice was stopped by the
            Furies.
Then, with a troubled heart, the swift Achilles addressed him:
    'Why dost thou prophesy so my death to me, Xanthus? It
        needs not.
I of myself know well, that here I am destined to perish,
Far from my father and mother dear: for all that, I will not
Stay this hand from fight, till the Trojans are utterly routed.'

So he spake, and drove with a cry his steeds into battle.

Here the only particular remark which I will make is, that
in the fourth and eighth lines the grammar is what I call a
loose and idiomatic grammar. In writing a regular and literary style, one would in the fourth line have to repeat before
'leave' the words 'that ye' from the second line, and to insert
the word 'do;' and in the eighth line one would not use such
an expression as 'he was given a voice.' But I will make one
general remark on the character of my own translations, as
I have made so many on that of the translations of others.

It is, that over the graver passages there is shed an air somewhat too strenuous and severe, by comparison with that
lovely ease and sweetness which Homer, for all his noble
and masculine way of thinking, never loses.

Here I stop. I have said so much, because I think that the
task of translating Homer into English verse both will be
re-attempted, and may be re-attempted successfully. There
are great works composed of parts so disparate that one
translator is not likely to have the requisite gifts for poetically rendering all of them. Such are the works of Shakespeare, and Goethe's *Faust;* and these it is best to attempt to
render in prose only. People praise Tieck and Schlegel's version of Shakespeare: I, for my part, would sooner read
Shakespeare in the French prose translation, and that is
saying a great deal; but in the German poets' hands Shakespeare so often gets, especially where he is humorous, an
air of what the French call *niaiserie!*[81] and can anything be
more un-Shakespearian than that? Again; Mr. Hayward's
prose translation of the first part of *Faust*—so good that it
makes one regret Mr. Hayward should have abandoned the
line of translation for a kind of literature which is, to say the
least, somewhat slight[82]—is not likely to be surpassed by
any translation in verse. But poems like the *Iliad,* which, in
the main, are in one manner, may hope to find a poetical
translator so gifted and so trained as to be able to learn that
one manner, and to reproduce it. Only, the poet who would
reproduce this must cultivate in himself a Greek virtue by
no means common among the moderns in general, and the
English in particular,—*moderation.* For Homer has not only
the English vigour, he has the Greek grace; and when one
observes the boisterous, rollicking way in which his English
admirers—even men of genius, like the late Professor Wilson[83]—love to talk of Homer and his poetry, one cannot
help feeling that there is no very deep community of nature
between them and the object of their enthusiasm. 'It is very
well, my good friends,' I always imagine Homer saying to
them, if he could hear them: 'you do me a great deal of
honour, but somehow or other you praise me too like bar-
barians.' For Homer's grandeur is not the mixed and turbid
grandeur of the great poets of the north, of the authors of
Othello and *Faust;* it is a perfect, a lovely grandeur. Certainly his poetry has all the energy and power of the poetry
of our ruder climates; but it has, besides, the pure lines of
an Ionian horizon, the liquid clearness of an Ionian sky.

Last Words

1862

'Multi, qui persequuntur me, et tribulant me: a testimoniis non declinavi.'[84]

BUFFON, the great French naturalist, imposed on himself the rule of steadily abstaining from all answer to attacks made upon him. 'Je n'ai jamais répondu à aucune critique,' he said to one of his friends who, on the occasion of a certain criticism, was eager to take up arms in his behalf; 'je n'ai jamais répondu à aucune critique, et je garderai le même silence sur celle-ci.'[85] On another occasion, when accused of plagiarism, and pressed by his friends to answer, 'Il vaut mieux,' he said, 'laisser ces mauvaises gens dans l'incertitude.'[86] Even when reply to an attack was made successfully, he disapproved of it, he regretted that those he esteemed should make it. Montesquieu, more sensitive to criticism than Buffon, had answered, and successfully answered, an attack made upon his great work, the *Esprit des Lois*, by the *Gazetier Janséniste*. This Jansenist Gazetteer was a periodical of those times,—a periodical such as other times, also, have occasionally seen,—very pretentious, very aggressive, and, when the point to be seized was at all a delicate one, very apt to miss it. 'Notwithstanding this example,' said Buffon,—who, as well as Montesquieu, had been attacked by the Jansenist Gazetteer,—'notwithstanding this example, I think I may promise my course will be different. I shall not answer a single word.'

And to any one who has noticed the baneful effects of controversy, with all its train of personal rivalries and hatreds, on men of letters or men of science; to any one who has observed how it tends to impair, not only their dignity and repose, but their productive force, their genuine

activity; how it always checks the free play of the spirit, and
often ends by stopping it altogether; it can hardly seem
doubtful, that the rule thus imposed on himself by Buffon
was a wise one. His own career, indeed, admirably shows
the wisdom of it. That career was as glorious as it was
serene; but it owed to its serenity no small part of its glory.
The regularity and completeness with which he gradually
built up the great work which he had designed, the air of
equable majesty which he shed over it, struck powerfully
the imagination of his contemporaries, and surrounded Buffon's fame with a peculiar respect and dignity. 'He is,' said
Frederick the Great of him, 'the man who has best deserved
the great celebrity which he has acquired.' And this regularity of production, this equableness of temper, he maintained by his resolute disdain of personal controversy.

Buffon's example seems to me worthy of all imitation, and
in my humble way I mean always to follow it. I never have
replied, I never will reply, to any literary assailant; in such
encounters tempers are lost, the world laughs, and truth is
not served. Least of all should I think of using this Chair[87]
as a place from which to carry on such a conflict. But when
a learned and estimable man thinks he has reason to complain of language used by me in this Chair,—when he attributes to me intentions and feelings towards him which are
far from my heart, I owe him some explanation,—and I am
bound, too, to make the explanation as public as the words
which gave offence. This is the reason why I revert once
more to the subject of translating Homer. But being thus
brought back to that subject, and not wishing to occupy you
solely with an explanation which, after all, is Mr. Newman's
affair and mine, not the public's, I shall take the opportunity,
—not certainly to enter into any conflict with any one,—but
to try to establish our old friend, the coming translator of
Homer, yet a little firmer in the positions which I hope we
have now secured for him; to protect him against the danger
of relaxing, in the confusion of dispute, his attention to those
matters which alone I consider important for him; to save
him from losing sight, in the dust of the attacks delivered
over it, of the real body of Patroclus.[88] He will, probably,
when he arrives, requite my solicitude very ill, and be in
haste to disown his benefactor: but my interest in him is so
sincere that I can disregard his probable ingratitude.

First, however, for the explanation. Mr. Newman has
published a reply[89] to the remarks which I made on his
translation of the *Iliad*. He seems to think that the respect
which at the outset of those remarks I professed for him

must have been professed ironically; he says that I use 'forms of attack against him which he does not know how to characterise;' that I 'speak scornfully' of him, treat him with 'gratuitous insult, gratuitous rancour;' that I 'propagate slanders' against him, that I wish to 'damage him with my readers,' to 'stimulate my readers to despise' him. He is entirely mistaken. I respect Mr. Newman sincerely; I respect him as one of the few learned men we have, one of the few who love learning for its own sake; this respect for him I had before I read his translation of the *Iliad*, I retained it while I was commenting on that translation, I have not lost it after reading his reply. Any vivacities of expression which may have given him pain I sincerely regret, and can only assure him that I used them without a thought of insult or rancour. When I took the liberty of creating the verb *to Newmanise*, my intentions were no more rancorous than if I had said to *Miltonise*; when I exclaimed, in my astonishment at his vocabulary, 'With whom can Mr. Newman have lived?' I meant merely to convey, in a familiar form of speech, the sense of bewilderment one has at finding a person to whom words one thought all the world knew seem strange, and words one thought entirely strange, intelligible. Yet this simple expression of my bewilderment Mr. Newman construes into an accusation that he is 'often guilty of keeping low company,' and says that I shall 'never want a stone to throw at him.' And what is stranger still, one of his friends gravely tells me that Mr. Newman 'lived with the fellows of Balliol.' As if that made Mr. Newman's glossary less inexplicable to me! As if he could have got his glossary from the fellows of Balliol! As if I could believe that the members of that distinguished society—of whose discourse, not so many years afterwards, I myself was an unworthy hearer—were in Mr. Newman's time so far removed from the Attic purity of speech which we all of us admired, that when one of them called a calf a *bulkin*, the rest 'easily understood' him; or, when he wanted to say that a newspaper-article was 'proudly fine,' it mattered little whether he said it was that or *bragly!* No; his having lived with the fellows of Balliol does not explain Mr. Newman's glossary to me. I will no longer ask 'with whom he can have lived,' since that gives him offence; but I must still declare that where he got his test of rarity or intelligibility for words is a mystery to me.

That, however, does not prevent me from entertaining a very sincere respect for Mr. Newman, and since he doubts it, I am glad to reiterate my expression of it. But the truth of the matter is this: I unfeignedly admire Mr. Newman's ability and learning; but I think in his translation of Homer he has employed that ability and learning quite amiss. I think he has chosen quite the wrong field for turning his ability and learning to account. I think that in England, partly from the want of an Academy, partly from a national habit of intellect to which that want of an Academy is itself due, there exists too little of what I may call a public force of correct literary opinion, possessing within certain limits a clear sense of what is right and wrong, sound and unsound, and sharply recalling men of ability and learning from any flagrant misdirection of these their advantages. I think, even, that in our country a powerful misdirection of this kind is often more likely to subjugate and pervert opinion than to be checked and corrected by it.* Hence a chaos of false tendencies, wasted efforts, impotent conclusions, works which ought never to have been undertaken. Any one who can introduce a little order into this chaos by establishing in any quarter a single sound rule of criticism, a single rule which clearly marks what is right as right, and what is wrong as wrong, does a good deed; and his deed is so much the better the greater force he counteracts of learning and ability applied to thicken the chaos. Of course no one can be sure that he has fixed any such rules; he can only do his best to fix them; but somewhere or other, in the literary opinion of Europe, if not in the literary opinion of one nation, in fifty years, if not in five, there is a final judgment on these matters, and the critic's work will at last stand or fall by its true merits.

Meanwhile, the charge of having in one instance misapplied his powers, of having once followed a false tendency, is no such grievous charge to bring against a man; it does not exclude a great respect for himself personally, or for his powers in the happier manifestation of them. False tendency is, I have said, an evil to which the artist or the man of letters in England is peculiarly prone; but everywhere in our time he is liable to it,—the greatest as well as the humblest. 'The first beginnings of my *Wilhelm Meister*,' says Goethe,

* 'It is the fact, that scholars of fastidious refinement, but of a judgment which I think far more masculine than Mr. Arnold's, have passed a most encouraging sentence on large specimens of my translation. I at present count eight such names.'—'Before venturing to print, I sought to ascertain how unlearned women and children would accept my verses. I could boast how children and half-educated women have extolled them, how greedily a working man has inquired for them, without knowing who was the translator.'— Mr. Newman's Reply, pp. 2, 12, 13. [M. A.]

'arose out of an obscure sense of the great truth that man will often attempt something for which nature has denied him the proper powers, will undertake and practise something in which he cannot become skilled. An inward feeling warns him to desist' (yes, but there are, unhappily, cases of absolute judicial blindness!), 'nevertheless he cannot get clear in himself about it, and is driven along a false road to a false goal, without knowing how it is with him. To this we may refer everything which goes by the name of false tendency, dilettantism, and so on. A great many men waste in this way the fairest portion of their lives, and fall at last into wonderful delusion.' Yet after all,—Goethe adds,—it sometimes happens that even on this false road a man finds, not indeed that which he sought, but something which is good and useful for him; 'like Saul, the son of Kish, who went forth to look for his father's asses, and found a kingdom.' And thus false tendency as well as true, vain effort as well as fruitful, go together to produce that great movement of life, to present that immense and magic spectacle of human affairs, which from boyhood to old age fascinates the gaze of every man of imagination, and which would be his terror, if it were not at the same time his delight.

So Mr. Newman may see how wide-spread a danger it is, to which he has, as I think, in setting himself to translate Homer, fallen a prey. He may be well satisfied if he can escape from it by paying it the tribute of a single work only. He may judge how unlikely it is that I should 'despise' him for once falling a prey to it. I know far too well how exposed to it we all are; how exposed to it I myself am. At this very moment, for example, I am fresh from reading Mr. Newman's Reply to my Lectures, a reply full of that erudition in which (as I am so often and so good-naturedly reminded, but indeed I know it without being reminded) Mr. Newman is immeasurably my superior. Well, the demon that pushes us all to our ruin is even now prompting me to follow Mr. Newman into a discussion about the digamma, and I know not what providence holds me back. And some day, I have no doubt, I shall lecture on the language of the Berbers, and give him his entire revenge.

But Mr. Newman does not confine himself to complaints on his own behalf, he complains on Homer's behalf too. He says that my 'statements about Greek literature are against the most notorious and elementary fact;' that I 'do a public wrong to literature by publishing them;' and that the Professors to whom I appealed in my three Lectures, 'would only lose credit if they sanctioned the use I make of their names.' He does these eminent men the kindness of adding, however, that 'whether they are pleased with this parading of their names in behalf of paradoxical error, he may well doubt,' and that 'until they endorse it themselves, he shall treat my process as a piece of forgery.' He proceeds to discuss my statements at great length, and with an erudition and ingenuity which nobody can admire more than I do. And he ends by saying that my ignorance is great.

Alas! that is very true. Much as Mr. Newman was mistaken when he talked of my rancour, he is entirely right when he talks of my ignorance. And yet, perverse as it seems to say so, I sometimes find myself wishing, when dealing with these matters of poetical criticism, that my ignorance were even greater than it is. To handle these matters properly there is needed a poise so perfect that the least overweight in any direction tends to destroy the balance. Temper destroys it, a crotchet destroys it, even erudition may destroy it. To press to the sense of the thing itself with which one is dealing, not to go off on some collateral issue about the thing, is the hardest matter in the world. The 'thing itself' with which one is here dealing,—the critical perception of poetic truth,—is of all things the most volatile, elusive, and evanescent; by even pressing too impetuously after it, one runs the risk of losing it. The critic of poetry should have the finest tact, the nicest moderation, the most free, flexible, and elastic spirit imaginable; he should be indeed the 'ondoyant et divers,' the *undulating and diverse* being of Montaigne.[90] The less he can deal with his object simply and freely, the more things he has to take into account in dealing with it,—the more, in short, he has to encumber himself,— so much the greater force of spirit he needs to retain his elasticity. But one cannot exactly have this greater force by wishing for it; so, for the force of spirit one has, the load put upon it is often heavier than it will well bear. The late Duke of Wellington said of a certain peer that 'it was a great pity his education had been so far too much for his abilities.' In like manner, one often sees erudition out of all proportion to its owner's critical faculty. Little as I know, therefore, I am always apprehensive, in dealing with poetry, lest even that little should prove 'too much for my abilities.'

With this consciousness of my own lack of learning,— nay, with this sort of acquiescence in it, with this belief that for the labourer in the field of poetical criticism learning has its disadvantages,—I am not likely to dispute with Mr. Newman about matters of erudition. All that he says on these matters in his Reply I read with great interest; in general I agree with him; but only, I am sorry to say, up to a certain point. Like all learned men, accustomed to desire definite rules, he draws his conclusions too absolutely; he wants to include too much under his rules; he does not quite perceive that in poetical criticism the shade, the fine distinction, is everything; and that, when he has once missed this, in all he says he is in truth but beating the air. For instance: because I think Homer noble, he imagines I must think him elegant; and in fact he says in plain words that I do think him so,— that to me Homer seems 'pervadingly elegant.' But he does not. Virgil is elegant,—'pervadingly elegant,'—even in passages of the highest emotion:

> O, ubi campi,
> Spercheosque, et virginibus bacchata Lacænis
> Taygeta!*

Even there Virgil, though of a divine elegance, is still elegant: but Homer is not elegant; the word is quite a wrong one to apply to him, and Mr. Newman is quite right in blaming any one he finds so applying it. Again; arguing against my assertion that Homer is not quaint, he says: 'It is quaint to call waves *wet*, milk *white*, blood *dusky*, horses *single-hoofed*, words *winged*, Vulcan *Lobfoot* (Κυλλοποδίων), a spear *longshadowy*,' and so on. I find I know not how many distinctions to draw here. I do not think it quaint to call waves *wet*, or milk *white*, or words *winged*; but I do think it quaint to call horses *single-hoofed*, or Vulcan *Lobfoot*, or a spear *longshadowy*. As to calling blood *dusky*, I do not feel quite sure; I will tell Mr. Newman my opinion when I see the passage in which he calls it so. But then, again, because it is quaint to call Vulcan *Lobfoot*, I cannot admit that it was quaint to call him Κυλλοποδίων; nor that, because it is quaint to call a spear *longshadowy*, it was quaint to call it δολιχόσκιον. Here Mr. Newman's erudition misleads him: he knows the literal value of the Greek so well, that he thinks his literal rendering identical with the Greek, and that the Greek must stand or fall along with his rendering. But the real question is, not whether he has given us, so to speak, full change for the Greek, but *how* he gives us our change: we want it in gold, and he gives it us in copper. Again: 'It is quaint,' says Mr. Newman, 'to address a young

* 'O for the fields of Thessaly and the streams of Spercheios! O for the hills alive with the dances of the Laconian maidens, the hills of Taygetus!'—*Georgics*, ii. 486. [M. A.]

friend as "O Pippin!"—it is quaint to compare Ajax to an
ass whom boys are belabouring.' Here, too, Mr. Newman
goes much too fast, and his category of quaintness is too
comprehensive. To address a young friend as 'O Pippin!' is,
I cordially agree with him, very quaint; although I do not
think it was quaint in Sarpedon to address Glaucus as ὦ
πέπον: but in comparing, whether in Greek or in English,
Ajax to an ass whom boys are belabouring, I do not see that
there is of necessity anything quaint at all. Again; because
I said that *eld, lief, in sooth,* and other words, are, as Mr.
Newman uses them in certain places, bad words, he imagines
that I must mean to stamp these words with an absolute
reprobation; and because I said that 'my Bibliolatry is excessive,' he imagines that I brand all words as ignoble which
are not in the Bible. Nothing of the kind: there are no such
absolute rules to be laid down in these matters. The Bible
vocabulary is to be used as an assistance, not as an authority.
Of the words which, placed where Mr. Newman places
them, I have called bad words, every one may be excellent
in some other place. Take *eld,* for instance: when Shakespeare, reproaching man with the dependence in which his
youth is passed, says:

> all thy blessed youth
> Becomes as aged, and doth beg the alms
> Of palsied *eld,* . . .[91]

it seems to me that *eld* comes in excellently there, in a passage of curious meditation; but when Mr. Newman renders
ἀγήρω τ' ἀθανάτω τε by 'from *Eld* and Death exempted,' it
seems to me he infuses a tinge of quaintness into the trans-
parent simplicity of Homer's expression, and so I call *eld* a
bad word in that place.

Once more. Mr. Newman lays it down as a general rule
that 'many of Homer's energetic descriptions are expressed
in coarse physical words.' He goes on: 'I give one illustration,—Τρῶες προὔτυψαν ἀολλέες. Cowper, misled by the *ignis
fatuus*[92] of "stateliness," renders it absurdly:

> The powers of Ilium gave the first assault
> Embattled close;[93]

but it is, strictly, 'The Trojans *knocked forward* (or,
thumped, butted forward) *in close pack."* The verb is too
coarse for later polished prose, and even the adjective is very
strong (*packed together*). I believe, that "forward in pack
the Trojans pitched," would not be really unfaithful to the
Homeric colour; and I maintain, that "forward in mass the

Trojans pitched," would be an irreprovable rendering.' He actually gives us all that as if it were a piece of scientific deduction; and as if, at the end, he had arrived at an incontrovertible conclusion. But, in truth, one cannot settle these matters quite in this way. Mr. Newman's general rule may be true or false (I dislike to meddle with general rules), but every part in what follows must stand or fall by itself, and its soundness or unsoundness has nothing at all to do with the truth or falsehood of Mr. Newman's general rule. He first gives, as a strict rendering of the Greek, 'The Trojans knocked forward (or, thumped, butted forward), in close pack.' I need not say that, as a 'strict rendering of the Greek,' this is good,—all Mr. Newman's 'strict renderings of the Greek' are sure to be, as such, good; but 'in close pack,' for δολλέες, seems to me to be what Mr. Newman's renderings are not always,—an excellent *poetical rendering* of the Greek; a thousand times better, certainly, than Cowper's 'embattled close.' Well, but Mr. Newman goes on: 'I believe, that "forward in pack the Trojans pitched," would not be really unfaithful to the Homeric colour.' Here, I say, the Homeric colour is half washed out of Mr. Newman's happy rendering of δολλέες; while in 'pitched' for προύτυψαν, the literal fidelity of the first rendering is gone, while certainly no Homeric colour has come in its place. Finally, Mr. Newman concludes: 'I maintain that "forward in mass the Trojans pitched," would be an irreprovable rendering.' Here, in what Mr. Newman fancies his final moment of triumph, Homeric colour and literal fidelity have alike abandoned him altogether; the last stage of his translation is much worse than the second, and immeasurably worse than the first.

All this to show that a looser, easier method than Mr. Newman's must be taken, if we are to arrive at any good result in these questions. I now go on to follow Mr. Newman a little further, not at all as wishing to dispute with him, but as seeking (and this is the true fruit we may gather from criticisms upon us) to gain hints from him for the establishment of some useful truth about our subject, even when I think him wrong. I still retain, I confess, my conviction that Homer's characteristic qualities are rapidity of movement, plainness of words and style, simplicity and directness of ideas, and, above all, nobleness, the grand manner. Whenever Mr. Newman drops a word, awakens a train of thought, which leads me to see any of these characteristics more clearly, I am grateful to him; and one or two suggestions of this kind which he affords, are all that now,—having expressed my sorrow that he should have misconceived my feelings towards him, and pointed out what I think the vice of his method of criticism,—I have to notice in his Reply.

Such a suggestion I find in Mr. Newman's remarks on my assertion that the translator of Homer must not adopt a quaint and antiquated style in rendering him, because the impression which Homer makes upon the living scholar is not that of a poet quaint and antiquated, but that of a poet perfectly simple, perfectly intelligible. I added that we cannot, I confess, really know how Homer seemed to Sophocles, but that it is impossible to me to believe that he seemed to him quaint and antiquated. Mr. Newman asserts, on the other hand, that I am absurdly wrong here; that Homer seemed 'out and out' quaint and antiquated to the Athenians; that 'every sentence of him was more or less antiquated to Sophocles, who could no more help feeling at every instant the foreign and antiquated character of the poetry than an Englishman can help feeling the same in reading Burns's poems.' And not only does Mr. Newman say this, but he has managed thoroughly to convince some of his readers of it. 'Homer's Greek,' says one of them, 'certainly seemed antiquated to the historical times of Greece. Mr. Newman, taking a far broader historical and philological view than Mr. Arnold, stoutly maintains that it did seem so.' And another says: 'Doubtless Homer's dialect and diction were as hard and obscure to a later Attic Greek as Chaucer to an Englishman of our day.'

Mr. Newman goes on to say, that not only was Homer antiquated relatively to Pericles, but he is antiquated to the living scholar; and, indeed, is in himself 'absolutely antique, being the poet of a barbarian age.' He tells us of his 'inexhaustible quaintnesses,' of his 'very eccentric diction;' and he infers, of course, that he is perfectly right in rendering him in a quaint and antiquated style.

Now this question,—whether or no Homer seemed quaint and antiquated to Sophocles,—I call a delightful question to raise. It is not a barren verbal dispute; it is a question 'drenched in matter,' to use an expression of Bacon; a question full of flesh and blood, and of which the scrutiny, though I still think we cannot settle it absolutely, may yet give us a directly useful result. To scrutinise it may lead us to see more clearly what sort of a style a modern translator of Homer ought to adopt.

Homer's verses were some of the first words which a young Athenian heard. He heard them from his mother or his nurse before he went to school; and at school, when he went there, he was constantly occupied with them. So much did he hear of them that Socrates proposes, in the interests of morality, to have selections from Homer made, and placed in the hands of mothers and nurses, in his model republic; in order that, of an author with whom they were sure to be so perpetually conversant, the young might learn only those parts which might do them good. His language was as familiar to Sophocles, we may be quite sure, as the language of the Bible is to us.

Nay, more. Homer's language was not, of course, in the time of Sophocles, the spoken or written language of ordinary life, any more than the language of the Bible, any more than the language of poetry, is with us; but for one great species of composition—epic poetry—it was still the current language; it was the language in which every one who made that sort of poetry composed. Every one at Athens who dabbled in epic poetry, not only understood Homer's language,—he possessed it. He possessed it as every one who dabbles in poetry with us, possesses what may be called the poetical vocabulary, as distinguished from the vocabulary of common speech and of modern prose: I mean, such expressions as *perchance* for *perhaps*, *spake* for *spoke*, *aye* for *ever*, *don* for *put on*, *charméd* for *charm'd*, and thousands of others.

I might go to Burns and Chaucer, and, taking words and passages from them, ask if they afforded any parallel to a language so familiar and so possessed. But this I will not do, for Mr. Newman himself supplies me with what he thinks a fair parallel, in its effect upon us, to the language of Homer in its effect upon Sophocles. He says that such words as *mon, londis, libbard, withouten, muchel,* give us a tolerable but incomplete notion of this parallel; and he finally exhibits the parallel in all its clearness, by this poetical specimen:—

> Dat mon, quhich hauldeth Kyngis-af
>   Londis yn féo, niver
> (I tell 'e) feereth aught; sith hee
>   Doth hauld hys londis yver.

Now, does Mr. Newman really think that Sophocles could, as he says, 'no more help feeling at every instant the foreign and antiquated character of Homer, than an Englishman can help feeling the same in hearing' these lines? Is he quite sure of it? He says he is; he will not allow of any doubt or hesitation in the matter. I had confessed we could not really

know how Homer seemed to Sophocles;—'Let Mr. Arnold
confess for himself,' cries Mr. Newman, 'and not for me,
who know perfectly well.' And this is what he knows!

Mr. Newman says, however, that I 'play fallaciously on
the words familiar and unfamiliar;' that 'Homer's words
may have been familiar to the Athenians (*i.e.* often heard)
even when they were either not understood by them or else,
being understood, were yet felt and known to be utterly
foreign. Let my renderings,' he continues, 'be heard, as Pope
or even Cowper has been heard, and no one will be "surprised." '

But the whole question is here. The translator must not
assume that to have taken place which has not taken place,
although, perhaps, he may wish it to have taken place,—
namely, that his diction is become an established possession
of the minds of men, and therefore is, in its proper place,
familiar to them, will not 'surprise' them. If Homer's language was familiar,—that is, often heard,—then to this
language words like *londis* and *libbard*, which are not familiar, offer, for the translator's purpose, no parallel. For some
purpose of the philologer they may offer a parallel to it; for
the translator's purpose they offer none. The question is not,
whether a diction is antiquated for current speech, but
whether it is antiquated for that particular purpose for
which it is employed. A diction that is antiquated for common speech and common prose, may very well not be
antiquated for poetry or certain special kinds of prose.
'Peradventure there shall be ten found there,'[94] is not antiquated for Biblical prose, though for conversation or for a
newspaper it is antiquated. 'The trumpet spake not to the
arméd throng,'[95] is not antiquated for poetry, although we
should not write in a letter, 'he *spake* to me,' or say, 'the
British soldier is *arméd* with the Enfield rifle.' But when
language is antiquated for that particular purpose for which
it is employed,—as numbers of Chaucer's words, for instance, are antiquated for poetry,—such language is a bad
representative of language which, like Homer's, was never
antiquated for that particular purpose for which it was employed. I imagine that Πηληϊάδεω for Πηηλειδου, in Homer, no
more sounded antiquated to Sophocles, than *arméd* for
arm'd, in Milton, sounds antiquated to us; but Mr. Newman's *withouten* and *muchel* do sound to us antiquated,
even for poetry, and therefore they do not correspond in
their effect upon us with Homer's words in their effect upon
Sophocles. When Chaucer, who uses such words, is to pass
current amongst us, to be familiar to us, as Homer was

familiar to the Athenians, he has to be modernised, as Wordsworth and others[96] set to work to modernise him; but an Athenian no more needed to have Homer modernised, than we need to have the Bible modernised, or Wordsworth himself.

Therefore, when Mr. Newman's words *bragly, bulkin*, and the rest, are an established possession of our minds, as Homer's words were an established possession of an Athenian's mind, he may use them; but not till then. Chaucer's words, the words of Burns, great poets as these were, are yet not thus an established possession of an Englishman's mind, and therefore they must not be used in rendering Homer into English.

Mr. Newman has been misled just by doing that which his admirer praises him for doing, by taking a 'far broader historical and philological view than' mine. Precisely because he has done this, and has applied the 'philological view' where it was not applicable, but where the 'poetical view' alone was rightly applicable, he has fallen into error.

It is the same with him in his remarks on the difficulty and obscurity of Homer. Homer, I say, is perfectly plain in speech, simple, and intelligible. And I infer from this that his translator, too, ought to be perfectly plain in speech, simple, and intelligible; ought not to say, for instance, in rendering

Οὔτε κε σὲ στέλλοιμι μάχην ἐς κυδιάνειραν . . .[97]

'Nor liefly thee would I advance to man-ennobling battle,' —and things of that kind. Mr. Newman hands me a list of some twenty hard words, invokes Buttmann, Mr. Malden, and M. Benfey, and asks me if I think myself wiser than all the world of Greek scholars, and if I am ready to supply the deficiencies of Liddell and Scott's *Lexicon!* But here, again, Mr. Newman errs by not perceiving that the question is one not of scholarship, but of a poetical translation of Homer. This, I say, should be perfectly simple and intelligible. He replies by telling me that ἀδινός, εἰλίποδες, and σιγαλόεις are hard words. Well, but what does he infer from that? That the poetical translator, in his rendering of them, is to give us a sense of the difficulties of the scholar, and so is to make his translation obscure? If he does not mean that, how, by bringing forward these hard words, does he touch the question whether an English version of Homer should be plain or not plain? If Homer's poetry, as poetry, is in its general effect on the poetical reader perfectly simple and intelligible, the uncertainty of the scholar about the true

meaning of certain words can never change this general
effect. Rather will the poetry of Homer make us forget his
philology, than his philology make us forget his poetry. It
may even be affirmed that every one who reads Homer perpetually for the sake of enjoying his poetry (and no one
who does not so read him will ever translate him well),
comes at last to form a perfectly clear sense in his own
mind for every important word in Homer, such as ἀδινὸς, or
ἠλίβατος, whatever the scholar's doubts about the word may
be. And this sense is present to his mind with perfect clearness and fulness, whenever the word recurs, although as a
scholar he may know that he cannot be sure whether this
sense is the right one or not. But poetically he feels clearly
about the word, although philologically he may not. The
scholar in him may hesitate, like the father in Sheridan's
play; but the reader of poetry in him is, like the governor,
fixed.[98] The same thing happens to us with our own language. How many words occur in the Bible, for instance, to
which thousands of hearers do not feel sure they attach the
precise real meaning; but they make out *a* meaning for them
out of what materials they have at hand; and the words,
heard over and over again, come to convey this meaning,
with a certainty which poetically is adequate, though not
philologically. How many have attached a clear and poetically adequate sense to 'the *beam*' and 'the *mote*,'[99] though
not precisely the right one! How clearly, again, have readers
got a sense from Milton's words, 'grate on their *scrannel*
pipes,'[100] who yet might have been puzzled to write a commentary on the word *scrannel* for the dictionary! So we get
a clear sense from ἀδινὸς as an epithet for grief, after often
meeting with it and finding out all we can about it, even
though that all be philologically insufficient; so we get a clear
sense from εἰλίποδες as an epithet for cows. And this his clear
poetical sense about the words, not his philological uncer-
tainties about them, is what the translator has to convey.
Words like *bragly* and *bulkin* offer no parallel to these
words; because the reader, from his entire want of familiarity with the words *bragly* and *bulkin,* has no clear sense of
them poetically.

Perplexed by his knowledge of the philological aspect of
Homer's language, encumbered by his own learning, Mr.
Newman, I say, misses the poetical aspect, misses that with
which alone we are here concerned. 'Homer *is* odd,' he per-
sists, fixing his eyes on his own philological analysis of
μῶνυξ, and μέροψ, and Κυλλοποδίων, and not on these words in
their synthetic character;—just as Professor Max Müller,

going a little farther back, and fixing his attention on the elementary value of the word θυγάτηρ, might say Homer was 'odd' for using *that* word;—'if the whole Greek nation, by long familiarity, had become inobservant of Homer's oddities,'—of the oddities of this 'noble barbarian,' as Mr. Newman elsewhere calls him, this 'noble barbarian' with the 'lively eye of the savage,'—'that would be no fault of mine. That would not justify Mr. Arnold's blame of me for rendering the words correctly.' *Correctly,*—ah, but what *is* correctness in this case? This correctness of his is the very rock on which Mr. Newman has split. He is so correct that at last he finds peculiarity everywhere. The true knowledge of Homer becomes at last, in his eyes, a knowledge of Homer's 'peculiarities, pleasant and unpleasant.' Learned men know these 'peculiarities,' and Homer is to be translated because the unlearned are impatient to know them too. 'That,' he exclaims, 'is just why people want to read an English Homer,—*to know all his oddities, just as learned men do.*' Here I am obliged to shake my head, and to declare that, in spite of all my respect for Mr. Newman, I cannot go these lengths with him. He talks of my 'monomaniac fancy that there is nothing quaint or antique in Homer.' Terrible learning,—I cannot help in my turn exclaiming,—terrible learning, which discovers so much!

Here, then, I take my leave of Mr. Newman, retaining my opinion that his version of Homer is spoiled by his making Homer odd and ignoble; but having, I hope, sufficient love for literature to be able to canvass works without thinking of persons, and to hold this or that production cheap, while retaining a sincere respect, on other grounds, for its author.

In fulfilment of my promise to take this opportunity for giving the translator of Homer a little further advice, I proceed to notice one or two other criticisms which I find, in like manner, *suggestive;* which give us an opportunity, that is, of seeing more clearly, as we look into them, the true principles on which translation of Homer should rest. This is all I seek in criticisms; and, perhaps (as I have already said) it is only as one seeks a positive result of this kind, that one can get any fruit from them. Seeking a negative result from them,—personal altercation and wrangling,—one gets no fruit; seeking a positive result,—the elucidation and establishment of one's ideas,—one may get much. Even bad criticisms may thus be made suggestive and fruitful. I declared, in a former lecture on this subject, my conviction that criticism is not the strong point of our national literature. Well, even the bad criticisms on our present topic which I meet with, serve to illustrate this conviction for me. And thus one is enabled, even in reading remarks which for Homeric criticism, for their immediate subject, have no value,—which are far too personal in spirit, far too immoderate in temper, and far too heavy-handed in style, for the delicate matter they have to treat,—still to gain light and confirmation for a serious idea, and to follow the Baconian injunction, *semper aliquid addiscere*, always to be adding to one's stock of observation and knowledge. Yes, even when we have to do with writers who,—to quote the words of an exquisite critic, the master of us all in criticism, M. Sainte-Beuve,—remind us, when they handle such subjects as our present, of 'Romans of the fourth or fifth century, coming to hold forth, all at random, in African style, on papers found in the desk of Augustus, Mæcenas, or Pollio,'—even then we may instruct ourselves if we regard ideas and not persons; even then we may enable ourselves to say, with the same critic describing the effect made upon him by D'Argenson's *Memoirs:* 'My taste is revolted, but I learn something;—*Je suis choqué mais je suis instruit.'*

But let us pass to criticisms which are suggestive directly and not thus indirectly only,—criticisms by examining which we may be brought nearer to what immediately interests us, —the right way of translating Homer.

I said that Homer did not rise and sink with his subject, was never to be called prosaic and low. This gives surprise to many persons, who object that parts of the *Iliad* are certainly pitched lower than others, and who remind me of a number of absolutely level passages in Homer. But I never denied that a *subject* must rise and sink, that it must have its elevated and its level regions; all I deny is, that a poet can be said to rise and sink when all that he, as a poet, can do, is perfectly well done; when he is perfectly sound and good, that is, perfect as a poet, in the level regions of his subject as well as in its elevated regions. Indeed, what distinguishes the greatest masters of poetry from all others is, that they are perfectly sound and poetical in these level regions of their subject,—in these regions which are the great difficulty of all poets but the very greatest, which they never quite know what to do with. A poet may sink in these regions by being falsely grand as well as by being low; he sinks, in short, whenever he does not treat his matter, whatever it is, in a perfectly good and poetic way. But, so long as he treats it in this way, he cannot be said to *sink*, whatever his matter

may do. A passage of the simplest narrative is quoted to me
from Homer:—

ὤτρυνεν δὲ ἕκαστον ἐποιχόμενος ἐπέεσσιν,
Μέσθλην τε, Γλαῦκόν τε, Μέδοντά τε, Θερσίλοχόν τε . . .*

and I am asked, whether Homer does not sink *there;* whether
he *'can* have intended such lines as those for poetry?' My
answer is: Those lines are very good poetry indeed, poetry of
the best class, *in that place*. But when Wordsworth, having
to narrate a very plain matter, tries *not* to sink in narrating
it, tries, in short, to be what is falsely called poetical, he
does sink, although he sinks by being pompous, not by
being low.

> Onward we drove beneath the Castle; caught
> While crossing Magdalene Bridge, a glimpse of Cam,
> And at the Hoop alighted, famous inn.[102]

That last line shows excellently how a poet may sink with
his subject by resolving not to sink with it. A page or two
farther on, the subject rises to grandeur, and then Wordsworth is nobly worthy of it:—

> The antechapel, where the statue stood
> Of Newton with his prism and silent face,
> The marble index of a mind for ever
> Voyaging through strange seas of thought, alone.

But the supreme poet is he who is thoroughly sound and
poetical, alike when his subject is grand, and when it is
plain: with him the subject may sink, but never the poet.
But a Dutch painter does not rise and sink with his subject,
—Defoe, in *Moll Flanders*, does not rise and sink with his
subject,—in so far as an artist cannot be said to sink who
is sound in his treatment of his subject, however plain it is:
yet Defoe, yet a Dutch painter, may in one sense be said to
sink with their subject, because though sound in their treatment of it, they are not *poetical*,—poetical in the true, not
the false sense of the word; because, in fact, they are not in
the grand style. Homer can in no sense be said to sink with
his subject, because his soundness has something more than
literal naturalness about it; because his soundness is the
soundness of Homer, of a great epic poet; because, in fact,
he is in the grand style. So he sheds over the simplest matter
he touches the charm of his grand manner; he makes everything noble. Nothing has raised more questioning among my

* *Iliad*, xvii. 216. [M. A.][101]

critics than these words,—*noble, the grand style.* People complain that I do not define these words sufficiently, that I do not tell them enough about them. 'The grand style,— but what *is* the grand style?'—they cry; some with an inclination to believe in it, but puzzled; others mockingly and with incredulity. Alas! the grand style is the last matter in the world for verbal definition to deal with adequately. One may say of it as is said of faith: 'One must feel it in order to know what it is.' But, as of faith, so too one may say of nobleness, of the grand style: 'Woe to those who know it not!' Yet this expression, though indefinable, has a charm; one is the better for considering it; *bonum est, nos hic esse;*[103] one loves to try to explain it, though one knows that one must speak imperfectly. For those, then, who ask the question,—What is the grand style?—with sincerity, I will try to make some answer, inadequate as it must be. For those who ask it mockingly I have no answer, except to repeat to them, with compassionate sorrow, the Gospel words: *Moriemini in peccatis vestris,*—Ye shall die in your sins.[104]

But let me, at any rate, have the pleasure of again giving, before I begin to try and define the grand style, a specimen of what it *is.*

> Standing on earth, not rapt above the pole,
> More safe I sing with mortal voice, unchanged
> To hoarse or mute, though fall'n on evil days,
> On evil days though fall'n, and evil tongues. . . .[105]

There is the grand style in perfection; and any one who has a sense for it, will feel it a thousand times better from repeating those lines than from hearing anything I can say about it.

Let us try, however, what *can* be said, controlling what we say by examples. I think it will be found that the grand style arises in poetry, *when a noble nature, poetically gifted, treats with simplicity or with severity a serious subject.* I think this definition will be found to cover all instances of the grand style in poetry which present themselves. I think it will be found to exclude all poetry which is not in the grand style. And I think it contains no terms which are obscure, which themselves need defining. Even those who do not understand what is meant by calling poetry noble, will understand, I imagine, what is meant by speaking of a noble nature in a man. But the noble or powerful nature—the *bedeutendes Individuum* of Goethe—is not enough. For instance, Mr. Newman has zeal for learning, zeal for thinking, zeal for liberty, and all these things are noble, they ennoble a man; but he has not the poetical gift: there must be the poetical gift, the 'divine faculty,' also. And, besides all this, the subject must be a serious one (for it is only by a kind of license that we can speak of the grand style in comedy); and it must be treated *with simplicity or severity*. Here is the great difficulty: the poets of the world have been many; there has been wanting neither abundance of poetical gift nor abundance of noble natures; but a poetical gift so happy, in a noble nature so circumstanced and trained, that the result is a continuous style, perfect in simplicity or perfect in severity, has been extremely rare. One poet has had the gifts of nature and faculty in unequalled fulness, without the circumstances and training which make this sustained perfection of style possible. Of other poets, some have caught this perfect strain now and then, in short pieces or single lines, but have not been able to maintain it through considerable works; others have composed all their productions in a style which, by comparison with the best, one must call secondary.

The best model of the grand style simple is Homer; perhaps the best model of the grand style severe is Milton. But Dante is remarkable for affording admirable examples of both styles; he has the grand style which arises from simplicity, and he has the grand style which arises from severity; and from him I will illustrate them both. In a former lecture I pointed out what that severity of poetical style is, which comes from saying a thing with a kind of intense compression, or in an allusive, brief, almost haughty way, as if the poet's mind were charged with so many and such grave matters, that he would not deign to treat any one of them explicitly. Of this severity the last line of the following stanza of the *Purgatory* is a good example. Dante has been telling Forese that Virgil had guided him through Hell, and he goes on:—

> Indi m' han tratto su gli suoi conforti,
> Salendo e rigirando la Montagna
> *Che drizza voi che il mondo fece torti.**

'Thence hath his comforting aid led me up, climbing and circling the Mountain, *which straightens you whom the world made crooked.*' These last words, 'la Montagna *che drizza voi che il mondo fece torti,*'—'the Mountain *which straightens you whom the world made crooked,*'—for the Mountain of Purgatory, I call an excellent specimen of the

* *Purgatory*, xxiii. 124. [M. A.]

grand style in severity, where the poet's mind is too full charged to suffer him to speak more explicitly. But the very next stanza is a beautiful specimen of the grand style in simplicity, where a noble nature and a poetical gift unite to utter a thing with the most limpid plainness and clearness:—

> Tanto dice di farmi sua compagna
> Ch' io sarò là dove fia Beatrice;
> Quivi convien che senza lui rimagna.*

'So long,' Dante continues, 'so long he (Virgil) saith he will bear me company, until I shall be there where Beatrice is; there it behoves that without him I remain.' But the noble simplicity of that in the Italian no words of mine can render.

Both these styles, the simple and the severe, are truly grand; the severe seems, perhaps, the grandest, so long as we attend most to the great personality, to the noble nature, in the poet its author; the simple seems the grandest when we attend most to the exquisite faculty, to the poetical gift. But the simple is no doubt to be preferred. It is the more *magical*: in the other there is something intellectual, something which gives scope for a play of thought which may exist where the poetical gift is either wanting or present in only inferior degree: the severe is much more imitable, and this a little spoils its charm. A kind of semblance of this style keeps Young going, one may say, through all the nine parts of that most indifferent production, the *Night Thoughts*.[106] But the grand style in simplicity is inimitable:

> αἰὼν ἀσφαλὴς
> οὐκ ἔγεντ' οὔτ' Αἰακίδᾳ παρὰ Πηλεῖ,
> οὔτε παρ' ἀντιθέῳ Κάδμῳ · λέγονται μὰν βροτῶν
> ὄλβον ὑπέρτατον οἳ σχεῖν, οἵ τε καὶ χρυσαμπύκων
> μελπομενᾶν ἐν ὄρει Μοισᾶν, καὶ ἐν ἑπταπύλοις
> ἄϊον Θήβαις . . .†

There is a limpidness in that, a want of salient points to seize and transfer, which makes imitation impossible, except by a genius akin to the genius which produced it.

Greek simplicity and Greek grace are inimitable; but it is said that the *Iliad* may still be ballad-poetry while infinitely

---

* *Purgatory*, xxiii. 127. [M. A.]

† 'A secure time fell to the lot neither of Peleus the son of Æacus, nor of the godlike Cadmus; howbeit these are said to have had, of all mortals, the supreme of happiness, who heard the golden-snooded Muses sing, one of them on the mountain (Pelion), the other in seven-gated Thebes.' [M. A.][107]

superior to all other ballads, and that, in my specimens of English ballad-poetry, I have been unfair. Well, no doubt there are better things in English ballad-poetry than

Now Christ thee save, thou proud portér, . . .

but the real strength of a chain, they say, is the strength of its weakest link; and what I was trying to show you was, that the English ballad-style is not an instrument of enough compass and force to correspond to the Greek hexameter; that, owing to an inherent weakness in it as an epic style, it easily runs into one of two faults,—either it is prosaic and humdrum, or, trying to avoid that fault, and to make itself lively (*se faire vif*), it becomes pert and jaunty. To show that, the passage about King Adland's porter serves very well. But these degradations are not proper to a true epic instrument, such as the Greek hexameter.

You may say, if you like, when you find Homer's verse, even in describing the plainest matter, neither humdrum nor jaunty, that this is because he is so incomparably better a poet than other balladists, because he is Homer. But take the whole range of Greek epic poetry,—take the later poets, the poets of the last ages of this poetry, many of them most indifferent,—Coluthus, Tryphiodorus, Quintus of Smyrna, Nonnus. Never will you find in this instrument of the hexameter, even in their hands, the vices of the ballad-style in the weak moments of this last: everywhere the hexameter —a noble, a truly epical instrument—rather resists the weakness of its employer than lends itself to it. Quintus of Smyrna is a poet of merit, but certainly not a poet of a high order; with him, too, epic poetry, whether in the character of its prosody or in that of its diction, is no longer the epic poetry of earlier and better times, nor epic poetry as again restored by Nonnus: but even in Quintus of Smyrna, I say, the hexameter is still the hexameter; it is a style which the ballad-style, even in the hands of better poets, cannot rival. And in the hands of inferior poets, the ballad-style sinks to vices of which the hexameter, even in the hands of a Tryphiodorus, never can become guilty.

But a critic, whom it is impossible to read without pleasure, and the disguise of whose initials I am sure I may be allowed to penetrate,—Mr. Spedding,[108]—says that he 'denies altogether that the metrical movement of the English hexameter has any resemblance to that of the Greek.' Of course, in that case, if the two metres in no respect correspond, praise accorded to the Greek hexameter as an epical instrument will not extend to the English. Mr. Spedding seeks to establish his proposition by pointing out that the system of accentuation differs in the English and in the Virgilian hexameter; that in the first, the accent and the long syllable (or what has to do duty as such) coincide, in the second they do not. He says that we cannot be so sure of the accent with which Greek verse should be read as of that with which Latin should; but that the lines of Homer in which the accent and the long syllable coincide, as in the English hexameter, are certainly very rare. He suggests a type of English hexameter in agreement with the Virgilian model, and formed on the supposition that 'quantity is as distinguishable in English as in Latin or Greek by any ear that will attend to it.' Of the truth of this supposition he entertains no doubt. The new hexameter will, Mr. Spedding thinks, at least have the merit of resembling, in its metrical movement, the classical hexameter, which merit the ordinary English hexameter has not. But even with this improved hexameter he is not satisfied; and he goes on, first to suggest other metres for rendering Homer, and finally to suggest that rendering Homer is impossible.

A scholar to whom all who admire Lucretius owe a large debt of gratitude,—Mr. Munro,[109]—has replied to Mr. Spedding. Mr. Munro declares that 'the accent of the old Greeks and Romans resembled our accent only in name, in reality was essentially different;' that 'our English reading of Homer and Virgil has in itself no meaning;' and that 'accent has nothing to do with the Virgilian hexameter.' If this be so, of course the merit which Mr. Spedding attributes to his own hexameter, of really corresponding with the Virgilian hexameter, has no existence. Again; in contradiction to Mr. Spedding's assertion that lines in which (in our reading of them) the accent and the long syllable coincide,* as in the ordinary English hexameter, are 'rare even in Homer,' Mr. Munro declares that such lines, 'instead of being rare, are among the very commonest types of Homeric rhythm.' Mr. Spedding asserts that 'quantity is as distinguishable in English as in Latin or Greek by any ear that will attend to it;' but Mr. Munro replies, that in English 'neither his ear nor his reason recognises any real distinction of quantity except that which is produced by accentuated and unaccentuated syllables.' He therefore arrives at the conclusion that in constructing English hexameters, 'quantity must be utterly discarded; and longer or shorter unac-

---

* Lines such as the first of the *Odyssey*:

Ἄνδρα μοι ἔννεπε, Μοῦσα, πολύτροπον, ὃς μάλα πολλὰ . . . [M. A.]

centuated syllables can have no meaning, except so far as they may be made to produce sweeter or harsher sounds in the hands of a master.'

It is not for me to interpose between two such combatants; and indeed my way lies, not up the highroad where they are contending, but along a bypath. With the absolute truth of their general propositions respecting accent and quantity, I have nothing to do; it is most interesting and instructive to me to hear such propositions discussed, when it is Mr. Munro or Mr. Spedding who discusses them; but I have strictly limited myself in these Lectures to the humble function of giving practical advice to the translator of Homer. He, I still think, must not follow so confidently, as makers of English hexameters have hitherto followed, Mr. Munro's maxim,—*quantity may be utterly discarded*. He must not, like Mr. Longfellow,[110] make *seventeen* a dactyl in spite of all the length of its last syllable, even though he can plead that in counting we lay the accent on the first syllable of this word. He may be far from attaining Mr. Spedding's nicety of ear;—may be unable to feel that 'while *quantity* is a dactyl *quiddity* is a tribrach,' and that '*rapidly* is a word to which we find no parallel in Latin;'—but I think he must bring himself to distinguish, with Mr. Spedding, between '*th' o'er*-wearied eyelid,' and '*the* wearied eyelid,' as being, the one a correct ending for a hexameter, the other an ending with a false quantity in it; instead of finding, with Mr. Munro, that this distinction 'conveys to his mind no intelligible idea.' He must temper his belief in Mr. Munro's dictum,—*quantity must be utterly discarded*,—by mixing with it a belief in this other dictum of the same author,— *two or more consonants take longer time in enunciating than one.* *

* Substantially, however, in the question at issue between Mr. Munro and Mr. Spedding, I agree with Mr. Munro. By the italicised words in the following sentence, 'The rhythm of the Virgilian hexameter depends entirely on *cæsura, pause,* and a due arrangement of words,' he has touched, it seems to me, in the constitution of this hexameter, the central point, which Mr. Spedding misses. The accent, or *heightened tone,* of Virgil in reading his own hexameters was probably far from being the same thing as the accent or *stress* with which we read them. The general effect of each line, in Virgil's mouth, was probably therefore something widely different from what Mr. Spedding assumes it to have been: an ancient's accentual reading was something which allowed the metrical beat of the Latin line to be far more perceptible than our accentual reading allows it to be.

On the question as to the *real* rhythm of the ancient hexameter, Mr. Newman has in his *Reply* a page quite admirable for force and precision. Here he is in his element, and his ability and acuteness

Criticism is so apt in general to be vague and impalpable, that when it gives us a solid and definite possession, such as is Mr. Spedding's parallel of the Virgilian and the English hexameter with their difference of accentuation distinctly marked, we cannot be too grateful to it. It is in the way in which Mr. Spedding proceeds to press his conclusions from the parallel which he has drawn out, that his criticism seems to me to come a little short. Here even he, I think, shows (if he will allow me to say so) a little of that want of pliancy and suppleness so common among critics, but so dangerous to their criticism; he is a little too absolute in imposing his metrical laws; he too much forgets the excellent maxim of Menander, so applicable to literary criticism:—

Καλὸν οἱ νόμοι σφόδρ' εἰσίν • ὁ δ' ὁρῶν τοὺς νόμους
λίαν ἀκριβῶς, συκοφάντης φαίνεται •

'Laws are admirable things; but he who keeps his eye too closely fixed upon them, runs the risk of becoming'—let us say, a purist. Mr. Spedding is probably mistaken in supposing that Virgil pronounced his hexameters as Mr. Spedding pronounces them. He is almost certainly mistaken in supposing that Homer pronounced his hexameters as Mr. Spedding pronounces Virgil's. But this, as I have said, is not a question for us to treat; all we are here concerned with is the imitation, by the English hexameter, of the ancient hexameter *in its effect upon us moderns*. Suppose we concede to Mr. Spedding that his parallel proves our accentuation of the English and of the Virgilian hexameter to be different: what are we to conclude from that; how will a criticism —not a formal, but a substantial criticism—deal with such a fact as that? Will it infer, as Mr. Spedding infers, that the English hexameter, therefore, must not pretend to reproduce better than other rhythms the movement of Homer's hexameter for us,—that there can be no correspondence at all between the movement of these two hexameters,—that if we want to have such a correspondence, we must abandon the current English hexameter altogether, and adopt in its place a new hexameter of Mr. Spedding's Anglo-Latin type, —substitute for lines like the

---

have their proper scope. But it is true that the *modern* reading of the ancient hexameter is what the modern hexameter has to imitate, and that the English reading of the Virgilian hexameter is as Mr. Spedding describes it. Why this reading has not been imitated by the English hexameter, I have tried to point out in the text. [M. A.]

Clearly the rest I behold of the dark-eyed sons of Achaia . . .

of Dr. Hawtrey, lines like the

> Procession, complex melodies, pause, quantity, accent,
> After Virgilian precedent and practice, in order . . .

of Mr. Spedding? To infer this, is to go, as I have complained of Mr. Newman for sometimes going, a great deal too fast. I think prudent criticism must certainly recognise, in the current English hexameter, a fact which cannot so lightly be set aside; it must acknowledge that by this hexameter the English ear, the genius of the English language, have, in their own way, adopted, have *translated* for themselves the Homeric hexameter; and that a rhythm which has thus grown up, which is thus, in a manner, the production of nature, has in its general type something necessary and inevitable, something which admits change only within narrow limits, which precludes change that is sweeping and essential. I think, therefore, the prudent critic will regard Mr. Spedding's proposed revolution as simply impracticable. He will feel that in English poetry the hexameter, if used at all, must be, in the main, the English hexameter now current. He will perceive that its having come into existence as the representative of the Homeric hexameter, proves it to have, for the English ear, a certain correspondence with the Homeric hexameter, although this correspondence may be, from the difference of the Greek and English languages, necessarily incomplete. This incompleteness he will endeavour,* as he may find or fancy himself able, gradually somewhat to lessen through minor changes, suggested by the

---

* Such a minor change I have attempted by occasionally shifting, in the first foot of the hexameter, the accent from the first syllable to the second. In the current English hexameter, it is on the first. Mr. Spedding, who proposes radically to subvert the constitution of this hexameter, seems not to understand that any one can propose to modify it partially; he can comprehend revolution in this metre, but not reform. Accordingly he asks me how I can bring myself to say '*Bé*tween that and the ships,' or '*Thére* sat fifty men;' or how I can reconcile such forcing of the accent with my own rule, that 'hexameters must *read themselves.*' Presently he says that he cannot believe I do pronounce these words so, but that he thinks I leave out the accent in the first foot altogether, and thus get a hexameter with only five accents. He will pardon me: I pronounce, as I suppose he himself does, if he reads the words naturally, 'Be*twéen* that and the ships,' and 'There *sát* fifty men.' Mr. Spedding is familiar enough with this accent on the second syllable in Virgil's hexameters; in 'et *té* montosæ,' or 'Ve*lóces* jaculo.' Such a change is an attempt to relieve the monotony of the current English hexameter by occasionally altering the position of one of its accents; it is not an attempt to make a

ancient hexameter, but respecting the general constitution of the modern: the notion of making it disappear altogether by the critic's inventing in his closet a new constitution of his own for the English hexameter, he will judge to be a chimerical dream.

When, therefore, Mr. Spedding objects to the English hexameter, that it imperfectly represents the movement of the ancient hexameters, I answer: We must work with the tools we have. The received English type, in its general outlines, is, for England, the necessary given type of this metre; it is by rendering the metrical beat of its pattern, not by rendering the accentual beat of it, that the English language has adapted the Greek hexameter. To render the metrical beat of its pattern is something; by effecting so much as this the English hexameter puts itself in closer relations with its original, it comes nearer to its movement than any other metre which does not even effect so much as this; but Mr. Spedding is dissatisfied with it for not effecting more still, for not rendering the accentual beat too. If he asks me *why* the English hexameter has not tried to render this too, *why* it has confined itself to rendering the metrical beat, *why*, in short, it is itself, and not Mr. Spedding's new hexameter,— that is a question which I, whose only business is to give practical advice to a translator, am not bound to answer; but I will not decline to answer it nevertheless. I will suggest to Mr. Spedding that, as I have already said, the modern hexameter is merely an attempt to imitate the effect of the ancient hexameter, as read by us moderns; that the great object of its imitation has been the hexameter of Homer; that of this hexameter such lines as those which Mr. Spedding declares to be so rare, even in Homer, but which are in truth so common,—lines in which the quantity and the reader's accent coincide,—are, for the English reader, just

wholly new English hexameter by habitually altering the position of four of them. Very likely it is an unsuccessful attempt; but at any rate it does not violate what I think is the fundamental rule for English hexameters,—that they be such as to *read themselves* without necessitating, on the reader's part, any non-natural putting-on or taking-off of accent. Hexameters like these of Mr. Longfellow,

'In that delightful land which is washed by the Delaware's waters,'

and,

'As if they fain would appease the Dryads, whose haunts they molested,'

violate this rule; and they are very common. I think the blemish of Mr. Dart's recent meritorious version of the *Iliad* is that it contains too many of them. [M. A.][111]

from that simplicity (for him) of rhythm which they owe to this very coincidence, the master-type; that so much is this the case, that one may again and again notice an English reader of Homer, in reading lines where his Virgilian accent would not coincide with the quantity, abandoning this accent, and reading the lines (as we say) *by quantity*, reading them as if he were scanning them; while foreigners neglect our Virgilian accent even in reading Virgil, read even Virgil by quantity, making the accents coincide with the long syllables. And no doubt the hexameter of a kindred language, the German, based on this mode of reading the ancient hexameter, has had a powerful influence upon the type of its English fellow. But all this shows how extremely powerful accent is for us moderns, since we find not even Greek and Latin quantity perceptible enough without it. Yet in these languages, where we have been accustomed always to look for it, it is far more perceptible to us Englishmen than in our own language, where we have not been accustomed to look for it. And here is the true reason why Mr. Spedding's hexameter is not and cannot be the current English hexameter, even though it is based on the accentuation which Englishmen give to all Virgil's lines, and to many of Homer's,—that the quantity which in Greek or Latin words we feel, or imagine we feel, even though it be unsupported by accent, we do not feel or imagine we feel in English words when it is thus unsupported. For example, in repeating the Latin line,

Ipsa tibi blandos *fundent* cunabula flores,[112]

an Englishman feels the length of the second syllable of *fundent*, although he lays the accent on the first; but in repeating Mr. Spedding's line,

Softly cometh slumber *closing* th' o'erwearied eyelid,

the English ear, full of the accent on the first syllable of *closing*, has really no sense at all of any length in its second. The metrical beat of the line is thus quite destroyed.

So when Mr. Spedding proposes a new Anglo-Virgilian hexameter he proposes an impossibility; when he 'denies altogether that the metrical movement of the English hexameter has *any* resemblance to that of the Greek,' he denies too much; when he declares that, 'were every other metre impossible, an attempt to translate Homer into English hexameters might be permitted, *but that such an attempt he himself would never read*,' he exhibits, it seems to me, a little of that obduracy and over-vehemence in liking and disliking,—a remnant, I suppose, of our insular ferocity,—to which English criticism is so prone. He ought to be enchanted to meet with a good attempt in any metre, even though he would never have advised it, even though its success be contrary to all his expectations; for it is the critic's first duty—prior even to his duty of stigmatising what is bad—*to welcome everything that is good.* In welcoming this, he must at all times be ready, like the Christian convert, even to burn what he used to worship, and to worship what he used to burn. Nay, but he need not be thus inconsistent in welcoming it; he may retain all his principles: principles endure, circumstances change; absolute success is one thing, relative success another. Relative success may take place under the most diverse conditions; and it is in appreciating the good in even relative success, it is in taking into account the change of circumstances, that the critic's judgment is tested, that his versatility must display itself. He is to keep his idea of the best, of perfection, and at the same time to be willingly accessible to every second best which offers itself. So I enjoy the ease and beauty of Mr. Spedding's stanza,

> Therewith to all the gods in order due . . .

I welcome it, in the absence of equally good poetry in another metre,* although I still think the stanza unfit to

---

* As I welcome another more recent attempt in stanza,—Mr. Worsley's version of the *Odyssey* in Spenser's measure. Mr. Worsley does me the honour to notice some remarks of mine on this measure: I had said that its greater intricacy made it a worse measure than even the ten-syllable couplet to employ for rendering Homer. He points out, in answer, that 'the more complicated the correspondences in a poetical measure, the less obtrusive and absolute are the rhymes.' This is true, and subtly remarked; but I never denied that the single shocks of rhyme in the couplet were more *strongly felt* than those in the stanza; I said that the more frequent recurrence of the same rhyme, in the stanza, necessarily made this measure more *intricate.* The stanza repacks Homer's matter yet more arbitrarily, and therefore changes his movement yet more radically, than the couplet. Accordingly, I imagine a nearer approach to a perfect translation of Homer is possible in the couplet, well managed, than in the stanza, however well managed. But meanwhile Mr. Worsley,—applying the Spenserian stanza, that beautiful romantic measure, to the most romantic poem of the ancient world; making this stanza yield him, too (what it never yielded to Byron), its treasures of fluidity and sweet ease; above all, bringing to his task a truly poetical sense and skill, —has produced a version of the *Odyssey* much the most pleasing of those hitherto produced, and which is delightful to read.

For the public this may well be enough, nay, more than enough; but for the critic even this is not yet quite enough. [M. A.][113]

render Homer thoroughly well,—although I still think other
metres fit to render him better. So I concede to Mr. Spedding
that every form of translation, prose or verse, must more or
less break up Homer in order to reproduce him; but then I
urge that that form which needs to break him up least is to
be preferred. So I concede to him that the test proposed by
me for the translator—a competent scholar's judgment
whether the translation more or less reproduces for him
the effect of the original—is not perfectly satisfactory; but
I adopt it as the best we can get, as the only test capable
of being really applied; for Mr. Spedding's proposed substitute—the translation's making the same effect, more or
less, upon the unlearned which the original makes upon
the scholar—is a test which can never really be applied at all.
These two impressions—that of the scholar, and that of the
unlearned reader—can, practically, never be accurately
compared; they are, and must remain, like those lines we
read of in Euclid, which, though produced ever so far, can
never meet. So, again, I concede that a good verse-translation of Homer, or, indeed, of any poet, is very difficult, and
that a good prose-translation is much easier; but then I urge
that a verse-translation, while giving the pleasure which
Pope's has given, might at the same time render Homer
more faithfully than Pope's; and that this being possible, we
ought not to cease wishing for a source of pleasure which no
prose-translation can ever hope to rival.

Wishing for such a verse-translation of Homer, believing
that rhythms have natural tendencies which, within certain
limits, inevitably govern them; having little faith, therefore,
that rhythms which have manifested tendencies utterly un-
Homeric can so change themselves as to become well-
adapted for rendering Homer,—I have looked about for
the rhythm which seems to depart least from the tendencies
of Homer's rhythm. Such a rhythm I think may be found
in the English hexameter, somewhat modified. I look with
hope towards continued attempts at perfecting and employing this rhythm; but my belief in the immediate success
of such attempts is far less confident than has been supposed. Between the recognition of this rhythm as ideally
the best, and the recommendation of it to the translator for
instant practical use, there must come all that consideration of circumstances, all that pliancy in foregoing, under
the pressure of certain difficulties, the absolute best, which I
have said is so indispensable to the critic. The hexameter is,
comparatively, still unfamiliar in England; many people
have a great dislike to it. A certain degree of unfamiliarity,

a certain degree of dislike, are obstacles with which it is not wise to contend. It is difficult to say at present whether the dislike to this rhythm is so strong and so widespread that it will prevent its ever becoming thoroughly familiar. I think not, but it is too soon to decide. I am inclined to think that the dislike of it is rather among the professional critics than among the general public; I think the reception which Mr. Longfellow's *Evangeline* has met with indicates this. I think that even now, if a version of the *Iliad* in English hexameters were made by a poet who, like Mr. Longfellow, has that indefinable quality which renders him popular,— something *attractive* in his talent, which communicates itself to his verses,—it would have a great success among the general public. Yet a version of Homer in hexameters of the *Evangeline* type would not satisfy the judicious, nor is the definite establishment of this type to be desired; and one would regret that Mr. Longfellow should, even to popularise the hexameter, give the immense labour required for a translation of Homer, when one could not wish his work to stand. Rather it is to be wished that by the efforts of poets like Mr. Longfellow in original poetry, and the efforts of less distinguished poets in the task of translation, the hexameter may gradually be made familiar to the ear of the English public; at the same time that there gradually arises, out of all these efforts, an improved type of this rhythm; a type which some man of genius may sign with the final stamp, and employ in rendering Homer; a hexameter which may be as superior to Voss's as Shakespeare's blank verse is superior to Schiller's. I am inclined to believe that all this travail will actually take place, because I believe that modern poetry is actually in want of such an instrument as the hexameter.

In the meantime, whether this rhythm be destined to success or not, let us steadily keep in mind what originally made us turn to it. We turned to it because we required certain Homeric characteristics in a translation of Homer, and because all other rhythms seemed to find, from different causes, great difficulties in satisfying this our requirement. If the hexameter is impossible, if one of these other rhythms must be used, let us keep this rhythm always in mind of our requirements and of its own faults, let us compel it to get rid of these latter as much as possible. It may be necessary to have recourse to blank verse; but then blank verse must *de-Cowperise* itself, must get rid of the habits of stiff self-retardation which make it say 'Not fewer shone,' for 'So many shone.' Homer moves swiftly: blank verse *can* move swiftly if it likes, but it must remember that the movement of such lines as

A thousand fires were burning, and by each . . .

is just the slow movement which makes us despair of it. Homer moves with noble ease: blank verse must not be suffered to forget that the movement of

Came they not over from sweet Lacedæmon . . .

is ungainly. Homer's expression of his thought is simple as light: we know how blank verse affects such locutions as

While the steeds *mouthed their corn aloof* . . .

and such modes of expressing one's thought are sophisticated and artificial.

One sees how needful it is to direct incessantly the English translator's attention to the essential characteristics of Homer's poetry, when so accomplished a person as Mr. Spedding, recognising these characteristics as indeed Homer's, admitting them to be essential, is led by the ingrained habits and tendencies of English blank verse thus repeatedly to lose sight of them in translating even a few lines. One sees this yet more clearly, when Mr. Spedding, taking me to task for saying that the blank verse used for rendering Homer 'must not be Mr. Tennyson's blank verse,' declares that in most of Mr. Tennyson's blank verse all Homer's essential characteristics—'rapidity of movement, *plainness of words and style, simplicity and directness of idea,* and, above all, nobleness of manner—are as conspicuous as in Homer himself.' This shows, it seems to me, how hard it is for English readers of poetry, even the most accomplished, to feel deeply and permanently what Greek plainness of thought and Greek simplicity of expression really are: they admit the importance of these qualities in a general way, but they have no ever-present sense of them; and they easily attribute them to any poetry which has other excellent qualities, and which they very much admire. No doubt there are plainer things in Mr. Tennyson's poetry than the three lines I quoted; in choosing them, as in choosing a specimen of ballad-poetry, I wished to bring out clearly, by a strong instance, the qualities of thought and style to which I was calling attention; but when Mr. Spedding talks of a plainness of thought *like Homer's,* of a plainness of speech *like Homer's,* and says that he finds these constantly in Mr. Tennyson's poetry, I answer that these I do not find there at all. Mr. Tennyson is a most distinguished and charming poet; but the very essential characteristic of his poetry is, it seems to me, an extreme subtlety and curious elaborateness of thought, an extreme subtlety and curious elaborateness of expression. In the best and most characteristic productions of his genius, these characteristics are most prominent. They are marked characteristics, as we have seen, of the Elizabethan poets; they are marked, though not the essential, characteristics of Shakespeare himself. Under the influences of the nineteenth century, under wholly new conditions of thought and culture, they manifest themselves in Mr. Tennyson's poetry in a wholly new way. But they are still there. The essential bent of his poetry is towards such expressions as—

> Now lies the Earth all Danaë to the stars;

>   O'er the sun's bright eye
> Drew the vast eyelid of an inky cloud;

> When the cairned mountain was a shadow, sunned
> The world to peace again;

> The fresh young captains flashed their glittering teeth,
> The huge bush-bearded barons heaved and blew;

> He bared the knotted column of his throat,
> The massive square of his heroic breast,
> And arms on which the standing muscle sloped
> As slopes a wild brook o'er a little stone,
> Running too vehemently to break upon it.[114]

And this way of speaking is the least *plain*, the most *un-Homeric*, which can possibly be conceived. Homer presents his thought to you just as it wells from the source of his mind: Mr. Tennyson carefully distils his thought before he will part with it. Hence comes, in the expression of the thought, a heightened and elaborate air. In Homer's poetry it is all natural thoughts in natural words; in Mr. Tennyson's poetry it is all distilled thoughts in distilled words. Exactly this heightening and elaboration may be observed in Mr. Spedding's

> While the steeds *mouthed their corn aloof,*

(an expression which might have been Mr. Tennyson's) on which I have already commented; and to one who is penetrated with a sense of the real simplicity of Homer, this subtle sophistication of the thought is, I think, very perceptible even in such lines as these,—

And drunk delight of battle with my peers,
Far on the ringing plains of windy Troy,——115

which I have seen quoted as perfectly Homeric. Perfect simplicity can be obtained only by a genius of which perfect
simplicity is an essential characteristic.

So true is this, that when a genius essentially subtle, or
a genius which, from whatever cause, is in its essence not
truly and broadly simple, determines to be perfectly plain,
determines not to admit a shade of subtlety or curiosity into
its expression, it cannot even then attain real simplicity; it
can only attain a semblance of simplicity.* French criticism,
richer in its vocabulary than ours, has invented a useful
word to distinguish this semblance (often very beautiful and
valuable) from the real quality. The real quality it calls
simplicité, the semblance *simplesse*. The one is natural
simplicity, the other is artificial simplicity. What is called
simplicity in the productions of a genius essentially not
simple, is, in truth, *simplesse*. The two are distinguishable
from one another the moment they appear in company.
For instance, let us take the opening of the narrative in
Wordsworth's "Michael:"——

> Upon the forest-side in Grasmere Vale
> There dwelt a shepherd, Michael was his name;
> An old man, stout of heart, and strong of limb.
> His bodily frame had been from youth to age
> Of an unusual strength; his mind was keen,
> Intense, and frugal, apt for all affairs;
> And in his shepherd's calling he was prompt
> And watchful more than ordinary men.

Now let us take the opening of the narrative in Mr. Tennyson's "Dora:"——

> With Farmer Allan at the farm abode
> William and Dora. William was his son,
> And she his niece. He often looked at them,
> And often thought, 'I'll make them man and wife.'

The simplicity of the first of these passages is *simplicité;*
that of the second, *simplesse*. Let us take the end of the same
two poems; first, of "Michael:"——

---

* I speak of poetic genius as employing itself upon narrative or
dramatic poetry,—poetry in which the poet has to go out of himself
and to create. In lyrical poetry, in the direct expression of personal
feeling, the most subtle genius may, under the momentary pressure
of passion, express itself simply. Even here, however, the native tendency will generally be discernible. [M. A.]

> The cottage which was named the Evening Star
> Is gone,—the ploughshare has been through the ground
> On which it stood; great changes have been wrought
> In all the neighbourhood: yet the oak is left
> That grew beside their door: and the remains
> Of the unfinished sheepfold may be seen
> Beside the boisterous brook of Green-head Ghyll.

And now, of "Dora:"—

> So those four abode
> Within one house together; and as years
> Went forward, Mary took another mate:
> But Dora lived unmarried till her death.

A heedless critic may call both of these passages simple if he will. Simple, in a certain sense, they both are; but between the simplicity of the two there is all the difference that there is between the simplicity of Homer and the simplicity of Moschus.[116]

But—whether the hexameter establish itself or not, whether a truly simple and rapid blank verse be obtained or not, as the vehicle for a standard English translation of Homer—I feel sure that this vehicle will not be furnished by the ballad-form. On this question about the ballad-character of Homer's poetry, I see that Professor Blackie[117] proposes a compromise: he suggests that those who say Homer's poetry is pure ballad-poetry, and those who deny that it is ballad-poetry at all, should split the difference between them; that it should be agreed that Homer's poems are ballads *a little*, but not so much as some have said. I am very sensible to the courtesy of the terms in which Mr. Blackie invites me to this compromise; but I cannot, I am sorry to say, accept it; I cannot allow that Homer's poetry is ballad-poetry at all. A want of capacity for sustained nobleness seems to me inherent in the ballad-form when employed for epic poetry. The more we examine this proposition, the more certain, I think, will it become to us. Let us but observe how a great poet, having to deliver a narrative very weighty and serious, instinctively shrinks from the ballad-form as from a form not commensurate with his subject-matter, a form too narrow and shallow for it, and seeks for a form which has more amplitude and impressiveness. Every one knows the "Lucy Gray" and the "Ruth" of Wordsworth. Both poems are excellent; but the subject-matter of the narrative of "Ruth" is much more weighty and impressive to the poet's own feeling than that of the narrative of

"Lucy Gray," for which latter, in its unpretending simplicity, the ballad-form is quite adequate. Wordsworth, at the time he composed "Ruth,"—his great time, his *annus mirabilis,* about 1800,—strove to be simple; it was his mission to be simple; he loved the ballad-form, he clung to it, because it was simple. Even in "Ruth" he tried, one may say, to use it; he would have used it if he could: but the gravity of his matter is too much for this somewhat slight form; he is obliged to give to his form more amplitude, more augustness, to shake out its folds.

> The wretched parents all that night
> Went shouting far and wide;
> But there was neither sound nor sight
> To serve them for a guide.

That is beautiful, no doubt, and the form is adequate to the subject-matter. But take this, on the other hand:—

> I, too, have passed her on the hills,
> Setting her little water-mills
> By spouts and fountains wild;
> Such small machinery as she turned,
> Ere she had wept, ere she had mourned,
> A young and happy child.

Who does not perceive how the greater fulness and weight of his matter has here compelled the true and feeling poet to adopt a form of more *volume* than the simple ballad-form?

It is of narrative poetry that I am speaking; the question is about the use of the ballad-form for *this.* I say that for this poetry (when in the grand style, as Homer's is) the ballad-form is entirely inadequate; and that Homer's translator must not adopt it, because it even leads him, by its own weakness, away from the grand style rather than towards it. We must remember that the matter of narrative poetry stands in a different relation to the vehicle which conveys it,—is not so independent of this vehicle, so absorbing and powerful in itself,—as the matter of purely emotional poetry. When there comes in poetry what I may call the *lyrical cry,* this transfigures everything, makes everything grand; the simplest form may be here even an advantage, because the flame of the emotion glows through and through it more easily. To go again for an illustration to Wordsworth;—our great poet, since Milton, by his performance, as Keats, I think, is our great

poet by his gift and promise;—in one of his stanzas to the
Cuckoo, we have:—

> And I can listen to thee yet;
> Can lie upon the plain
> And listen, till I do beget
> That golden time again.

Here the lyrical cry, though taking the simple ballad-form,
is as grand as the lyrical cry coming in poetry of an ampler
form, as grand as the

> An innocent life, yet far astray!

of "Ruth;" as the

> There is a comfort in the strength of love

of "Michael." In this way, by the occurrence of this lyrical
cry, the ballad-poets themselves rise sometimes, though not
so often as one might perhaps have hoped, to the grand
style.

> O lang, lang may their ladies sit,
> Wi' their fans into their hand,
> Or ere they see Sir Patrick Spence
> Come sailing to the land.

> O lang, lang may the ladies stand,
> Wi' their gold combs in their hair,
> Waiting for their ain dear lords,
> For they'll see them nae mair.

But from this impressiveness of the ballad-form, when its
subject-matter fills it over and over again,—is, indeed, in
itself, all in all,—one must not infer its effectiveness when
its subject-matter is not thus overpowering, in the great
body of a narrative.

But, after all, Homer is not a better poet than the balladists, because he has taken in the hexameter a better instrument; he took this instrument because he was a *different*
poet from them; so different,—not only so much better, but
so essentially different,—that he is not to be classed with
them at all. Poets receive their distinctive character, not
from their subject, but from their application to that subject of the ideas (to quote the *Excursion*)

> On God, on Nature, and on human life,[118]

which they have acquired for themselves. In the ballad-
poets in general, as in men of a rude and early stage of the

world, in whom their humanity is not yet variously and fully
developed, the stock of these ideas is scanty, and the ideas
themselves not very effective or profound. For them the
narrative itself is the great matter, not the spirit and significance which underlies the narrative. Even in later times
of richly developed life and thought, poets appear who
have what may be called a *balladist's mind;* in whom a fresh
and lively curiosity for the outward spectacle of the world
is much more strong than their sense of the inward significance of that spectacle. When they apply ideas to their
narrative of human events, you feel that they are, so to
speak, travelling out of their own province: in the best of
them you feel this perceptibly, but in those of a lower order
you feel it very strongly. Even Sir Walter Scott's efforts of
this kind,—even, for instance, the

> Breathes there the man with soul so dead,[119]

or the

> O woman! in our hours of ease,—[120]

even these leave, I think, as high poetry, much to be desired;
far more than the same poet's descriptions of a hunt or a
battle. But Lord Macaulay's

> Then out spake brave Horatius,
>   The captain of the gate:
> 'To all the men upon this earth
>   Death cometh soon or late,'

(and here, since I have been reproached with undervaluing
Lord Macaulay's *Lays of Ancient Rome,* let me frankly say
that, to my mind, a man's power to detect the ring of false
metal in those Lays is a good measure of his fitness to give
an opinion about poetical matters at all),—I say, Lord
Macaulay's

> To all the men upon this earth
>   Death cometh soon or late,

it is hard to read without a cry of pain. But with Homer it
is very different. This 'noble barbarian,' this 'savage with
the lively eye,'—whose verse, Mr. Newman thinks, would
affect us, if we could hear the living Homer, 'like an elegant
and simple melody from an African of the Gold Coast,'—
is never more at home, never more nobly himself, than in
applying profound ideas to his narrative. As a poet he belongs—narrative as is his poetry, and early as is his date—

to an incomparably more developed spiritual and intellectual order than the balladists, or than Scott and Macaulay; he is here as much to be distinguished from them, and in the same way, as Milton is to be distinguished from them. He is, indeed, rather to be classed with Milton than with the balladists and Scott; for what he has in common with Milton—the noble and profound application of ideas to life —is the most essential part of poetic greatness. The most essentially grand and characteristic things of Homer are such things as—

> ἔτλην δ', οἷ' οὔ πώ τις ἐπιχθόνιος βροτὸς ἄλλος,
> ἀνδρὸς παιδοφόνοιο ποτὶ στόμα χεῖρ' ὀρέγεσθαι,*

or as—

> καὶ σὲ, γέρον, τὸ πρὶν μὲν ἀκούομεν ὄλβιον εἶναι,†

or as—

> ὡς γὰρ ἐπεκλώσαντο θεοὶ δειλοῖσι βροτοῖσιν,
> ζώειν ἀχνυμένους · αὐτοὶ δέ τ' ἀκηδέες εἰσίν,‡

and of these the tone is given, far better than by anything of the balladists, by such things as the

> Io non piangeva: sì dentro impietrai:
> Piangevan elli . . .§

of Dante; or the

> Fall'n Cherub! to be weak is miserable[121]

of Milton.

I suppose I must, before I conclude, say a word or two about my own hexameters; and yet really, on such a topic, I am almost ashamed to trouble you. From those perishable objects I feel, I can truly say, a most Oriental detachment. You yourselves are witnesses how little importance, when I offered them to you, I claimed for them,—how humble a

---

* 'And I have endured—the like whereof no soul upon the earth hath yet endured—to carry to my lips the hand of him who slew my child.'—*Iliad*, xxiv. 505. [M. A.][122]

† 'Nay and thou too, old man, in times past wert, as we hear, happy.'—*Iliad*, xxiv. 543. In the original this line, for mingled pathos and dignity, is perhaps without a rival even in Homer. [M. A.]

‡ 'For so have the gods spun our destiny to us wretched mortals,— that we should live in sorrow; but they themselves are without trouble.'—*Iliad*, xxiv. 525. [M. A.]

§ '*I* wept not: so of stone grew I within:—*they* wept.'—*Hell*, xxxiii. 49 (Carlyle's Translation, slightly altered). [M. A.]

function I designed them to fill. I offered them, not as specimens of a competing translation of Homer, but as illustrations of certain canons which I had been trying to establish for Homer's poetry. I said that these canons they might very well illustrate by failing as well as succeeding: if they illustrate them in any manner, I am satisfied. I was thinking of the future translator of Homer, and trying to let him see as clearly as possible what I meant by the combination of characteristics which I assigned to Homer's poetry,—by saying that this poetry was at once rapid in movement, plain in words and style, simple and direct in its ideas, and noble in manner. I do not suppose that my own hexameters are rapid in movement, plain in words and style, simple and direct in their ideas, and noble in manner; but I am in hopes that a translator, reading them with a genuine interest in his subject, and without the slightest grain of personal feeling, may see more clearly, as he reads them, what I mean by saying that Homer's poetry is all these. I am in hopes that he may be able to seize more distinctly, when he has before him my

So shone forth, in front of Troy, by the bed of the Xanthus,

or my

  Ah, unhappy pair, to Peleus why did we give you?

or my

 So he spake, and drove with a cry his steeds into battle,

the exact points which I wish him to avoid in Cowper's

  So numerous seemed those fires the banks between,

or in Pope's

   Unhappy coursers of immortal strain,

or in Mr. Newman's

He spake, and, yelling, held a-front his single-hoofed horses.

At the same time there may be innumerable points in mine which he ought to avoid also. Of the merit of his own compositions no composer can be admitted the judge.

 But thus humbly useful to the future translator I still hope my hexameters may prove; and he it is, above all, whom one has to regard. The general public carries away little from discussions of this kind, except some vague notion that one advocates English hexameters, or that one has attacked Mr. Newman. On the mind of an adversary one never makes the faintest impression. Mr. Newman reads all one can say about diction, and his last word on the subject is, that he 'regards it as a question about to open hereafter, whether a translator of Homer ought not to adopt the old dissyllabic *landis, houndis, hartis*' (for lands, hounds, harts), and also 'the final *en* of the plural of verbs (we *dancen,* they *singen,* etc.),' which 'still subsists in Lancashire.' A certain critic reads all one can say about style, and at the end of it arrives at the inference that, 'after all, there is some style grander than the grand style itself, since Shakespeare has not the grand manner, and yet has the supremacy over Milton;' another critic reads all one can say about rhythm, and the result is, that he thinks Scott's rhythm, in the description of the death of Marmion, all the better for being *saccadé,* because the dying ejaculations of Marmion were likely to be 'jerky.' How vain to rise up early, and to take rest late, from any zeal for proving to Mr. Newman that he must not, in translating Homer, say *houndis* and *dancen;* or to the first of the two critics above quoted, that one poet may be a greater poetical force than another, and yet have a more unequal style; or to the second, that the best art, having to represent the death of a hero, does not set about imitating his dying noises! Such critics, however, provide for an opponent's vivacity the charming excuse offered by Rivarol[123] for his, when he was reproached with giving offence by it:—'Ah!' he exclaimed, 'no one considers how much pain every man of taste has had to *suffer,* before he ever inflicts any.'

It is for the future translator that one must work. The successful translator of Homer will have (or he cannot succeed) that true sense for his subject, and that disinterested love of it, which are, both of them, so rare in literature, and so precious; he will not be led off by any false scent; he will have an eye for the real matter, and, where he thinks he may find any indication of this, no hint will be too slight for him, no shade will be too fine, no imperfections will turn him aside,—he will go before his adviser's thought, and help it out with his own. This is the sort of student that a critic of Homer should always have in his thoughts; but students of this sort are indeed rare.

And how, then, can I help being reminded what a student of this sort we have just lost in Mr. Clough, whose name I have already mentioned in these lectures? He, too, was busy with Homer,[124] but it is not on that account that I now speak of him. Nor do I speak of him in order to call attention to his qualities and powers in general, admirable as these were. I mention him because, in so eminent a degree, he possessed these two invaluable literary qualities,—a true sense for his object of study, and a single-hearted care for it. He had both; but he had the second even more eminently than the first. He greatly developed the first through means of the second. In the study of art, poetry, or philosophy, he had the most undivided and disinterested love for his object in itself, the greatest aversion to mixing up with it anything accidental or personal. His interest was in literature itself; and it was this which gave so rare a stamp to his character, which kept him so free from all taint of littleness. In the saturnalia of ignoble personal passions, of which the struggle for literary success, in old and crowded communities, offers so sad a spectacle, he never mingled. He had not yet traduced his friends, nor flattered his enemies, nor disparaged what he admired, nor praised what he despised. Those who knew him well had the conviction that, even with time, these literary arts would never be his. His poem, of which I before spoke, has some admirable Homeric qualities;—out-of-doors freshness, life, naturalness, buoyant rapidity. Some of the expressions in that poem,—'*Dangerous Corrievreckan . . . Where roads are unknown to Loch Nevish,*'[125]—come back now to my ear with the true Homeric ring. But that in him of which I think oftenest is he Homeric simplicity of his literary life.

NOTES

On Translating Homer: Delivered at Oxford, October, 1860–January, 1861; published 1861.
Last Words: Delivered at Oxford, November, 1861; published 1862.

1. Juvenal, I. i: *Shall I never repay?*
2. Francis William Newman (1805–97), brother of John Henry Newman, published his translation of the *Iliad* in 1856.
3. Charles Wright (published 1859–65).
4. Respectively, E. C. Hawtrey; W. H. Thompson, Regius Professor of Greek at Cambridge; and Benjamin Jowett, Regius Professor of Greek at Oxford.
5. Richard Bentley (1662–1742), classical scholar.
6. Aristotle's *Nicomachean Ethics.*
7. J. H. Voss translated the *Odyssey* (1781) and the *Iliad* (1793) into German hexameters. Tennyson ridiculed Voss in "Experiments in Quantity: Hexameters and Pentameters."
8. October, 1860.
9. See p. 241.
10. *Modern Painters,* Part IV (1853), chapter xii.
11. Sainte-Beuve: *As each literary kind has its own peculiar pitfall, that of the romantic kind is falseness.*
12. "A fifth-century (B.C.) Athenian painter whose murals at

Delphi on the destruction of Troy and on Odysseus' visit to the underworld are described by Pausanias X. xxv–xxxi" (R. H. Super).

13. William Cowper (1731–1800), translation of the *Iliad* (1791).

14. *Iliad* (1715–20), *Odyssey* (1725–26).

15. William Sotheby (1831).

16. *Iliad* (1598–1611); *Odyssey* (1614–15).

17. "Reason" (1830).

18. *Iliad*, viii. 643–45.

19. *Iliad*, xix. 491–95.

20. *Let us go.*

21. By Samuel Johnson (1759).

22. Pope has "lighten."

23. To Scott, November 7, 1805 (R. H. Super).

24. Henry Hallam, *Introduction to the Literature of Europe* (1837; 2nd ed., 1843).

25. R. Hooper (1857).

26. "The epithet 'clearest-soul'd' is Arnold's own, from his early sonnet 'To a Friend' " (R. H. Super).

27. See p. 186.

28. *Iliad*, xix. 401–03.

29. Greek sculptor.

30. R. H. Super notes that Cowper has "unseasonably."

31. Prologue to *Troilus and Cressida* ("orgulous" and "Sperr" are eighteenth-century emendations for "orgillous" and "Stirre").

32. *Ars Poetica*, line 359.

33. "*Iliad*, ii. 211–77 and *Odyssey*, xviii. 1–109; both Thersites and Irus were vulgar characters" (R. H. Super).

34. William Maginn (1849).

35. *Paradise Lost*, iii. 35–36.

36. Nicholas Brady and Nahum Tate, metrical translation of the Psalms (1696).

37. Ancient Homeric scholar.

38. 1611 has *tast* (taste), though *haste* has been suggested as an emendation.

39. Chapman has "used."

40. *Lays of Ancient Rome* (1842).

41. Leader of the chorus.

42. Moss-troopers: marauders who infested the "mosses" of the Scottish Border.

43. *Iliad*, xvi. 74–79.

44. *A Defence of Poesie* (1595): "Certainly, I must confess my own barbarousness, I never heard the old song of Percy and Douglas that I found not my heart moved more than with a trumpet."

45. *John*, vi. 63.

46. Johnson, "The Vanity of Human Wishes," lines 351–52.

47. *Paradise Lost*, ii. 1–2.

48. H. F. Cary (completed 1814).

49. *Iliad*, i. 1: *The wrath do thou sing, O goddess.*

50. *Paradise Lost*, i. 1–6.

51. *Paradise Lost*, iv. 1–2.

52. *We are dust and shadows.*

53. *Rarely does Vengeance, albeit of halting gait, fail to o'ertake* (deseruit) *the guilty, though he gain the start.*

54. *The Task* (1785), i. 264–65.

55. "Ulysses" (1842), misquoting: "Yet all experience is an arch wherethrough / Gleams that untravelled world, whose margin fades / For ever and for ever when I move."

56. "Medea's magic spells rejuvenated Jason's aged father Æson; the daughters of Jason's wicked uncle Pelias, beholding the miracle, were induced to stab their father in the hope of effecting similar rejuvenation, but the experiment proved fatal.—Ovid, *Metamorphoses*, vii. 159–349" (R. H. Super).

57. *It is solved by walking.*

58. (1848), by Arthur Hugh Clough (1819–61); revised as *The Bothie of Tober-Na-Vuolich* (1862).

59. J. T. Freeman Mitford (1859).

60. Chapman's *Iliad*, i. 590.

61. In a letter to Gabriel Harvey, 1580 (R. H. Super).

62. *Macbeth*, I. vii. 12–14.

63. *As You Like It*, IV. i. 168.

64. Chapman's *Iliad*, ix. 307.

65. *Hamlet*, III. i. 77 ("weary life").

66. *Macbeth*, II. i. 58 ("my whereabout"), I. vii. 7, 20 ("the deep damnation"); *Hamlet*, III. i. 75–76.

67. III. i. 59.

68. I. vii. 66–68.

69. Charles Knight's edition (1839–43).

70. I. vii. 49–51.

71. "Il Penseroso" ("In scepter'd").

72. *Romeo and Juliet*, III. ii. 1.

73. "Elegy Written in a Country Churchyard."

74. *Iliad*, xiv. 83.

75. *Matthew*, xvi. 22.

76. *John*, xvi. 18.

77. *Iliad*, xvii. 441–47.

78. Proverbial: judge of the statue of Hercules by the size of the foot.

79. *"Psalms*, cxviii. 16, in the Prayer Book version" (R. H. Super).

80. *Antony and Cleopatra*, V. ii. 304–05.

81. *Silliness.*

82. "Abraham Hayward's prose translation of *Faust*, Part I, was first published in 1833 and remained current for many years. By the time Arnold spoke, however, Hayward was perhaps best known for *The Art of Dining; or, Gastronomy and Gastronomers* (1852)" (R. H. Super).

83. John Wilson ("Christopher North"), who wrote on Homer in *Blackwood's Magazine*, 1831–34.

84. *Psalms*, cxix. 157: "Many are my persecutors and mine enemies; yet do I not decline from thy testimonies."

85. *I have never replied to any criticism, and I shall preserve the same silence on this one.*

86. *It is better to leave these wretches in uncertainty.*

87. The Professorship of Poetry at Oxford.

88. *Iliad*, xvii. 384–99.

89. *Homeric Translation in Theory and Practice . . .* (1861).

90. Montaigne's essay "Des livres" speaks of Seneca as "plus ondoyant et divers" than Plutarch.

91. *Measure for Measure*, III. i. 34–36.

92. Will-o'-the-wisp.

93. *Iliad*, xiii. 136.

94. Adapting *Genesis*, xviii. 31–32.

95. Milton, "On the Morning of Christ's Nativity."

96. *Poems of Chaucer Modernized*, ed. R. H. Horne (1841).

97. *Iliad*, xii. 325.

98. R. H. Super cites *The Critic*, II. ii. 380–81: "The *father* softens—but the *governor* is fixed!"

99. *Matthew*, vii. 3–5.

101. "Lycidas."

101. *And going to and fro he spake and heartened each man, Mesthles and Glaucus and Medon and Thersilochus.*

102. *The Prelude*, iii. 15–17; followed by iii. 60–63.

103. *Matthew*, xvii. 4: "It is good for us to be here."

104. *John*, viii. 24.

105. *Paradise Lost*, vii. 23–26.

106. Edward Young (1683–1765), author of *Night Thoughts* (1742–45).

107. Pindar, *Pythian Odes*, iii. 86–91.

108. James Spedding (1808–81) wrote in *Fraser's Magazine* (June, 1861).

109. H. A. J. Munro (1819–85), edition of Lucretius (1864).

110. R. H. Super cites *Evangeline*, I. i. 46: "Fair was she to behold, that maiden of seventeen summers."

111. Quoting *Evangeline*, II. v. 1, 6. Also referring to J. H. Dart (1862).

112. Virgil, *Eclogues*, iv. 23: *The very cradle shall pour forth pleasing flowers to thee.*

113. P. S. Worsley (1861–62).

114. Respectively, *The Princess*, vii. 182; *Merlin and Vivien*, lines 633–34, 638–39 ("And the cairn'd"); *The Princess*, v. 20–21; *The Marriage of Geraint*, lines 74–78 ("And bared").

115. Tennyson, "Ulysses."

116. A pastoral poet of Syracuse, c. 150 B.C.

117. J. S. Blackie, *Macmillan's Magazine* (August, 1861).

118. From Wordsworth's fragment, "The Recluse," prefixed to *The Excursion* (read "On man").

119. *Lay of the Last Minstrel*, VI. i.

120. *Marmion*, VI. xxx.

121. *Paradise Lost*, i. 157.

122. "We pedants . . . know that the verse of Homer really means 'to reach forth my hand to the chin of him that slew my son' " (A. E. Housman).

123. Antoine Rivarol (1753–1801).

124. R. H. Super notes: "Clough turned to the translation of Homer into English hexameters at various times; during the last years of his life it was almost the only poetical work he was able to undertake. He submitted specimens of it to Arnold as early as 1849."

125. *The Bothie*, ix. 79, iv. 12.

DANTE AND BEATRICE

1863

THOSE CRITICS who allegorize the *Divine Comedy,* who exaggerate, or, rather, who mistake the supersensual element in Dante's work, who reduce to nothing the sensible and human element, are hardly worth refuting. They know nothing of the necessary laws under which poetic genius works, of the inevitable conditions under which the creations of poetry are produced. But, in their turn, those other critics err hardly less widely, who exaggerate, or, rather, who mistake the human and real element in Dante's poem; who see, in such a passion as that of Dante for Beatrice, an affection belonging to the sphere of actual domestic life, fitted to sustain the wear and tear of our ordinary daily existence. Into the error of these second critics an accomplished recent translator of Dante, Mr. Theodore Martin,[1] seems to me to have fallen. He has ever present to his mind, when he speaks of the Beatrice whom Dante adored, Wordsworth's picture of—

> The perfect woman, nobly planned
> To warm, to comfort, and command;
> And yet a spirit still, and bright
> With something of an angel light.[2]

He is ever quoting these lines in connexion with Dante's Beatrice; ever assimilating to this picture Beatrice as Dante conceived her; ever attributing to Dante's passion a character identical with that of the affection which Wordsworth, in the poem from which these lines are taken, meant to portray. The affection here portrayed by Wordsworth is, I grant, a substantial human affection, inhabiting the domain of real life, at the same time that it is poetical and beautiful. But in order to give this flesh-and-blood character to Dante's passion for Beatrice, what a task has Mr. Martin to perform! how much is he obliged to imagine! how much to shut his eyes to, or to disbelieve! Not perceiving that the vital impulse of Dante's soul is towards reverie and spiritual vision; that the task Dante sets himself is not the task of reconciling poetry and reality, of giving to each its due part, of supplementing the one by the other; but the task of sacrificing the world to the spirit, of making the spirit all in all, of effacing the world in presence of the spirit—Mr. Martin seeks to find a Dante admirable and complete in the life of the world as well as in the life of the spirit; and when he cannot find him, he invents him. Dante saw the world, and used in his poetry what he had seen; for he was a born artist. But he was essentially aloof from the world, and not complete in the life of the world; for he was a born spiritualist and solitary. Keeping in our minds this, his double character, we may seize the exact truth as to his relations with Beatrice, and steer a right course between the error of those who deliteralize them too much, on the one hand, and that of those who literalize them too much, on the other.

The *Divine Comedy*, I have already said, is no allegory, and Beatrice no mere personification of theology. Mr. Martin is quite right in saying that Beatrice is the Beatrice whom men turned round to gaze at in the streets of Florence; that she is no 'allegorical phantom,' no 'fiction purely ideal.' He is quite right in saying that Dante 'worships no phantoms,' that his passion for Beatrice was a real passion, and that his love-poetry does not deal 'in the attributes of celestial charms.' He was an artist—one of the greatest of artists; and art abhors what is vague, hollow, and impalpable.

Enough to make this fully manifest we have in the *Vita Nuova*. Dante there records how, a boy of ten, he first saw Beatrice, a girl of nine, dressed in crimson; how, a second time, he saw her, nine years later, passing along the street, dressed in white, between two ladies older than herself, and how she saluted him. He records how afterwards she once denied him her salutation; he records the profound impression which, at her father's death, the grief and beauty of Beatrice made on all those who visited her; he records his meeting with her at a party after her marriage, his emotion, and how some ladies present, observing his emotion, 'made a mock of him to that most gentle being;' he records her death, and how, a year afterwards, some gentlemen found him, on the anniversary of her death, 'sketching an angel on his tablets.' He tells us how, a little later, he had a vision of the dead Beatrice 'arrayed in the same crimson robe in which she had originally appeared to my eyes, and she seemed as youthful as on the day I saw her first.' He mentions how, one day, the sight of some pilgrims passing along a particular street in Florence brought to his mind the thought that perhaps these pilgrims, coming from a far country, had never even heard the name of her who filled his thoughts so entirely. And even in the *Divine Comedy,* composed many years afterwards, and treating of the glorified Beatrice only, one distinct trait of the earthly Beatrice is still preserved—her smile; the *santo riso* of the *Purgatory,* the *dolce riso* of the *Paradise.*

Yes, undoubtedly there was a real Beatrice, whom Dante had seen living and moving before him, and for whom he had felt a passion. This basis of fact and reality he took from the life of the outward world: this basis was indispensable to him, for he was an artist.

But this basis was enough for him as an artist: to have seen Beatrice two or three times, to have spoken to her two or three times, to have felt her beauty, her charm; to have had the emotion of her marriage, her death—this was enough. Art requires a basis of fact, but it also desires to treat this basis of fact with the utmost freedom; and this desire for the freest handling of its object is even thwarted when its object is too near, and too real. To have had his relations with Beatrice more positive, intimate and prolonged, to have had an affection for her into which there entered more of the life of this world, would have even somewhat impeded, one may say, Dante's free use of these relations for the purpose of art. And the artist nature in him was in little danger of being thus impeded; for he was a born solitary.

Thus the conditions of art do not make it necessary that Dante's relations with Beatrice should have been more close and real than the *Vita Nuova* represents them; and the conditions of Dante's own nature do not make it probable. Not the less do such admirers of the poet as Mr. Martin—misconceiving the essential characteristic of chivalrous passion in general, and of Dante's divinization of Beatrice in particular, misled by imagining this 'worship for woman,' as they call it, to be something which it was not, something involving modern relations in social life between the two sexes—insist upon making out of Dante's adoration of Beatrice a substantial modern love-story, and of arranging Dante's real life so as to turn it into the proper sort of real life for a 'worshipper of woman' to lead. The few real incidents of Dante's passion, enumerated in the *Vita Nuova*, sufficient to give to his great poem the basis which it required, are far too scanty to give to such a love-story as this the basis which it requires; therefore they must be developed and amplified. Beatrice was a living woman, and Dante had seen her; but she must become

> The creature not too bright and good
> For human nature's daily food,

of Wordsworth's poem: she must become 'pure flesh and blood—beautiful, yet substantial,' and 'moulded of that noble humanity wherewith Heaven blesses, not unfrequently, our common earth.' Dante had saluted Beatrice, had spoken to her; but this is not enough: he has surely omitted to 'record particulars:' it is 'scarcely credible that he should not have found an opportunity of directly declaring his attachment;' for 'in position, education, and appearance he was a man worth any woman,' and his face 'at that time of his life must have been eminently engaging.' Therefore 'it seems strange that his love should not have found its issue in marriage;' for 'he loved Beatrice as a man loves, and with the passion that naturally perseveres to the possession of its mistress.'

However, his love did *not* find its issue in marriage. Beatrice married Messer Simone dei Bardi, to whom, says Mr. Martin, 'her hand had been, perhaps lightly or to please her parents, pledged, in ignorance of the deep and noble passion which she had inspired in the young poet's heart.' But she certainly could not 'have been insensible to his profound tenderness and passion;' although whether 'she knew of it before her marriage,' and whether 'she, either then or afterwards, gave it her countenance and approval, and returned it in any way, and in what degree'—questions which, Mr. Martin says, 'naturally suggest themselves'—are, he confesses, questions for solving which 'the materials are most scanty and unsatisfactory.' 'Unquestionably,' he adds, 'it startles and grieves us to find Beatrice taking part with her friends' in laughing at Dante when he was overcome at first meeting her after her marriage. 'But there may,' he thinks, 'have been causes for this—causes for which, in justice to her, allowance must be made, even as we see that Dante made it.' Then, again, as to Messer Simone dei Bardi's feelings about this attachment of Dante to his wife. 'It is true,' says Mr. Martin, 'that we have no direct information on this point;' but 'the love of Dante was of an order too pure and noble to occasion distrust, even if the purity of Beatrice had not placed her above suspicion;' but Dante 'did what only a great and manly nature could have done—he triumphed over his pain; he uttered no complaint; his regrets were buried within his own heart.' 'At the same time,' Mr. Martin thinks, 'it is contrary to human nature that a love unfed by any tokens of favour should retain all its original force; and without wrong either to Beatrice or Dante, we may conclude that an understanding was come to between them, which in some measure soothed his heart, if it did not satisfy it.' And 'sooner or later, before Beatrice died, we cannot doubt that there came a day when words passed between them which helped to reconcile Dante to the doom that severed her from his side during her all too brief sojourn on earth, when the pent-up heart of the poet swept down the barriers within which it had so long struggled, and he

> Caught up the whole of love, and utter'd it,
> Then bade adieu for ever,[3]

if not to her, yet to all those words which it was no longer meet should be spoken to another's wife.'

But Dante married, as well as Beatrice; and so Dante's married life has to be *arranged* also. 'It is,' says Mr. Martin, 'only those who have observed little of human nature, or of their own hearts, who will think that Dante's marriage with Gemma Donati argues against the depth of[4] sincerity of his first love. Why should he not have sought the solace and the support of a generous woman's nature, who, knowing all the truth, was yet content with such affection as he was able to bring to a second love? Nor was that necessarily small. Ardent and affectionate as his nature was, the sympathies of such a woman must have elicited from him a satisfactory response; while, at the same time, without prejudice to the wife's claim on his regard, he might entertain his heaven-ward dream of the departed Beatrice.' The tradition is, how-ever, that Dante did not live happily with his wife; and some have thought that he means to cast a disparaging re-flection on his marriage in a passage of the *Purgatory*. I need not say that this sort of thing would never do for Mr. Martin's hero—that hero who can do nothing 'inconsistent with the purest respect to her who had been the wedded wife of another, on the one hand, or with his regard for the mother of his children, on the other.' Accordingly, 'are we to assume,' Mr. Martin cries, 'that the woman who gave herself to him in the full knowledge that she was not the bride of his imagination, was not regarded by him with the esteem which her devotion was calculated to inspire?' It is quite impossible. 'Dante was a true-hearted gentleman, and could never have spoken slightingly of her on whose breast he had found comfort amid many a sorrow, and who had borne to him a numerous progeny—the last a Beatrice.' Donna Gemma was a 'generous and devoted woman,' and she and Dante 'thoroughly understood each other.'

All this has, as applied to real personages, the grave defect of being entirely of Mr. Martin's own imagining. But it has a still graver defect, I think, as applied to Dante, in being so singularly inappropriate to its object. The grand, impracticable Solitary, with keen senses and ardent passions —for nature had made him an artist, and art must be, as Milton says, 'sensuous and impassioned'[5]—but with an irresistible bent to the inward life, the life of imagination, vision, and ecstacy; with an inherent impatience of the outward life, the life of distraction, jostling, mutual concession; this man 'of a humour which made him hard to get on with,' says Petrarch; 'melancholy and pensive,' says Boccaccio; 'by nature abstracted and taciturn, seldom speaking unless he was questioned, and often so absorbed in his own reflections that he did not hear the questions which were put to him;' who could not live with the Florentines, who could not live with Gemma Donati, who could not live with Can Grande della Scala; this lover of Beatrice, but of Beatrice a vision of his youth, hardly at all in contact with him in actual life, vanished from him soon, with whom his imagination could deal freely, whom he could divinize into a fit object for the spiritual longing which filled him—this Dante is transformed, in Mr. Martin's hands, into the hero of a sentimental, but strictly virtuous, novel! To make out Dante to have been eminent for a wise, complete conduct of his outward life, seems to me as unimportant as it is impossible. I can quite believe the tradition which represents him as not having lived happily with his wife, and attributes her not having joined him in his exile to this cause. I can even believe, without difficulty, an assertion of Boccaccio which excites Mr. Martin's indignation, that Dante's conduct, even in mature life, was at times exceedingly irregular. We know how the followers of the spiritual life tend to be antinomian in what belongs to the outward life: they do not attach much importance to such irregularity themselves; it is their fault, as complete men, that they do not; it is the fault of the spiritual life, as a complete life, that it allows this tendency: by dint of despising the outward life, it loses the control of this life, and of itself when in contact with it. My present business, however, is not to praise or blame Dante's practical conduct of his life, but to make clear his peculiar mental and spiritual constitution. This, I say, disposed him to absorb himself in the inner life, wholly to humble and efface before this the outward life. We may see this in the passage of the *Purgatory*[6] where he makes Beatrice reprove him for his backslidings after she, his visible symbol of spiritual perfection, had vanished from his eyes.

'For a while'—she says of him to the 'pious substances,' the angels—'for a while with my countenance I upheld him; showing to him my youthful eyes, with me I led him, turned towards the right way.

'Soon as I came on the threshold of my second age, and changed my life, this man took himself from me and gave himself to others.

'When that I had mounted from flesh to spirit, and beauty and spirit were increased unto me, I was to him less dear and less acceptable.

'He turned his steps to go in a way not true, pursuing after false images of good, which fulfil nothing of the promises which they give.

'Neither availed it me that I obtained inspirations to be granted me, whereby, both in dream and otherwise, I called him back; so little heed paid he to them.

'So deep he fell, that, for his salvation all means came short, except to show him the people of perdition.

'The high decree of God would be broken, could Lethe be passed, and that so fair aliment tasted, without some scot paid of repentance, which pours forth tears.'

Here, indeed, and in a somewhat similar passage of the next canto, Mr. Martin thinks that the 'obvious allusion' is to certain moral shortcomings, occasional slips, of which (though he treats Boccaccio's imputation as monstrous and incredible) 'Dante, with his strong and ardent passions, having, like meaner men, to fight the perennial conflict between flesh and spirit,' had sometimes, he supposes, been guilty. An Italian commentator gives at least as true an interpretation of these passages when he says that 'in them Dante makes Beatrice, as the representative of theology, lament that he should have left the study of divinity—in which, by the grace of Heaven, he might have attained admirable proficiency—to immerse himself in civil affairs with the parties of Florence.' But the real truth is, that all the life of the world, its pleasures, its business, its parties, its politics, all is alike hollow and miserable to Dante in comparison with the inward life, the ecstacy of the divine vision; every way which does not lead straight towards this is for him a *via non vera;* every good thing but this is for him a false image of good, fulfilling none of the promises which it gives; for the excellency of the knowledge of this he counts all things but loss. Beatrice leads him to this; herself symbolises for him the ineffable beauty and purity for which he longs. Even to Dante at twenty-one, when he yet sees the living Beatrice with his eyes, she already symbolises this for him, she is already not the 'creature not too bright and good' of Wordsworth, but a spirit far more than a woman; to Dante at twenty-five composing the *Vita Nuova* she is still more a spirit; to Dante at fifty, when his character has taken its bent, when his genius is come to its perfection, when he is composing his immortal poem, she is a spirit altogether.

NOTES

Dante and Beatrice: Based on a lecture delivered at Oxford, March, 1862; published in *Fraser's Magazine* (May, 1863); not reprinted by Arnold.

1. This translation of Dante's *Vita Nuova* had appeared in 1861 (title page "1862").
2. "She was a phantom of delight" (as quoted by Martin).
3. Tennyson, "Love and Duty" ("And bade").
4. R. H. Super notes that Martin has "or."
5. "Of Education" (1644): poetry as "more simple, sensuous, and passionate" than rhetoric.
6. From *Purgatorio,* xxx. 101–45.

from HAMLET ONCE MORE

1884

FOR ME the interest of this discovery[1] does not lie in its showing that Shakespeare thought Montaigne a dangerous author, and meant to give in *Hamlet* a shocking example of what Montaigne's teaching led to. It lies in its explaining how it comes about that *Hamlet*, in spite of the prodigious mental and poetic power shown in it, is really so tantalising and ineffective a play. To the common public *Hamlet* is a famous piece by a famous poet, with crime, a ghost, battle, and carnage; and that is sufficient. To the youthful enthusiast *Hamlet* is a piece handling the mystery of the universe, and having throughout cadences, phrases, and words full of divinest Shakespearian magic; and that, too, is sufficient. To the pedant, finally, *Hamlet* is an occasion for airing his psychology; and what does pedant require more? But to the spectator who loves true and powerful drama, and can judge whether he gets it or not, *Hamlet* is a piece which opens, indeed, simply and admirably, and then: 'The rest is puzzle'!

The reason is, apparently, that Shakespeare conceived this play with his mind running on Montaigne, and placed its action and its hero in Montaigne's atmosphere and world. What is that world? It is the world of man viewed as a being *ondoyant et divers*,[2] balancing and indeterminate, the plaything of cross motives and shifting impulses, swayed by a thousand subtle influences, physiological and pathological. Certainly the action and hero of the original Hamlet story are not such as to compel the poet to place them in this world and no other, but they admit of being placed there, Shakespeare resolved to place them there, and they lent themselves to his resolve. The resolve once taken to place the action in this world of problem, the problem became brightened by all the force of Shakespeare's faculties, of Shakespeare's subtlety. *Hamlet* thus comes at last to be not a drama followed with perfect comprehension and profoundest emotion, which is the ideal for tragedy, but a problem soliciting interpretation and solution.

It will never, therefore, be a piece to be seen with pure satisfaction by those who will not deceive themselves. But such is its power and such is its fame that it will always continue to be acted, and we shall all of us continue to go and see it.

NOTES

from *Hamlet Once More:* Published *Pall Mall Gazette* (October 23, 1884); not reprinted by Arnold.

1. Jacob Feis, in *Shakspere and Montaigne* (1884), had—in Arnold's words—"proved the preoccupation of Shakespeare's mind when he made *Hamlet* with Montaigne's *Essays*," but took the critical view here rejected by Arnold.
2. See p. 299, note 90.

A FRENCH CRITIC
ON MILTON

1877

MR. TREVELYAN'S[1] Life of his uncle must have induced many people to read again Lord Macaulay's *Essay on Milton*. With the *Essay on Milton* began Macaulay's literary career, and, brilliant as the career was, it had few points more brilliant than its beginning. Mr. Trevelyan describes with animation that decisive first success. The essay appeared in the *Edinburgh Review* in 1825. Mr. Trevelyan says, and quite truly:—

> The effect on the author's reputation was instantaneous. Like Lord Byron, he awoke one morning and found himself famous. The beauties of the work were such as all men could recognise, and its very faults pleased. . . . The family breakfast-table in Bloomsbury was covered with cards of invitation to dinner from every quarter of London. . . . A warm admirer of Robert Hall, Macaulay heard with pride how the great preacher, then wellnigh worn out with that long disease, his life, was discovered lying on the floor, employed in learning by aid of grammar and dictionary enough Italian to enable him to verify the parallel between Milton and Dante. But the compliment that, of all others, came most nearly home,—the only commendation of his literary talent which even in the innermost domestic circle he was ever known to repeat,—was the sentence with which Jeffrey[2] acknowledged the receipt of his manuscript: 'The more I think, the less I can conceive where you picked up that style.'

And already, in the *Essay on Milton*, the style of Macaulay is, indeed, that which we know so well. A style to dazzle,

311

to gain admirers everywhere, to attract imitators in multitude! A style brilliant, metallic, exterior; making strong points, alternating invective with eulogy, wrapping in a robe of rhetoric the thing it represents; not, with the soft play of life, following and rendering the thing's very form and pressure. For, indeed, in rendering things in this fashion, Macaulay's gift did not lie. Mr. Trevelyan reminds us that in the preface to his collected Essays Lord Macaulay himself 'unsparingly condemns the redundance of youthful enthusiasm' of the *Essay on Milton*. But the unsoundness of the essay does not spring from its 'redundance of youthful enthusiasm.' It springs from this: that the writer has not for his aim to see and to utter the real truth about his object. Whoever comes to the *Essay on Milton* with the desire to get at the real truth about Milton, whether as a man or as a poet, will feel that the essay in nowise helps him. A reader who only wants rhetoric, a reader who wants a panegyric on Milton, a panegyric on the Puritans, will find what he wants. A reader who wants criticism will be disappointed.

This would be palpable to all the world, and everyone would feel, not pleased, but disappointed, by the *Essay on Milton*, were it not that the readers who seek for criticism are extremely few; while the readers who seek for rhetoric, or who seek for praise and blame to suit their own already established likes and dislikes, are extremely many. A man who is fond of rhetoric may find pleasure in hearing that in *Paradise Lost* 'Milton's conception of love unites all the voluptuousness of the Oriental haram, and all the gallantry of the chivalric tournament, with all the pure and quiet affection of an English fireside.' He may glow at being told that 'Milton's thoughts resemble those celestial fruits and flowers which the Virgin Martyr of Massinger[3] sent down from the gardens of Paradise to the earth, and which were distinguished from the productions of other souls not only by superior bloom and sweetness, but by miraculous efficacy to invigorate and to heal.' He may imagine that he has got something profound when he reads that, if we compare Milton and Dante in their management of the agency of supernatural beings,—'the exact details of Dante with the dim intimations of Milton,'—the right conclusion of the whole matter is this:—

Milton wrote in an age of philosophers and theologians. It was necessary, therefore, for him to abstain from giving such a shock to their understandings as might break the charm which it was his object to throw over their imaginations. It was impossible for him to adopt altogether the material or the immaterial system. He therefore took his stand on the debateable ground. He left the whole in ambiguity. He has doubtless, by so doing, laid himself open to the charge of inconsistency. But though philosophically in the wrong he was poetically in the right.'

Poor Robert Hall, 'wellnigh worn out with that long disease, his life,' and, in the last precious days of it, 'discovered lying on the floor, employed in learning, by aid of grammar and dictionary, enough Italian to enable him to verify' this ingenious criticism! Alas! even had his life been prolonged like Hezekiah's,[4] he could not have verified it, for it is unverifiable. A poet who, writing 'in an age of philosophers and theologians,' finds it 'impossible for him to adopt altogether the material or the immaterial system,' who, therefore, 'takes his stand on the debateable ground,' who 'leaves the whole in ambiguity,' and who, in doing so, 'though philosophically in the wrong, was poetically in the right'! Substantial meaning such lucubrations have none. And in like manner, a distinct and substantial meaning can never be got out of the fine phrases about 'Milton's conception of love uniting all the voluptuousness of the Oriental haram, and all the gallantry of the chivalric tournament, with all the pure and quiet affection of an English fireside;' or about 'Milton's thoughts resembling those celestial fruits and flowers which the Virgin Martyr of Massinger sent down from the gardens of Paradise to the earth;' the phrases are mere rhetoric. Macaulay's writing passes for being admirably clear, and so externally it is; but often it is really obscure, if one takes his deliverances seriously, and seeks to find in them a definite meaning. However, there is a multitude of readers, doubtless, for whom it is sufficient to have their ears tickled with fine rhetoric; but the tickling makes a serious reader impatient.

Many readers there are, again, who come to an Essay on Milton with their minds full of zeal for the Puritan cause, and for Milton as one of the glories of Puritanism. Of such readers the great desire is to have the cause and the man, who are already established objects of enthusiasm for them, strongly praised. Certainly Macaulay will satisfy their desire. They will hear that the Civil War was 'the great conflict between Oromasdes and Arimanes,[5] liberty and despotism, reason and prejudice;' the Puritans being Oromasdes, and the Royalists Arimanes. They will be told that the great Puritan poet was worthy of the august cause which he served. 'His radiant and beneficent career resembled that of the god of light and fertility.' 'There are a few characters which have

stood the closest scrutiny and the severest tests, which have
been tried in the furnace and have proved pure, which have
been declared sterling by the general consent of mankind,
and which are visibly stamped with the image and super-
scription of the Most High. Of these was Milton.' To descend a little to particulars. Milton's temper was especially
admirable. 'The gloom of Dante's character discolours all
the passions of men and all the face of nature, and tinges
with its own livid hue the flowers of Paradise and the glories
of the eternal throne.' But in our countryman, although 'if
ever despondency and asperity could be excused in any man,
they might have been excused in Milton,' nothing 'had
power to disturb his sedate and majestic patience.' All this
is just what an ardent admirer of the Puritan cause and of
Milton would most wish to hear, and when he hears it he is
in ecstasies.

But a disinterested reader, whose object is not to hear
Puritanism and Milton glorified, but to get at the truth about
them, will surely be dissatisfied. With what a heavy brush,
he will say to himself, does this man lay on his colours! The
Puritans Oromasdes, and the Royalists Arimanes? What a
different strain from Chillingworth's,[6] in his sermon at Oxford at the beginning of the Civil War! 'Publicans and sin-
ners on the one side,' said Chillingworth, 'scribes and Phari-
sees on the other.' Not at all a conflict between Oromasdes
and Arimanes, but a good deal of Arimanes on both sides.
And as human affairs go, Chillingworth's version of the
matter is likely to be nearer the truth than Macaulay's. Indeed, for anyone who reads thoughtfully and without bias,
Macaulay himself, with the inconsistency of a born rhetorician, presently confutes his own thesis. He says of the Royalists: 'They had far more both of profound and of polite
learning than the Puritans. Their manners were more engaging, their tempers more amiable, their tastes more elegant,
and their households more cheerful.' Is being more kindly
affectioned such an insignificant superiority? The Royalists
too, then, in spite of their being insufficiently jealous for
civil and ecclesiastical liberty, had in them something of Oromasdes, the principle of light.

And Milton's temper! His 'sedate and majestic patience;'
his freedom from 'asperity'! If there is a defect which, above
all others, is signal in Milton, which injures him even intellectually, which limits him as a poet, it is the defect common
to him with the whole Puritan party to which he belonged,—
the fatal defect of *temper*. He and they may have a thousand
merits, but they are *unamiable*. Excuse them how one will,

Milton's asperity and acerbity, his want of sweetness of temper, of the Shakespearian largeness and indulgence, are undeniable. Lord Macaulay in his Essay regrets that the prose writings of Milton should not be more read. 'They abound,' he says in his rhetorical way, 'with passages, compared with which the finest declamations of Burke sink into insignificance.' At any rate, they enable us to judge of Milton's temper, of his freedom from asperity. Let us open the *Doctrine and Discipline of Divorce* and see how Milton treats an opponent. 'How should he, a serving man both by nature and function, an idiot by breeding, and a solicitor by presumption, ever come to know or feel within himself what the meaning is of *gentle?*' What a gracious temper! 'At last, and in good hour, we come to his farewell, which is to be a concluding taste of his jabberment in law, the flashiest and the fustiest that ever corrupted in such an unswilled hogshead.' How 'sedate and majestic'!

Human progress consists in a continual increase in the number of those, who, ceasing to live by the animal life alone and to feel the pleasures of sense only, come to participate in the intellectual life also, and to find enjoyment in the things of the mind. The enjoyment is not at first very discriminating. Rhetoric, brilliant writing, gives to such persons pleasure for its own sake; but it gives them pleasure, still more, when it is employed in commendation of a view of life which is on the whole theirs, and of men and causes with which they are naturally in sympathy. The immense popularity of Macaulay is due to his being pre-eminently fitted to give pleasure to all who are beginning to feel enjoyment in the things of the mind. It is said that the traveller in Australia, visiting one settler's hut after another, finds again and again that the settler's third book, after the Bible and Shakespeare, is some work by Macaulay. Nothing can be more natural. The Bible and Shakespeare may be said to be imposed upon an Englishman as objects of his admiration; but as soon as the common Englishman, desiring culture, begins to choose for himself, he chooses Macaulay. Macaulay's view of things is, on the whole, the view of them which he feels to be his own also; the persons and causes praised are those which he himself is disposed to admire; the persons and causes blamed are those with which he himself is out of sympathy; and the rhetoric employed to praise or to blame them is animating and excellent. Macaulay is thus a great civiliser. In hundreds of men he hits their nascent taste for the things of the mind, possesses himself of it and stimulates it, draws it powerfully forth and confirms it.

But with the increasing number of those who awake to the intellectual life, the number of those also increases, who, having awoke to it, go on with it, follow where it leads them. And it leads them to see that it is their business to learn the real truth about the important men, and things, and books, which interest the human mind. For thus is gradually to be acquired a stock of sound ideas, in which the mind will habitually move, and which alone can give to our judgments security and solidity. To be satisfied with fine writing about the object of one's study, with having it praised or blamed in accordance with one's own likes or dislikes, with any conventional treatment of it whatever, is at this stage of growth seen to be futile. At this stage, rhetoric, even when it is so good as Macaulay's, dissatisfies. And the number of people who have reached this stage of mental growth is constantly, as things now are, increasing; increasing by the very same law of progress which plants the beginnings of mental life in more and more persons who, until now, have never known mental life at all. So that while the number of those who are delighted with rhetoric such as Macaulay's is always increasing, the number of those who are dissatisfied with it is always increasing too.

And not only rhetoric dissatisfies people at this stage, but conventionality of any kind. This is the fault of Addison's Miltonic criticism,[7] once so celebrated; it rests almost entirely upon convention. Here is *Paradise Lost,* 'a work which does an honour to the English nation,' a work claiming to be one of the great poems of the world, to be of the highest moment to us. 'The *Paradise Lost,*' says Addison, 'is looked upon by the best judges as the greatest production, or at least the noblest work of genius, in our language, and therefore deserves to be set before an English reader in its full beauty.' The right thing, surely, is for such a work to prove its own virtue by powerfully and delightfully affecting us as we read it, and by remaining a constant source of elevation and happiness to us for ever. But the *Paradise Lost* has not this effect certainly and universally; therefore Addison proposes to 'set before an English reader, in its full beauty,' the great poem. To this end he has 'taken a general view of it under these four heads: the fable, the characters, the sentiments, and the language.' He has, moreover,

> endeavoured not only to prove that the poem is beautiful in general, but to point out its particular beauties and to determine wherein they consist. I have endeavoured to show how some passages are beautiful by being sublime, others by

being soft, others by being natural; which of them are recom-
mended by the passion, which by the moral, which by the
sentiment, and which by the expression. I have likewise endeavoured to show how the genius of the poet shines by a
happy invention, or distant allusion, or a judicious imitation;
how he has copied or improved Homer or Virgil, and raises
his own imagination by the use which he has made of several
poetical passages in Scripture. I might have inserted also several passages in Tasso[8] which our author has imitated; but
as I do not look upon Tasso to be a sufficient voucher, I
would not perplex my reader with such quotations as might
do more honour to the Italian than the English poet.

This is the sort of criticism which held our grandfathers
and great-grandfathers spell-bound in solemn reverence. But
it is all based upon convention, and on the positivism of the
modern reader it is thrown away. Does the work which you
praise, he asks, affect me with high pleasure and do me good,
when I try it as fairly as I can? The critic who helps such a
questioner is one who has sincerely asked himself, also, this
same question; who has answered it in a way which agrees,
in the main, with what the questioner finds to be his own
honest experience in the matter, and who shows the reasons
for this common experience. Where is the use of telling a
man, who finds himself tired rather than delighted by *Paradise Lost,* that the incidents in that poem 'have in them all
the beauties of novelty, at the same time that they have all
the graces of nature:' that 'though they are natural, they are
not obvious, which is the true character of all fine writing'?
Where is the use of telling him that 'Adam and Eve are
drawn with such sentiments as do not only interest the
reader in their afflictions, but raise in him the most melting
passions of humanity and commiseration'? His own experience, on the other hand, is that the incidents in *Paradise Lost*
are such as awaken in him but the most languid interest;
and that the afflictions and sentiments of Adam and Eve
never melt or move him passionately at all. How is he advanced by hearing that 'it is not sufficient that the language
of an epic poem be perspicuous, unless it be also sublime;'
and that Milton's language is both? What avails it to assure
him that 'the first thing to be considered in an epic poem is
the fable, which is perfect or imperfect, according as the
action which it relates is more or less so;' that 'this action
should have three qualifications, should be but one action,
an entire action, and a great action;' and that if we 'consider
the action of the *Iliad, Æneid,* and *Paradise Lost,* in these

three several lights, we shall find that Milton's poem does not fall short in the beauties which are essential to that kind of writing'? The patient whom Addison thus doctors will reply, that he does not care two straws whether the action of *Paradise Lost* satisfies the proposed test or no, if the poem does not give him pleasure. The truth is, Addison's criticism rests on certain conventions: namely, that incidents of a certain class *must* awaken keen interest; that sentiments of a certain kind *must* raise melting passions; that language of a certain strain, and an action with certain qualifications, *must* render a poem attractive and effective. Disregard the convention; ask solely whether the incidents *do* interest, whether the sentiments *do* move, whether the poem *is* attractive and effective, and Addison's criticism collapses.

Sometimes the convention is one which in theory ought, a man may perhaps admit, to be something more than a convention; but which yet practically is not. Milton's poem is of surpassing interest to us, says Addison, because in it 'the principal actors are not only our progenitors but our representatives. We have an actual interest in everything they do, and no less than our utmost happiness is concerned, and lies at stake, in all their behaviour.' Of ten readers who may even admit that in theory this is so, barely one can be found whose practical experience tells him that Adam and Eve do really, as his representatives, excite his interest in this vivid manner. It is by a mere convention, then, that Addison supposes them to do so, and claims an advantage for Milton's poem from the supposition.

The theological speeches in the third book of *Paradise Lost* are not, in themselves, attractive poetry. But, says Addison:—

> The passions which they are designed to raise are a divine love and religious fear. The particular beauty of the speeches in the third book consists in that shortness and perspicuity of style in which the poet has couched the greatest mysteries of Christianity. . . . He has represented all the abstruse doctrines of predestination, free-will, and grace, as also the great points of incarnation and redemption (which naturally grow up in a poem that treats of the fall of man) with great energy of expression, and in a clearer and stronger light than I ever met with in any other writer.

But nine readers out of ten feel that, as a matter of fact, their religious sentiments of 'divine love and religious fear' are wholly ineffectual even to reconcile them to the poetical tiresomeness of the speeches in question; far less can they render them interesting. It is by a mere convention, then, that Addison pretends that they do.

The great merit of Johnson's criticism on Milton is that from rhetoric and convention it is free. Mr. Trevelyan says that the enthusiasm of Macaulay's *Essay on Milton* is, at any rate, 'a relief from the perverted ability of that elaborate libel on our great epic poet, which goes by the name of Dr. Johnson's *Life of Milton*.' This is too much in Lord Macaulay's own style. In Johnson's *Life of Milton* we have the straightforward remarks, on Milton and his works, of a very acute and robust mind. Often they are thoroughly sound. 'What we know of Milton's character in domestic relations is that he was severe and arbitrary. His family consisted of women; and there appears in his books something like a Turkish contempt of females as subordinate and inferior beings.' Mr. Trevelyan will forgive our saying that the truth is here much better hit, than in Lord Macaulay's sentence telling us how Milton's 'conception of love unites all the voluptuousness of the Oriental haram, and all the gallantry of the chivalric tournament, with all the pure and quiet affection of an English fireside.' But Johnson's mind, acute and robust as it was, was at many points bounded, at many points warped. He was neither sufficiently disinterested, nor sufficiently flexible, nor sufficiently receptive, to be a satisfying critic of a poet like Milton. 'Surely no man could have fancied that he read "Lycidas" with pleasure, had he not known the author!' Terrible sentence for revealing the deficiencies of the critic who utters it.

A completely disinterested judgment about a man like Milton is easier to a foreign critic than to an Englishman. From conventional obligation to admire 'our great epic poet' a foreigner is free. Nor has he any bias for or against Milton because he was a Puritan,—in his political and ecclesiastical doctrines to one of our great English parties a delight, to the other a bugbear. But a critic must have the requisite knowledge of the man and the works he is to judge; and from a foreigner,—particularly, perhaps, from a Frenchman,—one hardly expects such knowledge. M. Edmond Scherer, however, whose essay on Milton lies before me,[9] is an exceptional Frenchman. He is a senator of France and one of the directors of the *Temps* newspaper. But he was trained at Geneva, that home of large instruction and lucid intelligence. He was in youth the friend and hearer of Alexandre Vinet,[10] —one of the most salutary influences a man in our times can have experienced, whether he continue to think quite with Vinet or not. He knows thoroughly the language and literature of England, Italy, Germany, as well as of France. Well-informed, intelligent, disinterested, open-minded, sympathetic, M. Scherer has much in common with the admirable critic whom France has lost,—Sainte-Beuve. What he has not, as a critic, is Sainte-Beuve's elasticity and cheerfulness. He has not that gaiety, that radiancy, as of a man discharging with delight the very office for which he was born, which, in the *Causeries,* make Sainte-Beuve's touch so felicitous, his sentences so crisp, his effect so charming. But M. Scherer has the same open-mindedness as Sainte-Beuve, the same firmness and sureness of judgment; and having a much more solid acquaintance with foreign languages than Sainte-Beuve, he can much better appreciate a work like *Paradise Lost* in the only form in which it can be appreciated properly,—in the original.

We will commence, however, by disagreeing with M. Scherer. He sees very clearly how vain is Lord Macaulay's sheer laudation of Milton, or Voltaire's sheer disparagement of him.[11] Such judgments, M. Scherer truly says, are not judgments at all. They merely express a personal sensation of like or dislike. And M. Scherer goes on to recommend, in the place of such 'personal sensations,' the method of historical criticism,—that great and famous power in the present day. He sings the praises of 'this method at once more conclusive and more equitable, which sets itself to understand things rather than to class them, to explain rather than to judge them; which seeks to account for a work from the genius of its author, and for the turn which this genius has taken from the circumstances amidst which it was developed;'—the old story of 'the man and the *milieu,*' in short. 'For thus,' M. Scherer continues, 'out of these two things, the analysis of the writer's character and the study of his age, there spontaneously issues the right understanding of his work. In place of an appreciation thrown off by some chance comer, we have the work passing judgment, so to speak, upon itself, and assuming the rank which belongs to it among the productions of the human mind.'

The advice to study the character of an author and the circumstances in which he has lived, in order to account to oneself for his work, is excellent. But it is a perilous doctrine, that from such a study the right understanding of his work will 'spontaneously issue.' In a mind qualified in a certain manner it will, not in all minds. And it will be that mind's 'personal sensation.' It cannot be said that Macaulay had not studied the character of Milton, and the history of the times in which he lived. But a right understanding of Milton did not 'spontaneously issue' therefrom in the mind of Macaulay, because Macaulay's mind was that of a rhetorician, not of a disinterested critic. Let us not confound the method with the result intended by the method,—right judgments. The critic who rightly appreciates a great man or a great work, and who can tell us faithfully, life being short and art long and false information very plentiful, what we may expect from their study and what they can do for us, he is the critic we want, by whatever methods, intuitive or historical, he may have managed to get his knowledge.

M. Scherer begins with Milton's prose works, from which he translates many passages. Milton's sentences can hardly know themselves again in clear modern French, and with all their inversions and redundancies gone. M. Scherer does full justice to the glow and mighty eloquence with which Milton's prose, in its good moments, is instinct and alive; to the 'magnificences of his style,' as he calls them:—

> The expression is not too strong. There are moments when, shaking from him the dust of his arguments, the poet bursts suddenly forth, and bears us away in a torrent of incomparable eloquence. We get, not the phrase of the orator, but the glow of the poet, a flood of images poured around his arid theme, a rushing flight carrying us above his paltry controversies. The polemical writings of Milton are filled with such beauties. The prayer which concludes the treatise on Reformation in England, the praise of zeal in the Apology for Smectymnuus, the portrait of Cromwell in the Second Defence of the English People, and, finally, the whole tract on the Liberty of Unlicensed Printing from beginning to end, are some of the most memorable pages in English literature, and some of the most characteristic products of the genius of Milton.

Macaulay himself could hardly praise the eloquence of Milton's prose writings more warmly. But it is a very inadequate criticism which leaves the reader, as Macaulay's rhetoric would leave him, with the belief that the total impression to be got from Milton's prose writings is one of enjoyment and admiration. It is not; we are misled, and our time is wasted, if we are sent to Milton's prose works in the expectation of finding it so. Grand thoughts and beautiful language do not form the staple of Milton's controversial treatises, though they occur in them not unfrequently. But the total impression from those treatises is rightly given by M. Scherer:—

In all of them the manner is the same. The author brings into play the treasures of his learning, heaping together testimonies from Scripture, passages from the Fathers, quotations from the poets; laying all antiquity, sacred and profane, under contribution; entering into subtle discussions on the sense of this or that Greek or Hebrew word. But not only by his undigested erudition and by his absorption in religious controversy does Milton belong to his age; he belongs to it, too, by the personal tone of his polemics. Morus and Salmasius had attacked his morals, laughed at his low stature, made unfeeling allusions to his loss of sight: Milton replies by reproaching them with the wages they have taken and with the servant-girls they have debauched. All this mixed with coarse witticisms, with terms of the lowest abuse. Luther and Calvin, those virtuosos of insult, had not gone farther.

No doubt there is, as M. Scherer says, 'something indescribably heroical and magnificent which overflows from Milton, even when he is engaged in the most miserable discussions.' Still, for the mass of his prose treatises, 'miserable discussion' is the final and right word. Nor, when Milton passed to his great epic, did he altogether leave the old man of these 'miserable discussions' behind him.

In his soul he is a polemist and theologian; a Protestant Schoolman. He takes delight in the favourite dogmas of Puritanism: original sin, predestination, free-will. Not that even here he does not display somewhat of that independence which was in his nature. But his theology is, nevertheless, that of his epoch, tied and bound to the letter of Holy Writ, without grandeur, without horizons, without philosophy. He never frees himself from the bondage of the letter. He settles the most important questions by the authority of an obscure text, or a text isolated from its context. In a word, Milton is a great poet with a Salmasius or a Grotius bound up along with him; a genius nourished on the marrow of lions, of Homer, Isaiah, Virgil, Dante, but also, like the serpent of Eden, eating dust, the dust of dismal polemics. He is a doctor, a preacher, a man of didactics; and when the day shall arrive when he can at last realise the dreams of his youth and bestow on his country an epic poem, he will compose it of two elements, gold and clay, sublimity and scholasticism, and will bequeath to us a poem which is at once the most wonderful and the most insupportable poem in existence.

From the first, two conflicting forces, two sources of inspiration, had contended with one another, says M. Scherer, for the possession of Milton,—the Renascence and Puritanism. Milton felt the power of both:—

Elegant poet and passionate disputant, accomplished humanist and narrow sectary, admirer of Petrarch, of Shakespeare, and hair-splitting interpreter of Bible-texts, smitten with pagan antiquity and smitten with the Hebrew genius; and all this at once, without effort, naturally;—an historical problem, a literary enigma!

Milton's early poems, such as the *Allegro,* the *Penseroso,* are poems produced while a sort of equilibrium still prevailed in the poet's nature; hence their charm, and that of their youthful author:—

Nothing morose or repellent, purity without excess of rigour, gravity without fanaticism. Something wholesome and virginal, gracious and yet strong. A son of the North who has passed the way of Italy; a last fruit of the Renascence, but a fruit filled with a savour new and strange!

But Milton's days proceeded, and he arrived at the latter years of his life, a life which in its outward fortunes darkened more and more, *alla s'assombrissant de plus en plus,* towards its close. He arrived at the time when 'his friends had disappeared, his dreams had vanished, his eyesight was quenched, the hand of old age was upon him.' It was then that, 'isolated by the very force of his genius,' but full of faith and fervour, he 'turned his eyes towards the celestial light' and produced *Paradise Lost.* In its form, M. Scherer observes, in its plan and distribution, the poem follows Greek and Roman models, particularly the *Æneid.* 'All in this respect is regular and classical; in this fidelity to the established models we recognise the literary superstitions of the Renascence.' So far as its form is concerned, *Paradise Lost* is, says M. Scherer, 'the copy of a copy, a tertiary formation. It is to the Latin epics what these are to Homer.' The most important matter, however, is the contents of the poem, not the form. The contents are given by Puritanism. But let M. Scherer speak for himself:—

Paradise Lost is an epic, but a theological epic; and the theology of the poem is made up of the favourite dogmas of the Puritans,—the Fall, justification, God's sovereign decrees. Milton, for that matter, avows openly that he has a thesis to maintain; his object is, he tells us at the outset, to 'assert Eternal Providence and justify the ways of God to man.'[12] *Paradise Lost,* then, is two distinct things in one—an epic and a theodicy. Unfortunately, these two elements, which correspond to the two men of whom Milton was composed and to the two tendencies which ruled his century, these two elements have not managed to get amalgamated. Far from doing so, they clash with one another, and from their juxtaposition there results a suppressed contradiction which extends to the whole work, impairs its solidity, and compromises its value.

M. Scherer gives his reasons for thinking that the Christian theology is unmanageable in an epic poem, although the gods may come in very well in the *Iliad* and *Æneid*. Few will differ from him here, so we pass on. A theological poem is a mistake, says M. Scherer; but to call *Paradise Lost* a theological poem is to call it by too large a name. It is really a commentary on a biblical text,—the first two or three chapters of Genesis. Its subject, therefore, is a story, taken literally, which many of even the most religious people nowadays hesitate to take literally; while yet, upon our being able to take it literally, the whole real interest of the poem for us depends. Merely as matter of poetry, the story of the Fall has no special force or effectiveness; its effectiveness for us comes, and can only come, from our taking it all as the literal narrative of what positively happened.

Milton, M. Scherer thinks, was not strong in invention. The famous allegory of Sin and Death may be taken as a specimen of what he could do in this line, and the allegory of Sin and Death is uncouth and unpleasing. But invention is dangerous when one is dealing with a subject so grave, so strictly formulated by theology, as the subject of Milton's choice. Our poet felt this, and allowed little scope to free poetical invention. He adhered in general to data furnished by Scripture, and supplemented somewhat by Jewish legend. But this judicious self-limitation had, again, its drawbacks:—

If Milton has avoided factitious inventions, he has done so at the price of another disadvantage; the bareness of his story, the epic poverty of his poem. It is not merely that the reader is carried up into the sphere of religious abstractions, where man loses power to see or breathe. Independently of this, everything is here too simple, both actors and actions. Strictly speaking, there is but one personage before us, God the Father; inasmuch as God cannot appear without effacing everyone else, nor speak without the accomplishment of his will. The Son is but the Father's double. The angels and archangels are but his messengers, nay, they are less; they are but his decrees personified, the supernumeraries of a drama which would be transacted quite as well without them.

Milton has struggled against these conditions of the subject which he had chosen. He has tried to escape from them, and has only made the drawback more visible. The long speeches with which he fills up the gaps of the action are sermons, and serve but to reveal the absence of action. Then, as, after all, some action, some struggle, was necessary, the poet had recourse to the revolt of the angels. Unfortunately, such is the fundamental vice of the subject, that the poet's instrument has, one may say, turned against him. What his action has gained from it in movement it has lost in probability. We see a battle, indeed, but who can take either the combat or the combatants seriously? Belial shows his sense of this, when in the infernal council he rejects the idea of engaging in any conflict whatever, open or secret, with Him who is Allseeing and Almighty; and really one cannot comprehend how his mates should have failed to acquiesce in a consideration so evident. But, I repeat, the poem was not possible save at the price of this impossibility. Milton, therefore, has courageously made the best of it. He has gone with it all lengths, he has accepted in all its extreme consequences the most inadmissible of fictions. He has exhibited to us Jehovah apprehensive for his omnipotence, in fear of seeing his position turned, his residence surprised, his throne usurped. He has drawn the angels hurling mountains at one another's heads, and firing cannon at one another. He has shown us the victory doubtful until the Son appears armed with lightnings, and standing on a car horsed by four Cherubim.

The fault of Milton's poem is not, says M. Scherer, that, with his Calvinism of the seventeenth century, Milton was a man holding other beliefs than ours. Homer, Dante, held other beliefs than ours:—

But Milton's position is not the same as theirs. Milton has something he wants to prove, he supports a thesis. It was his intention, in his poem, to do duty as theologian as well as poet; at any rate, whether he meant it or not, *Paradise Lost* is a didactic work, and the form of it, therefore, cannot be separated from the substance. Now, it turns out that the idea of the poem will not bear examination; that its solution for the problem of evil is almost burlesque; that the character of its heroes, Jehovah and Satan, has no coherence; that what happens to Adam interests us but little; finally, that the action takes place in regions where the interests and passions of our common humanity can have no scope. I have already insisted on this contradiction in Milton's epic; the story on which it turns can have meaning and value only so long as it preserves its dogmatic weight, and, at the same time, it cannot preserve this without falling into theology, —that is to say, into a domain foreign to that of art. The subject of the poem is nothing if it is not real, and if it does not touch us as the turning-point of our destinies; and the more the poet seeks to grasp this reality, the more it escapes from him.

In short, the whole poem of *Paradise Lost* is vitiated, says M. Scherer, 'by a kind of antinomy, by the conjoint necessity and impossibility of taking its contents literally.'

M. Scherer then proceeds to sum up. And in ending, after having once more marked his objections and accentuated them, he at last finds again that note of praise, which the reader will imagine him to have quite lost:—

> To sum up: *Paradise Lost* is a false poem, a grotesque poem, a tiresome poem; there is not one reader out of a hundred who can read the ninth and tenth books without smiling, or the eleventh and twelfth without yawning. The whole thing is without solidity; it is a pyramid resting on its apex, the most solemn of problems resolved by the most puerile of means. And, notwithstanding, *Paradise Lost* is immortal. It lives by a certain number of episodes which are for ever famous. Unlike Dante, who must be read as a whole if we want really to seize his beauties, Milton ought to be read only by passages. But these passages form part of the poetical patrimony of the human race.

And not only in things like the address to light, or the speeches of Satan, is Milton admirable, but in single lines and images everywhere:—

> *Paradise Lost* is studded with incomparable lines. Milton's poetry is, as it were, the very essence of poetry. The author seems to think always in images, and these images are grand and proud like his soul, a wonderful mixture of the sublime and the picturesque. For rendering things he has the unique word, the word which is a discovery. Everyone knows his *darkness visible*.[13]

M. Scherer cites other famous expressions and lines, so familiar that we need not quote them here. Expressions of the kind, he says, not only beautiful, but always, in addition to their beauty, striking one as the absolutely right thing (*toujours justes dans leur beauté*), are in *Paradise Lost* innumerable. And he concludes:—

> Moreover, we have not said all when we have cited particular lines of Milton. He has not only the image and the word, he has the period also, the large musical phrase, somewhat long, somewhat laden with ornaments and intricate with inversions, but bearing all along with it in its superb undulation. Lastly, and above all, he has a something indescribably serene and victorious, an unfailing level of style,

power indomitable. He seems to wrap us in a fold of his robe, and to carry us away with him into the eternal regions where is his home.

With this fine image M. Scherer takes leave of Milton. Yet the simple description of the man in Johnson's life of him touches us more than any image; the description of the old poet 'seen in a small house, neatly enough dressed in black clothes, sitting in a room hung with rusty green, pale but not cadaverous, with chalk stones in his hands. He said that, if it were not for the gout his blindness would be tolerable.'

But in his last sentences M. Scherer comes upon what is undoubtedly Milton's true distinction as a poet, his 'unfailing level of style.' Milton has always the sure, strong touch of the master. His power both of diction and of rhythm is unsurpassable, and it is characterised by being always present—not depending on an access of emotion, not intermittent, but, like the grace of Raphael, working in its possessor as a constant gift of nature. Milton's style, moreover, has the same propriety and soundness in presenting plain matters, as in the comparatively smooth task for a poet of presenting grand ones. His rhythm is as admirable where, as in the line

And Tiresias and Phineus, prophets old—[14]

it is unusual, as in such lines as—

With dreadful faces throng'd and fiery arms—[15]

where it is simplest. And what high praise this is, we may best appreciate by considering the ever-recurring failure, both in rhythm and in diction, which we find in the so-called Miltonic blank verse of Thomson, Cowper, Wordsworth. What leagues of lumbering movement! what desperate endeavours, as in Wordsworth's

And at the 'Hoop' alighted, famous inn,[16]

to render a platitude endurable by making it pompous! Shakespeare himself, divine as are his gifts, has not, of the marks of the master, this one: perfect sureness of hand in his style. Alone of English poets, alone in English art, Milton has it; he is our great artist in style, our one first-rate master in the grand style. He is as truly a master in this style as the great Greeks are, or Virgil, or Dante. The number of such masters is so limited that a man acquires a world-rank in poetry and art, instead of a mere local rank, by being counted among them. But Milton's importance to us Englishmen, by virtue of this distinction of his, is incalculable. The charm of a master's unfailing touch in diction and in rhythm, no one, after all, can feel so intimately, so profoundly, as his own countrymen. Invention, plan, wit, pathos, thought, all of them are in great measure capable of being detached from the original work itself, and of being exported for admiration abroad. Diction and rhythm are not. Even when a foreigner can read the work in its own language, they are not, perhaps, easily appreciable by him. It shows M. Scherer's thorough knowledge of English, and his critical sagacity also, that he has felt the force of them in Milton. We natives must naturally feel it yet more powerfully. Be it remembered, too, that English literature, full of vigour and genius as it is, is peculiarly impaired by gropings and inadequacies in form. And the same with English art. Therefore for the English artist in any line, if he is a true artist, the study of Milton may well have an indescribable attraction. It gives him lessons which nowhere else from an Englishman's work can he obtain, and feeds a sense which English work, in general, seems bent on disappointing and baffling. And this sense is yet so deep-seated in human nature,—this sense of style,—that probably not for artists alone, but for all intelligent Englishmen who read him, its gratification by Milton's poetry is a large though often not fully recognised part of his charm, and a very wholesome and fruitful one.

As a man, too, not less than as a poet, Milton has a side of unsurpassable grandeur. A master's touch is the gift of nature. Moral qualities, it is commonly thought, are in our own power. Perhaps the germs of such qualities are in their greater or less strength as much a part of our natural constitution as the sense for style. The range open to our own will and power, however, in developing and establishing them, is evidently much larger. Certain high moral dispositions Milton had from nature, and he sedulously trained and developed them until they became habits of great power.

Some moral qualities seem to be connected in a man with his power of style. Milton's power of style, for instance, has for its great character *elevation;* and Milton's elevation clearly comes, in the main, from a moral quality in him,—his pureness. 'By pureness, by kindness!' says St. Paul.[17] These two, pureness and kindness, are, in very truth, the two signal Christian virtues, the two mighty wings of Christianity, with which it winnowed and renewed, and still winnows and renews, the world. In kindness, and in all which that word conveys or suggests, Milton does not shine.

He had the temper of his Puritan party. We often hear the
boast, on behalf of the Puritans, that they produced 'our
great epic poet.' Alas! one might not unjustly retort that
they spoiled him. However, let Milton bear his own burden;
in his temper he had natural affinities with the Puritans. He
has paid for it by limitations as a poet. But, on the other
hand, how high, clear, and splendid is his pureness; and
how intimately does its might enter into the voice of his
poetry! We have quoted some ill-conditioned passages from
his prose, let us quote from it a passage of another stamp:—

> And long it was not after, when I was confirmed in this
> opinion, that he, who would not be frustrate of his hope to
> write well hereafter in laudable things, ought himself to be a
> true poem; that is, a composition and pattern of the best
> and honourablest things; not presuming to sing high praises
> of heroic men, or famous cities, unless he have in himself
> the experience and the practice of all that which is praise-
> worthy. These reasonings, together with a certain niceness
> of nature, an honest haughtiness and self-esteem, either of
> what I was or what I might be (which let envy call pride),
> and lastly that modesty whereof here I may be excused to
> make some beseeming profession; all these uniting the sup-
> ply of their natural aid together kept me still above low
> descents of mind. Next (for hear me out now, readers), that
> I may tell you whither my younger feet wandered; I betook
> me among those lofty fables and romances which recount
> in solemn cantos the deeds of knighthood founded by our
> victorious kings, and from hence had in renown over all
> Christendom. There I read it in the oath of every knight,
> that he should defend to the expense of his best blood, or of
> his life if it so befell him, the honour and chastity of virgin
> or matron; from whence even then I learnt what a noble
> virtue chastity sure must be, to the defence of which so
> many worthies by such a dear adventure of themselves had
> sworn. Only this my mind gave me, that every free and gen-
> tle spirit, without that oath, ought to be born a knight, nor
> needed to expect the gilt spur, or the laying of a sword upon
> his shoulder, to stir him up both by his counsel and his arm
> to secure and protect the weakness of any attempted
> chastity.[18]

Mere fine professions are in this department of morals
more common and more worthless than in any other. What
gives to Milton's professions such a stamp of their own is
their accent of absolute sincerity. In this elevated strain of
moral pureness his life was really pitched; its strong, immortal beauty passed into the diction and rhythm of his
poetry.

But I did not propose to write a criticism of my own upon Milton. I proposed to recite and compare the criticisms on him by others. Only one is tempted, after our many extracts from M. Scherer, in whose criticism of Milton the note of blame fills so much more place than the note of praise, to accentuate this note of praise, which M. Scherer touches indeed with justness, but hardly perhaps draws out fully enough or presses firmly enough. As a poet and as a man, Milton has a side of grandeur so high and rare, as to give him rank along with the half-dozen greatest poets who have ever lived, although to their masterpieces his *Paradise Lost* is, in the fulfilment of the complete range of conditions which a great poem ought to satisfy, indubitably inferior.

Nothing is gained by huddling on 'our great epic poet,' in a promiscuous heap, every sort of praise. Sooner or later the question: How does Milton's masterpiece really stand to us moderns, what are we to think of it, what can we get from it? must inevitably be asked and answered. We have marked that side of the answer which is and will always remain favourable to Milton. The unfavourable side of the answer is supplied by M. Scherer. '*Paradise Lost* lives; but none the less is it true that its fundamental conceptions have become foreign to us, and that if the work subsists it is in spite of the subject treated by it.'

The verdict seems just, and it is supported by M. Scherer with considerations natural, lucid, and forcible. He, too, has his conventions when he comes to speak of Racine and Lamartine. But his judgments on foreign poets, on Shakespeare, Byron, Goethe, as well as on Milton, seem to me to be singularly uninfluenced by the conventional estimates of these poets, and singularly rational. Leaning to the side of severity, as is natural when one has been wearied by choruses of ecstatic and exaggerated praise, he yet well and fairly reports, I think, the real impression made by these great men and their works on a modern mind disinterested, intelligent, and sincere. The English reader, I hope, may have been interested in seeing how Milton and his *Paradise Lost* stand such a survey. And those who are dissatisfied with what has been thus given upon them may always revenge themselves by falling back upon their Addison, and by observing sarcastically that 'a few general rules extracted out of the French authors, with a certain cant of words, has sometimes set up an illiterate heavy writer for a most judicious and formidable critic.'[19]

NOTES

A French Critic on Milton: Published in *Quarterly Review* (January, 1877); *Mixed Essays* (1879).

1. G. O. Trevelyan (1838–1928), nephew of Macaulay and author of *The Life and Letters of Lord Macaulay* (1876).

2. Francis Jeffrey, Lord Jeffrey (1773–1850), founder of the *Edinburgh Review.*

3. The martyred Dorothea (in Massinger's play, 1622) sends fruit and flowers from Heaven to her persecutor.

4. *Isaiah,* xxxviii. 5: "Thus saith the Lord, the God of David thy father, I have heard thy prayer, I have seen thy tears: behold, I will add unto thy days fifteen years."

5. Ormazd, the good principle and highest god, and Ahriman, the evil principle or devil, in the Zoroastrian religion.

6. William Chillingworth (1602–44), theologian.

7. Joseph Addison (1672–1719), in *The Spectator,* January 5–May 3, 1712.

8. Torquato Tasso (1544–95), author of the romantic epic *Gerusalemme Liberata* (1576).

9. Scherer (1815–89) collected his *Études critiques de littérature* in 1876; he had previously collected his *Études sur la littérature contemporaine* (from 1863).

10. (1797–1847), Swiss critic and theologian.

11. *An Essay on Epic Poetry* (1727).

12. *Paradise Lost,* i. 26 ("to men").

13. *Paradise Lost,* i. 63.

14. *Paradise Lost,* iii. 36.

15. *Paradise Lost,* xii. 644.

16. See p. 273.

17. *2 Corinthians,* vi. 6.

18. *An Apology for Smectymnuus* (1642).

19. *The Spectator,* February 2, 1712.

from MILTON

1888

IF to our English race an inadequate sense for perfection of work is a real danger, if the discipline of respect for a high and flawless excellence is peculiarly needed by us, Milton is of all our gifted men the best lesson, the most salutary influence. In the sure and flawless perfection of his rhythm and diction he is as admirable as Virgil or Dante, and in this respect he is unique amongst us. No one else in English literature and art possesses the like distinction.

Thomson, Cowper, Wordsworth, all of them good poets who have studied Milton, followed Milton, adopted his form, fail in their diction and rhythm if we try them by that high standard of excellence maintained by Milton constantly. From style really high and pure Milton never departs; their departures from it are frequent.

Shakespeare is divinely strong, rich, and attractive. But sureness of perfect style Shakespeare himself does not possess. I have heard a politician express wonder at the treasures of political wisdom in a certain celebrated scene of *Troilus and Cressida;* for my part I am at least equally moved to wonder at the fantastic and false diction in which Shakespeare has in that scene clothed them. Milton, from one end of *Paradise Lost* to the other, is in his diction and rhythm constantly a great artist in the great style. Whatever may be said as to the subject of his poem, as to the conditions under which he received his subject and treated it, that praise, at any rate, is assured to him.

For the rest, justice is not at present done, in my opinion, to Milton's management of the inevitable matter of a Puritan epic, a matter full of difficulties, for a poet. Justice is

not done to the *architectonics,* as Goethe would have called
them, of *Paradise Lost;* in these, too, the power of Milton's
art is remarkable. But this may be a proposition which requires discussion and development for establishing it, and
they are impossible on an occasion like the present.

That Milton, of all our English race, is by his diction and
rhythm the one artist of the highest rank in the great style
whom we have; this I take as requiring no discussion, this
I take as certain.

The mighty power of poetry and art is generally admitted.
But where the soul of this power, of this power at its best,
chiefly resides, very many of us fail to see. It resides chiefly
in the refining and elevation wrought in us by the high and
rare excellence of the great style. We may feel the effect
without being able to give ourselves clear account of its
cause, but the thing is so. Now, no race needs the influences
mentioned, the influences of refining and elevation, more
than ours; and in poetry and art our grand source for them
is Milton.

To what does he owe this supreme distinction? To nature
first and foremost, to that bent of nature for inequality
which to the worshippers of the average man is so unacceptable; to a gift, a divine favour. 'The older one grows,'
says Goethe, 'the more one prizes natural gifts, because by
no possibility can they be procured and stuck on.' Nature
formed Milton to be a great poet. But what other poet has
shown so sincere a sense of the grandeur of his vocation,
and a moral effort so constant and sublime to make and keep
himself worthy of it? The Milton of religious and political
controversy, and perhaps of domestic life also, is not seldom
disfigured by want of amenity, by acerbity. The Milton of
poetry, on the other hand, is one of those great men 'who
are modest'—to quote a fine remark of Leopardi,[1] that
gifted and stricken young Italian, who in his sense for poetic
style is worthy to be named with Dante and Milton—'who
are modest, because they continually compare themselves,
not with other men, but with that idea of the perfect which
they have before their mind.' The Milton of poetry is the
man, in his own magnificent phrase, of 'devout prayer to
that Eternal Spirit that can enrich with all utterance and
knowledge, and sends out his Seraphim with the hallowed
fire of his altar, to touch and purify the lips of whom he
pleases.' And finally, the Milton of poetry is, in his own
words again, the man of 'industrious and select reading.'[2]
Continually he lived in companionship with high and rare
excellence, with the great Hebrew poets and prophets, with

the great poets of Greece and Rome. The Hebrew compositions were not in verse, and can be not inadequately represented by the grand, measured prose of our English Bible. The verse of the poets of Greece and Rome no translation can adequately reproduce. Prose cannot have the power of verse; verse-translation may give whatever of charm is in the soul and talent of the translator himself, but never the specific charm of the verse and poet translated. In our race are thousands of readers, presently there will be millions, who know not a word of Greek and Latin, and will never learn those languages. If this host of readers are ever to gain any sense of the power and charm of the great poets of antiquity, their way to gain it is not through translations of the ancients, but through the original poetry of Milton, who has the like power and charm, because he has the like great style.

Through Milton they may gain it, for, in conclusion, Milton is English; this master in the great style of the ancients is English.

NOTES

from *Milton:* Delivered at the unveiling of a Memorial Window at St. Margaret's Church, Westminster, February 13, 1888; published in *Essays in Criticism* [Second Series] (1888).

1. Giacomo Leopardi (1798–1837).
2. *The Reason of Church Government* (1642).

THOMAS GRAY

1880

JAMES BROWN, Master of Pembroke Hall at Cambridge, Gray's friend and executor, in a letter written a fortnight after Gray's death to another of his friends, Dr. Wharton of Old Park, Durham, has the following passage:—

'Everything is now dark and melancholy in Mr. Gray's room, not a trace of him remains there; it looks as if it had been for some time uninhabited, and the room bespoke for another inhabitant. The thoughts I have of him will last, and will be useful to me the few years I can expect to live. He never spoke out, but I believe from some little expressions I now remember to have dropped from him, that for some time past he thought himself nearer his end than those about him apprehended.'

He never spoke out. In these four words is contained the whole history of Gray, both as a man and as a poet. The words fell naturally, and as it were by chance, from their writer's pen; but let us dwell upon them, and press into their meaning, for in following it we shall come to understand Gray.

He was in his fifty-fifth year when he died,[1] and he lived in ease and leisure, yet a few pages hold all his poetry; *he never spoke out* in poetry. Still, the reputation which he has achieved by his few pages is extremely high. True, Johnson speaks of him with coldness and disparagement. Gray disliked Johnson, and refused to make his acquaintance; one might fancy that Johnson wrote with some irritation from this cause. But Johnson was not by nature fitted to do justice to Gray and to his poetry; this by itself is a sufficient ex-

planation of the deficiencies of his criticism of Gray. We
may add a further explanation of them which is supplied by
Mr. Cole's papers.[2] 'When Johnson was publishing his Life
of Gray,' says Mr. Cole, 'I gave him several anecdotes, *but
he was very anxious as soon as possible to get to the end of
his labours.*' Johnson was not naturally in sympathy with
Gray, whose life he had to write, and when he wrote it he
was in a hurry besides. He did Gray injustice, but even Johnson's authority failed to make injustice, in this case, prevail.
Lord Macaulay calls the Life of Gray the worst of Johnson's
Lives, and it had found many censurers before Macaulay.
Gray's poetical reputation grew and flourished in spite of it.
The poet Mason,[3] his first biographer, in his epitaph
equalled him with Pindar. Britain has known, says Mason,

> '. . . a Homer's fire in Milton's strains,
> A Pindar's rapture in the lyre of Gray.'

The immense vogue of Pope and of his style of versification
had at first prevented the frank reception of Gray by the
readers of poetry. The "Elegy" pleased; it could not but
please: but Gray's poetry, on the whole, astonished his contemporaries at first more than it pleased them; it was so unfamiliar, so unlike the sort of poetry in vogue. It made its
way, however, after his death, with the public as well as
with the few; and Gray's second biographer, Mitford,[4] remarks that 'the works which were either neglected or ridiculed by their contemporaries have now raised Gray and
Collins[5] to the rank of our two greatest lyric poets.' Their
reputation was established, at any rate, and stood extremely
high, even if they were not popularly read. Johnson's disparagement of Gray was called 'petulant,' and severely
blamed. Beattie,[6] at the end of the eighteenth century, writing to Sir William Forbes, says: 'Of all the English poets of
this age Mr. Gray is most admired, and I think with justice.'
Cowper[7] writes: 'I have been reading Gray's works, and
think him the only poet since Shakespeare entitled to the
character of sublime. Perhaps you will remember that I once
had a different opinion of him. I was prejudiced.' Adam
Smith[8] says: 'Gray joins to the sublimity of Milton the
elegance and harmony of Pope; and nothing is wanting to
render him, perhaps, the first poet in the English language,
but to have written a little more.' And, to come nearer to
our own times, Sir James Mackintosh[9] speaks of Gray thus:
'Of all English poets he was the most finished artist. He attained the highest degree of splendour of which poetical
style seemed to be capable.'

In a poet of such magnitude, how shall we explain his scantiness of production? Shall we explain it by saying that to make of Gray a poet of this magnitude is absurd; that his genius and resources were small, and that his production, therefore, was small also, but that the popularity of a single piece, the "Elegy",—a popularity due in great measure to the subject,—created for Gray a reputation to which he has really no right? He himself was not deceived by the favour shown to the "Elegy". 'Gray told me with a good deal of acrimony,' writes Dr. Gregory,[10] 'that the "Elegy" owed its popularity entirely to the subject, and that the public would have received it as well if it had been written in prose.' This is too much to say; the "Elegy" is a beautiful poem, and in admiring it the public showed a true feeling for poetry. But it is true that the "Elegy" owed much of its success to its subject, and that it has received a too unmeasured and unbounded praise.

Gray himself, however, maintained that the "Elegy" was not his best work in poetry, and he was right. High as is the praise due to the "Elegy," it is yet true that in other productions of Gray he exhibits poetical qualities even higher than those exhibited in the "Elegy". He deserves, therefore, his extremely high reputation as a poet, although his critics and the public may not always have praised him with perfect judgment. We are brought back, then, to the question: How, in a poet so really considerable, are we to explain his scantiness of production?

Scanty Gray's production, indeed, is; so scanty that to supplement our knowledge of it by a knowledge of the man is in this case of peculiar interest and service. Gray's letters and the records of him by his friends have happily made it possible for us thus to know him, and to appreciate his high qualities of mind and soul. Let us see these in the man first, and then observe how they appear in his poetry; and why they cannot enter into it more freely and inspire it with more strength, render it more abundant.

We will begin with his acquirements. 'Mr. Gray was,' writes his friend Temple, 'perhaps the most learned man in Europe. He knew every branch of history both natural and civil; had read all the original historians of England, France, and Italy; and was a great antiquarian. Criticism, metaphysics, morals, politics, made a principal part of his study. Voyages and travels of all sorts were his favourite amusements; and he had a fine taste in painting, prints, architecture, and gardening.' The notes in his interleaved copy of Linnæus remained to show the extent and accuracy of his knowledge in the natural sciences, particularly in botany, zoology, and entomology. Entomologists testified that his account of English insects was more perfect than any that had then appeared. His notes and papers, of which some have been published, others remain still in manuscript, give evidence, besides, of his knowledge of literature ancient and modern, geography and topography, painting, architecture and antiquities, and of his curious researches in heraldry. He was an excellent musician. Sir James Mackintosh remains us, moreover, that to all the other accomplishments and merits of Gray we are to add this: 'That he was the first discoverer of the beauties of nature in England, and has marked out the course of every picturesque journey that can be made in it.'

Acquirements take all their value and character from the power of the individual storing them. Let us take, from amongst Gray's observations on what he read, enough to show us his power. Here are criticisms on three very different authors, criticisms without any study or pretension, but just thrown out in chance letters to his friends. First, on Aristotle:—

> 'In the first place he is the hardest author by far I ever meddled with. Then he has a dry conciseness that makes one imagine one is perusing a table of contents rather than a book; it tastes for all the world like chopped hay, or rather like chopped logic; for he has a violent affection to that art, being in some sort his own invention; so that he often loses himself in little trifling distinctions and verbal niceties, and what is worse, leaves you to extricate yourself as you can. Thirdly, he has suffered vastly by his transcribers, as all authors of great brevity necessarily must. Fourthly and lastly, he has abundance of fine, uncommon things, which make him well worth the pains he gives one. You see what you have to expect.'

Next, on Isocrates:—

> 'It would be strange if I should find fault with you for reading Isocrates; I did so myself twenty years ago, and in an edition at least as bad as yours. The Panegyric, the De Pace, Areopagitic, and Advice to Philip, are by far the noblest remains we have of this writer, and equal to most things extant in the Greek tongue; but it depends on your judgment to distinguish between his real and occasional opinion of things, as he directly contradicts in one place what he has advanced in another; for example, in the Panathenaic and the De Pace, on the naval power of Athens; the latter of the two is undoubtedly his own undisguised sentiment.'

After hearing Gray on Isocrates and Aristotle, let us hear him on Froissart:—

'I rejoice you have met with Froissart, he is the Herodotus of a barbarous age; had he but had the luck of writing in as good a language, he might have been immortal. His locomotive disposition (for then there was no other way of learning things), his simple curiosity, his religious credulity, were much like those of the old Grecian. When you have *tant chevauché*[11] as to get to the end of him, there is Monstrelet waits to take you up, and will set you down at Philip de Commines; but previous to all these, you should have read Villehardouin and Joinville.'

Those judgments, with their true and clear ring, evince the high quality of Gray's mind, his power to command and use his learning. But Gray was a poet; let us hear him on a poet, on Shakespeare. We must place ourselves in the full midst of the eighteenth century and of its criticism; Gray's friend, West,[12] had praised Racine for using in his dramas 'the language of the times and that of the purest sort'; and he had added: 'I will not decide what style is fit for our English stage, but I should rather choose one that bordered upon *Cato*,[13] than upon Shakespeare.' Gray replies:—

'As to matter of style, I have this to say: The language of the age is never the language of poetry; except among the French, whose verse, where the thought does not support it, differs in nothing from prose. Our poetry, on the contrary, has a language peculiar to itself, to which almost every one that has written has added something. In truth, Shakespeare's language is one of his principal beauties; and he has no less advantage over your Addisons and Rowes[14] in this, than in those other great excellences you mention. Every word in him is a picture. Pray put me the following lines into the tongue of our modern dramatics—

"But I, that am not shaped for sportive tricks,
    Nor made to court an amorous looking-glass"—[15]

and what follows? To me they appear untranslatable; and if this be the case, our language is greatly degenerated.'

It is impossible for a poet to lay down the rules of his own art with more insight, soundness, and certainty. Yet at the moment in England there was perhaps not one other man, besides Gray, capable of writing the passage just quoted.

Gray's quality of mind, then, we see; his quality of soul will no less bear inspection. His reserve, his delicacy, his distaste for many of the persons and things surrounding him in the Cambridge of that day,—'this silly, dirty place,' as he calls it,—have produced an impression of Gray as being a man falsely fastidious, finical, effeminate. But we have already had that grave testimony to him from the Master of Pembroke Hall: 'The thoughts I have of him will last, and will be useful to me the few years I can expect to live.' And here is another to the same effect from a younger man, from Gray's friend Nicholls:—

'You know,' he writes to his mother, from abroad, when he heard of Gray's death, 'that I considered Mr. Gray as a second parent, that I thought only of him, built all my happiness on him, talked of him for ever, wished him with me whenever I partook of any pleasure, and flew to him for refuge whenever I felt any uneasiness. To whom now shall I talk of all I have seen here? Who will teach me to read, to think, to feel? I protest to you, that whatever I did or thought had a reference to him. If I met with any chagrins, I comforted myself that I had a treasure at home; if all the world had despised and hated me, I should have thought myself perfectly recompensed in his friendship. There remains only one loss more; if I lose you, I am left alone in the world. At present I feel that I have lost half of myself.'

Testimonies such as these are not called forth by a fastidious effeminate weakling; they are not called forth, even, by mere qualities of mind; they are called forth by qualities of soul. And of Gray's high qualities of soul, of his σπουδαιότης, his excellent seriousness, we may gather abundant proof from his letters. Writing to Mason who had just lost his father, he says:—

'I have seen the scene you describe, and know how dreadful it is; I know too I am the better for it. We are all idle and thoughtless things, and have no sense, no use in the world any longer than that sad impression lasts; the deeper it is engraved the better.'

And again, on a like occasion to another friend:—

'He who best knows our nature (for he made us what we are) by such afflictions recalls us from our wandering thoughts and idle merriment, from the insolence of youth and prosperity, to serious reflection, to our duty, and to himself; nor need we hasten to get rid of these impressions. Time (by appointment of the same Power) will cure the smart and in some hearts soon blot out all the traces of sorrow; but such as preserve them longest (for it is partly left in our own power) do perhaps best acquiesce in the will of the chastiser.'

And once more to Mason, in the very hour of his wife's death; Gray was not sure whether or not his letter would reach Mason before the end:—

> 'If the worst be not yet past, you will neglect and pardon me; but if the last struggle be over, if the poor object of your long anxieties be no longer sensible to your kindness or to her own sufferings, allow me, at least an idea (for what could I do, were I present, more than this?) to sit by you in silence and pity from my heart not her, who is at rest, but you, who lose her. May he, who made us, the Master of our pleasures and of our pains, support you! Adieu.'

Seriousness, character, was the foundation of things with him; where this was lacking he was always severe, whatever might be offered to him in its stead. Voltaire's literary genius charmed him, but the faults of Voltaire's nature he felt so strongly that when his young friend Nicholls was going abroad in 1771, just before Gray's death, he said to him: 'I have one thing to beg of you which you must not refuse.' Nicholls answered: 'You know you have only to command; what is it?'—'Do not go to see Voltaire,' said Gray; and then added: 'No one knows the mischief that man will do.' Nicholls promised compliance with Gray's injunction; 'But what,' he asked, 'could a visit from me signify?'—'Every tribute to such a man signifies,' Gray answered. He admired Dryden, admired him, even, too much; had too much felt his influence as a poet. He told Beattie 'that if there was any excellence in his own numbers he had learned it wholly from that great poet'; and writing to Beattie afterwards he recurs to Dryden, whom Beattie, he thought, did not honour enough as a poet: 'Remember Dryden,' he writes, 'and be blind to all his faults.' Yes, his faults as a poet; but on the man Dryden, nevertheless, his sentence is stern. Speaking of the Poet-Laureateship, 'Dryden,' he writes to Mason, 'was as disgraceful to the office from his character, as the poorest scribbler could have been from his verses.' Even where crying blemishes were absent, the want of weight and depth of character in a man deprived him, in Gray's judgment, of serious significance. He says of Hume:[16] 'Is not that *naïveté* and good-humour, which his admirers celebrate in him, owing to this, that he has continued all his days an infant, but one that has unhappily been taught to read and write?'

And with all this strenuous seriousness, a pathetic sentiment, and an element, likewise, of sportive and charming humour. At Keswick, by the lakeside on an autumn evening, he has the accent of the *Rêveries*,[17] or of Obermann,[18] or Wordsworth:—

> 'In the evening walked down alone to the lake by the side of Crow Park after sunset and saw the solemn colouring of light draw on, the last gleam of sunshine fading away on the hill-tops, the deep serene of the waters, and the long shadows of the mountains thrown across them, till they nearly touched the hithermost shore. At distance heard the murmur of many waterfalls, not audible in the daytime. Wished for the Moon, but she was *dark to me and silent, hid in her vacant interlunar cave.'* [19]

Of his humour and sportiveness his delightful letters are full; his humour appears in his poetry too, and is by no means to be passed over there. Horace Walpole[20] said that 'Gray never wrote anything easily but things of humour; humour was his natural and original turn.'

Knowledge, penetration, seriousness, sentiment, humour, Gray had them all; he had the equipment and endowment for the office of poet. But very soon in his life appear traces of something obstructing, something disabling; of spirits failing, and health not sound; and the evil increases with years. He writes to West in 1737:—

> 'Low spirits are my true and faithful companions; they get up with me, go to bed with me, make journeys and returns as I do; nay, and pay visits and will even affect to be jocose and force a feeble laugh with me; but most commonly we sit alone together, and are the prettiest insipid company in the world.'

The tone is playful, Gray was not yet twenty-one. 'Mine,' he tells West four or five years later, 'mine, you are to know, is a white Melancholy, or rather *Leucocholy*,[21] for the most part; which, though it seldom laughs or dances, nor ever amounts to what one calls joy or pleasure, yet is a good easy sort of a state.' But, he adds in this same letter:—

> 'But there is another sort, black indeed, which I have now and then felt, that has something in it like Tertullian's rule of faith, *Credo quia impossibile est;*[22] for it believes, nay, is sure of everything that is unlikely, so it be but frightful; and on the other hand excludes and shuts its eyes to the most possible hopes, and everything that is pleasurable; from this the Lord deliver us! for none but he and sunshiny weather can do it.'

Six or seven years pass, and we find him writing to Wharton from Cambridge thus:—

'The spirit of laziness (the spirit of this place) begins to possess even me, that have so long declaimed against it. Yet has it not so prevailed, but that I feel that discontent with myself, that *ennui*, that ever accompanies it in its beginnings. Time will settle my conscience, time will reconcile my languid companion to me; we shall smoke, we shall tipple, we shall doze together, we shall have our little jokes, like other people, and our long stories. Brandy will finish what port began; and, a month after the time, you will see in some corner of a London Evening Post, "Yesterday died the Rev. Mr. John Gray, Senior-Fellow of Clare Hall, a facetious companion, and well-respected by all who knew him." '

The humorous advertisement ends, in the original letter, with a Hogarthian touch which I must not quote.[23] Is it Leucocholy or is it Melancholy which predominates here? at any rate, this entry in his diary, six years later, is black enough:—

'Insomnia crebra, atque expergiscenti surdus quidam doloris sensus; frequens etiam in regione sterni oppressio, et cardialgia gravis, fere sempiterna.'[24]

And in 1757 he writes to Hurd:—[25]

'To be employed is to be happy. This principle of mine (and I am convinced of its truth) has, as usual, no influence on my practice. I am alone, and *ennuyé* to the last degree, yet do nothing. Indeed I have one excuse; my health (which you have so kindly inquired after) is not extraordinary. It is no great malady, but several little ones, that seem brewing no good to me.'

From thence to the end his languor and depression, though still often relieved by occupation and travel, keep fatally gaining on him. At last the depression became constant, became mechanical. 'Travel I must,' he writes to Dr. Wharton, 'or cease to exist. Till this year I hardly knew what *mechanical* low spirits were; but now I even tremble at an east wind.' Two months afterwards he died.

What wonder, that with this troublous cloud, throughout the whole term of his manhood, brooding over him and weighing him down, Gray, finely endowed though he was, richly stored with knowledge though he was, yet produced so little, found no full and sufficient utterance, *'never,'* as the Master of Pembroke Hall said, *'spoke out.'* He knew well enough, himself, how it was with him.

'My *verve*[26] is at best, you know' (he writes to Mason), 'of so delicate a constitution, and has such weak nerves, as not to stir out of its chamber above three days in a year.'

And to Horace Walpole he says: 'As to what you say to me civilly, that I ought to write more, I will be candid, and avow to you, that till fourscore and upward, whenever the humour takes me, I will write; because I like it, and because I like myself better when I do so. If I do not write much, it is because I cannot.' How simply said, and how truly also! Fain would a man like Gray speak out if he could, he 'likes himself better' when he speaks out; if he does not speak out, 'it is because I cannot.'

Bonstetten, that mercurial Swiss who died in 1832 at the age of eighty-seven, having been younger and livelier from his sixtieth year to his eightieth than at any other time in his life, paid a visit in his early days to Cambridge, and saw much of Gray, to whom he attached himself with devotion. Gray, on his part, was charmed with his young friend; 'I never saw such a boy,' he writes; 'our breed is not made on this model.' Long afterwards Bonstetten published his reminiscences of Gray. 'I used to tell Gray,' he says, 'about my life and my native country, but *his* life was a sealed book to me; he never would talk of himself, never would allow me to speak to him of his poetry. If I quoted lines of his to him, he kept silence like an obstinate child. I said to him sometimes: "Will you have the goodness to give me an answer?" But not a word issued from his lips.' *He never spoke out*. Bonstetten thinks that Gray's life was poisoned by an unsatisfied sensibility, was withered by his having never loved; by his days being passed in the dismal cloisters of Cambridge, in the company of a set of monastic book-worms, 'whose existence no honest woman ever came to cheer.' Sainte-Beuve, who was much attracted and interested by Gray, doubts whether Bonstetten's explanation of him is admissible; the secret of Gray's melancholy he finds rather in the sterility of his poetic talent, 'so distinguished, so rare, but so stinted'; in the poet's despair at his own unproductiveness.

But to explain Gray, we must do more than allege his sterility, as we must look further than to his reclusion at Cambridge. What caused his sterility? Was it his ill-health, his hereditary gout? Certainly we will pay all respect to the powers of hereditary gout for afflicting us poor mortals. But Goethe, after pointing out that Schiller, who was so productive, was 'almost constantly ill,' adds the true remark that it is incredible how much the spirit can do, in these cases, to keep up the body. Pope's animation and activity through all the course of what he pathetically calls 'that long disease, my life,'[27] is an example presenting itself signally, in Gray's own country and time, to confirm what Goethe here says. What gave the power to Gray's reclusion and ill-health to induce his sterility?

The reason, the indubitable reason as I cannot but think it, I have already given elsewhere. Gray, a born poet, fell upon an age of prose. He fell upon an age whose task was such as to call forth in general men's powers of understanding, wit and cleverness, rather than their deepest powers of mind and soul. As regards literary production, the task of the eighteenth century in England was not the poetic interpretation of the world, its task was to create a plain, clear, straight-forward, efficient prose. Poetry obeyed the bent of mind requisite for the due fulfilment of this task of the century. It was intellectual, argumentative, ingenious; not seeing things in their truth and beauty, not interpretative. Gray, with the qualities of mind and soul of a genuine poet, was isolated in his century. Maintaining and fortifying them by lofty studies, he yet could not fully educe and enjoy them; the want of a genial atmosphere, the failure of sympathy in his contemporaries, were too great. Born in the same year with Milton, Gray would have been another man; born in the same year with Burns, he would have been another man. A man born in 1608 could profit by the larger and more poetic scope of the English spirit in the Elizabethan age; a man born in 1759 could profit by that European renewing of men's minds of which the great historical manifestation is the French Revolution. Gray's alert and brilliant young friend, Bonstetten, who would explain the void in the life of Gray by his having never loved, Bonstetten himself loved, married, and had children. Yet at the age of fifty he was bidding fair to grow old, dismal and torpid like the rest of us, when he was roused and made young again for some thirty years, says M. Sainte-Beuve, by the events of 1789. If Gray, like Burns, had been just thirty years old when the French Revolution broke out, he would have shown, probably, productiveness and animation in plenty. Coming when he did, and endowed as he was, he was a man born out of date, a man whose full spiritual flowering was impossible. The same thing is to be said of his great contemporary, Butler,[28] the author of the *Analogy*. In the sphere of religion, which touches that of poetry, Butler was impelled by the endowment of his nature to strive for a profound and adequate conception of religious things, which was not pursued by his contemporaries, and which at that time, and in that atmosphere of mind, was not fully attainable. Hence, in Butler too, a dissatisfaction, a weariness, as in Gray; 'great labour and weariness, great disappointment, pain and even vexation of mind.' A sort of spiritual east wind was at that time blowing; neither Butler nor Gray could flower. They *never spoke out.*

Gray's poetry was not only stinted in quantity by reason of the age wherein he lived, it suffered somewhat in quality also. We have seen under what obligation to Dryden Gray professed himself to be—'if there was any excellence in his numbers, he had learned it wholly from that great poet.' It was not for nothing that he came when Dryden had lately 'embellished,' as Johnson says, English poetry; had 'found it brick and left it marble.' It was not for nothing that he came just when 'the English ear,' to quote Johnson again, 'had been accustomed to the mellifluence of Pope's numbers, and the diction of poetry had grown more splendid.' Of the intellectualities, ingenuities, personifications, of the movement and diction of Dryden and Pope, Gray caught something, caught too much. We have little of Gray's poetry, and that little is not free from the faults of his age. Therefore it was important to go for aid, as we did, to Gray's life and letters, to see his mind and soul there, and to corroborate from thence that high estimate of his quality which his poetry indeed calls forth, but does not establish so amply and irresistibly as one could desire.

For a just criticism it does, however, clearly establish it. The difference between genuine poetry and the poetry of Dryden, Pope, and all their school, is briefly this: their poetry is conceived and composed in their wits, genuine poetry is conceived and composed in the soul. The difference between the two kinds of poetry is immense. They differ profoundly in their modes of language, they differ profoundly in their modes of evolution. The poetic language of our eighteenth century in general is the language of men composing *without their eye on the object,* as Wordsworth[29] excellently said of Dryden; language merely recalling the object, as the common language of prose does, and then dressing it out with a certain smartness and brilliancy for the fancy and understanding. This is called 'splendid diction.' The evolution of the poetry of our eighteenth century is likewise intellectual; it proceeds by ratiocination, antithesis, ingenious turns and conceits. This poetry is often eloquent, and always, in the hands of such masters as Dryden and Pope, clever; but it does not take us much below the surface of things, it does not give us the emotion of seeing things in their truth and beauty. The language of genuine poetry, on the other hand, is the language of one composing with his eye on the object; its evolution is that of a thing which has been plunged in the poet's soul until it comes forth naturally and necessarily. This sort of evolution is infinitely simpler than the other, and infinitely more satisfying; the same thing is true of the genuine poetic language likewise. But they are both of them also infinitely harder of attainment; they come only from those who, as Emerson says, 'live from a great depth of being.'

Goldsmith disparaged Gray who had praised his *Traveller*,[30] and indeed in the poem on the "Alliance of Education and Government" had given him hints which he used for it. In retaliation let us take from Goldsmith himself a specimen of the poetic language of the eighteenth century.

> 'No cheerful murmurs fluctuate in the gale'—[31]

there is exactly the poetic diction of our prose century! rhetorical, ornate,—and, poetically, quite false. Place beside it a line of genuine poetry, such as the

> 'In cradle of the rude, imperious surge'[32]

of Shakespeare; and all its falseness instantly becomes apparent.

Dryden's poem on the death of Mrs. Killigrew is, says Johnson, 'undoubtedly the noblest ode that our language ever has produced.' In this vigorous performance Dryden has to say, what is interesting enough, that not only in poetry did Mrs. Killigrew excel, but she excelled in painting also. And thus he says it—

> 'To the next realm she stretch'd her sway,
>   For Painture near adjoining lay—
> A plenteous province and alluring prey.
> A Chamber of Dependencies was framed
> (As conquerors will never want pretence
>   When arm'd, to justify the offence),
> And the whole fief, in right of Poetry, she claim'd.'

The intellectual, ingenious, superficial evolution of poetry of this school could not be better illustrated. Place beside it Pindar's

> αἰὼν ἀσφαλὴς
> οὐκ ἔγεντ' οὔτ' Αἰακίδᾳ παρὰ Πηλεῖ,
> οὔτε παρ' ἀντιθέῳ Κάδμῳ . . .

'A secure time fell to the lot neither of Peleus the son of Æacus, nor of the godlike Cadmus; howbeit these are said to have had, of all mortals, the supreme of happiness, who heard the golden-snooded Muses sing,—on the mountain the one heard them, the other in seven-gated Thebes.'[33]

There is the evolution of genuine poetry, and such poetry kills Dryden's the moment it is put near it.

Gray's production was scanty, and scanty, as we have seen, it could not but be. Even what he produced is not always pure in diction, true in evolution. Still, with whatever drawbacks, he is alone, or almost alone (for Collins has something of the like merit) in his age. Gray said himself that 'the style he aimed at was extreme conciseness of expression, yet pure, perspicuous, and musical.' Compared, not with the work of the great masters of the golden ages of poetry, but with the poetry of his own contemporaries in general, Gray's may be said to have reached, in style, the excellence at which he aimed; while the evolution also of such a piece as his "Progress of Poesy" must be accounted not less noble and sound than its style.

NOTES

Thomas Gray: Published as preface to the selection from Gray in T. H. Ward's *The English Poets* (1880); *Essays in Criticism* [Second Series] (1888).

1. 1716–71.
2. William Cole (1714–82), Cambridge antiquary.
3. William Mason (1724–97), *Memoirs of Gray* (1775).
4. John Mitford edited Gray (1814 and subsequently).
5. William Collins (1721–59).
6. James Beattie (1735–1803), poet and professor.
7. William Cowper (1731–1800), poet.
8. (1723–90), author of *The Wealth of Nations* (1776).
9. (1765–1832), historian and thinker.
10. Dr. John Gregory (1724–73), physician.
11. *Journeyed on horseback so much.*
12. Richard West (1716–42).
13. Addison's tragedy, *Cato* (1713).
14. Nicholas Rowe (1674–1718), dramatist.
15. *Richard* III, I. i. 14–15.
16. David Hume (1711–76), philosopher.
17. Probably *Rêveries du promeneur solitaire*, written 1777 by Jean-Jacques Rousseau.
18. See p. 66, note 5.
19. Adapting *Samson Agonistes*, lines 86–89.
20. (1717–97), man of letters.
21. A nonce-word coined by Gray, *melancholy* being from the Greek for "black bile," and *leuco-* being "white."
22. *I believe because it is impossible.*

23. Gray to Wharton, April 25, 1749: "his death is supposed to have been occasion'd by a Fit of an Apoplexy, being found fall'n out of Bed with his Head in the Chamber-Pot."

24. *Frequent bouts of sleeplessness, and on waking a certain dull sense of pain; also constant pressure in the region of the breast-bone, and severe heartburn, almost perpetual.*

25. Richard Hurd (1720–1808), bishop and critic.

26. Special bent, talent.

27. "Epistle to Arbuthnot" (1735), line 132 ("this long").

28. Bishop Joseph Butler (1692–1752), *Analogy of Religion* (1736).

29. *Essay Supplementary to the Preface to Poems* (1815); see also p. 208.

30. Goldsmith (1764).

31. *The Deserted Village* (1770), line 126.

32. See p. 178.

33. See p. 276.

JOHNSON'S LIVES

1878

Da mihi, Domine, scire quod sciendum est—"Grant that the knowledge I get may be the knowledge which is worth having!"—the spirit of that prayer ought to rule our education. How little it does rule it, every discerning man will acknowledge. Life is short, and our faculties of attention and of recollection are limited; in education we proceed as if our life were endless, and our powers of attention and recollection inexhaustible. We have not time or strength to deal with half of the matters which are thrown upon our minds, and they prove a useless load to us. When some one talked to Themistocles of an art of memory, he answered: "Teach me rather to forget!" The sarcasm well criticises the fatal want of proportion between what we put into our minds and their real needs and powers.

From the time when first I was led to think about education, this want of proportion is what has most struck me. It is the great obstacle to progress, yet it is by no means remarked and contended against as it should be. It hardly begins to present itself until we pass beyond the strict elements of education—beyond the acquisition, I mean, of reading, of writing, and of calculating so far as the operations of common life require. But the moment we pass beyond these, it begins to appear. Languages, grammar, literature, history, geography, mathematics, the knowledge of nature—what of these is to be taught, how much, and how? There is no clear, well-grounded consent. The same with religion. Religion is surely to be taught, but what of it is to be taught, and how? A clear, well-grounded consent is again wanting. And taught in such fashion as things are now, how often must a candid and sensible man, if he could be offered an art of memory to secure all that he has learned of them, as to a very great deal of it be inclined to say with Themistocles: "Teach me rather to forget!"

In England the common notion seems to be that education is advanced in two ways principally: by for ever adding fresh matters of instruction, and by preventing uniformity. I should be inclined to prescribe just the opposite course; to prescribe a severe limitation of the number of matters taught, a severe uniformity in the line of study followed. Wide ranging, and the multiplication of matters to be investigated, belong to private study, to the development of special aptitudes in the individual learner, and to the demands which they raise in him. But separate from all this should be kept the broad plain lines of study for almost universal use. I say *almost* universal, because they must of necessity vary a little with the varying conditions of men. Whatever the pupil finds set out for him upon these lines, he should learn; therefore it ought not to be too much in quantity. The essential thing is that it should be well chosen. If once we can get it well chosen, the more uniformly it can be kept to, the better. The teacher will be more at home; and besides, when we have got what is good and suitable, there is small hope of gain, and great certainty of risk, in departing from it.

No such lines are laid out, and perhaps no one could be trusted to lay them out authoritatively. But to amuse oneself with laying them out in fancy is a good exercise for one's thoughts. One may lay them out for this or that description of pupil, in this or that branch of study. The wider the interest of the branch of study taken, and the more extensive the class of pupils concerned, the better for our purpose. Suppose we take the department of letters. It is interesting to lay out in one's mind the ideal line of study to be followed by all who have to learn Latin and Greek. But it is still more interesting to lay out the ideal line of study to be followed by all who are concerned with that body of literature which exists in English, because this class is so much more numerous amongst us. The thing would be, one imagines, to begin with a very brief introductory sketch of our subject; then to fix a certain series of works to serve as what the French, taking an expression from the builder's business, call *points de repère*—points which stand as so many natural centres, and by returning to which we can always find our way again, if we are embarrassed; finally, to mark out a number of illustrative and representative works, connecting themselves with each of these *points de repère*. In the introductory sketch we are amongst generalities, in the group of illustrative works we are amongst details; generalities and details have, both of them, their perils for the learner. It is evident that, for purposes of education, the most important parts by far in our scheme are what we call the *points de repère*. To get these rightly chosen and thoroughly known is the great matter. For my part, in thinking of this or that line of study which human minds follow, I feel always prompted to seek, first and foremost, the leading *points de repère* in it.

In editing for the use of the young the group of chapters which are now commonly distinguished as those of the Babylonian Isaiah,[1] I drew attention to their remarkable fitness for serving as a point of this kind to the student of universal history. But a work which by many is regarded as simply and solely a document of religion, there is difficulty, perhaps, in employing for historical and literary purposes. With works of a secular character one is on safer ground. And for years past, whenever I have had occasion to use Johnson's *Lives of the Poets,* the thought has struck me how admirable a *point de repère,* or fixed centre of the sort described above, these lives might be made to furnish for the student of English literature. If we could but take, I have said to myself, the most important of the lives in Johnson's volumes, and leave out all the rest, what a text-book we should have! The volumes at present are a work to stand in a library, "a work which no gentleman's library should be without." But we want to get from them a text-book, to be in the hands of every one who desires even so much as a general acquaintance with English literature;—and so much acquaintance as this who does not desire? The work as Johnson published it is not fitted to serve as such a text-book; it is too extensive, and contains the lives of many poets quite insignificant. Johnson supplied lives of all whom the booksellers proposed to include in their collection of British Poets; he did not choose the poets himself, although he added two or three to those chosen by the booksellers.[2] Whatever Johnson did in the department of literary biography and criticism possesses interest and deserves our attention. But in his *Lives of the Poets* there are six of pre-eminent interest; the lives of six men who, while the rest in the collection are of inferior rank, stand out as names of the first class in English literature—Milton, Dryden, Swift, Addison, Pope, Gray. These six writers differ among themselves, of course, in power and importance, and every one can see, that, if we were following certain modes of literary classification, Milton would have to be placed on a solitary eminence far above any of them. But if, without seeking a close view of individual differences, we form a large and liberal first class among English writers, all these six personages—Milton, Dryden, Swift, Addison, Pope, Gray—must, I think, be placed in it. Their lives cover a space of more than a century and a half, from 1608, the year of Milton's birth, down to 1771, the date of the death of Gray. Through this space of more than a century and a half the six lives conduct us. We follow the course of what Warburton well calls "the most agreeable subject in the world, which is literary history," and follow it in the lives of men of letters of the first class. And the writer of their lives is himself, too, a man of letters of the first class. Malone calls Johnson "the brightest ornament of the eighteenth century." He is justly to be called, at any rate, a man of letters of the first class, and the greatest power in English letters during the eighteenth century. And in these characteristic lives, not finished until 1781, and "which I wrote," as he himself tells us, "in my usual way, dilatorily and hastily, unwilling to work and working with vigour and haste," we have Johnson mellowed by years, Johnson in his ripeness and plenitude, treating the subject which he loved best and knew best. Much of it he could treat with the knowledge and sure tact of a contemporary; even from Milton and Dryden he was scarcely further separated than our generation is from Burns and Scott. Having all these recommendations, his *Lives of the Poets* do indeed truly stand for what Boswell calls them, "the work which of all Dr. Johnson's writings will perhaps be read most generally and with most pleasure." And in the lives of the six chief personages of the work, the lives of Milton, Dryden, Swift, Addison, Pope, and Gray, we have its very kernel and quintessence; we have the work relieved of whatever is less significant, retaining nothing which is not highly significant, brought within easy and convenient compass, and admirably fitted to serve as a *point de repère*, a fixed and thoroughly known centre of departure and return, to the student of English literature.

I know of no such first-rate piece of literature, for supplying in this way the wants of the literary student, existing at all in any other language; or existing in our own language, for any period except the period which Johnson's six lives cover. A student cannot read them without gaining from them, consciously or unconsciously, an insight into the history of English literature and life. He would find great benefit, let me add, from reading in connection with each biography something of the author with whom it deals; the first two books, say, of *Paradise Lost,* in connection with the life of Milton; *Absalom and Achitophel,* and the *Dedication of the Æneis,* in connection with the life of Dryden; in connection with Swift's life, the *Battle of the Books;* with Addison's, the *Coverley Papers;* with Pope's, the imitations of the *Satires* and *Epistles* of Horace. The *Elegy in a Country Churchyard* everybody knows, and will have it present to his mind when he reads the life of Gray. But of the other works which I have mentioned how little can this be said; to how many of us are Pope and Addison and Dryden and Swift, and even Milton himself, mere names, about whose date and history and supposed characteristics of style we may have learnt by rote something from a handbook, but of the real men and of the power of their works we know nothing! From Johnson's biographies the student will get a sense of what the real men were, and with this sense fresh in his mind he will find the occasion propitious for acquiring also, in the way pointed out, a sense of the power of their works.

This will seem to most people a very unambitious discipline. But the fault of most of the disciplines proposed in education is that they are by far too ambitious. Our improvers of education are almost always for proceeding by way of augmentation and complication; reduction and simplification, I say, is what is rather required. We give the learner too much to do, and we are over-zealous to tell him what he ought to think. Johnson himself has admirably marked the real line of our education through letters. He says in his life of Pope:—"Judgment is forced upon us by experience. He that reads many books must compare one opinion or one style with another; and when he compares, must necessarily distinguish, reject, and prefer." The aim and end of education through letters is to get this experience. Our being told by another what its results will properly be found to be, is not, even if we are told aright, at all the same thing as getting the experience for ourselves. The discipline, therefore, which puts us in the way of getting it, cannot be called an inconsiderable or inefficacious one. We should take care not to imperil its acquisition by refusing to trust to it in its simplicity, by being eager to add, set right, and annotate. It is much to secure the reading, by young English people, of the lives of the six chief poets of our nation between the years 1650 and 1750, related by our foremost man of letters of the eighteenth century. It is much to secure their reading, under the stimulus of Johnson's interesting recital and forcible judgments, famous specimens of the authors whose lives are before them. Do not let us insist on also reviewing in detail and supplementing Johnson's work for them, on telling them what they ought really and definitively to think about the six authors and about the exact place of each in English literature. Perhaps our pupils are not ripe for it; perhaps, too, we have not Johnson's interest and Johnson's force; we are not the power in letters for our century which he was for his. We may be pedantic, obscure, dull, everything that bores, rather than everything that attracts; and so Johnson and his lives will repel, and will not be received, because we insist on being received along with them. Again, as we bar a learner's approach to Homer and Virgil by our *chevaux de frise*[3] of elaborate grammar, so we are apt to stop his way to a piece of English literature by imbedding it in a mass of notes and additional matter. Mr. Croker's edition of Boswell's *Life of Johnson* is a good example of the labour and ingenuity which may be spent upon a masterpiece, with the result, after all, really of rather encumbering than illustrating it. All knowledge may be in itself good, but this kind of editing seems to proceed upon the notion that we have only one book to read in the course of our life, or else that we have eternity to read in. What can it matter to our generation whether it was Molly Aston or Miss Boothby whose preference for Lord Lyttelton made Johnson jealous, and produced in his *Life of Lyttelton* a certain tone of disparagement? With the young reader, at all events, our great endeavour should be to bring him face to face with masterpieces, and to hold him there, not distracting or rebutting him with needless excursions or trifling details.

I should like, therefore, to reprint Johnson's six chief lives, simply as they are given in the edition in four volumes octavo,—the edition which passes for being the first to have a correct and complete text,—and to leave the lives, in that natural form, to have their effect upon the reader. I should like to think that a number of young people might thus be brought to know an important period of our literary and intellectual history, by means of the lives of six of its leading and representative authors, told by a great man. I should like to think that they would go on, under the stimulus of the lives, to acquaint themselves with some leading and representative work of each author. In the six lives they would at least have secured, I think, a most valuable *point de repère* in the history of our English life and literature, a point from which afterwards to find their way; whether they might desire to ascend upwards to our anterior literature, or to come downwards to the literature of yesterday and of the present.

The six lives cover a period of literary and intellectual movement in which we are all profoundly interested. It is the passage of our nation to prose and reason; the passage to a type of thought and expression, modern, European, and which on the whole is ours at the present day, from a type antiquated, peculiar, and which is ours no longer. The period begins with a prose like this of Milton:[4] "They who to states and governors of the commonwealth direct their speech, high court of parliament! or wanting such access in a private condition, write that which they foresee may advance the public good; I suppose them, if at the beginning of no mean endeavour, not a little altered and moved inwardly in their minds." It ends with a prose like this of Smollet:[5] "My spirit began to accommodate itself to my beggarly fate, and I became so mean as to go down towards Wapping, with an intention to inquire for an old schoolfellow, who, I understood, had got the command of a small coasting vessel then in the river, and implore his assistance." These are extreme instances; but they give us no unfaithful notion of the change in our prose between the reigns of Charles I. and of George III. Johnson has recorded his own impression of the extent of the change and of its salutariness. Boswell gave him a book to read, written in 1702 by the English chaplain of a regiment stationed in Scotland. "It is sad stuff, sir," said Johnson, after reading it; "miserably written, as books in general then were. There is now an elegance of style universally diffused. No man now writes so ill as Martin's *Account of the Hebrides* is written. A man could not write so ill if he should try. Set a merchant's clerk now to write, and he'll do better."

It seems as if a simple and natural prose were a thing which we might expect to come easy to communities of men, and to come early to them; but we know from experience that it is not so. Poetry and the poetic form of expression naturally precede prose. We see this in ancient Greece. We see prose forming itself there gradually and with labour; we see it passing through more than one stage before it attains to thorough propriety and lucidity, long after forms of consummate adequacy have already been reached and used in poetry. It is a people's growth in practical life, and its native turn for developing this life and for making progress in it, which awaken the desire for a good prose—a prose plain, direct, intelligible, serviceable. A dead language, the Latin, for a long time furnished the nations of Europe with an instrument of the kind, superior to any which they had yet discovered in their own. But nations such as England and France, called to a great historic life, and with powerful interests and gifts either social or practical, were sure to feel the need of having a sound prose of their own, and to bring such a prose forth. They brought it forth in the seventeenth century; France first, afterwards England.

The Restoration marks the real moment of birth of our modern English prose. Men of lucid and direct mental habit there were, such as Chillingworth,[6] in whom before the Restoration the desire and the commencements of a modern prose show themselves. There were men like Barrow,[7] weighty and powerful, whose mental habit the old prose suited, who continued its forms and locutions after the Restoration. But the hour was come for the new prose, and it grew and prevailed. In Johnson's time its victory had long been assured, and the old style seemed barbarous. The prose writers of the eighteenth century have indeed their mannerisms and phrases which are no longer ours. Johnson says of Milton's blame of the universities for allowing young men designed for Orders in the Church to act in plays, "This is sufficiently peevish in a man, who, when he mentions his exile from college, relates, with great luxuriance, the compensation which the pleasures of the theatre afford him. Plays were therefore only criminal when they were acted by academics." We should now-a-days not say *peevish* here, nor *luxuriance,* nor *academics.* Yet the style is ours by its organism, if not by its phrasing. It is by its organism—an organism opposed to length and involvement, and enabling us to be clear, plain, and short—that English style after the Restoration breaks with the style of the times preceding it, finds the true law of prose, and becomes modern; becomes, in spite of superficial differences, the style of our own day.

Burnet[8] has pointed out how we are under obligations in this matter to Charles II., whom Johnson described as "the last king of England who was a man of parts." A king of England by no means fulfils his whole duty by being a man of parts, or by loving and encouraging art, science, and literature. Yet the artist and the student of the natural sciences will always feel a kindness towards the two Charleses for their interest in art and science; and modern letters, too, have their debt to Charles II., although it may be quite true that that prince, as Burnet says, "had little or no literature." "The King had little or no literature, but true and good sense, and had got a right notion of style; for he was in France at the time when they were much set on reforming their language. It soon appeared that he had a true taste. So this helped to raise the value of these men (Tillotson[9] and others), when the king approved of the style their discourses generally ran in, which was clear, plain, and short."

It is the victory of this prose style, "clear, plain, and short" over what Burnet calls "the old style, long and heavy," which is the distinguishing achievement, in the history of English letters, of the century following the Restoration. From the first it proceeded rapidly and was never checked. Burnet says of the Chancellor Finch, Earl of Nottingham— "He was long much admired for his eloquence, but it was laboured and affected, and he saw it much despised before he died." A like revolution of taste brought about a general condemnation of our old prose style, imperfectly disengaged from the style of poetry. By Johnson's time the new style, the style of prose, was altogether paramount in its own proper domain, and in its pride of victorious strength had invaded also the domain of poetry.

That invasion is now visited by us with a condemnation not less strong and general than the condemnation which the eighteenth century passed upon the unwieldy prose of its predecessors. But let us be careful to do justice while we condemn. A thing good in its own place may be bad out of it. Prose requires a different style from poetry. Poetry, no doubt, is more excellent in itself than prose. In poetry man finds the highest and most beautiful expression of that which is in him. We had far better poetry than the poetry of the eighteenth century before that century arrived, we have had better since it departed. Like the Greeks, and unlike the French, we can point to an age of poetry anterior to our age of prose, eclipsing our age of prose in glory, and fixing the future character and conditions of our literature. We do well to place our pride in the Elizabethan age and Shakespeare, as the Greeks placed theirs in Homer. We did well to return in the present century to the poetry of that older age for illumination and inspiration, and to put aside, in a great measure, the poetry and poets intervening between Milton and Wordsworth. Milton, in whom our great poetic age expired, was the last of the immortals. Of the five poets whose lives follow his in our proposed volume, three, Dryden, Addison, and Swift, are eminent prose-writers as well as poets; two of the three, Swift and Addison, far more distinguished as prose-writers than as poets. The glory of

English literature is in poetry, and in poetry the strength of the eighteenth century does not lie.

Nevertheless, the eighteenth century accomplished for us an immense literary progress, and even its shortcomings in poetry were an instrument to that progress, and served it. The example of Germany may show us what a nation loses from having no prose style. The practical genius of our people could not but urge irresistibly to the production of a real prose style, because for the purposes of modern life the old English prose, the prose of Milton and Taylor,[10] is cumbersome, unavailable, impossible. A style of regularity, uniformity, precision, balance, was wanted. These are the qualities of a serviceable prose style. Poetry has a different *logic*, as Coleridge said, from prose; poetical style follows another law of evolution than the style of prose. But there is no doubt that a style of regularity, uniformity, precision, balance, will acquire a yet stronger hold upon the mind of a nation, if it is adopted in poetry as well as in prose, and so comes to govern both. This is what happened in France. To the practical, modern, and social genius of the French, a true prose was indispensable. They produced one of conspicuous excellence, one marked in the highest degree by the qualities of regularity, uniformity, precision, balance. With little opposition from any deep-seated and imperious poetic instincts, they made their poetry conform to the law which was moulding their prose. French poetry became marked with the qualities of regularity, uniformity, precision, balance. This may have been bad for French poetry, but it was good for French prose. It heightened the perfection with which those qualities, the true qualities of prose, were impressed upon it. When England, at the Restoration, desired a modern prose, and began to create it, our writers turned naturally to French literature, which had just accomplished the very process which engaged them. The King's acuteness and taste, as we have seen, helped. Indeed, to the admission of French influence of all kinds, Charles the Second's character and that of his court were but too favourable. But the influence of the French writers was at that moment on the whole fortunate, and seconded what was a vital and necessary effort in our literature. Our literature required a prose which conformed to the true law of prose; and that it might acquire this the more surely, it compelled poetry, as in France, to conform itself to the law of prose likewise. The classic verse of French poetry was the Alexandrine, a measure favourable to the qualities of regularity, uniformity, precision, balance. Gradually a measure favourable to those very same qualities—the ten-syllable couplet—established itself as the classic verse of England, until in the eighteenth century it had become the ruling form of our poetry. Poetry, or rather the use of verse, entered in a remarkable degree, during that century, into the whole of the daily life of the civilised classes; and the poetry of the century was a perpetual school of the qualities requisite for a good prose, the qualities of regularity, uni-formity, precision, balance. This may have been of no great service to English poetry, although to say that it has been of no service at all, to say that the eighteenth century has in no respect changed the conditions of English poetical style, or that it has changed them for the worse, would be untrue. But it was undeniably of signal service to that which was the great want and work of the hour, English prose.

Do not let us, therefore, hastily despise Johnson and his century for their defective poetry and criticism of poetry. True, Johnson is capable of saying: "Surely no man could have fancied that he read *Lycidas* with pleasure had he not known the author!" True, he is capable of maintaining "that the description of the temple in Congreve's *Mourning Bride* was the finest poetical passage he had ever read—he recol-lected none in Shakespeare equal to it." But we are to con-ceive of Johnson and of his century as having a special task committed to them, the establishment of English prose; and as capable of being warped and narrowed in their judgments of poetry by this exclusive task. Such is the common course and law of progress; one thing is done at a time, and other things are sacrificed to it. We must be thankful for the thing done, if it is valuable, and we must put up with the tempo-rary sacrifice of other things to this one. The other things will have their turn sooner or later. Above all, a nation with profound poetical instincts, like the English nation, may be trusted to work itself right again in poetry after periods of mistaken poetical practice. Even in the midst of an age of such practice, and with his style frequently showing the bad influence of it, Gray was saved, we may say, and remains a poet whose work has high and pure worth, simply by know-ing the Greeks thoroughly, more thoroughly than any En-glish poet had known them since Milton. Milton was a survivor from the great age of poetry; Dryden, Addison, Pope, and Swift were mighty workers for the age of prose. Gray, a poet in the midst of the age of prose, a poet, more-over, of by no means the highest force and of scanty pro-ductiveness, nevertheless claims a place among the six chief personages of Johnson's lives, because it was impossible for an English poet, even in that age, who knew the great Greek masters intimately, not to respond to their good influence, and to be rescued from the false poetical practice of his contemporaries. Of such avail to a nation are deep poetical instincts even in an age of prose. How much more may they be trusted to assert themselves after the age of prose has ended, and to remedy any poetical mischief done by it! And meanwhile the work of the hour, the necessary and appointed work, has been done, and we have got our prose.

Let us always bear in mind, therefore, that the century so well represented by Dryden, Addison, Pope, and Swift, and of which the literary history is so powerfully written by Johnson in his lives, is a century of prose—a century of which the great work in literature was the formation of English prose. Johnson was himself a labourer in this great and needful work, and was ruled by its influences. His blame of genuine poets like Milton and Gray, his over-praise of artificial poets like Pope, are to be taken as the utterances of a man who worked for an age of prose, who was ruled by its influences, and could not but be ruled by them. Of poetry he speaks as a man whose sense for that with which he is dealing is in some degree imperfect.

Yet even on poetry Johnson's utterances are valuable, because they are the utterances of a great and original man. That indeed he was; and to be conducted by such a man through an important century cannot but do us good, even though our guide may in some places be less competent than in others. Johnson was the man of an age of prose. Furthermore, he was a strong force of conservation and concentration, in an epoch which by its natural tendencies seemed moving towards expansion and freedom. But he was a great man, and great men are always instructive. The more we study him, the higher will be our esteem for the power of his mind, the width of his interests, the largeness of his knowledge, the freshness, fearlessness, and strength of his judgments. The higher, too, will be our esteem for his character. His well-known lines on Levett's death, beautiful and touching lines, are still more beautiful and touching because they recall a whole history of Johnson's goodness, tenderness, and charity. Human dignity, on the other hand, he maintained, we all know how well, through the whole long and arduous struggle of his life, from his servitor days at Oxford, down to the *Jam moriturus*[11] of his closing hour. His faults and strangenesses are on the surface, and catch every eye. But on the whole we have in him a good and admirable type, worthy to be kept in our view for ever, of "the ancient and inbred integrity, piety, good-nature and good-humour of the English people."

A volume giving us Johnson's Lives of Milton, Dryden, Swift, Addison, Pope, Gray, would give us, therefore, the compendious story of a whole important age in English literature, told by a great man, and in a performance which is itself a piece of English literature of the first class. If such a volume could but be prefaced by Lord Macaulay's *Life of Johnson*,[12] it would be perfect.

NOTES

Johnson's Lives: Published in *Macmillan's Magazine* (June, 1878); *The Six Chief Lives from Johnson's "Lives of the Poets"* with Macaulay's *"Life of Johnson"* (1878).

1. *A Bible-Reading for Schools* (1872, revised 1875).
2. Blackmore, Watts, Pomfret, and Yalden (also, apparently, Thomson); Boswell's *Life of Johnson,* ed. Hill, rev. Powell, iii. 370.
3. Spiked defenses against cavalry.
4. The opening of *Areopagitica,* 1644 ("I suppose them as at the . . .").
5. Tobias Smollett (1721–71), *Roderick Random* (1748), chapter xxiv.
6. See p. 331, note 6.
7. See p. 91, note 35.
8. Gilbert Burnet (1643–1715), historian.
9. John Tillotson (1630–94), Archbishop of Canterbury.
10. Jeremy Taylor (1613–67), theologian.
11. *Now on the point of death.*
12. (1831).

from A FRENCH CRITIC

ON GOETHE

1878

I DO NOT agree with all M. Scherer's[1] criticisms on Goethe's literary work. I do not myself feel, in reading the *Gedichte,* the truth of what M. Scherer says,—that Goethe has corrected and retouched them till he has taken all the warmth out of them. I do not myself feel the irritation in reading Goethe's Memoirs, and his prose generally, which they provoke in M. Scherer. True, the prose has none of those positive qualities of style which give pleasure, it is not the prose of Voltaire or Swift; it is loose, ill-knit, diffuse; it bears the marks of having been, as it mostly was, dictated, —and dictating is a detestable habit. But it is absolutely free from affectation; it lets the real Goethe reach us.

In other respects I agree in the main with the judgments passed by M. Scherer upon Goethe's works. Nay, some of them, such as *Tasso*[2] and *Iphigeneia,*[3] I should hesitate to extol so highly as he does. In that peculiar world of thought and feeling, wherein *Tasso* and *Iphigeneia* have their existence, and into which the reader too must enter in order to understand them, there is something factitious; something devised and determined by the thinker, not given by the necessity of nature herself; something too artificial, therefore, too deliberately studied,—as the French say, *trop voulu.* They cannot have the power of works where we are in a world of thought and feeling not invented but natural, —of works like the *Agamemnon* or *Lear. Faust,*[4] too, suffers by comparison with works like the *Agamemnon* or *Lear.*

M. Scherer says, with perfect truth, that the first part of *Faust* has not a single false tone or weak line. But it is a work, as he himself observes, 'of episodes and detached scenes,' not a work where the whole material together has been fused in the author's mind by strong and deep feeling, and then poured out in a single jet. It can never produce the single, powerful total-impression of works which have thus arisen.

The first part of *Faust* is, however, undoubtedly Goethe's best work. And it is so for the plain reason that, except his *Gedichte,* it is his most straightforward work in poetry. Mr. Hayward's[5] is the best of the translations of *Faust* for the same reason,—because it is the most straightforward. To be simple and straightforward is, as Milton[6] saw and said, of the essence of first-rate poetry. All that M. Scherer says of the ruinousness, to a poet, of 'symbols, hieroglyphics, mystifications,' is just. When Mr. Carlyle praises the *Helena* for being 'not a type of one thing, but a vague, fluctuating, fitful adumbration of many,' he praises it for what is in truth its fatal defect. The *Mährchen,* again, on which Mr. Carlyle heaps such praise, calling it 'one of the notablest performances produced for the last thousand years,' a performance 'in such a style of grandeur and celestial brilliancy and life as the Western imagination has not elsewhere reached;' the *Mährchen,* woven throughout of 'symbol, hieroglyphic, mystification,' is by that very reason a piece of solemn inanity, on which a man of Goethe's powers could never have wasted his time, but for his lot having been cast in a nation which has never lived.

Mr. Carlyle has a sentence on Goethe which we may turn to excellent account for the criticism of such works as the *Mährchen* and *Helena:*—

> We should ask (he says) what the poet's aim really and truly was, and how far this aim accorded, not with us and our individual crotchets and the crotchets of our little senate where we give or take the law, but with human nature and the nature of things at large; with the universal principles of poetic beauty, not as they stand written in our text-books, but in the hearts and imaginations of all men.

To us it seems lost labour to inquire what a poet's *aim* may have been; but for aim let us read *work,* and we have here a sound and admirable rule of criticism. Let us ask how a poet's work accords, not with any one's fancies and crotchets, but 'with human nature and the nature of things at large, with the universal principles of poetic beauty as they stand written in the hearts and imaginations of all men,' and we shall have the surest rejection of symbol, hieroglyphic, and mystification in poetry. We shall have the surest condemnation of works like the *Mährchen* and the second part of *Faust*.

It is by no means as the greatest of poets that Goethe deserves the pride and praise of his German countrymen. It is as the clearest, the largest, the most helpful thinker of modern times. It is not principally in his published works, it is in the immense Goethe-literature of letter, journal, and conversation, in the volumes of Riemer, Falk, Eckermann, the Chancellor von Müller, in the letters to Merck and Madame von Stein and many others, in the correspondence with Schiller, the correspondence with Zelter, that the elements for an impression of the truly great, the truly significant Goethe are to be found. Goethe is the greatest poet of modern times, not because he is one of the half-dozen human beings who in the history of our race have shown the most signal gift for poetry, but because, having a very considerable gift for poetry, he was at the same time, in the width, depth, and richness of his criticism of life, by far our greatest modern man. He may be precious and important to us on this account above men of other and more alien times, who as poets rank higher. Nay, his preciousness and importance as a clear and profound modern spirit, as a master-critic of modern life, must communicate a worth of their own to his poetry, and may well make it erroneously seem to have a positive value and perfectness as poetry, more than it has. It is most pardonable for a student of Goethe, and may even for a time be serviceable, to fall into this error. Nevertheless, poetical defects, where they are present, subsist, and are what they are. And the same with defects of character. Time and attention bring them to light; and when they are brought to light, it is not good for us, it is obstructing and retarding, to refuse to see them. Goethe himself would have warned us against doing so.

NOTES

from *A French Critic on Goethe:* Published in *Quarterly Review* (January, 1878); *Mixed Essays* (1879).

1. See p. 331, note 9.
2. *Torquato Tasso* (1790), on the poet Tasso at Ferrara.
3. *Iphigenie auf Tauris* (1787), based on Euripides.
4. Part I (1808); Part II (1832).
5. See p. 299, note 82.
6. See p. 308, note 5.

WORDSWORTH

1879

I REMEMBER hearing Lord Macaulay say, after Wordsworth's death, when subscriptions were being collected to found a memorial of him, that ten years earlier more money could have been raised in Cambridge alone, to do honour to Wordsworth, than was now raised all through the country. Lord Macaulay had, as we know, his own heightened and telling way of putting things, and we must always make allowance for it. But probably it is true that Wordsworth has never, either before or since, been so accepted and popular, so established in possession of the minds of all who profess to care for poetry, as he was between the years 1830 and 1840, and at Cambridge. From the very first, no doubt, he had his believers and witnesses. But I have myself heard him declare that, for he knew not how many years, his poetry had never brought him in enough to buy his shoe-strings. The poetry-reading public was very slow to recognise him, and was very easily drawn away from him. Scott effaced him with this public, Byron effaced him.

The death of Byron, seemed, however, to make an opening for Wordsworth. Scott, who had for some time ceased to produce poetry himself, and stood before the public as a great novelist; Scott, too genuine himself not to feel the profound genuineness of Wordsworth, and with an instinctive recognition of his firm hold on nature and of his local truth, always admired him sincerely, and praised him generously. The influence of Coleridge upon young men of ability was then powerful, and was still gathering strength; this influence told entirely in favour of Wordsworth's poetry. Cambridge was a place where Coleridge's influence had great action, and where Wordsworth's poetry, therefore, flourished especially. But even amongst the general public its sale grew large, the eminence of its author was widely recognised, and Rydal Mount became an object of pilgrimage. I remember Wordsworth relating how one of the pilgrims, a clergyman, asked him if he had ever written anything besides the *Guide to the Lakes*. Yes, he answered modestly, he had written verses. Not every pilgrim was a reader, but the vogue was established, and the stream of pilgrims came.

Mr. Tennyson's decisive appearance dates from 1842.[1] One cannot say that he effaced Wordsworth as Scott and Byron had effaced him. The poetry of Wordsworth had been so long before the public, the suffrage of good judges was so steady and so strong in its favour, that by 1842 the verdict of posterity, one may almost say, had been already pronounced, and Wordsworth's English fame was secure. But the vogue, the ear and applause of the great body of poetry-readers, never quite thoroughly perhaps his, he gradually lost more and more, and Mr. Tennyson gained them. Mr. Tennyson drew to himself, and away from Wordsworth, the poetry-reading public, and the new generations. Even in 1850, when Wordsworth died, this diminution of popularity was visible, and occasioned the remark of Lord Macaulay which I quoted at starting.

The diminution has continued. The influence of Coleridge has waned, and Wordsworth's poetry can no longer draw succour from this ally. The poetry has not, however, wanted eulogists; and it may be said to have brought its eulogists luck, for almost every one who has praised Wordsworth's poetry has praised it well. But the public has remained cold, or, at least, undetermined. Even the abundance of Mr. Palgrave's fine and skilfully chosen specimens of Wordsworth, in the *Golden Treasury*, surprised many readers, and gave offence to not a few. To tenth-rate critics and compilers, for whom any violent shock to the public taste would be a temerity not to be risked, it is still quite permissible to speak of Wordsworth's poetry, not only with ignorance, but with impertinence. On the Continent he is almost unknown.

I cannot think, then, that Wordsworth has, up to this time, at all obtained his deserts. 'Glory,' said M. Renan[2] the other day, 'glory after all is the thing which has the best chance of not being altogether vanity.' Wordsworth was a homely man, and himself would certainly never have thought of talking of glory as that which, after all, has the best chance of not being altogether vanity. Yet we may well allow that few things are less vain than *real* glory. Let us conceive of the whole group of civilised nations as being, for intellectual and spiritual purposes, one great confederation, bound to a joint action and working towards a common result; a confederation whose members have a due knowledge both of the past, out of which they all proceed, and of one another. This was the ideal of Goethe, and it is an ideal which will impose itself upon the thoughts of our modern societies more and more. Then to be recognised by the verdict of such a confederation as a master, or even as a seriously and eminently worthy workman, in one's own line of intellectual or spiritual activity, is indeed glory; a glory which it would be difficult to rate too highly. For what could be more beneficent, more salutary? The world is forwarded by having its attention fixed on the best things; and here is a tribunal, free from all suspicion of national and provincial partiality, putting a stamp on the best things, and recommending them for general honour and acceptance. A nation, again, is furthered by recognition of its real gifts and successes; it is encouraged to develop them further. And here is an honest verdict, telling us which of our supposed successes are really, in the judgment of the great impartial world, and not in our own private judgment only, successes, and which are not.

It is so easy to feel pride and satisfaction in one's own things, so hard to make sure that one is right in feeling it! We have a great empire. But so had Nebuchadnezzar. We extol the 'unrivalled happiness'[3] of our national civilisation. But then comes a candid friend, and remarks that our upper class is materialised, our middle class vulgarised, and our lower class brutalised. We are proud of our painting, our music. But we find that in the judgment of other people our painting is questionable, and our music non-existent. We are proud of our men of science. And here it turns out that the world is with us; we find that in the judgment of other people, too, Newton among the dead, and Mr. Darwin among the living, hold as high a place as they hold in our national opinion.

Finally, we are proud of our poets and poetry. Now poetry is nothing less than the most perfect speech of man, that in which he comes nearest to being able to utter the truth. It is no small thing, therefore, to succeed eminently in poetry. And so much is required for duly estimating success here, that about poetry it is perhaps hardest to arrive at a sure general verdict, and takes longest. Meanwhile, our own conviction of the superiority of our national poets is not decisive, is almost certain to be mingled, as we see constantly in English eulogy of Shakespeare, with much of provincial infatuation. And we know what was the opinion current amongst our neighbours the French—people of taste, acuteness, and quick literary tact—not a hundred years ago, about our great poets. The old *Biographie Universelle* notices the pretension of the English to a place for their poets among the chief poets of the world, and says that this is a pretension which to no one but an Englishman can ever seem admissible. And the scornful, disparaging things said by foreigners about Shakespeare and Milton, and about our national over-estimate of them, have been often quoted, and will be in every one's remembrance.

A great change has taken place, and Shakespeare is now generally recognised, even in France, as one of the greatest of poets. Yes, some anti-Gallican cynic will say, the French rank him with Corneille and with Victor Hugo! But let me have the pleasure of quoting a sentence about Shakespeare, which I met with by accident not long ago in the *Correspondant,* a French review which not a dozen English people, I suppose, look at. The writer is praising Shakespeare's prose. With Shakespeare, he says, 'prose comes in whenever the subject, being more familiar, is unsuited to the majestic English iambic.' And he goes on: 'Shakespeare is the king of poetic rhythm and style, as well as the king of the realm of thought; along with his dazzling prose, Shakespeare has succeeded in giving us the most varied, the most harmonious verse which has ever sounded upon the human ear since the verse of the Greeks.' M. Henry Cochin, the writer of this sentence, deserves our gratitude for it; it would not be easy to praise Shakespeare, in a single sentence, more justly. And when a foreigner and a Frenchman writes thus of Shakespeare, and when Goethe says of Milton, in whom there was so much to repel Goethe rather than to attract him, that 'nothing has been ever done so entirely in the sense of the Greeks as *Samson Agonistes,'* and that 'Milton is in very truth a poet whom we must treat with all reverence,' then we understand what constitutes a European recognition of poets and poetry as contradistinguished from a merely national recognition, and that in favour both of Milton and of Shakespeare the judgment of the high court of appeal has finally gone.

I come back to M. Renan's praise of glory, from which I started. Yes, real glory is a most serious thing, glory authenticated by the Amphictyonic Court[4] of final appeal, definitive glory. And even for poets and poetry, long and difficult as may be the process of arriving at the right award, the right award comes at last, the definitive glory rests where it is deserved. Every establishment of such a real glory is good and wholesome for mankind at large, good and wholesome for the nation which produced the poet crowned with it. To the poet himself it can seldom do harm; for he, poor man, is in his grave, probably, long before his glory crowns him.

Wordsworth has been in his grave for some thirty years, and certainly his lovers and admirers cannot flatter themselves that this great and steady light of glory as yet shines over him. He is not fully recognised at home; he is not recognised at all abroad. Yet I firmly believe that the poetical performance of Wordsworth is, after that of Shakespeare and Milton, of which all the world now recognises the worth, undoubtedly the most considerable in our language from the Elizabethan age to the present time. Chaucer is anterior; and on other grounds, too, he cannot well be brought into the comparison. But taking the roll of our chief poetical names, besides Shakespeare and Milton, from the age of Elizabeth downwards, and going through it,—Spenser, Dryden, Pope, Gray, Goldsmith, Cowper, Burns, Coleridge, Scott, Campbell, Moore, Byron, Shelley, Keats (I mention those only who are dead),—I think it certain that Wordsworth's name deserves to stand, and will finally stand, above them all. Several of the poets named have gifts and excellences which Wordsworth has not. But taking the performance of each as a whole, I say that Wordsworth seems to me to have left a body of poetical work superior in power, in interest, in the qualities which give enduring freshness, to that which any one of the others has left.

But this is not enough to say. I think it certain, further, that if we take the chief poetical names of the Continent since the death of Molière, and, omitting Goethe, confront the remaining names with that of Wordsworth, the result is the same. Let us take Klopstock, Lessing, Schiller, Uhland, Rückert, and Heine for Germany; Filicaia, Alfieri, Manzoni, and Leopardi for Italy; Racine, Boileau, Voltaire, André Chenier, Béranger, Lamartine, Musset, M. Victor Hugo (he has been so long celebrated that although he still lives I may be permitted to name him) for France. Several of these, again, have evidently gifts and excellences to which Wordsworth can make no pretension. But in real poetical achievement it seems to me indubitable that to Wordsworth, here again, belongs the palm. It seems to me that Wordsworth has left behind him a body of poetical work which wears, and will wear, better on the whole than the performance of any one of these personages, so far more brilliant and celebrated, most of them, than the homely poet of Rydal. Wordsworth's performance in poetry is on the whole, in power, in interest, in the qualities which give enduring freshness, superior to theirs.

This is a high claim to make for Wordsworth. But if it is a just claim, if Wordsworth's place among the poets who have appeared in the last two or three centuries is after Shakespeare, Molière, Milton, Goethe, indeed, but before all the rest, then in time Wordsworth will have his due. We shall recognise him in his place, as we recognise Shakespeare and Milton; and not only we ourselves shall recognise him, but he will be recognised by Europe also. Meanwhile, those who recognise him already may do well, perhaps, to ask themselves whether there are not in the case of Wordsworth certain special obstacles which hinder or delay his due recognition by others, and whether these obstacles are not in some measure removable.

The *Excursion* and the *Prelude,* his poems of greatest bulk, are by no means Wordsworth's best work. His best work is in his shorter pieces, and many indeed are there of these which are of first-rate excellence. But in his seven volumes the pieces of high merit are mingled with a mass of pieces very inferior to them; so inferior to them that it seems wonderful how the same poet should have produced both. Shakespeare frequently has lines and passages in a strain quite false, and which are entirely unworthy of him. But one can imagine his smiling if one could meet him in the Elysian Fields and tell him so; smiling and replying that he knew it perfectly well himself, and what did it matter? But with Wordsworth the case is different. Work altogether inferior, work quite uninspired, flat and dull, is produced by him with evident unconsciousness of its defects, and he presents it to us with the same faith and seriousness as his best work. Now a drama or an epic fill the mind, and one does not look beyond them; but in a collection of short pieces the impression made by one piece requires to be continued and sustained by the piece following. In reading Wordsworth the impression made by one of his fine pieces is too often dulled and spoiled by a very inferior piece coming after it.

Wordsworth composed verses during a space of some sixty years; and it is no exaggeration to say that within one single decade of those years, between 1798 and 1808, almost all his really first-rate work was produced. A mass of inferior work remains, work done before and after this golden prime, imbedding the first-rate work and clogging it, obstructing our approach to it, chilling, not unfrequently, the high-wrought mood with which we leave it. To be recognised far and wide as a great poet, to be possible and receivable as a classic, Wordsworth needs to be relieved of a great deal of the poetical baggage which now encumbers him. To administer this relief is indispensable, unless he is to continue to be a poet for the few only,—a poet valued far below his real worth by the world.

There is another thing. Wordsworth classified his poems not according to any commonly received plan of arrangement, but according to a scheme of mental physiology. He has poems of the fancy, poems of the imagination, poems of sentiment and reflection, and so on. His categories are ingenious but far-fetched, and the result of his employment of them is unsatisfactory. Poems are separated one from another which possess a kinship of subject or of treatment far more vital and deep than the supposed unity of mental origin, which was Wordsworth's reason for joining them with others.

The tact of the Greeks in matters of this kind was infallible. We may rely upon it that we shall not improve upon the classification adopted by the Greeks for kinds of poetry; that their categories of epic, dramatic, lyric, and so forth, have a natural propriety, and should be adhered to. It may sometimes seem doubtful to which of two categories a poem belongs; whether this or that poem is to be called, for instance, narrative or lyric, lyric or elegiac. But there is to be found in every good poem a strain, a predominant note, which determines the poem as belonging to one of these kinds rather than the other; and here is the best proof of the value of the classification, and of the advantage of adhering to it. Wordsworth's poems will never produce their due effect until they are freed from their present artificial arrangement, and grouped more naturally.

Disengaged from the quantity of inferior work which now obscures them, the best poems of Wordsworth, I hear many people say, would indeed stand out in great beauty, but they would prove to be very few in number, scarcely more than half a dozen. I maintain, on the other hand, that what strikes me with admiration, what establishes in my opinion Wordsworth's superiority, is the great and ample body of powerful work which remains to him, even after all his inferior work has been cleared away. He gives us so much to rest upon, so much which communicates his spirit and engages ours!

This is of very great importance. If it were a comparison of single pieces, or of three or four pieces, by each poet, I do not say that Wordsworth would stand decisively above Gray, or Burns, or Coleridge, or Keats, or Manzoni, or Heine. It is in his ampler body of powerful work that I find his superiority. His good work itself, his work which counts, is not all of it, of course, of equal value. Some kinds of poetry are in themselves lower kinds than others. The ballad kind is a lower kind; the didactic kind, still more, is a lower kind. Poetry of this latter sort counts, too, sometimes, by its biographical interest partly, not by its poetical interest pure and simple; but then this can only be when the poet producing it has the power and importance of Wordsworth, a power and importance which he assuredly did not establish by such didactic poetry alone. Altogether, it is, I say, by the great body of powerful and significant work which remains to him, after every reduction and deduction has been made, that Wordsworth's superiority is proved.

To exhibit this body of Wordsworth's best work, to clear away obstructions from around it, and to let it speak for itself, is what every lover of Wordsworth should desire. Until this has been done, Wordsworth, whom we, to whom he is dear, all of us know and feel to be so great a poet, has not had a fair chance before the world. When once it has been done, he will make his way best, not by our advocacy of him, but by his own worth and power. We may safely leave him to make his way thus, we who believe that a superior worth and power in poetry finds in mankind a sense responsive to it and disposed at last to recognise it. Yet at the outset, before he has been duly known and recognised, we may do Wordsworth a service, perhaps, by indicating in what his superior power and worth will be found to consist, and in what it will not.

Long ago, in speaking of Homer, I said that the noble and profound application of ideas to life is the most essential part of poetic greatness. I said that a great poet receives his distinctive character of superiority from his application, under the conditions immutably fixed by the laws of poetic beauty and poetic truth, from his application, I say, to his subject, whatever it may be, of the ideas

'On man, on nature, and on human life,'[5]

which he has acquired for himself. The line quoted is

Wordsworth's own; and his superiority arises from his powerful use, in his best pieces, his powerful application to his subject, of ideas 'on man, on nature, and on human life.'

Voltaire, with his signal acuteness, most truly remarked that 'no nation has treated in poetry moral ideas with more energy and depth than the English nation.' And he adds: 'There, it seems to me, is the great merit of the English poets.' Voltaire does not mean, by 'treating in poetry moral ideas,' the composing moral and didactic poems;—that brings us but a very little way in poetry. He means just the same thing as was meant when I spoke above 'of the noble and profound application of ideas to life'; and he means the application of these ideas under the conditions fixed for us by the laws of poetic beauty and poetic truth. If it is said that to call these ideas *moral* ideas is to introduce a strong and injurious limitation, I answer that it is to do nothing of the kind, because moral ideas are really so main a part of human life. The question, *how to live,* is itself a moral idea; and it is the question which most interests every man, and with which, in some way or other, he is perpetually occupied. A large sense is of course to be given to the term *moral.* Whatever bears upon the question, 'how to live,' comes under it.

> 'Nor love thy life, nor hate; but, what thou liv'st,
> Live well; how long or short, permit to heaven.'[6]

In those fine lines Milton utters, as every one at once perceives, a moral idea. Yes, but so too, when Keats consoles the forward-bending lover on the Grecian Urn, the lover arrested and presented in immortal relief by the sculptor's hand before he can kiss, with the line,

> 'For ever wilt thou love, and she be fair'—

he utters a moral idea. When Shakespeare says, that

> 'We are such stuff
> As dreams are made of, and our little life
> Is rounded with a sleep,'[7]

he utters a moral idea.

Voltaire was right in thinking that the energetic and profound treatment of moral ideas, in this large sense, is what distinguishes the English poetry. He sincerely meant praise, not dispraise or hint of limitation; and they err who suppose that poetic limitation is a necessary consequence of the fact, the fact being granted as Voltaire states it. If what distinguishes the greatest poets is their powerful and profound application of ideas to life, which surely no good critic will deny, then to prefix to the term ideas here the term moral makes hardly any difference, because human life itself is in so preponderating a degree moral.

It is important, therefore, to hold fast to this: that poetry is at bottom a criticism of life; that the greatness of a poet lies in his powerful and beautiful application of ideas to life,—to the question: How to live. Morals are often treated in a narrow and false fashion; they are bound up with systems of thought and belief which have had their day; they are fallen into the hands of pedants and professional dealers; they grow tiresome to some of us. We find attraction, at times, even in a poetry of revolt against them; in a poetry which might take for its motto Omar Kheyam's[8] words: 'Let us make up in the tavern for the time which we have wasted in the mosque.' Or we find attractions in a poetry indifferent to them; in a poetry where the contents may be what they will, but where the form is studied and exquisite. We delude ourselves in either case; and the best cure for our delusion is to let our minds rest upon that great and inexhaustible word *life,* until we learn to enter into its meaning. A poetry of revolt against moral ideas is a poetry of revolt against *life;* a poetry of indifference towards moral ideas is a poetry of indifference towards *life.*

Epictetus[9] had a happy figure for things like the play of the senses, or literary form and finish, or argumentative ingenuity, in comparison with 'the best and master thing' for us, as he called it, the concern, how to live. Some people were afraid of them, he said, or they disliked and undervalued them. Such people were wrong; they were unthankful or cowardly. But the things might also be over-prized, and treated as final when they are not. They bear to life the relation which inns bear to home. 'As if a man, journeying home, and finding a nice inn on the road, and liking it, were to stay for ever at the inn! Man, thou hast forgotten thine object; thy journey was not *to* this, but *through* this. "But this inn is taking." And how many other inns, too, are taking, and how many fields and meadows! but as places of passage merely. You have an object, which is this: to get home, to do your duty to your family, friends, and fellow-countrymen, to attain inward freedom, serenity, happiness, contentment. Style takes your fancy, arguing takes your fancy, and you forget your home and want to make your abode with them and to stay with them, on the plea that they are taking. Who denies that they are taking? but as places of passage, as inns. And when I say this, you suppose me to be attacking the care for style, the care for argument. I am not; I attack the resting in them, the not looking to the end which is beyond them.'

Now, when we come across a poet like Théophile Gautier,[10] we have a poet who has taken up his abode at an inn, and never got farther. There may be inducements to this or that one of us, at this or that moment, to find delight in him, to cleave to him; but after all, we do not change the truth about him,—we only stay ourselves in his inn along with him. And when we come across a poet like Wordsworth, who sings

'Of truth, of grandeur, beauty, love and hope,
And melancholy fear subdued by faith,
Of blessed consolations in distress,
Of moral strength and intellectual power,
Of joy in widest commonalty spread'—[11]

then we have a poet intent on 'the best and master thing,' and who prosecutes his journey home. We say, for brevity's sake, that he deals with *life,* because he deals with that in which life really consists. This is what Voltaire means to praise in the English poets,—this dealing with what is really life. But always it is the mark of the greatest poets that they deal with it; and to say that the English poets are remarkable for dealing with it, is only another way of saying, what is true, that in poetry the English genius has especially shown its power.

Wordsworth deals with it, and his greatness lies in his dealing with it so powerfully. I have named a number of celebrated poets above all of whom he, in my opinion, deserves to be placed. He is to be placed above poets like Voltaire, Dryden, Pope, Lessing, Schiller, because these famous personages, with a thousand gifts and merits, never, or scarcely ever, attain the distinctive accent and utterance of the high and genuine poets—

'Quique pii vates et Phœbo digna locuti,'[12]

at all. Burns, Keats, Heine, not to speak of others in our list, have this accent;—who can doubt it? And at the same time they have treasures of humour, felicity, passion, for which in Wordsworth we shall look in vain. Where, then, is Wordsworth's superiority? It is here; he deals with more of *life* than they do; he deals with *life*, as a whole, more powerfully.

No Wordsworthian will doubt this. Nay, the fervent Wordsworthian will add, as Mr. Leslie Stephen[13] does, that Wordsworth's poetry is precious because his philosophy is sound; that his 'ethical system is as distinctive and capable of exposition as Bishop Butler's'; that his poetry is informed by ideas which 'fall spontaneously into a scientific system of thought.' But we must be on our guard against the Wordsworthians, if we want to secure for Wordsworth his due rank as a poet. The Wordsworthians are apt to praise him for the wrong things, and to lay far too much stress upon what they call his philosophy. His poetry is the reality, his philosophy,—so far, at least, as it may put on the form and habit of 'a scientific system of thought,' and the more that it puts them on,—is the illusion. Perhaps we shall one day learn to make this proposition general, and to say: Poetry is the reality, philosophy the illusion. But in Wordsworth's case, at any rate, we cannot do him justice until we dismiss his formal philosophy.

The *Excursion* abounds with philosophy, and therefore the *Excursion* is to the Wordsworthian what it never can be to the disinterested lover of poetry,—a satisfactory work. 'Duty exists,' says Wordsworth, in the *Excursion;* and then he proceeds thus—

> '. . . Immutably survive,
> For our support, the measures and the forms,
> Which an abstract Intelligence supplies,
> Whose kingdom is, where time and space are not.'[14]

And the Wordsworthian is delighted, and thinks that here is a sweet union of philosophy and poetry. But the disinterested lover of poetry will feel that the lines carry us really not a step farther than the proposition which they would interpret; that they are a tissue of elevated but abstract verbiage, alien to the very nature of poetry.

Or let us come direct to the centre of Wordsworth's philosophy, as 'an ethical system, as distinctive and capable of systematical exposition as Bishop Butler's'—

> '. . . One adequate support
> For the calamities of mortal life
> Exists, one only;—an assured belief
> That the procession of our fate, howe'er
> Sad or disturbed, is ordered by a Being
> Of infinite benevolence and power;

> Whose everlasting purposes embrace
> All accidents, converting them to good.'15

That is doctrine such as we hear in church too, religious and philosophic doctrine; and the attached Wordsworthian loves passages of such doctrine, and brings them forward in proof of his poet's excellence. But however true the doctrine may be, it has, as here presented, none of the characters of *poetic* truth, the kind of truth which we require from a poet, and in which Wordsworth is really strong.

Even the 'intimations' of the famous Ode, those corner-stones of the supposed philosophic system of Wordsworth,— the idea of the high instincts and affections coming out in childhood, testifying of a divine home recently left, and fading away as our life proceeds,—this idea, of undeniable beauty as a play of fancy, has itself not the character of poetic truth of the best kind; it has no real solidity. The instinct of delight in Nature and her beauty had no doubt extraordinary strength in Wordsworth himself as a child. But to say that universally this instinct is mighty in child-hood, and tends to die away afterwards, is to say what is extremely doubtful. In many people, perhaps with the ma-jority of educated persons, the love of nature is nearly imperceptible at ten years old, but strong and operative at thirty. In general we may say of these high instincts of early childhood, the base of the alleged systematic philosophy of Wordsworth, what Thucydides says of the early achieve-ments of the Greek race: 'It is imposible to speak with certainty of what is so remote; but from all that we can really investigate, I should say that they were no very great things.'

Finally, the 'scientific system of thought' in Wordsworth gives us at last such poetry as this, which the devout Words-worthian accepts—

> 'O for the coming of that glorious time
> When, prizing knowledge as her noblest wealth
> And best protection, this Imperial Realm,
> While she exacts allegiance, shall admit
> An obligation, on her part, to *teach*
> Them who are born to serve her and obey;
> Binding herself by statute to secure,
> For all the children whom her soil maintains,
> The rudiments of letters, and inform
> The mind with moral and religious truth.'16

Wordsworth calls Voltaire dull, and surely the production of these un-Voltairian lines must have been imposed on him as a judgment! One can hear them being quoted at a Social Science Congress; one can call up the whole scene. A great room in one of our dismal provincial towns; dusty air and jaded afternoon daylight; benches full of men with bald heads and women in spectacles; an orator lifting up his face from a manuscript written within and without to declaim these lines of Wordsworth; and in the soul of any poor child of nature who may have wandered in thither, an unutterable sense of lamentation, and mourning, and woe!

'But turn we,' as Wordsworth[17] says, 'from these bold, bad men,' the haunters of Social Science Congresses. And let us be on our guard, too, against the exhibitors and extollers of a 'scientific system of thought' in Wordsworth's poetry. The poetry will never be seen aright while they thus exhibit it. The cause of its greatness is simple, and may be told quite simply. Wordsworth's poetry is great because of the extraordinary power with which Wordsworth feels the joy offered to us in nature, the joy offered to us in the simple primary affections and duties; and because of the extraordinary power with which, in case after case, he shows us this joy, and renders it so as to make us share it.

The source of joy from which he thus draws is the truest and most unfailing source of joy accessible to man. It is also accessible universally. Wordsworth brings us word, therefore, according to his own strong and characteristic line, he brings us word

'Of joy in widest commonalty spread.'

Here is an immense advantage for a poet. Wordsworth tells of what all seek, and tells of it at its truest and best source, and yet a source where all may go and draw for it.

Nevertheless, we are not to suppose that everything is precious which Wordsworth, standing even at this perennial and beautiful source, may give us. Wordsworthians are apt to talk as if it must be. They will speak with the same reverence of "The Sailor's Mother," for example, as of "Lucy Gray." They do their master harm by such lack of discrimination. "Lucy Gray" is a beautiful success; "The Sailor's Mother" is a failure. To give aright what he wishes to give, to interpret and render successfully, is not always within Wordsworth's own command. It is within no poet's command; here is the part of the Muse, the inspiration, the God, the 'not ourselves.'[18] In Wordsworth's case, the accident, for so it may almost be called, of inspiration, is of peculiar importance. No poet, perhaps, is so evidently filled with a new and sacred energy when the inspiration is upon him;

no poet, when it fails him, is so left 'weak as is a breaking wave.'[19] I remember hearing him say that 'Goethe's poetry was not inevitable enough.' The remark is striking and true; no line in Goethe, as Goethe said himself, but its maker knew well how it came there. Wordsworth is right, Goethe's poetry is not inevitable; not inevitable enough. But Wordsworth's poetry, when he is at his best, is inevitable, as inevitable as Nature herself. It might seem that Nature not only gave him the matter for his poem, but wrote his poem for him. He has no style. He was too conversant with Milton not to catch at times his master's manner, and he has fine Miltonic lines; but he has no assured poetic style of his own, like Milton. When he seeks to have a style he falls into ponderosity and pomposity. In the *Excursion* we have his style, as an artistic product of his own creation; and although Jeffrey completely failed to recognise Wordsworth's real greatness, he was yet not wrong in saying of the *Excursion*, as a work of poetic style: 'This will never do.'[20] And yet magical as is that power, which Wordsworth has not, of assured and possessed poetic style, he has something which is an equivalent for it.

Every one who has any sense for these things feels the subtle turn, the heightening, which is given to a poet's verse by his genius for style. We can feel it in the

'After life's fitful fever, he sleeps well'—[21]

of Shakespeare; in the

'. . . though fall'n on evil days,
On evil days though fall'n, and evil tongues'—[22]

of Milton. It is the incomparable charm of Milton's power of poetic style which gives such worth to *Paradise Regained*, and makes a great poem of a work in which Milton's imagination does not soar high. Wordsworth has in constant possession, and at command, no style of this kind; but he had too poetic a nature, and had read the great poets too well, not to catch, as I have already remarked, something of it occasionally. We find it not only in his Miltonic lines; we find it in such a phrase as this, where the manner is his own, not Milton's—

'. . . the fierce confederate storm
Of sorrow barricadoed evermore
Within the walls of cities;'[23]

although even here, perhaps, the power of style, which is

undeniable, is more properly that of eloquent prose than the subtle heightening and change wrought by genuine poetic style. It is style, again, and the elevation given by style, which chiefly makes the effectiveness of "Laodameia."[24] Still the right sort of verse to choose from Wordsworth, if we are to seize his true and most characteristic form of expression, is a line like this from "Michael"—

> 'And never lifted up a single stone.'

There is nothing subtle in it, no heightening, no study of poetic style, strictly so called, at all; yet it is expression of the highest and most truly expressive kind.

Wordsworth owed much to Burns, and a style of perfect plainness, relying for effect solely on the weight and force of that which with entire fidelity it utters, Burns could show him.

> 'The poor inhabitant below
> Was quick to learn and wise to know,
> And keenly felt the friendly glow
> And softer flame;
> But thoughtless follies laid him low
> And stain'd his name.'[25]

Every one will be conscious of a likeness here to Wordsworth; and if Wordsworth did great things with this nobly plain manner, we must remember, what indeed he himself would always have been forward to acknowledge, that Burns used it before him.

Still Wordsworth's use of it has something unique and unmatchable. Nature herself seems, I say, to take the pen out of his hand, and to write for him with her own bare, sheer, penetrating power. This arises from two causes; from the profound sincereness with which Wordsworth feels his subject, and also from the profoundly sincere and natural character of his subject itself. He can and will treat such a subject with nothing but the most plain, first-hand, almost austere naturalness. His expression may often be called bald, as, for instance, in the poem of "Resolution and Independence"; but it is bald as the bare mountain tops are bald, with a baldness which is full of grandeur.

Wherever we meet with the successful balance, in Wordsworth, of profound truth of subject with profound truth of execution, he is unique. His best poems are those which most perfectly exhibit this balance. I have a warm admiration for "Laodameia" and for the great "Ode"; but if I am to tell the very truth, I find "Laodameia" not wholly free from something artificial, and the great "Ode" not wholly free from something declamatory. If I had to pick out poems of a kind most perfectly to show Wordsworth's unique power, I should rather choose poems such as "Michael," "The Fountain," "The Highland Reaper." And poems with the peculiar and unique beauty which distinguishes these, Wordsworth produced in considerable number; besides very many other poems of which the worth, although not so rare as the worth of these, is still exceedingly high.

On the whole, then, as I said at the beginning, not only is Wordsworth eminent by reason of the goodness of his best work, but he is eminent also by reason of the great body of good work which he has left to us. With the ancients I will not compare him. In many respects the ancients are far above us, and yet there is something that we demand which they can never give. Leaving the ancients, let us come to the poets and poetry of Christendom. Dante, Shakespeare, Molière, Milton, Goethe, are altogether larger and more splendid luminaries in the poetical heaven than Wordsworth. But I know not where else, among the moderns, we are to find his superiors.

To disengage the poems which show his power, and to present them to the English-speaking public and to the world, is the object of this volume. I by no means say that it contains all which in Wordsworth's poems is interesting. Except in the case of "Margaret," a story composed separately from the rest of the *Excursion*, and which belongs to a different part of England, I have not ventured on detaching portions of poems, or on giving any piece otherwise than as Wordsworth himself gave it. But under the conditions imposed by this reserve, the volume contains, I think, everything, or nearly everything, which may best serve him with the majority of lovers of poetry, nothing which may disserve him.

I have spoken lightly of Wordsworthians; and if we are to get Wordsworth recognised by the public and by the world, we must recommend him not in the spirit of a clique, but in the spirit of disinterested lovers of poetry. But I am a Wordsworthian myself. I can read with pleasure and edification 'Peter Bell', and the whole series of *Ecclesiastical Sonnets*, and the address to Mr. Wilkinson's spade,[26] and even the "Thanksgiving Ode";—everything of Wordsworth, I think, except "Vaudracour and Julia". It is not for nothing that one has been brought up in the veneration of a man so truly worthy of homage; that one has seen him and heard him, lived in his neighbourhood, and been familiar with his country. No Wordsworthian has a tenderer affection for this pure and sage master than I, or is less really offended by his defects. But Wordsworth is something more than the pure and sage master of a small band of devoted followers, and we ought not to rest satisfied until he is seen to be what he is. He is one of the very chief glories of English Poetry; and by nothing is England so glorious as by her poetry. Let us lay aside every weight which hinders our getting him recognised as this, and let our one study be to bring to pass, as widely as possible and as truly as possible, his own word[27] concerning his poems: 'They will co-operate with the benign tendencies in human nature and society, and will, in their degree, be efficacious in making men wiser, better, and happier.'

NOTES

Wordsworth: Published as preface to Arnold's selection from Wordsworth, 1879; *Essays in Criticism* [Second Series] (1888).

1. *Poems,* two volumes.
2. Ernest Renan (1823–92), French thinker.
3. See p. 104.
4. The supreme judicial court of the Hellenic league under Philip II of Macedonia (382-336 B. C.).
5. See p. 300, note 8.
6. *Paradise Lost,* xi. 549–50.
7. *The Tempest,* IV. i. 156–58.
8. Omar Khayyám, Persian poet whose *Rubáiyát* was translated by Edward FitzGerald (1859).
9. Stoic philosopher (c. 60–140 A.D.).
10. (1811–72), poet and novelist.
11. The fragment "The Recluse," prefixed to *The Excursion* (1814), lines 14–18.
12. *Aeneid,* vi. 662: *and the honorable poets whose speech abased not Apollo.*
13. "Wordsworth's Ethics," *Hours in a Library,* vol. ii.
14. *The Excursion,* iv. 73–76.
15. *The Excursion,* iv. 10–17.
16. *The Excursion,* ix. 293–302.
17. "Blest is this Isle," line 81.
18. Arnold, *Literature and Dogma* (1873), chapter viii: "that root and ground of religion, that element of awe and gratitude which fills religion with emotion, and makes it other and greater than morality—the *not ourselves.*"
19. "A Poet's Epitaph."
20. Arnold quotes the opening words of Francis Jeffrey's review of *The Excursion.*
21. *Macbeth,* III. ii. 23.

22. *Paradise Lost*, vii. 25–26.
23. "The Recluse," lines 78–80.
24. "Laodamia" (1815).
25. "A Bard's Epitaph."
26. "To the Spade of a Friend."
27. Letter to Lady Beaumont, May 21, 1807 ("society, wherever found; and that they will. . . .").

COLERIDGE AND
"MEN OF GENIUS":
from JOUBERT

1864

WHY SHOULD we ever treat of any dead authors but
the famous ones? Mainly for this reason: because, from
these famous personages, home or foreign, whom we all
know so well, and of whom so much has been said, the
amount of stimulus which they contain for us has been in a
great measure disengaged; people have formed their opinion
about them, and do not readily change it. One may write of
them afresh, combat received opinions about them, even
interest one's readers in so doing; but the interest one's
readers receive has to do, in general, rather with the treatment than with the subject; they are susceptible of a lively
impression rather of the course of the discussion itself,—
its turns, vivacity, and novelty,—than of the genius of the
author who is the occasion of it. And yet what is really
precious and inspiring, in all that we get from literature,
except this sense of an immediate contact with genius itself,
and the stimulus towards what is true and excellent which
we derive from it? Now in literature, besides the eminent
men of genius who have had their deserts in the way of
fame, besides the eminent men of ability who have often had
far more than their deserts in the way of fame, there are a
certain number of personages who have been real men of
genius,—by which I mean, that they have had a genuine
gift for what is true and excellent, and are therefore capable

of emitting a life-giving stimulus,—but who, for some reason or other, in most cases for very valid reasons, have remained obscure, nay, beyond a narrow circle in their own country, unknown. It is salutary from time to time to come across a genius of this kind, and to extract his honey. Often he has more of it for us, as I have already said, than greater men; for, though it is by no means true that from what is new to us there is most to be learnt, it is yet indisputably true that from what is new to us we in general learn most.

* * *

I have likened Joubert to Coleridge; and indeed the points of resemblance between the two men are numerous. Both of them great and celebrated talkers, Joubert attracting pilgrims to his upper chamber in the Rue St.-Honoré, as Coleridge attracted pilgrims to Mr. Gilman's[1] at Highgate; both of them desultory and incomplete writers,—here they had an outward likeness with one another. Both of them passionately devoted to reading in a class of books, and to thinking on a class of subjects, out of the beaten line of the reading and thought of their day; both of them ardent students and critics of old literature, poetry, and the metaphysics of religion; both of them curious explorers of words, and of the latent significance hidden under the popular use of them; both of them, in a certain sense, conservative in religion and politics, by antipathy to the narrow and shallow foolishness of vulgar modern liberalism;—here they had their inward and real likeness. But that in which the essence of their likeness consisted is this,—that they both had from nature an ardent impulse for seeking the genuine truth on all matters they thought about, and a gift for finding it and recognising it when it was found. To have the impulse for seeking this truth is much rarer than most people think; to have the gift for finding it is, I need not say, very rare indeed. By this they have a spiritual relationship of the closest kind with one another, and they become, each of them, a source of stimulus and progress for all of us.

Coleridge had less delicacy and penetration than Joubert, but more richness and power; his production, though far inferior to what his nature at first seemed to promise, was abundant and varied. Yet in all his production how much is there to dissatisfy us! How many reserves must be made in praising either his poetry, or his criticism, or his philosophy! How little either of his poetry, or of his criticism, or of his philosophy, can we expect permanently to stand! But that which will stand of Coleridge is this: the stimulus of his continual effort,—not a moral effort, for he had no morals, —but of his continual instinctive effort, crowned often with rich success, to get at and to lay bare the real truth of his matter in hand, whether that matter were literary, or philosophical, or political, or religious; and this in a country where at that moment such an effort was almost unknown; where the most powerful minds threw themselves upon poetry, which conveys truth, indeed, but conveys it indirectly; and where ordinary minds were so habituated to do without thinking altogether, to regard considerations of established routine and practical convenience as paramount, that any attempt to introduce within the domain of these the disturbing element of thought, they were prompt to resent as an outrage. Coleridge's great usefulness lay in his supplying in England, for many years and under critical circumstances, by the spectacle of this effort of his, a stimulus to all minds capable of profiting by it, in the generation which grew up around him. His action will still be felt as long as the need for it continues. When, with the cessation of the need, the action too has ceased, Coleridge's memory, in spite of the disesteem—nay, repugnance—which his character may and must inspire, will yet for ever remain invested with that interest and gratitude which invests the memory of founders.

M. de Rémusat,[2] indeed, reproaches Coleridge with his *jugements saugrenus;* the criticism of a gifted truth-finder ought not to be *saugrenu,* so on this reproach we must pause for a moment. *Saugrenu* is a rather vulgar French word, but, like many other vulgar words, very expressive; used as an epithet for a judgment, it means something like *impudently absurd.* The literary judgments of one nation about another are very apt to be *saugrenus.* It is certainly true, as M. Sainte-Beuve remarks in answer to Goethe's complaint against the French that they have undervalued Du Bartas,[3] that as to the estimate of its own authors every nation is the best judge; the *positive* estimate of them, be it understood, not, of course, the estimate of them in comparison with the authors of other nations. Therefore a foreigner's judgments about the intrinsic merit of a nation's authors will generally, when at complete variance with that nation's own, be wrong; but there is a permissible wrongness in these matters, and to that permissible wrongness there is a limit. When that limit is exceeded, the wrong judgment becomes more than wrong, it becomes *saugrenu,* or impudently absurd. For instance, the high estimate which the French have of Racine is probably in great measure deserved; or, to take a yet stronger case, even the high estimate which Joubert had of the Abbé Delille[4] is probably in great measure deserved; but the common disparaging judgment passed on Racine by English readers is not *saugrenu*, still less is that passed by them on the Abbé Delille *saugrenu*, because the beauty of Racine, and of Delille too, so far as Delille's beauty goes, is eminently in their language, and this is a beauty which a foreigner cannot perfectly seize.

* * *

Joubert was not famous while he lived, and he will not be famous now that he is dead. But, before we pity him for this, let us be sure what we mean, in literature, by *famous*. There are the famous men of genius in literature,—the Homers, Dantes, Shakespeares: of them we need not speak; their praise is for ever and ever. Then there are the famous men of ability in literature: their praise is in their own generation. And what makes this difference? The work of the two orders of men is at the bottom the same,—*a criticism of life*. The end and aim of all literature, if one considers it attentively, is, in truth, nothing but that. But the criticism which the men of genius pass upon human life is permanently acceptable to mankind; the criticism which the men of ability pass upon human life is transitorily acceptable. Between Shakespeare's criticism of human life and Scribe's[5] the difference is there;—the one is permanently acceptable, the other transitorily. Whence then, I repeat, this difference? It is that the acceptableness of Shakespeare's criticism depends upon its inherent truth: the acceptableness of Scribe's upon its suiting itself, by its subject-matter, ideas, mode of treatment, to the taste of the generation that hears it. But the taste and ideas of one generation are not those of the next. This next generation in its turn arrives;—first its sharpshooters, its quick-witted, audacious light troops; then the elephantine main body. The imposing array of its predecessor it confidently assails, riddles it with bullets, passes over its body. It goes hard then with many once popular reputations, with many authorities once oracular. Only two kinds of authors are safe in the general havoc. The first kind are the great abounding fountains of truth, whose criticism of life is a source of illumination and joy to the whole human race for ever,—the Homers, the Shakespeares. These are the sacred personages, whom all civilised warfare respects. The second are those whom the out-skirmishers of the new generation, its forerunners,—quick-witted soldiers, as I have said, the select of the army,—recognise, though the bulk of their comrades behind might not, as of the same family and character with the sacred personages, exercising like them an immortal function, and like them inspiring a permanent interest. They snatch them up, and set them in a place of shelter, where the on-coming multitude may not overwhelm them. These are the Jouberts. They will never, like the Shakespeares, command the homage of the multitude; but they are safe; the multitude will not trample them down. Except these two kinds, no author is safe. Let us consider, for example, Joubert's famous contemporary, Lord Jeffrey. All his vivacity and accomplishment avail him nothing; of the true critic he had in an eminent degree no quality, except one,—curiosity. Curiosity he had, but he had no gift for truth; he cannot illuminate and rejoice us; no intelligent out-skirmisher of the new generation cares about him, cares to put him in safety; at this moment we are all passing over his body. Let us consider a greater than Jeffrey, a critic whose reputation still stands firm,—will stand, many people think, for ever,—the great apostle of the Philistines, Lord Macaulay. Lord Macaulay was, as I have already said, a born rhetorician; a splendid rhetorician doubtless, and, beyond that, an *English* rhetorician also, an *honest* rhetorician; still, beyond the apparent rhetorical truth of things he never could penetrate; for their vital truth, for what the French call the *vraie vérité*, he had absolutely no organ; therefore his reputation, brilliant as it is, is not secure. Rhetoric so good as his excites and gives pleasure; but by pleasure alone you cannot permanently bind men's spirits to you. Truth illuminates and gives joy, and it is by the bond of joy, not of pleasure, that men's spirits are indissolubly held. As Lord Macaulay's own generation dies out, as a new generation arrives, without those ideas and tendencies of its predecessor which Lord Macaulay so deeply shared and so happily satisfied, will he give the same pleasure? and, if he ceases to give this, has he enough of light in him to make him last? Pleasure the new generation will get from its own novel ideas and tendencies; but light is another and a rarer thing, and must be treasured wherever it can be found. Will Macaulay be saved, in the sweep and pressure of time, for his light's sake, as Johnson has already been saved by two generations, Joubert by one? I think it very doubtful.

NOTES

Coleridge and "Men of Genius": From *Joubert:* Delivered at Oxford, November, 1863; published in *National Review* (January, 1864); *Essays in Criticism* (1865). Joseph Joubert (1754–1824), French thinker.

1. R. H. Super corrects this to "Gillman's." Coleridge lived from 1816 in the house of the physician James Gillman.
2. Charles de Rémusat, in *Revue des deux mondes,* October 1, 1856 (R. H. Super).
3. (1544–90), author of an epic on the Creation (1578).
4. Jacques Delille (1738–1813), poet and translator who enjoyed a great reputation in his day.
5. Eugène Scribe (1791–1861), popular dramatist.

BYRON

1881

WHEN at last I held in my hand the volume of poems
which I had chosen from Wordsworth, and began to turn
over its pages, there arose in me almost immediately the
desire to see beside it, as a companion volume, a like collection of the best poetry of Byron. Alone amongst our poets
of the earlier part of this century, Byron and Wordsworth
not only furnish material enough for a volume of this kind,
but also, as it seems to me, they both of them gain considerably by being thus exhibited. There are poems of Coleridge and Keats equal, if not superior, to anything of Byron
or Wordsworth; but a dozen pages or two will contain them,
and the remaining poetry is of a quality much inferior.
Scott never, I think, rises as a poet to the level of Byron
and Wordsworth at all. On the other hand, he never falls
below his own usual level very far; and by a volume of
selections from him, therefore, his effectiveness is not increased. As to Shelley there will be more question; and indeed Mr. Stopford Brooke, whose accomplishments, eloquence, and love of poetry we must all recognise and
admire, has actually given us Shelley in such a volume.
But for my own part I cannot think that Shelley's poetry,
except by snatches and fragments, has the value of the good
work of Wordsworth and Byron; or that it is possible for
even Mr. Stopford Brooke to make up a volume of selections from him which, for real substance, power, and
worth, can at all take rank with a like volume from Byron
or Wordsworth.

Shelley knew quite well the difference between the
achievement of such a poet as Byron and his own. He

praises Byron too unreservedly, but he sincerely felt, and he was right in feeling, that Byron was a greater poetical power than himself. As a man, Shelley is at a number of points immeasurably Byron's superior; he is a beautiful and enchanting spirit, whose vision, when we call it up, has far more loveliness, more charm for our soul, than the vision of Byron. But all the personal charm of Shelley cannot hinder us from at last discovering in his poetry the incurable want, in general, of a sound subject-matter, and the incurable fault, in consequence, of unsubstantiality. Those who extol him as the poet of clouds, the poet of sunsets, are only saying that he did not, in fact, lay hold upon the poet's right subject-matter; and in honest truth, with all his charm of soul and spirit, and with all his gift of musical diction and movement, he never, or hardly ever, did. Except, as I have said, for a few short things and single stanzas, his original poetry is less satisfactory than his translations, for in these the subject-matter was found for him. Nay, I doubt whether his delightful Essays and Letters, which deserve to be far more read than they are now, will not resist the wear and tear of time better, and finally come to stand higher, than his poetry.

There remain to be considered Byron and Wordsworth. That Wordsworth affords good material for a volume of selections, and that he gains by having his poetry thus presented, is an old belief of mine which led me lately to make up a volume of poems chosen out of Wordsworth, and to bring it before the public. By its kind reception of the volume, the public seems to show itself a partaker in my belief. Now Byron also supplies plenty of material for a like volume, and he too gains, I think, by being so presented. Mr. Swinburne urges, indeed, that 'Byron, who rarely wrote anything either worthless or faultless, can only be judged or appreciated in the mass; the greatest of his works was his whole work taken together.' It is quite true that Byron rarely wrote anything either worthless or faultless; it is quite true also that in the appreciation of Byron's power a sense of the amount and variety of his work, defective though much of his work is, enters justly into our estimate. But although there may be little in Byron's poetry which can be pronounced either worthless or faultless, there are portions of it which are far higher in worth and far more free from fault than others. And although, again, the abundance and variety of his production is undoubtedly a proof of his power, yet I question whether by reading everything which he gives us we are so likely to acquire an admiring sense even of his variety and abundance, as by reading what he gives us at his happier moments. Varied and abundant he amply proves himself even by this taken alone. Receive him absolutely without omission or compression, follow his whole outpouring stanza by stanza and line by line from the very commencement to the very end, and he is capable of being tiresome.

Byron has told us himself that the *Giaour* 'is but a string of passages.' He has made full confession of his own negligence. 'No one,' says he, 'has done more through negligence to corrupt the language.' This accusation brought by himself against his poems is not just; but when he goes on to say of them, that 'their faults, whatever they may be, are those of negligence and not of labour,' he says what is perfectly true. *'Lara,'* he declares, 'I wrote while undressing after coming home from balls and masquerades, in the year of revelry, 1814. The *Bride* was written in four, the *Corsair* in ten days.'[1] He calls this 'a humiliating confession, as it proves my own want of judgment in publishing, and the public's in reading, things which cannot have stamina for permanence.' Again he does his poems injustice; the producer of such poems could not but publish them, the public could not but read them. Nor could Byron have produced his work in any other fashion; his poetic work could not have first grown and matured in his own mind, and then come forth as an organic whole; Byron had not enough of the artist in him for this, nor enough of self-command. He wrote, as he truly tells us, to relieve himself, and he went on writing because he found the relief become indispensable. But it was inevitable that works so produced should be, in general, 'a string of passages,' poured out, as he describes them, with rapidity and excitement, and with new passages constantly suggesting themselves, and added while his work was going through the press. It is evident that we have here neither deliberate scientific construction, nor yet the instinctive artistic creation of poetic wholes; and that to take passages from work produced as Byron's was is a very different thing from taking passages out of the *Œdipus* or the *Tempest,* and deprives the poetry far less of its advantage.

Nay, it gives advantage to the poetry, instead of depriving it of any. Byron, I said, has not a great artist's profound and patient skill in combining an action or in developing a character,—a skill which we must watch and follow if we are to do justice to it. But he has a wonderful power of vividly conceiving a single incident, a single situation; of throwing himself upon it, grasping it as if it were real and he saw and felt it, and of making us see and feel it too. The *Giaour* is, as he truly called it, 'a string of passages,' not a work moving by a deep internal law of development to a necessary end; and our total impression from it cannot but receive from this, its inherent defect, a certain dimness and indistinctness. But the incidents of the journey and death of Hassan, in that poem, are conceived and presented with a vividness not to be surpassed; and our impression from them is correspondingly clear and powerful. In *Lara,* again, there is no adequate development either of the character of the chief personage or of the action of the poem; our total impression from the work is a confused one. Yet such an incident as the disposal of the slain Ezzelin's body passes before our eyes as if we actually saw it. And in the same way as these bursts of incident, bursts of sentiment also, living and vigorous, often occur in the midst of poems which must be admitted to be but weakly-conceived and loosely-combined wholes. Byron cannot but be a gainer by having attention concentrated upon what is vivid, powerful, effective in his work, and withdrawn from what is not so.

Byron, I say, cannot but be a gainer by this, just as Wordsworth is a gainer by a like proceeding. I esteem Wordsworth's poetry so highly and the world, in my opinion, has done it such scant justice, that I could not rest satisfied until I had fulfilled, on Wordsworth's behalf, a long-cherished desire;—had disengaged, to the best of my power, his good work from the inferior work joined with it, and had placed before the public the body of his good work by itself. To the poetry of Byron the world has ardently paid homage; full justice from his contemporaries, perhaps even more than justice, his torrent of poetry received. His poetry was admired, adored, 'with all its imperfections on its head,'[2]—in spite of negligence, in spite of diffuseness, in spite of repetitions, in spite of whatever faults it possessed. His name is still great and brilliant. Nevertheless the hour of irresistible vogue has passed away for him; even for Byron it could not but pass away. The time has come for him, as it comes for all poets, when he must take his real and permanent place, no longer depending upon the vogue of his own day and upon the enthusiasm of his contemporaries. Whatever we may think of him, we shall not be subjugated by him as they were; for, as he cannot be for us what he was for them, we cannot admire him so hotly and indiscriminately as they. His faults of negligence, of diffuseness, of repeti-

tion, his faults of whatever kind, we shall abundantly feel
and unsparingly criticise; the mere interval of time between
us and him makes disillusion of this kind inevitable. But
how then will Byron stand, if we relieve him too, so far
as we can, of the encumbrance of his inferior and weakest
work, and if we bring before us his best and strongest work
in one body together? That is the question which I, who can
even remember the latter years of Byron's vogue, and have
myself felt the expiring wave of that mighty influence, but
who certainly also regard him, and have long regarded
him, without illusion, cannot but ask myself, cannot but
seek to answer. The present volume is an attempt to provide
adequate data for answering it.

Byron has been over-praised, no doubt. 'Byron is one of
our French superstitions,' says M. Edmond Scherer; but
where has Byron not been a superstition? He pays now the
penalty of this exaggerated worship. 'Alone among the
English poets his contemporaries, Byron,' said M. Taine,[3]
'atteint à la cîme,—gets to the top of the poetic mountain.'
But the idol that M. Taine had thus adored M. Scherer is
almost for burning. 'In Byron,' he declares, 'there is a remarkable inability ever to lift himself into the region of real
poetic art,—art impersonal and disinterested,—at all. He has
fecundity, eloquence, wit, but even these qualities themselves
are confined within somewhat narrow limits. He has treated
hardly any subject but one,—himself; now the man, in
Byron, is of a nature even less sincere than the poet. This
beautiful and blighted being is at bottom a coxcomb. He
posed all his life long.'

Our poet could not well meet with more severe and un-
sympathetic criticism. However, the praise often given to
Byron has been so exaggerated as to provoke, perhaps, a
reaction in which he is unduly disparaged. 'As various in
composition as Shakespeare himself, Lord Byron has em-
braced,' says Sir Walter Scott, 'every topic of human life,
and sounded every string on the divine harp, from its slightest to its most powerful and heart-astounding tones.' It is
not surprising that some one with a cool head should re-
taliate, on such provocation as this, by saying: 'He has
treated hardly any subject but one, *himself.*' 'In the very
grand and tremendous drama of *Cain*,' says Scott, 'Lord
Byron has certainly matched Milton on his own ground.'
And Lord Byron has done all this, Scott adds, 'while managing his pen with the careless and negligent ease of a man
of quality.' Alas, 'managing his pen with the careless and

negligent ease of a man of quality,' Byron wrote in his
Cain—

> 'Souls that dare look the Omnipotent tyrant in
> His everlasting face, and tell him that
> His evil is not good;'

or he wrote—

> '. . . And *thou* would'st go on aspiring
> To the great double Mysteries! the *two Principles!*'*

One has only to repeat to oneself a line from *Paradise Lost*
in order to feel the difference.

Sainte-Beuve, speaking of that exquisite master of language, the Italian poet Leopardi, remarks how often we see
the alliance, singular though it may at first sight appear, of
the poetical genius with the genius for scholarship and
philology. Dante and Milton are instances which will occur
to every one's mind. Byron is so negligent in his poetical
style, he is often, to say the truth, so slovenly, slipshod, and
infelicitous, he is so little haunted by the true artist's fine
passion for the correct use and consummate management
of words, that he may be described as having for this
artistic gift the insensibility of the barbarian;—which is
perhaps only another and a less flattering way of saying, with
Scott, that he 'manages his pen with the careless and negligent ease of a man of quality.' Just of a piece with the
rhythm of

> 'Dare you await the event of a few minutes'
> Deliberation?'

or of

> 'All shall be void—
> Destroy'd!'

is the diction of

> 'Which now is painful to these eyes,
> Which have not seen the sun to rise;'

or of

> '. . . there let him lay!'

or of the famous passage beginning

> 'He who hath bent him o'er the dead;'[5]

* The italics are in the original. [M. A.][4]

with those trailing relatives, that crying grammatical sole-
cism, that inextricable anacolouthon! To class the work of
the author of such things with the work of the authors of
such verse as

> 'In the dark backward and abysm of time'—[6]

or as

> 'Presenting Thebes, or Pelops' line,
> Or the tale of Troy divine'[7]

is ridiculous. Shakespeare and Milton, with their secret of
consummate felicity in diction and movement, are of another and an altogether higher order from Byron, nay, for
that matter, from Wordsworth also; from the author of
such verse as

> 'Sol hath dropt into his harbour'—[8]

or (if Mr. Ruskin pleases) as

> 'Parching summer hath no warrant'—[9]

as from the author of

> 'All shall be void—
> Destroy'd!'

With a poetical gift and a poetical performance of the very
highest order, the slovenliness and tunelessness of much of
Byron's production, the pompousness and ponderousness
of much of Wordsworth's are incompatible. Let us admit
this to the full.

Moreover, while we are hearkening to M. Scherer, and
going along with him in his fault-finding, let us admit, too,
that the man in Byron is in many respects as unsatisfactory
as the poet. And, putting aside all direct moral criticism of
him,—with which we need not concern ourselves here,—
we shall find that he is unsatisfactory in the same way.
Some of Byron's most crying faults as a man,—his vulgarity, his affectation,—are really akin to the faults of commonness, of want of art, in his workmanship as a poet. The
ideal nature for the poet and artist is that of the finely
touched and finely gifted man, the εὐφυής of the Greeks;
now, Byron's nature was in substance not that of the εὐφυής
at all, but rather, as I have said, of the barbarian. The want
of fine perception which made it possible for him to formu-
late either the comparison between himself and Rousseau,[10]
or his reason for getting Lord Delawarr excused from a

'licking' at Harrow,[11] is exactly what made possible for him also his terrible dealings in, *An ye wool; I have redde thee; Sunburn me; Oons, and it is excellent well.* It is exactly, again, what made possible for him his precious dictum that Pope is a Greek temple, and a string of other criticisms of the like force; it is exactly, in fine, what deteriorated the quality of his poetic production. If we think of a good representative of that finely touched and exquisitely gifted nature which is the ideal nature for the poet and artist,—if we think of Raphael, for instance, who truly is εὐφυής just as Byron is not,—we shall bring into clearer light the connection in Byron between the faults of the man and the faults of the poet. With Raphael's character Byron's sins of vulgarity and false criticism would have been impossible, just as with Raphael's art Byron's sins of common and bad workmanship.

Yes, all this is true, but it is not the whole truth about Byron nevertheless; very far from it. The severe criticism of M. Scherer by no means gives us the whole truth about Byron, and we have not yet got it in what has been added to that criticism here. The negative part of the true criticism of him we perhaps have; the positive part, by far the more important, we have not. Byron's admirers appeal eagerly to foreign testimonies in his favour. Some of these testimonies do not much move me; but one testimony there is among them which will always carry, with me at any rate, very great weight,—the testimony of Goethe. Goethe's sayings about Byron were uttered, it must however be remembered, at the height of Byron's vogue, when that puissant and splendid personality was exercising its full power of attraction. In Goethe's own household there was an atmosphere of glowing Byron-worship; his daughter-in-law was a passionate admirer of Byron, nay, she enjoyed and prized his poetry, as did Tieck[12] and so many others in Germany at that time, much above the poetry of Goethe himself. Instead of being irritated and rendered jealous by this, a nature like Goethe's was inevitably led by it to heighten, not lower, the note of his praise. The Time-Spirit, or *Zeit-Geist*, he would himself have said, was working just then for Byron. This working of the *Zeit-Geist* in his favour was an advantage added to Byron's other advantages, an advantage of which he had a right to get the benefit. This is what Goethe would have thought and said to himself; and so he would have been led even to heighten somewhat his estimate of Byron, and to accentuate the emphasis of praise.

Goethe speaking of Byron at that moment was not and could not be quite the same cool critic as Goethe speaking of Dante, or Molière, or Milton. This, I say, we ought to remember in reading Goethe's judgments on Byron and his poetry. Still, if we are careful to bear this in mind, and if we quote Goethe's praise correctly,—which is not always done by those who in this country quote it,—and if we add to it that great and due qualification added to it by Goethe himself,—which so far as I have seen has never yet been done by his quoters in this country at all,—then we shall have a judgment on Byron, which comes, I think, very near to the truth, and which may well command our adherence.

In his judicious and interesting Life of Byron, Professor Nichol quotes Goethe as saying that Byron 'is undoubtedly to be regarded as the greatest genius of our century.' What Goethe did really say was 'the greatest *talent*,' not 'the greatest *genius*.' The difference is important, because, while talent gives the notion of power in a man's performance, genius gives rather the notion of felicity and perfection in it; and this divine gift of consummate felicity by no means, as we have seen, belongs to Byron and to his poetry. Goethe said that Byron 'must unquestionably be regarded as the greatest talent of the century.'* He said of him moreover: 'The English may think of Byron what they please, but it is certain that they can point to no poet who is his like. He is different from all the rest, and in the main greater.' Here, again, Professor Nichol translates: 'They can show no (living) poet who is to be compared to him;'—inserting the word *living*, I suppose, to prevent its being thought that Goethe would have ranked Byron, as a poet, above Shakespeare and Milton. But Goethe did not use, or, I think, mean to imply, any limitation such as is added by Professor Nichol. Goethe said simply, and he meant to say, '*no* poet.' Only the words which follow† ought not, I think, to be rendered, 'who is to be compared to him,' that is to say, '*who is his equal as a poet.*' They mean rather, 'who may properly be compared with him,' '*who is his parallel.*' And when Goethe said that Byron was 'in the main greater' than all the rest of the English poets, he was not so much thinking of the strict rank, as poetry, of Byron's production; he was thinking of that wonderful personality of Byron which so enters into his poetry, and which Goethe called 'a per-

* 'Der ohne Frage als das grösste Talent des Jahrhunderts anzusehen ist.' [M. A.]
† 'Der ihm zu vergleichen wäre.' [M. A.]

sonality such, for its eminence, as has never been yet, and such as is not likely to come again.' He was thinking of that 'daring, dash, and grandiosity,'* of Byron, which are indeed so splendid; and which were, so Goethe maintained, of a character to do good, because 'everything great is formative,' and what is thus formative does us good.

The faults which went with this greatness, and which impaired Byron's poetical work, Goethe saw very well. He saw the constant state of warfare and combat, the 'negative and polemical working,' which makes Byron's poetry a poetry in which we can so little find rest; he saw the *Hang zum Unbegrenzien*, the straining after the unlimited, which made it impossible for Byron to produce poetic wholes such as the *Tempest* or *Lear*; he saw the *zu viel Empirie*, the promiscuous adoption of all the matter offered to the poet by life, just as it was offered, without thought or patience for the mysterious transmutation to be operated on this matter by poetic form. But in a sentence which I cannot, as I say, remember to have yet seen quoted in any English criticism of Byron, Goethe lays his finger on the cause of all these defects in Byron, and on his real source of weakness both as a man and as a poet. 'The moment he reflects, he is a child,' says Goethe;—*'sobald er reflectirt ist er ein Kind.'*[13]

Now if we take the two parts of Goethe's criticism of Byron, the favourable and the unfavourable, and put them together, we shall have, I think, the truth. On the one hand, a splendid and puissant personality—a personality 'in eminence such as has never been yet, and is not likely to come again'; of which the like, therefore, is not to be found among the poets of our nation, by which Byron 'is different from all the rest, and in the main greater.' Byron is, moreover, 'the greatest talent of our century.' On the other hand, this splendid personality and unmatched talent, this unique Byron, 'is quite too much in the dark about himself;'† nay, 'the moment he begins to reflect, he is a child.' There we have, I think, Byron complete; and in estimating him and ranking him we have to strike a balance between the gain which accrues to his poetry, as compared with the productions of other poets, from his superiority, and the loss which accrues to it from his defects.

A balance of this kind has to be struck in the case of all poets except the few supreme masters in whom a profound

---

* 'Bryon's Kühnheit, Keckheit und Grandiositat, ist das nicht bildend?—Alles Grosse bildet, sobald wir es gewahr werden.' [M. A.]
† 'Gar zu dunkel über sich selbst.' [M. A.]

criticism of life exhibits itself in indissoluble connection with the laws of poetic truth and beauty. I have seen it said that I allege poetry to have for its characteristic this: that it is a criticism of life; and that I make it to be thereby distinguished from prose, which is something else. So far from it, that when I first used this expression, *a criticism of life,* now many years ago,[14] it was to literature in general that I applied it, and not to poetry in especial. 'The end and aim of all literature,' I said, 'is, if one considers it attentively, nothing but that: *a criticism of life.*' And so it surely is; the main end and aim of all our utterance, whether in prose or in verse, is surely a criticism of life. We are not brought much on our way, I admit, towards an adequate definition of poetry as distinguished from prose by that truth; still a truth it is, and poetry can never prosper if it is forgotten. In poetry, however, the criticism of life has to be made conformably to the laws of poetic truth and poetic beauty. Truth and seriousness of substance and matter, felicity and perfection of diction and manner, as these are exhibited in the best poets, are what constitute a criticism of life made in conformity with the laws of poetic truth and poetic beauty; and it is by knowing and feeling the work of those poets, that we learn to recognise the fulfilment and non-fulfilment of such conditions.

The moment, however, that we leave the small band of the very best poets, the true classics, and deal with poets of the next rank, we shall find that perfect truth and seriousness of matter, in close alliance with perfect truth and felicity of manner, is the rule no longer. We have now to take what we can get, to forego something here, to admit compensation for it there; to strike a balance, and to see how our poets stand in respect to one another when that balance has been struck. Let us observe how this is so.

We will take three poets, among the most considerable of our century: Leopardi, Byron, Wordsworth. Giacomo Leopardi was ten years younger than Byron, and he died thirteen years after him; both of them, therefore, died young—Byron at the age of thirty-six, Leopardi at the age of thirty-nine. Both of them were of noble birth, both of them suffered from physical defect, both of them were in revolt against the established facts and beliefs of their age; but here the likeness between them ends. The stricken poet of Recanati had no country, for an Italy in his day did not exist; he had no audience, no celebrity. The volume of his poems, published in the very year of Byron's death, hardly sold, I suppose, its tens, while the volumes of Byron's poetry were selling their tens of thousands. And yet Leopardi has the very qualities which we have found wanting to Byron; he has the sense for form and style, the passion for just expression, the sure and firm touch of the true artist. Nay, more, he has a grave fulness of knowledge, an insight into the real bearings of the questions which as a sceptical poet he raises, a power of seizing the real point, a lucidity, with which the author of *Cain* has nothing to compare. I can hardly imagine Leopardi reading the

> '. . . And *thou* would'st go on aspiring
> To the great double Mysteries! the *two Principles!*'

or following Byron in his theological controversy with Dr. Kennedy,[15] without having his features overspread by a calm and fine smile, and remarking of his brilliant contemporary, as Goethe did, that 'the moment he begins to reflect, he is a child.' But indeed whoever wishes to feel the full superiority of Leopardi over Byron in philosophic thought, and in the expression of it, has only to read one paragraph of one poem, the paragraph of *La Ginestra*, beginning

> 'Sovente in queste piagge,'

and ending

> 'Non so se il riso o la pietà prevale.'[16]

In like manner, Leopardi is at many points the poetic superior of Wordsworth too. He has a far wider culture than Wordsworth, more mental lucidity, more freedom from illusions as to the real character of the established fact and of reigning conventions; above all, this Italian, with his pure and sure touch, with his fineness of perception, is far more of the artist. Such a piece of pompous dulness as

> 'O for the coming of that glorious time,'[17]

and all the rest of it, or such lumbering verse as Mr. Ruskin's enemy,

> 'Parching summer hath no warrant'—

would have been as impossible to Leopardi as to Dante. Where, then, is Wordsworth's superiority? for the worth of what he has given us in poetry I hold to be greater, on the whole, than the worth of what Leopardi has given us. It is in Wordsworth's sound and profound sense

'Of joy in widest commonalty spread;'[18]

whereas Leopardi remains with his thoughts ever fixed upon the *essenza insanabile,* upon the *acerbo, indegno mistero delle cose.*[19] It is in the power with which Wordsworth feels the resources of joy offered to us in nature, offered to us in the primary human affections and duties, and in the power with which, in his moments of inspiration, he renders this joy, and makes us, too, feel it; a force greater than himself seeming to lift him and to prompt his tongue, so that he speaks in a style far above any style of which he has the constant command, and with a truth far beyond any philosophic truth of which he has the conscious and assured possession. Neither Leopardi nor Wordsworth are of the same order with the great poets who made such verse as

Τλητὸν γὰρ Μοῖραι θυμὸν θέσαν ἀνθρώποισιν·[20]

or as

'In la sua volontade e nostra pace;'[21]

or as

'. . . Men must endure
Their going hence, even as their coming hither;
Ripeness is all.'[22]

But as compared with Leopardi, Wordsworth, though at many points less lucid, though far less a master of style, far less of an artist, gains so much by his criticism of life being, in certain matters of profound importance, healthful and true, whereas Leopardi's pessimism is not, that the value of Wordsworth's poetry, on the whole, stands higher for us than that of Leopardi's, as it stands higher for us, I think, than that of any modern poetry except Goethe's.

Byron's poetic value is also greater, on the whole, than Leopardi's; and his superiority turns in the same way upon the surpassing worth of something which he had and was, after all deduction has been made for his shortcomings. We talk of Byron's *personality,* 'a personality in eminence such as has never been yet, and is not likely to come again;' and we say that by this personality Byron is 'different from all the rest of English poets, and in the main greater.' But can we not be a little more circumstantial, and name that in which the wonderful power of this personality consisted? We can; with the instinct of a poet Mr. Swinburne has seized upon it and named it for us. The power of Byron's personality lies in 'the splendid and imperishable excellence which covers all his offences and outweighs all his defects: *the excellence of sincerity and strength.*'

Byron found our nation, after its long and victorious struggle with revolutionary France, fixed in a system of established facts and dominant ideas which revolted him. The mental bondage of the most powerful part of our nation, of its strong middle-class, to a narrow and false system of this kind, is what we call British Philistinism. That bondage is unbroken to this hour, but in Byron's time it was even far more deep and dark than it is now. Byron was an aristocrat, and it is not difficult for an aristocrat to look on the prejudices and habits of the British Philistine with scepticism and disdain. Plenty of young men of his own class Byron met at Almack's or at Lady Jersey's,[23] who regarded the established facts and reigning beliefs of the England of that day with as little reverence as he did. But these men, disbelievers in British Philistinism in private, entered English public life, the most conventional in the world, and at once they saluted with respect the habits and ideas of British Philistinism as if they were a part of the order of creation, and as if in public no sane man would think of warring against them. With Byron it was different. What he called the *cant* of the great middle part of the English nation, what we call its Philistinism, revolted him; but the cant of his own class, deferring to this Philistinism and profiting by it, while they disbelieved in it, revolted him even more. 'Come what may,' are his own words, 'I will never flatter the million's canting in any shape.' His class in general, on the other hand, shrugged their shoulders at this cant, laughed at it, pandered to it, and ruled by it. The falsehood, cynicism, insolence, misgovernment, oppression, with their consequent unfailing crop of human misery, which were produced by this state of things, roused Byron to irreconcilable revolt and battle. They made him indignant, they infuriated him; they were so strong, so defiant, so maleficent,—and yet he felt that they were doomed. 'You have seen every trampler down in turn,' he comforts himself with saying, 'from Buonaparte to the simplest individuals.' The old order, as after 1815 it stood victorious, with its ignorance and misery below, its cant, selfishness, and cynicism above, was at home and abroad equally hateful to him. 'I have simplified my politics,' he writes, 'into an utter detestation of all existing governments.' And again: 'Give me a republic. The king-times are fast finishing; there will be blood shed like water and tears like mist, but the peoples will conquer in the end. I shall not live to see it, but I foresee it.'

Byron himself gave the preference, he tells us, to politicians and doers, far above writers and singers. But the politics of his own day and of his own class,—even of the Liberals of his own class,—were impossible for him. Nature had not formed him for a Liberal peer, proper to move the Address in the House of Lords, to pay compliments to the energy and self-reliance of British middle-class Liberalism, and to adapt his politics to suit it. Unfitted for such politics, he threw himself upon poetry as his organ; and in poetry his topics were not Queen Mab, and the Witch of Atlas, and the Sensitive Plant—they were the upholders of the old order, George the Third and Lord Castlereagh and the Duke of Wellington and Southey, and they were the canters and tramplers of the great world, and they were his enemies and himself.

Such was Byron's personality, by which 'he is different from all the rest of English poets, and in the main greater.' But he posed all his life, says M. Scherer. Let us distinguish. There is the Byron who posed, there is the Byron with his affectations and silliness, the Byron whose weakness Lady Blessington, with a woman's acuteness, so admirably seized: 'His great defect is flippancy and a total want of self-possession.' But when this theatrical and easily criticised personage betook himself to poetry, and when he had fairly warmed to his work, then he became another man; then the theatrical personage passed away; then a higher power took possession of him and filled him; then at last came forth into light that true and puissant personality, with its direct strokes, its ever-welling force, its satire, its energy, and its agony. This is the real Byron; whoever stops at the theatrical preludings does not know him. And this real Byron may well be superior to the stricken Leopardi, he may well be declared 'different from all the rest of English poets, and in the main greater,' in so far as it is true of him, as M. Taine well says, that 'all other souls, in comparison with his, seem inert'; in so far as it is true of him that with superb, exhaustless energy, he maintained, as Professor Nichol well says, 'the struggle that keeps alive, if it does not save, the soul;' in so far, finally, as he deserves (and he does deserve) the noble praise of him which I have already quoted from Mr. Swinburne; the praise for 'the splendid and imperishable excellence which covers all his offences and outweighs all his defects: *the excellence of sincerity and strength.*'

True, as a man, Byron could not manage himself, could not guide his ways aright, but was all astray. True, he has no light, cannot lead us from the past to the future; 'the moment he reflects, he is a child.' The way out of the false state of things which enraged him he did not see,—the slow and laborious way upward; he had not the patience, knowledge, self-discipline, virtue, requisite for seeing it. True, also, as a poet, he has no fine and exact sense for word and structure and rhythm; he has not the artist's nature and gifts. Yet a personality of Byron's force counts for so much in life, and a rhetorician of Byron's force counts for so much in literature! But it would be most unjust to label Byron, as M. Scherer is disposed to label him, as a rhetorician only. Along with his astounding power and passion he had a strong and deep sense for what is beautiful in nature, and for what is beautiful in human action and suffering. When he warms to his work, when he is inspired, Nature herself seems to take the pen from him as she took it from Wordsworth, and to write for him as she wrote for Wordsworth, though in a different fashion, with her own penetrating simplicity. Goethe has well observed of Byron, that when he is at his happiest his representation of things is as easy and real as if he were improvising. It is so; and his verse then exhibits quite another and a higher quality from the rhetorical quality,—admirable as this also in its own kind of merit is,—of such verse as

'Minions of splendour shrinking from distress,'[24]

and of so much more verse of Byron's of that stamp. Nature, I say, takes the pen for him; and then, assured master of a true poetic style though he is not, any more than Wordsworth, yet as from Wordsworth at his best there will come such verse as

'Will no one tell me what she sings?'[25]

so from Byron, too, at his best, there will come such verse as

'He heard it, but he heeded not; his eyes
Were with his heart, and that was far away.'[26]

Of verse of this high quality, Byron has much; of verse of a quality lower than this, of a quality rather rhetorical than truly poetic, yet still of extraordinary power and merit, he has still more. To separate, from the mass of poetry which Byron poured forth, all this higher portion, so superior to the mass, and still so considerable in quantity, and to present it in one body by itself, is to do a service, I believe, to Byron's reputation, and to the poetic glory of our country.

Such a service I have in the present volume attempted to perform. To Byron, after all the tributes which have been paid to him, here is yet one tribute more—

'Among thy mightier offerings here are mine!'[27]

not a tribute of boundless homage certainly, but sincere; a tribute which consists not in covering the poet with eloquent eulogy of our own, but in letting him, at his best and greatest, speak for himself. Surely the critic who does most for his author is the critic who gains readers for his author himself, not for any Lucubrations on his author;—gains more readers for him, and enables those readers to read him with more admiration.

And in spite of his prodigious vogue, Byron has never yet, perhaps, had the serious admiration which he deserves. Society read him and talked about him, as it reads and talks about *Endymion* to-day; and with the same sort of result. It looked in Byron's glass as it looks in Lord Beaconsfield's,[28] and sees, or fancies that it sees, its own face there; and then it goes its way, and straightway forgets what manner of man it saw. Even of his passionate admirers, how many never got beyond the theatrical Byron, from whom they caught the fashion of deranging their hair, or of knotting their neck-handkerchief, or of leaving their shirt-collar unbuttoned; how few profoundly felt his vital influence, the influence of his splendid and imperishable excellence of sincerity and strength!

His own aristocratic class, whose cynical make-believe drove him to fury; the great middle-class, on whose impregnable Philistinism he shattered himself to pieces,—how little have either of these felt Byron's vital influence! As the inevitable break-up of the old order comes, as the English middle-class slowly awakens from its intellectual sleep of two centuries, as our actual present world, to which this sleep has condemned us, shows itself more clearly,—our world of an aristocracy materialised and null, a middle-class purblind and hideous, a lower class crude and brutal,—we shall turn our eyes again, and to more purpose, upon this passionate and dauntless soldier of a forlorn hope, who, ignorant of the future and unconsoled by its promises, nevertheless waged against the conservation of the old impossible world so fiery battle; waged it till he fell,—waged it with such splendid and imperishable excellence of sincerity and strength.

Wordsworth's value is of another kind. Wordsworth has an insight into permanent sources of joy and consolation for mankind which Byron has not; his poetry gives us more which we may rest upon than Byron's,—more which we can rest upon now, and which men may rest upon always. I place Wordsworth's poetry, therefore, above Byron's on the whole, although in some points he was greatly Byron's inferior, and although Byron's poetry will always, probably, find more readers than Wordsworth's, and will give pleasure more easily. But these two, Wordsworth and Byron, stand, it seems to me, first and preeminent in actual performance, a glorious pair, among the English poets of this century. Keats had probably, indeed, a more consummate poetic gift than either of them; but he died having produced too little and being as yet too immature to rival them. I for my part can never even think of equalling with them any other of their contemporaries;—either Coleridge, poet and philosopher wrecked in a mist of opium; or Shelley, beautiful and ineffectual angel, beating in the void his luminous wings in vain. Wordsworth and Byron stand out by themselves. When the year 1900 is turned, and our nation comes to recount her poetic glories in the century which has then just ended, the first names with her will be these.

NOTES

Byron: Published as preface to Arnold's selection from Byron, 1881; *Essays in Criticism* [Second Series] (1888).

1. Byron "wrote to Moore from Italy in 1822: 'Do you recollect, in the year of revelry 1814, the pleasantest parties and balls all over London?' " (Leslie A. Marchand, *Byron,* 1957, i. 455). *The Bride of Abydos* (1813).
2. Adapting *Hamlet,* I. v. 79.
3. Hippolyte Taine (1828–93), author of a history of English literature.
4. *Cain,* I. i. and II. ii.
5. *Werner,* V. 383-84; *Heaven and Earth,* I. iii; *The Prisoner of Chillon,* lines 42–43 ("sun so rise"); *Childe Harold,* IV. clxxx; *The Giaour,* line 68.
6. *The Tempest,* I. ii. 50.
7. Milton, "Il Penseroso."
8. Wordsworth, "The Longest Day" (1820); in 1843, Wordsworth had revised the line to: "For the sun is in his harbour."
9. Wordsworth, "Inscriptions, iv"; discussed by Ruskin in *Fiction, Fair and Foul* (1880).

10. "He has a bad memory, I a good one. He was of the people; I of the aristocracy" (quoted in John Nichol, *Bryon*, 1880, p. 38).

11. " 'Pray don't lick him.' 'Why not?' 'Why, I don't know, except that he is a brother peer; but pray don't,' etc. . . ." Hobhouse wrote in the margin opposite this in his copy of Moore: "I do not believe Byron would be such a fool as to say this" (Marchand, i. 89-90). The story is given in Nichol.

12. J. L. Tieck (1773–1853), German man of letters.

13. "Arnold misuses the quotation. Goethe was speaking not of Byron's poetry and its reflective parts, but of Byron's wild surmises on the sources of *Faust*. See Eckermann, ed. H. H. Houben (Leipzig, 1948), p. 111" (René Wellek).

14. See p. 388.

15. James Kennedy, who tried to convert Byron.

16. *Often upon these slopes . . . I know not whether pity or laughter wins.*

17. See p. 378.

18. See p. 376.

19. *Incurable essence; harsh unworthy mystery of things.*

20. *Iliad*, xxiv. 49: *an enduring soul have the Fates given unto men.*

21. See p. 178.

22. *King Lear*, v. ii. 9–11.

23. "As a leading patroness of the fashionable balls at Almack's, the most exclusive social center of the West End, she had tremendous power as arbiter of taste and manners" (Marchand, i. 347–48).

24. *Childe Harold's Pilgrimage*, II. xxvi. 5.

25. "The Solitary Reaper."

26. *Childe Harold*, IV. cxli.

27. *Childe Harold's Pilgrimage*, IV. cxxxi. 3.

28. Benjamin Disraeli (1804–81), statesman and novelist, author of *Endymion* (1880).

from SHELLEY

1888

TO ALL this we have to add the charm of the man's writings—of Shelley's poetry. It is his poetry, above everything else, which for many people establishes that he is an angel. Of his poetry I have not space now to speak. But let no one suppose that a want of humour and a self-delusion such as Shelley's have no effect upon a man's poetry. The man Shelley, in very truth, is not entirely sane, and Shelley's poetry is not entirely sane either. The Shelley of actual life is a vision of beauty and radiance, indeed, but availing nothing, affecting nothing. And in poetry, no less than in life, he is 'a beautiful *and ineffectual* angel, beating in the void his luminous wings in vain'.[1]

NOTES

From *Shelley:* Published in the *Nineteenth Century* (January, 1888); *Essays in Criticism* [Second Series] (1888). In a letter, Arnold said: "In this article on Shelley I have spoken of his life, not his poetry" (*Letters*, ii. 372).

1. See p. 408.

JOHN KEATS

1880

POETRY, according to Milton's famous saying, should be 'simple, sensuous, impassioned.'[1] No one can question the eminency, in Keats's poetry, of the quality of sensuousness. Keats as a poet is abundantly and enchantingly sensuous; the question with some people will be, whether he is anything else. Many things may be brought forward which seem to show him as under the fascination and sole dominion of sense, and desiring nothing better. There is the exclamation in one of his letters: 'O for a life of sensations rather than of thoughts!' There is the thesis, in another, 'that with a great Poet the sense of Beauty overcomes every other consideration, or rather obliterates all consideration.' There is Haydon's[2] story of him, how 'he once covered his tongue and throat as far as he could reach with Cayenne pepper, in order to appreciate the delicious coldness of claret in all its glory—his own expression.' One is not much surprised when Haydon further tells us, of the hero of such a story, that once for six weeks together he was hardly ever sober. 'He had no decision of character,' Haydon adds; 'no object upon which to direct his great powers.'

Character and self-control, the *virtus verusque labor*[3] so necessary for every kind of greatness, and for the great artist, too, indispensable, appear to be wanting, certainly, to this Keats of Haydon's portraiture. They are wanting also to the Keats of the *Letters to Fanny Brawne*.[4] These letters make as unpleasing an impression as Haydon's anecdotes. The editor of Haydon's journals could not well omit what Haydon said of his friend, but for the publication of the *Letters to Fanny Brawne* I can see no good reason whatever. Their publication appears to me, I confess, inexcusable; they ought never to have been published. But published they are, and we have to take notice of them. Letters written when Keats was near his end, under the throttling and unmanning grasp of mortal disease, we will not judge. But here is a letter written some months before he was taken ill. It is printed just as Keats wrote it.

> 'You have absorb'd me. I have a sensation at the present moment as though I was dissolving—I should be exquisitely miserable without the hope of soon seeing you. I should be afraid to separate myself far from you. My sweet Fanny, will your heart never change? My love, will it? I have no limit now to my love. . . . Your note came in just here. I cannot be happier away from you. 'Tis richer than an Argosy of Pearles. Do not threat me even in jest. I have been astonished that Men could die Martyrs for religion—I have shuddered at it. I shudder no more—I could be martyred for my Religion—Love is my religion—I could die for that. I could die for you. My Creed is Love and you are its only tenet. You have ravished me away by a Power I cannot resist; and yet I could resist till I saw you; and even since I have seen you I have endeavoured often "to reason against the reasons of my Love." I can do that no more—the pain would be too great. My love is selfish. I cannot breathe without you.'

A man who writes love-letters in this strain is probably predestined, one may observe, to misfortune in his love-affairs; but that is nothing. The complete enervation of the writer is the real point for remark. We have the tone, or rather the entire want of tone, the abandonment of all reticence and all dignity, of the merely sensuous man, of the man who 'is passion's slave.'[5] Nay, we have them in such wise that one is tempted to speak even as Blackwood or the Quarterly were in the old days wont to speak; one is tempted to say that Keats's love-letter is the love-letter of a surgeon's apprentice. It has in its relaxed self-abandonment something underbred and ignoble, as of a youth ill brought up, without the training which teaches us that we must put some constraint upon our feelings and upon the expression of them. It is the sort of love-letter of a surgeon's apprentice which one might hear read out in a breach of promise case, or in the Divorce Court. The sensuous man speaks in it, and the sensuous man of a badly bred and badly trained sort. That many who are themselves also badly bred and badly trained should enjoy it, and should even think it a beautiful and characteristic production of him whom they call their 'lovely and beloved Keats,' does not make it better. These

are the admirers whose pawing and fondness does not good
but harm to the fame of Keats; who concentrate attention
upon what in him is least wholesome and most questionable; who worship him, and would have the world worship
him too, as the poet of

> 'Light feet, dark violet eyes, and parted hair,
> Soft dimpled hands, white neck, and creamy breast.'[6]

This sensuous strain Keats had, and a man of his poetic
powers could not, whatever his strain, but show his talent
in it. But he has something more, and something better.
We who believe Keats to have been by his promise, at any
rate, if not fully by his performance, one of the very greatest of English poets, and who believe also that a merely
sensuous man cannot either by promise or by performance
be a very great poet, because poetry interprets life, and so
large and noble a part of life is outside of such a man's ken,
—we cannot but look for signs in him of something more
than sensuousness, for signs of character and virtue. And
indeed the elements of high character Keats undoubtedly
has, and the effort to develop them; the effort is frustrated
and cut short by misfortune, and disease, and time, but for
the due understanding of Keats's worth the recognition of
this effort, and of the elements on which it worked, is necessary.

Lord Houghton,[7] who praises very discriminatingly the
poetry of Keats, has on his character also a remark full of
discrimination. He says: 'The faults of Keats's disposition
were precisely the contrary of those attributed to him by
common opinion.' And he gives a letter written after the
death of Keats by his brother George, in which the writer,
speaking of the fantastic *Johnny Keats* invented for common
opinion by Lord Byron and by the reviewers, declares indignantly: 'John was the very soul of manliness and courage,
and as much like the Holy Ghost as *Johnny Keats.*' It is
important to note this testimony, and to look well for whatever illustrates and confirms it.

Great weight is laid by Lord Houghton on such a direct
profession of faith as the following: 'That sort of probity
and disinterestedness,' Keats writes to his brothers, 'which
such men as Bailey[8] possess, does hold and grasp the tip-
top of any spiritual honours that can be paid to anything
in this world.' Lord Houghton says that 'never have words
more effectively expressed the conviction of the superiority
of virtue above beauty than those.' But merely to make a
profession of faith of the kind here made by Keats is not

difficult; what we should rather look for is some evidence of the instinct for character, for virtue, passing into the man's life, passing into his work.

Signs of virtue, in the true and large sense of the word, the instinct for virtue passing into the life of Keats and strengthening it, I find in the admirable wisdom and temper of what he says to his friend Bailey on the occasion of a quarrel between Reynolds[9] and Haydon:—

> 'Things have happened lately of great perplexity; you must have heard of them; Reynolds and Haydon retorting and re-criminating, and parting for ever. The same thing has happened between Haydon and Hunt.[10] It is unfortunate; men should bear with each other; there lives not the man who may not be cut up, aye, lashed to pieces, on his weakest side. The best of men have but a portion of good in them. . . . The sure way, Bailey, is first to know a man's faults, and then be passive. If, after that, he insensibly draws you to-wards him, then you have no power to break the link. Before I felt interested in either Reynolds or Haydon, I was well read in their faults; yet, knowing them, I have been cement-ing gradually with both. I have an affection for them both, for reasons almost opposite; and to both must I of necessity cling, supported always by the hope that when a little time, a few years, shall have tried me more fully in their esteem, I may be able to bring them together.'

Butler[11] has well said that 'endeavouring to enforce upon our own minds a practical sense of virtue, or to beget in others that practical sense of it which a man really has himself, is a virtuous *act*.' And such an 'endeavouring' is that of Keats in those words written to Bailey. It is more than mere words; so justly thought and so discreetly urged as it is, it rises to the height of a virtuous *act*. It is proof of character.

The same thing may be said of some words written to his friend Charles Brown, whose kindness, willingly ex-erted whenever Keats chose to avail himself of it, seemed to free him from any pressing necessity of earning his own living. Keats felt that he must not allow this state of things to continue. He determined to set himself to 'fag on as others do' at periodical literature, rather than to endanger his independence and his self-respect; and he writes to Brown:—

> 'I had got into a habit of mind of looking towards you as a help in all difficulties. This very habit would be the parent of idleness and difficulties. You will see it is a duty I owe to

myself to break the neck of it. I do nothing for my subsistence —make no exertion. At the end of another year you shall applaud me, not for verses, but for conduct.'

He had not, alas, another year of health before him when he announced that wholesome resolve; it then wanted but six months of the day of his fatal attack. But in the brief time allowed to him he did what he could to keep his word.

What character, again, what strength and clearness of judgment, in his criticism of his own productions, of the public, and of 'the literary circles'! His words after the severe reviews of *Endymion* have often been quoted; they cannot be quoted too often:—

'Praise or blame has but a momentary effect on the man whose love of beauty in the abstract makes him a severe critic on his own works. My own criticism has given me pain without comparison beyond what *Blackwood* or the *Quarterly* could possibly inflict; and also, when I feel I am right, no external praise can give me such a glow as my own solitary reperception and ratification of what is fine. J. S. is perfectly right in regard to the "slip-shod Endymion." That it is so is no fault of mine. No! though it may sound a little paradoxical, it is as good as I had power to make it by myself.'[12]

And again, as if he had foreseen certain of his admirers gushing over him, and was resolved to disengage his responsibility:—

'I have done nothing, except for the amusement of a few people who refine upon their feelings till anything in the ununderstandable way will go down with them. I have no cause to complain, because I am certain anything really fine will in these days be felt. I have no doubt that if I had written *Othello* I should have been cheered. I shall go on with patience.'

Young poets almost inevitably over-rate what they call 'the might of poesy,' and its power over the world which now is. Keats is not a dupe on this matter any more than he is a dupe about the merit of his own performances:—

'I have no trust whatever in poetry. I don't wonder at it; the marvel is to me how people read so much of it.'

His attitude towards the public is that of a strong man, not of a weakling avid of praise, and made to 'be snuff'd out by an article':[13]—

'I shall ever consider the public as debtors to me for verses, not myself to them for admiration, which I can do without.'

And again, in a passage where one may perhaps find fault with the capital letters, but surely with nothing else:—

> 'I have not the slightest feel of humility towards the public or to anything in existence but the Eternal Being, the Principle of Beauty, and the Memory of great Men. . . . I would be subdued before my friends, and thank them for subduing me, but among multitudes of men I have no feel of stooping; I hate the idea of humility to them. I never wrote one single line of poetry with the least shadow of thought about their opinion. Forgive me for vexing you, but it eases me to tell you: I could not live without the love of my friends; I would jump down Etna for any great public good—but I hate a mawkish popularity. I cannot be subdued before them. My glory would be to daunt and dazzle the thousand jabberers about pictures and books.'

Against these artistic and literary 'jabberers,' amongst whom Byron fancied Keats, probably, to be always living, flattering them and flattered by them, he has yet another outburst:—

> 'Just so much as I am humbled by the genius above my grasp, am I exalted and look with hate and contempt upon the literary world. Who could wish to be among the commonplace crowd of the little famous, who are each individually lost in a throng made up of themselves?'

And he loves Fanny Brawne the more, he tells her, because he believes that she has liked him for his own sake and for nothing else. 'I have met with women who I really think would like to be married to a Poem and to be given away by a Novel.'

There is a tone of too much bitterness and defiance in all this, a tone which he with great propriety subdued and corrected when he wrote his beautiful preface to *Endymion*. But the thing to be seized is, that Keats had flint and iron in him, that he had character; that he was, as his brother George says, 'as much like the Holy Ghost as *Johnny Keats*,' —as that imagined sensuous weakling, the delight of the literary circles of Hampstead.

It is a pity that Byron, who so misconceived Keats, should never have known how shrewdly Keats, on the other hand, had characterised *him*, as 'a fine thing' in the sphere of 'the worldly, theatrical, and pantomimical.' But indeed nothing is more remarkable in Keats than his clear-sightedness, his lucidity; and lucidity is in itself akin to character and to high and severe work. In spite, therefore, of his overpowering feeling for beauty, in spite of his sensuousness, in spite

of his facility, in spite of his gift of expression, Keats could
say resolutely:—

> 'I know nothing, I have read nothing; and I mean to fol-
> low Solomon's directions: "Get learning,[14] get understand-
> ing." There is but one way for me. The road lies through
> application, study, and thought. I will pursue it.'

And of Milton, instead of resting in Milton's incomparable phrases, Keats could say, although indeed all the
while 'looking upon fine phrases,' as he himself tells us,
'like a lover'—

> 'Milton had an exquisite passion for what is properly, in
> the sense of ease and pleasure, poetical luxury; and with that,
> it appears to me, he would fain have been content, if he
> could, so doing, preserve his self-respect and feeling of duty
> performed; but there was working in him, as it were, that
> same sort of thing which operates in the great world to the
> end of a prophecy's being accomplished. Therefore he de-
> voted himself rather to the ardours than the pleasures of
> song, solacing himself at intervals with cups of old wine.'

In his own poetry, too, Keats felt that place must be
found for 'the ardours rather than the pleasures of song,'
although he was aware that he was not yet ripe for it—

> 'But my flag is not unfurl'd
> On the Admiral-staff, and to philosophise
> I dare not yet.'[15]

Even in his pursuit of 'the pleasures of song,' however,
there is that stamp of high work which is akin to character,
which is character passing into intellectual production. *'The
best sort of poetry*—that,' he truly says, 'is all I care for,
all I live for.' It is curious to observe how this severe addiction of his to the best sort of poetry affects him with a
certain coldness, as if the addiction had been to mathematics, towards those prime objects of a sensuous and
passionate poet's regard, love and women. He speaks of 'the
opinion I have formed of the generality of women, who
appear to me as children to whom I would rather give a
sugar-plum than my time.' He confesses 'a tendency to class
women in my books with roses and sweetmeats—they never
see themselves dominant'; and he can understand how the
unpopularity of his poems may be in part due to 'the offence
which the ladies,' not unnaturally 'take at him' from this
cause. Even to Fanny Brawne he can write 'a flint-worded
letter,' when his 'mind is heaped to the full' with poetry:—

'I know the generality of women would hate me for this; that I should have so unsoftened, so hard a mind as to forget them; forget the brightest realities for the dull imaginations of my own brain. . . . My heart seems now made of iron— I could not write a proper answer to an invitation to Idalia.'[16]

The truth is that 'the yearning passion for the Beautiful,' which was with Keats, as he himself truly says, the master-passion, is not a passion of the sensuous or sentimental man, is not a passion of the sensuous or sentimental poet. It is an intellectual and spiritual passion. It is 'connected and made one,' as Keats declares that in his case it was, 'with the ambition of the intellect.' It is, as he again says, 'the mighty *abstract idea* of Beauty in all things.' And in his last days Keats wrote: 'If I should die, I have left no immortal work behind me—nothing to make my friends proud of my memory; *but I have loved the principle of beauty in all things,* and if I had had time I would have made myself remembered.' He *has* made himself remembered, and remembered as no merely sensuous poet could be; and he has done it by having 'loved the principle of beauty in all things.'

For to see things in their beauty is to see things in their truth, and Keats knew it. 'What the Imagination seizes as Beauty must be Truth,' he says in prose; and in immortal verse he has said the same thing—

> 'Beauty is truth, truth beauty,—that is all
> Ye know on earth, and all ye need to know.'[17]

No, it is not all; but it is true, deeply true, and we have deep need to know it. And with beauty goes not only truth, joy goes with her also; and this too Keats saw and said, as in the famous first line of his *Endymion* it stands written—

> 'A thing of beauty is a joy for ever.'

It is no small thing to have so loved the principle of beauty as to perceive the necessary relation of beauty with truth, and of both with joy. Keats was a great spirit, and counts for far more than many even of his admirers suppose, because this just and high perception made itself clear to him. Therefore a dignity and a glory shed gleams over his life, and happiness, too, was not a stranger to it. 'Nothing startles me beyond the moment,' he says; 'the setting sun will always set me to rights, or if a sparrow come before my window I take part in its existence and pick about the gravel.' But he had terrible bafflers,—consuming disease and early death. 'I think,' he writes to Reynolds, 'if I had a free and healthy and lasting organisation of heart, and lungs as strong as an ox's, so as to be able to bear unhurt the shock of extreme thought and sensation without weariness, I could pass my life very nearly alone, though it should last eighty years. But I feel my body too weak to support me to the height; I am obliged continually to check myself, and be nothing.' He had against him even more than this; he had against him the blind power which we call Fortune. 'O that something fortunate,' he cries in the closing months of his life, 'had ever happened to me or my brothers!—then I might hope,—but despair is forced upon me as a habit.' So baffled and so sorely tried,—while laden, at the same time, with a mighty formative thought requiring health, and many days, and favouring circumstances, for its adequate manifestation,—what wonder if the achievement of Keats be partial and incomplete?

Nevertheless, let and hindered as he was, and with a short term and imperfect experience,—'young,' as he says of himself, 'and writing at random, straining after particles of light in the midst of a great darkness, without knowing the bearing of any one assertion, of any one opinion,'—notwithstanding all this, by virtue of his feeling for beauty and of his perception of the vital connection of beauty with truth, Keats accomplished so much in poetry, that in one of the two great modes by which poetry interprets, in the faculty of naturalistic interpretation, in what we call natural magic, he ranks with Shakespeare. 'The tongue of Kean,'[18] he says in an admirable criticism of that great actor and of his enchanting elocution, 'the tongue of Kean must seem to have robbed the Hybla bees and left them honeyless. There is an indescribable *gusto* in his voice;—in *Richard*, "Be stirring with the lark to-morrow, gentle Norfolk!"[19] comes from him as through the morning atmosphere towards which he yearns.' This magic, this 'indescribable *gusto* in the voice,' Keats himself, too, exhibits in his poetic expression. No one else in English poetry, save Shakespeare, has in expression quite the fascinating felicity of Keats, his perfection of loveliness. 'I think,' he said humbly, 'I shall be among the English poets after my death.' He is; he is with Shakespeare.

For the second great half of poetic interpretation, for that faculty of moral interpretation which is in Shakespeare, and is informed by him with the same power of beauty as his naturalistic interpretation, Keats was not ripe. For the architectonics of poetry, the faculty which presides at the evolution of works like the *Agamemnon* or *Lear,* he was not ripe. His *Endymion,* as he himself well saw, is a failure, and his

Hyperion, fine things as it contains, is not a success. But in shorter things, where the matured power of moral interpretation, and the high architectonics which go with complete poetic development, are not required, he is perfect. The poems which follow prove it,—prove it far better by themselves than anything which can be said about them will prove it. Therefore I have chiefly spoken here of the man, and of the elements in him which explain the production of such work. Shakespearian work it is; not imitative, indeed, of Shakespeare, but Shakespearian, because its expression has that rounded perfection and felicity of loveliness of which Shakespeare is the great master. To show such work is to praise it. Let us now end by delighting ourselves with a fragment of it, too broken to find a place among the pieces which follow, but far too beautiful to be lost. It is a fragment of an ode for May-day. O might I, he cries to May, O might I

> '. . . thy smiles
> Seek as they once were sought, in Grecian isles,
> By bards who died content on pleasant sward,
> Leaving great verse unto a little clan!
> O, give me their old vigour, and unheard
> Save of the quiet primrose, and the span
>   Of heaven, and few ears,
> Rounded by thee, my song should die away,
>   Content as theirs,
> Rich in the simple worship of a day!'

NOTES

John Keats: Published as preface to the selection from Keats in T. H. Ward's *The English Poets* (1880); *Essays in Criticism* [Second Series] (1888).

1. See p. 308, note 5.
2. Benjamin Robert Haydon (1786–1846), painter.
3. *Manliness and real labour.*
4. Published 1878.
5. Adapting *Hamlet,* III. ii. 74.
6. "Woman! when I behold thee flippant, vain."
7. Richard Monckton Milnes (1809–85), who edited *The Life, Letters and Literary Remains of Keats* (1848, revised 1867).
8. Keats's friend, Benjamin Bailey.
9. John Hamilton Reynolds (1796–1852), poet and friend of Keats.
10. Leigh Hunt (1784–1859), poet and editor.
11. Bishop Joseph Butler, in his *Analogy of Religion,* Part I, chapter v.
12. Letter to J. A. Hessey, October 9, 1818. "J. S." wrote a letter about Keats to the *Morning Chronicle,* October 3, 1818.

13. Byron's *Dan Juan*, XI. lx, on "John Keats, who was kill'd off by one critique. . . ./ 'Tis strange the mind, that very fiery particle, /Should let itself be snuff'd out by an article."

14. Keats wrote "Get Wisdom" (from *Proverbs*, iv. 5).

15. "Epistle to Reynolds."

16. Aphrodite, goddess of love and beauty.

17. "Ode on a Grecian Urn."

18. Edmund Kean (1789–1833).

19. *Richard III*, V. iii. 56: "Stir with the lark tomorrow, gentle Norfolk."

HEINRICH HEINE

1863

"I KNOW NOT if I deserve that a laurel-wreath should one day be laid on my coffin. Poetry, dearly as I have loved it, has always been to me but a divine plaything. I have never attached any great value to poetical fame; and I trouble myself very little whether people praise my verses or blame them. But lay on my coffin a *sword;* for I was a brave soldier in the Liberation War of humanity."

Heine had his full share of love of fame, and cared quite as much as his brethren of the *genus irritabile*[1] whether people praised his verses or blamed them. And he was very little of a hero. Posterity will certainly decorate his tomb with the emblem of the laurel rather than with the emblem of the sword. Still, for his contemporaries, for us, for the Europe of the present century, he is significant chiefly for the reason which he himself in the words just quoted assigns. He is significant because he was, if not pre-eminently a brave, yet a brilliant, a most effective soldier in the Liberation War of humanity.

To ascertain the master-current in the literature of an epoch, and to distinguish this from all minor currents, is one of the critic's highest functions; in discharging it he shows how far he possesses the most indispensable quality of his office,—justness of spirit. The living writer who has done most to make England acquainted with German authors, a man of genius, but to whom precisely this one quality of justness of spirit is perhaps wanting,—I mean Mr. Carlyle,—seems to me in the result of his labours on German literature to afford a proof how very necessary to the critic this quality is. Mr. Carlyle has spoken admirably of Goethe; but then Goethe stands before all men's eyes, the manifest centre of German literature; and from this central source many rivers flow. Which of these rivers is the main stream? which of the courses of spirit which we see active in Goethe is the course which will most influence the future, and attract and be continued by the most powerful of Goethe's successors?—that is the question. Mr. Carlyle attaches, it seems to me, far too much importance to the romantic school of Germany,—Tieck, Novalis, Jean Paul Richter,—and gives to these writers, really gifted as two, at any rate, of them are, an undue prominence. These writers, and others with aims and a general tendency the same as theirs, are not the real inheritors and continuators of Goethe's power; the current of their activity is not the main current of German literature after Goethe. Far more in Heine's works flows this main current; Heine, far more than Tieck or Jean Paul Richter, is the continuator of that which, in Goethe's varied activity, is the most powerful and vital; on Heine, of all German authors who survived Goethe, incomparably the largest portion of Goethe's mantle fell. I do not forget that when Mr. Carlyle was dealing with German literature, Heine, though he was clearly risen above the horizon, had not shone forth with all his strength; I do not forget, too, that after ten or twenty years many things may come out plain before the critic which before were hard to be discerned by him; and assuredly no one would dream of imputing it as a fault to Mr. Carlyle that twenty years ago he mistook the central current in German literature, overlooked the rising Heine, and attached undue importance to that romantic school which Heine was to destroy; one may rather note it as a misfortune, sent perhaps as a delicate chastisement to a critic, who,—man of genius as he is, and no one recognises his genius more admiringly than I do,—has, for the functions of the critic, a little too much of the self-will and eccentricity of a genuine son of Great Britain.

Heine is noteworthy, because he is the most important German successor and continuator of Goethe in Goethe's most important line of activity. And which of Goethe's lines of activity is this?—His line of activity as "a soldier in the war of liberation of humanity."

Heine himself would hardly have admitted this affiliation, though he was far too powerful-minded a man to decry, with some of the vulgar German liberals, Goethe's genius. "The wind of the Paris Revolution," he writes after the three days of 1830, "blew about the candles a little in the dark night of Germany, so that the red curtains of a German throne or two caught fire; but the old watchmen, who do the police of the German kingdoms, are already bringing out the fire engines, and will keep the candles closer snuffed for the future. Poor, fast-bound German people, lose not all heart in thy bonds! The fashionable coating of ice melts off from my heart, my soul quivers and my eyes burn, and that is a disadvantageous state of things for a writer, who should control his subject-matter and keep himself beautifully objective, as the artistic school would have us, and as Goethe has done; he has come to be eighty years old doing this, and minister, and in good condition:—poor German people! that is thy greatest man!"

But hear Goethe himself: "If I were to say what I had really been to the Germans in general, and to the young German poets in particular, I should say I had been their *liberator.*"

Modern times find themselves with an immense system of institutions, established facts, accredited dogmas, customs, rules, which have come to them from times not modern. In this system their life has to be carried forward; yet they have a sense that this system is not of their own creation, that it by no means corresponds exactly with the wants of their actual life, that, for them, it is customary, not rational. The awakening of this sense is the awakening of the modern spirit. The modern spirit is now awake almost everywhere; the sense of want of correspondence between the forms of modern Europe and its spirit, between the new wine of the eighteenth and nineteenth centuries, and the old bottles of the eleventh and twelfth centuries, or even of the sixteenth and seventeenth, almost every one now perceives; it is no longer dangerous to affirm that this want of correspondence exists; people are even beginning to be shy of denying it. To remove this want of correspondence is beginning to be the settled endeavour of most persons of good sense. Dissolvents of the old European system of dominant ideas and facts we must all be, all of us who have any power of working; what we have to study is that we may not be acrid dissolvents of it.

And how did Goethe, that grand dissolvent in an age when there were fewer of them than at present, proceed in his task of dissolution, of liberation of the modern European from the old routine? He shall tell us himself. "Through me the German poets have become aware that, as man must live from within outwards, so the artist must work from within outwards, seeing that, make what contortions he will, he can only bring to light his own individuality. I can clearly mark where this influence of mine has made itself felt; there arises out of it a kind of poetry of nature, and only in this way is it possible to be original."

My voice shall never be joined to those which decry Goethe, and if it is said that the foregoing is a lame and impotent conclusion to Goethe's declaration that he had been the liberator of the Germans in general, and of the young German poets in particular, I say it is not. Goethe's profound, imperturbable naturalism is absolutely fatal to all routine thinking; he puts the standard, once for all, inside every man instead of outside him; when he is told, such a thing must be so, there is immense authority and custom in favour of its being so, it has been held to be so for a thousand years, he answers with Olympian politeness, "But *is* it so? is it so to *me?*" Nothing could be more really subversive of the foundations on which the old European order rested; and it may be remarked that no persons are so radically detached from this order, no persons so thoroughly modern, as those who have felt Goethe's influence most deeply. If it is said that Goethe professes to have in this way deeply influenced but a few persons, and those persons poets, one may answer that he could have taken no better way to secure, in the end, the ear of the world; for poetry is simply the most beautiful, impressive, and widely effective mode of saying things, and hence its importance. Nevertheless the process of liberation, as Goethe worked it, though sure, is undoubtedly slow; he came, as Heine says, to be eighty years old in thus working it, and at the end of that time the old Middle-Age machine was still creaking on, the thirty German courts and their chamberlains subsisted in all their glory; Goethe himself was a minister, and the visible triumph of the modern spirit over prescription and routine seemed as far off as ever. It was the year 1830; the German sovereigns had passed the preceding fifteen years in breaking the promises of freedom they had made to their subjects when they wanted their help in the final struggle with Napoleon. Great events were happening in France; the revolution, defeated in 1815, had arisen from its defeat, and was wresting from its adversaries the power. Heinrich Heine, a young man of genius, born at Hamburg, and with all the culture of Germany, but by race a Jew; with warm sympathies for France, whose revolution[2] had given to his race the rights of citizenship, and whose rule had been, as is well known, popular in the Rhine provinces, where he passed his youth; with a passionate admiration for the great French Emperor, with a passionate contempt for the sovereigns who

had overthrown him, for their agents, and for their policy,—
Heinrich Heine was in 1830 in no humour for any such
gradual process of liberation from the old order of things
as that which Goethe had followed. His counsel was for
open war. Taking that terrible modern weapon, the pen, in
his hand, he passed the remainder of his life in one fierce
battle. What was that battle? the reader will ask. It was a
life and death battle with Philistinism.

Philistinism!—we have not the expression in English.
Perhaps we have not the word because we have so much of
the thing. At Soli, I imagine, they did not talk of solecisms;[3]
and here, at the very headquarters of Goliath, nobody talks
of Philistinism. The French have adopted the term *épicier*
(grocer), to designate the sort of being whom the Germans
designate by the term Philistine; but the French term,—besides that it casts a slur upon a respectable class, composed
of living and susceptible members, while the original Philistines are dead and buried long ago,—is really, I think, in
itself much less apt and expressive than the German term.
Efforts have been made to obtain in English some term
equivalent to *Philister* or *épicier;* Mr. Carlyle has made
several such efforts: "respectability with its thousand gigs,"[4]
he says;—well, the occupant of every one of these gigs is,
Mr. Carlyle means, a Philistine. However, the word *respectable* is far too valuable a word to be thus perverted from its
proper meaning; if the English are ever to have a word for
the thing we are speaking of,—and so prodigious are the
changes which the modern spirit is introducing, that even
we English shall perhaps one day come to want such a word,
—I think we had much better take the term *Philistine* itself.

Philistine must have originally meant, in the mind of those
who invented the nickname, a strong, dogged, unenlightened
opponent of the chosen people, of the children of the light.
The party of change, the would-be remodellers of the old
traditional European order, the invokers of reason against
custom, the representatives of the modern spirit in every
sphere where it is applicable, regarded themselves, with the
robust self-confidence natural to reformers, as a chosen people, as children of the light. They regarded their adversaries
as humdrum people, slaves to routine, enemies to light;
stupid and oppressive, but at the same time very strong. This
explains the love which Heine, that Paladin of the modern
spirit, has for France; it explains the preference which he
gives to France over Germany: "the French," he says, "are
the chosen people of the new religion, its first gospels and

dogmas have been drawn up in their language; Paris is the new Jerusalem, and the Rhine is the Jordan which divides the consecrated land of freedom from the land of the Philistines." He means that the French, as a people, have shown more accessibility to ideas than any other people; that prescription and routine have had less hold upon them than upon any other people; that they have shown most readiness to move and to alter at the bidding (real or supposed) of reason. This explains, too, the detestation which Heine had for the English: "I might settle in England," he says, in his exile, "if it were not that I should find there two things, coal-smoke and Englishmen; I cannot abide either." What he hated in the English was the "ächt britische Beschränktheit," as he calls it,—the *genuine British narrowness*. In truth, the English, profoundly as they have modified the old Middle-Age order, great as is the liberty which they have secured for themselves, have in all their changes proceeded, to use a familiar expression, by the rule of thumb; what was intolerably inconvenient to them they have suppressed, and as they have suppressed it, not because it was irrational, but because it was practically inconvenient, they have seldom in suppressing it appealed to reason, but always, if possible, to some precedent, or form, or letter, which served as a convenient instrument for their purpose, and which saved them from the necessity of recurring to general principles. They have thus become, in a certain sense, of all people the most inaccessible to ideas and the most impatient of them; inaccessible to them, because of their want of familiarity with them; and impatient of them because they have got on so well without them, that they despise those who, not having got on as well as themselves, still make a fuss for what they themselves have done so well without. But there has certainly followed from hence, in this country, somewhat of a general depression of pure intelligence: Philistia has come to be thought by us the true Land of Promise, and it is anything but that; the born lover of ideas, the born hater of commonplaces, must feel in this country, that the sky over his head is of brass and iron. The enthusiast for the idea, for reason, values reason, the idea, in and for themselves; he values them, irrespectively of the practical conveniences which their triumph may obtain for him; and the man who regards the possession of these practical conveniences as something sufficient in itself, something which compensates for the absence or surrender of the idea, of reason, is, in his eyes, a Philistine. This is why Heine so often and so mercilessly attacks the liberals; much as he hates conservatism he hates Philistinism even more, and whoever attacks conservatism itself ignobly, not as a child of light, not in the name of the idea, is a Philistine. Our Cobbett is thus for him, much as he disliked our clergy and aristocracy whom Cobbett attacked, a Philistine with six fingers on every hand and on every foot six toes, four-and-twenty in number: a Philistine, the staff of whose spear is like a weaver's beam. Thus he speaks of him:—

"While I translate Cobbett's words, the man himself comes bodily before my mind's eye, as I saw him at that uproarious dinner at the Crown and Anchor Tavern, with his scolding red face and his radical laugh, in which venomous hate mingles with a mocking exultation at his enemies' surely approaching downfall. He is a chained cur, who falls with equal fury on every one whom he does not know, often bites the best friend of the house in his calves, barks incessantly, and just because of this incessantness of his barking cannot get listened to, even when he barks at a real thief. Therefore the distinguished thieves who plunder England do not think it necessary to throw the growling Cobbett a bone to stop his mouth. This makes the dog furiously savage, and he shows all his hungry teeth. Poor old Cobbett! England's dog! I have no love for thee, for every vulgar nature my soul abhors; but thou touchest me to the inmost soul with pity, as I see how thou strainest in vain to break loose and to get at those thieves, who make off with their booty before thy very eyes, and mock at thy fruitless springs and thine impotent howling."

There is balm in Philistia as well as in Gilead. A chosen circle of children of the modern spirit, perfectly emancipated from prejudice and commonplace, regarding the ideal side of things in all its efforts for change, passionately despising half-measures and condescension to human folly and obstinacy,—with a bewildered, timid, torpid multitude behind,—conducts a country to the government of Herr von Bismarck.[5] A nation regarding the practical side of things in its efforts for change, attacking not what is irrational, but what is pressingly inconvenient, and attacking this as one body, "moving altogether if it move at all," and treating children of light like the very harshest of stepmothers, comes to the prosperity and liberty of modern England. For all that, however, Philistia (let me say it again) is not the true promised land, as we English commonly imagine it to be; and our excessive neglect of the idea, and consequent inaptitude for it, threatens us, at a moment when the idea is beginning to exercise a real power in human society, with serious future inconvenience, and, in the meanwhile, cuts us off from the sympathy of other nations, which feel its power more than we do.

But, in 1830, Heine very soon found that the fire-engines of the German governments were too much for his direct efforts at incendiarism. "What demon drove me," he cries, "to write my *Reisebilder,* to edit a newspaper, to plague myself with our time and its interests, to try and shake the poor German Hodge out of his thousand years' sleep in his hole? What good did I get by it? Hodge opened his eyes, only to shut them again immediately; he yawned, only to begin snoring again the next minute louder than ever; he stretched his stiff ungainly limbs, only to sink down again directly afterwards, and lie like a dead man in the old bed of his accustomed habits. I must have rest; but where am I to find a resting-place? In Germany I can no longer stay."

This is Heine's jesting account of his own efforts to rouse Germany: now for his pathetic account of them; it is because he unites so much wit with so much pathos that he is so effective a writer:—

"The Emperor Charles the Fifth sate in sore straits, in the Tyrol, encompassed by his enemies. All his knights and courtiers had forsaken him; not one came to his help. I know not if he had at that time the cheese face with which Holbein has painted him for us. But I am sure that under lip of his, with its contempt for mankind, stuck out even more than it does in his portraits. How could he but contemn the tribe which in the sunshine of his prosperity had fawned on him so devotedly, and now, in his dark distress, left him all alone? Then suddenly his door opened, and there came in a man in disguise, and, as he threw back his cloak, the Kaiser recognised in him his faithful Conrad von der Rosen, the court jester. This man brought him comfort and counsel, and he was the court jester!

"O German fatherland! dear German people! I am thy Conrad von der Rosen. The man whose proper business was to amuse thee, and who in good times should have catered only for thy mirth, makes his way into thy prison in time of need; here, under my cloak, I bring thee thy sceptre and crown; dost thou not recognise me, my Kaiser? If I cannot free thee, I will at least comfort thee, and thou shalt at least have one with thee who will prattle with thee about thy sorest affliction, and whisper courage to thee, and love thee, and whose best joke and best blood shall be at thy service. For thou, my people, art the true Kaiser, the true lord of the land; thy will is sovereign, and more legitimate far than that purple *Tel est notre plaisir*, which invokes a divine right with no better warrant than the anointings of shaven and shorn jugglers; thy will, my people, is the sole rightful source of power. Though now thou liest down in thy bonds, yet in the end will thy rightful cause prevail; the day of deliverance is at hand, a new time is beginning. My Kaiser, the night is over, and out there glows the ruddy dawn.

" 'Conrad von der Rosen, my fool, thou art mistaken; perhaps thou takest a headsman's gleaming axe for the sun, and the red of dawn is only blood.'

" 'No, my Kaiser, it is the sun, though it is rising in the west; these six thousand years it has always risen in the east; it is high time there should come a change.'

" 'Conrad von der Rosen, my fool, thou hast lost the bells out of thy red cap, and it has now such an odd look, that red cap of thine!'

" 'Ah, my Kaiser, thy distress has made me shake my head so hard and fierce, that the fool's bells have dropped off my cap; the cap is none the worse for that.'

" 'Conrad von der Rosen, my fool, what is that noise of breaking and cracking outside there?'

" 'Hush! that is the saw and the carpenter's axe, and soon the doors of thy prison will be burst open, and thou wilt be free, my Kaiser!'

" 'Am I then really Kaiser? Ah, I forgot, it is the fool who tells me so!'

" 'Oh, sigh not, my dear master, the air of thy prison makes thee so desponding! when once thou hast got thy rights again, thou wilt feel once more the bold imperial blood in thy veins, and thou wilt be proud like a Kaiser, and violent, and gracious, and unjust, and smiling, and ungrateful, as princes are.'

" 'Conrad von der Rosen, my fool, when I am free, what wilt thou do then?'

" 'I will then sew new bells on to my cap.'

" 'And how shall I recompense thy fidelity?'

" 'Ah, dear master, by not leaving me to die in a ditch!' "

I wish to mark Heine's place in modern European literature, the scope of his activity, and his value. I cannot attempt to give here a detailed account of his life, or a description of his separate works. In May 1831 he went over his Jordan, the Rhine, and fixed himself in his new Jerusalem, Paris. There, henceforward, he lived, going in general to some French watering-place in the summer, but making only one or two short visits to Germany during the rest of his life. His works, in verse and prose, succeeded each other without stopping; a collected edition of them, filling seven closely-printed octavo volumes, has been published in America;* in the collected editions of few people's works is there so little to skip. Those who wish for a single good specimen of him should read his first important work, the work which made his reputation, the *Reisebilder*, or "Travelling Sketches:" prose and verse, wit and seriousness, are mingled in it, and the mingling of these is characteristic of Heine, and is nowhere to be seen practised more naturally and happily than in his *Reisebilder*. In 1847 his health, which till then had always been perfectly good, gave way. He had a kind of paralytic stroke. His malady proved to be a softening of the spinal marrow: it was incurable; it made rapid progress. In May 1848, not a year after his first attack, he went out of doors for the last time; but his disease took more than eight years to kill him. For nearly eight years he lay helpless on a couch, with the use of his limbs gone, wasted almost to the proportions of a child, wasted so that a woman could carry him about; the sight of one eye lost, that of the other greatly dimmed, and requiring, that it might be exercised, to have the palsied eyelid lifted and held up by the finger; all this, and, besides this, suffering at short intervals paroxysms of nervous agony. I have said he was not pre-eminently brave; but in the astonishing force of spirit with which he retained his activity of mind, even his gaiety, amid all his suffering, and went on composing with undiminished fire to the last, he was truly brave. Nothing could clog that aërial lightness. "Pouvez-vous siffler?" his doctor asked him one day, when he was almost at his last gasp;— "siffler," as every one knows, has the double meaning of *to whistle* and *to hiss:*—"Hélas! non," was his whispered answer; "pas même une comédie de M. Scribe!" M. Scribe is, or was, the favourite dramatist of the French Philistine. "My nerves," he said to some one who asked him about them in 1855, the year of the Great Exhibition in Paris, "my nerves are of that quite singularly remarkable miserableness of nature, that I am convinced they would get at the Exhibition the grand medal for pain and misery." He read all the medical books which treated of his complaint. "But," said he to some one who found him thus engaged, "what good this reading is to do me I don't know, except that it will qualify me to give lectures in heaven on the ignorance of doctors on earth about diseases of the spinal

* A complete edition has at last appeared in Germany. [M. A.]

marrow." What a matter of grim seriousness are our own ailments to most of us! yet with this gaiety Heine treated his to the end. That end, so long in coming, came at last. Heine died on the 17th of February 1856, at the age of fifty-eight. By his will he forbade that his remains should be transported to Germany. He lies buried in the cemetery of Montmartre, at Paris.

His direct political action was null, and this is neither to be wondered at nor regretted; direct political action is not the true function of literature, and Heine was a born man of letters. Even in his favourite France the turn taken by public affairs was not at all what he wished, though he read French politics by no means as we in England, most of us, read them. He thought things were tending there to the triumph of communism; and to a champion of the idea like Heine, what there is gross and narrow in communism was very repulsive. "It is all of no use," he cried on his deathbed, "the future belongs to our enemies, the Communists, and Louis Napoleon is their John the Baptist." "And yet,"— he added with all his old love for that remarkable entity, so full of attraction for him, so profoundly unknown in England, the French people,—"do not believe that God lets all this go forward merely as a grand comedy. Even though the Communists deny him to-day, he knows better than they do, that a time will come when they will learn to believe in him." After 1831, his hopes of soon upsetting the German Governments had died away, and his propagandism took another, a more truly literary, character. It took the character of an intrepid application of the modern spirit to literature. To the ideas with which the burning questions of modern life filled him, he made all his subject-matter minister. He touched all the great points in the career of the human race, and here he but followed the tendency of the wide culture of Germany; but he touched them with a wand which brought them all under a light where the modern eye cares most to see them, and here he gave a lesson to the culture of Germany,—so wide, so impartial, that it is apt to become slack and powerless, and to lose itself in its materials for want of a strong central idea round which to group all its other ideas. So the mystic and romantic school of Germany lost itself in the Middle Ages, was overpowered by their influence, came to ruin by its vain dreams of renewing them. Heine, with a far profounder sense of the mystic and romantic charm of the Middle Ages than Görres, or Brentano, or Arnim,[6] Heine the chief romantic poet of

Germany, is yet also much more than a romantic poet; he is a great modern poet, he is not conquered by the Middle Age, he has a talisman by which he can feel,—along with but above the power of the fascinating Middle Age itself,—the power of modern ideas.

A French critic of Heine thinks he has said enough in saying that Heine proclaimed in German countries, with beat of drum, the ideas of 1789, and that at the cheerful noise of his drum the ghosts of the Middle Age took to flight. But this is rather too French an account of the matter. Germany, that vast mine of ideas, had no need to import ideas, as such, from any foreign country; and if Heine had carried ideas, as such, from France into Germany, he would but have been carrying coals to Newcastle. But that for which France, far less meditative than Germany, is eminent, is the prompt, ardent, and practical application of an idea, when she seizes it, in all departments of human activity which admit it. And that in which Germany most fails, and by failing in which she appears so helpless and impotent, is just the practical application of her innumerable ideas. "When Candide,"[7] says Heine himself, "came to Eldorado, he saw in the streets a number of boys who were playing with gold-nuggets instead of marbles. This degree of luxury made him imagine that they must be the king's children, and he was not a little astonished when he found that in Eldorado gold-nuggets are of no more value than marbles are with us, and that the schoolboys play with them. A similar thing happened to a friend of mine, a foreigner, when he came to Germany and first read German books. He was perfectly astounded at the wealth of ideas which he found in them; but he soon remarked that ideas in Germany are as plentiful as gold-nuggets in Eldorado, and that those writers whom he had taken for intellectual princes, were in reality only common schoolboys." Heine was, as he calls himself, a "Child of the French Revolution," an "Initiator," because he vigorously assured the Germans that ideas were not counters or marbles, to be played with for their own sake; because he exhibited in literature modern ideas applied with the utmost freedom, clearness, and originality. And therefore he declared that the great task of his life had been the endeavour to establish a cordial relation between France and Germany. It is because he thus operates a junction between the French spirit, and German ideas and German culture, that he founds something new, opens a fresh period, and deserves the attention of criticism far more than the German poets his contemporaries, who merely continue an old period till it expires. It may be predicted that in the literature of other countries, too, the French spirit is destined to make its influence felt,—as an element, in alliance with the native spirit, of novelty and movement,—as it has made its influence felt in German literature; fifty years hence a critic will be demonstrating to our grandchildren how this phenomenon has come to pass.

We in England, in our great burst of literature during the first thirty years of the present century, had no manifestation of the modern spirit, as this spirit manifests itself in Goethe's works or Heine's. And the reason is not far to seek. We had neither the German wealth of ideas, nor the French enthusiasm for applying ideas. There reigned in the mass of the nation that inveterate inaccessibility to ideas, that Philistinism,—to use the German nickname,—which reacts even on the individual genius that is exempt from it. In our greatest literary epoch, that of the Elizabethan age, English society at large was accessible to ideas, was permeated by them, was vivified by them, to a degree which has never been reached in England since. Hence the unique greatness in English literature of Shakespeare and his contemporaries. They were powerfully upheld by the intellectual life of their nation; they applied freely in literature the then modern ideas,—the ideas of the Renascence and the Reformation. A few years afterwards the great English middle class, the kernel of the nation, the class whose intelligent sympathy had upheld a Shakespeare, entered the prison of Puritanism, and had the key turned on its spirit there for two hundred years. *He enlargeth a nation,* says Job, *and straiteneth it again.*[8]

In the literary movement of the beginning of the nineteenth century the signal attempt to apply freely the modern spirit was made in England by two members of the aristocratic class, Byron and Shelley. Aristocracies are, as such, naturally impenetrable by ideas; but their individual members have a high courage and a turn for breaking bounds; and a man of genius, who is the born child of the idea, happening to be born in the aristocratic ranks, chafes against the obstacles which prevent him from freely developing it. But Byron and Shelley did not succeed in their attempt freely to apply the modern spirit in English literature; they could not succeed in it; the resistance to baffle them, the want of intelligent sympathy to guide and uphold them, were too great. Their literary creation, compared with the literary creation of Shakespeare and Spenser, compared with the literary creation of Goethe and Heine, is a failure. The best literary creation of that time in England proceeded from men who did not make the same bold attempt as Byron and Shelley. What, in fact, was the career of the chief English men of letters, their contemporaries? The greatest of them, Wordsworth, retired (in Middle-Age phrase) into a monastery. I mean, he plunged himself in the inward life, he voluntarily cut himself off from the modern spirit. Coleridge took to opium. Scott became the historiographer-royal of feudalism. Keats passionately gave himself up to a sensuous genius, to his faculty for interpreting nature; and he died of consumption at twenty-five. Wordsworth, Scott, and Keats have left admirable works; far more solid and complete works than those which Byron and Shelley have left. But their works have this defect,—they do not belong to that which is the main current of the literature of modern epochs, they do not apply modern ideas to life; they constitute, therefore, *minor currents*, and all other literary work of our day, however popular, which has the same defect, also constitutes but a minor current. Byron and Shelley will long be remembered, long after the inadequacy of their actual work is clearly recognised, for their passionate, their Titanic effort to flow in the main stream of modern literature; their names will be greater than their writings; *stat magni nominis umbra*.[9]

Heine's literary good fortune was superior to that of Byron and Shelley. His theatre of operations was Germany, whose Philistinism does not consist in her want of ideas, or in her inaccessibility to ideas, for she teems with them and loves them, but, as I have said, in her feeble and hesitating application of modern ideas to life. Heine's intense modernism, his absolute freedom, his utter rejection of stock classicism and stock romanticism, his bringing all things under the point of view of the nineteenth century, were understood and laid to heart by Germany, through virtue of her immense, tolerant intellectualism, much as there was in all Heine said to affront and wound Germany. The wit and ardent modern spirit of France Heine joined to the culture, the sentiment, the thought of Germany. This is what makes him so remarkable; his wonderful clearness, lightness, and freedom, united with such power of feeling, and width of range. Is there anywhere keener wit than in his story of the French abbé who was his tutor, and who wanted to get from him that *la religion* is French for *der Glaube*: "Six times did he ask me the question: 'Henry, what is *der Glaube* in French?' and six times, and each time with a greater burst of tears, did I answer him—'It is *le crédit.*' And at the seventh time, his face purple with rage, the infuriated questioner screamed out: 'It is *la religion;*' and a rain of cuffs descended upon me, and all the other boys burst out laughing. Since that day I have never been able to hear *la religion* mentioned, without feeling a tremor run through my back, and my cheeks grow red with shame." Or in that comment on the fate of Professor Saalfeld, who had been addicted to writing furious pamphlets against Napoleon, and who was a professor at Göttingen, a great seat, according to Heine, of pedantry and Philistinism: "It is curious," says Heine, "the three greatest adversaries of Napoleon have all of them ended miserably. Castlereagh cut his own throat; Louis the Eighteenth rotted upon his throne; and Professor Saalfeld is still a professor at Göttingen." It is impossible to go beyond that.

What wit, again, in that saying which every one has heard: "The Englishman loves liberty like his lawful wife, the Frenchman loves her like his mistress, the German loves her like his old grandmother." But the turn Heine gives to this incomparable saying is not so well known; and it is by that turn he shows himself the born poet he is,—full of delicacy and tenderness, of inexhaustible resource, infinitely new and striking:—

"And yet, after all, no one can ever tell how things may turn out. The grumpy Englishman, in an ill-temper with his wife, is capable of some day putting a rope round her neck, and taking her to be sold at Smithfield. The inconstant Frenchman may become unfaithful to his adored mistress, and be seen fluttering about the Palais Royal after another. *But the German will never quite abandon his old grandmother;* he will always keep for her a nook by the chimney-corner, where she can tell her fairy stories to the listening children."

Is it possible to touch more delicately and happily both the weakness and the strength of Germany;—pedantic, simple, enslaved, free, ridiculous, admirable Germany?

And Heine's verse,—his *Lieder?* Oh, the comfort, after dealing with French people of genius, irresistibly impelled to try and express themselves in verse, launching out into a deep which destiny has sown with so many rocks for them, —the comfort of coming to a man of genius, who finds in verse his freest and most perfect expression, whose voyage over the deep of poetry destiny makes smooth! After the rhythm, to us, at any rate, with the German paste in our composition, so deeply unsatisfying, of—

> "Ah! que me dites-vous, et que vous dit mon âme?
> Que dit le ciel à l'aube et la flamme à la flamme?"[10]

what a blessing to arrive at rhythms like—

> "Take, oh, take those lips away,
> That so sweetly were forsworn—"[11]

or—

> "Siehst sehr sterbeblässlich aus,
> Doch getrost! du bist zu Haus—"[12]

in which one's soul can take pleasure! The magic of Heine's poetical form is incomparable; he chiefly uses a form of old German popular poetry, a ballad-form which has more rapidity and grace than any ballad-form of ours; he employs this form with the most exquisite lightness and ease, and yet it has at the same time the inborn fulness, pathos, and old-world charm of all true forms of popular poetry. Thus in Heine's poetry, too, one perpetually blends the impression of French modernism and clearness, with that of German sentiment and fulness; and to give this blended impression is, as I have said, Heine's great characteristic. To feel it, one must read him; he gives it in his form as well as in his contents, and by translation I can only reproduce it so far as his contents give it. But even the contents of many of his poems are capable of giving a certain sense of it. Here, for instance, is a poem in which he makes his profession of faith to an innocent beautiful soul, a sort of Gretchen, the child of some simple mining people having their hut among the pines at the foot of the Hartz Mountains, who reproaches him with not holding the old articles of the Christian creed:—

"Ah, my child, while I was yet a little boy, while I yet sate upon my mother's knee, I believed in God the Father, who rules up there in Heaven, good and great;

"Who created the beautiful earth, and the beautiful men and women thereon; who ordained for sun, moon, and stars their courses.

"When I got bigger, my child, I comprehended yet a great deal more than this, and comprehended, and grew intelligent; and I believe on the Son also;

"On the beloved Son, who loved us, and revealed love to us; and, for his reward, as always happens, was crucified by the people.

"Now, when I am grown up, have read much, have travelled much, my heart swells within me, and with my whole heart I believe on the Holy Ghost.

"The greatest miracles were of his working, and still greater miracles doth he even now work; he burst in sunder the oppressor's stronghold, and he burst in sunder the bondsman's yoke.

"He heals old death-wounds, and renews the old right; all mankind are one race of noble equals before him.

"He chases away the evil clouds and the dark cobwebs of the brain, which have spoilt love and joy for us, which day and night have loured on us.

"A thousand knights, well harnessed, has the Holy Ghost chosen out to fulfil his will, and he has put courage into their souls.

"Their good swords flash, their bright banners wave; what, thou wouldst give much, my child, to look upon such gallant knights?

"Well, on me, my child, look! kiss me, and look boldly upon me! one of those knights of the Holy Ghost am I."

One has only to turn over the pages of his *Romancero*,—a collection of poems written in the first years of his illness, with his whole power and charm still in them, and not, like his latest poems of all, painfully touched by the air of his *Matratzengruft*, his "mattress-grave,"—to see Heine's width of range; the most varied figures succeed one another,—Rhampsinitus, Edith with the Swan Neck, Charles the First, Marie Antoinette, King David, a heroine of *Mabille*, Melisanda of Tripoli, Richard Cœur de Lion, Pedro the Cruel, Firdusi, Cortes, Dr. Döllinger;—but never does Heine attempt to be *hübsch objectiv*, "beautifully objective," to become in spirit an old Egyptian, or an old Hebrew, or a Middle-Age knight, or a Spanish adventurer, or an English royalist; he always remains Heinrich Heine, a son of the nineteenth century. To give a notion of his tone, I will quote a few stanzas at the end of the *Spanish Atridæ*, in which he describes, in the character of a visitor at the court of Henry of Transtamare at Segovia, Henry's treatment of the children of his brother, Pedro the Cruel. Don Diego Albuquerque, his neighbour, strolls after dinner through the castle with him:

"In the cloister-passage, which leads to the kennels where are kept the king's hounds, that with their growling and yelping let you know a long way off where they are,

"There I saw, built into the wall, and with a strong iron grating for its outer face, a cell like a cage.

"Two human figures sate therein, two young boys; chained by the leg, they crouched in the dirty straw.

"Hardly twelve years old seemed the one, the other not much older; their faces fair and noble, but pale and wan with sickness.

"They were all in rags, almost naked; and their lean bodies showed wounds, the marks of ill-usage; both of them shivered with fever.

"They looked up at me out of the depth of their misery; 'Who,' I cried in horror to Don Diego, 'are these pictures of wretchedness?'

"Don Diego seemed embarrassed; he looked round to see that no one was listening; then he gave a deep sigh; and at last, putting on the easy tone of a man of the world, he said:

" 'These are a pair of king's sons, who were early left orphans; the name of their father was King Pedro, the name of their mother, Maria de Padilla.

" 'After the great battle of Navarette, when Henry of Transtamare had relieved his brother, King Pedro, of the troublesome burden of the crown,

" 'And likewise of that still more troublesome burden, which is called life, then Don Henry's victorious magnanimity had to deal with his brother's children.

" 'He has adopted them, as an uncle should; and he has given them free quarters in his own castle.

" 'The room which he has assigned to them is certainly rather small, but then it is cool in summer, and not intolerably cold in winter.

" 'Their fare is rye-bread, which tastes as sweet as if the goddess Ceres had baked it express for her beloved Proserpine.

" 'Not unfrequently, too, he sends a scullion to them with garbanzos, and then the young gentlemen know that it is Sunday in Spain.

" 'But it is not Sunday every day, and garbanzos do not come every day; and the master of the hounds gives them the treat of his whip.

" 'For the master of the hounds, who has under his superintendence the kennels and the pack, and the nephews' cage also,

" 'Is the unfortunate husband of that lemon-faced woman with the white ruff, whom we remarked to-day at dinner.

" 'And she scolds so sharp, that often her husband snatches his whip, and rushes down here, and gives it to the dogs and to the poor little boys.

" 'But his majesty has expressed his disapproval of such

proceedings, and has given orders that for the future his nephews are to be treated differently from the dogs.

" 'He has determined no longer to entrust the disciplining of his nephews to a mercenary stranger, but to carry it out with his own hands.'

"Don Diego stopped abruptly; for the seneschal of the castle joined us, and politely expressed his hope that we had dined to our satisfaction."

Observe how the irony of the whole of that, finishing with the grim innuendo of the last stanza but one, is at once truly masterly and truly modern.

No account of Heine is complete which does not notice the Jewish element in him. His race he treated with the same freedom with which he treated everything else, but he derived a great force from it, and no one knew this better than he himself. He has excellently pointed out how in the sixteenth century there was a double renascence,—a Hellenic renascence and a Hebrew renascence,—and how both have been great powers ever since. He himself had in him both the spirit of Greece and the spirit of Judæa; both these spirits reach the infinite, which is the true goal of all poetry and all art,—the Greek spirit by beauty, the Hebrew spirit by sublimity. By his perfection of literary form, by his love of clearness, by his love of beauty, Heine is Greek; by his intensity, by his untamableness, by his "longing which cannot be uttered,"[13] he is Hebrew. Yet what Hebrew ever treated the things of the Hebrews like this?—

"There lives at Hamburg, in a one-roomed lodging in the Baker's Broad Walk, a man whose name is Moses Lump; all the week he goes about in wind and rain, with his pack on his back, to earn his few shillings; but when on Friday evening he comes home, he finds the candlestick with seven candles lighted, and the table covered with a fair white cloth, and he puts away from him his pack and his cares, and he sits down to table with his squinting wife and yet more squinting daughter, and eats fish with them, fish which has been dressed in beautiful white garlic sauce, sings therewith the grandest psalms of King David, rejoices with his whole heart over the deliverance of the children of Israel out of Egypt, rejoices, too, that all the wicked ones who have done the children of Israel hurt, have ended by taking themselves off; that King Pharaoh, Nebuchadnezzar, Haman, Antiochus, Titus, and all such people, are well dead, while he, Moses Lump, is yet alive, and eating fish with wife and daughter; and I can tell you, Doctor, the fish is delicate and the man is happy, he has no call to torment himself about culture, he sits contented in his religion and in his green bedgown, like Diogenes in his tub, he contemplates with satisfaction his candles, which he on no account will snuff for himself; and I can tell you, if the candles burn a little dim, and the snuffers-woman, whose business it is to snuff them, is not at hand, and Rothschild the Great were at that moment to come in, with all his brokers, bill discounters, agents, and chief clerks, with whom he conquers the world, and Rothschild were to say: 'Moses Lump, ask of me what favour you will, and it shall be granted you;'—Doctor, I am convinced, Moses Lump would quietly answer: 'Snuff me those candles!' and Rothschild the Great would exclaim with admiration: 'If I were not Rothschild, I would be Moses Lump.'"

There Heine shows us his own people by its comic side; in the poem of the *Princess Sabbath* he shows it to us by a more serious side. The Princess Sabbath, "the *tranquil Princess,* pearl and flower of all beauty, fair as the Queen of Sheba, Solomon's bosom friend, that blue-stocking from Ethiopia, who wanted to shine by her *esprit,* and with her wise riddles made herself in the long run a bore" (with Heine the sarcastic turn is never far off), this princess has for her betrothed a prince whom sorcery has transformed into an animal of lower race, the Prince Israel.

"A dog with the desires of a dog, he wallows all the week long in the filth and refuse of life, amidst the jeers of the boys in the street.

"But every Friday evening, at the twilight hour, suddenly the magic passes off, and the dog becomes once more a human being.

"A man with the feelings of a man, with head and heart raised aloft, in festal garb, in almost clean garb, he enters the halls of his Father.

"'Hail, beloved halls of my royal Father! Ye tents of Jacob, I kiss with my lips your holy door-posts!'"

Still more he shows us this serious side in his beautiful poem on Jehuda ben Halevy, a poet belonging to "the great golden age of the Arabian, Old-Spanish, Jewish school of poets," a contemporary of the troubadours:—

"He, too,—the hero whom we sing,—Jehuda ben Halevy, too, had his lady-love; but she was of a special sort.

"She was no Laura, whose eyes, mortal stars, in the cathedral on Good Friday kindled that world-renowned flame.

"She was no châtelaine, who in the blooming glory of her youth presided at tourneys, and awarded the victor's crown.

"No casuistess in the Gay Science was she, no lady *doc-*

trinaire, who delivered her oracles in the judgment-chamber of a Court of Love.

"She, whom the Rabbi loved, was a woe-begone poor darling, a mourning picture of desolation . . . and her name was Jerusalem."

Jehuda ben Halevy, like the Crusaders, makes his pilgrimage to Jerusalem; and there, amid the ruins, sings a song of Sion which has become famous among his people:—

"That lay of pearled tears is the wide-famed Lament, which is sung in all the scattered tents of Jacob throughout the world,

"On the ninth day of the month which is called Ab, on the anniversary of Jerusalem's destruction by Titus Vespasianus.

"Yes, that is the song of Sion, which Jehuda ben Halevy sang with his dying breath amid the holy ruins of Jerusalem.

"Barefoot, and in penitential weeds, he sate there upon the fragment of a fallen column; down to his breast fell,

"Like a gray forest, his hair; and cast a weird shadow on the face which looked out through it,—his troubled pale face, with the spiritual eyes.

"So he sate and sang, like unto a seer out of the foretime to look upon; Jeremiah, the Ancient, seemed to have risen out of his grave.

"But a bold Saracen came riding that way, aloft on his barb, lolling in his saddle, and brandishing a naked javelin;

"Into the breast of the poor singer he plunged his deadly shaft, and shot away like a winged shadow.

"Quietly flowed the Rabbi's life-blood, quietly he sang his song to an end; and his last dying sigh was Jerusalem!"

But, most of all, Heine shows us this side in a strange poem describing a public dispute, before King Pedro and his Court, between a Jewish and a Christian champion, on the merits of their respective faiths. In the strain of the Jew all the fierceness of the old Hebrew genius, all its rigid defiant Monotheism, appear:—

"Our God has not died like a poor innocent lamb for mankind; he is no gushing philanthropist, no declaimer.

"Our God is not love, caressing is not his line; but he is a God of thunder, and he is a God of revenge.

"The lightnings of his wrath strike inexorably every sinner, and the sins of the fathers are often visited upon their remote posterity.

"Our God, he is alive, and in his hall of heaven he goes on existing away, throughout all the eternities.

"Our God, too, is a God in robust health, no myth, pale and thin as sacrificial wafers, or as shadows by Cocytus.

"Our God is strong. In his hand he upholds sun, moon, and stars; thrones break, nations reel to and fro, when he knits his forehead.

"Our God loves music, the voice of the harp and the song of feasting; but the sound of church-bells he hates, as he hates the grunting of pigs."

Nor must Heine's sweetest note be unheard,—his plaintive note, his note of melancholy. Here is a strain which came from him as he lay, in the winter night, on his "mattress-grave" at Paris, and let his thoughts wander home to Germany, "the great child, entertaining herself with her Christmas-tree." "Thou tookest,"—he cries to the German exile,—

"Thou tookest thy flight towards sunshine and happiness; naked and poor returnest thou back. German truth, German shirts,—one gets them worn to tatters in foreign parts.

"Deadly pale are thy looks, but take comfort, thou art at home! one lies warm in German earth, warm as by the old pleasant fireside.

"Many a one, alas, became crippled, and could get home no more! longingly he stretches out his arms; God have mercy upon him!"

God have mercy upon him! for what remain of the days of the years of his life are few and evil. "Can it be that I still actually exist? My body is so shrunk that there is hardly anything of me left but my voice, and my bed makes me think of the melodious grave of the enchanter Merlin, which is in the forest of Broceliand in Brittany, under high oaks whose tops shine like green flames to heaven. Ah, I envy thee those trees, brother Merlin, and their fresh waving! for over my mattress-grave here in Paris no green leaves rustle; and early and late I hear nothing but the rattle of carriages, hammering, scolding, and the jingle of the piano. A grave without rest, death without the privileges of the departed, who have no longer any need to spend money, or to write letters, or to compose books. What a melancholy situation!"

He died, and has left a blemished name; with his crying faults,—his intemperate susceptibility, his unscrupulousness in passion, his inconceivable attacks on his enemies, his still more inconceivable attacks on his friends, his want of generosity, his sensuality, his incessant mocking,—how could it be otherwise? Not only was he not one of Mr. Carlyle's "respectable" people, he was profoundly *dis*respectable; and not even the merit of not being a Philistine can make up for a man's being that. To his intellectual deliverance there was an addition of something else wanting, and that something else was something immense; the old-fashioned, laborious, eternally needful moral deliverance. Goethe says that he was deficient in *love*;[14] to me his weakness seems to be not so much a deficiency in love as a deficiency in self-respect, in true dignity of character. But on this negative side of one's criticism of a man of great genius, I for my part, when I have once clearly marked that this negative side is and must be there, have no pleasure in dwelling. I prefer to say of Heine something positive. He is not an adequate interpreter of the modern world. He is only a brilliant soldier in the Liberation War of humanity. But, such as he is, he is (and posterity too, I am quite sure, will say this), in the European poetry of that quarter of a century which follows the death of Goethe, incomparably the most important figure.

What a spendthrift, one is tempted to cry, is Nature! With what prodigality, in the march of generations, she employs human power, content to gather almost always little result from it, sometimes none! Look at Byron, that Byron whom the present generation of Englishmen are forgetting; Byron, the greatest natural force, the greatest elementary power, I cannot but think, which has appeared in our literature since Shakespeare. And what became of this wonderful production of nature? He shattered himself, he inevitably shattered himself to pieces against the huge, black, cloud-topped, interminable precipice of British Philistinism. But Byron, it may be said, was eminent only by his genius, only by his inborn force and fire; he had not the intellectual equipment of a supreme modern poet; except for his genius he was an ordinary nineteenth-century English gentleman, with little culture and with no ideas. Well, then, look at Heine. Heine had all the culture of Germany; in his head fermented all the ideas of modern Europe. And what have we got from Heine? A half-result, for want of moral balance, and of nobleness of soul and character. That is what I say; there is so much power, so many seem able to run well, so many give promise of running well;—so few reach the goal, so few are chosen. *Many are called, few chosen.*[15]

NOTES

Heinrich Heine: Delivered at Oxford, June, 1863; published in *Cornhill Magazine* (August, 1863); *Essays in Criticism* (1865). Heinrich Heine (1797–1856), German poet. For details of the works by Heine which Arnold translates and quotes, see R. H. Super. Arnold said in a letter: "My object is not so much to give a literary history of Heine's works, as to mark his place in modern European letters, and the special tendency and significance of what he did."

1. Horace, *Epistles*, II. ii. 102: *fretful tribe.*
2. Under Napoleon.
3. "Grammatical impropriety, said by ancient writers to refer to the corruption of the Attic dialect by Athenian colonists at *Soloi* in Cilicia" (*Oxford Dictionary of English Etymology*).
4. R. H. Super notes that Carlyle speaks of respectability and gigs in his essay "Count Cagliostro" (1833).
5. (1815–98), chancellor of the German empire.
6. Three scholars of medievalism, contemporaries of Heine.
7. Voltaire, *Candide* (1759), chapter xvii.
8. *Job*, xii. 23.
9. Lucan, *Pharsalia*, i. 135: *The mere shadow of a mighty name he stood.*
10. From the *Journal* (1862) of Eugénie de Guérin: *Ah, what do you say to me, and what does my soul say to you? What does the sky say to the dawn, and the flame to the flame?*
11. *Measure for Measure*, IV. i. 1–2.
12. "Lazarus": *You're deathly pale! But come, take heart, you are at home.*
13. *Romans*, viii. 26 ("*groanings which*").
14. This remark by Goethe in 1825, mistakenly but widely thought to be about Heine, was in fact about the poet Platen (for details, see R. H. Super).
15. *Matthew*, xxii. 14.

EMERSON AND CARLYLE:

from EMERSON

1884

MILTON[1] SAYS that poetry ought to be simple, sensuous, impassioned. Well, Emerson's poetry is seldom either
simple, or sensuous, or impassioned. In general it lacks
directness; it lacks concreteness; it lacks energy. His grammar is often embarrassed; in particular, the want of clearly
marked distinction between the subject and the object of
his sentence is a frequent cause of obscurity in him. A poem
which shall be a plain, forcible, inevitable whole he hardly
ever produces. Such good work as the noble lines graven
on the Concord Monument is the exception with him; such
ineffective work as the 'Fourth of July Ode' or the 'Boston
Hymn' is the rule. Even passages and single lines of thorough plainness and commanding force are rare in his poetry.
They exist, of course; but when we meet with them they
give us a slight shock of surprise, so little has Emerson
accustomed us to them. Let me have the pleasure of quoting
one or two of these exceptional passages:—

> 'So nigh is grandeur to our dust,
>   So near is God to man,
> When Duty whispers low, *Thou must,*
>   The youth replies, *I can.*'[2]

Or again this:—

> 'Though love repine and reason chafe,
>   There came a voice without reply:

446

" 'Tis man's perdition to be safe,
   When for the truth he ought to die." '3

Excellent! but how seldom do we get from him a strain
blown so clearly and firmly! Take another passage where
his strain has not only clearness, it has also grace and
beauty:—

'And ever, when the happy child
  In May beholds the blooming wild,
  And hears in heaven the bluebird sing,
"Onward," he cries, "your baskets bring!
  In the next field is air more mild,
  And in yon hazy west is Eden's balmier spring." '

In the style and cadence here there is a reminiscence, I
think, of Gray; at any rate the pureness, grace, and beauty
of these lines are worthy even of Gray. But Gray holds his
high rank as a poet, not merely by the beauty and grace of
passages in his poems; not merely by a diction generally
pure in an age of impure diction: he holds it, above all, by
the power and skill with which the evolution of his poems
is conducted. Here is his grand superiority to Collins, whose
diction in his best poem, the 'Ode to Evening,' is purer than
Gray's; but then the 'Ode to Evening' is like a river which
loses itself in the sand, whereas Gray's best poems have an
evolution sure and satisfying. Emerson's 'Mayday,' from
which I just now quoted, has no real evolution at all; it
is a series of observations. And, in general, his poems have
no evolution. Take, for example, his 'Titmouse.' Here he has
an excellent subject; and his observation of Nature, moreover, is always marvellously close and fine. But compare
what he makes of his meeting with his titmouse with what
Cowper or Burns makes of the like kind of incident! One
never quite arrives at learning what the titmouse actually
did for him at all, though one feels a strong interest and
desire to learn it; but one is reduced to guessing, and cannot
be quite sure that after all one has guessed right. He is not
plain and concrete enough,—in other words, not poet
enough,—to be able to tell us. And a failure of this kind
goes through almost all his verse, keeps him amid symbo-
lism and allusion and the fringes of things, and, in spite of
his spiritual power, deeply impairs his poetic value. Through
the inestimable virtue of concreteness, a simple poem like
'The Bridge' of Longfellow, or the 'School Days' of Mr.
Whittier, is of more poetic worth, perhaps, than all the
verse of Emerson.

*　*　*

Yet even Carlyle is not, in my judgment, to be called a great writer; one cannot think of ranking him with men like Cicero and Plato and Swift and Voltaire. Emerson freely promises to Carlyle immortality for his histories. They will not have it. Why? Because the materials furnished to him by that devouring eye of his, and that portraying hand, were not wrought in and subdued by him to what his work, regarded as a composition for literary purposes, required. Occurring in conversation, breaking out in familiar correspondence, they are magnificent, inimitable; nothing more is required of them; thus thrown out anyhow, they serve their turn and fulfil their function. And, therefore, I should not wonder if really Carlyle lived, in the long run, by such an invaluable record as that correspondence between him and Emerson, of which we owe the publication to Mr. Charles Norton,—by this and not by his works, as Johnson lives in Boswell, not by his works. For Carlyle's sallies, as the staple of a literary work, become wearisome; and as time more and more applies to Carlyle's works its stringent test, this will be felt more and more. Shakespeare, Molière, Swift,— they, too, had, like Carlyle, the devouring eye and the portraying hand. But they are great literary masters, they are supreme writers, because they knew how to work into a literary composition their materials, and to subdue them to the purposes of literary effect. Carlyle is too wilful for this, too turbid, too vehement.

*　*　*

One can scarcely overrate the importance of thus holding fast to happiness and hope. It gives to Emerson's work an invaluable virtue. As Wordsworth's poetry is, in my judgment, the most important work done in verse, in our language, during the present century, so Emerson's *Essays* are, I think, the most important work done in prose. His work is more important than Carlyle's. Let us be just to Carlyle, provoking though he often is. Not only has he that genius of his which makes Emerson say truly of his letters, that 'they savour always of eternity.' More than this may be said of him. The scope and upshot of his teaching are true; 'his guiding genius,' to quote Emerson again, is really 'his moral sense, his perception of the sole importance of truth and justice.' But consider Carlyle's temper, as we have been considering Emerson's! take his own account of it! 'Perhaps London is the proper place for me after all, seeing all places are *im*proper: who knows? Meanwhile, I lead a most dyspeptic, solitary, self-shrouded life; consuming, if possible, in silence, my considerable daily allotment of pain; glad when any strength is left in me for writing, which is the only use I can see in myself,—too rare a case of late. The ground of my existence is black as death; too black, when all *void* too; but at times there paint themselves on it pictures of gold, and rainbow, and lightning; all the brighter for the black ground, I suppose. Withal, I am very much of a fool.'—No, not a fool, but turbid and morbid, wilful and perverse. 'We judge of a man's wisdom by his hope.'

Carlyle's perverse attitude towards happiness cuts him off from hope. He fiercely attacks the desire for happiness; his grand point in *Sartor*,[4] his secret in which the soul may find rest, is that one shall cease to desire happiness, that one should learn to say to oneself: 'What if thou wert born and predestined not to be happy, but to be unhappy!' He is wrong; Saint Augustine is the better philosopher, who says: 'Act we *must* in pursuance of what gives us most delight.' Epictetus and Augustine can be severe moralists enough; but both of them know and frankly say that the desire for happiness is the root and ground of man's being. Tell him and show him that he places his happiness wrong, that he seeks for delight where delight will never be really found; then you illumine and further him. But you only confuse him by telling him to cease to desire happiness; and you will not tell him this unless you are already confused yourself.

Carlyle preached the dignity of labour, the necessity of righteousness, the love of veracity, the hatred of shams. He is said by many people to be a great teacher, a great helper for us, because he does so. But what is the due and eternal result of labour, righteousness, veracity?—Happiness. And how are we drawn to them by one who, instead of making us feel that with them is happiness, tells us that perhaps we were predestined not to be happy but to be unhappy?

You will find, in especial, many earnest preachers of our popular religion to be fervent in their praise and admiration of Carlyle. His insistence on labour, righteousness, and veracity, pleases them; his contempt for happiness pleases them too. I read the other day a tract against smoking, although I do not happen to be a smoker myself. 'Smoking,' said the tract, 'is liked because it gives agreeable sensations. Now it is a positive objection to a thing that it gives agreeable sensations. An earnest man will expressly avoid what gives agreeable sensations.' Shortly afterwards I was inspecting a school, and I found the children reading a piece of poetry on the common theme that we are here to-day and gone to-morrow. I shall soon be gone, the speaker in this poem was made to say,—

> 'And I shall be glad to go,
> For the world at best is a dreary place,
> And my life is getting low.'

How usual a language of popular religion that is, on our side of the Atlantic at any rate! But then our popular religion, in disparaging happiness here below, knows very well what it is after. It has its eye on a happiness in a future life above the clouds, in the New Jerusalem, to be won by disliking and rejecting happiness here on earth. And so long as this ideal stands fast, it is very well. But for very many it now stands fast no longer; for Carlyle, at any rate, it had failed and vanished. Happiness in labour, righteousness, and veracity,—in the life of the spirit,—here was a gospel still for Carlyle to preach, and to help others by preaching. But he baffled them and himself by preferring the paradox that we are not born for happiness at all.

NOTES

Emerson and Carlyle: From *Emerson:* Delivered at Boston, December, 1883; published in *Macmillan's Magazine* (May, 1884); *Discourses in America* (1885).

1. See p. 308, note 5.
2. "Voluntaries iii."
3. "Sacrifice."
4. *Sartor Resartus* (1833).

David Copperfield:

from THE INCOMPATIBLES

1881

MUCH AS I have published, I do not think it has ever yet happened to me to comment in print upon any production of Charles Dickens. What a pleasure to have the opportunity of praising a work so sound, a work so rich in merit, as *David Copperfield!* 'Man lese nicht die mitstrebende, mitwirkende!' says Goethe: 'Do not read your fellow-strivers, your fellow-workers!' Of the contemporary rubbish which is shot so plentifully all round us, we can, indeed, hardly read too little. But to contemporary work so good as *David Copperfield* we are in danger of perhaps not paying respect enough, of reading it (for who could help reading it?) too hastily, and then putting it aside for something else and forgetting it. What treasures of gaiety, invention, life, are in that book! what alertness and resource! what a soul of good nature and kindness governing the whole! Such is the admirable work which I am now going to call in evidence.

Intimately, indeed, did Dickens know the middle class; he was bone of its bone and flesh of its flesh. Intimately he knew its bringing up. With the hand of a master he has drawn for us a type of the teachers and trainers of its youth, a type of its places of education. Mr. Creakle and Salem House are immortal. The type itself, it is to be hoped, will perish; but the drawing of it which Dickens has given cannot die. Mr. Creakle, the stout gentleman with a bunch of watch-chain and seals, in an arm-chair, with the fiery face and the thick veins in his forehead; Mr. Creakle sitting at his breakfast with the cane, and a newspaper, and the buttered toast before him, will sit on, like Theseus, for ever. For ever will last the recollection of Salem House, and of 'the daily strife and struggle' there; the recollection 'of the frosty mornings when we were rung out of bed, and the cold, cold smell of the dark nights when we were rung into bed again; of the evening schoolroom dimly lighted and indifferently warmed, and the morning schoolroom which was nothing but a great shivering machine; of the alternation of boiled beef with roast beef, and boiled mutton with roast mutton; of clods of bread and butter, dog's-eared lesson-books, cracked slates, tear-blotted copy-books, canings, rulerings, hair-cuttings, rainy Sundays, suet-puddings, and a dirty atmosphere of ink surrounding all.'

*   *   *

We may even go further still in our use of that charming and instructive book, the *History of David Copperfield*. We may lay our finger there on the very types in adult life which are the natural product of Salem House and of Mr. Creakle; the very types of our middle class, nay of Englishmen and the English nature in general, as to the Irish imagination they appear. We have only to recall, on the one hand, Mr. Murdstone. Mr. Murdstone may be called the natural product of a course of Salem House and of Mr. Creakle, acting upon hard, stern, and narrow natures. Let us recall, then, Mr. Murdstone; Mr. Murdstone with his firmness and severity; with his austere religion and his tremendous visage in church; with his view of the world as 'a place for action, and not for moping and droning in'; his view of young Copperfield's disposition as 'requiring a great deal of correcting, and to which no greater service can be done than to force it to conform to the ways of the working world, and to bend it and break it'. We may recall, too, Miss Murdstone, his sister, with the same religion, the same tremendous visage in church, the same firmness; Miss Murdstone with her 'hard steel purse', and her 'uncompromising hard black boxes with her initials on the lids in hard black nails'; severe and formidable like her brother, 'whom she greatly resembled in face and voice'. These two people, with their hardness, their narrowness, their want of consideration for other people's feelings, their inability to enter into them, are just the type of the Englishman and his civilisation as he presents himself to the Irish mind[1] by his serious side. His energy, firmness, industry, religion, exhibit themselves with these unpleasant features; his bad qualities exhibit themselves without mitigation or relief.

*   *   *

But in Murdstone we see English middle-class civilisation by its severe and serious side only. That civilisation has undoubtedly also its gayer and lighter side. And this gayer and lighter side, as well as the other, we shall find, wonderful to relate, in that all-containing treasure-house of ours, the *History of David Copperfield*. Mr. Quinion, with his gaiety, his chaff, his rough coat, his incessant smoking, his brandy and water, is the jovial, genial man of our middle-class civilisation, prepared by Salem House and Mr. Creakle, as Mr. Murdstone is its severe man. Quinion, we are told in our *History,* was the manager of Murdstone's business, and he is truly his pendant. He is the answer of our middle-class civilisation to the demand in man for beauty and enjoyment, as Murdstone is its answer to the demand for temper and manners. But to a quick, sentimental race, Quinion can hardly be more attractive than Murdstone. Quinion produces our towns considered as seats of pleasure, as Murdstone produces them considered as seats of business and religion.

NOTES

David Copperfield: From *The Incompatibles:* "The Incompatibles" was published in the *Nineteenth Century* (April and June, 1881); *Irish Essays* (1882).

1. Arnold's essay is on the relations of the English and the Irish, "the quick sentimental race" referred to below.

COUNT LEO TOLSTOI

1887

IN REVIEWING at the time of its first publication,
thirty years ago, Flaubert's remarkable novel of *Madame
Bovary*, Sainte-Beuve observed that in Flaubert we come
to another manner, another kind of inspiration, from those
which had prevailed hitherto; we find ourselves dealing, he
said, with a man of a new and different generation from
novelists like George Sand. The ideal has ceased, the lyric
vein is dried up; the new men are cured of lyricism and the
ideal; 'a severe and pitiless truth has made its entry, as the
last word of experience, even into art itself.' The characters of the new literature of fiction are 'science, a spirit
of observation, maturity, force, a touch of hardness.' *L'idéal
a cessé, le lyrique a tari.*

The spirit of observation and the touch of hardness (let
us retain these mild and inoffensive terms) have since been
carried in the French novel very far. So far have they been
carried, indeed, that in spite of the advantage which the
French language, familiar to the cultivated classes everywhere, confers on the French novel, this novel has lost
much of its attraction for those classes; it no longer commands their attention as it did formerly. The famous English
novelists have passed away, and have left no successors of
like fame. It is not the English novel, therefore, which has
inherited the vogue lost by the French novel. It is the novel
of a country new to literature, or at any rate unregarded,
till lately, by the general public of readers: it is the novel
of Russia. The Russian novel has now the vogue, and deserves to have it. If fresh literary productions maintain this
vogue and enhance it, we shall all be learning Russian.

The Slav nature, or at any rate the Russian nature, the Russian nature as it shows itself in the Russian novels, seems marked by an extreme sensitiveness, a consciousness most quick and acute both for what the man's self is experiencing, and also for what others in contact with him are thinking and feeling. In a nation full of life, but young, and newly in contact with an old and powerful civilisation, this sensitiveness and self-consciousness are prompt to appear. In the Americans, as well as in the Russians, we see them active in a high degree. They are somewhat agitating and disquieting agents to their possessor, but they have, if they get fair play, great powers for evoking and enriching a literature. But the Americans, as we know, are apt to set them at rest in the manner of my friend Colonel Higginson[1] of Boston. 'As I take it, Nature said, some years since: "Thus far the English is my best race; but we have had Englishmen enough; we need something with a little more buoyancy than the Englishman; let us lighten the structure, even at some peril in the process. Put in one drop more of nervous fluid, and make the American." With that drop, a new range of promise opened on the human race, and a lighter, finer, more highly organised type of mankind was born.' People who by this sort of thing give rest to their sensitive and busy self-consciousness may very well, perhaps, be on their way to great material prosperity, to great political power; but they are scarcely on the right way to a great literature, a serious art.

The Russian does not assuage his sensitiveness in this fashion. The Russian man of letters does not make Nature say: 'The Russian is my best race.' He finds relief to his sensitiveness in letting his perceptions have perfectly free play, and in recording their reports with perfect fidelity. The sincereness with which the reports are given has even something childlike and touching. In the novel of which I am going to speak there is not a line, not a trait, brought in for the glorification of Russia, or to feed vanity; things and characters go as nature takes them, and the author is absorbed in seeing how nature takes them and in relating it. But we have here a condition of things which is highly favourable to the production of good literature, of good art. We have great sensitiveness, subtlety, and finesse, addressing themselves with entire disinterestedness and simplicity to the representation of human life. The Russian novelist is thus master of a spell to which the secrets of human nature—both what is external and what is internal, gesture and manner no less than thought and feeling—willingly make themselves known. The crown of literature is poetry, and the Russians have not yet had a great poet. But in that form of imaginative literature which in our day is the most popular and the most possible, the Russians at the present moment seem to me to hold, as Mr. Gladstone would say, the field. They have great novelists, and of one of their great novelists I wish now to speak.

Count Leo Tolstoi is about sixty years old,[2] and tells us that he shall write novels no more. He is now occupied with religion and with the Christian life. His writings concerning these great matters are not allowed, I believe, to obtain publication in Russia, but instalments of them in French and English reach us from time to time.[3] I find them very interesting, but I find his novel of *Anna Karénine* more interesting still. I believe that many readers prefer to *Anna Karénine* Count Tolstoi's other great novel, *La Guerre et la Paix*. But in the novel one prefers, I think, to have the novelist dealing with the life which he knows from having lived it, rather than with the life which he knows from books or hearsay. If one has to choose a representative work of Thackeray, it is *Vanity Fair* which one would take rather than *The Virginians*. In like manner I take *Anna Karénine* as the novel best representing Count Tolstoi. I use the French translation; in general, as I long ago said, work of this kind is better done in France than in England, and *Anna Karénine* is perhaps also a novel which goes better into French than into English, just as Frederika Bremer's[4] *Home* goes into English better than into French. After I have done with *Anna Karénine* I must say something of Count Tolstoi's religious writings. Of these too I use the French translation, so far as it is available. The English translation,[5] however, which came into my hands late, seems to be in general clear and good. Let me say in passing that it has neither the same arrangement, nor the same titles, nor altogether the same contents, with the French translation.

There are many characters in *Anna Karénine*—too many if we look in it for a work of art in which the action shall be vigorously one, and to that one action everything shall converge. There are even two main actions extending throughout the book, and we keep passing from one of them to the other—from the affairs of Anna and Wronsky to the affairs of Kitty and Levine. People appear in connection with these two main actions whose appearance and proceedings do not in the least contribute to develop them; incidents are multiplied which we expect are to lead to something important, but which do not. What, for instance, does the episode of

Kitty's friend Warinka and Levine's brother Serge Ivanitch, their inclination for one another and its failure to come to anything, contribute to the development of either the character or the fortunes of Kitty and Levine? What does the incident of Levine's long delay in getting to church to be married, a delay which as we read of it seems to have significance, really import? It turns out to import absolutely nothing, and to be introduced solely to give the author the pleasure of telling us that all Levine's shirts had been packed up.

But the truth is we are not to take *Anna Karénine* as a work of art; we are to take it as a piece of life. A piece of life it is. The author has not invented and combined it, he has seen it; it has all happened before his inward eye, and it was in this wise that it happened. Levine's shirts were packed up, and he was late for his wedding in consequence; Warinka and Serge Ivanitch met at Levine's country-house and went out walking together; Serge was very near proposing, but did not. The author saw it all happening so—saw it, and therefore relates it; and what his novel in this way loses in art it gains in reality.

For this is the result which, by his extraordinary fineness of perception, and by his sincere fidelity to it, the author achieves; he works in us a sense of the absolute reality of his personages and their doings. Anna's shoulders, and masses of hair, and half-shut eyes; Alexis Karénine's up-drawn eyebrows, and tired smile, and cracking finger-joints; Stiva's eyes suffused with facile moisture—these are as real to us as any of those outward peculiarities which in our own circle of acquaintance we are noticing daily, while the inner man of our own circle of acquaintance, happily or unhappily, lies a great deal less clearly revealed to us than that of Count Tolstoi's creations.

I must speak of only a few of these creations, the chief personages and no more. The book opens with 'Stiva,' and who that has once made Stiva's acquaintance will ever forget him? We are living, in Count Tolstoi's novel, among the great people of Moscow and St. Petersburg, the nobles and the high functionaries, the governing class of Russia. Stépane Arcadiévitch—'Stiva'—is Prince Oblonsky, and descended from Rurik, although to think of him as anything except 'Stiva' is difficult. His *air souriant*, his good looks, his satisfaction; his 'ray,' which made the Tartar waiter at the club joyful in contemplating it; his pleasure in oysters and champagne, his pleasure in making people happy and in rendering services; his need of money, his attachment to the French governess, his distress at his wife's distress, his affection for her and the children; his emotion and suffused eyes, while he quite dismisses the care of providing funds for household expenses and education; and the French attachment, contritely given up to-day only to be succeeded by some other attachment to-morrow—no, never, certainly, shall we come to forget Stiva. Anna, the heroine, is Stiva's sister. His wife Dolly (these English diminutives are common among Count Tolstoi's ladies) is daughter of the Prince and Princess Cherbatzky, grandees who show us Russian high life by its most respectable side; the Prince, in particular, is excellent—simple, sensible, right-feeling; a man of dignity and honour. His daughters, Dolly and Kitty, are charming. Dolly, Stiva's wife, is sorely tried by her husband, full of anxieties for the children, with no money to spend on them or herself, poorly dressed, worn and aged before her time. She has moments of despairing doubt whether the gay people may not be after all in the right, whether virtue and principle answer; whether happiness does not dwell with adventuresses and profligates, brilliant and perfectly dressed adventuresses and profligates, in a land flowing with roubles and champagne. But in a quarter of an hour she comes right again and is herself—a nature straight, honest, faithful, loving, sound to the core; such she is and such she remains; she can be no other. Her sister Kitty is at bottom of the same temper, but she has her experience to get, while Dolly, when the book begins, has already acquired hers. Kitty is adored by Levine, in whom we are told that many traits are to be found of the character and history of Count Tolstoi himself. Levine belongs to the world of great people by his birth and property, but he is not at all a man of the world. He has been a reader and thinker, he has a conscience, he has public spirit and would ameliorate the condition of the people, he lives on his estate in the country, and occupies himself zealously with local business, schools, and agriculture. But he is shy, apt to suspect and to take offence, somewhat impracticable, out of his element in the gay world of Moscow. Kitty likes him, but her fancy has been taken by a brilliant guardsman, Count Wronsky, who has paid her attentions. Wronsky is described to us by Stiva; he is 'one of the finest specimens of the *jeunesse dorée* of St. Petersburg; immensely rich, handsome, aide-de-camp to the emperor, great interest at his back, and a good fellow notwithstanding; more than a good fellow, intelligent besides and well read—a man who has a splendid career before him.' Let us complete the picture by adding that Wronsky is a powerful man, over thirty, bald at the top of his head, with irreproachable manners, cool and calm, but a little haughty. A hero, one murmurs to oneself, too much of the Guy Livingstone[6] type, though without the bravado and exaggeration. And such is, justly enough perhaps, the first impression, an impression which continues all through the first volume; but Wronsky, as we shall see, improves towards the end.

Kitty discourages Levine, who retires in misery and confusion. But Wronsky is attracted by Anna Karénine, and ceases his attentions to Kitty. The impression made on her heart by Wronsky was not deep; but she is so keenly mortified with herself, so ashamed, and so upset, that she falls ill, and is sent with her family to winter abroad. There she regains health and mental composure, and discovers at the same time that her liking for Levine was deeper than she knew, that it was a genuine feeling, a strong and lasting one. On her return they meet, their hearts come together, they are married; and in spite of Levine's waywardness, irritability, and unsettlement of mind, of which I shall have more to say presently, they are profoundly happy. Well, and who could help being happy with Kitty? So I find myself adding impatiently. Count Tolstoi's heroines are really so living and charming that one takes them, fiction though they are, too seriously.

But the interest of the book centres in Anna Karénine. She is Stiva's sister, married to a high official at St. Petersburg, Alexis Karénine. She has been married to him nine years, and has one child, a boy named Serge. The marriage had not brought happiness to her, she had found in it no satisfaction to her heart and soul, she had a sense of want and isolation; but she is devoted to her boy, occupied, calm. The charm of her personality is felt even before she appears, from the moment when we hear of her being sent for as the good angel to reconcile Dolly with Stiva. Then she arrives at the Moscow station from St. Petersburg, and we see the gray eyes with their long eyelashes, the graceful carriage, the gentle and caressing smile on the fresh lips, the vivacity restrained but waiting to break through, the fulness of life, the softness and strength joined, the harmony, the bloom, the charm. She goes to Dolly, and achieves, with infinite tact and tenderness, the task of reconciliation. At a ball a few days later, we add to our first impression of Anna's beauty, dark hair, a quantity of little curls over her temples and at the back of her neck, sculptural shoulders, firm throat, and beautiful arms. She is in a plain dress of black velvet with a pearl necklace, a bunch of forget-me-nots in the front of her dress, another in her hair. This is Anna Karénine.

She had travelled from St. Petersburg with Wronsky's mother; had seen him at the Moscow station, where he came to meet his mother; had been struck with his looks and manner, and touched by his behaviour in an accident which happened, while they were in the station, to a poor workman crushed by a train. At the ball she meets him again; she is fascinated by him and he by her. She had been told of Kitty's fancy, and had gone to the ball meaning to help Kitty; but Kitty is forgotten, or at any rate neglected; the spell which draws Wronsky and Anna is irresistible. Kitty finds herself opposite to them in a quadrille together:—

> 'She seemed to remark in Anna the symptoms of an over-excitement which she herself knew from experience—that of success. Anna appeared to her as if intoxicated with it. Kitty knew to what to attribute that brilliant and animated look, that happy and triumphant smile, those half-parted lips, those movements full of grace and harmony.'

Anna returns to St. Petersburg, and Wronsky returns there at the same time; they meet on the journey, they keep meeting in society; and Anna begins to find her husband, who before had not been sympathetic, intolerable. Alexis Karénine is much older than herself, a bureaucrat, a formalist, a poor creature; he has conscience, there is a root of goodness in him, but on the surface and until deeply stirred he is tiresome, pedantic, vain, exasperating. The change in Anna is not in the slightest degree comprehended by him; he sees nothing which an intelligent man might in such a case see, and does nothing which an intelligent man would do. Anna abandons herself to her passion for Wronsky.

I remember M. Nisard saying to me many years ago at the École Normale in Paris, that he respected the English because they are *une nation qui sait se gêner*—people who can put constraint on themselves and go through what is disagreeable. Perhaps in the Slav nature this valuable faculty is somewhat wanting; a very strong impulse is too much regarded as irresistible, too little as what can be resisted and ought to be resisted, however difficult and disagreeable the resistance may be. In our high society with its pleasure and dissipation, laxer notions may to some extent prevail; but in general an English mind will be startled by Anna's suffering herself to be so overwhelmed and irretrievably carried away by her passion, by her almost at once regarding it, apparently, as something which it was hopeless to fight against. And this I say irrespectively of the worth of her lover. Wronsky's gifts and graces hardly qualify him, one might think, to be the object of so instantaneous and mighty a passion on the part of a woman like Anna. But that is not the question. Let us allow that these passions are incalculable; let us allow that one of the male sex scarcely does justice, perhaps, to the powerful and handsome guardsman and his attractions. But if Wronsky had been even such a lover as Alcibiades[7] or the Master of Ravenswood,[8] still that Anna, being what she is and her circumstances being what they are, should show not a hope, hardly a thought, of conquering her passion, of escaping from its fatal power, is to our notions strange and a little bewildering.

I state the objection; let me add that it is the triumph of Anna's charm that it remains paramount for us nevertheless; that throughout her course, with its failures, errors, and miseries, still the impression of her large, fresh, rich, generous, delightful nature, never leaves us—keeps our sympathy, keeps even, I had almost said, our respect.

To return to the story. Soon enough poor Anna begins to experience the truth of what the Wise Man told us long ago, that 'the way of transgressors is hard.' Her agitation at a steeple-chase where Wronsky is in danger attracts her husband's notice and provokes his remonstrance. He is bitter and contemptuous. In a transport of passion Anna declares to him that she is his wife no longer; that she loves Wronsky, belongs to Wronsky. Hard at first, formal, cruel, thinking only of himself, Karénine, who, as I have said, has a conscience, is touched by grace at the moment when Anna's troubles reach their height. He returns to her to find her with a child just born to her and Wronsky, the lover in the house and Anna apparently dying. Karénine has words of kindness and forgiveness only. The noble and victorious effort transfigures him, and all that her husband gains in the eyes of Anna, her lover Wronsky loses. Wronsky comes to Anna's bedside, and standing there by Karénine, buries his face in his hands. Anna says to him, in the hurried voice of fever:—

' " Uncover your face; look at that man; he is a saint. Yes, uncover your face; uncover it," she repeated with an angry air. "Alexis, uncover his face; I want to see him."

'Alexis took the hands of Wronsky and uncovered his face, disfigured by suffering and humiliation.

' "Give him your hand; pardon him."

'Alexis stretched out his hand without even seeking to restrain his tears.

' "Thank God, thank God!" she said; "all is ready now. How ugly those flowers are," she went on, pointing to the wall-paper; "they are not a bit like violets. My God, my God! when will all this end? Give me morphine, doctor—I want morphine. Oh, my God, my God!" '

She seems dying, and Wronsky rushes out and shoots himself. And so, in a common novel, the story would end. Anna would die, Wronsky would commit suicide, Karénine would survive, in possession of our admiration and sympathy. But the story does not always end so in life; neither does it end so in Count Tolstoi's novel. Anna recovers from her fever, Wronsky from his wound. Anna's passion for Wronsky reawakens, her estrangement from Karénine returns. Nor does Karénine remain at the height at which in the forgiveness scene we saw him. He is formal, pedantic, irritating. Alas! even if he were not all these, perhaps even his *pince-nez*, and his rising eyebrows, and his cracking finger-joints, would have been provocation enough. Anna and Wronsky depart together. They stay for a time in Italy, then return to Russia. But her position is false, her disquietude incessant, and happiness is impossible for her. She takes opium every night, only to find that 'not poppy nor mandragora shall ever medicine her to that sweet sleep which she owed yesterday.'⁹ Jealousy and irritability grow upon her; she tortures Wronsky, she tortures herself. Under these trials Wronsky, it must be said, comes out well, and rises in our esteem. His love for Anna endures; he behaves, as our English phrase is, 'like a gentleman'; his patience is in general exemplary. But then Anna, let us remember, is to the last, through all the fret and misery, still Anna; always with something which charms; nay, with something, even, something in her nature, which consoles and does good. Her life, however, was becoming impossible under its existing conditions. A trifling misunderstanding brought the inevitable end. After a quarrel with Anna, Wronsky had gone one morning into the country to see his mother; Anna summons him by telegraph to return at once, and receives an answer from him that he cannot return before ten at night. She follows him to his mother's place in the country, and at the station hears what leads her to believe that he is not coming back. Maddened with jealousy and misery, she descends the platform and throws herself under the wheels of a goods train passing through the station. It is over—the graceful head is untouched, but all the rest is a crushed, formless heap. Poor Anna!

We have been in a world which misconducts itself nearly as much as the world of a French novel all palpitating with 'modernity.' But there are two things in which the Russian novel—Count Tolstoi's novel at any rate—is very advantageously distinguished from the type of novel now so much in request in France. In the first place, there is no fine sentiment, at once tiresome and false. We are not told to believe, for example, that Anna is wonderfully exalted and ennobled by her passion for Wronsky. The English reader is thus saved from many a groan of impatience. The other thing is yet more important. Our Russian novelist deals abundantly with criminal passion and with adultery, but he does not seem to feel himself owing any service to the goddess Lubricity, or bound to put in touches at this goddess's dictation. Much in *Anna Karénine* is painful, much is unpleasant, but nothing is of a nature to trouble the senses, or to please those who wish their senses troubled. This taint is wholly absent. In the French novels where it is so abundantly present its baneful effects do not end with itself. Burns long ago remarked with deep truth that it *petrifies feeling*.[10] Let us revert for a moment to the powerful novel of which I spoke at the outset, *Madame Bovary*. Undoubtedly the taint in question is present in *Madame Bovary,* although to a much less degree than in more recent French novels, which will be in every one's mind. But *Madame Bovary,* with this taint, is a work of *petrified feeling;* over it hangs an atmosphere of bitterness, irony, impotence; not a personage in the book to rejoice or console us; the springs of freshness and feeling are not there to create such personages. Emma Bovary follows a course in some respects like that of Anna, but where, in Emma Bovary, is Anna's charm? The treasures of compassion, tenderness, insight, which alone, amid such guilt and misery, can enable charm to subsist and to emerge, are wanting to Flaubert. He is cruel, with the cruelty of petrified feeling, to his poor heroine; he pursues her without pity or pause, as with malignity; he is harder upon her himself than any reader even, I think, will be inclined to be.

But where the springs of feeling have carried Count Tolstoi, since he created Anna ten or twelve years ago, we have now to see.

We must return to Constantine Dmitrich Levine. Levine, as I have already said, thinks. Between the age of twenty and that of thirty-five he had lost, he tells us, the Christian belief in which he had been brought up, a loss of which examples nowadays abound certainly everywhere, but which in Russia, as in France, is among all young men of the upper and cultivated classes more a matter of course, perhaps, more universal, more avowed, than it is with us. Levine had adopted the scientific notions current all round him; talked of cells, organisms, the indestructibility of matter, the conservation of force, and was of opinion, with his comrades of the university, that religion no longer existed. But he was of a serious nature, and the question what his life meant, whence it came, whither it tended, presented themselves to him in moments of crisis and affliction with irresistible importunity, and getting no answer, haunted him, tortured him, made him think of suicide.

Two things, meanwhile, he noticed. One was, that he and his university friends had been mistaken in supposing that Christian belief no longer existed; they had lost it, but they were not all the world. Levine observed that the persons to whom he was most attached, his own wife Kitty amongst the number, retained it and drew comfort from it; that the women generally, and almost the whole of the Russian common people, retained it and drew comfort from it. The other was, that his scientific friends, though not troubled like himself by questionings about the meaning of human life, were untroubled by such questionings, not because they had got an answer to them, but because, entertaining themselves intellectually with the consideration of the cell theory, and evolution, and the indestructibility of matter, and the conservation of force, and the like, they were satisfied with this entertainment, and did not perplex themselves with investigating the meaning and object of their own life at all.

But Levine noticed further that he himself did not actually proceed to commit suicide; on the contrary, he lived on his lands as his father had done before him, busied himself with all the duties of his station, married Kitty, was delighted when a son was born to him. Nevertheless he was indubitably not happy at bottom, restless and disquieted, his disquietude sometimes amounting to agony.

Now on one of his bad days he was in the field with his peasants, and one of them happened to say to him, in answer to a question from Levine why one farmer should in a certain case act more humanely than another: 'Men are not all alike; one man lives for his belly, like Mitiovuck, another for his soul, for God, like old Plato.'*—'What do you call,'

---

* A common name among Russian peasants. [M. A.]

cried Levine, 'living for his soul, for God?' The peasant answered: 'It's quite simple—living by the rule of God, of the truth. All men are not the same, that's certain. You yourself, for instance, Constantine Dmitrich, you wouldn't do wrong by a poor man.' Levine gave no answer, but turned away with the phrase, *living by the rule of God, of the truth,* sounding in his ears.

Then he reflected that he had been born of parents professing this rule, as their parents again had professed it before them; that he had sucked it in with his mother's milk; that some sense of it, some strength and nourishment from it, had been ever with him although he knew it not; that if he had tried to do the duties of his station it was by help of the secret support ministered by this rule; that if in his moments of despairing restlessness and agony, when he was driven to think of suicide, he had yet not committed suicide, it was because this rule had silently enabled him to do his duty in some degree, and had given him some hold upon life and happiness in consequence.

The words came to him as a clue of which he could never again lose sight, and which with full consciousness and strenuous endeavour he must henceforth follow. He sees his nephews and nieces throwing their milk at one another and scolded by Dolly for it. He says to himself that these children are wasting their subsistence because they have not to earn it for themselves and do not know its value, and he exclaims inwardly: 'I, a Christian, brought up in the faith, my life filled with the benefits of Christianity, living on these benefits without being conscious of it, I, like these children, I have been trying to destroy what makes and builds up my life.' But now the feeling has been borne in upon him, clear and precious, that what he has to do is to *be good;* he has 'cried to *Him.'* What will come of it?

'I shall probably continue to get out of temper with my coachman, to go into useless arguments, to air my ideas unseasonably; I shall always feel a barrier between the sanctuary of my soul and the soul of other people, even that of my wife; I shall always be holding her responsible for my annoyances and feeling sorry for it directly afterwards. I shall continue to pray without being able to explain to myself why I pray; but my inner life has won its liberty; it will no longer be at the mercy of events, and every minute of my existence will have a meaning sure and profound which it will be in my power to impress on every single one of my actions, that of *being good.'*

With these words the novel of *Anna Karénine* ends. But in Levine's religious experiences Count Tolstoi was relating his own, and the history is continued in three autobiographical works translated from him, which have within the last two or three years been published in Paris: *Ma Confession, Ma Religion,* and *Que Faire*. Our author announces further, 'two great works,' on which he has spent six years: one a criticism of dogmatic theology, the other a new translation of the four Gospels, with a concordance of his own arranging. The results which he claims to have established in these two works, are however, indicated sufficiently in the three published volumes which I have named above.

These autobiographical volumes show the same extraordinary penetration, the same perfect sincerity, which are exhibited in the author's novel. As autobiography they are of profound interest, and they are full, moreover, of acute and fruitful remarks. I have spoken of the advantages which the Russian genius possesses for imaginative literature. Perhaps for Biblical exegesis, for the criticism of religion and its documents, the advantage lies more with the older nations of the West. They will have more of the experience, width of knowledge, patience, sobriety, requisite for these studies; they may probably be less impulsive, less heady.

Count Tolstoi regards the change accomplished in himself during the last half-dozen years, he regards his recent studies and the ideas which he has acquired through them, as epoch-making in his life and of capital importance:—

'Five years ago faith came to me; I believed in the doctrine of Jesus, and all my life suddenly changed. I ceased to desire that which previously I desired, and, on the other hand, I took to desiring what I had never desired before. That which formerly used to appear good in my eyes appeared evil, that which used to appear evil appeared good.'

The novel of *Anna Karénine* belongs to that past which Count Tolstoi has left behind him; his new studies and the works founded on them are what is important; light and salvation are there. Yet I will venture to express my doubt whether these works contain, as their contribution to the cause of religion and to the establishment of the true mind and message of Jesus, much that had not already been given or indicated by Count Tolstoi in relating, in *Anna Karénine,* Levine's mental history. Points raised in that history are developed and enforced; there is an abundant and admirable exhibition of knowledge of human nature, penetrating insight, fearless sincerity, wit, sarcasm, eloquence, style. And we have too the direct autobiography of a man not only interesting to us from his soul and talent, but highly interesting also from his nationality, position, and course of proceeding. But to light and salvation in the Christian religion we are not, I think, brought very much nearer than in Levine's history. I ought to add that what was already present in that history seems to me of high importance and value. Let us see what it amounts to.

I must be general and I must be brief; neither my limits nor my purpose permit the introduction of what is abstract. But in Count Tolstoi's religious philosophy there is very little which is abstract, arid. The idea of *life* is his master idea in studying and establishing religion. He speaks impatiently of St. Paul as a source, in common with the Fathers and the Reformers, of that ecclesiastical theology which misses the essential and fails to present Christ's Gospel aright. Yet Paul's 'law of the spirit of life in Christ Jesus freeing me from the law of sin and death'[11] is the pith and ground of all Count Tolstoi's theology. Moral life is the gift of God, is God, and this true life, this union with God to which we aspire, we reach through Jesus. We reach it through union with Jesus and by adopting his life. This doctrine is proved true for us by the life in God, to be acquired through Jesus, being what our nature feels after and moves to, by the warning of misery if we are severed from it, the sanction of happiness if we find it. Of the access for *us*, at any rate, to the spirit of life, us who are born in Christendom, are in touch, conscious or unconscious, with Christianity, this is the true account. Questions over which the churches spend so much labour and time—questions about the Trinity, about the godhead of Christ, about the procession of the Holy Ghost, are not vital; what is vital is the doctrine of access to the spirit of life through Jesus.

Sound and saving doctrine, in my opinion, this is. It may be gathered in a great degree from what Count Tolstoi had already given us in the novel of *Anna Karénine*. But of course it is greatly developed in the special works which have followed. Many of these developments are, I will repeat, of striking force, interest, and value. In *Anna Karénine* we had been told of the scepticism of the upper and educated classes in Russia. But what reality is added by such an anecdote as the following from *Ma Confession:*—

'I remember that when I was about eleven years old we had a visit one Sunday from a boy, since dead, who announced to my brother and me, as great news, a discovery just made at his public school. This discovery was to the effect that God had no existence, and that everything which we were taught about Him was pure invention.'

Count Tolstoi touched, in *Anna Karénine,* on the failure of science to tell a man what his life means. Many a sharp stroke does he add in his latter writings:—

> 'Development is going on, and there are laws which guide it. You yourself are a part of the whole. Having come to understand the whole so far as is possible, and having comprehended the law of development, you will comprehend also your place in that whole, you will understand yourself.
>
> 'In spite of all the shame the confession costs me, there was a time, I declare, when I tried to look as if I was satisfied with this sort of thing!'

But the men of science may take comfort from hearing that Count Tolstoi treats the men of letters no better than them, although he is a man of letters himself:—

> 'The judgment which my literary companions passed on life was to the effect that life in general is in a state of progress, and that in this development we, the men of letters, take the principal part. The vocation of us artists and poets is to instruct the world; and to prevent my coming out with the natural question, "What am I, and what am I to teach?" it was explained to me that it was useless to know that, and that the artist and the poet taught without perceiving how. I passed for a superb artist, a great poet, and consequently it was but natural I should appropriate this theory. I, the artist, the poet—I wrote, I taught, without myself knowing what. I was paid for what I did. I had everything: splendid fare and lodging, women, society; I had *la gloire.* Consequently, what I taught was very good. This faith in the importance of poetry and of the development of life was a religion, and I was one of its priests—a very agreeable and advantageous office.
>
> 'And I lived ever so long in this belief, never doubting but that it was true!'

The adepts of this literary and scientific religion are not numerous, to be sure, in comparison with the mass of the people, and the mass of the people, as Levine had remarked, find comfort still in the old religion of Christendom; but of the mass of the people our literary and scientific instructors make no account. Like Solomon and Schopenhauer, these gentlemen, and 'society' along with them, are, moreover, apt to say that life is, after all, vanity: but then they all know of no life except their own.

'It used to appear to me that the small number of cultivated, rich, and idle men, of whom I was one, composed the
whole of humanity, and that the millions and millions of
other men who had lived and are still living were not in
reality men at all. Incomprehensible as it now seems to me,
that I should have gone on considering life without seeing the
life which was surrounding me on all sides, the life of humanity; strange as it is to think that I should have been so
mistaken, and have fancied my life, the life of the Solomons
and the Schopenhauers, to be the veritable and normal life,
while the life of the masses was but a matter of no importance—strangely odd as this seems to me now, so it was, notwithstanding.'

And this pretentious minority, who call themselves 'society,' 'the world,' and to whom their own life, the life of 'the
world,' seems the only life worth naming, are all the while
miserable! Our author found it so in his own experience:—

'In my life, an exceptionally happy one from a worldly
point of view, I can number such a quantity of sufferings endured for the sake of "the world," that they would be enough
to furnish a martyr for Jesus. All the most painful passages
in my life, beginning with the orgies and duels of my student
days, the wars I have been in, the illnesses, and the abnormal
and unbearable conditions in which I am living now—all this
is but one martyrdom endured in the name of the doctrine
of the world. Yes, and I speak of my own life, exceptionally
happy from the world's point of view.

'Let any sincere man pass his life in review, and he will
perceive that never, not once, has he suffered through practising the doctrine of Jesus; the chief part of the miseries of
his life have proceeded solely from his following, contrary
to his inclination, the spell of the doctrine of the world.'

On the other hand, the simple, the multitudes, outside of
this spell, are comparatively contented:—

'In opposition to what I saw in our circle, where life without faith is possible, and where I doubt whether one in a
thousand would confess himself a believer, I conceive that
among the people (in Russia) there is not one sceptic to
many thousands of believers. Just contrary to what I saw in
our circle, where life passes in idleness, amusements, and discontent with life, I saw that of these men of the people the
whole life was passed in severe labour, and yet they were
contented with life. Instead of complaining like the persons
in our world of the hardship of their lot, these poor people
received sickness and disappointments without any revolt,
without opposition, but with a firm and tranquil confidence

that so it was to be, that it could not be otherwise, and that it was all right.'

All this is but development, sometimes rather surprising, but always powerful and interesting, of what we have already had in the pages of *Anna Karénine*. And like Levine in that novel, Count Tolstoi was driven by his inward struggle and misery very near to suicide. What is new in the recent books is the solution and cure announced. Levine had accepted a provisional solution of the difficulties oppressing him; he had lived right on, so to speak, obeying his conscience, but not asking how far all his actions hung together and were consistent:—

'He advanced money to a peasant to get him out of the clutches of a money-lender, but did not give up the arrears due to himself; he punished thefts of wood strictly, but would have scrupled to impound a peasant's cattle trespassing on his fields; he did not pay the wages of a labourer whose father's death caused him to leave work in the middle of harvest, but he pensioned and maintained his old servants; he let his peasants wait while he went to give his wife a kiss after he came home, but would not have made them wait while he went to visit his bees.'

Count Tolstoi has since advanced to a far more definite and stringent rule of life—the positive doctrine, he thinks, of Jesus. It is the determination and promulgation of this rule which is the novelty in our author's recent works. He extracts this essential doctrine, or rule of Jesus, from the Sermon on the Mount, and presents it in a body of commandments—Christ's commandments; the pith, he says, of the New Testament, as the Decalogue is the pith of the Old. These all-important commandments of Christ are 'commandments of peace,' and five in number. The first commandment is: 'Live in peace with all men; treat no one as contemptible and beneath you. Not only allow yourself no anger, but do not rest until you have dissipated even unreasonable anger in others against yourself.' The second is: 'No libertinage and no divorce; let every man have one wife and every woman one husband.' The third: 'Never on any pretext take an oath of service of any kind; all such oaths are imposed for a bad purpose.' The fourth: 'Never employ force against the evil-doer; bear whatever wrong is done to you without opposing the wrong-doer or seeking to have him punished.' The fifth and last: 'Renounce all distinction of nationality; do not admit that men of another nation may ever be treated by you as enemies; love all men alike as alike near to you; do good to all alike.'

If these five commandments were generally observed, says Count Tolstoi, all men would become brothers. Certainly the actual society in which we live would be changed and dissolved. Armies and wars would be renounced; courts of justice, police, property, would be renounced also. And whatever the rest of us may do, Count Tolstoi at least will do his duty and follow Christ's commandments sincerely. He has given up rank, office, and property, and earns his bread by the labour of his own hands. 'I believe in Christ's commandments,' he says, 'and this faith changes my whole former estimate of what is good and great, bad and low, in human life.' At present—

'Everything which I used to think bad and low—the rusticity of the peasant, the plainness of lodging, food, clothing, manners—all this has become good and great in my eyes. At present I can no longer contribute to anything which raises me externally above others, which separates me from them. I cannot, as formerly, recognise either in my own case or in that of others any title, rank, or quality beyond the title and quality of man. I cannot seek fame and praise; I cannot seek a culture which separates me from men. I cannot refrain from seeking in my whole existence—in my lodging, my food, my clothing, and my ways of going on with people— whatever, far from separating me from the mass of mankind, draws me nearer to them.'

Whatever else we have or have not in Count Tolstoi, we have at least a great soul and a great writer. In his Biblical exegesis, in the criticism by which he extracts and constructs his Five Commandments of Christ which are to be the rule of our lives, I find much which is questionable along with much which is ingenious and powerful. But I have neither space, nor, indeed, inclination, to criticise his exegesis here. The right moment, besides, for criticising this will come when the 'two great works,' which are in preparation, shall have appeared.

For the present I limit myself to a single criticism only— a general one. Christianity cannot be packed into any set of commandments. As I have somewhere or other said, 'Christianity is a *source;* no one supply of water and refreshment that comes from it can be called the sum of Christianity. It is a mistake, and may lead to much error, to exhibit any series of maxims, even those of the Sermon on the Mount, as the ultimate sum and formula into which Christianity may be run up.'

And the reason mainly lies in the character of the Founder of Christianity and in the nature of his utterances. Not less important than the teachings given by Jesus is the *temper* of their giver, his temper of sweetness and reasonableness, of *epieikeia.* Goethe calls him a *Schwärmer,* a fanatic; he may much more rightly be called an opportunist. But he is an opportunist of an opposite kind from those who in politics, that 'wild and dreamlike trade' of insincerity, give themselves this name. They push or slacken, press their points hard or let them be, as may best suit the interests of their self-aggrandisement and of their party. Jesus has in view simply 'the rule of God, of the truth.' But this is served by waiting as well as by hasting forward, and sometimes served better.

Count Tolstoi sees rightly that whatever the propertied and satisfied classes may think, the world, ever since Jesus Christ came, is judged; 'a new earth' is in prospect. It was ever in prospect with Jesus, and should be ever in prospect with his followers. And the ideal in prospect has to be realised. 'If ye know these things, happy are ye if ye do them.' But they are to be done through a great and widespread and long-continued change, and a change of the inner man to begin with. The most important and fruitful utterances of Jesus, therefore, are not things which can be drawn up as a table of stiff and stark external commands, but the things which have most soul in them; because these can best sink down into our soul, work there, set up an influence, form habits of conduct, and prepare the future. The Beatitudes are on this account more helpful than the utterances from which Count Tolstoi builds up his Five Commandments. The very *secret* of Jesus, 'He that loveth his life shall lose it, he that will lose his life shall save it,' does not give us a command to be taken and followed in the letter, but an idea to work in our mind and soul, and of inexhaustible value there.

Jesus paid tribute to the government and dined with the publicans, although neither the empire of Rome nor the high finance of Judea were compatible with his ideal and with the 'new earth' which that ideal must in the end create. Perhaps Levine's provisional solution, in a society like ours, was nearer to 'the rule of God, of the truth,' than the more trenchant solution which Count Tolstoi has adopted for himself since. It seems calculated to be of more use. I do not know how it is in Russia, but in an English village the determination of 'our circle' to earn their bread by the work of their hands would produce only dismay, not fraternal joy, amongst that 'majority' who are so earning it already. 'There are plenty of us to compete as things stand,' the gardeners, carpenters, and smiths would say; 'pray stick to your articles, your poetry, and nonsense; in manual labour you will interfere with us, and be taking the bread out of our mouths.'

So I arrive at the conclusion that Count Tolstoi has perhaps not done well in abandoning the work of the poet and artist, and that he might with advantage return to it. But whatever he may do in the future, the work which he has already done, and his work in religion as well as his work in imaginative literature, is more than sufficient to signalise him as one of the most marking, interesting, and sympathy-inspiring men of our time—an honour, I must add, to Russia, although he forbids us to heed nationality.

NOTES

Count Leo Tolstoi: Published in *Fortnightly Review* (December, 1887); *Essays in Criticism* [Second Series] (1888).

1. T. W. S. Higginson (1823–1911). Arnold returned to this quotation in "Civilisation in the United States" (1888).
2. Born 1828.
3. *Anna Karenina* (1875–78) was translated into French in 1885, and into English in 1886. *War and Peace* (1865–73) was translated into French in 1879, and into English in 1886.
4. (1801–65), Swedish novelist.
5. *Christ's Christianity* (1885).
6. The hero of G. A. Lawrence's *Guy Livingstone* (1857).
7. In Plato's *Symposium.*
8. The hero of Scott's *The Bride of Lammermoor* (1819).
9. Adapting *Othello,* III. iii. 335–38.
10. See p. 190.
11. *Romans,* viii. 2.

from ARNOLD'S LETTERS

TO ARTHUR HUGH CLOUGH, *c.* DECEMBER 6, 1847

I do think however that rare as individuality is you have to be on your guard against it—you particularly:—though indeed I do not really know that I think so. Shakespeare[1] says that if imagination would apprehend some joy it comprehends some bringer of that joy: and this latter operation which makes palatable the bitterest or most arbitrary original apprehension you seem to me to despise. Yet to *solve* the Universe as you try to do is as irritating as Tennyson's dawdling with its painted shell is fatiguing to me to witness: and yet I own that to *re-construct* the Universe is not a satisfactory attempt either—I keep saying, Shakespeare, Shakespeare, you are as obscure as life is: yet this unsatisfactoriness goes against the poetic office in general: for this must I think certainly be its end. But have I been inside you, or Shakespeare? Never. Therefore heed me not, but come to what you can.

TO CLOUGH, *c.* DECEMBER, 1847

One does not always remember that one of the signs of the Decadence of a literature, one of the factors of its decadent condition indeed, is this—that new authors attach themselves to the poetic expression the founders of a literature have flowered into, which may be *learned* by a sensitive person, to the neglect of an inward poetic life. The strength of the German literature consists in this—that having no national models from whence to get an idea of *style* as half the work, they were thrown upon themselves, and driven to make the fulness of the content of a work atone for deficiencies of form. Even Goethe at the end of his life has not the inversions, the taking *tourmenté*[2] style we admire in the Latins, in some of the Greeks, and in the great French and English authors. And had Shakespeare and Milton lived in the atmosphere of modern feeling, had they had the multitude of new thoughts and feelings to deal with a modern has, I think it likely the style of each would have been far less *curious* and exquisite. For in a *man* style is the saying in the best way *what you have to say.* The *what you have to say* depends on your age. In the seventeenth century it was *a smaller harvest than now,* and sooner to be reaped: and therefore to its reaper was left time to stow it more finely and curiously. Still more was this the case in the ancient world. The poet's matter being *the hitherto experience of the world, and his own,* increases with every century.

TO CLOUGH, 1848-49

What a brute you were to tell me to read Keats' Letters. However it is over now: and reflexion resumes her power over agitation.

What harm he has done in English Poetry. As Browning is a man with a moderate gift passionately desiring movement and fulness, and obtaining but a confused multitudinousness, so Keats with a very high gift, is yet also consumed by this desire: and cannot produce the truly living and moving, as his conscience keeps telling him. They will not be patient neither understand that they must begin with an Idea of the world in order not to be prevailed over by the world's multitudinousness: or if they cannot get that, at least with isolated ideas: and all other things shall (perhaps) be added unto them.

TO CLOUGH, FEBRUARY, 1849

If I were to say the real truth as to your poems in general, as they impress me—it would be this—that they are not *natural.*

Many persons with far lower gifts than yours yet seem to find their natural mode of expression in poetry, and though the contents may not be very valuable they appeal with justice from the judgment of the mere thinker to the world's general appreciation of naturalness—i.e.—an absolute propriety—of form, as the sole *necessary* of Poetry as such: whereas the greatest wealth and depth of matter is merely a superfluity in the Poet *as such.*

—Form of Conception comes by nature certainly, but is

generally developed late: but this lower form, of expression, is found from the beginning amongst all born poets, even feeble thinkers, and in an unpoetical age: as Collins,[3] Green[4] and fifty more, in England only.

The question is not of congruity between conception and expression: which when both are poetical, is the poet's highest result:—you say what you mean to say: but in such a way as to leave it doubtful whether your mode of expression is not quite arbitrarily adopted.

I often think that even a slight gift of poetical expression which in a common person might have developed itself easily and naturally, is overlaid and crushed in a profound thinker so as to be of no use to him to help him to express himself. —The trying to go into and to the bottom of an object instead of grouping *objects* is as fatal to the sensuousness of poetry as the mere painting, (for, *in Poetry*, this is not *grouping*) is to its airy and rapidly moving life.

TO ARNOLD'S SISTER, MRS. FORSTER, 1849, ON THE PUBLICATION OF *The Strayed Reveller*.

At Oxford particularly many complain that the subjects treated do not interest them. But as I feel rather as a reformer in poetical matters, I am glad of this opposition. If I have health and opportunity to go on, I will shake the present methods until they go down, see if I don't. More and more I feel bent against the modern English habit (too much encouraged by Wordsworth) of using poetry as a channel for thinking aloud, instead of making anything.

TO MRS. FORSTER, c. JULY, 1849

Fret not yourself to make my poems square in all their parts, but like what you can my darling. The true reason why parts suit you while others do not is that my poems are fragments —*i.e.* that I am fragments, while you are a whole; the whole effect of my poems is quite vague and indeterminate—this is their weakness; a person therefore who endeavoured to make them accord would only lose his labour; and a person who has any inward completeness can at best only like parts of them; in fact such a person stands firmly and knows what he is about while the poems stagger weakly and are at their wits end. I shall do better some day I hope—meanwhile change nothing, resign nothing that you have in deference to me or my oracles; and do not plague yourself to find a consistent meaning for these last, which in fact they do not possess through my weakness.

TO CLOUGH, OCTOBER 28, 1852

More and more I feel that the difference between a mature and a youthful age of the world compels the poetry of the former to use great plainness of speech as compared with that of the latter: and that Keats and Shelley were on a false track when they set themselves to reproduce the exuberance of expression, the charm, the richness of images, and the felicity, of the Elizabethan poets. Yet critics cannot get to learn this, because the Elizabethan poets are our greatest, and our canons of poetry are founded on their works. They still think that the object of poetry is to produce exquisite bits and images—such as Shelley's *clouds shepherded by the slow unwilling wind,*[5] and Keats passim: whereas modern poetry can only subsist by its *contents:* by becoming a complete *magister vitae*[6] as the poetry of the ancients did: by including, as theirs did, religion with poetry, instead of existing as poetry only, and leaving religious wants to be supplied by the Christian religion, as a power existing independent of the poetical power. But the language, style and general proceedings of a poetry which has such an immense task to perform, must be very plain direct and severe: and it must not lose itself in parts and episodes and ornamental work, but must press forwards to the whole.

TO CLOUGH, NOVEMBER 30, 1853

I am glad you like the 'Gipsy Scholar'[7]—but what does it *do* for you? Homer *animates*—Shakespeare *animates*—in its poor way I think 'Sohrab and Rustum' *animates*—the 'Gipsy Scholar' at best awakens a pleasing melancholy. But this is not what we want.

> The complaining millions of men
> Darken in labour and pain—[8]

what they want is something to *animate* and *ennoble* them— not merely to add zest to their melancholy or grace to their dreams.—I believe a feeling of this kind is the basis of my nature—and of my poetics.

* * *

My poems, however, viewed *absolutely*, are certainly little or nothing.

TO MRS. FORSTER, APRIL, 1856

My poems are making their way, I think, though slowly, and
perhaps never to make way very far. There must always be
some people, however, to whom the literalness and sincerity
of them has a charm. After all that American review, which
hit upon this last—their sincerity—as their most interesting
quality, was not far wrong. It seems to me strange sometimes to hear of people taking pleasure in this or that poem
which was written years ago, which then nobody took pleasure in but you, which I then perhaps wondered that nobody
took pleasure in, but since had made up my mind that nobody was likely to. The fact is, however, that the state of
mind expressed in many of the poems is one that is becoming more common, and you see that even the Obermann
stanzas[9] are taken up with interest by some.

TO W. B. FORSTER, JANUARY 11, 1858

As to *Merope*[10] not exciting you—on the stage (for which
these things are meant) I think the chief situations would
excite you; and it is easy to over-write a situation for acting.
For an unconscious testimony to this truth, see that masterpiece of bad criticism, the *Times'* remarks on Rachel's[11] acting. But we must beware of taking our notions of excitement from the modern *drame* or from the modern novel—
from *Adrienne Lecouvreur* or from *Night and Morning*.[12]
Certainly the Greek tragic drama does not excite and harrow
us to the extent that these do; I think, neither does Shakespeare. Not one hundredth part of the excitement have I
ever felt at seeing *Lear* or *Othello* on the stage that I have
felt at *The Corsican Brothers*[13] or *Adrienne Lecouvreur*.
And, perhaps, this is necessary. For in good tragedy the poet
must control his matter—and in the drama and novel the
matter is uncontrollable. There is a kind of pity and fear
(Kotzebue[14] is a great master of it) which cannot be puri-
fied, it is the most agitating and overwhelming, certainly, but,
for the sake of a higher result, we must renounce this. Pity
and fear of a certain kind—say commiseration and awe and
you will perhaps better feel what I mean—I think *Merope*
does excite—as does Greek tragedy in general; I allow, however, that the problem for the poet is, or should be, to unite
the highest degree of agitatingness on the part of his subject-
matter, with the highest degree of control and assuagement

on the part of his own exhibition of it—Shakespeare, under immense difficulties, goes further in this respect than the Greeks, and so far he is an advance upon them.

TO MRS. FORSTER, SEPTEMBER 6, 1858

I should like to send you a letter which I had from Froude[15] about *Merope,* just at the same time that your record of Kingsley's[16] criticisms reached me. If I can find it when I return to England I will send it to you. It was to beg me to discontinue the *Merope* line, but entered into very interesting developments, as the French say, in doing so. Indeed, if the opinion of the general public about my poems were the same as that of the leading literary men, I should make more money by them than I do. But, more than this, I should gain the stimulus necessary to enable me to produce my best—all that I have in me, whatever that may be,—to produce which is no light matter with an existence so hampered as mine is. People do not understand what a temptation there is, if you cannot bear anything not *very good,* to transfer your operations to a region where form is everything. Perfection of a certain kind may there be attained, or at least approached, without knocking yourself to pieces, but to attain or approach perfection in the region of thought and feeling, and to unite this with perfection of form, demands not merely an effort and a labour, but an actual tearing of oneself to pieces, which one does not readily consent to (although one is sometimes forced to it) unless one can devote one's whole life to poetry. Wordsworth could give his whole life to it, Shelley and Byron both could, and were besides driven by their demon to do so. Tennyson, a far inferior natural power to either of the three, can; but of the moderns Goethe is the only one, I think, of those who have had an *existence assujettie,*[17] who has thrown himself with a great result into poetry. And even he felt what I say, for he could, no doubt, have done more, *poetically,* had he been freer; but it is not so light a matter, when you have other grave claims on your powers, to submit voluntarily to the exhaustion of the best poetical production in a time like this. Goethe speaks somewhere of the endless matters on which he had employed himself, and says that with the labour he had given to them he might have produced half a dozen more good tragedies; but to produce these, he says, I must have been *sehr zerrissen.*[18] It is only in the best poetical epochs (such as the Elizabethan) that you can descend into yourself and produce the best of your thought and feeling naturally, and without an overwhelming and in some degree morbid effort; for then all the people around you are more or less doing the same thing. It is natural, it is the bent of the time to do it; its being the bent of the time, indeed, is what makes the time a *poetical* one.

TO ARNOLD'S MOTHER, DECEMBER 17, 1860

I have a strong sense of the irrationality of that period ["the Middle Age"], and of the utter folly of those who take it seriously, and play at restoring it; still, it has poetically the greatest charm and refreshment possible for me. The fault I find with Tennyson in his *Idylls of the King* is that the peculiar charm and aroma of the Middle Age he does not give in them. There is something magical about it, and I will do something with it before I have done. The real truth is that Tennyson, with all his temperament and artistic skill, is deficient in intellectual power; and no modern poet can make very much of his business unless he is pre-eminently strong in this. Goethe owes his grandeur to his strength in this, although it even hurt his poetical operations by its immense predominance.

TO J. DYKES CAMPBELL, SEPTEMBER 22, 1864

I am much tempted to say something about the *Enoch Arden* volume. I agree with you in thinking "Enoch Arden" itself very good indeed—perhaps the best thing Tennyson has done; "Tithonus" I do not like quite so well. But is it possible for one who has himself published verses to print a criticism on Tennyson in which perfect freedom shall be used? And without perfect freedom, what is a criticism worth? I do not think Tennyson a great and powerful spirit in any line—as Goethe was in the line of modern thought, Wordsworth in that of contemplation, Byron even in that of passion; and unless a poet, especially a poet at this time of day, is that, my interest in him is only slight, and my conviction that he will not finally stand high is firm. But is it possible or proper for me to say this about Tennyson, when my saying it would inevitably be attributed to odious motives?

TO J. C. SHAIRP, APRIL 12, 1866

"Thyrsis" is a very quiet poem, but I think solid and sincere. It will not be popular, however. It had long been in my head to connect Clough with the Cumner country, and when I began I was carried irresistibly into this form; you say, truly, however, that there is much in Clough (the whole *prophet* side, in fact) which one cannot deal with in this way, and one has the feeling, if one reads the poem as a memorial poem, that not enough is said about Clough in it; I feel this so much that I do not send the poem to Mrs. Clough. Still Clough *had* this idyllic side, too; to deal with this suited my desire to deal again with that Cumner country: anyway only so could I treat the matter this time.

TO ARNOLD'S MOTHER, JUNE 5, 1869

My poems represent, on the whole, the main movement of mind of the last quarter of a century, and thus they will probably have their day as people become conscious to themselves of what that movement of mind is, and interested in the literary productions which reflect it. It might be fairly urged that I have less poetical sentiment than Tennyson, and less intellectual vigour and abundance than Browning; yet, because I have perhaps more of a fusion of the two than either of them, and have more regularly applied that fusion to the main line of modern development, I am likely enough to have my turn, as they have had theirs.

NOTES

From *Arnold's Letters:*

1. *Midsummer Night's Dream,* V. i. 19–21.
2. See p. 212.
3. William Collins (1721–59).
4. Matthew Green (1696–1737), author of *The Spleen* (1737), living in the same "unpoetical age" as Collins. H. F. Lowry mistakenly changes the spelling to indicate the Elizabethan Robert Greene (*Letters of Arnold to Clough,* 1932, p. 25 and index).
5. *Prometheus Unbound,* II. i. 147.
6. *Master (teacher) of life.*
7. Arnold's "The Scholar" (1853).
8. Arnold, "The Youth of Nature," lines 51–52.
9. "Stanzas in Memory of the Author of 'Obermann'" (1852).
10. See p. 58.
11. The French actress Élisa Felix (Rachel) had died January 3, 1858.
12. Two nineteenth-century dramas; see Allardyce Nicoll, *A History of English Drama 1600–1900* (vol. vi, 1959).

13. Melodrama (1848) by Dion Boucicault.
14. August von Kotzebue (1761–1819), German dramatist.
15. J. A. Froude (1818–94), historian.
16. Charles Kingsley (1819–75), man of letters.
17. *Hampered existence* (Arnold's words above).
18. *Very torn.*

SELECTED
BIBLIOGRAPHY

The most useful bibliography is the sixty pages by F. E. Faverty
in *The Victorian Poets: A Guide to Research* (2nd ed.,
1968). The indispensable edition of Arnold is that by R. H.
Super, *The Complete Prose Works of Matthew Arnold*
(1960–   ), seven volumes of which have appeared to
date (1970). There is a very useful edition of *Essays in
Criticism* [First Series] by Sister Thomas Marion Hoctor
(1968). Some out-of-the-way pieces by Arnold have been
brought together by Fraser Neiman: *Essays, Letters, and
Reviews by Matthew Arnold* (1960). *The Poems of Matthew Arnold* (1965, Longman Annotated English Poets)
have been excellently edited by Kenneth Allott.

Letters of Matthew Arnold, 1848–88, ed. G. W. E. Russell
(1895).

Unpublished Letters of Matthew Arnold, ed. A. Whitridge
(1923).

The Letters of Matthew Arnold to Arthur Hugh Clough, ed.
H. F. Lowry (1932).

Warren D. Anderson, *Matthew Arnold and the Classical Tradition* (1965).

Louis Bonnerot, *Matthew Arnold, Poète: Essai de biographie
psychologique* (1947).

S. M. B. Coulling, "Matthew Arnold's 1853 Preface: Its Origin
and Aftermath," *Victorian Studies* (1964).

A. Dwight Culler, *Imaginative Reason: The Poetry of Matthew
Arnold* (1966).

T. S. Eliot, "Arnold and Pater" (1930), *Selected Essays* (1932):
and *The Use of Poetry and the Use of Criticism* (1933).

H. W. Garrod, *Poetry and the Criticism of Life* (1931).

John Holloway, *The Victorian Sage* (1953).

E. D. H. Johnson, *The Alien Vision of Victorian Poetry* (1952).

J. D. Jump, *Matthew Arnold* (1955).

F. R. Leavis, "Arnold as Critic," *Scrutiny* (1938); reprinted in
A Selection from Scrutiny (1968).

William A. Madden, *Matthew Arnold: A Study of the Aesthetic Temperament in Victorian England* (1967).

G. Robert Stange, *Matthew Arnold: The Poet as Humanist* (1967).

Lionel Trilling, *Matthew Arnold* (1939).

Arnold figures importantly in histories of literary criticism, most notably in the following:

George Watson, *The Literary Critics* (1962).

René Wellek, *A History of Modern Criticism,* volume iv (1966).

W. K. Wimsatt, Jr., and Cleanth Brooks, *Literary Criticism: A Short History* (1957).

INDEX

Ⓒ

The SIGNET CLASSIC SHAKESPEARE

Superlatively edited paperbound volumes of the complete works of Shakespeare are now being added to the Signet Classic list. Under the general editorship of Sylvan Barnet of the English Department of Tufts University, each volume features a general introduction by Dr. Barnet; special introduction and Notes by an eminent Shakespearean scholar; critical commentary from past and contemporary authorities, and when possible, the original source material, in its entirety or in excerpt, on which Shakespeare based his work.

☐ **THE SONNETS.** Edited by William Burto. Introduction by W. H. Auden.   (#CT554—75¢)
☐ **ANTONY AND CLEOPATRA.** Edited by Barbara Everett.
                                                       (#CT392—75¢)
☐ **AS YOU LIKE IT.** Edited by Albert Gilman.
                                                       (#CT520—75¢)
☐ **HAMLET.** Edited by Edward Hubler.   (#CT528—75¢)
☐ **JULIUS CAESAR.** Edited by William and Barbara Rosen.
                                                       (#CT529—75¢)
☐ **KING LEAR.** Edited by Russell Fraser.   (#CD160)
☐ **MACBETH.** Edited by Sylvan Barnet.   (#CD161)
☐ **MEASURE FOR MEASURE.** Edited by S. Nagarajan.
                                                       (#CT541—75¢)
☐ **A MIDSUMMER NIGHT'S DREAM.** Edited by Wolfgang Clemen.   (#CT518—75¢)
☐ **MUCH ADO ABOUT NOTHING.** Edited by David Stevenson.   (#CD173)
☐ **OTHELLO.** Edited by Alvin Kernan.   (#CD162)
☐ **RICHARD II.** Edited by Kenneth Muir.   (#CD163)
☐ **RICHARD III.** Edited by Mark Eccles.   (#CD175)
☐ **THE TEMPEST.** Edited by Robert Langbaum.
                                                       (#CT527—75¢)
☐ **TITUS ANDRONICUS.** Edited by Sylvan Barnet.
                                                       (#CD197)

THE NEW AMERICAN LIBRARY, INC., P.O. Box 999, Bergenfield, New Jersey 07621

Please send me the SIGNET CLASSICS I have checked above. I am enclosing $_____(check or money order—no currency or C.O.D.'s). Please include the list price plus 15¢ a copy to cover handling and mailing costs. (Prices and numbers are subject to change without notice.)

Name_____

Address_____

City_____State_____Zip Code_____
        Allow at least 3 weeks for delivery

THE SIGNET CLASSIC POETRY SERIES

presents, in inexpensive format, comprehensive, authoritative, and up-to-date editions of the works of the major British and American poets. Prepared under the general editorship of John Hollander, Professor of English at Hunter College, each volume in the series is devoted to a single poet, and edited by a noted scholar. Included in each volume is an Introduction by the individual editor, a bibliography, a textual noted, and detailed footnotes. Among the volumes already available are:

☐ **THE SELECTED POETRY OF BYRON.** Edited by W. H. Auden. (#CQ346—95¢)

☐ **THE SELECTED POETRY OF DONNE.** Edited by Marius Bewley. (#CQ343—95¢)

☐ **THE SELECTED POETRY OF KEATS.** Edited by Paul de Man. (#CQ325—95¢)

☐ **THE SELECTED POETRY OF HERBERT.** Edited by Joseph H. Summers. (#CY366—$1.25)

☐ **THE SELECTED POETRY OF MARVELL.** Edited by Frank Kermode. (#CQ363—95¢)

☐ **SAMSON AGONISTES AND THE SHORTER POEMS OF MILTON.** Edited by Isabel Gamble MacCaffrey. (#CT323—75¢)

☐ **THE SELECTED POETRY OF SHELLEY.** Edited by Harold Bloom. (#CQ342—95¢)

☐ **THE SELECTED POETRY OF SPENSER.** Edited by A. C. Hamilton. (#CY350—$1.25)

THE NEW AMERICAN LIBRARY, INC., P.O. Box 999, Bergenfield, New Jersey 07621

Please send me the SIGNET CLASSICS I have checked above. I am enclosing $_____(check or money order—no currency or C.O.D.'s). Please include the list price plus 15¢ a copy to cover handling and mailing costs. (Prices and numbers are subject to change without notice.)

Name_____

Address_____

City_____State_____Zip Code_____

Allow at least 3 weeks for delivery